# ORDINARY ETHICS

# Ordinary Ethics

## Anthropology, Language, and Action

*Edited by*

Michael Lambek

FORDHAM UNIVERSITY PRESS

*New York* 2010

Fordham University Press has no responsibility for the persistence or accuracy of URLs for external or third-party Internet websites referred to in this publication and does not guarantee that any content on such websites is, or will remain, accurate or appropriate.

Fordham University Press also publishes its books in a variety of electronic formats. Some content that appears in print may not be available in electronic books.

Library of Congress Cataloging-in-Publication Data

Ordinary ethics : anthropology, language, and action / edited by Michael Lambek.—1st ed.
p.   cm.
Includes bibliographical references and index.
ISBN 978-0-8232-3316-8 (cloth : alk. paper)
ISBN 978-0-8232-3317-5 (pbk. : alk. paper)
ISBN 978-0-8232-3318-2 (ebook)
1. Anthropological ethics.   I. Lambek, Michael.
GN33.6.O74   2011
303.3'72—dc22
2010033983

Printed in the United States of America
12      5 4 3 2
First edition

*For Aram Yengoyan*
*and in memory of Roy (Skip) Rappaport*

# CONTENTS

The Ghosts of War and the Ethics of Memory

ACKNOWLEDGMENTS

This book had its germ in a graduate seminar entitled Subjects of Speech, conceived and taught jointly with Paul Antze and Jack Sidnell at the University of Toronto in fall 2006. Paul and Jack were central in planning the subsequent workshop and book. Their intellectual curiosity and acuity have been inspirational and their advice indispensable and reassuring. Members of the original seminar included Donna Young and Shirley Yeung, and their rich contributions helped prompt us to move on to the next stage. Veena Das and Bill Hanks visited the seminar and inspired all of us.

Fortuitously, that fall Alan Rumsey approached me with the suggestion that we co-organize a workshop on ethics. Together with Francesca Merlan, we made a bid to the Wenner Gren Foundation. Their initial response led us to realize that a more viable course of action would be for me to seek support from a variety of sources and hold the workshop at the University of Toronto; Alan and Francesca remained staunch supporters behind the scenes. Held on October 3 to 6, 2008, at the University of Toronto's Centre for Ethics, the workshop received generous funding from: the Connaught Foundation and the Centre for Ethics, both at the University of Toronto; the Canada Research Chair fund, University of Toronto at Scarborough; the Social Science and Humanities Research Council of Canada; and the Wenner Gren Foundation. In addition, the cost of this book is partially subsidized by the CRC fund. I am very grateful to each of these institutions.

The first versions of most of the essays in this volume were discussed at the Toronto workshop.[1] Unfortunately, three of the participants, Jennifer Jackson, Elinor Ochs, and Robin Shoaps, had already promised their excellent papers elsewhere. The workshop was greatly enriched by a series of appointed discussants, including Joshua Barker, Girish Daswani, and Valentina Napolitano, as well as some of the authors, and by the session

---

1. Naisargi Dave served as a discussant and was subsequently invited to submit a paper. The chapter by Veena Das is different from the one she presented.

chairs, including Janice Boddy, Mieke de Gelder, Sarah Gould, Pamela Klassen, Amira Mittermaier, Andrea Muehlebach, Maureen Murney, and Jackie Solway. Together they showcase the rich environment in which anthropology subsists in Toronto, and they must stand in here for all my wonderful colleagues and students. We were honored to have as summary discussants political theorist Melissa Williams and philosophers Judith Baker and Ian Hacking. Melissa graciously hosted the event at the Centre for Ethics she has created at the University of Toronto, and Ian persevered despite the flu. Mark Reczkiewicz was an excellent graduate assistant, and Audrey Glasbergen and Gail Copland each provided, as usual, unstinting administrative support, as did Sam Grey with the Web page.

My deep appreciation goes to Charles Hirschkind and an anonymous reviewer for agreeing to read an unruly set of papers in draft form and for offering generous and insightful comments, and to Helen Tartar for being such an intelligent and enabling editor. Esther Kühn helped very ably in compiling the bibliography, as did Peter Skrivanic with the index and proofing.

At arm's length from workshop and book, Maurice Bloch serves as a disturber of my intellectual peace and as host, cook, and conversationalist extraordinaire. Stephan Feuchtwang and Megan Vaughan, among many other friends, have been wonderful interlocutors. Olivia Harris was an inestimable and irrepressible intellectual companion and is very much missed.

The book is dedicated to Aram Yengoyan and the late Roy (Skip) Rappaport, who, in their different ways, have taught me most of what I know about the conjunction of anthropology and ethics. They are, of course, not responsible for any infelicities.

Finally, I have the great good fortune to be able to count on the support and critical approbation of Jackie Solway and Nadia and Simon Lambek. Jackie has been my companion for the past thirty years, while Nadia and Simon are leading us into the next thirty.

**Paul Antze** is Associate Professor in the Department of Social Science and the Graduate Programs in Social and Political Thought and Social Anthropology at York University. His research examines cultural aspects of contemporary therapeutic movements and has focused primarily on psychoanalysis, trauma, memory, dissociation, and addiction. He is co-editor, with Michael Lambek, of *Tense Past: Cultural Essays in Trauma and Memory* (1996) and *Illness and Irony: On the Ambiguity of Suffering in Culture* (2004).

**Judith Baker** is Associate Professor in the Department of Philosophy at Glendon College, York University. Her most recent article is "Rationality Without Reasons" (*Mind*, 2008). She is currently writing on trust and commitment.

**Steven C. Caton** is Professor of Contemporary Arab Studies in the Department of Anthropology at Harvard University. For thirty years, his ethnographic focus has been on the Arabian Peninsula, in particular, on Yemen, Saudi Arabia, and the Gulf. His interests range broadly, including anthropological linguistics, film and media studies, urbanism and the environment, and the anthropology of water. His major publications include *Peaks of Yemen I Summon: Poetry as Cultural Practice in a North Yemeni Tribe* (1990), *Lawrence of Arabia: A Films' Anthropology* (1999), and *Yemen Chronicle: An Anthropology of War and Mediation* (2005).

**Veena Das** is Krieger-Eisenhower Professor at The Johns Hopkins University, where she teaches in the Department of Anthropology. She is a Foreign Fellow of the American Academy of Arts and Sciences and the Third World Academy of Sciences. She has published widely on questions of social suffering and violence. The last two books she has authored are *Life and Words: Violence and the Descent into the Ordinary* (2006) and *Critical Events: An Anthropological Perspective on Contemporary India* (1995).

**Naisargi N. Dave** is Assistant Professor of Anthropology at the University of Toronto. Her research concerns emergent forms of politics and relationality in contemporary urban India, including activism around queer rights and animal welfare. Her work has been published in *Signs* (2010), and she is completing a book entitled *Queer Activism in India: A Story in the Anthropology of Ethics*.

**Sophie Day** is Professor of Anthropology at Goldsmiths College, the University of London. She is the author of *On the Game: Women and Sex Work* (2007) and the co-editor, with Helen Ward, of *Sex Work, Mobility and Health in Europe* (2004) and, with Michael Stewart and Evthymios Papataxiarchis, *Lilies of the Field: Marginal People Who Live for the Moment* (1999).

**James D. Faubion** is Professor of Anthropology at Rice University. His interests include the formation and maintenance of epistemic authority, heterodoxy and radicalism, and the modalities of temporal consciousness. He is the author of *Modern Greek Lessons: A Primer in Historical Constructivism* (1993), *The Shadows and Lights of Waco: Millennialism Today* (2001), and *What Becomes a Subject: An Anthropology of Ethics* (forthcoming). He is the co-editor, with George E. Marcus, of *Fieldwork Is Not What It Used to Be: Learning Anthropology's Method in a Time of Transition* (2008) and the editor of two volumes of *Essential Works of Michel Foucault* (1998 and 2000).

**Webb Keane** is Professor of Anthropology at the University of Michigan (Ann Arbor). He is the author of *Signs of Recognition: Powers and Hazards of Representation in an Indonesian Society* (1997) and *Christian Moderns: Freedom and Fetish in the Mission Encounter* (2007).

**Heonik Kwon** is Reader in Anthropology at the London School of Economics. He is the author of the prize-winning *After the Massacre: Commemoration and Consolation in Ha My and My Lai* (2006) and *Ghosts of War in Vietnam* (2008). His new book is *The Other Cold War* (2010).

**James Laidlaw** is a Fellow of King's College, Cambridge, and University Lecturer in the Department of Social Anthropology at the University of Cambridge. He has conducted research in India, Inner Mongolia, and Taiwan. His publications include a study of Jain religious and ethical life in northern India, *Riches and Renunciation* (1995), and, with Caroline Humphrey, *The Archetypal Actions of Ritual* (1994), as well as *The Essential Edmund Leach* (2001) and two collections on the anthropology of religion, psychology, and cognitive science, both co-edited with Harvey White-house: *Ritual and Memory* (2004) and *Religion, Anthropology, and Cognitive Science* (2007).

**Michael Lambek** is Professor of Anthropology at the University of To-ronto and holds a Canada Research Chair in the Department of Social Sciences at the University of Toronto at Scarborough. He is the author of *Human Spirits: A Cultural Account of Trance in Mayotte* (1981, reissued 2009), *Knowledge and Practice in Mayotte* (1993), and *The Weight of the Past: Living with History in Mahajanga, Madagascar* (2002). Among the volumes he has edited is *A Reader in the Anthropology of Religion* (2002, 2nd ed. 2008).

**Carlos David Londoño Sulkin** is Associate Professor of Anthropology at the University of Regina. Most of his published research—several articles and a book titled *Muinane: Un proyecto moral a perpetuidad* (2004)—stems from his ethnographic fieldwork among the indigenous People of the Center (Colombian Amazon) and engages in the anthropological study of morality.

**Francesca Merlan** is Professor of Anthropology at Australian National University. She has pursued research on social transformation through the exploration of language in social action (*Ku Waru: Language and Segmentary Politics in the Western Nebilyer Valley, Papua New Guinea*, co-authored with Alan Rumsey, 1991), change in indigenous social orders and their relations to Australian state and society (*Caging the Rainbow: Places, Politics and Aborigines in a North Australian Town*, 1998), change in landed livelihoods and lifeworlds (*Tracking Rural Change: Community, Policy and Technology in Australia, New Zealand and Europe*, co-edited with David Raftery, 2009), and anthropology's engagement with economy (*Economic Anthropology: Transforming Economies, Changing States*, special issue of *The Australian Journal of Anthropology*, 2009).

**Justin B. Richland** is Associate Professor and Vice Chair in the Department of Criminology, Law, and Society at the University of California, Irvine. His areas of research interest include legal discourse analysis and semiotics, anthropology of law, contemporary Native American law and politics, and North American colonialism. He is the author of several works on the contemporary legal systems and practices of Native American Nations, including *Arguing with Tradition: The Language of Law in Hopi*

*Tribal Court* (2008) and, with Sarah Deer, *Introduction to Tribal Legal Studies* (2nd ed., 2009).

**Alan Rumsey** is a Senior Fellow and Head of Anthropology in the College of Asia and the Pacific at Australian National University. His research fields are Highland New Guinea and Aboriginal Australia, with a focus on relations among language, culture, and intersubjectivity. Recent publications include "Rhetoric, Truth and the Work of Trope" (in *Rhetoric and Culture*, ed. Ivo Strecker and Stephen Tyler, 2009) and, with Joel Robbins, *Anthropology and the Opacity of Other Minds* (special issue of *Anthropological Quarterly*, 2008). He is currently involved in a major research project on social cognition and language (http://rspas.anu.edu.au/~tomhoney/soccog/index.html).

**Jack Sidnell** is Associate Professor of Anthropology at the University of Toronto. His current research focuses on conversation in Vietnamese. He is the author of *Conversation Analysis: An Introduction* (2010) and the editor of *Conversation Analysis: Comparative Perspectives* (2009).

**Charles Stafford** is Professor of Anthropology at the London School of Economics and a specialist on China and Taiwan. Most of his research has focused on questions related to learning, cognition, and child development; his most recent work examines economic psychology from a cognitive anthropological perspective. He is the author of *The Roads of Chinese Childhood* (1995) and *Separation and Reunion in Modern China* (2000), the editor of *Living with Separation in China* (2003), and the co-editor, with Rita Astuti and Jonathan Parry, of *Questions of Anthropology* (2007).

**Nireka Weeratunge** is Senior Scientist (Gender and Social Development) at The WorldFish Center in Penang, Malaysia. Her research focuses on discourses and sociocultural practices relating to livelihoods, micro- and small enterprise, poverty, well-being, gender, and the environment in the context of globalization and change in rural communities in Asia and the Pacific. Her publications include *Aspects of Ethnicity and Gender among the Rodi of Sri Lanka* (1988, reissue 2002), "Nature, Harmony and the Kaliyugaya: Global/local Discourses on the Human-Environment Relationship" (*Current Anthropology*, 2000), as well as work on entrepreneurship in Sri Lanka.

**Shirley Yeung** is a Ph.D. student in the Department of Anthropology at the University of Chicago. She has co-authored articles on the life histories of Philippine migrants in Toronto and has also written on "liberation" psychology in the Philippines and therapeutic practice in Alcoholics Anonymous. Her current research focuses on questions of citizenship, health and healing, and multilingualism in present-day Switzerland.

**Donna J. Young** teaches anthropology at the University of Toronto, Scarborough. She is the co-editor, with Anne Meneley, of *Auto-ethnographies: The Anthropology of Academic Practices* (2005). She has written on the subject of memory and narrative in Atlantic Canada, most recently in *Ethnos* (2008). Her current work explores the intersection of religion and ethics for Christian pilgrims in Israel and Palestine.

# ORDINARY ETHICS

# INTRODUCTION

## *Michael Lambek*

Ethnographers commonly find that the people they encounter are trying to do what they consider right or good, are being evaluated according to criteria of what is right and good, or are in some debate about what constitutes the human good. Yet anthropological theory tends to overlook all this in favor of analyses that emphasize structure, power, and interest. The essays collected in this volume demonstrate the centrality of ethical practice, judgment, reasoning, responsibility, cultivation, and questioning in social life. They develop a cumulative argument for attending to the ethical in the anthropological study of social action and, indeed, in the human condition, and hence recast discussion "in ways that will force a rethinking of 'power.'"[1]

The phrase "ordinary ethics" signals several things. First, contributors argue that ethics is part of the human condition; human beings cannot avoid being subject to ethics, speaking and acting with ethical consequences, evaluating our actions and those of others, acknowledging and refusing acknowledgment, caring and taking care, but also being aware of our failure to do so consistently. As a species, given our consciousness, our socialization and sociality, and our use of language, we are fundamentally ethical; as Signe Howell puts it, "humans everywhere are cognitively and emotionally predisposed toward moral sensibility" (1997: 10). I argue below that ethics is intrinsic to speech and action, and other contributors show how it is specified through cultural values and social projects. Moreover, as Alan Rumsey argues in his chapter (supported by arguments in Webb Keane's), the bases of the ethical predisposition are no doubt both ontogenetic and phylogenetic. Indeed, recent work by developmental psychologists more or less corroborates long-standing arguments by psychoanalysts that ethics is intrinsic to human character formation. Freudians argue that healthy socialization entails the development of a conscience,

1. The phrase is Webb Keane's (pers. comm.). Thanks to him, James Laidlaw, and Shirley Yeung for very helpful comments on the penultimate draft, and Kristina Kyser for superbly insightful editing.

and they have observed the significant operations of guilt—at both conscious and unconscious levels.[2] Moving beyond drive theory, psychoanalytic object relations theorists (e.g., Mitchell 1988) analyze the ontogeny of moral selves with respect to a relational matrix. In being acknowledged and in internalizing the acknowledgment of others, infants grow capable of acknowledging others and themselves. Concomitantly, ethology has begun to shift from neo-evolutionary obsessions with aggression and selfishness toward the ethical (Warneken and Tomasello 2006).

Aristotle saw ethics as indicative of the human telos; humans strive for excellence and well-being, asking everywhere "How ought I to live?" But insofar as ethics is in all these respects basic to the human condition, it need not be singled out as an explicit category or department of human thought nor constituted, as Maurice Bloch (1992 and elsewhere) sees religion and as some philosophers have seen metaphysics, at the expense of the ordinary. A call for "ordinary ethics" echoes arguments of Wittgenstein and Austin with respect to "ordinary language." We may find the wellsprings of ethical insight deeply embedded in the categories and functions of language and ways of speaking, in the commonsense ways we distinguish among various kinds of actors or characters, kinds of acts and manners of acting; in specific nouns and adjectives, verbs and adverbs, or adverbial phrases, respectively; thus, in the shared criteria we use to make ourselves intelligible to one another, in "what we say when."[3] At least we can say that "only ordinary language is powerful enough to overcome its own inherent tendency to succumb to metaphysical denunciations of its apparent vagueness, imprecision, superstition—not overcome this once and for all, but in each incidence of our intellectual and spiritual chagrin" (Cavell 2004: 8).

Second, then, the "ordinary" implies an ethics that is relatively tacit, grounded in agreement rather than rule, in practice rather than knowledge or belief, and happening without calling undue attention to itself. When, by contrast, ethics does become explicit, that is generally (1) in respect to its breaches; (2) with regard to ethical problems or issues in which the right thing to do is unknown or hotly contested; (3) in prophetic movements of social and ethical renewal; and (4) among priestly classes attempting to rationalize and educate. Historically, ethics has been closely related

---

2. For a classic ethnographic assimilation of these ideas, see Obeyesekere (1981).

3. Wittgenstein's and Austin's invocations of the ordinary are not identical, and Cavell's own profound exploration is largely beyond the scope of this essay. Austin's attention to the spoken word is most straightforward; his "A Plea for Excuses" (1961b) is a classic locus.

to religion, to theodicy and the problem of evil. Through religion, the ordinary is transcended and ethics intellectualized, materialized, or transcendentalized. Today, in a context one can loosely call "secular" (bearing in mind the debates that currently swirl around the concept), the subject of "ethics" is more closely connected to law and regulation, with respect to such matters as professional conduct, human rights, refuge and citizenship, retributive and redistributive justice, reproduction, and bioethics. However, the present book intends to go deeper; the focus is less on special cases, unusual circumstances, new horizons, professional rationalizations, or contested forms of authorization than on everyday comportment and understanding. Some chapters do touch on such matters, but precisely to show how they are drawn into and draw from the ordinary.[4] One of the questions implicitly raised is whether and how ordinary ethical sensibilities are coarsened or heightened with respect to broad social forces such as consumer capitalism, media advertising, inequality, violence, and specific forms of discipline, such as boot-camp army training (or other ascetic practices).[5]

The ordinary might be compared to Aristotle's concept of actuality (*energeia*) and the unity of means and ends. Consider Hannah Arendt's gloss on this. Actuality designates "all activities that do not pursue an end and leave no work behind, but exhaust their full meaning in the performance itself" (1998: 206, Greek omitted).[6] This is life as lived for itself.

> This specifically human achievement lies altogether outside the category of means and ends; the "work of man" is no end because the means to achieve it—the virtues, or *aretai*—are not qualities which may or may not be actualized, but are themselves "actualities." In other words, the means to achieve the end would already be the end; and this "end," conversely, cannot be considered a means in some other respect, because there is nothing higher to attain than this actuality itself. (ibid. 207)

In this sense, the ordinary is intrinsically ethical and ethics intrinsically ordinary.

---

4. Contributors were instructed not to focus on bioethical regimes, human rights, or the ethics of anthropology. Naturally, these topics creep back in, as it is a feature of ordinary ethics that it cannot be compartmentalized, and likewise a feature of anthropological practice that it cannot be divorced from its subject matter.

5. Under certain circumstances, everyday acts of humiliation may come to seem very ordinary indeed. A comparison of Caton and Young's chapters with those by Das and Kwon is instructive.

6. *Energeia*—full actuality—"effects and produces nothing besides itself" (Arendt 1998: 206n37).

Insofar as ordinary ethics refers to the actual and circumstantial—specific instances of conduct, insight, action, or dilemma—anthropology, in its ethnographic refraction, can usefully respond to Austin's request for "fieldwork in philosophy." Ethnography supplies case material that speaks to the urgency and immediacy yet ordinariness of the ethical rather than reverting to hypothetical instances and ultimately to reified abstractions.[7] "What we say when" is not always what armchair philosophers, or even seasoned fieldworkers, imagine. When a granary collapsed on a senior man in a village in Mayotte, people spoke not of witchcraft but of his survival as a sign of God's mercy; yet the death of his daughter (who had not been anywhere near the granary) some years later was attributed to the man's conduct while pinned under it (Lambek 1993). The individual incident is located within the stream of particular lives and the narratives that are constituted from them, changing its valence in relation to the further unfolding of those lives and narratives and never fully determined or predictable. Jack Sidnell's chapter uses microscopic conversational analysis to show what we actually do say when—and how this saying is ethical to its roots.

Finally, ordinary ethics recognizes human finitude but also hope. Ordinary experience encompasses the inevitable cracks and ruptures in the actual and the ubiquity of responses to the ever-present limits of criteria and paradoxes of the human condition, hence the attempts in everyday practice and thought to inhabit and persevere in light of uncertainty, suffering, injustice, incompleteness, inconsistency, the unsayable, the unforgivable, the irresolvable, and the limits of voice and reason.[8]

## Conversing with Philosophy

This book emerges from a workshop on the anthropology of ordinary ethics held at the University of Toronto, October 6 to 9, 2008.[9] The workshop was organized to explore the significance of ethics for social theory and ethnographic depiction, and also to encourage conversation between anthropology and philosophy. Similar endeavors have been suggested in

---

7. Philosophers have generally preferred the texts of literature to those of ethnography as source material, but see Lear (2006). Hacking (1998) has pursued actual fieldwork to brilliant philosophical effect.

8. See the compelling essays by Das (2007).

9. Papers were pre-circulated and intensively discussed at the workshop. For further details, please see the Acknowledgments to this volume.

recent articles by James Faubion (2001a) and James Laidlaw (2002), and are evident in their respective contributions here. To do this, it turns out, also requires building a bridge between certain trends in sociocultural anthropology, on the one side, and linguistic anthropology, on the other. That is because ethics is intrinsically linked to speaking as much as it is to action, and indeed, the move in linguistic anthropology has been to understand speech not only within the context of action but *as* action. Linguistically oriented anthropologists have taken the lead both in identifying the ethical quality of action and in engaging with philosophy of language. A notable feature of this book is that it convenes scholars who start from the analysis of speech or language ("linguistic anthropologists") together those who start from social action or relations or specific cultural practices ("sociocultural anthropologists"). However, rather than reproducing or defending distinct subdisciplinary paradigms, we attempt a collective conversation. Together we are concerned with the ethical entailments of speech and action and, as noted, of speech as action.

Compared with the long and distinguished traditions of Aristotelian, Kantian, and consequentialist ethics within philosophy, anthropologists, with some notable exceptions, have had relatively little to say explicitly about ethics and the ethical, or at least have not woven their insights into a full picture. This situation is rapidly changing.[10] *Ordinary Ethics* brings together for the first time several anthropologists who have independently initiated this "ethical turn" and begun to theorize and document the centrality of ethics for human life. Moreover, contributors recognize that an adequate approach to ethics must be philosophically informed. Collectively, we draw from the insights of philosophers and engage in closer dialogue with philosophy than has been the norm in anthropology.[11] In the interests of interdisciplinary polylogue, we include a chapter by an

---

10. The impetus thus overlaps, but does not coincide, with the "turn to ethics" as critically observed within the Humanities (Garber et al. 2000). For pioneering anthropological works, see Burridge (1960, 1969), Edel and Edel (1970), Fortes (1987), Read (1955), Vogt and Albert (1966). Significant recent contributions include Barker (2007), Evens (2008), Hirschkind (2006), Howell ed. (1997), R. Kelly (1993), Laidlaw (1995), Lambek (1993), Mahmood (2005), Meneley (1996), Overing ed. (1985), Parry and Bloch (1989), Robbins (2004), Shoaps (2004), Sykes (2005), and Zigon (2008).

11. Again, worthy predecessors abound. See, inter alia, Crapanzano (2004), Geertz (2000a), Hollis and Lukes (1982), Jackson (1989), Lévi-Strauss (1966), Needham (1972), Rabinow (1996), Wilson ed. (1970), and other works by these authors.

analytic philosopher, Judith Baker, written in response to chapters by
Francesca Merlan and Charles Stafford.

This book is not a comparative or descriptive study of ethics but a series
of reflections on the place of ethics in human life and the ways in which
attention to the ethical can enrich theory and deepen ethnographic analyses. Our intention is both to draw from the debates of moral philosophy
and to contribute an anthropological voice to them. Our ethics is neither
prescriptive nor universalist, in the sense of advocating uniform global
rights or straining for a version of the common good. We try to be vigilant
lest ethics replace politics and at the same time we remain skeptical of
moralism. We do not begin with a definition of ethics itself. Because contributors draw from a variety of philosophical traditions and arguments,
we vary accordingly the emphasis we give to various themes associated
with the subject—freedom, judgment, responsibility, dignity, self-fashioning, care, empathy, character, virtue, truth, reasoning, justice, and the
good life for humanity. While not speaking in unanimity, we share a general perspective from which we can fruitfully build, but also debate one
other. We have in common an unease with reigning theoretical paradigms,
whether grounded in evolutionary psychology or political economy, that
begin or rest with individual or sectional group interest or competition. In
this respect, we follow in the tradition of broadly Aristotelian political
philosophers, like Canadian theorist C. B. Macpherson, who wrote of
human capacities (1973) and Arendt, who developed ideas of creative action and forgiveness (1998), but also in the tradition of analytic philosophy
(Wittgenstein, Austin, Grice, Strawson, Cavell, Williams) that attends
closely to the ethical entailments of speech and language, to the fine discriminations among, and weighty consequences of, what we say and do.
Attention to such thinkers can sharpen and deepen ethnographic portraits
and cultural analyses.

While each of us attends to language, a number of the contributors
evoke a sense of ethics that precedes, exceeds, or escapes specific words
and acts, suggesting a productive tension between more formal and more
existential concerns in any full account of the ethical. Many of the chapters
locate ethics in the dialectical movement between the spoken and the unspoken or, more generally, between objectification and embodiment—
between words, rules, and objects and tacit bodily disposition,
comportment, affect, and character. This is paralleled by, if not quite the
same thing as, trying to catch the leap between the ostensible and the
subjunctive, to dress up the old distinction between the "is" and the
"ought." This moment of the creative act, insight, initiative, or coming

into being might be celebrated as the human condition of (or capacity for) "natality," following Arendt (1988: 8–9); Faubion (below) terms it the Weberian primal scene. In any case, where Kantian ethics begins with reason and its objectification in propositional language, many of us try to evade Kantian oppositions between sense and reason by returning to Aristotle and locating ethics first in practice and action. Broadly speaking, recourse to Aristotle enables one to evade what Faubion (2001a) in a striking pun calls the "two mutually repellent extremes" of decisionism (economic or Sartrean) and determinism, with their polarizations of agency and structure, or choice and compulsion. Equally, it evades excessive polarizations between the rational and irrational, objective and subjective, rule and behavior (Lambek 2000, 2010). This, in turn, suggests how attention to ethics may contribute to thinking through the relation of culture to social action.

As the various chapters show, attending to the ethical provokes reconsideration of the basic terms in the anthropological tool kit—language, culture, politics, social structure, practice, agency, and the like. We do not attempt to distinguish ethics as something discrete and thus in explicit relationship to other objects of inquiry but rather explore how attention to the ethical might shift or deepen our understanding of social life more generally. A question faced by all the contributors is how to bridge gaps in scale of inquiry and which tools to use to cross between the mind and the social, or between philosophy and history. The point is less to purify a notion of ethics or delimit its province than to recognize the ethical dimensions—including the uncertainty, polyvalence, or ambivalence—of selfhood, social encounters, and action. In general, we locate the ethical in the conjunction or movement between explicit local pronouncements and implicit local practices and circumstances. We also want to discern its place within specific events and histories, which then become no longer simply either the idealized reenactments of key scenarios or the cynical playing out of strategies and interests in competitive games of power and prestige. In any case, the respective strengths and weaknesses of both structuralism and practice theory are placed on the table in a number of the chapters, and the question to what degree a focus on the ethical enables us to transcend or reformulate their dialectic is raised.

While a central goal of this volume is to enhance communication between anthropology and philosophy, we do not anticipate that "ethics" could become a central topic or scholarly specialty in anthropology analogous to its position within philosophy (without thereby becoming philosophy). This is both because of the different ways in which the disciplines constitute their objects of inquiry and because of their respective histories. If philosophy has the advantage over anthropology in maintaining a long tradition of studying ethics, it has inherited the problem that alternative subtraditions are often understood as mutually exclusive. One is a deontologist or a virtue theorist, an analytic or a continental philosopher, etc., and one defends one's position. While some philosophers seem to think it their task to purify highly specific arguments about ethics—thereby emphasizing the contrasts between various thinkers—anthropologists, qua outsiders, can afford a more pragmatic approach. Indeed, one of the foundational texts in anthropology, Marcel Mauss's *The Gift*, is informed in roughly equal measure by Aristotelian and Kantian ideas, while explicitly firmly rejecting utilitarian ones.

In sum, the chapters offer an exploration of the significance of the ethical in human speech, action, and thought, and concomitantly of selected strands from the broad philosophical tradition for grasping that significance. We argue the indispensability of the ethical for social theory and ethnography, and we demonstrate how ethnographic encounter and anthropological analysis might in turn enrich a philosophical understanding of ethics.

## *Constituting a Subject—or Identifying a Category Error?*

In writing about "ethics" as anthropologists we must be aware of whether we are simply adopting the natives' term and arguments—in this case our own or those of our philosophers—or attempting to take some distance from them. Insofar as we are conversing with philosophers rather than conducting an anthropological account of philosophy,[12] we do not begin by deconstructing the basic terms or putting them in a yet more abstract meta-language. When we write of "philosophy" and "philosophers," we do not address the question of whether this refers to a specifically "Western" tradition; this important task is best left to other occasions.

Were we doing an anthropological account of philosophy, we would immediately discern the presence of two key but overlapping terms, namely, *ethics* and *morality*. In this work, except where some contributors specifically distinguish them, we use the terms interchangeably, though

---

12. For two quite different attempts at the latter, see Kresse (2007) and Sahlins (1996).

with preference for *ethics*. The reason for this is simple—the many interesting distinctions made between "ethics" and "morality" in the philosophical and, to a lesser extent, the social science literature are not consistent with one another. Maintaining such a distinction is thus bound either to lead to confusion or to limit discussion to the province of one particular thinker. We prefer *ethics* to *morality* due to its prominence in philosophy and its possibly greater association with action than propriety and with "the good" than "the right." A further convention of this book is much simpler: we treat *ethics* as a singular noun.

There is a more basic ambiguity. The word *ethical* is used in common speech to refer both to the field in which criteria are applied or practical judgment enacted and to the positive valence put on certain acts. In the latter case, ethical and unethical acts are specifically distinguished from one another, but it is not so clear what is the "other" to the ethical in the former sense. For the most part, we are using *ethical* in the broader sense, referring to the field of action or practical judgment rather than to what is specifically right or good, but the reader has to exercise some discernment.

Most broadly, we use *ethics* as a cover term for recognizing the complexity and perhaps inconsistency of human action and intention, a complexity that we think is neglected in much social theory, leading to various kinds of reduction and caricature. This complexity is the subject of philosophy; within contemporary social science its recognition may be most readily found in the fine-grained analyses of anthropological linguists and also in certain phenomenologically or hermeneutically oriented ethnographic accounts. In this sense, ethics is far from the presumptions of moral codes and prescriptions and closer to irony, particularly in the sense of recognizing the limits of self-understanding (Nehamas 1998: 67) and that one cannot fully know that one means what one says or does (Cavell 1976).[13] In this formulation (and in contrast to ordinary usages of the word *irony*), the

---

13. Irony recognizes the burden of making truth and clarity central to ethics. Understood as "acknowledged concealment," irony moves interpretation away from the question of truth versus deceit since, "Like truthfulness, concealment does not distort the truth; like lying, it does not reveal it" (Nehamas 1998: 62). Additionally, "irony often insinuates that something is taking place inside you that your audience is not allowed to see, but it does not always entail that you see it yourself. Irony often communicates that only part of a picture is visible to an audience, but it does not always entail that the speaker sees the whole. Sometimes, it does not even imply that a whole picture exists." (ibid. 67, cf. Lambek 2003a: 51–52).

ironic is opposed to neither the serious nor the well intentioned.[14] This is a lesson I have drawn from studying spirit possession, which always and of necessity operates at multiple levels, simultaneously of startling direction and impressive indirection, presence and absence, said and unsaid, insight and self-deception.

While some scholars have proposed an "anthropology of ethics" and there has been discussion (notably by some contributors to this volume) as to why its appearance is belated, we do not collectively advocate the formulation of another explicit object of study or another subfield, but rather seek to acknowledge the ubiquity of the ethical and to explore the ways in which it pervades ordinary speech, action, and the situation of persons living together. It makes as little (or as much) sense to speak of an anthropology of ethics as of an anthropology of power, interest, or desire. The anthropology of ethics, in this sense, is hardly a subdisciplinary equivalent to the anthropology of economy, religion, medicine, or politics.[15] And even if it were, the status of all such subfields is questionable, running against anthropology's central tenets of holism, particularism, and genealogical skepticism. The task is to recognize the ethical dimension of human life—of the human condition—without objectifying ethics as a natural organ of society, universal category of human thought, or distinct kind of human practice. In sum, it is preferable to see the ethical as a modality of social action or of being in the world than as a modular component of society or mind. Of course, this is not to ignore the historical dimensions of ethical thought, practices in which the ethical dimension is particularly salient, and accounts that discern the priestly objectification of morality, the philosophical objectification of ethics, the rearticulating of ethics to religion and law in modernity, or the new arena of "expertise" that is bioethics.

In late-nineteenth-century Scotland, as MacIntyre pithily describes (1990: 26), morality was conceived as a distinct compartment of social life, one concerned with observing rules—or rather, negative prohibitions—and responding with condemnation to their breaches; this was mirrored in its depiction as an object of study at the onset of anthropology. Today the temptation to objectify ethics—and hence an anthropology of ethics—is

---

14. Nehamas discusses Socrates, Plato, and Nietzsche. But perhaps Kierkegaard is the predecessor who most explicitly recognizes and deeply explores the relationship of irony to seriousness. Geertz (2000b) elucidates what he calls "anthropological irony" precisely in a discussion of the ethics of fieldwork.

15. However, like these categories, "ethics" becomes objectified within modernity; see the chapter by Webb Keane.

enhanced by our own subjection to a growing objectified ethics of anthropology, inscribed in professional codes and constituted through bureaucratic institutions and auditing procedures like ethics review boards and informed consent forms (practices that are as much about passing on liability as cultivating an ethical disposition). Insofar as we could mistake such discursive formations for a natural ethics, assume a discrete institution of ethics characteristic of all human societies, or, conversely, praise ourselves for ethical advancement above and beyond other societies or professions, we would be guilty of parochialism or ethnocentrism. We would thereby also be tempted to clarify rules and certainties in a domain that is characterized by uncertainty.

More than all this, I think that in distinguishing the ethical as a distinct realm of human thought or action we might be guilty of committing what Gilbert Ryle (1949) famously described as a category mistake. Rather than attempting to locate and specify a domain of ethics, we ought to clarify and deepen our understanding of the ethical quality or dimension of the full range of human action and practice. Insofar as ethics is a dimension, feature, quality, or entailment of action (acts and utterances), it becomes a false problem, a category mistake, to distinguish what is covered by ethics from what is not, that is, to distinguish the ethical as a particular domain of social life or human experience. We cannot say of something that it was an act and also a subject for ethics as if those were distinct. Formally, the relation of ethics to action is analogous to the mind/body problem as discerned by Ryle. Ethics : action :: mind : body.

However, while it may be relatively easy to identify category mistakes, it is much harder to correct them, and in some cases it may be impossible. Some category errors may be imposed on us by the human condition, and the best we can do is to recognize them at times. Indeed, the attempt to do so might be described as ethical. Put another way, category errors—or the paradoxes of incommensurability—may provoke us to ethical agitation, for example, around matters of intentionality and the final locus of responsibility.

Instead of identifying a fixed object or locus of study, an anthropological account of ethics might be characterized by its attention to the following matters, among others: the indexical qualities of language; the entailments of speaking, speech acts, and ritual performances; the establishment and recognition of criteria as well as the angst, anomie, vertigo, and, possibly, freedom incurred in their failure or absence; the means of attribution and acknowledgment—public and private, tacit and explicit—of intention, responsibility, and reasons for action; the exercise of practical judgment; the forms of sustained attention and labor subsumed under the concept or practice of "care"; the virtues embedded in or constitutive of any given set of cultural practices and of local depictions of character; the socialization or cultivation of ethical persons; and the confrontation with paradox, chiasm, guilt, rupture, otherness, violence, the intractable, destiny, and evil. However, before turning to some of these issues here and in the next chapter, I will briefly attend to the two main modes of addressing ethics from within anthropology.

## Durkheimian and Boasian Alternatives

Any new approach to ethics ought to avoid the corners that earlier anthropological accounts—informed by either the Durkheimian concern with rules and obligation ("morality") or the Boasian focus on discrete values—ostensibly paint us into. Laidlaw (2002) has suggested why the British Durkheimian route proved sterile. Associating the ethical with the obligatory and identifying the latter as the criterion for social facts meant that anthropologists were unable to distinguish the ethical from the entire realm of the social; moreover, this limited the field to the "moral" one of constraint and conformity, thereby excluding, as Laidlaw, following Bernard Williams, puts it, the "ethical" one of freedom and creativity. The first of these criticisms should serve as a caution to my own enterprise. With respect to the second, in fact, Durkheim and many of his followers, such as Mauss, Evans-Pritchard, or Meyer Fortes, were subtler than their critics would imply. Thus, for example, Eduardo Archetti, in an otherwise delightful and illuminating essay, notes that ethics should be conceived more dynamically and advises that "Morality requires compassion, fervour and a sense of engagement" (1997: 100), without noticing that he is actually adapting a phrase from Bryan Turner's depiction of Durkheim in his preface to Durkheim's *Professional Ethics and Civic Morals* (1992: xxvi). And far from resting with order and propriety, Franz Steiner (1956), Mary Douglas (1966), and others were able to show the far-reaching implications of its violation. Moreover, one of the attractions of Durkheim is his dualism, which, like Freud's, recognizes an internal rift and hence a tragic dimension of human being. Ethics is not a matter of smoothly following the rules but of the exhilaration of self-transcendence, as well as the struggle with ambivalence and conflict. Society "obliges us to surpass ourselves" (Durkheim 1973: 163); we may do so willingly, even joyfully, but we do so always with a residue of tension. Nevertheless, it is true that Durkheim offers little room for action and hence for "dilemma, reasoning, decision, and doubt" (Laidlaw 2002: 315). In the chapters that follow there are echoes of "multiple Durkheims."

By contrast, the American Boasian route foundered on the specter of relativism. The often-compelling identification of particular cultural values produced overly homogeneous and bounded portraits, objectifying both individual values and the cultures they composed. This appeared to reduce questions of ethics to debates over cultural relativism, then to move rapidly from cultural to ethical relativism, and to distort the question of relativism itself. In fact, however, the Boasians left room for internal cultural debate; after all, Paul Radin wrote a book called Primitive Man as Philosopher (1957 [1927]). Boas and others balanced their particularism with universalism.[16] Moreover, to recognize something as ethical for someone or to see how it fits into a particular context need not entail advocating it. Relativism itself becomes less of a threat once it is understood in its own terms, namely, relatively. The fact that relativism can never be either fully consistent or complete is part of its own self-understanding (rather than a devastating critique), and relativism is in fact more realistic about mind, nature, and society than its antithesis. Geertz was absolutely (or relatively) correct to advocate not relativism but what he called "anti-anti-relativism" (2000c). In any case, Geertz was a particularist, not specifically a relativist. In his early essays (especially 1973b), it is evident he is trying, not to support relativism as opposed to universalism, but rather to explore how we might find the universal within the particular. He supports his philosophical position on evolutionary grounds (1973c), namely, that human biology is shaped by dependence on culture—and culture is by its nature always (universally) particular, that is, can only manifest itself particularly (as with language—we don't speak language in general, but one particular version of it at a time).

This volume attempts to discern a path that is neither relativist nor antirelativist and that does not oppose particularism to universalism. Such an opposition would be another instance of a category mistake. This is easier said than understood, and when it was said (or implied) by Geertz, he was generally misunderstood.

## From Kantian Reason to Aristotelian Activity

Both the Boasian and the Durkheimian approaches have strong roots in Kant. There is much that is admirable in Kant, but it could be said that he focuses too heavily on the rational. Kantian dualisms of man and

---

16. I thank Maurice Bloch for the reminder.

nature, reason and sensory perception, freedom and constraint, get transformed in a variety of ways within anthropology but in general remain too much at the level of the ideal at the expense of the material, embodied, emotional, or practical. One way to attempt to avoid this path is to go back and start before Kant made his interventions.[17] Specifically, by returning to Aristotle, we can take ethics to be fundamentally a property or function of action rather than (only) of abstract reason. Aristotle does not begin with a primary distinction between reason and its other but rather distinguishes among several equally human forms of activity, namely, making (creation, poiesis), doing (action, praxis), and thinking (contemplation, theoria). Aristotle locates ethics as a dimension of action, whereas many philosophers, not surprisingly, given their vocation, have preferred to see it as an aspect of thought. (Indeed, Aristotle himself ended by favoring the contemplative life.) The latter path leads not only to critique but rapidly to portraying ethics as a set of values, rules, or conventions, and hence raises questions of their universality or correctness. I take the elaboration of values or rules to be already an abstraction or rationalization of what is found in ordinary action. It not only objectifies ethics but risks literalizing ethical insight and rendering it static.

I will return shortly to ethics as a function of action, but first inquire whether ethics is not also a function of making. Some have argued, as did Edmund Leach, "logically, aesthetics and ethics are identical" (1954: 12). Leach cites Wittgenstein, whose actual words were:

> It is clear that ethics cannot be expressed.
> Ethics is transcendental.
> (Ethics and aesthetics are one.)[18]

---

17. This is a turn that a number of philosophers have also made since the eighties. Kant, too, saw ethics as a matter of practical reason; see note 22, below, for further discussion.

18. This is the 1922 translation by C. K. Ogden from Wittgenstein's *Tractatus* 6.421:

> Es ist klar, dass sich die Ethik nicht aussprechen laesst.
> Die Ethik ist transzendental.
> (Ethik und Aesthetik sind eins.)

An alternate translation, by D. F. Pears and R. F. McGuinness (Wittgenstein 1961), reads:

> It is clear that ethics cannot be put into words.
> Ethics is transcendental.
> (Ethics and aesthetics are one and the same.)

I am indebted to Ian Hacking for providing these sources.

Without pursuing Wittgenstein's meaning or investigating aesthetics directly (but see the chapter by Justin Richland), I note instead how Arendt's significant emendation of the Aristotelian triad of making, doing, and thinking inflects the question. In *The Human Condition* (1998 [1958]), she distinguishes between two forms of making, namely, "work" and "labor." "Work" refers to the production of finished products, durable "works," notably works of art (of which, following the classical Greeks, her exemplary case is sculpture, perhaps the most durable) but also applies to the field of economic production more generally.[19] By "labor" Arendt indicates the daily chores characteristic of the private household or farm in contrast to exemplary productions and interventions in the public sphere. Labor refers to continuous or repetitive life-reproducing activities rather than marked spurts of work productive of discrete and durable objects. Thus one may contrast the "work of art" with a "labor of love." Perhaps cleaning is the exemplary form of labor; it is "never done" and leaves nothing to show for itself.

Although Arendt seems more or less to agree with the Greek devaluation of private labor in favor of public works, she anticipates feminist attention to processes of reproduction. Critical to reproductive labor is not only the literal process of giving birth (which, as Arendt astutely notes, Indo-European languages refer to as "labor" rather than "work") but also childcare. In feminist ethics, "care" itself has become a central concept (Noddings 1984). In fact, the Arendtian category of labor both undermines any clear distinction between production and action (hence aesthetics and ethics) and locates itself firmly in the sphere of the ordinary.[20] Care signifies, in the first instance, looking after, or looking out for, the well-being of others, and as such it both is central to what anthropologists have constructed as the domain of kinship and serves to remind us that kinship is fundamentally a realm of ethical activity (Faubion 2001b). Care also transcends any distinction between the rational and the sensory. But more than this, "care" can serve, like "seriousness" or "sincerity," as a significant felicity condition or at least as an attribute of practice, in the manner

---

19. More specifically, work produces goods for use, while labor produces goods for consumption. Arendt argues that the industrial revolution has replaced work with labor, leading to the decline of durable objects. Thus, "the ideals of *homo faber*, the fabricator of the world, which are permanence, stability, and durability, have been sacrificed to abundance, the ideal of the *animal laborans*" (1998: 126).

20. Many thinkers have noted that, on close inspection, the distinction between doing and making is hard to maintain. Thus we say in English that to "execute" a judgment is to "make" it.

that we "take care" not only to say and do the right thing but to say and do things well, to do them carefully. This is an affirmation of both Aristotelian notions of virtue as excellence and Heideggerian concern with being, as well as a reminder that practice theory's focus on routinized disposition needs to be supplemented with the disposition to take care, to carry out one's tasks with due attention and consideration.

In his late work, Michel Foucault also draws on Greek ideas of making or creation in his discussion of ethics, which he conceives in terms of care of the self, self-fashioning, and making one's life a work of art. Faubion argues that Foucault restores the "poetic pitch" to what Aristotle restricts to a form of doing, and thus "the genuine complexity of ethical subject-formation" (2001a: 94). Nevertheless, I prefer Nehamas's phrase of "the art of living" (1998), which could combine autopoiesis with Arendt's attention to care and to cleaning up after oneself and others, and could also be understood as a kind of practice of practices.[21] A focus on self-fashioning can open up questions concerning how much each of us is part of others and how much my self is determined by the self-making projects or the acts of others, as well as the acts I carry out for, in respect to, or inextricably interconnected with others, and to what degree such "dividualism" (Marriott 1976, Strathern 1988) or intersubjectivity is locally recognized or occluded. Thinking through the contrast between an individualist "Western" or "modern" subject and a dividualistic "non-Western" one, as well as the typically gendered opposition between self- and other-oriented subjects, might benefit from attention to matters of ethical cultivation and self-fashioning, and conversely. These matters are variously taken up in the chapters by Francesca Merlan, Carlos Londoño Sulkin, and Paul Antze, among others.

## From Categorical Imperative to Foundational Act

I now return to the significance of an action-centered approach to ethics. The implications of the shift in focus from Kantian reason, Durkheimian rules, or Boasian values to Aristotelian practices and acts can be illustrated by treatments of the lie. Kant famously addressed the lie by saying that the only rational course for humans is to demand that everyone keep his

---

21. Arendt herself replaces the solipsism of Heidegger with attention to human plurality. As one sympathetic commentator puts it, "she has disclosed *the deep structure of human action as interaction*" (Benhabib 2003: 111, italics in original).

word. It would be illogical and lead to chaos if people routinely did not keep their promises; indeed, it would make the very concept of the promise contradictory. For Kant, if I expect other people to keep their word, then I must demand the same of myself. Hence keeping one's word is a categorical imperative. It is imperative or obligatory not because it is imposed by society but because it is imposed by reason.

Whatever the ripostes to Kant's rationalism, idealism, and universalism may be,[22] it is probably empirically the case that every known society values honesty and expects people to honor their promises and keep their word. However, as Rappaport (1999) notes, the possibility of the lie always lurks in the background (if it didn't, priests and jurists wouldn't come up with explicit injunctions); moreover, it is also the case that, for various reasons, people often fail to keep their word. Simply asserting the rule or value is insufficient to explain what happens. Specifically, the theory of language available to him makes it impossible for Kant to distinguish fully the ethical issues entailed in the prohibition against lying from those entailed in the act of promising (and perhaps from those entailed in the act of promising from the fact of keeping one's word).

To begin with, the promise is inherently interpersonal. Many theorists have seen it as an instance of a collective and legal construct they have termed the contract. In *The Gift* (1990 [1925]), Mauss both describes the historical roots of the contract in acts of exchange and considers what the unwritten or unstated rules or conditions are that make any given contract possible. Henri Hubert and Mauss had many years earlier written a book on sacrifice (1964 [1898]), in which they describe sacrifice as a ritual act and hence to be distinguished from any simple notion of a gift. But the lesson Mauss eventually took from this was that, if sacrifice is more than an instrumental gift, then in the end all gifts entail something of the sacramental or sacrificial. In other words, in the course of his thinking sacrifice became the model for the gift. Purely instrumental reason is rejected; in explicitly Durkheimian terms, impulses determined by human nature (needs or interests) are transcended by higher ideals afforded and demanded by society. In addition, what Mauss implicitly shows by the comparison with sacrifice is that giving and receiving are performative acts.

---

22. In fact, Kant distinguishes between what he calls perfect obligations, like refraining from false promises or coercion, and imperfect obligations, such as not failing to help others or developing your own potential. Imperfect obligations cannot prescribe universal performance. We can't help everyone in need or develop all our capacities equally, but we can "refuse to make indifference of either sort basic to our lives" (O'Neill 1991: 179). Insofar as imperfect obligations are a matter of judgment, they approximate the Aristotelian virtues.

Thus, *The Gift* is not simply a structural model of circulation or the found-ing text of practice theory but also an account of ritual action.

Explicitly, Mauss's essay is about the obligations to give, to return, and, perhaps most interestingly, to receive gifts. Yet it is the actual circulation of gifts in a given society or social world that underpins any particular instance of donation or reception. Moreover, in the societies that he exam-ines most closely, such acts of giving and receiving are carried out publicly. As "total social facts" they are at once economic and political, domestic and public, otherworldly and this-worldly, necessary and pleasurable. They are a matter of some formality and often of spectacle. Participants in the event acknowledge the actions of the central participants, thereby granting them dignity. In all this there is apparent the recognition of a close, if not intrinsic, relation between ritual and ethics. Giving and receiv-ing are not merely Durkheimian (or Kantian) moral *obligations*, but the active and formalized fulfillment of those obligations. Hence they are si-multaneously *acts*, embedded in a cycle of the production and cancellation of particular personal, interpersonal, and collective states and reestablish-ing the criteria through which persons and relationships are constituted and evaluated and the world renewed. Moreover, it is the ritual framework that establishes the authority and meaningfulness of any given act, that is, the "the contract behind the contract."[23]

If there is a contract behind the contract, perhaps there is also a debt behind the debt. Ethics must be grounded in prior acts, and specifically, ethics must address the rupture, wound, or fall of a debt already incurred, "an originary guilt or incrimination, a guilt or responsibility (*Schuldigsein*, as the German can luckily say in one word), the theme of a debt, an indebt-edness, a being-indebted, all originary, prior to any contract, prior to con-tracting anything" (Derrida 2008: 319–20). It is not only in the Abrahamic religions that this is articulated as some sort of primordial act of sacrifice that founds the system of value and exchange (Lambek 2007c, 2008).

In sum, I have moved here from a focus on an absolute prohibition against lying as seen through a Kantian lens to the ways in which promises or contracts, as interpersonal forms of relation, are instantiated. I suggest that what ritual acts like making sacrifices or giving and receiving gifts do is to initiate or cancel particular ethical criteria, conditions, or states,

---

23. See Rappaport (1999) for the larger argument about ritual founding the contract. This is not infinitely recursive (contracts behind contracts), as in Ryle's account of intentionality, because the process is grounded in a hierarchy of sanc-tity, whose first or final level is expressed in what Rappaport calls ultimate sacred postulates.

minimally of living under a promise, obligation, or debt but usually also connected to the production and circulation of value and to transformations in social status, relationship, honor, and the like. This argument about the ethical consequentiality of ritual action will be elucidated in my own chapter.

## Practice and Virtue

Implicit in this discussion has been a distinction between singular, irreversible acts and ongoing practice. It can be a distinctive task for an Aristotelian anthropology of ethics to articulate their relationship. Acts percolate from or disrupt the stream of practice, and they have consequences for subsequent practice. In moving from the performance of individuated acts to practice more generally—thus from specific acts of piety, generosity, etc. to practicing piety or generosity, and hence to acquiring or manifesting a pious or generous disposition and being or becoming a pious person—we enter the realm of virtue theory as initiated by Aristotle. Virtues are qualities of actions or practice and ultimately of actors (character). Virtues cannot be defined in an absolute sense but only insofar as they are contingently applied to specific actions, in specific circumstances. We judge an act courageous if a man jumps in the water to assist a flailing swimmer, but the same act is foolhardy if the current is too strong or the jumper does not know how to swim.

The point of virtue ethics is not to criticize or demand conformity of others but to guide us to live well. As Jonathan Lear (1988: 170) puts it, acting virtuously has three conditions. First, the actor must have practical knowledge, knowing what is right to do in the circumstances; second, she must choose the act, and for its own sake, because in the circumstances it is the right thing to do, rather than for some ulterior motive; and third, the act should flow from her character and not be a matter of chance.[24] These conditions are rather stiff, such that we might observe people acting more or less virtuously rather than completely or consistently so. Yet Aristotle is somewhat more realistic than Kant, since he grounds ethics in human motivation and desire rather than detached reasoning (ibid. 156–57). Aristotelian virtues are never abstractions or categorical but always a matter of judging the right balance to fit the immediate circumstances.

---

24. For another notable reading of Aristotelian ethics, see Gadamer (1975, 1979) and recapitulation in R. Bernstein (1983).

Every virtue thus presupposes two vices, one of insufficiency and the other of excess. Thus, generosity is not manifest in giving away everything one has but in the balance between prodigality and meanness. For Aristotle, the meta-virtue is that of *phronesis*, or temperance, that is, knowing how to find the judicious middle path between opposing extremes. *Phronesis* is central because it describes what practical judgment is, though here a closer translation is "wisdom."[25] In general, then, rather than attempting to discern or objectify specific virtues, an anthropological account of ordinary ethics might do better simply to observe ongoing practice, including local accounts of it.

Whereas an ethics of the extraordinary might posit freedom as its end or even its condition, an ethics of ordinary practice does better to stick with happiness (though as James Laidlaw [pers. comm.] points out, any exercise of judgment presupposes some measure of freedom). For Aristotle, acting ethically, like being healthy, is not a means to an end but constitutes a happy life (ibid. 158).[26] To be happy is for people to realize their nature, thus to exercise their capacities (Macpherson 1973).[27] However, "it seems part of man's nature to transcend nature" (Lear 1988: 165; note the parallel with Durkheim) and this entails organizing desires in order to develop character so that one is disposed to act virtuously. Character comes not from "internalizing a set of rules, for there are no rules to internalize" (ibid. 158), but rather from developing the capacity for doing good. "Habits . . . do not merely instill a disposition to engage in certain types of behavior: they instill a sensitivity as to how to act in various circumstances" (ibid. 166).

Aristotelian judicious practice has been elaborated in various ways by modern thinkers. In *The Gift*, Mauss demonstrates that giving entails a balance of interest and disinterest (Parry 1986), thereby exemplifying exactly what Aristotle said was intrinsic to the exercise of the virtues (Myhre 1998) and offering a more realistic formulation than an ethics of either

---

25. Virtue theorists debate whether the virtues are consistent or whether the virtuous person must judge between competing virtues to apply to the circumstances.

26. Aristotle may be too optimistic, but even for Freud, whose more modest goal is to reduce neurotic misery to ordinary unhappiness, the result is to be manifested through satisfaction in love and work.

27. These insights are taken up (if somewhat watered down) in the contemporary social science literature on "capabilities" (Sen 1999) and "well-being." See Corsín (2007) for an instructive set of essays.

pure self-denial or pure self-fashioning. Evans-Pritchard (1969) memorably describes as the lesson of *The Gift* that one belongs to others, not to oneself.[28] Bourdieu (1977), in turn, draws implicitly on Aristotle (perhaps via Mauss), yet it might be questioned whether, for Bourdieu, practice is any longer a matter of ethics. For one thing, it is much more individuated than in either Arendt or Mauss. For another, whereas the master virtue for Aristotle is temperance or wisdom (*phronesis*), it might be said that, for Bourdieu (although he does not actually draw on the language of the virtues), the master virtue would be cleverness or skill. That is because Bourdieu's model for practice is that of a game. Games have players, and hence winners and losers. The game is played in order to win or at least to get or stay ahead (ahead of others, ahead of the game). Life is a competition and ends are not always identified with means.

MacIntyre is helpful in clarifying what is at stake here.[29] He distinguishes the goods internal to a given practice from those external to it (1984: 187ff). In his sense, Bourdieu's practitioners can be said to be seeking goods external to their practice—fame, fortune, mastery over others, etc. (but also honor), whereas MacIntyre argues that the virtues should be understood with respect to goods internal to a specific practice—and, more generally, the good entailed in stretching one's capacities or the pleasure of playing well. This implies not that means are more important than ends ("it's not whether you win or lose but how you play the game") but that means and ends are one and the same, the means are the end ("being honest for honesty's sake," etc.). In effect, the means/end dichotomy is transcended, as we saw in Arendt's discussion of "actuality." Phrased another way, a practice is ethical insofar as the goal is not instrumental but reaching for excellence within the particular practice—and for human good or happiness overall in the practice of practices.

One field in which this can readily be observed is that of music. If not constrained by economic necessity to make money from their music, most people play for the pleasure of it and strive to play better for the rewards

---

28. *The Gift* also implicitly understands life as a kind of practice of practices and recognizes the significance of giving as itself an end. On a more collective level, Mauss addresses questions of the distribution of social goods and well-being in the modern state in an argument that links up with socialist theory and welfare economics (Graeber 2001).

29. MacIntyre does not specifically address Bourdieu, but his criticisms of Goffman are to the point (MacIntyre 1984: 115–16). See the chapters by Keane and Sidnell for a different take on Goffman.

that playing better and extending their skill entail in and of themselves. These are goals internal to the practice (musical goals) as opposed to the external goals of earning a contract or winning a competition.[30] Of course, these distinctions are not absolute, and it is not always easy to discern what is internal or external to a given practice. Moreover, one practice can draw upon or be embedded within another. Thus, if we listen to music for pleasure or instruction, we may cultivate our ear in order to become a better person. In the case described by Charles Hirschkind (2006), the means and virtues of listening to Islamic sermons are elaborated (often in the sermons themselves) according to a long tradition of auditory aesthetics. Here, listening well is a modality of piety, simultaneously a means and an end.

In the end, this approximates Aristotle's picture of realizing one's human nature. However, MacIntyre's distinction between goods internal and external to a given practice directs attention away from practice in the abstract toward the appreciation of specific *practices* in their complex social actuality, in a manner analogous to Geertz's shift from "culture" in general to "cultures" in their particularity (1973a) and to Wittgenstein's attention to specific language games. Practices are conceived as distinct and distinctive cultural phenomena entailing their own criteria. Playing string quartets is a practice, but so is embodying spirits or raising children. One of the things anthropology contributes is description and evocation of the diverse practices that passionately engage people in particular settings, such as piety in contemporary Cairo (Mahmood 2005, Hirschkind 2006), *kula* in the Trobriand Islands (as observed by Malinowski and many others since), art and pageantry in Bali (Geertz 1980 and others), or even a sort of negative practice like the discernment and disarming of witchcraft (as Evans-Pritchard records for the Azande [1937]) or the intensity of head-hunting for the Ilongot (Rosaldo 1980). Our own engagement in scholarship is a practice comparable to these. These are each cultural fields of "play" (played seriously), and some instantiate total social facts in Mauss's sense. Indeed, the practices described in *The Gift* are prototypes of this sort of thing. Such practices may afford internal competition and also external rewards for success—as Mauss indicates, practical judgment always

---

30. The situation is somewhat different with respect to intrinsically competitive sports, like football or tennis, but even here we recognize something like MacIntyre's distinction in the difference between amateurs and professionals, though presumably professionals too seek and experience the goods internal to their practice. Archetti (1997) vividly illustrates how football players in Argentina debate the respective values of playing beautifully and playing to win.

entails a balance of self-interest with disinterest—but above all, they provide orientation, motivation, and pleasure, and make life absorbing, worthwhile, and even exciting.

In attending to the goods embedded in practices, the study of ethics contributes to the understanding of culture by elaborating its vectoral qualities. As an ensemble of practices rather than texts, culture is a matter of passionate engagement rather than passive contemplation (though the latter may itself be a valued practice). Conversely, it is through the study of such cultural practices rather than of "values" taken in the abstract and external to any given practice that we can carry out a comparative cultural ethics (hence, in this respect, departing from a Boasian approach). Such an ethics is not relativist in an overarching sense, since the values are already internal to the practices concerned.[31]

Nevertheless, this picture is still too abstract. In real life, practices impinge on one another, and judgment must be exercised continuously between, for example, expending time on earning a living to feed your children and playing with them, or between playing with them and having time for yourself. Thus, while many Aristotelians have tried to inculcate or ascertain specific virtues, the master or meta-virtue for Aristotle remains simply finding the right balance both in the circumstances and in life overall. It is too easy, for example, simply to advocate or cultivate piety; one must know not only what the pious thing to do is in any given circumstance but also how to balance between being pious, nurturing, industrious, etc. Within a given social world, practices and their specific values and virtues may be articulated hierarchically with respect to one another. Judgment is also entailed in balancing or moving between incommensurable practices or, as Stafford notes in his chapter, between competing claims or private and public values.[32] As noted, practices are embedded within practices; living one's life may be the broadest, most encompassing practice of all, the practice of practices. In other words, we cannot simply limit ethics to the goods internal to a set of discrete bounded practices but must examine the juxtaposition of practices and the exercise of judging among incommensurable goods in "the art of living."

---

31. Moreover, while practices enable the exercise of certain human capacities for some members of society, they need to be balanced with opportunities for the exercise of other capacities (e.g., love in addition to musical skill) and for other members of society—servants, assistants, and clients as well as aristocrats, experts, and patrons, men as well as women, etc.

32. Elsewhere (Lambek 2008) I elaborate on hierarchies of value and distinguish judgment from choice according to the criterion of commensurability.

I briefly mention the contributions of two other thinkers with respect to practice. As is often the case, Weber appears to anticipate much of contemporary discussion. He formulates the vectoral qualities of ethical practice, especially in his notion of a "calling," and he mediates between goods internal and external to specific practices in his elaboration of four modes of orientation to social action, namely, rational orientation toward individual ends (*Zweckrationalität*), rational orientation toward an absolute value (*Wertrationalität*), affectual orientation, and traditional or habitual orientation (Weber 1947: 115ff). These are not necessarily mutually exclusive (ibid. 117), but Weber is more sociologically rigorous than any of the other thinkers mentioned, insofar as he attempts to associate particular orientations with particular social strata.[33] However, Weber possibly makes too sharp a distinction between the rational and the nonrational, and his concept of tradition here is insufficient. It could be replaced by MacIntyre's discussion of the way *all* meaningful practices are located within a tradition. For MacIntyre, tradition is "a historically extended community in which practices relevant to the fulfillment of human nature can be carried out" (Gutting 1999: 526–27). In MacIntyre's own words (1984: 222), "A living tradition . . . is an historically extended, socially embodied argument, and an argument precisely in part about the goods which constitute that tradition. Within a tradition the pursuit of goods extends through generations. . . . Hence the individual's search for his or her good is generally and characteristically conducted within a context defined by those traditions of which the individual's life is a part, and this is true both of those goods which are internal to practices and of the goods of a single life." Note that not only does MacIntyre allow here for the relevance to an individual of multiple traditions, but he also describes traditions as "arguments" and asserts that vital traditions "embody continuities of conflict" (ibid.).

Finally, Foucault considerably elaborates the dimensions of practice with respect to the self-constitution of ethical subjects. He delineates four aspects of relation to oneself, namely: the part of oneself that is singled out for concern; the mode of subjection or principle that legitimates or rationalizes one's self-subjection (reason, divine law, natural law, etc.); the means available for self-fashioning as an ethical subject; and the goal or kind of being subjects aspire to become (purity, devotion, self-mastery, etc.). The point here is how we constitute ourselves as the moral subjects of our own desires and actions (Foucault 1984: 352). However, Foucault

---

33. For sociological work on action theory, see Joas (1996).

is not studying the exigencies of actual practice, which, as both Arendt and Bourdieu remind us, always entails articulation with other persons, nor, perhaps, is he attending sufficiently to those dimensions of virtues like responsibility or cohabitation that respond in the first instance to the call of the other.[34]

## *Freedom and Judgment*

A practice approach raises the question of human freedom in a different manner from that of Kant, and here Foucault has been extremely helpful. Foucault's orientation is broadly similar to Weber's insofar as he emphasizes the disciplining and self-disciplinary dimensions of ethical subjects and is always attentive to the workings of power. In his later writing, Foucault shifts emphasis from governmentality to the power individuals exercise independently on themselves, in which self-regulation is seen as a freely chosen project involving available and imagined cultural models rather than being fully imposed or externally derived. As Laidlaw cogently notes, Foucault "does persistently distance himself from two utopian ideas about freedom (ideas which, being utopian, often lead in practice to the opposite of freedom): the idea that to act freely is to act in conformity with reason (or one's 'true' interests—this is the idea that lurks behind much anthropological use of 'agency'), and the idea that freedom is only possible in the total absence of constraint or relations of power" (Laidlaw 2002: 323). With respect to the first idea, Foucault's concept of freedom attempts to evade the Kantian dichotomy, still evident in Weber, between reason and sensory experience. With respect to the second idea, the pervasiveness of power must color the distinction between radical "ethics" and conventional "morality" that existentialists and some Foucauldians (after Nietzsche) wish to make.

Indeed, insofar as I am correct that ethics is intrinsic to the human condition, to the ordinary, to action, to self-fashioning, and to the presence of criteria, a distinction between ethics and morality as, respectively, freedom and convention, could be only relative. But this is less because of problems with the idea of an original or radically free ethical act than because ordinary acts are rarely the mere following of convention. As already implied, the tension between obligation or convention and freedom

---

34. This places Foucault in contrast with Levinas, a philosopher who deserves greater attention than he receives here.

is mediated by the concept of judgment. Here again Arendt makes an interesting intervention—following Heidegger, she distinguishes judgment from thinking. Judgment is perspectival and situated, in comparison to thinking, which is ostensibly neutral and objective.

> Judgment requires the moral-cognitive capacities for worldliness, that is, an interest in the world and in the human beings who constitute the world, and a firm grasp of where one's own boundaries lie and where those of others begin. . . . Whereas thinking requires autonomy, consistency, tenacity, independence, and steadfastness, judging requires worldliness, an interest in one's fellow human beings, and the capacity to appreciate the standpoint of others without projection, idealization, and distortion. (Benhabib 2003: 191; compare Steven Caton's chapter)

Judgment is neither as "free" as Kantian reason nor as constrained as conventional morality (there is such a thing as "poor judgment"). Moreover, Arendt's discernment of judgment is resolutely nonindividualistic; judgment occurs "in an anticipated communication with others with whom I know I must finally come to some agreement" (as cited by Benhabib 2003: 189). I suggest that judgment may be more appropriate than either freedom or convention as the fulcrum of everyday ethics.

However, this is not the end of the story, insofar as actors are obligated to live with the consequences of their acts. Specifically, they are subject to both the criteria that define their actions as acts of a certain kind and to the criteria their acts have specifically made relevant. Even acts that are relatively novel, momentous, and unconstrained, that mark new beginnings and definitive departures from what has preceded them, with consequences as yet unknown, are subject to definition and judgment after the fact.[35]

Let me take a concrete ethnographic example. Laidlaw (2002) has argued that, insofar as taking up ascetic practices is a choice for Jains rather than an obligation, it is a practice of freedom. Yet while it is true that the judgment to practice as an ascetic may be made more or less freely (but what of unconscious motivation and what of alternatives that have been cut off for reasons of birth, education, poverty, etc.?), as Laidlaw also shows (1995), the set of practices such a decision entails clearly are not free, and ascetics are judged according to how well they conform to them. Thus, if ascetics freely choose their acts, the means by which they carry

---

35. On acts of beginning, see, in addition to Arendt, Lambek (2007c), Said (1975), as well as the chapters by Faubion and Dave.

them out and what they commit or submit to fall within a given order that constitutes the acts as acts of a certain kind. This is clearly indicated by means of the vows that initiate the acts. Once they are engaged in the performance, as Maurice Bloch long ago remarked of religious ritual more generally (1989 [1974]), actors are obliged to follow quite a narrow path, and indeed there is hardly anything more regulated than Jain ascetic practice (Vallely 2002). This conjunction of being freely present to one's act and submitting to an order that is not of one's own making are the two dimensions that in Rappaport's analysis (1999) are intrinsic to ritual and that he refers to as the indexical and the canonical, respectively. To commit an act is a unique event, but only in terms of the relatively unchanging order that defines it as an act of a certain kind or declares it indefinable.

The assumption of ascetic practice surely does not make sense without understanding the broader "ethical" project. Moreover, ascetic practice entails sustained reflection; it is neither a product of pure habit nor self-evident and may be accompanied by some uncertainty. Indeed, asceticism proceeds along a number of stages, from each of which novices can choose to proceed further or take a reasonably graceful exit out of the whole process (Laidlaw 1995, Vallely 2002). As Laidlaw shows, prospective ascetics do not come to their position out of the blue, and they weigh the ascetic project alongside other alternatives. They must take into account their relationships with others and balance what is entailed in breaking off from the life of a householder with what is given back. In sum, taking up and maintaining the practice of asceticism, which is certainly not for everyone, is based on a combination of both judgment in Arendt's sense and freedom in Foucault's, and it also entails acceptance of the order in which acts are made possible, in Rappaport's sense. Indeed, in Laidlaw's summation (pers. comm.), the practice of freedom intrinsically entails the exercise of judgment. Jains do this through rituals that involve the optional adoption of compulsory orders and obligations.

Practice is continuous—a matter of living one's life—but also discontinuous, insofar as the exercise of judgment responds to changing circumstances and contingencies. For many thinkers, the discontinuities are more salient, hence a matter of discrete acts, of beginnings and endings, of shifting between states in which different combinations of criteria apply or apply differently. The greater the emphasis on discontinuity, the greater the salience of freedom. However, it is striking how often a central, primary, or salient feature of ethics is identified as keeping one's word, following through on what one has committed to, finishing what one has begun, or at least acknowledging that one has changed direction. This may be as ordinary and implicit as adhering to the conversational implicatures of speaking (as set forth by Grice or equivalent ones in a given speech community), as everyday as carrying through the obligations of kinship, or as grand and explicit as adhering to the Abrahamic covenant or redeeming the Christian sacrifice. Acknowledging one's commitments is what the obligations to receive, to give, and to return the gift are, what the Maussian gift describes. Judgment entails discerning when to follow one's commitments and when to depart from them, or how to evaluate competing or incommensurable commitments; thus a focus on judgment transcends a divide between freedom and obligation, between conventional morality and charismatic innovation, or between performative felicity and subjective sincerity.

To conclude, I hope I have shown that there is no great methodological danger in dissolving the ethical into the social once the social is conceived as (Aristotelian) activity, practice, and judgment rather than (Kantian/Durkheimian) rule or obligation. The ethical does not simply go without saying. Indeed, ethics can be found not only in the balance between continuity and innovation but in the movement or tension between the ostensible (manifest, explicit, conspicuous, declared, avowed, certain, normative, necessary) and the tacit (latent, implicit, ambiguous, subjunctive, aporetic, paradoxical, uncertain, transgressive, possible), and between the application of criteria and the recognition of their limits.

The chapters that follow draw various threads from this general picture. If ethics submerges into habit or habitus, into Durkheimian convention or Aristotelian disposition, there are going to be performances, practices, projects, and events that recall it to consciousness, whether with respect to punishment (Stafford's chapter), the giving of reasons (Keane), attributions of responsibility (Laidlaw), moments of activism and radical hope (Dave; compare Lear 2006), etc. Pervasiveness obviously need not entail agreement with respect to either what constitutes an ethical field or what the ethical thing to do is in any given instance. Chapters by Paul Antze, Sophie Day, Nireka Weeratunge, and Shirley Yeung demonstrate that making an ethical life or being seen as an ethical person often takes work and entails attention. Justin Richland illustrates what happens when ethical differences emerge in legal battles, Heonik Kwon when ethics becomes a matter of recuperation, Veena Das when it is a matter of neighborliness across religious divides, Francesca Merlan when, by Euro-American standards, it appears submerged. The "right thing to do" is going to be a matter of the conjunction of criteria with character, circumstance, genre, discursive field, tradition, event, institution, affect, and standpoint. As

Donna Young suggests, it may take a "holy fool" to see it. People not only differ from their friends and neighbors with respect to specific judgments, they struggle internally; indeed, that is how, in common parlance, we often recognize something as a matter for ethics, a dilemma. The depictions in Webb Keane's chapter of the multiplicity of internal voices, in Steven Caton's of what to do in the face of evil, and in Das's of the heterogeneity of concepts and the uncertainty of moral striving are useful correctives to an overly smooth application of an Aristotelian model of the kind I have presented here.

## The Chapters

Contributors were invited to address the following questions:

What is the place of the ethical in human life?

How might attention to the ethical contribute to anthropological theory and enrich our understanding of thought, speech, and social action?

Insofar as the ethical is implicit in human action, how do we render it visible?

Which anthropological approaches and philosophical formulations are most helpful for the project?

How can anthropology best draw from and contribute to philosophical debate and to a broader conceptualization and demonstration of the ethical in human life?

Together the responses speak to the nature and grounds of ethics and its relation to language, politics, religion, and desire. Although the chapters naturally differ from one another with respect to emphasis, there are many cross-cutting themes; they could have been organized in multiple ways—and can be read in any sequence.

The arguments initiated in the Introduction are continued in Part I. The chapters here offer a set of diverse perspectives on how to distinguish and depict the ethical. In my chapter, I argue that ethics is, in the first instance, neither a compartment of social life nor a specific category of human thought but entailed in all speech and action. I bring ideas about practice and judgment together with theories of act and utterance—though both lines of thought, perhaps, find their origins in Aristotle. To phrase this schematically, the task is to articulate the relationship between practice and performance (used here primarily in the sense of performative acts). Speech act theory demonstrates how particular ethical states and the criteria to evaluate subsequent practice are brought into being. Such acts are consequential and irreversible; their effects can only be changed by further speech acts arising from the stream of practice. Subsequently, in confronting the forthrightness of action with the cautiousness of skepticism, I move toward what might become an ethics of history.

Webb Keane offers a lucid account of the sociality of ethics. He is interested in the various cultural modalities through which the ethical becomes manifest on the surface of things, discernible and objectifiable. He moves from explicitly material modalities like the gift and bookkeeping, through aspects of speaking in which questions of stance and voice, including multivocality and what he calls dysfluencies, are central, to the explicit giving of reasons or justifications for action. Thus his argument concerns the relationship between what is tacit, embodied, or "inside" and what is explicit, objectified, and "outside," or between individuals. Keane furthermore historicizes his argument (as developed more fully in *Christian Moderns* [2007]), suggesting that the ideology of modernity, with its value given to objectifying explicit reasons, produces a demarcation of the "ethical" and disembeds it from other spheres. In effect, ethics and religion become associated with the giving of certain kinds of reasons as opposed to others.

James Faubion is concerned with elaborating a more rigorous approach to the ethical, in which it can be discerned through specific diagnostic categories. Drawing from an impressive range of scholarship, from a philological analysis of Aristotle's key terms through Weber, Foucault, and Luhmann, Faubion argues for a depiction of the ethical in much more specific, and indeed stronger, terms than those developed in this Introduction. Faubion proposes an original distinction between the ethical and what he calls, to avoid the ambiguity accruing to the word *moral*, the themitical. If the themitical is the dimension of the ethical field concerned with orderly reproduction, the ethical in its pure form is for Faubion quite literally the *extra*-ordinary. Ethics lies in the acts of charismatic leaders, marking moments of sheer and original departure. Faubion thus articulates the relationships of ethics to power and to innovation.

The essays in Part II elaborate Keane's point that "linguistic interaction is perhaps one of the chief domains in which everyday ethics lives." They advance the argument by means of close attention to language and, in particular, to sequences of speech and bodily movements in social interaction. Alan Rumsey provides both phylogenetic and ontogenetic arguments for the centrality of the ethical dimension to human sociality. A particularly original part of Rumsey's argument concerns the triadic quality of human interaction, a feature that follows from primatological studies as well as his own careful fieldwork in Papua New Guinea on both early childhood socialization and political oratory, and that also resonates with the best psychoanalytically informed work (Crapanzano 1992).

Like Rumsey, Jack Sidnell takes the initiation and acknowledgment of ethical action to the level of everyday interaction and conversation. Through the fine-grained methodology of conversational analysis as initiated by Erving Goffman, he is able to tease out minute and often tacit adjustments of position that nevertheless are consequential. As he said in the discussion that followed the delivery of his paper, ethics occurs by the microsecond. Sidnell thus demonstrates the pervasiveness of the ethical at a fundamental level of human sociality, deeper than that of explicit performatives like introducing or promising. He shows the primordial importance of recognition and ratification in the most informal of conversations and sequences of social interaction.

The essays in Part III turn their attention to questions of accountability that have a long standing within anthropology, at least since Evans-Pritchard. James Laidlaw offers a forceful argument concerning agency and its limitations as a concept for social theory. He suggests that the conflation of agency with subjectivity or consciousness has obscured the way that responsible agents and reflective selves constitute each other. Agency is not an intrinsic attribute or capacity of persons and therefore something of which one could have more or less, but a function of specific kinds of arguments concerning liability and responsibility. Thus, following Williams, ethical concepts cannot be reduced to psychological states. Laidlaw illustrates with an instructive contrast between Nuer and Azande modes, respectively, of concentrating responsibility on the victims of misfortune or dispersing it outward to others (ostensible witches). Quite fascinatingly, he likens the contemporary Euro-American situation to the Azande of Evans-Pritchard's classic description with respect to calculations of risk and the proliferation of forms of collective agency.

Steven Caton provides an illustration of Laidlaw's general points about the distribution of agency and its relation to law. Caton forces us to turn our eyes to the uncomfortable photographs from Abu Ghraib, or rather, to the photographers, asking in what sense the "ordinary" American soldiers who took the pictures or posed in them could be held accountable for their actions. One of the issues concerns understanding Abu Ghraib as a node in a "security apparatus," with its demand for improvisation on the part of personnel rather than in a more rigidly rule-based bureaucratic order. Caton shows the inadequacy of analyses based on concepts of either intentionality or contingency, drawing instead on Arendt's notions of responsibility and will. But Caton goes further and asks (after Arendt) how to consider the actions that took place at Abu Ghraib as not merely unethical, but sheer evil.

The chapters in Part IV address matters of punishment and personal dignity. Drawing on a disconcerting event during his own fieldwork, in which he was punished for attending a Taiwanese funeral and inadvertently polluting himself, Charles Stafford takes the perspective of the person who is chastised or punished for ostensibly bad behavior. Stafford argues that such a person might be attempting to do good (acting "ethically") while at the same time breaking the norms or conventions of society (acting "immorally"). Insofar as this paradox is widespread, it returns us to the questions of judgment and accountability, but Stafford takes us in the direction of the subjectivity constituted in the experience of being punished and asks what people could learn from it.

Francesca Merlan links the question of ordinary ethics to the anthropological literature on relational personhood. While anthropological models of personhood among Aboriginal Australians have tended to argue for the significance and predominance of relationality, or identification with others, Merlan demonstrates beautifully that interactional styles cannot be seen simply in terms of continuous relationality but are characterized by particular kinds of reserve and regard, human dignity that is shaped both structurally and experientially. Relationality may perhaps be best understood as having properties that, within the overall terms of Aboriginal life settings to date, have enabled continuity over time and space, renewability, and potentiality for further inclusion.

Judith Baker offers a thoughtful response to Stafford's and Merlan's essays from the perspective of an analytic philosopher. Following Keane's assertion that ethics entails the giving of reasons, Baker points out that ordinary people attempt to discriminate between ethical and other kinds of reasons for action; ethical practice, thereby, always entails meta-ethics, reflection upon itself *as* ethical. In considering why Stafford should have resented being punished for having done what he thought right, she brings the voice of Peter Strawson and his important essay "Freedom and Resentment" to the table. Strawson discerns the inextricable connection between the emotional and the ethical as people respond with gratitude or resentment when they are subject to the intentional acts of others, with indignation with respect to acts applied to others, or with satisfaction or remorse as they reflect on their own acts.

I began my paper with Rappaport's analysis of how ritual instantiates new moral states. For Rappaport, formality is a key feature of ritual, and it can be found, to a lesser degree, in everyday performative statements, like greetings, described by Austin. The essays in Part V address the question of formality head on. Shirley Yeung explores the relationship of etiquette to ethics, a question that is much more profound than simple dismissal of propriety would imply. Yeung's focus is on nineteenth-century North American etiquette manuals, which were popular in somewhat the way that self-help manuals are today. While, on the one hand, they can be seen as indicative of social anxiety and, perhaps, as a means for social climbing, Yeung offers a more subtle interpretation in which the acquisition of proper etiquette is a form of ethical cultivation, a kind of secular version of the practices characteristic of the piety movement in Egypt, analyzed so well by Mahmood (2005) and Hirschkind (2006). Indeed, Yeung shows the deep affinity, if not intrinsic connection, between etiquette and ethics, while also maintaining the sense of their difference. As Yeung says eloquently, "Of the perfectly executed performative, one might still ask, as Austin does, 'Agreed, I spoke in all sincerity . . . I was fully justified perhaps, but was I right?' (1963: 31)."

Justin Richland addresses the question of formality by exploring what he calls the relationship between ethics and aesthetics. He draws on the ceremoniousness and propriety characteristic of Hopi ritual and social interaction to show that the relationship between form and substance, or outward performance and inner feeling, may differ from that characteristic of mainstream contemporary Western ideology. Richland supplies segments of legal transcripts to show the intersection of Hopi reasoning with the hegemonic legal system. In addition, he makes a very important supplement to my argument, namely, that we are not just subject to performative effects but dependent on other people accepting the legitimacy of specific performative acts. The ethical and the political/legal or religious are thus folded into one another.

Part VI offers a closer inspection of the ways in which ethical subjects are depicted and depict themselves in specific contexts. It is probably a human universal that people enjoy specifying, evaluating, and even deliberately performing character, as Carlos Londoño Sulkin's paper makes clear, and observing one another's moral careers. I suspect that *hypocrite* is a word that translates widely; so also, *braggart* or *show off*. I have often had occasion to reflect on the proverb printed on a cloth given me in Madagascar: *feno tsy mikobaña*, "full containers don't rattle." Among Sakalava, such observation of character is linked to a theory of the discretion, silence, or invisibility of true power. Londoño Sulkin's paper opens up a whole other way to think about forms of posturing and imposture. He illustrates both the intense sociality characteristic of everyday life (Overing 2000) and the cosmological perspectivism (Viveiros de Castro 1998) that have so impressed anthropologists of Amazonian societies. Most interestingly, he demonstrates how the ethical qualities of personhood are understood materially and hence conveyed indexically and iconically in substances such as tobacco paste and chili. Participants at the workshop had the pleasure of tasting these intense foods.

The next two chapters examine the cases of persons who are perceived by society to be at the borders of the ethical. The question, then, is how such persons enact, manage, or represent their own dignity as ethical persons. Sophie Day takes us to a world that appears to many outsiders to be ethically predetermined. She offers a compelling portrait of female sex workers in London, who strive to maintain the taboo against mixing love and money and hence to maintain boundaries between their clients and working lives, on the one side, and friends, family, and partners, on the other. Yet events often take unexpected directions, and, as she well puts it, "Acknowledging, even taking responsibility for the unanticipated consequences of their earlier activities, women trod a knife-edge between recognizing and contaminating significant relationships."

Paul Antze explores people diagnosed with autism who are able to reject the label of disability placed on them while embracing the condition. Antze confronts the question of whether empathy is a necessary attribute of ethical action and how people who are said to lack empathy—the ability to read the face of the other or follow the sorts of cues in social interaction described by Rumsey and Sidnell—are able to establish and legitimate moral claims. In particular, Antze points to an interesting distinction between the constative and performative dimensions of ethical appeals, between what is said and what is performed in the saying of it.

Nireka Weeratunge takes us to a question embedded in the history of Western thought, namely, the ethics of making a profit or, indeed, living by means of trade. However, her context is not Christian Europe but the Buddhist tradition of Sri Lanka. Drawing from extensive interviews, Weeratunge addresses the ways in which business people and their clients describe and enact practices that they can consider "just" or "fair." The argument is relevant for considering how the profits from trade may be redirected into other circuits of social or religious significance and thus how business people can demonstrate and establish moral dignity.

If religion forms a domain in which material gain can be transformed into ethical action and profit taking be made right, it also often forms a context that highlights ethical difference and shapes political conflict. The chapters in Part VII direct us to places where the ordinary remains very much an achievement in the aftermath or ever-present threat of violence. These are the hot spots of religious, ethnic, or political tensions where, it is important to affirm, ethical life continues beneath and beyond the political events that fill the news. Hence the chapters challenge us to consider the relationship between "religion" and the ethical.

Donna Young takes us on a tour of Jerusalem, deftly shifting perspective as she juxtaposes the irreconcilable claims of inhabitants and pilgrims, Muslims and Jews, Palestinians and Israelis, with the voices and actions of those who have the privilege, but also the wisdom, to act as what she calls (Christian) holy fools. The Sisters of Zion are "fools" in the sense that their ethics remains ordinary—unrationalized and unconstrained by the dominant competing modes of ascription. Young's essay also exemplifies a narrative mode of ethnographic exposition, provoking reflection on the relevance of genre to ethical insight and perhaps of foolishness to anthropology.

Naisargi Dave returns us to a theoretical landscape quite close to that of Faubion and offers a clear elaboration of Foucault's distinction between ethics and morality, specifically, of ethics as a work of self-production rather than self-discovery or acknowledgment of normative limits. In reflecting on social activism as a form of ethical practice, Dave speaks to an ethics of possibility and shows with great clarity "the struggle . . . between imaginative possibility [ethics] and moral imperative." She illustrates this not only by means of the activities of the queer activists in India with whom she was engaged but through her realization in the midst of fieldwork that ethics was in fact the subject of her own research project. Like Young's, her essay thus invites reflection on both the relationship of ethics to politics and the ways in which fieldwork itself can be a site of ethical formation.

Veena Das offers a profound meditation on what it takes to be neighbors in a period and place of violence. Inspired by the thought of Stanley Cavell, she illuminates the struggle for moral perfectionism in mixed neighborhoods of Muslims and Hindus in urban India, illustrating both the resources and the uncertainties for moral life, and the improvisations to which they give rise. As she argues, the central questions concern not "belief" or following rules but rather the sensibility entailed in receiving the claims of the other—ethical demands that arise from sheer proximity and a common history, and sometimes from romantic love. Here passionate or tacit modes of acceptance and adjustment are more germane to ethics than formulations of judgment in the abstract. Close attention to the often tentative, uncertain, and circumstantial ways in which people receive and respond to one another offers a very different picture from the irruptions of communal violence or pronouncements of national and religious exclusion.

Drawing on Kantian ideas of universal hospitality and Hegelian ones of the tension between kinship and the state, Heonik Kwon describes the ways in which Vietnamese villagers attempt to do right by the war dead, in the first instance, by attempting to treat them all equally. In contrast to the degradation of bodies at Abu Ghraib, in Vietnam, some thirty years after the American war, the dead—former allies and former foes, the heroic and the frightened, and all those whose actions and experiences serve to undermine these distinctions—are all treated with hospitality. Kwon calls this an ethics of memory, but one could equally call it an ethics of hope.

It is with hope as an ethical object, but without thereby disparaging the ethical qualities of despair, that the reader is invited into the ordinary world of this book.

# PART ONE

# Theoretical Frameworks

# Toward an Ethics of the Act

## Michael Lambek

Where is the ethical located? I shall argue that it is intrinsic to action. I look at action in two related ways—as specific acts (performance) and ongoing judgment (practice)—and show that ethics is a function of each. Criteria for practical judgment are established and acknowledged in performative acts, while acts emerge from the stream of practice. Performance draws on previously established criteria, or felicity conditions, in order to produce its effects. These effects can be understood as committing performers to one particular alternative or set of alternatives out of many, and these commitments in turn inform subsequent evaluations of practice, and thus practical judgment itself, but do not determine practice. A simple illustration: insofar as the performance of a wedding instantiates the state of marriage, it provides criteria for evaluating the actors' subsequent practice as spouses. The act of marriage does not determine whether people remain "faithful" or practice "adultery," but it entails that their actions fall under such descriptions. If practice is rendered possible and meaningful through performative acts, practice also inevitably reveals the inadequacy of such acts and the limits of criteria and descriptions, especially their vulnerability to skepticism, and hence the need to start anew. Ethics, then, is not only about executing acts, establishing criteria, and practicing judgment, but also about confronting their limits, and ours.

## A Personal Prolegomenon

The ethical has come to seem central and even necessary for my work along at least three overlapping routes. First, there has been my experience in the field, experiences (*erlebnis*) that across different sites and over many decades have, in this respect, not changed in the slightest, except insofar as it is *my* experience (*erfahrung*) that has grown or ripened.[1] Very simply, the people I encountered have attempted, routinely—but also anything but routinely—to do what they think right or good, sometimes as a matter of course, sometimes in a struggle to know what the right path was, and sometimes ineffectively, infelicitously, inconsistently, incontinently, or not at all, but then with respect to what they or others think or have established as right or good. They also interpreted the actions and characters of others by criteria similar to those they applied to themselves. Put another way, they have acted largely from a sense of their own dignity; they have refused positions or attributions of indignity, and they have treated, or understood that they ought to treat, others as bearing dignity of their own. I do not think the Malagasy speakers I have met are exceptional in this regard, yet social theory has focused almost exclusively on rules, power, interest, and desire as forces or motivations for action.[2]

Second, and to move up a level of abstraction, in trying to interpret and account for the acts and practices I encountered, I discovered the inadequacy or limited nature of previous theoretical models that attempt to explain a rich cultural tradition and set of practices with respect to the needs and intentions of its participants and that, as noted, reduce intention to interest, compulsion, obligation, competition, or imitation, hence to a kind of social or psychobiological mechanics, or, in the least mechanical of cases, to deception or game playing, thus formulating action either too automatically, too strategically, too self-consciously, or too self-interestedly, but never seriously, complexly, judiciously, passionately, or even ambivalently.[3] Spirit possession, for example, became an epiphenomenon rather than a practice,

---

1. The German distinction between *erfahrung* and *erlebnis* captures something not directly available in English *experience*; see Martin Jay's (2005) comprehensive account.

2. I do recognize that the attempt to do right or good is often distorted by rationalization, self-deception, or denying the humanity of others. As Jackie Solway (pers. comm.) has pointed out, particular distortions may be characteristic of specific regimes of power, such as capitalism, slavery, etc. My thanks to Solway, James Laidlaw, Veena Das, and the other workshop participants for helpful discussion of an earlier draft and to Kristina Kyser for excellent editing.

3. Weber, of course, is a partial exception, but most Weberian-inspired anthropologists have been impatient with Geertz's attention to meaning and ambiguity and have searched for more muscular kinds of explanation (Ortner 2006).

genre, tradition, or form of life that exists in its own right and that enables human creativity and skill in no less a fashion than any artistic or religious tradition that scholars of the humanities hold dear.[4] Moreover, as I have come to understand it, in its combination of passion and action, playfulness and seriousness, spirit possession itself is replete with moral insight.[5] Indeed, no less than Islam, Christianity, or Hinduism, spirit possession offers the means (for those who accept it) to cultivate an ethical disposition or sensibility.

Third, and moving to a yet higher level of abstraction, I have been deeply influenced by the later work of Roy Rappaport on the illocutionary function of ritual and hence from ritual back to ordinary language as formulated in J. L. Austin. From my other teacher, Aram Yengoyan, I was directed thirty years ago to *Must We Mean What We Say?* by Austin's student, Stanley Cavell, though twenty-five years were to pass before I took Yengoyan's advice, or perhaps was only then able to begin to understand what Cavell meant by what he wrote. Whereas Rappaport informed me of his own impatience with the hair-splitting of philosophers, I was taken by Cavell's complex style (evident in a lesser key in Geertz). Such a style adds to the locutionary, illocutionary, and perlocutionary means of language what I have the conceit to think of as the circumlocutionary. In the right hands, the fineness of insight expressed through circumlocution is no less than that to be found in the directness and clarity of Austin; Cavell speaks truth to the consequentiality of speaking despite the recursiveness of human experience.[6] Rather than providing specific lessons that could be

---

4. It seems odd to keep making the point. This is, in a nutshell, the critique of Lewis (1971) as set forth in Lambek (1981) and Boddy (1989), as well as by a number of other scholars. The argument can be found at a more abstract level (with no reference to spirit possession per se) in Sahlins (1976), but structural or cultural mediation says nothing about the forces underlying or stemming from specific actions.

5. Again, see Lambek (1981). On the ethical practice of spirit mediums, see Lambek (1993, 2002a, 2002b); on various other ethical dimensions of possession, Lambek (1988, 1992, 1996, 2002c, 2003a, 2003b, 2007a, and 2010). When I say "spirit possession," I refer in the first instance to the traditions and sets of practices I have encountered and described on the island of Mayotte and in northwest Madagascar in fieldwork since 1975. I leave open to what degree this might be exemplary of some broader category or family of traditions and practices of "spirit possession" that are not culturally specific, thus embracing forms of life found in West Africa, Brazil, Malaysia, etc. (Boddy 1994, Johnson forthcoming).

6. One might distinguish between two ideologies (or ethics) of writing— Austinian plain speaking, in which one's word is one's bond and therefore clarity is of the essence (though Austin himself is also deeply ironic), and the circumlocutionary or otherwise indirect forms characteristic of Socrates (Plato), Derrida, or

summarized from their texts, writers like Cavell and Derrida offer their readers, as Cavell puts it, the opportunity of being read by their texts (somewhat as attentive participants are "read" by their observation of spirit possession or students of traditional Qur'anic recitation come to embody the text). This is reading as ethical experience. Immersion in ethnographic fieldwork is similar as the fieldworker is "read" or tested in multiple ways. Irrespective of any insight or wisdom forged in this manner, the interpretation of ethnographic phenomena should contribute to the expansion and refinement of philosophy's attempts to reformulate and address classic problems.

Having criticized reductionist arguments, I am equally uneasy about jumping to a position directly in opposition to them, namely, to seeing the human condition as essentially one of freedom (or reason) and, as a corollary, where this primary freedom is constrained, as inevitably one of resistance (ending, thereby, exactly back in a reductionist position). That is to forget all we know about structure, cultural mediation, social interpellation, violence, subjectivity, and psychic conflict. Recognizing that people want to do good and that attending to intention or motivation is critical for understanding human life is necessary but insufficient. Such insights cannot account for all the contexts in which good intention is derailed or misguided. Nor can they displace the analysis of particular cultural models and social practices or the general ways in which speech and action work. I argue that ethics is an intrinsic dimension of human activity and interpretation irrespective of whether people are acting in ways that they or we consider specifically "ethical" or ethically positive at any given moment. One can neither reduce human motivation to the ethical nor, as Laidlaw argues in his chapter, reduce the ethical to human psychology.

## How to Recognize and Produce Ethical Criteria and Judgment Through Ritual Performance

Ethics entails judgment (evaluation)[7] with respect to situations, actions, and, cumulatively, actors, persons, or character. The exercise of judgment

---

Cavell, in which wisdom is to recognize what (or that) one does not know or cannot put into direct words. However, the work of the reader includes avoiding "an act of pious merger with Cavell's . . . all-but-inimitable sensitivity" (Gould 2003: 54).

7. I use "judgment" to similar ends but in virtually the opposite sense from Veena Das (this volume), for whom "the crucial requirement is that we should be able to take an abstract, nonsubjective vantage position from which we can orient

is prospective (evaluating what to do, how to live), immediate (doing the right thing, drawing on what is at hand, jumping in), and retrospective (acknowledging what has been done for what it was and is). Articulated more strongly as forms of action, these can be epitomized, respectively, as promising, beginning, and forgiving (Arendt 1998: 237–46). Judgment is both of others, thus social and conventional, and for oneself, thus linked to freedom and self-fashioning, but also to responsibility, care, guilt, forgiveness, and insight, and to recognizing the limits of what one can know or do or understand.

In order to exercise judgment, there must be criteria. Whence come criteria? I assume some come from mind and some from experience. But criteria are also instantiated through human speech and action. Ethics is intrinsic because there are always criteria already in place, because speaking entails and generates criteria, and because there are always places where disagreement over criteria or their absence is troubling. Criteria serve as the basis for judging how to conduct oneself, whether to commit or exercise specific acts, to what ends and in what manner—but also for deciding what constitutes a given act or kind of act, where specific acts begin and end, whether acts have in fact been committed correctly, completely, and legitimately (Austin's felicity conditions), and how to evaluate one's own and others' actions. In the ordinary course of events, criteria are implicit, internal to judgment itself, but they are also available for conscious discernment and deliberation. It should be evident that criteria are not rules for using words that can guarantee the correctness or success of our claims but "rather, criteria bring out what we claim by using the words we do . . . in making claims to knowledge, undertaking actions, and forming interpersonal relationships" (Guyer 1999: 128). As Cavell notes (1979: 30), if in ordinary usage (as in prize juries or admissions committees) agreement over criteria makes possible agreement over judgments, for Wittgenstein it appears that the ability to establish criteria is based on prior agreement in judgment. Wittgenstein's "appeal to criteria is meant, one might say, exactly to call to consciousness the astonishing fact of the astonishing extent to which we *do* agree in judgment; eliciting criteria goes to show therefore that our judgments *are* public, that is, shared" (ibid. 31). However, for that reason, criteria do not often need to be publicly enunciated; we appeal to criteria only when the sense of mutual attunement is threatened (ibid. 34). As Shiner helpfully explicates, for Cavell,

ourselves to the world." My usage is thus not that of the definitive attributive actions of the courts. Thanks to Carolyn Hamilton for urging the clarification.

Wittgenstein's criteria are in the nature of things, not a matter of imposed convention. "Criterial rules . . . are not external to, but *internal to* the human form of life" (1986: 364, italics in original). To call them conventional, "alienates us from them, and thus from ourselves, for our form of life and our criteria are one" (ibid).[8]

I take this to indicate the fundamental givenness of ethics. Nevertheless, while certain criteria are continuous or perduring, others are contingent. If criteria define contexts of action, there must be the means to transform the context and hence the relevant criteria. There are times when new criteria must be brought into effect or applied to new persons or new contexts and hence when they must be made relatively explicit. Rappaport (1999) shows how ritual operates as a central means through which this happens. Among Tsembaga Maring of highland Papua New Guinea, rituals effect—bring into being—particular states of war and peace. These can be considered ethical states, since any aggressive or non-aggressive act is interpreted and evaluated as such in their light (that is, differently according to whether the current state is one of peace or war). Likewise, acts may be discerned as cooperative or uncooperative among those constituted as allies by having undergone the ritual together. More generally, rituals effect states of ethical personhood and relation, transforming a biological infant into a named social person, a man and woman into a married couple, a novice into a monk, a profane condition into one of blessing, a breach into a reconciliation, and so forth. To each of these persons, relationships, and states, criteria departing or renewed from or additional to what has hitherto been the case apply.

Whereas Austin argued that criteria of truth and falsity do not apply to illocutionary statements, Rappaport showed that in a sense they do, but in an inverted fashion. A locutionary statement is judged true or false according to whether it is in conformity with the state of affairs that it purports to describe or refer to (it is raining, Sarah Palin is president). However, following a felicitously enacted illocutionary utterance, it is the state of affairs or the subsequent actions that are to be judged as true or false according to whether they are in conformity with the utterance (you are false not to keep your promise or the peace; the drought is false once the rain magic has been performed). These are faults—falsehoods, lies, errors, sins, etc.—insofar as they are not in conformity with the moral condition that has been brought into effect. When the state of affairs is in conformity

---

8. The depth of human agreement is acknowledged in Cavell's phrase "the conventionality of human nature itself" (1979: 111, as cited by Hammer 2002: 28).

with the performative act, then the state can be said to be "true" (or correct, right, or good). Once I am inaugurated as president, my conduct is judged with respect to my status as an office holder and no longer as a contender. It is my conduct that is in question, not the act of inauguration or the office. If I serve as witness to a marriage, I cannot henceforward deny that the couple are married, nor act toward them or evaluate their actions as if they were not. To undergo a ritual is to commit, says Rappaport, both to the specific effects or conditions it produces (thereby agreeing to apply to them the relevant criteria) and to commit more generally to the relevance of the criteria that the ritual underwrites or reproduces, as well as the means of producing them (the nature of marriage, the legitimacy of weddings). Thus, the performance of a ritual initiates or transforms a specific moral state or condition relative to the participants, while also reproducing the felicity conditions or criteria that apply to such a transformation. Hence Rappaport says that ritual is simultaneously performative and meta-performative.[9]

The performance of a ritual, argues Rappaport, is characterized by the conjunction of indexical and canonical dimensions—that it is me undergoing it here and now ("indexical"), and that it is these previously inscribed and relatively unchangeable ("canonical") utterances and acts, part of a perduring liturgical order, that I hereby repeat. Rappaport argues that, by their submission to its bodily demands (of presence, posture, endurance, etc.), the participants performing or undergoing a ritual demonstrate to others and to themselves their acceptance of both its message and its form. They do so whether or not they "believe" in any specific propositions associated with it; hence the outward, public consequences prevail irrespective of the inner states of the participants. This evades the problem of recursiveness inherent to theories of intentionality, as well as the instability of subjectivity. In these respects Rappaport is very close to Austin and somewhat akin to what Derrida means by "tethering" or avowal, or Cavell means by acknowledgment, and quite distinct from what is commonly meant by sincerity. I can pray effectively, for example, without being certain that I believe in God, that I want to do so, or that prayer is the means to address God; I can successfully ask for forgiveness without feeling particularly contrite.[10] Indeed, in Rappaport's view, I am *likely* to be uncertain;

---

9. Here and below I severely condense what is actually a highly elaborated and systematic argument (Rappaport 1999).

10. The matter of sincerity has been the subject of considerable debate, especially over the interpretation of Austin's citation of the words Euripides gives to Hippolytus, "my tongue swore to, but my heart did not" (Austin 1965: 9–10, Cavell 1995b, 1996). Presumably its salience as a felicity condition depends on the

the point of ritual is to substitute public clarity for private obscurity or ambiguity, that is, to establish beyond question the relevant criteria. The central criterion—being accountable for what one says and does—is virtually universal, by contrast to the substantive criteria put into effect by specific rituals. Definitive ethical commitments and criteria are thus produced publicly and irrespective of personal doubt.

Rappaport begins his book not by acknowledging the universality of acknowledgment but by asserting that recognizing lies is a human problem. Insofar as symbols form the basis for human language and culture, hence for creativity, speculation, and so forth, hence, following Kant, for freedom from immediate sensations and circumstance, thought and communication by means of symbols raise two enormous problems. These are the problem of the lie and the problem of the alternative. The problem of the alternative can be seen as the flip side to Geertz's observation that culture always manifests itself as particular (1973a); it is always in some specific form and thereby in contrast to alternative forms. This raises the following questions. On what basis should I follow one alternative rather than another? Is the choice mutually exclusive? (Does the acceptance of one entail the rejection of all others?[11]) How do I indicate which alternative I have chosen? How do I come to accept that I have made the (right) choice and hence stick to it? Rappaport attends more explicitly in his subsequent argument to the way ritual addresses the problem of the lie (How can we be reasonably sure that we are not lying to each other or establish commitments in the face of possible insincerity?) than to how it addresses alternatives. But in a sense the lie is a subspecies of alternative, and the focus in the subsequent argument on how ritual produces (relative) certainty is a way of reducing alternatives and specifying a particular path or

---

"semiotic ideology" in place (Keane 2007; compare Lambek 2007a). Mahmood (2004) and Hirschkind (2006) have pointed interestingly to an ideology in which the "inside" of a person is part of the context that is expected to be transformed by performative acts and utterances. Here, then, is the reverse of the idea that a "good" or "true" utterance corresponds to an existing interior state. Rather, a person becomes better insofar as his interior state is appropriately shaped by the right acts and utterances: for example, contrition would follow from rather than precede an act of apology. Prevalent among pious Muslims in Cairo, such an argument draws from (and elaborates) Aristotle's ideas about the cultivation of character through education and good deeds.

11. Alternatives thus come in the form of either/or and both /and. The tension between them exemplifies a central feature of human thought (Lambek 1998, 2007b).

set of criteria as much as it is one of assuring the truthfulness of any given utterance or set of propositions or, as noted above, of moving from the assertion's conformity to the facts to the facts' conformity to the assertion.[12] Rituals commit their performers to taking up specific alternatives and therefore rejecting competing or contradictory ones (you cannot be simultaneously married and unmarried or alternate between these states at will) and to ignoring incommensurable ones (alternative views of what constitutes "marriage"). Moreover, they render such acts of commitment difficult, and sometimes impossible, to take back, as in acts of scarification, circumcision, and other forms of sacrifice (Lambek 2007c). (Cavell's problem of finding a voice is thus partially obviated by inhabiting and suffering a body.) A critical point here is that, while the unfolding of events enables us to reinterpret earlier events in light of subsequent ones through the ongoing construction of narrative, it is more difficult to reinterpret after the fact the commitments entered into and the moral conditions brought into effect through the performance of rituals and, indeed, of everyday performative utterances of all kinds.

Truthfulness and committing to specific ways of doing or being are fundamentally ethical matters. The questions are not only how human society responds to the possibility of the lie or adjudicates among competing alternatives but how we accept specific statements, alternatives, responsibilities, and courses of action as *ours*, how we become committed to them (such that they become a part of us and we of them), and how we demonstrate and acknowledge to ourselves and to others that we (and that others) mean what they say. The broader issues are less ones of distinguishing lies from truth than of enacting and recognizing acceptance (or accepting one's nomination) to certain positions and committing to one's utterances, to the courses of action established and initiated in public moments, and to the criteria by which such courses of action are identified as such and the means by which they are taken up and evaluated. Temporality is critical—whether we stick with things long enough to make our statements and actions coherent and reasonably predictable, available for development, interpretation, evaluation, and response. Ultimately we must acknowledge our identification with the person we have, through a series of marked and unmarked acts and utterances, become.

---

12. The most salient and succinct form of the question of commitment is that of making a pledge or promise, a matter that, as noted in the Introduction, is central to and often materialized as the gift.

## From Performance of Ritual to Performance
## of Everyday Speech and Action

For Rappaport, ritual lies at one end of a continuum of formality. Yet many of his arguments apply to acts and events of lesser formality. While the "conjunction of the indexical and canonical," and especially the invocation of relatively unchanging "canonical" phrases (like the *B'ismillah*) and sequences of action (like the Catholic communion), are depicted as characterizing ritual, in fact virtually all speaking entails a similar conjunction. What Rappaport calls the indexical dimension is each time original, linear, and consequential—a threshold crossed and an act that happens and cannot readily be retracted (my words uttered, the "reply all" button fatefully pushed), while what he calls the canonical dimension is highly iterative or citational, comprising words or phrases that have been said before, and will be again, by other people.[13] Many ordinary utterances bring the performative and iterative dimension to the fore, so that Austin originally referred to them as performatives, as when I thank or introduce someone, or simply say "yes." As Austin subsequently realized, all utterances contain an illocutionary dimension, insofar as they make statements, describe a state of affairs, refer to a person or place, ask or respond to a question, and so forth. In so doing, and in announcing that they are statements or other specific acts of communication, all utterances entail simultaneously a commitment on the part of the speaker to be understood (somehow) and a commitment to stand by the message, semiotic code, and conversational implicatures (Grice 1976; Ochs Keenan 1976) that are ostensibly in use. We must, as Cavell puts it, mean what we say. Or, as Hent de Vries explicates Cavell's reading of Wittgenstein, "No a priori principles or axioms, no conventional maxims or norms, could ever relieve us of that responsibility—'commitment'—to the language and singular terms we use. . . . What holds true for promising and for moral judgment governs all actions and passions, events and encounters" (2008: 85).

Particular genres of speech and action in various cultural milieus refine such commitment—the ostensive relations between the speaker's intentionality and the code or message—in various ways. We can refer here to the field of metapragmatics as elaborated by Michael Silverstein (1976). Thus the displacement of intentionality is central to a practice like spirit possession, in which there are explicit shifts in voice (Boddy 1989, Lambek

---

13. Thus, ritual action entails the conjunction of what Lévi-Strauss has called reversible and irreversible time.

1981). The perception of a possible gap between what is said and what is meant is also heightened in certain discursive regimes, such as Calvinist Protestantism, with respect to what Webb Keane (2007) has usefully identified as semiotic ideologies. Nevertheless, insofar as there is an illocutionary dimension and it is felicitously enacted, so too the consequences that Austin and Rappaport attribute to performative utterances follow—namely, that they usher in a state of affairs (criteria) according to which the speakers, participants, and context are henceforth to be judged.

Language is central to the ethical and the ethical to language, both to language in the abstract, in the sense of grammar and semantics (*langue*), and to acts of speaking, pragmatics, and meta-pragmatics (*parole*)—to the names and pronouns that I take on, by which I am addressed and respond, by which I address others or refer to others, and which I link to specific actions. The ethical is intrinsic to utterances by which I acknowledge (or repudiate) words and acts as mine or yours, ours or theirs; by which I accuse, command, condemn, confess, congratulate, criticize, defer, defy, denounce, encourage, excuse, exonerate, honor, insult, ignore, injure, obey, praise, pronounce, refuse, swear, sympathize, etc.; but also by which I agree, answer, argue, denote, describe, disagree, exclaim, imply, question, refer, request, state, suggest, and so forth.[14] The ethical is embedded in the relations produced and presupposed among the nominative, the accusative, the dative, the ablative, and the genitive attributions of persons and things as the subjects and objects of action—as people nominate and accept nomination, accuse and receive accusation, act on and are acted upon directly and indirectly, toward and by means of other persons and things, and attribute similar actions and causes to others. Adverbs and adverbial phrases specifically refine aspects of means and intention, as memorably illustrated in Austin's (1961b) elaboration of the distinction between shooting a donkey and dropping a tea tray by accident or by mistake. Ethics is grammatical, grammar ethical.

Of course, the distinct verbs and adverbs of English or nominal cases of Latin or Russian, no less than the speech genres in which they are embedded, express refinements of ethical stance and perspective that in

---

14. In our joint seminar (2006), Jack Sidnell remarked on the large number of performative verbs in a single paragraph from Jane Austen. So far as I know, no one has investigated whether there has been a decline in the presence, number, or quality of explicitly performative verbs in English, whether and how their presence is related to such matters as genre and social class, what the implications are for infusing sociality with an ethical tenor (or whether this is mere propriety), or how closely the set of English performative verbs is replicated in other languages.

other languages may be performed by means of other grammatical categories and functions, including modes of address (such as tecknonyms), allusion, metaphor, avoidance, shifts between transitive and intransitive or
active and passive verbs, morphemes indicative of agency, authorship versus animation (Goffman 1981), evidentiality (Hill and Irvine, eds., 1993),
indexical discernments of context (Hanks 1990), genres or modes of speaking that enable degrees of quotation or de-quotation (Urban 1989), turn
taking, and various forms of oral and gestural punctuation.

### *Ethical Consequences of the Irreversibility of Action: Forgiveness and Acknowledgment*

Taking speech to be a subcategory of acts (or, perhaps, acts to be a subcategory of speaking),[15] I turn to some of the general features of human action
as discerned by Arendt, followed by some remarks on Cavell. Despite radical differences in style, sources, and temperament, there are interesting
parallels between these two thinkers, each of whom attends to the irreversibility and ethical consequentiality of action. I begin with Arendt, even
though, unlike Cavell, she writes without the benefit of speech act theory
and hence introduces something of a break in my larger argument.[16]

Arendt celebrates the *vita activa*, in which public action is really the
highest or best form of activity. The fundamental feature of an act is that
it brings into play something new in the world. "To act" she says, "means
to take an initiative, to begin" (1998: 177). She writes, "The life span of
man running toward death would inevitably carry everything human to
ruin and destruction if it were not for the faculty of interrupting it and
beginning something new, a faculty which is inherent in action like an
ever-present reminder that men, though they must die, are not born in
order to die but in order to begin" (ibid. 246). Arendt identifies "the principle of beginning" with "the principle of freedom" (ibid. 177). However,
the condition of humanity is one of plurality. Hence she cautions that
"Because the actor always moves among and in relation to other acting

---

15. Elsewhere (Lambek 1992) I have described the maintenance of taboos as a
kind of performative activity, in which speech may be largely irrelevant; gendered
comportment would be another instance (Butler 1989). However, to ascribe an act
as performative is to acknowledge its categorization in words.

16. My remarks on Arendt are restricted entirely to *The Human Condition*.

beings, he is never merely a 'doer' but always and at the same time a sufferer. To do and to suffer are like opposite sides of the same coin" (ibid. 190).

If human labor stems from necessity and work is prompted by utility, by contrast, Arendt argues, speech and action spring from us as a kind of spontaneous disclosure of the agent. However, such disclosure retains a certain ambiguity insofar as action reveals its consequences only after the fact. Illuminating action is the province of the storyteller, not the agent; it cannot be captured in the intentionality of the actor. "This unpredictability of outcome is closely related to the revelatory character of action and speech, in which one discloses one's self without either knowing himself or being able to calculate beforehand whom he reveals" (ibid. 192).[17] Hence the burden of the consequentiality of action is "the burden of irreversibility and unpredictability" (ibid. 233).

Arendt honors the act more than the actor; indeed, for her, the relationship between the two is characterized by a kind of opacity:

> Men have always known . . . that he who acts never quite knows what he is doing, that he always becomes 'guilty' of consequences he never intended or even foresaw, that no matter how disastrous and unexpected the consequences of his deed he can never undo it, that the process he starts is never consummated unequivocally in one single deed or event, and that its very meaning never discloses itself to the actor but only to the backward glance of the historian who himself does not act. (ibid. 233)

This produces a paradox with respect to freedom insofar as it makes the actor appear "more the victim and the sufferer than the author and doer of what he has done" (ibid. 234). Arendt remarks provocatively, "Nowhere, in other words, neither in labor, subject to the necessity of life, nor in fabrication, dependent upon given material, does man appear to be less free than in those capacities whose very essence is freedom and in that realm which owes its existence to nobody and nothing but man" (ibid. 234).

The solution lies in the act and reception of the other. Arendt writes, "The possible redemption from the predicament of irreversibility—of being unable to undo what one has done though one did not, and could not, have known what he was doing—is the faculty of forgiving" (ibid. 237). Moreover, forgiving cannot be predicted and thus "is the only reaction [that] . . . retains . . . something of the original character of action";

---

17. This speaks directly to the condition of irony I discussed in the Introduction and is illustrated there in my anecdote of the fallen granary.

indeed, forgiving is a new, unconditioned act (ibid. 241). Furthermore, in a remark that returns us to Rappaport, "The remedy for unpredictability, for the chaotic uncertainty of the future, is contained in the faculty to make and keep promises" (ibid. 237). In these two quintessential expressions of freedom—forgiving and promising—we are back to preeminently illocutionary acts and the criteria they establish.

Both forgiving and promising are performative acts, one retrospectively redressing the past and the other prospectively charting a future. Ethics in this vision is resolutely historical. It is not maintained by means of individual reason or internal self-control (ibid. 238), nor does it emerge directly from a form of Durkheimian social regulation or transcendence. Both promising and forgiving depend on the fact of human plurality, "for no one can forgive himself and no one can feel bound by a promise made only to himself" (ibid. 237). In a striking phrase that distills the wisdom acquired by her own experience, Arendt writes that "men are unable to forgive what they cannot punish and . . . unable to punish what has turned out to be unforgivable" (ibid. 241).

Arendt's ability to forgive was no doubt compromised by Martin Heidegger's inability to acknowledge his own actions. This weight of acknowledgment is a central subject for Cavell, who goes so far as to say that speaking is apt to become unbearable. Here Arendt's miracle of natality produces labor pains and struggles over both detachment from the words of others so as to find one's own voice and the weight of attachment to one's own words. Cavell advocates finding one's voice, yet recognizes that one "moves between owning one's words and being abandoned to them" (Szafraniec 2008: 379). We must mean what we say and yet recognize that we cannot always do so completely or consistently. The world would be incoherent if we did not stand by what we say, but to do so inflexibly leads inevitably to tragedy, so well exemplified in the figure of King Lear, or, for that matter, the unfolding of the *Hippolytus*.

Thus, if Cavell reads Austin as "affirming that I am abandoned to [my words]" (Szafraniec 2008: 371–72, citing Cavell 1996: 125), Cavell himself would not exactly follow suit. Cavell would not condone Hippolytus for keeping his word to the bitter end:

> To live is to engage in a movement between controlling one's words and being controlled by them. To act as if these two sides of the movement were the same, as Hippolytus does, is to have, in Cavell's terms, a petrified imagination. To mean every word one says is to assume responsibility for the (criterial) implications of what one says, while in full awareness that

these implications may change, that they remain in need of our future interventions, and that they are potentially infinite, so that what we say exceeds our control, so that we will always mean more and less than we do. (Ibid. 372)

That is to say, it is to acknowledge Arendt's "burden of irreversibility and unpredictability."

To take responsibility for one's words is not to refuse ever to take them back. But to redeem a change of direction, one must acknowledge it for what it is. We are faced with the challenges not only of keeping our commitments and answering to the names we have been given and accepted but also of acknowledging our failures, thoughtlessness, infelicities, incontinence, and changes of heart and direction—and forgiving those of others, as well as accepting their forgiveness. As Stephen Mulhall helpfully puts it, it is not that a person is or isn't responsible for all the consequences of her utterances or actions, could have foreseen them all, etc. but rather that "she is then flatly responsible for determining her relation to them—whether and how to claim them as unforeseeable or simply unforeseen, to accept them as meant or excuse them as unintended" (1996: 17). The point is recognizing and living with the consequences of one's words.

Thus, whereas some thinkers focus on the lie, on promising, or on keeping one's promise, Cavell adds that, whether one promises or fails to keep a promise, the issue is acknowledging that one has done so. Whereas silence has its functions, sometimes speech is "essentially *owed*. Flowers are not a substitute" (Cavell 2005b: 191). Moreover, as he notes in *The Claim of Reason* (p. 298, as cited by De Vries 2008: 83), "there are any number of ways, other than promising, for committing yourself to a course of action: the expression or declaration of an intention, the giving of an impression, not correcting someone's misapprehension . . . and so on."

I take the ethics of the ordinary to be entailed in these performative and practical qualities of speech and action, promising and beginning, forgiveness and acknowledgment. Not only are speaking and acting intrinsically or formally ethical (committing, executing, evaluating, and becoming subject to evaluation), but the particular substance of ethics (criteria, values, commitments) is specified, instantiated, and informed through specific utterances and acts. Original utterances nevertheless contain quotation or citation of some kind. Ritual performances may differ from everyday acts and utterances with respect to the degree of canonical citation, formality, legitimacy, publicity, conventionality, spectacle, consequentiality, and, as Rappaport (1999) argues, the relative certainty, perdurance, and sanctity of what is iterated. As noted, ritual performances more clearly establish and specify criteria for judgment than do less formal utterances, leaving less room for the kinds of qualifications that Cavell describes. However, the distinctions are not absolute, and all speaking carries some of the weight that Rappaport attributes to ritual, just as ritual carries the weight Cavell attributes to speaking. Moreover, certain relatively informal utterances, such as accusations and invective (*sale juif*), but also repeated praise or affirmations of love, may prove equally if not more momentous for addressees, and perhaps for speakers.[18] One implication of the work of Arendt, Cavell, and Rappaport is that the ethical is to be distinguished not only from what is specifically unethical but also, and perhaps more fundamentally, from simple indifference.

Finally, it is worth underlining that action finds its complement in passion; as Aristotle realized, virtue finds the right balance of passion and action to suit the circumstances. Arendt, as I have indicated, speaks of the complementarity of acting and suffering. Cavell (2005b) argues that the criteria for passionate utterances are not the same as those for performative utterances, emphasizing that a passionate utterance is one in which I do not know in advance how my statement will be received or what my standing is.[19] Radically to separate the ethical from the passionate would reproduce the Kantian dichotomy between reason and the senses as one between freedom and constraint. This is one of the places where a close analysis of spirit possession could prove instructive (Boddy 1989, Lambek 2010).

## From Performance to Practice and Back: Toward an Ethics of History

While ritual performance produces states of affairs, the descriptions under which people act, and the criteria for judgment, it cannot determine either who participates or the subsequent actions (including acts of evaluation) of the participants. How, when, and whether people act is a product of

---

18. In fact, invectives often carry the features of being low in informational content and high in meaning that Rappaport attributes to sacred utterances.

19. Thanks to Veena Das for clarifying the point. In addition, many emotion words or invocations carry ethical weight (Lutz 1988; see also Lutz and Abu Lughod, eds., 1990, Myers 1988, Lambek and Solway 2001, Hirschkind 2006, and chapters below by Stafford and Baker).

their exercise of judgment to fit the circumstances, an exercise that is in turn related to character, acquired disposition, and accumulated wisdom.[20] Hence one may distinguish analytically the ethics of practice from that of performance. As a theorist of performance, Rappaport has relatively little to say about practice, how it is that *I* come to perform *this* ritual *now*, how I orient my conduct subsequently, whether or how I fulfill the obligations I have just committed myself to, or what happens if I do not. Bourdieu is the primary theorist of practice, discriminating the manner in which actions are undertaken and paying specific attention to response and timing. It is not simply a matter of playing by rules but, as Bourdieu puts it so well, of having a feel for the game, of simply doing the right or best thing under the circumstances (1977). If a theory of performativity describes the establishment of criteria, practice theory recognizes that criteria are not usually applied explicitly, as in following a set of rules or bureaucratic procedures, but are implicit in both the game and the disposition to exercise (and the ability to recognize) good judgment.

What counts as ethical is a matter not only of choosing freely or judging wisely but of sustaining commitment to a specific direction, order, goal, discipline, set of criteria, or Weberian "absolute value." Not to follow through on what one has committed to is, in at least some respect (but bearing in mind Cavell's strong qualifications), to place oneself in the wrong. Moreover, we are back to the problem of alternatives. To take up one alternative or to go down one path entails passing up opportunities that other paths could have afforded and even explicitly rejecting some. Having married one woman, given my blessing to one child, or shown my devotion to one jealous god, I cannot readily go ahead and pursue other alternatives.[21] Not only can we not explore all paths at once, or even in succession, but there is something to the fact that we ought to keep to certain paths or commitments once we have initiated or started to follow them, at least long enough for our companions to be able to count on us to be there. The freedom of starting something new entails the judgment of what kinds of compromises that will make with the old and reconciling the new direction with what is being left behind.

---

20. Material constraints and political and discursive factors can also prevent people from carrying out certain desirable acts or from carrying them out in a specific manner.

21. Yet one should continuously exercise judgment; it would be unethical to be rigid, to stop thinking after one has made one's first commitment. The point is that subsequent acts need to be made in light of previous commitments.

If performance establishes the criteria by which subsequent practice is engaged and evaluated, so too practical judgment generates new perform-ances, that is, relatively formal acts and utterances that recalibrate the cri-teria and shift the ethical context. Thus there is a whole ethics to history and social change.

The emergence of new performances within the stream of practice may be understood with the assistance of a distinction made by Cavell.[22] Cavell describes appeals to criteria as having two moments, which he calls predi-cation and proclamation, namely, having something to say about some-thing, and actually saying it:

> In ordinary cases, a set of specifications or features is established that set the terms of, are the "means" or basis of, the judgment; and then there are standards on the basis of which to assign the degree to which the object satisfies the criteria of judgment, or to determine whether an object *counts* under the criteria at all. We may think of the former moment as the judgment's *predication*, its saying something *about* something; we may think of the latter moment as the judgment's *proclamation*, its saying it out. (1979: 34)

Further, "Whether to speak (proclaim) has two aspects: determining whether you are willing to count something as something; and determin-ing when, if ever, you wish, or can, enter your accounting into a particular occasion" (ibid. 35). Wittgenstein, says Cavell, moves between observ-ing—"it is what human beings *say* that is true or false," the predicative moment—and communication as "agreement in judgments," the procla-matory moment (ibid. 35).

A broad concern with acknowledging and reconciling with the past and bearing witness to departures from it has been evident in the practices of people I have encountered in fieldwork and hence has become a theme of my work (Lambek 1996, 2002a, 2002b, 2004). Here, however, I offer two brief illustrations drawn from recent essays by younger scholars of the way that judgment is predicated in practice and proclaimed in performance, in acts of acknowledgement (as pointed to by Cavell) and in forgiveness and natality (as emphasized by Arendt).

Catherine Allerton reports the various ways that people of Manggarai in Western Flores, Indonesia, are performatively rooted in their localities,

---

22. In light of Cavell's account of opera as an exemplary locus of voice, I am tempted to speak of my ethnographic illustrations as a kind of Cavelleria Rustic-ana. Mascagni's *Cavalleria Rusticana* is itself a drama of failed acknowledgment.

through ritual acts performed as infants. As youths setting out to live elsewhere for high school or university, they perform another ritual, of "rooting the feet," acknowledging where they come from in order to travel safely forward. People of Manggarai must also formally say farewell to the dead. Allerton recounts how:

> Maria . . . once described to me a time when she briefly visited a house in another village. As she sat down, she became aware of a terrible smell of rotting. She called out to the women of the house, "Quick, pass me a betel quid!" and then "offered betel" (*waré sepa*) to the ghost of a woman of that house. Maria told me that she had known this woman fairly well, but had not been able to visit the house to formally offer her "tears" (*waé lu'u*) [money] after the woman's death. The terrible smell was that of the corpse of the deceased woman, who Maria had not yet formally "remembered." Finally remembering the woman by offering betel caused the smell to disappear, as the ghost returned to the realm of the ancestors. (Forthcoming)

We see here both the named acts of conventional acknowledgment and the circumstantiality of initially having forgotten to carry them out. Maria both proclaims her omission (as manifest or predicated in the smell) and redresses it by acknowledging the deceased person. Her act is accepted and the omission forgiven as the smell disperses.

The second example illustrates how an act of acknowledgement resolves a traumatic historical event and a political stalemate. In 2002 a heavily laden ferry capsized en route from Ziguinchor in the Casamance region of Senegal to the capital, Dakar. As Ferdinand de Jong describes, after unsatisfactory attempts at memorializing the nearly two thousand people who drowned, some citizens of Ziguinchor began to feel that the cause of the accident was their unresolved struggle for independence of the Casamance. Women referred back to an earlier event, predicating the shipwreck as part of a moral state of struggle they had proclaimed in 1982. They then attempted to undo what they had begun, to terminate the state of being and close off the chapter. The women of the sacred groves, who twenty years earlier had assisted militants to utter oaths of commitment to the insurgent movement, now asked the men to take them back. As one of the women explained to de Jong, "*Il faut passer là où tu es passé.* We have to return along the same path that has taken us here" (n.d.: 6). Most remarkably, at the signing of the peace treaty that soon followed, the leader of the separatist movement publicly "apologized for the victims of the shipwreck" (ibid.).

These events indicate how Rappaport's account of ritual can be taken out of the structural and functionalist framework in which he largely places it and applied directly to specific historical occasions. The performance of taking back the oaths is a novel, historical event, actually making history, and doing so by publicly transforming the ethical state of affairs in Casamance so that new criteria apply. This offers another dimension to the much-discussed question of the relationship of structure to event (Sahlins 1985).

What is equally exciting and so productive of peace here is the performance of an apology. The actors in the conflict take responsibility for the tragedy rather than displacing it onto other people, actions, or forces (which one could readily imagine). There is a lesson of wide relevance here. Taking responsibility for historical events, acknowledging our role in them, is not only the way to make peace but also turns people from the victims of history into its agents and finds in suffering not resentment or *ressentiment* but forgiveness and conciliation.

The simultaneous profundity and fragility of such acts leads directly to the final phase of my argument.


## *Skepticism*

Rappaport argues that the clarity and certainty produced in the performance of ritual is necessary in light of the ambiguity and uncertainty that would reign in its absence; this is clearly illustrated in these ethnographic vignettes. But sometimes ambiguity appears more salient or powerful than what is achieved in ritual, persisting in the face of the performance or having no performance that could resolve it. Despite the evident and positive effects of acknowledgment, apology, and forgiveness, it sometimes rises to consciousness not only that the proclamation might be at odds with what we feel but that the very predication is difficult or impossible to make; that we cannot get to the bottom of where we stand or who we are, of our original or current intentions or deepest desires; that the right words or even the criteria for knowing, saying, or doing something are absent. An account of ethics must recognize limitations to acts of acknowledgment, the inevitable infelicities that accompany and undermine them, and the difficulties encountered in remaining consistent and complete with respect to one's criteria and acknowledgments.

Assuming we have the freedom or potential of which some philosophers speak, how shall we know what to do with it, what to choose, or how to recognize on what basis we have made our choice (or chosen to have it made for us)? Were we responsible for a given act of omission or commission? Where does responsibility begin and end? Did we know what we were doing or mean what we said? Are conventional words and actions sufficient to our meaning? Did we do it in intentionally, seriously, unconsciously, by accident? Are your criteria commensurate with mine? How are we to recognize the meaning of our words or the consequences of our acts? How, at the end of the day, are we even to know who "we" are, or even that we are? Sometimes we simply feel the absence of criteria to know. Performance then takes place on thin ice, appearing as "mere" or "staged" performance, and sometimes the ice begins to melt.

In sum, what if skepticism creeps into performance or practice, if criteria are no longer unambiguous or disambiguating (or, conversely, too discriminating), if felicity conditions lose their authority, become fragmented or incoherent, if practices are no longer satisfying or sufficient, if there is a perceived rupture between means and ends, if competing or contradictory ends and means nominate us or override each other? These are problems not only of individual or collective incontinence and failure but also of genuine human paradox. Cavell describes the condition as "the absence or withdrawal of the world, that is, the withdrawal of my presentness to it; which for me means the withdrawal of my presentness to (the denial of our inheritance of) language" (1988: 174–75). Presence to the world is replaced by mourning its loss.

How could one have an answer for the disappointment of criteria? Only by concluding that ethical insight must *begin* in mourning the loss of the world—and thereby recognizing the courage entailed in speaking and acting at all, including the act of refusing to do so. (As Derrida indicates, disavowal is also an act of a kind of avowal.)

Most fundamentally, if ethics entails acknowledgement or avowal, who am *I* to make such acknowledgment? How is it that I find my voice or acknowledge myself, that I am who I say I am, who others say I am (or that I am other than who others say I am), that I hear my nomination, that I accept what has been entailed in that nomination, that I can be sure it is me who has been nominated, that I have not mistaken myself for another or been so mistaken by another? Reflecting on Abraham's answer to God's call to sacrifice his son, these are the questions with which Derrida begins a late essay.[23]

---

23. Derrida is drawing on a parable by Kafka, who imagines "another Abraham" who was unsure whether he was the one called and doesn't want to appear ridiculous by accepting the call too readily.

the first Abrahamic teaching . . . that if everything begins for us with the response, if everything begins with the "yes" implied in all responses ("yes, I respond," "yes, here I am," even if the response is "no"), then any response, even the most modest, the most mundane of responses, remains an acquiescence given to some self-presentation. Even if, during the response, in the determined content of a reply, I were to say "no"; even if I were to declare "no, no, and no. I am not here, I will not come, I am leaving, I withdraw, I desert, I'm going to the desert, I am not one of your own nor am I facing you," or "no, I deny, abjure, refuse, disavow, and so on," well then, this "no" will have said "yes," "yes, I am here to speak to you, I am addressing you in order to answer 'no,' here I am to deny, disavow, or refuse" (Derrida 2008: 313)

How Abraham should answer when he is called by God is not so different a question from how Derrida himself should answer the call of the other, as a child in Algeria and since. What is it to be Jewish, or to be "a Jew," because others have called him Jew? And why him, rather than another? Derrida's "Jewish question" is at once exemplary and ordinary, applying to each of us.[24] This is because we come to be persons "under a description," hence ethical subjects, precisely by means of such nominations or interpellations, performative acts that begin even before we are born. For Derrida, to answer, to avow or disavow, provokes "an ethics of decision, an ethics of responsibility, exposed to the endurance of the undecidable, to the law of *my* decision as *decision of the other* in me" (ibid. 324).

Derrida answers "yes," but he avows that he does not know what he means when he does so. He points to the

> essential difficulty . . . in underwriting and in countersigning [*à soussigner et à contresigner*] an utterance of the type: "Me, I am jew" . . . To say "I am jew," as I do, while knowing and meaning what one says, is very difficult and vertiginous. One can only attempt to think it after having said it, and therefore, in a certain manner, without yet knowing what one does there, the *doing* [*le* faire] preceding the *knowing* [*le* savoir]. (Ibid. 333)[25]

Derrida answers "yes," but he refuses to choose or to authorize whether this answer (in response to Sartre) is authentic or inauthentic. Such undecidability, "far from being a suspending and paralyzing neutrality, I hold to be the very condition . . . within which decision, and any responsibility worthy of the name . . . must breathe" (ibid. 335):

---

24. Cavell responds to his own "Jewish question" in the remarkable autobiographical essay in *A Pitch of Philosophy* (1996).

25. Note how Derrida addresses Cavell's fundamental question *Must We Mean What We Say?* and places "proclamation" ahead of "predication."

anyone responding to the call must continue to doubt, to ask himself whether he has heard right, whether there is no original misunderstanding; whether in fact it was his name that was heard, whether he is the only or the first addressee of the call; whether he is not in the process of substituting himself violently for another; whether the law of substitution, which is also the law of responsibility, does not call for an infinite increase of vigilance and concern. It is possible that I have not been called, me, and it is not even excluded that no one, no One, nobody, ever called any One, any unique one, anybody. The possibility of an originary misunderstanding in destination is not an evil, it is the structure, perhaps the very vocation of any call worthy of that name, of all nomination, of all response and responsibility. (Ibid. 337).

In the beginning was the word, but the word was simultaneously a deed, an act, a call uttered without an intention we can fully understand but the effects of whose proclamation we must continue to acknowledge.

## Conclusion

By contrast to those who have seen the substance of ethics as either values or rules, or as the freedom to break away from the obligation of adhering to rules, I have argued that the ethical is intrinsic to human action, to meaning what one says and does and to living according to the criteria thereby established. Ethics is a property of speech and action, as mind is a property of body (or, action is a manifestation of ethics as body is an extension of mind). Ethics is not a discrete object, not best understood as a kind or set of things. Taking such an approach has avoided explaining ethics in universal rational, instrumental, psychological, or biological terms. And while acknowledging cultural difference, it has equally avoided depicting such difference according to distinctive values and thus stumbling over problems of relativism.

If I have advocated the exercise of practical judgment at the expense of following (or rejecting) rules, that is in large part because it is a more accurate description of how we live. And if I have taken up the concept of virtue at the expense of values, that is largely because virtue pertains to the qualities of acts and practical judgment rather than to the depiction of discrete objects or cultures. The substance of a virtue is never fixed but is a function of contingent circumstances; virtues are attributions in context, not things in themselves.[26] Whether a specific act is to be described as virtuous is a matter not of adherence to a rule but of the quality of judgment it exhibits. The judgments entailed in ongoing practice (when and in what manner to act), no less than the judgments entailed in evaluating acts and character after the fact, are rendered possible by the criteria at hand. Criteria are embedded in our use of language or established by means of the relatively formal orders of acts and utterances that anthropologists describe as ritual and that have as their core the illocutionary function of speech acts.[27] Criteria can be found in a hierarchy or continuum—from the fundamental, constant, comprehensive, or certain to those specific to the moral states, persons, and relations that have been brought into effect (under description) through immediate performances and acts of commitment. Criteria shape but do not determine how we act. We are never free insofar as we are always already spoken, spoken to, and spoken for; we are always free insofar as we are always already responsible for exercising our practical judgment.

Aristotle's conception of virtue as a function of ongoing practical judgment (*phronesis*) needs to be supplemented with an understanding of how criteria are established and how they come to apply to specific circumstances, contingencies, subjects, objects, and means of action. It is in the definitive acts and utterances we refer to as ritual that particular criteria are simultaneously established, acknowledged in principle, and rendered applicable in practice. To establish criteria is to acknowledge them both as valid generally and as relevant and relative to particular persons and circumstances. To live ethically is to accept specific criteria and nominations, to acknowledge such acceptance, to live in accord with such acceptance, to recognize the fragility of that acceptance and those criteria, and, finally, in the least felicitous circumstances, to acknowledge when one has failed and to forgive others their failures. Among the most significant and pervasive criteria are those that establish the basic humanity of persons—as beings mutually subject to criteria and hence to be acknowledged as ethical subjects in their own right, thereby, as Kant put it, having dignity, not price. However, this is also an area both subject to abuse and vulnerable to skepticism.

---

26. Of course, they often do become objectified as values. For an earlier and somewhat different attempt to articulate the relation of virtue to value, see Lambek 2008.

27. I have not addressed the place of criteria established through law, and hence the tension between ritual performance and legal act.

Speaking and acting entail the predication and appropriation of voice—speaking and acting as oneself (to someone, in the sight or hearing of someone, with reference to someone . . . )—and as such are intrinsically constitutive of ethical subjects and relations. We must (in this sense) mean what we say and do. In addition, we are required to acknowledge what we have said and done. And yet, at the same time, we cannot always mean what we say, insofar as we do not fully know the consequences of our actions, the depths of our intentions, the specificity of our path, or even that it is we who are called upon to speak and act now. We must speak and act seriously and commit to the paths we have begun, to which we are held (and hold ourselves) accountable—and also recognize that full certainty and consistency are not possible. Ethics is vulnerable to—but also achieved in the face of—rupture, erosion, and skepticism.

Speech and action, understood as illocutionary performance, establish the criteria according to which practice, understood as the ongoing exercise of judgment, takes place. We are judged and we judge according to the commitments we make and have made (including those that others have made on our behalf). Ritual acts establish moral states in which new or renewed criteria apply. Ritual serves to increase clarity, certainty, consistency and completeness in what is accomplished in speech and action. Yet it can never fully overcome skepticism or the work of time.

Since every utterance entails a commitment to our words, we are continually put to the test to keep, as it were, our promises. But in the face of circumstance this is often hard to do, and so we are also faced with the challenges of acknowledging our failures, thoughtlessness, misdeeds, infelicities, and changes of heart—and forgiving those of others. It might be said, then, that promising, acknowledging, and forgiving are meta-ethical acts.

Such acts are intrinsically temporal and historical. Indeed, insofar as taking responsibility, rather than apportioning blame, serves as the motor of history, it not inconsequentially produces a subject position of agent rather than victim (except insofar as one is victim to one's own acts).

Insofar as these are features intrinsic to human speech and action, criteria of being human, they will be culturally recognized, a part of the store of human wisdom transmitted in distinctive traditions, cultivated through forms of discipline, embedded in the fine discriminations of ordinary language, and enunciated more explicitly in proverbs and narratives, and sometimes in the rationalized bodies of argument we call philosophy, theology, and even "ethics."

# Minds, Surfaces, and Reasons in the Anthropology of Ethics

*Webb Keane*

Whether they are trying to understand such things as global religious or political movements, ethnic clashes, state violence, diasporas, or biotechnology, or are faced with calls for social activism and political engagement, anthropologists may find familiar ethnographic habits serve them poorly and discover old questions acquiring new force. Does the specificity of cultural context mark a limit to the claims of universal justice and human rights? Or is the deployment of these very ideas merely the work of power? And if so, must we ultimately understand social relations in purely instrumental terms? But then to what ends? What makes one kind of self-formation or social project worth undertaking and another not? The giving of justifications for our political, ethical, or epistemic commitments eventually comes to an end point: What do we find there? These questions are not provoked only by new circumstances or extreme situations. They can arise in the most ordinary reaches of everyday life.

Concepts like society, culture, ideology, and power were meant to help answer questions like these. Should they fail to do so, triumphant explanations derived from genetics, rational-choice modeling, neo-liberal economics, cognitive science, evolutionary psychology, and neurophysiology are eagerly poised to take their place. But whatever else the latter approaches may offer, their effect is often to render out of court some problems with which actually existing people still need to contend. Part (but only part) of the distinctive mandate of anthropology is to encounter people in the midst of things. This mandate suggests one way to think about ethical experience as an irreducible component of the politics and pragmatics of ordinary life.[1]

Although many social scientists are skeptical of the vocabulary of morality and ethics, it speaks to some of the fundamental challenges their practices have long posed, not least to the very societies that produced them. Darwin and Nietzsche can stand for two poles from which natural science and humanistic scholarship threatened to undermine the assurance of human self-mastery, if not of divine sanction itself, on which much nineteenth-century European religious and moral thought rested. But situated between them were emerging disciplines that became the social sciences. Their claim to be sciences of something distinctively human was often staked on the assertion that their knowledge concerned objects of an entirely different status from those of natural science, what Emile Durkheim (1938 [1895]) called "social facts." For Max Weber (1978), sociology's purview was limited to purposeful actions oriented to those of other persons. Thus in *The Protestant Ethic*, Weber (1958) portrays what I would call a "virtue system," a more or less coherent vision of ultimate goods that gave rise to a coordinated set of socially supported and institutionally organized means of self-cultivation.

Varied though the heirs of Durkheim and Weber may be, an empirical focus on the domain of values helps characterize disciplines such as anthropology, with their own implications for prevailing ideas about morality (Keane 2003a; cf. Howell 1997, Lambek 2000, and this volume). After all, many philosophical and theological traditions have held some variation of the idea that the ethical act presupposes a degree of autonomy on the part of the actor, since it must be the outcome of a choice made from among alternative possible courses of action (Schneewind 1998).[2] This is

---

1. For purposes of this chapter, I will follow Ian Hacking's advice, during discussion in the Toronto conference, and treat "morality" and "ethics" as interchangeable. Although I find Williams's distinction between deontological morality and socially situated ethics useful in principle, in practice I have found it unwieldy to keep the words themselves clearly separated. Indeed, this difficulty may ultimately reflect the dialectical relations between modalities that this chapter addresses.

2. Anthropology's own relation to sociological and other kinds of determinism has been highly ambivalent (see Keane 2003a). Laidlaw (2002; see also his contribution to this volume) has argued that anthropologists' overemphasis on social norms has obscured their view of the freedom that defines moral agency; con-

why Adam's Fall is a moral story, not merely a causal one. Once transcendental mandate is eliminated, morality often seems to depend on the autonomy of individual minds. But if humans are products of natural processes over which they have no power, of social forces beyond their ken, and internally, if their very self-knowledge is limited and untrustworthy, then what could ground moral responsibility? Posed against autonomy seems to be what we might call, in the old phrase of C. Wright Mills (1959), the sociological imagination. This denotes the observation that we live among other people, and that this condition is no mere happenstance. We do not just discover ourselves already fully formed among others, with whom we must then contend. Rather, we come to be who we are within, and by virtue of, relationships with others, their bodies, their possessions, their languages, their ways of inhabiting our imaginations and emotions. What follows from this claim, however, is far from settled.

## In the Midst of the Action

In a recent iteration of the contest between mental autonomy and scientific explanation, Anthony Appiah (2008) reviews psychological research showing that the accounts people give of their own behavior are not reliable. Cues below the subjects' threshold of awareness frame their interpretations of and reactions to different situations that call for ethical decisions. As a result, not only do actors lack full consciousness of the real causes of their actions, their actions are also not consistent across contexts. Such "situationist" explanations seem to eliminate the element of self-awareness and intentionality on which many familiar accounts of moral responsibility depend. They suggest that we cannot take individuals' stated reasons for their choices at face value, which seems to jeopardize the deliberative component of much moral philosophy. By raising doubts about consistency of character, they also seem to undermine a key premise of virtue ethics.

Having accepted these findings enthusiastically, Appiah nonetheless defends the philosophical enterprise: "Moral thought aspires to a register that is universal without being impersonal. . . . it has to be intelligible to us ordinary persons. That's why an explanation cannot supplant a moral

---

versely, others like Sperber (1996) assert that an overemphasis on cultural self-invention has led anthropologists to ignore important causal explanations for human behavior.

justification" (ibid. 117). These words portray the psychologist and the philosopher as united in their quest for universals, a goal many cultural anthropologists habitually dismiss. But suppose we grant them their goal and accept their empirical findings—we may still say that something important eludes our understanding. We might even start with Appiah's own assertion that justification is not something that stands apart from moral action, since "the act of describing a situation, and thus determining that there's a decision to be made—is itself a moral task. It's often *the* moral task. Learning how to recognize what is and isn't an option is part of our ethical development" (ibid. 196). For Appiah, this recognition seems to be largely a matter of personal insight, ultimately grounded in psychological processes. But the sociological imagination suggests that the presence of other people is a crucial element of any ethical "situation." And no empirically known community has ever in practice been able to rely entirely on either the individual intuitions described by psychology or the general principles sought by philosophy (or, we might add, the explicit rules of theology and law, or even the tacit ones of custom).

Bernard Williams takes up the challenge the sociological imagination poses to the Kantian traditions of Western moral thought by stipulating a distinction within the moral domain. What he calls the "morality system" centers on deontological obligations that are held to be universal, context free, and wholly binding. But in confronting the experience of practical necessity and the decisions it involves, Williams says, "the agent's conclusions will not usually be solitary or unsupported, because they are part of an ethical life that is to an important degree shared with others. In this respect, the morality system . . . conceals the dimension in which ethical life lies outside the individual" (1985: 191). Theorists of virtue and moral community like Alasdair MacIntyre (2007) and Charles Taylor (1985, 1989) make similar points. In these views, morality is not founded on structures of pure reason or on psychological universals but is the product of an encompassing social order, oriented to a distinct vision of human flourishing, and the historically specific habits and disciplines it inculcates. And, of course, it was precisely the goal of some classic anthropological concepts of culture (e.g., Benedict 1959, Sahlins 1972, 1988) to show that particular notions of human flourishing or ultimate goods are formed within and sustained by the totalizing frame of historically specific communities.

But, put this way, the sociological imagination runs into some well-known problems. Faced with a world that seems irremediably conflictual, relentlessly unstable, and powerfully constraining while also shaped by purposeful actions, anthropologists have long since abandoned models of self-contained social worlds and their holistic systems of meaning. Yet, if communities are not totalizing, how do we understand the force and efficacy of the social facts they create? And, given the force and efficacy of those social facts, how do we also understand doubt, innovation, protest, and sheer indifference? To say that morality is inseparable from the very nature of people's lives with one another—that it is not reducible to some context-free explanation in terms of innate drives, economic interests, rational first principles, or evolutionarily adaptive functions—should not lead to the conclusion that morality must be a pure social construction, continually reinvented from scratch and shared by a group of like-minded people. The sociological imagination works against strong claims to derive ethics entirely from universal reason or moral psychology. But historical and ethnographic realism warns us against trying to do so by appeal to seamless cultural traditions or cohesive moral communities instead.

I will argue that the descriptions to which Appiah refers typically arise in the midst of acts like deliberating, making excuses, and offering justifications instigated by the demands and expectations of social interaction, especially in cases of disagreement and conflict. Their intelligibility to the participants derives, in part, from available vocabularies, material practices, norms for argumentation, and the authority to take them up. But vocabularies, practices, norms, and authority are not sufficient to account for the outcomes of interaction. There are several reasons for this, including the effects of differing individual interests, dispositions, and capacities, as well as the ineluctable specificity of circumstance. The approach I sketch here starts elsewhere. To one who is in the midst of the action, the entire range of possible explanations for other people's actions and possible outcomes of one's own can never be fully apparent. Lacking the view from nowhere, people are likely to find themselves responding to the surfaces of things, to their forms or semiotic modalities.[3]

Within the limits of this chapter, I will develop this claim: if a significant part of ethical life lies outside the individual, as Williams puts it, then

---

3. By *semiotic* I mean this: people draw inferences about their circumstances on the basis of their perceptible experience of material forms, including the forms of language (see Keane 2003b, 2008c). Those inferences are not necessarily conventional—thus they do not treat things as "symbols"—nor are they necessarily fully cognizable—thus they are not always "interpretative" nor are the results necessarily "meaningful" (see Engelke and Tomlinson eds. 2006). Since material forms have *causal* sources, a semiotic approach is not to be confused with idealism or social constructionism. Since the inferences are usually informed by cultural knowledge, this approach is also not a pure phenomenology.

it is an individual who attends to the surface of things. After all, being unable to read minds, we are, in a sense, surfaces to one another. I want to argue that ethics takes a variety of semiotic modalities and that these interact with one another. Ethics is not all of one order. Sometimes we are in the midst of the action; sometimes we seem to stand apart from it. If the ethical life centers on the tacit competences of the individual embedded in a social world, under certain social circumstances that individual undertakes explicit deliberation and justification. Sometimes ethics *does* act, in certain respects, like Williams's "moral system," and as obligations that one can justify in words. But those words do not *explain* either morality or action. Justifications respond to the way some social contexts require the giving of reasons. The giving of reasons is itself a practice that requires certain competences, certain capacities for objectification. Objectification is an endemic feature of social life overall (Keane 2003b, 2007, 2008a). It has effects across the spectrum from silent bodily habitus to self-conscious verbalization. Objectification permits certain kinds of reflexivity. A capacity to reflect on agency itself—to take actions and their purported agents as objects of thought, discourse, and manipulation—may be a prerequisite for what Williams called the morality system. It facilitates praise and blame, explanation and excuses, and the disciplining of self and other.

This chapter will briefly sketch some of the dimensions a contemporary anthropology of morality might consider by looking at different modalities that ethically marked practices can take. It begins with forms that help endow material and verbal exchanges with their ethical character and concludes with contexts that encourage or demand the explicit giving of reasons. This is not meant to be an exhaustive typology, and these modalities are often thoroughly entangled with one another. But by focusing on these different aspects of ethical action, I hope to show what we can learn by attending to the surfaces of things and the interactions they mediate.

## The Shape of Things

One of the founding texts for the anthropology of morality, Marcel Mauss's *The Gift* (1967) focuses on social interactions that are mediated by material things. In Mauss's view, the morality of the gift derives from the way it seems to confound the distinction between the domain of practical functions and value judgments. It interposes a rule that interrupts the logic of economic utility. On its first page, *The Gift* points to the importance of semiotic modality to the ethical act: "The form usually taken is that of the gift generously offered; but the accompanying behaviour is formal pretence and social deception, while the transaction itself is based on obligation" (ibid. 1). What endows a particular kind of transaction with moral weight may be obligation, but it is the formal properties of the action that frame it as a gift. As people on the Indonesian island of Sumba made clear in talking to me about their own exchanges, a horse given without the due forms is not a gift at all. An object may pass hands, and certainly there will be material results: one more horse in one person's corral, one less in another's. But if the link between objects, acts, and persons is not established by certain physical and verbal expressions, the transaction has no *moral* consequences, no socially binding debt, no ethical virtue accrued to the giver, no recognition accorded to the recipient.

Some procedural norms look like rules. The ability to refer actions to the domain of rules places them *publicly* under a certain description, as instances of a recognizable type of action and thus, as Sumbanese see it, as something more than willful behavior driven by personal desires. These norms are central to the performance of disinterestedness. If the gift is not best understood in terms of following a rule (Bourdieu 1977, Taylor 1993), what gives it the moral character that people engaged in gift exchange clearly accord it? And what are we to make of the fact that people some-times *do* use the language of rules to talk about exchange? If we look at the concrete activities that constitute Sumbanese exchange, it becomes appar-ent that they take their value within a larger field of unmarked transac-tions, against which they are made to stand out by virtue of their formal character. The formality that registers a transaction as an instance of gift exchange marks the way people sit facing one another; two-part dialogue structure and the ritual couplets naming the gift, identifying the responsi-ble agent and the target; preliminary tokens conveyed in betel dishes; re-ciprocal tokens given in acknowledgment of receipt; and so forth (see Keane 1997). Sumbanese explicitly draw a contrast to the marketplace, where often the same items (horses, cloth, machetes, and so forth) will change hands, but without any of the formality. This formality frames acts of exchange as transpiring within a domain of evaluations of people, their actions, and their material goods. To be completed, a transaction must be recognized as valid by an exchange partner. If it is valid, then certain things follow. The presence of horses in a man's corral, or gold in his storage chest, is considered to be proof of a transaction recognized by an other, and all the moral standing that retrospectively conveys. The semi-otic forms of the interaction and of the objects that flow through it form a moral metalanguage. The goods that result index the mutual recognition of both parties; the horse in my corral indexes a moral bond between its source and me. Talk about rules is a way of establishing value judgments, rendering material goods traces of past actions of a certain knowable type.

Sometimes the suppression of certain ways of talking helps constitute acts as moral. In some societies people typically claim it is impossible to know what is in the mind of another person. Melanesian research suggests this "opacity claim" is less a theory of mind than an ethic of *talk about* minds (Duranti 2008, Rumsey 2008, Schieffelin 1990). That is, when people deny they can tell what others intend, they are expressing a strong cultural norm about who has the right to put inner thoughts into words. This has consequences for the forms that acts can take in order to be morally recognizable. These forms stress material transactions over the verbalizing of purposes, and thus place great weight on inferences drawn by the recipient rather than on explications offered by the giver. Opacity statements sometimes manifest a local moral theory, that the privacy of inner thought guarantees the individual's relative autonomy (Stasch 2008). The combined focus on things and silence around intentions helps constitute certain acts as morally consequential and demands attentiveness to the forms those acts take.

Mauss saw gift exchange as characteristic of "archaic societies." He took it, in part, as a counter-ideal he posed against liberal capitalist modernity, manifesting a world prior to individualism, alienation, and the drawing of boundaries among such distinct value spheres as religion, economics, government, and kinship. But even in the most liberal economies, some things such as children, spouses, body parts, sex, good grades in school, and even political office are not supposed to be for sale (Sharp 2000, Zelizer 2005). And they are cordoned off for reasons different from the prohibition on selling dangerous drugs or military secrets. They concern the ethical boundaries that distinguish persons from things, ends from means (Keane 2007: 223–51).

The relation between form and ethics is not confined to supposedly traditional economies or to the domestic sphere in capitalism. As I have argued elsewhere (Keane 2008b), marketplace bargaining typically follows rules that derive some of their ethical force from the interactive norms of social etiquette (see Yeung in this volume). The norms often remain tacit, but, as the metalanguages that can emerge amidst marketplace negotiations above might suggest, the move into explicitness can draw moral authority from that implicit domain. Drawing on the early history of capitalism, Mary Poovey (1998) has suggested that double-entry book-keeping manifested ethical values such as transparency. Among contemporary futures traders in Tokyo, according to Hiro Miyazaki, people can self-consciously respond to the values suggested by such forms. Miyazaki writes:

> In the Japanese business world, storytelling is an important genre of speech. . . . Typically delivered in monologue form by a senior to a junior while drinking and eating late into the night, this speech consists of a retrospective account of the senior's reflection on his career. The account always has a slightly moral overtone. It also usually culminates in a revelation of the speaker's "dreams" for the future. The dreams are presented as if they were secrets, as truthful presentations of who one is. (2006: 150)

These revelations are inseparable from ideas about finance. According to Miyazaki, "In [Japan] in the late 1990s, the move to calculate one's own worth was one of the characteristic activities of the 'strong individual.' . . . This practice was evidence, in the popular imagination, of the strong individual's rationality, risk taking, and self-responsibility" (ibid. 151). The very instrumentality of this practice imposed what I think we can call an ethical value, as an external discipline on the willful self. One of these men, Tada, uses a spreadsheet to calculate his worth. "From Tada's point of view," Miyazaki writes, "the power of logic inhered in its use as a constraint on intuitive impulses. Tada demanded that traders should do exactly what their models were telling them to do even if this contradicted their intuition" (ibid. 154). Like the Maussian gift, certain forms, such as spreadsheets and financial models, can be used to impose a rule on the willful actor. Submission to them is a virtue. Their moral standing derives from the experience of externality that their materiality makes possible. This externality allows (but does not determine) a sharpening of ethical awareness.

In material transactions ranging from the ordinary etiquette of hospitality (Shryock 2008) to formal exchange, from marketplace haggling to high-end financial operations, the material or transactional forms that govern ordinary commercial interactions give an ethical shape to actions and, characteristically, embody a moral metalanguage rendering them available for judgments by others. The very externality of things and forms to the subjective life of those who wield them seems to be part of that morality. Their semiotic form materializes that externality and its difference from the subject's unself-conscious habits and desires. Yet physical objects remain mute. That is also part of their power—they enter into the projects of their recipients bearing a proliferation of possible futures (see Keane 2003b). That muteness is also a source of moral ambiguity: gifts, for example, do not make intentions transparent, and they can be diverted to alien purposes. In response, people often try to channel and control those possibilities by using words. But words, like things, have surfaces. Speech does not have to be either ritualized or ethically explicit to have moral implications; those implications can saturate the very forms that ordinary conversation takes.

## Others' Words and Other Minds

Acts such as justifying, accusing, and persuading cannot be understood outside the context of interaction with other persons. Close study of inter-actions shows how human cognitive and affective endowments are brought to bear on, and respond to, the realm of those public concepts and values that are most salient to consciousness. It is in interactions that we can begin to tease out the relations between the universalizing assertions of psychology or philosophy and the particularities of history and ethnogra-phy. Certain basic components of moral psychology, such as empathy, helpfulness, fairness, and an ability to distinguish intentional from nonin-tentional actions, appear very early in childhood (Tomasello 1999). The cognitive capacity to take another's perspective—both to see things from his or her point of view and to see oneself from the outside—is often taken to be an essential precondition for morality (see Rumsey 2003a and in this volume). Indeed, this capacity is presupposed by Weber's definition of so-cial actions, which take their meaning from their orientation to those of other actors. Reciprocity of perspectives is evident early on, in the prelin-guistic child's ability to direct her gaze in parallel with others and later to point. Linked to this ability is the subsequent emergence of an awareness that what others know and desire may differ from one's own knowledge and desires, which are prerequisites for the distinctly human "theory of mind" (Baron-Cohen 1995, Gopnik and Meltzoff 1997, Wellman 2002). Language seems to play a critical role in the full development of the reci-procity of perspectives (Lucy ed. 1993). According to the developmental psychologist Michael Tomasello, "to understand that other persons have beliefs about the world that differ from their own, children need to engage them in discourse in which these different perspectives are clearly appar-ent—either in a disagreement, a misunderstanding, a request for clarifica-tion, or a reflective dialogue" (1999: 182). Once a basic theory of mind has been established, children can internalize explicit rules they have learned from adults, using them for self-regulation. Further developments include metacognition (being able to discuss one's own reasoning) and representational redescription (being able to present knowledge in different formats, to represent representations as such). The latter ability is presupposed by many familiar theories of morality, since, according to Tomasello (1999: 191–95), it allows people to generalize about ethical principles and to apply them flexibly across different contexts. But as suggested above, morality is not only, or even primarily, a matter of rules and reasons.

Empirical observation bears out classical theory: one does not develop morality all by oneself. Studies of children's language socialization (Ochs 1988, Schieffelin 1990; see also Ochs and Kremer-Sadlik 2007) have shown that the habits and emotions we can identify with moral virtues are shaped and given coherence in ongoing social interactions over the course of a lifetime. This process occurs across a range of interactions with distinct kinds of persons, giving it a socially distributed character. Research on responsibility attribution, negotiation, and didactic talk (e.g., Hill and Irvine eds. 1992, Hill and Zepeda 1992, Hanks 2000, Keane 1997, Shoaps 2007, Sacks 1974) shows the importance of collaborative acts of framing— precisely that which Appiah, as noted above, calls *the* moral task. Typically, over the course of an interaction, lexical, grammatical, and pragmatic linguistic devices specify what kind of action is in question and who the agents are, such that responsibility, praise, or blame is even in question at all (Silverstein 1993). Framing is also crucial to the identification of acts and agents as belonging to socially recognized types, such as cheating and cheater, bravery and the brave, which contributes to the perception that traits are coherent and stable. As conversation analysis shows (e.g., Sidnell in this volume), framing is an outcome of the emergent properties of interaction as a shared activity. Close analysis of interaction demonstrates how ongoing sociability provides the continuous external reinforcement that not only sustains ethical intuitions and moral virtues but also shapes them in ways that make them recognizable to other people within the same community.

Palpable objectifications make the individual's character available for evaluations and responses by other people and serve as feedback to the individual him- or herself. Self-knowledge thus draws on some of the same resources as knowledge of others (see Rumsey in this volume). Ordinary interaction is saturated with the subtle acts of evaluation and judgment linguistic anthropologists categorize as stance. Stance refers to the ways people assign value to objects of interest, position themselves, and invoke personal and cultural systems of goods (Du Bois 2007: 139). In conversation analysis, "moral stance" has been defined rather narrowly as "action [taken] in such a way as to reveal to others that the actor can be trusted to assume the alignments and do the cognitive work required for the appropriate accomplishment of the collaborative tasks they are pursuing in concert with each other, that is to act as a moral member of the community being sustained through the actions currently in progress" (Goodwin 2007: 70–71). As Veena Das suggests (2007, and in this volume), moral dilemmas can arise out of the small exchanges that make or undo neighborliness. Like attributions of responsibility, stance is not entirely in the hands of a single actor, for "the very act of taking a stance becomes fair game to serve as a target for the next speaker's stance" (Du Bois 2007: 141). In this way, the ethical character imputed to individuals is shaped by such things as publicly circulating stereotypes and speakers' institutional positions (Irvine 2009). Thus many linguistic anthropologists are coming to describe stance more broadly than the local collaborations Goodwin invokes, as "a way of categorizing and judging experience particular to a group or individual that turns on some notion of the good or true" (Kockelman 2004: 129). But to have moral consequences that endure beyond the moment of interaction, notions of the good must become part of what people are to one another, and to themselves.

## Moral Voicing

Social interactions are mediated by processes of objectification that contribute to actors' experience of living in knowable, relatively stable realities. Typification (Schutz 1967) produces widely recognized character types or figures within a particular social context (Agha 2007, Silverstein 2003). The embodied and discursive figures available in any moral community serve as public models or exemplars with respect to which actions can be oriented, reasons given, and justifications made. People are shaped as publicly known moral characters over the course of their interactions with others—this becomes part of the frame through which subsequent actions are interpreted. Lies are expected of known liars, charity of the generous. Taking on certain figures during interaction can itself become a process of moral self-discovery that contributes to the formation and systematization of virtues. Since these internalized figures are objectified, they are manifestly available to other people to respond to and evaluate. The feedback may help consolidate bodily habits, affective dispositions, ways of speaking, and styles of reasoning that persist or recur across contexts. But interaction also threatens that consolidation. As Erving Goffman wrote, "The divination of moral character by adducing indicators from the past is one of the major preoccupations of everyday life. And the treacherous feature is that 'a case can be made,' and at the same time there is no foolproof way of determining whether it is made correctly" (1974b: 453).

The divination of moral character to which Goffman refers depends on the surfaces of things, such as the quality of the gift and the timing of the countergift, the tone of the voice and the choice of the words. Choices among linguistic forms, for example, can play a crucial role in defining speakers' character and even the ethical options available to them. Consider Jane Hill's (1995) close analysis of a narrative by Don Gabriel, a speaker of the Native American language known as Mexicano, who lived in a farming village of central Mexico. Don Gabriel recounts the events surrounding the murder of his adult son, who was involved in a small business, by envious neighbors. The narrative, which culminates in the father viewing his son's corpse, implicitly stages a contest of value systems. It pits Indian-identified subsistence farmers, who are committed to relations of kinship and reciprocity in the village, against the Spanish-oriented world of individualistic urban capitalists.

Virtually none of the ethical contest takes explicit propositional form in Don Gabriel's talk. It emerges in code switching between Mexicano and Spanish, in different kinds of dysfluency (false starts, stutters, verbal slips, memory gaps, and so forth), shifts in the use of tenses, and changes in intonation contour. Hill finds that several distinct voices can be identified with Don Gabriel himself. He embodies by turns a neutral narrator, an engaged narrator, an emotionally overcome protagonist, and a moral commentator on the events. The latter offers his commentary to the listener through direct address, marked by other techniques of immediacy as well, such as historical present verb tenses and certain intonation contours.

Hill's analysis is of particular interest because it is strongly influenced by Goffman, whose portrayal of social interaction Alasdair MacIntyre took to exemplify the peculiarly amoral condition of modernity. According to MacIntyre, in Goffman's world "imputations of merit are themselves part of the contrived social reality whose function is to aid or to contain some striving role-playing will. Goffman's is a sociology which by intention deflates the pretensions of appearance to be anything more than appearance" (2007: 116). But although Don Gabriel is attentive to how he is presenting himself, the surface appearances he is trying to manage involve serious ethical commitments and the difficulties that their contradictions pose for him. The linguistic variations in his speech index both a cast of social types that manifest distinct moral stances and visions of the good life, and the speaker's identification with or estrangement from them. Hill, following Bakhtin (1981, 1984), says that insofar as discourse is replete with references to the words of others, by allusion, implication, or reported speech, it is constantly judging the words of others. The speaker's relationship to the words of a typified other is always one of taking a position, or stance. To speak dialogically is both to respond to others and to evaluate them in some way. This is why variations in speech style can reflect choices among ethical positions and moral commitments.

Don Gabriel is not in full control of the voices in his narrative. The very limit faced by his mastery registers the ethical gravity of the options he faces. The presentation of self is a kind of ethical work on the self. Don Gabriel tries to establish a coherent ethical position among conflicting ways of speaking. He cannot, for example, simply eliminate the presence of the voices of the profit seekers—his son is one of them—but he can locate them as far from the ethical center of the narrative as possible. Just as he participates in a social world that includes both agrarian collectivism and profit seeking, so too the voices that index that social world remain part of his own discursive repertoire. It appears that the struggle for dominance among the voices and the dysfluencies that result arises from a condition endemic to social existence: Don Gabriel cannot wholly identify with only a single voice. His dysfluencies may exemplify something about the ordinary ethics of everyday life.

Don Gabriel's encounter with the moral universe is neither created ex nihilo nor scripted in advance but works with the materials at hand. His moral intuitions are surely his own. That is, following the psychologists mentioned above, we can assume those intuitions are not merely imposed from without onto an otherwise empty space. It is those intuitions, presumably, that motivate and direct his struggles among the figures available to him. Yet those intuitions must be articulated in some manifest form, such as actions, habits, or voices. In this case, his self-knowledge depends upon those very voices. The need to choose among the options available in the public space within which the voices circulate is crucial to the production of consciousness. If we consider consciousness to be a component of a fully ethical person, then that person depends upon the existence of differing, even clashing, voices and upon the possibility of choosing among varieties of semiotic form: without those conflicts and without the objective materials of semiotic form, perhaps there is no occasion for ethical consciousness.

## Giving Reasons

Don Gabriel lays out his ethical *apologia* not in the form of overt self-justification but by embodying certain moral figures. This may be one of the most common modes of ethical stance taking. But it is certainly not the only discursive option. It is not just professional moralists who talk explicitly about ethics; such talk is ubiquitous. The invocation of rules and principles that Bernard Williams identifies with the morality system is instigated by all sorts of social interactions. Let us suppose that actions are characteristically evaluated ethically by virtue of being understood "under a description." Identifying an act as an instance of a knowable social or ethical type, a description implicitly must take into account the perspective of others, those for whom it would also be recognizable. In some cases, like excuses, the actor explicitly appeals to others to accept a certain description. In either case, there is thus an inherently dialogic feature in *any* judgment of action. The description of an action is perhaps usually only tacitly understood. But, what is tacitly understood can, under some circumstances, be put into words. Objectification can be a crucial—although not necessary—moment within the dialectic of action.

Sometimes people are called to give an account of themselves by the very nature of their activity. The giving of reasons is itself a kind of consequential action, to be understood like any other social practice. Among other things, the practice of giving reasons can enter into those of making moral claims- and of ethical self-formation. This kind of talk characteristically responds to the demands posed by social distance and moral or ideological differences. But the differences are not absolute, since they separate one from others who must be persuaded or to whom one owes self-justification. I don't owe an accounting of myself to just anyone. And I don't try to persuade people whom I consider utterly alien to me. As in gift exchange, explanations involve differences that constitute certain possible kinds of relationship.

In the contemporary world, one of the fields of activity in which ethical argument and moral justification are expected is religion. Indeed, in certain respects, religious institutions have come to be identified with morality. This is an aspect of the differentiation of spheres that both Durkheim and Weber saw as characteristic of modernity. James Laidlaw (2002) has criticized the Durkheimian tradition for so wholly equating morality with society that no distinctly moral sphere can be identified. But, of course, the lack of distinctions among social spheres was part of the point of the Durkheimian concept of "total social fact." It was meant to characterize societies before modern institutions and categories. Thus any attempt to understand "archaic" exchange by way of the modern categories—to see it as merely economic—would miss most of its significance; moreover, the same might be true of contemporary commercial activity as well. For Mauss, at least, the concept of the gift was also meant to reveal the underlying moral dimensions of social life, even in the contemporary world (Graeber 2001).

But in the contemporary world, morality *is* often treated as the special concern of religion. According to what I've called the "moral narrative of modernity" (Keane 2007), to treat economics, politics, or even education in moral terms too seriously exhibits a failure to be modern. By the same logic (and vastly oversimplifying), religion retains an instrumental function in otherwise secular societies because it justifies and inculcates morality. If economic rationality should prevail in the marketplace, strategic calculation in politics, and sentiment in the family, then moral reasoning is proper to religious institutions. As I have argued elsewhere (Keane 2007), the creedal and evangelistic practices of the northern Reformation contributed to the Enlightenment model, which takes the rational capacity for deliberation to be a condition for moral actions. The demand that one be responsible for one's thoughts can translate into a demand that those thoughts be objectifiable, available for rendering in propositional form.[4] But the high value often placed on the propositional stance toward one's thoughts has become a general expectation within the frame of secularism. As Michael Warner has put it, "the trend toward the personalization of belief in the long history of Christian reform is a trend toward intensification and propositionalization simultaneously, and it is the latter that liberalism stems from" (2008: 612).

As I have suggested, the need for explicit ethical justification and the giving of moral reasons characteristically arises across some social or conceptual gap. In contexts of religious difference and change, people may

---

4. John Calvin, for example, held that all humans know moral law but this knowledge is obscured; therefore we need the written law of scripture (see Keane 2007: 109). In this view, the need for verbal explicitness that motivates scripture, prayers, sermons, and creeds is a direct effect of a condition specific to humanity due to Adam's fall.

draw on speech genres such as inculcation, proselytization, casuistry, and apologetics directed at others. They can also be directed at oneself, for instance, as speaking a religious creed helps discipline one's thoughts (Keane 2007: 67–72). In my closing example, I want to look at what seems to be an especially hard case, a piety movement defined in opposition to the rationalistic discourse of justifications usually identified with Enlightenment modernity (or its imagined Greek predecessors). Charles Hirschkind has analyzed men in contemporary Cairo who strenuously engage in ethical self-cultivation. They aspire to virtue in the form of embodied and affective dispositions. To this end, they regularly listen to cassette recordings of sermons. In contrast to sermons delivered in state-sponsored mosques, these sermons do not justify faith and offer up reasons. They are shaped within a tradition that is "relatively unconcerned with . . . devising techniques to ensure the persuasiveness of a preacher's discourse" (2006: 33). In this semiotic ideology (see Keane 2007), listening is not a rational engagement with concepts but an aesthetic one with sound. The stress is on the moral receptivity of the listener, which is located above all in bodily and affective responses to the spoken word. In this tradition, "all moral action is in some sense a listening, the reverberation of the words of God within human souls and actions" (Hirschkind 2006: 37).

This twentieth-century movement responds to the challenges posed to piety by the everyday conditions of life in a secular nation state. Moreover, its adherents are characteristically people who have in some sense converted; they have chosen the disciplines to which they subject themselves. Within that context, it is no surprise to discover them to be highly articulate exponents of their practices and the justifications for them. One man tells Hirschkind that, when you listen, it "makes you want to pray, read the Quran . . . to think more about religion" (ibid. 68). For many, this listening "serves as a constant reminder to monitor their behavior for vices and virtues, . . . to maintain a level of self-scrutiny" (ibid. 71). Thus, while the sermon does not necessarily work by virtue of persuasive arguments, it does contribute to modes of heightened awareness in which the self is transformed into an object of observation. If the goal is the inculcation of habits, they are instigated by a purposeful break from the unreflecting flow of a previous way of life. And, in the end, the sermons *do* provide the language by which these men portray themselves and try to persuade one another. Moreover, in persuading others they are also speaking to themselves. Their own explicit discourse helps guide their self-transformation, helping sustain an emerging habitus.

Just as Tada, the Japanese trader, externalizes himself in an objective form in order to subject himself to an ethical discipline, so too the act of giving an account of oneself to others can be at the same moment an act of self-formation. It is an ethical act that depends on those others and on the semiotic forms demanded by their presence. These men have undergone a kind of conversion, which provides them with the social space across which reasons may be demanded. We may find such social spaces in all sorts of contexts. As Michael Warner has suggested, for example, the American practice of stating publicly who one is has its roots in the models of individual conversion that emerged in evangelical Protestantism. Speaking of American evangelical testimony, he writes, "one way that fundamentalists have contributed to the culture of minority identities is by developing the performative genres of identity-talk. Sentences like . . . 'We're here, we're queer, get used to it' take for granted a context in which people are accorded the power of declaring what they are" (1993: 75). He says this capacity is based, in part, on the conviction of one's separateness from mainstream society. (But, I should add, it's still a society that can be addressed and ought to listen; this is not the separatism of, say, the Amish.) The conversion experience and the sense of separateness it can induce, or to which it can respond, is one basis for a position in which the critic might stand somewhat apart from the community. It might provide a position from which the giving of reasons and the mobilization of a knowable typology of persons and practices are necessary components of any act that would be deemed ethical.

## Ethics, Others, and Objects

I suggested that Don Gabriel's own ethical self-consciousness is a function of the differing voices he is trying to master. I proposed that without those differences, although there would still be basic moral intuitions, there might be no basis for a full-fledged ethical *consciousness* per se. Similarly, the purposeful self-cultivation that Hirschkind describes is also a product of divergent possibilities. And even Maussian exchange works to define an other and to specify the distance between the giver and recipient of the gift. Potential conflict and difference are ubiquitous within even fairly unremarkable social circumstances and can belie the shared and taken for granted background values, the habitual character, and the embedded lack of self-consciousness that both the communitarians and their critics sometimes imagine a cultural account of ethics must require. The ethical modalities I have sketched out here allow certain kinds of self-distancing.

They involve distinct modalities of objectification by which people and their relations to other people are mediated by semiotic forms. The futures trader's spread sheet imposes a formal rule on a willful self. The Sumbanese gift enmeshes high moral claims with the causal consequences of material transactions. The grammatical forms with which Don Gabriel cannot help but speak resist his full mastery and express the role other people play within his own ethical self-formation. The Muslim sermonic cassette tape fuses emotion and argument; it instills passion with reasons. If ethics is a function of life with others, those others are neither wholly other to the self (Don Gabriel's others speak *within* his own words) nor do they snuggle down comfortably together with it (Marcel Mauss pointed out that gift exchange can verge on *warfare*). The moment of objectification can turn in any number of directions.

I started by suggesting that the sociological imagination would put the bare fact of life with others at the heart of ethics. If this is so, I then proposed, we should attend to the surface of things. The dialectics of objectification makes possible a wide range of stances, a host of different ways of acting morally and being ethically aware that are in continual interaction with one another. The empirical study of actually existing moral worlds will cast doubt on any effort to reduce ethics to individuals taken in isolation, whether to their self-interest, instrumental rationality, abstract principles, cognitive proclivities, or affective dispositions. The sociological imagination suggests there is no source of goods or goals wholly antecedent to the context out of which the actor's motives and options have been formed. Thus there is no Archimedean point from which either one's self-interest or means-ends calculations can be objectively perceived and evaluated. Although morality is not *reducible* to experience—this chapter is not making a case for a strict phenomenology—the first and second person character of ethical experience is not something we should or can eliminate from our analysis. This conclusion does not, however, throw us back to the seamless determinism of a tradition or the structured order of a Durkheimian social morality. Ethics are not *only* tacit competences. Moral life is lived in, and moves among, different modalities. There is a space for deliberation, practices of objectification, for critique and invention, and for socially embedded demands for the giving of reasons. Even the smallest spaces of routine face-to-face interaction can foster moments of difference and distance that may demand an articulate morality. Both the tacit intimacy of habit and the vociferous distance of estrangement, the first person stance and the possibility of departing from it, are everyday conditions of life with other people.

ACKNOWLEDGMENTS

Versions of this chapter were presented at the conference Ordinary Ethics at the University of Toronto, at Princeton University, and as the Annette B. Weiner Memorial Lecture at New York University and the D. R. Sharpe Lecture on Social Ethics at the University of Chicago. I am grateful to my hosts for inviting me to these events, to the other participants and audiences for their comments, and to Victor Caston, Veena Das, Charles Hirschkind, Matthew Hull, Michael Lambek, Adela Pinch, Alan Rumsey, and Kathryn Tanner for their astute criticism.

# From the Ethical to the Themitical (and Back): Groundwork for an Anthropology of Ethics

*James D. Faubion*

The ethical domain is very much a part of contemporary anthropological horizons, and not merely because anthropologists continue to worry over their own professional ethics or because a number of them suffuse their own research and writing with the ethical position that they personally hold most dear. Ethical anxiety is a marked feature of the broader intellectual and practical ecumene. Unsurprisingly, the best of recent contributions to an anthropology of ethics tend to acknowledge Michel Foucault as at least one near forerunner. Talal Asad's *Genealogies of Religion* (1993) is among these, as are Heather Paxson's exploration of reproduction and mothering in Greece (2004), Saba Mahmood's study of a women's pietistic movement in Egypt (2005), certain of the essays that Michael Fischer includes in his *Emergent Forms of Life and the Anthropological Voice* (2003) and Joel Robbins's *Becoming Sinners* (2004; see also Howell 1997b, Humphrey 1997, Lambek 2002a). I have made three previous forays of my own. The first brought a blend of Foucault and Aristotle to the outlining of the general program of an anthropology of ethics (Faubion 2001a). The second, far more empirically engaged, explored the works and days of a Branch Davidian claimant to prophetic authority (Faubion 2001c: 115–59). The third brought a similar blend of Aristotle and Foucault to a consideration of the claims, the duties, and the existential hallmarks of kinship (Faubion 2001b; cf. Faubion and Hamilton 2007).

The extant anthropology of ethics—my own past interventions into it included—does not, however, quite articulate or give full analytical attention to a distinction that I now consider intrinsic to what, following Foucault, I think of as the ethical domain and thus as crucial to any approach to the anthropology of ordinary ethics (cf. Foucault 1985). I approach that domain diagnostically, as an array of cases, some but not all of whose features might be generalizable. At the very least, I think the distinction in question is diagnostically stable and diagnostically useful. If it survives the test of Occam's razor, which would trim any conceptual apparatus of all but the presumptions that are strictly necessary to it, then it should be part of the explicit diagnostic infrastructure of an anthropology of ethics. That distinction—which I develop at greater length in the opening chapters of a book from which this paper is a refigured excerpt (Faubion, forthcoming)—has its ground in an important and related series of cognitive, affective, semiotic, and structural differences between the more dynamic and the more homeostatic aspects of what I think of systems theoretically as ethical autopoiesis—the production and the maintenance of the ethical subject. My fashioning of it has certain elements in common with Jarrett Zigon's recently circulating intuition that ethics is peculiarly visible in moments of "moral breakdown" (Zigon 2007) but ultimately differs from his distinction between the ethical and the moral. Above all, and counter to what Zigon suggests, I resist both semantically and diagnostically any construal of the dynamic (or productive) and the homeostatic (or reproductive) dimensions of the ethical field as contradictory. My own distinction is more closely related but still not equivalent to the distinction that has reemerged in the Anglo-American analytical tradition of philosophy in the past couple of decades between an "ethics" centered on the concept of virtue and the rest of "moral philosophy" (see, e.g., MacIntyre 1984, Nussbaum 1992).

Rendering what I have in mind, I turn once again to Aristotle, who does not term his enterprise in *Nicomachaean Ethics ēthika* (an editor's titular intervention) but instead an inquiry into *to anthrōpinon agathon*, "the human good" or, as several translators have (not altogether fortunately) preferred, "the good for man." In his introductory remarks in that work, however, Aristotle makes an incisive and, for my purposes, particularly relevant distinction between what I am calling ethics and the "architectonic" (Aristotle 1934: 4–5 [NE 1093b.ii.4–6]) or "science," for which the resolution of what constitutes the human good is propaideutic. The term he assigns to that architectonic is *politikē*. One usually finds the term glossed into English as "politics," which serves if nothing else to make for a contrast of a very stark sort. Few if any of us would confuse "ethics" with "politics" today. Yet *politikē* does not mean "politics" as we have come to know it. It rather denoted—and for many scholars of political theory, still does denote—the care and maintenance of the *polis*, of the Greek city-state, which was for Aristotle the teleological culmination of the development of civilized human life and within which alone human life could be fully worth living (and then fully only for wealthy, free adult men).

*Politikē* has ethics as one of its cardinal concerns, because the maintenance of the polis requires the existence of citizens equipped intellectually with the judgment to govern it and characterologically with the dispositions affinate to the civilization it realizes. In a definitional effort to avoid the unhappy consequences that Plato had revealed would follow from the Socratic understanding of the exercise of virtue by way of analogy with the plying of a craft, Aristotle insists that ethics is not concerned with *poiesis*, with "making" or "creating," but instead with *praxis*, with "doing." If every ethical practitioner has something of a natural history, moreover, he is not, in Aristotle's considered judgment, born with his agency fully realized any more than a sculpture is already complete in the block of marble from which it is carved. Aristotle is explicit: the virtues that are the dispositional ground of ethical agency do not reside in human beings by nature but can and must be cultivated only in and through practice. Grown men might be left largely to their own exercises. Children, however, require ethical pedagogues.

Hence, *politikē* rests largely in the order of the homeostatic, or more simply, in being. In this respect, it is on a par with what I would formerly have designated as "morality." Discussion and commentary at the workshop in which Michael Lambek graciously invited me to participate has convinced me, however, that yet another stipulative foray into the semantics of "ethics" versus those of "morality" is likely to become entangled—and sooner rather than later—in the thick and inconsistent morass of the forays that have preceded it. I see no other alternative, in consequence, than to resort to coinage. I propose accordingly to designate the homeostatic dimension of the ethical domain its "themitical" dimension—after the Greek *themitos*, "allowed by the laws of the gods and of men, righteous," as Liddell and Scott's venerable *English-Greek Lexicon* has it. The themitical dimension of the ethical field is hardly without its own dynamics, of course, but they belong largely to the order of reproduction. The broader ethical field, however, must always also have one foot at least in the dynamics of production, of becoming. This is Foucault's particular illumination of that field, but he fails to do full justice to the themitical. Indeed, his illumination is in need of refinement and elaboration in order to sharpen and broaden its anthropological reach. The most secure starting point in doing so must, to my mind, be as near as possible to absolute zero, to the collective situation in which the ethical domain and a fortiori its themitical dimension do not (yet) exist. I turn to Max Weber to find it.

### The Charismatic and the Ethical

Weber articulates at various junctures something of a sociological primal scene, a scene in which rationalization approaches absolute zero and the divide between the anethical and the ethical domains, between the one and the other ecology, has yet to be made. We find it in what in English is his best-known and methodologically most thorough ideal-typification (and one must stress that it is an ideal-typification) of charismatic authority. In that scene, the typically subliminal normativity of everyday routine is suspended. It is a scene of the unfamiliar or of disturbance, in which the experience of the disruption or failure of the reproduction of the routine is also the impetus to thought and action, to urgent response. Weber appropriates the historical sociology of charisma and charismatic authority from the first volume of Rudolph Sohm's *Kirchenrecht* (1892), which departs from Paul's evocation of the *kharisma* or "gift of divine grace" in his first epistle to the Corinthians (12:4), in an analysis of the peculiarly counter-ecclesiastic— counter-institutional, even anti-institutional—authority upon which the Christian movement claimed to stand as it was establishing itself. Weber undertakes a "political" expansion of Sohm's conceptualization of charisma, putting the warlord, raging Achilles, shoulder to shoulder with the prophet, with Jesus himself.

These are odd bedfellows, but are for Weber a proper pair for at least three of their ideal-typical characteristics. First, both are (for those who deem them charismatic) literally extraordinary, endowed with powers and capable of actions beyond the abilities of the merely mortal. Second, both are radically indifferent if not positively opposed to the routine demands of any given institutional order, above all of economic routine. Hence, the sociological hallmark of charismatic authority is that it is sensu stricto non-normative. It is thus both logically and practically antithetical to any of the normative regimes—whether traditional or rational-legal—that might transpire through one or another process of routinization. The only criteria for its justification are performative. Charismatic authority stands or falls with the charismatic leader's continuous conjuration of extraordinary effects.

Finally, both the warlord and the prophet are of the same political mind or, in any event, of the same political ethos. Both are sovereign in refusing to recognize any compromise or co-domination of the realm they claim as their own. They reject any laws, or at least any laws other than those they themselves decree. Weber is very fond of paraphrasing the central rhetorical device of Jesus' Sermon on the Mount (Matt. 5–7): "It is written . . . but I say unto you . . ." (1946: 250). If charismatic authority is "revolutionary," this is precisely because the charismatic leader (ideal-typically, to repeat) reveals, to those who follow or revere him or her or it, the inadequacy of the established social and cultural order. As leader, however, the charismatic acknowledges and can acknowledge only the powers with which he or she is invested, whether by a god or in essence. Hence, charismatic leadership entails a relationship with the charismatic following that is homologous to that between master and slave. A relationship there must be, since charisma is a social fact, not, ultimately, a psychological one. Yet charismatic leadership can accommodate the other only in one mode: as follower. Here, what Foucault terms *assujetissement* as the potentially ethical condition of "subjectivation" dissolves into *assujetissement* as the ethically abject condition of "subjection" (cf. Faubion 2001a: 125–27).

We are thus warranted in inferring that in Weberian sociology's primal scene—ideal-typically at least and to the extent that it is ever realized in fact—there is no such thing as ethics. That his "value-free" methodology does not inhibit him from considering whether Mormon prophet Joseph Smith might not simply have accomplished a "hoax" (1946: 246) strongly suggests that Weber himself would license the same inference. That he also finds and takes the opportunity to fashion the ecstatic warriors retained in Byzantium as the "blond beasts" of Nietzsche's *Genealogy of Morals* only reinforces that suggestion (ibid.; cf. Nietzsche 1956: 175). The logical and practical agon on the charismatic stage pits sovereignty against ethics, but in a quite specific sense. Following Carl Schmitt's currently fashionable conception, the sovereign actor is an anethical or sur-ethical actor because he or she stands as the arbiter of the "state of exception" and so of the always somewhat magical crossing of the divide between ought and is, fact and value (Schmitt 1985 [1922]). That conception is, however, more narrow than its Weberian counterpart. The berserk warrior is not sovereign in so strictly a political-theoretic sense, and the prophet who teaches by example rather than by decree resists or perhaps even defies classification as an executive or legislator. The Weberian contradiction between the sovereign and the ethical is also ontological, but in just this sense: in the sovereign's cosmos, there is no one to serve as an ethical other. Such a cosmos, of course, includes others; it is always a social cosmos. Yet, it includes them only as instruments or as enemies to the death. What is absent from the sovereign's cosmos is any other with any recognized chrism of his or her or its own.

Whatever its (properly) philosophical or political-theoretic implications may be, Weber's primal scene thus generates a sociological lemma that seems to me as fit as any available to serve as a basic working postulate of an anthropology of ethics. Put in terms of its Weberian semiotics, it would go something like this: ethics emerges within the primal scene of charismatic performance at the moment at which the charismatic leader recognizes and accommodates the chrism of the other. Clarification is urgent. First, though the contradiction between the sovereign and the ethical is inherent in the Weberian primal scene, its overcoming in the charismatic's gesture of accommodation is still within the bounds of the primal scene, at least to the extent that the accommodation of the chrism of the other does not yet constitute an act of routinization, the establishment of normativity. To be frank, it is unclear whether Weber himself would agree with this formulation. His stipulation that the charismatic leader's mission must prove itself in bringing about the well-being of his followers (1946: 249) is compatible with it. Yet just such a pragmatic understanding of charismatic proof leads him to cast such apparent failures of success as Jesus' crucifixion in terms perhaps too close to the letter of those of Matthew's and Mark's Jesus himself—as the deprivation of a chrism and so of the loss of the authority it had conferred (1946: 248). The semiotics of charismatic authority is more complex and so, in consequence, is its pragmatics.

One can make little sense of the charisma of the typical Christian martyr, much less of the enduring charisma of Jesus himself, if one rests with interpreting suffering and the sacrifice of the self as evidence only of having been forsaken by one's god and deprived of one's formerly miraculous powers. On the contrary, in the Christian interpretation, through the crucifixion charisma is not lost but miraculously distributed. The Christ who dies for the sins of the other, for the sins of every other, radically extends the election that was formerly the privilege of his fellow Jews. On the cross, but still entirely enclosed within the extraordinary noise and thunder of, indeed at the moment of, the denouement of the charismatic agon, the Christ renounces his sovereignty in favor of ethical universality. Nor, for that matter, is it Achilles the slayer of Hector and conqueror of Troy alone who is the most charismatic of the heroes of the *Iliad*; it is also Achilles enraged and desperate with grief over the death of his beloved Patroclus and the Achilles who, returned to his senses, finds it in himself to pay honor to Hector's grieving father, Priam, the father of Patroclus's killer.

## Modes of Ethical Evaluation

In the Western philosophical tradition alone, the ethical acknowledgment and accommodation of the other exhibits impressive semiotic—or, as the philosophers would have it, ontological or metaphysical—variety. The ground of the obligation to pay the other ethical regard may be logocentric in the classical circle, but it is not purely that of logos even there. In the background even of a cosmology as logophilic as Aristotle's, the ethical subject that remains under the aegis of the gods still asserts its sacral inviolability. In Greece and widely beyond it, the identification of the ethical subject can also include such concrete, mundane, or at least experiential considerations as whether someone lives or pursues his or her own interests or appears capable of suffering, among many others. Whether or not a subject counts as an ethical subject can hinge on such heady and transcendental criteria as the possession of dignity, belonging to the kingdom of ends, or being an end in itself or an end for itself or indeed an Other (Levinas 2003; Løgstrup 1997). In contrast to these more inclusive categories and qualities, ordinary ethical regard—in the West and elsewhere—often remains resolutely local, extending effective acknowledgment and accommodation no farther than kin and friends and perhaps the occasional urchin or foundling. Whatever might be expected of the ideal ethical subject, the ethical everyman and everywoman are, frankly, not striking for their ardent logicism in the West or anywhere else. An anthropologist of ethics does well to keep this in mind.

One or another grounding of the demand of ethical regard, one or another postulation of criteria for or an essence of ethical value, is nevertheless constitutive of the ethical domain as an ecological domain, a domain that, in other words, encompasses the ethical field, its environment, and the interfaces between the two. Hence, it needs to be advanced as a formal dimension of a diagnostics of that domain. Call it the dimension of the mode of ethical valuation. Logically, any such mode is a mode of valuation only within a given ethical semiotics. The anthropologist of ethics should not slip into a naturalistic fallacy in presuming that such value actually resides in an empirically available condition functioning as a criterion of the ethical agent or locus of ethical value. Nor should he or she slip into a metaphysical fallacy, a fallacy of pure reason, in accepting that one or another idealization of ethical value is in fact its real essence, and semiotic alternatives be damned.

That discursive formations do not provide the anthropologist with inferential passes outside of them does not constrain him or her to the vapid relativism that would simply see a thousand flowers blooming and think them all equally worthy members of the whole grand bouquet. Diversity isn't everything. As a causal-analytical enterprise, an anthropology of ethics should endeavor to account for both the scope—which is impressive— and the sensible limits of ethical valuation. To put the same point differently, ethical value is an irreducibly semiotic phenomenon. Thus it belongs to the realm of the intersubjective and to the realm of Wittgensteinian language games and forms of life. But not all language games and forms of life work equally well. All the anthropological evidence agrees that human beings can elaborate codes at a far remove from the stubborn this-worldly requirements and constraints of sustainable autopoiesis. All the instruments agree that human beings are capable of finding and do indeed often find meaning in the most extravagant of ideas. Anthropological instruments might nevertheless provide a measure of that extravagance, without in any way presuming semiotically to invalidate or logically to reduce to absurdity anything short of patent contradiction (or even that) in doing so.

The anthropologist of ethics can, accordingly, make rather short work of the ethics of the lachrymose doctrines of Karl Robert Eduard von Hartmann, who was born in Berlin at the cusp of the bourgeois revolutions and died in the same city just a few years after the turn of the nineteenth into the twentieth century. He was a prolific writer, but his works sit largely uncelebrated on library shelves, perhaps for good anthropological reason. He argued (not altogether unreasonably) that, because human happiness is impossible, either in this or in any other world, the only fully rational course of human action consists in the radical pursuit of nonaction, not least, in the nonaction of a passive genocide, a refusal to reproduce that would in a few generations leave the world free of human striving and human suffering alike (Anonymous 1911). Hartmann is not a radical ascetic. It is not sex that he rejects but the further proliferation of the species. Nor is he a Zen mystic with a gloomy, Teutonic, fin-de-siècle bearing. His despairing anti-eudaimonism recommends a more material and global end to our orbit on the wheel of desire than does the Buddhist advocate of satori. For all this, it is far from incoherent. Its problem is, rather, that it is autopoietically bankrupt.

The sovereign regard of human beings as being mere instruments is logically incompatible with their being attributed ethical value. The Hartmannean regard of the ethically appropriate destiny of the human species is causally incompatible with sociocultural autopoiesis. Were it adopted as the themitical core of the ethical field, it would press human action in a direction contrary to that of autopoiesis and so contrary to the very condition of the sustenance of any ethical field as such. This point is indeed functionalist. The anthropologist of ethics should not rest with functionalism, but functionalist assessment seems inescapable here. Hartmannean ethics is maladaptive. This does not deprive it of meaning. Not merely for Hartmann himself but for his considerable late-nineteenth-century readership, such Swinburnean or Schopenhauerean pessimism was all the more existentially revelatory for being so bleak. Nor is it inconceivable that the whole of the human species might have embraced it. That it did not do so and has not done so is, nevertheless, what one might expect. On the anthropological metric of extravagance, Hartmannean pessimism is moderately extreme, but his endorsement of passive genocide is genuinely "far out."

## *Ethical Value*

That ethical value remains within the Weberian primal scene and that its semiotics in that scene partakes of the semiotics of the chrism suggests a strategy through which to characterize ethical value in general. Any attempt at a substantive rendering of ethical value, at pursuing in its auratic and atmospheric mist any particular molecular code, is clearly misguided. The substantive variability of conceptions of ethical value merely within the Western tradition already militates against such an approach. The extraordinary and unroutinized powers of the charismatic—in failure as in success—positively preclude it. Semiotically, the schematic of ethical value, like that of charisma, can only allow so much substantive variation because it is fundamentally substantively indeterminate. A placeholder for the extraordinary, for that which is not profane, for the Durkheimian "sacred" (Durkheim 1995:35–39), the schematic of ethical value thus approximates what, after Roman Jakobson and Claude Lévi-Strauss, one could call the "zero-phonemic." In his introduction to Marcel Mauss's collected papers, Lévi-Strauss expands Jakobson's concept of a phoneme that has no distinct differential value (Jakobson and Lotz 1949) into the concept of the "floating signifier," a meaning-bearing unit that nevertheless has no distinct meaning and so is capable of bearing any meaning, operating within any given linguistic system as the very possibility of signification (Lévi-Strauss 1950: xlix–l). Lévi-Strauss's example is "mana," which generations of anthropologists have struggled to define, largely without success. In its operation, it is very close to charisma—all the more so now that, as Matthew Tomlinson has shown, it has come to serve contemporary Fijians as an index not just of human and divine blessedness but also of the power of failure and loss (Tomlinson 2006; cf. Graeber 2001: 170–72).

Any rush simply to identify ethical value in its schematic indeterminacy with the value of signification would, however, lead precipitously to the commission of a semiotic fallacy, the mistaken inference that from significance in a linguistic sense significance in an ethical sense results. Yet the homology between the semiotics of so many of the signifiers of ethical value—"logos" included—and that of both "charisma" and "mana" cannot be diagnostically overlooked. Two features of the floating signifier in particular are worth emphasizing. The first is that, because it lacks any precise semiotic determination, it becomes all the more effectively a contrary of any sign of instrumentality or contingency. As semiotic systems around the world attest, the floating signifier is an especially effective carrier of conceptions of the transcendent and the absolute. Second, in lacking determination, the floating signifier also positively conveys an omnipotentiality that remains not merely undifferentiated but also auratic, atmospheric, ineffable, beyond articulation. The floating signifier is thus made for the mystic as the semiotic abyss that is also a plenitude and thus a topos of the excess that can only be experienced, never pinned down or spelled out. Roy Rappaport has made a similar point, recently reaffirmed by Michael Lambek (Lambek 2008; Rappaport 1999).

No substantive conception of determinate ethical value can preserve the semiotic limitlessness of the floating signifier. Ethics demands judgment, which demands justification, which demands criteria for the rectitude of both diction and declamation, which demands functional language games (Wittgenstein 1958: 5–13). So perhaps such modern mystics as Agehananda Bharati (cf. Kripal 2001: 207–49) are correct in drawing a sharp divide between mystical experience and ethical practice. Yet in doing so, they are in danger of obscuring not merely the semiotic but also the experiential aura and atmosphere that surround ethical value, and the aura and atmosphere that it frequently inspires. Nor is this merely the aura of the charismatic, the extraordinary man or woman made for extraordinary times. In one of its anthropologically best-known manifestations, it is also the aura that surrounds the initiate passing into and dwelling within the liminal phase of the rite of passage. For Victor Turner, the liminal is the contradiction and contraversion of the determinacy and definition of ordinary social life. It is "anti-structural," and, in its dissolution of the inevitable divisions and compartments of ordinary social life, it is a momentary liberation from social constraint and a window into our common humanity. So, at least, the humanist Turner would have it (1969: 105–11). We do not need to follow Turner, either in his dialectical or in his humanist interpretation of liminality—which can often be full of the worst unpleasantries, as Turner certainly knows—in order to recognize rites of passage as technologies of the transformation of the subject, targeting its ethical substance, doing their work to displace the subject from its former position and ready it for placement into a position that will define some part at least of its social future. We do not have to be Turnerians to recognize in that transformative process the subject's immersion in or infusion with the overflowing abyss of a significance that is never merely semiotic, but also always that of the ethical itself.

## From the Ethical to the Themitical (and Back)

On the plane of working diagnostic postulates, the homology between the schematic of mana and that of ethical value, and the attachment of the latter to the primal scene of charismatic anointment, encourage an analytical distinction between the ethical and the themitical, in two steps. Step one: the ethical field encompasses the themitical. Its themitical features are most apparent when one considers the ethical subject's mode of subjectivation to norms and values. The second step can be formulated in terms of systems theory, once systems theory is freed from the naturalistic conception, dear to Niklas Luhmann and others, of the system as always ultimately closed and so ultimately closed off from any direct or unmediated interaction with its environment. The organizationally open system troubles Luhmann because it slips from the natural to the historical. It is messy. It does not allow precise definition, and its definitional fuzziness can lead to paradox. As I argue at length in my forthcoming book, the anthropologist of ethics must learn to live with all this, on good empirical grounds, because sociocultural systems are in fact historical, messy, and definable only through analytical reification. There are advantages to doing so. Working with the concept of the open system, systems theory can render the second step as follows. In its primal (and thus inchoate) moment, ethics does not belong to the anatomy, the physiology, or the psychology of system maintenance or to the autopoietic reproduction of systemic structure or even organization. It is instead among the constituents of the restructuration and even reorganization of a system that thenceforth will not altogether be the system it used to be. Its specific difference lies in the ethical subject's effecting the sort of adjustment in which, neither closing itself off the sociocultural system in which it resides from any engagement with its environment nor approaching either the environment or that system simply as hostile or instrumental, the system itself moves or might move toward (a better, or worse, or in any event different) ecological accommodation. With that move, the themitical is likely not to be everything that it used to be.

So general a distinction—namely, between the ethical and the themitical—might be thought of as the first taxonomical step beyond the even more basic distinction between system and environment. From the concept of the system, it inherits the qualitative distinctions between code and behavior or, more precisely, between meaning and the structure and organization of action. It is relieved, however, of the burden of accepting among its provisional axiomatics the axiom of the existence of discrete traditions, cultures, or societies. It considers the existence and the definition of any and all of these to be an empirical and provisional matter, though it is quite capable of including them. It accordingly avoids falling by axiomatic fiat into discursive, cultural, or social relativism as we currently know and have known them (cf. Hatch 1983). Technically speaking, a system-theoretic approach to the ethical domain is thus axiomatically and ontologically weaker—it assumes less; it is more parsimonious—than its familiar relativist counterparts, whether anthropological or philosophical. It is free, for example, of the analytical and anthropological impasses that commitment to a Heideggerian ontology of tradition or historical Being would entail. It is also able to leave undecided even the more open-ended ontology of traditions that informs the otherwise congenial and relativistically tempered philosophical programs of such "virtue ethicists" as MacIntyre and, in particular, the ontological requisite that any tradition worthy of the name be of narrative tissue, be storied. That requirement might very plausibly be imposed on the traditions with which MacIntyre is specifically concerned—those of distinctively human beings. Whether it should be imposed on all autopoietic systems capable of occupying ethical subject positions is more ambiguous and, once again, thus best left to be empirically decided.

The very generality of the concept of the system and its autopoiesis further points toward an account—not a normative justification—of some at least of the universalistic criteria offered for the ethical and the moral by humanist and deontological philosophies over the centuries. It also points toward an account of why at least some human actions and human practices meet with disapproval and negative sanctions more or less everywhere we find them. Habermas's formal pragmatics of communicative action looks, for example, to be a formal rationalization (a.k.a. reification) of autopoiesis as a communicative process, despite Habermas's skepticism concerning systems theory. His three criteria for the validity of any communicative act oriented toward mutual understanding—its truth (functionality), its normative rectitude, and its sincerity or truthfulness—echo Kant, but they belong to our phenomenal world and they are meant to articulate not the necessary conditions of coherent thinking and autonomous action but rather the necessary conditions of the maintenance of ongoing intersubjectively intelligible interaction. As Habermas clearly recognizes, they are purely formal criteria—"syntactic" or procedural, not "semantic" or substantive. Substantively, they remain or are compatible with remaining relativistic, since the means of determining the truth, of determining proper authority, and of determining what constitutes and assessing truthfulness may vary from one communicative (sub)system to another. Habermas is probably correct to identify such procedural criteria as at least highly advantageous to systemic autopoiesis. Perhaps they are even necessarily in force. If so, however, they are so only as a rule or in the long run. That they are required of every single instance of action oriented toward mutual understanding is flatly false—and would be extraordinarily inefficient as well. The naturalistic fallacy thus admits of no overcoming here, either.

Of course, actions or practices that run against the grain of the sustenance of communication are also costly, and the general features of autopoiesis would suggest that arbitrariness might rank among the most universal of autopoietic irritants. This might help us to account for why, across so many socioculturally specific communicative regions, the arbitrary actor is likely to be labeled mad—not merely bad or evil, but positively mad. However, systemic irritants are not autopoetically deleterious without qualification; anthropologists and historians can report that even the mad occasionally find an audience. Whether or not arbitrary, acts or practices that abruptly or persistently disrupt the maintenance of communication might also be expected to be met with disapprobation the communicative world over. Murder is plausibly one such act or practice. Lying is another. Even with murder and certainly with lying, however, "extenuating circumstances" are in great supply—and often in the name of the maintenance of autopoiesis rather than because of any systemic laxity or decadence. The requirements of communicative autopoiesis might, finally, go some way toward explaining why the nonparticipant and the freeloader tend ubiquitously to be met with disfavor and disesteem—or at the very least, toward explaining why crafting an effective response to the question of why one should participate and shouldn't freeload has been a philosophical obsession in the West ever since the first rationally self-interested actor appeared on the scene (for which, see Plato's *Republic*). A system-theoretic approach to autopoiesis can at best advise such an actor that nonparticipation and freeloading are very likely to increase the complexity of the environment with which he or she or it must accordingly cope and hence are likely to be inefficient and cybernetically costly modes of being in the communicative world. Likelihoods are not, however, guarantees, and actors with a taste for risk or the increase of complexity or both thus have no self-interestedly rational reason to be deterred from pursuing their penchants. The philosophers' work is thus never done.

Luhmann also distinguishes between ethics and "morality," though in a manner that seems to have far less motivation in systems theory than in his own antipathy toward moralisms of any sort. When at his most consistent, and especially when distinguishing himself from Durkheim, he is fully aware that no ethical conclusions, or at least no ethical imperatives, can be drawn from his or any other social theory (Luhmann 1996: 32). Yet, as William Rasch appropriately notes, Luhmann's sociological characterization of modernity often fades into affirmation and often does so to antimoralistic ends (Rasch 2000: 145). For Luhmann—at whose conception of ethics I will arrive shortly—morality consists not in the anointed normativity of the system but instead in a discourse grounded in the binary opposition between esteem and disesteem (1996: 29) that concerns "the whole person as communicative agent" (Moeller 2006: 111) and is governed by the interdiction of self-exemption (Luhmann 1996: 29; the moralist thus cannot escape his or her or its own standards of evaluation). Yet in contrast, say, to economic, political, or legal discourse, morality has no correlative institutional locus. It floats systemically and for Luhmann, its origin is "pathological" precisely because it arises out of circumstances of "uncertainty, disunity and conflict" (1989: 140). Echoes of the Weberian primal scene here—but where I see an ecology of the ethical and a fortiori the themitical *in potentia*, Luhmann sees only confusion in and the confusion of the system itself. The intrasystemic incitement of such confusion is above all religion, whose regulative idea is for Luhmann the idea of transcendence and whose self-referential dynamics is accordingly a dynamics of self-transcendence in which the deconstructive dominates the constructive in the long term, often to "ruinous" effect. Morality is just the "invention" that constrains the play of secrets and paradoxes providing religion with its imaginative wellspring—but at its most "successful" and "productive" constrains but does not quash it (Luhmann 2001: 555–63).

The modern or functionally differentiated social system depends for its ongoing autopoiesis on the capacity of its subsystems to "recognize themselves" in terms of the binary codes that are specific to each of them. The recognition and maintenance of those codes is a necessary condition of the effective functioning of the subsystems jointly and severally. That condition is incompatible with "the moral integration of society" because, as Luhmann emphatically puts it, maintenance of these codes "*excludes the identification of the code values of the function systems* with the positive/negative values" that typically constitute the apparatus of justification or "program" of the moral code (1996: 35). Indeed, the genuinely modern moralist would object on moral grounds to the fusion of the codes of the functional subsystems with that of the moral coding of esteem and disesteem, since such a fusion would render what is economically profitable "good" and unprofitable "bad" in a moral as well as an economic sense, what is worthy of an A+ "good" and worthy of an F "bad" in a moral as well as a pedagogical sense, and so on. This indicates to Luhmann that "the moral itself accepts and even postulates" its "loss of sovereignty," its "negative self-restraint as a condition of its autonomy" (1996: 35). Otherwise said, the themitically modern attests, to Luhmann's mind, to the anointment of the functional differentiation of a system whose normativity is precisely that of functional differentiation. This is the cardinal systemic source of the distinctive complexity of what are for Luhmann distinctively modern ethical practices.

The same anointment constitutes the cardinal reason for the emergence in the eighteenth century of what Luhmann understands as the "reformulation of the meaning of ethics" as a "reflection on the grounds of [distinctively] moral judgment" (1996: 35). Ethics thus construed is, in short, a "reflection theory of morality" (1989: 141) whose two great polar alternatives remain for Luhmann Kantian deontology (of which he surely deems Habermas to be an heir) and Benthamite utilitarianism (1996: 33; cf.

Moeller 2006: 111). They are alternatives that by their very existence betray each other's inadequacies. Luhmann thinks there is ample empirical evidence—to be found in the fractious history of moral philosophy (or ethics) from the eighteenth century on—of the impossibility of a fully adequate, fully comprehensive, and self-consistent ethics. After the fall of theology, the sources of moral semantics are irreducibly plural (cf. Moeller 2006: 111). Ethical absolutism is thus—system-theoretically, in any case—out of the question. Inspired, perhaps, by the experience of the many forms of exclusion and disenfranchisement that are themselves products of functional differentiation, such absolutism is, of course, everywhere. Wherever it is, however, what it communicates can only be registered à la Luhmann (and by all means as what in his terms would constitute a moral failing) as antimodern (cf. Rasch 2000: 122–23). Such disdain betrays Luhmann's tendency to enclose autopoiesis solely within the problematic of organizational reproduction, which in turn betrays the restriction of what he calls morality and ethics alike to the themitical dimension of the ethical field. Equipped with the concept of the open system and the distinction between the ethical (or productive) and the themitical (or reproductive) that it allows, however, the anthropologist is by no means obliged to agree with him.

What anthropologists used to consider culture as a whole is, *pace* Malinowski (1939), probably not best or even adequately approached as some vast repertoire of devices of "adaptation." Ethics, however, must be so approached—recall von Hartmann—even if it can be adequately comprehended neither as practice nor as discourse through an adaptationist framework alone. On the plane of working postulates, then, ethical spacetime has one of its absolute limits when and where any adjustment to, any accommodation of the environment is impossible. Then and there, one might well find the charismatic leader at his or her most despotically sovereign. It has the other of its limits when and where the environment, and not least the other subjects that in part constitute that environment, are reduced—as subjects or as tools—to being nothing more than instruments, to being forced to accommodate without benefiting from any accommodation in return. In its purest expressions, it is precisely what the Greeks recognized it to be: enslavement. There is no need to review here the long, long list of the nonethical, the barely ethical, or the sur-ethical practices of which human beings have proven capable. It is still possible to conclude anthropologically that if ethics did not exist, we would surely have had to invent it.

It is, finally, possible to advance the basic diagnostic virtue of distinguishing between the ethical and the themitical, for which the Weberian primal scene once again provides the key. It is worth noting, first of all, that even Weber's exemplars betray elements of their own routinization, the beginnings of their transformation from exemplars of the anethical-becoming-ethical response to extraordinary circumstances into exemplars of the practices best suited to the themitical dimensions of autopoietic systems. The Jesus who works miracles remains charismatically pure. His crucifixion is diagnostically quintessential of the flood of ethical value that the rite of passage might unleash. In his broader life, however, as it is variously recorded in the synoptic gospels, Jesus is well on the way from the system-adjusting interventions of a charismatic becoming ethicist to the ethical attendant of the themitical. Not least, in practicing precisely what he preaches and so routinizing through concrete conduct what Paul will develop into the code of a fully fledged Christian life, he delivers to posterity the precedent for a normativity no longer proper only to the son of god but incorporable into the structure of the values and the obligations of the merely mortal woman and man.

Achilles' charisma is also routinized, if only weakly, for he has the benefit of being the son of a goddess. Though he indeed elects it, his destiny will remain on the side of the always extraordinary circumstances of the battles of which not just ancient Greek legends are made. Yet when he participates with his fellow heroes in the victory games, as in his treatment of Priam, his conduct is of a piece with the normativity of an ethical field that has routinized the apportionment and accommodation of every other subject's portion of honor and, in its cosmological warning that the beggar at one's door might be Zeus in disguise, has come as close to an ethical humanism as it ever would (cf. Pitt-Rivers 1977). Rather like Jesus at his most purely charismatic, the purely charismatic Achilles is hardly a picture of stability, even dynamic stability. He is anything but methodical. This remains true even when, his rage spent, he comes again to recognize that there are others in his environs with grief to bear and bodies to be given themitically proper burial.

As a matter of generalization, then, one can expect the ethical field to exhibit a certain lack of fixity, an indeterminacy echoing that of the semiotics of ethical value, the more its circumstances are extraordinary and the more pressing the need for ecological adjustment or restructuration or reorganization. The themitical tends by contrast—but not dichotomous contrast—to be less mutable. It partakes of the established. It partakes at least of whatever longevity the autopoietic system of whose normativity it is the valorization can boast. Again, the anthropologist of ethics slips into yet another modality of the naturalistic fallacy should he or she mistake the normativity—the structural-functional principles—of the organization of autopoiesis for ethics itself, or even its themitical dimension. The diagnostics that Foucault and Weber help us bring to the ethical domain, however, allows two further working postulates. One of these, with which Zigon would perhaps also agree (2007: 138), is that ethical value and the normatively established stand in a weakly dialectic relationship to one another.

Autopoietic creation ex nihilo belongs beyond the reaches of our actual horizons and so should remain beyond our diagnostic horizons as well. Yet we can further postulate that, however inextricable their relationship may be, the ethical retains a certain priority over the themitical (here reversing the Aristotelian relation between *ēthos* and *politikē*). Its priority is that, in the Weberian primal scene, ethical value remains resolutely indefinite. Within its semiotically and practically unroutinized ideal-typical ambit, the signifier of the ethical continues and can only continue to float. Only through routinization—which is to say, a rendering normative, but by no means a rendering habitual or subliminal—of one or another of its possible semiotic qualifications or criteria can ethical value be adapted to the temporal requirements of autopoiesis as a process of system maintenance. Hence, ethical value becomes themitical normativity and the ethical encounter of crisis a themitically oriented practice of deliberative decision through a translation that is also a reduction at once of complexity and of the scope of the ethical imagination. Contrary to what Zigon has suggested, however (2007: 138), such a reduction cannot be conceived as the telos of ethics but must rather be conceived as its ecological retraction. From the vantage of the ethical apostate, in any event, any given themitical system can only appear partial in its valuation. This in itself can and does stimulate the undertaking of adjustments, even in the absence of any properly environmental irritation and very much at the level of ordinary ethical life. It thus provides the energies for an increase of ethico-moral complexity that stands against the reduction of ethical complexity as its always potential counter-current. It is itself a part of what gives the ethical field and a fortiori its themitical dimension sociocultural variety. It is part of what gives both their histories.

# PART TWO

# The Ethics of Speaking

# Ethics, Language, and Human Sociality

*Alan Rumsey*

In the spirit of interdisciplinary collaboration that has inspired this volume, I will discuss some of the ways in which I think recent work in linguistic anthropology and related fields has shown that elements of the ethical are built into language at its core and how this work can shed new light on the role played by language in ethical thought and action. First, what do we mean by "ethics"? Whatever else the notion may involve, a wide range of philosophers (e.g., Hume 1957 [1751], Smith 1976, Rousseau 1979, B. Williams 1985: 12, Ricoeur 1992: 172, Levinas 1998) agree that ethics necessarily involves acting with regard for another person or people.[1] Another point of widespread if not universal agreement is that, across the range of natural species, the ethical is a uniquely human capacity. This conjunction seems unlikely to be an accidental one. While I am hardly the first to suspect as much, it seems to me that the conjunction itself is not too obvious to be worth pointing out and that there is more to be said about why it is a necessary one in light of some basic features of

---

1. Others, such as Nietzsche, Foucault, and perhaps Aristotle, place more emphasis on regard for the self, but this and a capacity for acting with regard for others are not mutually exclusive. Indeed, the former may even presuppose the latter.

language and its relation to human sociality. For a start, consider the following classic statement by linguist Emile Benveniste concerning a kind of grammatical category that is found in every human language, the category of *person*:

> I use *I* only when I am speaking to someone who will be a *you* in my address. It is this condition of dialogue that is constitutive of *person*, for it implies that reciprocally *I* becomes *you* in the address of the one who in turn designates himself as *I*. Language is possible only because each speaker sets himself up as a *subject* by referring to himself as *I* in his discourse. Because of this, *I* posits another person, the one who, being, as he is, completely exterior to "me," becomes my echo, to whom I say *you* and who says *you* to me. This polarity of persons is the fundamental condition in language [and] ... offers a type of opposition whose equivalent is offered nowhere outside language. This polarity does not mean either equality or symmetry: "ego" always has a position of transcendence with regard to *you*. Nevertheless, neither of the terms can be conceived without the other: they are complementary, though according to an "interior/exterior" opposition, and, at the same time, are reversible. If we seek a parallel to this, we will not find it. The condition of man in language is unique. (Benveniste 1971: 224–25)

## Ethics and Human Sociality: A Natural History

Whatever else may be entailed by the notion of "ethics," surely the reversibility of perspectives that Benveniste points to is an essential element of it. And insofar as ethics involves acting with regard for others, it is something that is not only enabled by language but is positively required by it, since ordinary use of the "person" categories that are found in every language is impossible without it. Below I will discuss other categories of language besides person and show how this pertains to them also, but first I will step back from the focus on language per se and turn to a consideration of a more wide-ranging body of recent work to which Benveniste's observations on language can be related. I refer to the newly emerging interdisciplinary synthesis concerning what Nicholas Enfield and Stephen Levinson (2006) call the "roots of human sociality." In their introduction to the volume by that name, which came out of the 2005 Wenner-Gren Symposium that they organized on the topic, Enfield and Levinson begin by declaring that "At the heart of the uniquely human way of life is our peculiarly intense, mentally mediated, and highly structured way of interacting with one another. This rests on participation in a common mental world, a world in which we have detailed expectations about each other's knowledge, intentions and motivations" (Enfield and Levinson 2006: 1).

How is that world constructed, and what is the nature of the uniquely human capacity that enables it? Obviously language plays a big part, and until recently its evolution would have been cited by nearly everyone—in line with Benveniste—as the single most important enabling condition for the forms of social interaction and mental life to which Enfield and Levinson point. But this view has had to be modified in recent years in light of new work by a number of researchers in developmental psychology, primatology, and evolutionary anthropology, such as Daniel Stern, Colwyn Trevarthen, Peter Hobson, and Michael Tomasello. Of particular relevance is the work of Tomasello and his colleagues, who work both with children and with nonhuman primates and whose findings compare interestingly with those of Peter Hobson and others working with autistic children (and who, on basis of far more substantial empirical work than most evolutionary psychologists have done, find themselves radically at odds with most of their views[2]).

Corroborating the earlier findings of M. C. Bateson (1979), Tomasello and his team have found that, long before children begin to speak, they engage in "proto-conversations" with adults and older children in which they exchange roles and perspectives with them. What is most distinctively human about those interactions is that many of them are not just dyadic but triadic, involving joint attention to a third person or object outside of the immediate circuit of interaction between infant and other. At nine to twelve months of age, still before beginning to speak, children show an operational capacity to understand that other humans are intentional beings like themselves, to construe their actions as goal-directed ones, to understand their point, and to collaborate with others in triadic interactions, in the course of which they attend both to the object of shared attention and to the person with whom they are jointly attending to it, whom they understand to be doing the same with respect to themselves. Many of the triadic interactions that infants engage in before speech are

---

2. A basic tenet of evolutionary psychology is that, as a result of evolved psychological adaptations to aspects of the ancestral environment, the human brain is hardwired with a number distinct cognitive "modules," or specialized capacities (e.g., to acquire language, numeracy, knowledge of certain kinds of objects, etc.). By contrast, Tomasello (1999: 203ff) posits a single adaptation—a new way of identifying with and understanding conspecifics as intentional beings—as a general capacity that has allowed for the development of all the others by enabling "cultural learning."

ones they themselves initiate, including, from about nine or ten months of age, acts of pointing to objects during which they attend both to the object and to the gaze direction of the person with whom they are interacting. Other primates too—especially our closest relatives the chimpanzees and bonobos—show a "sophistication in understanding many important aspects of intentional action" but by contrast with humans, they "seem to lack the motivations and skills for even the most basic forms of sharing psychological states with others. . . . Similarly, . . . systematic observations of chimpanzees and bonobo mothers and infants with objects reveals very little triadic engagement, and none that appears to involve a shared goal" (Tomasello et al. 2005: 685).

These observations have profound implications for our understanding of human sociality, for at least two reasons.

1. They show that some of its basic features, which are often thought of (by Benveniste, for example) as being dependent on language— mutuality of perspective, capacity for shared intentionality and role reversal—in fact begin to develop in infants long before language does and are quite highly developed by the time that children begin to speak.

2. They show that those features are, nonetheless, distinctive to the human species—as distinctive to it as language is.

Based largely on these two facts, and on the fact that the features in question are built into the nature of language, Tomasello (1999; cf. Tomasello et al. 2005) argues that the relevant human capacities actually evolved before language and were what made it and "cultural learning" possible. Whether or not that conclusion is correct, the research findings on which it is based are directly relevant for our understanding of the ethical dimension of human social life, as they show that some of its basic elements are, ontogenetically at least, even more basic than language and, indeed, part of a special capacity for taking into account the intentions of others that underlies not only language use but other forms of human communication as well.[3] The same conclusion is supported by researchers who contributed to the Enfield-Levinson symposium from a number of different fields besides psychology and primatology, including linguistic pragmatics, conversational analysis, and linguistic anthropology (Enfield and Levinson 2006).

---

3. It is perhaps needless to say that the same capacity allows humans to act *un*ethically, greatly increasing our ability to deceive and exploit each other for selfish purposes, as has been extensively explored in the literature on "Machiavellian intelligence."

I cannot review any of that other work here. Rather, I turn to a consideration of some aspects of language that are especially relevant for understanding how the ethical is implicated in language use. Of special interest here are the kinds of grammatical categories that are ubiquitous across the languages of the world—most or all of the relevant ones being indexical categories in the sense that their referential values are intrinsically linked to aspects of the contexts in which they are used.[4]

## *Ethics and Language: A Review of Some Relevant Grammatical Categories*

### PERSON

This category has already been introduced above by the quote from Benveniste and my discussion of it. But some further remarks are in order. First, the category of person itself is realized not only by personal pronouns, as in Benveniste's examples involving the pronouns *I* and *you*, but also, in many languages, including the Papuan one to be discussed below, by the form of the verb (as in Spanish: *voy*, "I go"; *vas*, "you go"; *va*, "he/she/it goes," etc.). Moreover, many of the world's languages encode finer distinctions of person and number than Indo-European ones do, including, for example, a dual number and "inclusive" versus "exclusive" distinction in the first person, so that, for example, instead of a single first person plural form, such as English "we," there may be four distinct pronouns or person categories corresponding to "I and thou," "I and you (plural)," "I and one other person who is not you," "I and at least two other persons, neither of whom is you." Also relevant is the phenomenon found in many languages of the world, including almost all European ones other than English, whereby the choice of pronouns and person categories used in reference to the addressee indexes aspects of the social relationship between her and the speaker, such as the degree of imputed social distance and/or hierarchical disparity between them (Brown and Gilman 1960, Agha 2007: 278–300). And in some Australian Aboriginal languages, different personal pronouns are used according to the classificatory kin relationship not only between speaker and addressee but among the people

---

4. This brief review of grammatical categories does not by any means include all the ethically pertinent ones, only those that are taken up in the ethnographic examples below. Among other relevant categories, one that has had to be excluded here for length reasons is (socio)spatial deixis, for which see Hanks (1990), Rumsey (2003a:174–75).

referred to by the various nonsingular forms in all the nonaddressee categories as well (Hercus and White 1973, cf. Merlan 1989).

In all of these cases, we can see that the choice that must be made among person categories in order to speak necessarily requires the speaker to take up a position within a complex social field. Especially if we take into consideration the fact that many of these choices are not entirely determined by preexisting social "facts" but are part of what establishes them as such, we can see that these choices are by nature ethical ones. And even where the relevant social facts are solidly established in advance of the act of pronoun use, for example, by the Tamil caste system (Levinson 1977) or Australian Aboriginal protocols for dealing with one's mother-in-law (e.g., Haviland 1979, 220–21, Rumsey 1982: 168), the relevant norms are, inter alia, ethical ones, whose observance is evaluated accordingly.

### REPORTED (A.K.A. ''PROJECTED'') SPEECH

It is a remarkable fact that every known language includes formal means for placing any given speech event into a kind of dialogical relationship with another one, whether real or imagined. The available forms of reported speech in any given language seem always to include what is known as "direct discourse" or "quotation," in which all the indexical categories of the "reported" utterance—person, spatial deixis, tense, etc.—are grounded in the "reported" speech event, for example, "Arthur said 'Mr. Tite Barnacle is a buttoned-up man, and consequently a weighty one.'" In many languages they also include various varieties of "indirect" discourse, in which some or all of the indexical categories are shifted so as to ground them in the "reporting" speech event, for example, "Arthur remarked that Mr. Tite Barnacle was a buttoned up man, and consequently a weighty one.'" The brilliant work of Bakhtin (1981) and Vološinov (1973) has both shown how pervasive a role is played by reported speech in the creation of evaluative stances in discourse, and placed it in relation to the wider range of discursive phenomena that have been studied under the rubric of "voicing."

These include not only explicit attributions of speech or thought by one speaker to another, as in the above examples, but also implicit ones, such as the one by Charles Dickens—or, perhaps more accurately, by the implied author of *Little Dorrit*—when he says about one of his characters "Mr. Tite Barnacle was a buttoned-up man, and consequently a weighty one."[5] Though the author does not frame this statement explicitly as reported speech, even of the "indirect" variety, other, more subtle aspects of the framing make it clear, at least to readers familiar with the mores of Victorian England, that this statement is being voiced from the point of view of a particular element of Victorian society, which the author is holding up to ridicule for, among other things, the assumption he imputes to them that "clothes make the man." Though this is done in a humorous way, the evaluative stance behind it is a serious one and exemplifies both the centrality of the ethical dimension in Dickens's works and, more generally, the way in which reported speech and the more general phenomenon of voicing is tied up with ethics. Below I will be discussing some other examples from actual speech rather than written fiction. For others I refer the reader to the excellent discussion of voice as a modality of the ethical in the essay by Webb Keane in this volume.

## MOOD AND MODALITY

Another set of ubiquitous grammatical categories that require the speaker to take up a position in relation to others are those of "mood" and "modality." With respect to their meanings, these fall into two broad classes known to grammarians and logicians as "epistemic" modality and "deontic" modality. Epistemic modality concerns the nature and degree of the speaker's avowed commitment to the factual status of what she is saying and is expressed through grammatical categories such as the indicative ("John came"), subjunctive ("John might have come"), and negative ("John didn't come"); deontic modality has to do with the speaker's commitment to the desirability or necessity of what she is predicating and is expressed through categories such as the optative ("May John always come"), obligative ("John must come"), and imperative ("John, come!").

Among formal grammatical categories associated with deontic modality, in many ways the most basic is the imperative mood. As has often been pointed out, (e.g., Palmer 1986: 29, 108), across the world's languages, there is a strong tendency for the imperative form of the verb to be the simplest one. The imperative is basic in another, related way: it is one of the first grammatical categories that infants learn to use and understand. In a preliminary study based on language-acquisition data from four languages around the world (Rumsey 2003a: 174–83), I have found that in all of them the imperative was not only one of the first forms of the verb to

---

5. This example is taken from Bakhtin (1981: 305).

be acquired but it was acquired well before the category of person. This is especially interesting with respect to the phenomenon of reciprocity of perspective and its relation to language, because the ordinary use of the imperative involves precisely the sort of commutability that Benveniste took to be associated with pronouns and the linguistic category of person. To grasp the force of "Stop!" or "Eat your sweet potato!" for example, a child must be able to understand that the wish being expressed is the speaker's and that he or she, the addressee, is the one being enjoined to perform the action. To use the imperative the child must be able to understand that these roles are thereby reversed.

Having reviewed three of the basic categories in terms of which the ethical is implicated in language I now turn to some ethnographic examples of how it works in practice, which are drawn from my work over the past three decades, partly in collaboration with Francesca Merlan, in the Ku Waru region of Highland Papua New Guinea.

### *Case 1: Taka and Laplin*

The following is an excerpt from a conversation that took place near the public meeting ground at Kailge in the western Nebilyer Valley. The speakers are a man named Taka and his fifteen-month old son, Laplin.

1. Taka: *mawa          wi        to*
        (boy's name) call out do(imperative)
        Call out to Mawa.

2. Laplin: [shouts] *mawai!*
            Hey Mawa!

3. Taka: *kar-na        pabiyl            wa!            kar!*
         car(locative) go(optative;    come(imperative) The car!
                       first person dual)
       Come, let's you and me go in the car! The car!

4. Laplin: *wa*
           come(imperative)
           Come!

Laplin here has had a directive addressed to him with an imperative verb, telling him to call out to a boy called Mawa, who is passing by. Laplin does so, using the correct vocative ending *ai* and intonation *ai!* In the words spoken by Taka to Laplin in the next line (3), the assumed speaker associated with the first person dual subject marking on the verb *pabiyl* ("Let's go!") is not the person from whose mouth they come, Taka, but his addressee, Laplin. Taka is, as we say, putting words into Laplin's mouth, prompting him to shout them out to Mawa. Laplin responds to this by repeating a single word of the grammatically complex utterance with which he has been prompted, the imperative form *wa* "come."

In grammatical terms, these few lines of speech involving a very young child already include all three of the categories discussed above: *person* (in the first person dual subject marking on the verb *pabiyl* in line 3), *mood* (the imperative verbs in lines 1, 3, and 4 and the optative in line 3), and *projected speech* (in line 3). In interactional terms, what is going on here involves triadic relations at two distinct levels. Line 1 involves one among the speaker Taka, the addressee Laplin, and the referent Mawa. Its effect is to bring Laplin into a circuit of joint attention between him and Taka, whose object is Mawa and to enjoin an action to be directed at him by Taka, namely, the action of calling out Mawa's name. Laplin's response in line 2 shows that he has understood this and in turn establishes the ground for the second triadic interaction, which Taka projects in line 3.

That projected interaction is at a meta-level in relation to the one between Taka and Laplin in that the third term that is involved in the exchange between the two of them is not just the boy Mawa but another projected triad: a ventriloquized exchange between Laplin and Mawa in which the third term is the car—or, more precisely, a proposed trip in the car that Laplin and Mawa would make together. In other words, there are two interactional frames here: the initial one involving Taka and Laplin, and another one involving Laplin and Mawa. Both of Laplin's utterances belong to both of those frames at once, in that they are positioned both as responses to Taka and as utterances addressed to Mawa, as prompted in ventriloquized form by Taka.

As shown by Bambi Schieffelin's (1990) detailed study of child language socialization among the nearby Kaluli people, this kind of ventriloquizing is ubiquitous in speech to infants, not only by adults but also by older children, often at the prompting of adults. It is a powerful form of subjectification, especially when the action being enjoined is speech to another, in that it presents to the child not only a model of interaction in which his or her subjectivity is virtually aligned with that of the caregiver, but also a model of what to expect in engagements with others. In the ventriloquized words in line 3, for example, Taka is presenting to Laplin a model of what, in order to get Mawa's attention, he can assume will be an alluring prospect

for him, namely, a trip in the community's only motor vehicle to the pro-
vincial capital Mount Hagen. In other words, through a directive that
Laplin is enjoined to issue to another, Laplin is himself being placed within
an established landscape—an ethical landscape—of differentially valued
places and kinds of movement within it, and ways of feeling about it.

The main point I want to draw from this example is that, from the
very earliest stages of language acquisition, children here as elsewhere are
inducted into forms of language use and associated grammatical categories
that require them to act with regard for others. The example also shows
the important role played by modality, in particular the imperative mood,
in speech to and by children. At that earliest stage, the imperative plays a
more important role than the category of person. This is interesting in
relation to questions of ethics in that the imperative is, par excellence, the
form that speakers use to make demands on one another, and it shows
that, in developmental terms at least, these are more basic than acts of
reference to the self and other by whom those demands are voiced and on
whom they are enjoined. They are also more basic than overt reference to
ethical precepts—a point to which I will return below.


## Case 2: *Warfare, Ceremonial Exchange, and the
Ethics of Bigmanship at Kailge*

I turn now to some examples of the role played by the grammatical categories I have reviewed above in the speech of adults and in their ethical
positioning of themselves in relation to one another. The examples come
from speeches made at two intergroup exchange events arising from the
Marsupial Road War of 1982, at which compensation payments were
made by one of the belligerent groups to another that had fought alongside them as allies.

One of the distinctive features of the oratory at such events is the use
of what Francesca Merlan and I (1991) call "segmentary person" forms, in
which singular and dual pronouns and verb forms are used to personify
the relevant social identities (e.g., "I killed you" means "My clan fought
with your clan and killed some people in it," even if the fighting took place
before the speaker and addressee were born). Such usages are by nature
ethically charged in that they entail taking responsibility for the actions of
the group over the long term and attributing it to others on the same basis.

The first example concerns the role of a leading "big man," Kujilyi, who played a role both in the recruitment by his tribe cluster, which I will call Cluster A, of tribe pair B to the fighting and in organizing the compensation payment that was owed by A to B for injuries they suffered in it. In Kujilyi's speeches (as transcribed in Merlan and Rumsey 1991: 247–54, 260–71), he works to position himself as a mediator rather than a *pul* ("owner," "source," "base") of the fight. In order to do this, he makes subtle use of shifts between the group-personifying "segmentary" sense of the first person singular and a more ordinary sense in which he is referring to himself as a single person. At the group level, he resists the characterization that has been made of him as a "fight source" in two ways. The first is by pointing out that, as everyone knows, the fight originally broke out as a dispute within another tribe pair, D, as a result of which one of the disputants fled from D and moved in with cluster A.

Having first traced the etiology of the fight back to a source that is not even within his own tribe cluster, Kujilyi then in effect denies ultimate responsibly for it in another way, by recourse to finer gradations of segmentary difference than are evident in my unitary reference to "cluster A." Kujilyi points out that only one of the tribes within that cluster, Epola, first took up the dispute, because of their affinal link to the refugee from tribe pair D. But then, because the Epola were on the verge of defeat, says Kujilyi, "I sort of took it [the fight] up and put it on my own skin [i.e., made myself liable for it].[6] The "I" in this formulation can be taken to refer either to Kujilyi himself, to his tribe, the Midipu, or to the Midipu together with its paired tribe, the Kusika. As in many uses of the first person singular by big men, this formulation obviates the difference between the segmentary sense of "I" and the ordinary one, since, Kujilyi being the principal big man of this tribe or tribe pair, insofar as he acts, it acts, and vice versa.

While thus denying that he was an original "owner" or "source" of the fight, Kujilyi owns up to having taken responsibility for his own tribe's having come to the aid of the Epola and Alya, and for then soliciting aid from pair B, the Kopia and Kubuka tribes. That act is subject to conflicting construals by various subsequent speakers, mostly notably by a series of Kopia speakers, who liken Kujilyi's solicitation of military aid to the work

---

6. For the Ku Waru original, see Merlan and Rumsey (1991: 291, l. 1135). For a detailed account of Kujilyi's role in these events and the speeches made by and about him, see Merlan and Rumsey (1991: 130–36).

of a prostitute, casting his recruitment of their tribe pair as an opportunistic one, which is by implication unlikely to turn into a real "marriage." Interestingly, this figure is introduced in reported speech, by a Kopia orator, Kupena, who attributes it to Kujilyi himself, as something he has supposedly either said or thought to himself. Later on in his speech, Kupena develops the image further in what are patently his own words, saying that Kujilyi "copulated with us all and brought us into the fight."[7] This figure is picked up by subsequent orators from Kopia and elaborated in various ways, describing how Kujilyi as prostitute had washed himself off and prettied himself up in preparation for his task, etc. Kujilyi in his subsequent speeches neither acknowledges nor denies having likened himself to a prostitute, but he gives the image a more positive spin by likening himself to an unmarried young women, presumably one to whom Kopia-Kubuka had been attracted on a more honorable basis and to whom they would stay "married" as a continuing ally.

In all of this give and take, Kujilyi's actions are made the subject of intense ethical labor, both by himself and others, at this, the first of several exchange events that were precipitated by those actions.

## Case 3: The Intervention of the Kulka Women's Club

The war from which the above-discussed compensation claims arose was ended by a remarkable intervention by a local women's cooperative work group. On September 13, 1982 women from the club, all wearing shirts bearing the national emblem of Papua New Guinea, marched in between the opposing armies and exhorted the men in both to lay down their arms and go home. The women brought with them garden produce, money, cigarettes, and bottled soft drinks, which they offered as gifts to both sides in equal measure. They also brought with them the national flag, which they planted on the battlefield. The men accepted their offer and did as they were told. It was a bold act, which no one expected at the time. Elsewhere Merlan and I (1991; Rumsey 2000, 2003b) have analyzed the women's action in detail, arguing that it was made possible by a particular set of circumstances, including the group's perceived association with "government law" and "business," its identification with a neutral tribe, and

---

7. More literally, and more interestingly, what Kupena says, using the group-personifying "segmentary" first person singular, is that Kujilyi "copulated with all of me" (*na payl topa*), where the understood referent of "I/me" is the Kopia tribe of the pair of Kopia and Kubuka.

the interstitial position of women in general with respect to the male-dominated order of segmentary groups in the region.

To say that these were enabling conditions is not to say that the group's success followed automatically from them. Rather, the group demonstrated a profound capacity for what I would call "ethical imagination," whereby, even in the total absence of any direct precedent for their intervention, the women recognized the novel circumstances they were in as ones that might empower them to act in ways that everyone could see the good in, and they did so with implacable resolve and stunning éclat.

At two exchange events subsequent to the one in Case 2, where each of the principal combatant sides gave compensation to their allies, payments were also presented to the women's group, and its leaders appeared as orators—the first time that women had ever done so at such an event. Examining the women's speeches in detail, Merlan and I (1991) have shown how they drew upon both the newly established rhetorics of "government law" and "business," and upon features of traditional male oratory, creating for themselves a new, hybrid speaking position that was both subversive of the segmentary order and complexly entangled with it. One of the features of traditional oratory the women drew upon was the totalizing use of grammatical person categories that I have discussed above, as in the following lines from one of their speeches:

elti el tiringl-kiyl-o kanilka-o
you two fought, and I, seeing it

kapola naa mel tirim kanap-o
I, seeing that it was not a good thing

el kani-yl yi te-n mol-o
that fight, no man

na-ni gai punya-na konturud-o
but I in the sweet potato garden stopped it (Merlan and Rumsey 1991: 186)

This excerpt contains, in the first line, a segmentary second person dual reference "You two fought," referring to whole tribes, and in the second and fourth lines, first person singular forms that can be taken, in the characteristic segmentary person manner, as referring both to the speaker and to the social totality with which she is identified.

But exactly what is the social totality of identification here? In this case the indeterminacy is not just a matter of the scope of the social identity in question (tribe *versus* tribe pair, etc.) but of its very nature. To be sure, the woman's group has a segmentary identity, Kulka, but not because the women themselves are of the Kulka tribe. Most of them are not, but rather have married into it. Rather, given the range of interests and identities in which the Kulka women's group's action is grounded, Kopil's totalizing "I" cannot be construed in any single way, but rather in any or all of the following:

> I, Kopil, a leader of the Kulka women's group
> We the Kulka women's group, which I embody as its leader.
> We, the forces of "government law"
> We women.

The fact that there is an established Ku Waru genre employing segmentary person reference provides a way for Kopil to cast her person references as totalizing ones. Yet the fact that the references were being spoken by *her* in these particular circumstances meant that the social totalities being invoked could not be of the usual segmentary sort: they must instead be construed in novel ways such as the above, creating a mutual alignment among these various identities. This creative act, and the novel political intervention in which it figured, are a prime example of what I mean by the "ethical imagination."

For understanding how this works, I find useful a distinction made by Bernard Williams between two different kinds of ethical consideration (one broadly Kantian and the other Aristotelian). The first is based on obligation and duty, which by nature

> look backwards, or at least sideways. The acts they require, supposing that one is deliberating about what to do, lie in the future, but the reasons for those acts lie in the fact that I have already promised, the job I have undertaken, the position I am already in. Another kind of ethical consideration looks forward, to the outcomes of the acts open to me. "It will be for the best" may be taken as the general form of this kind of consideration. (B. Williams 1985: 8)

It seems to me that especially in deliberations about what will be for the best the ethical imagination can come to the fore and in some cases lead to action that creates an expanded sense of what can be. The Kulka Women's Club's action was clearly forward looking in this way, rather than being grounded in any existing obligation or duty. And what Williams (1985: 14 *et passim*) would have called a relevant "ethical constituency" deemed it to have opened up new possibilities for the future.

## Conclusion

In this essay I have explored the ethical dimension of human social life from three very different perspectives: the phylogeny of the human species; ontogeny as exemplified from my work with children in Highland Papua New Guinea; and, from the same region, the ethics of intergroup politics and wealth exchange. From the first of these perspectives, drawing on recent work in primatology and evolutionary anthropology, I have established that crucial prerequisites of the ethical—the ability to understand and participate in the psychological states of others and the propensity for doing so—are distinctively human traits. Crucial in this regard is the ability to participate in triadic interactions in which the interacting parties jointly focus their attention on a common object, share and exchange intentions with respect to it, and collaborate in joint action with respect to it.

As for ontogeny, through their interaction with older conspecifics, human infants acquire these skills before they learn to speak. As they begin to acquire a language, the skills are put to new uses. At the same time, they are developed in new ways by the child's entry into language. This is true in part because, as I have discussed above, there are certain grammatical categories within every language that require interlocutors to exchange perspectives with each other.[8] These include the categories of person, mood, and reported speech. Using a sample of conversational interaction involving an infant, I have shown how each of these categories figures in such exchanges of perspective, and how in the process, from the very earliest stages of language acquisition, these perspectives and the messages conveyed from them are charged with ethical import.

Especially important in this respect are imperatives—not the abstract imperatives of moral philosophers, and certainly not the lofty "categorical imperative" of Kant—but ordinary everyday imperative verbs, like the ones that figure in Bourdieu's famous "implicit pedagogy, capable of instilling a whole cosmology, an ethic, a metaphysic, a political philosophy, through injunctions as insignificant as 'stand up straight' or 'don't hold your knife in your left hand'" (Bourdieu 1977: 94). While I would not go as far as Bourdieu does in suggesting that whole cosmologies, metaphysical

---

8. Another huge difference that language makes is that, as Webb Keane reminded us at the Toronto conference, it allows actions to be construed and evaluated as actions of a given *type*. Though I cannot go into that point here, it is richly exemplified in cases 2 and 3 above.

systems, or political philosophies can be instilled *solely* through such injunctions—or indeed, that they ever are instilled in toto—I would agree with, for example, Schieffelin (1990) and Don Kulick (1992) that mundane communicative practices and interactional routines provide one of the main bases on which more enduring sociocultural forms are reproduced and transformed, and through which subjectivity is constituted as social being.

Among humans beyond the age of about twenty to twenty-four months, a crucial role is also played in this process by the person categories of language, as discerned by Benveniste and as is evident in all the examples discussed above. But the examples also show that this is rather more complicated than Benveniste (1971: 225) allows when he says that "each speaker sets himself up as a subject by referring to himself as *I* in his discourse" and thereby posits another person (the *you*) who is "completely exterior to 'me.'" As we have seen in case 1, even in speech to an infant Taka uses a first person form in ventriloquized speech that in effect posits another person as himself and vice versa. In case 2, similar considerations apply to Kupena's use of the first person when attributing to Kujilyi the thought that he, Kujiyli, had acted like a prostitute. In both of these cases, there is not a simple relation of "exteriority" between the "I" and the "you" but an interplay between them within the speech of a single person. In cases 2 and 3, we have seen examples of the segmentary "I," in which the relation is not only one of interplay—for example, between the segmentary sense of Kujilyi's "I" and the personal one—but also one of "amplification" and "personification," whereby the "I" personifies an enduring segmentary group identity and takes responsibility for its actions, as seen in those examples.

Of course, none of this takes place entirely in language or speech. At the exchange events from which my oratorical examples are taken, for instance, equally important is the grounding of the interactions in a public performance space that is constructed as an oriented microcosm of the larger surrounding space of tribal and clan territories with which the participating groups are identified (Merlan and Rumsey 1991: 125–28, 163–67) and in a long history involving macro-level institutions and processes that are only in part linguistic or semiotic (ibid.: 34–87, 198–220, 239–44; cf. Keane 1997, and in this volume). Without in any way discounting the importance of such embedding of the verbal within more inclusive interactional frames and sociocultural contexts, the main focus of this chapter has been on the ways in which some central aspects of language itself provide part of the basis for ethical action by engaging its users in forms of regard for the other.

The main way in which I hope my treatment of these phenomena will have pushed the boundaries of existing work in linguistic and sociocultural anthropology is through my focus on joint attention and shared intentionality as providing a pivot in relation to which the exchange of perspectives is grounded. Though I cannot go into the matter here (but see, e.g., Crapanzano 1992: 70–90, Tomasello 1999, Hobson 2004), I believe that triadic interactions of that kind provide an essential bridge between the consciousness, intentionality, and agency of particular persons and the larger lifeworld they inhabit. With regard to the ethical domain (among others), a very important fact about that bridge is that the traffic across it runs in both directions. So, for example, in the Marsupial Road War of 1982, the Kulka women's group acted out of shared concern for what was happening on the battlefield and took an action that altered the ethical horizon for everyone involved.

At the second exchange event of 1983, in which tribe cluster A as the "owners" of the fight paid compensation to pair B, the Kulka Women's Club participated as one of the parties to whom a payment was also owed for their role in stopping the fight. There is a tacit protocol whereby the staging of such events often reenacts the ones for which the compensation is owed. So at this event there was a mock charge, in which men from B ran onto the display ground in battle dress, shouting as they had at the fight and brandishing spears and bows and arrows. Likewise, the Kulka Women's Club appeared, wearing their club shirts with the national insignia and carrying the national flag, which they planted on the display ground just as they had done on the battlefield. A leading Kulka big man, Pokea, whose daughter was one of the group's leaders, in his speech referred to them as *ab kupari* "mad women," "insane women." He nonetheless commended them for their action, saying, "Now we are living in changed conditions, in new and different conditions," and that, just as the women had planted the flag on the battlefield, "we people" (*olyo yab*, an expression that includes both men and women) would be doing so in the future and "acting according to your different way of doing things."

Like Charles Dickens's use of the word *consequently* in my example of free indirect discourse above, Pokea's use of the word *kupari*, "mad" in this speech can only be understood as an instance of what Bakhtin called "heteroglossia," that is, as partially echoing the speech of another. But in this case the "other" implicitly includes Pokea himself, in an earlier incarnation in which he had thought and acted according to the older way of doing things. Here, I would say, is another instance of the ethical imagination at work, acting within the new horizon that had been opened up by the women's bold act on the battlefield. And here in the use of free indirect discourse is another instance of the way in which the ethical is tied up with the power of language to enable multiple perspectives and to allow and even compel speakers to place their own in relation to others'— and indeed, in relation to their own, as shown by this example and illuminated by Hegel, Freud, Peirce, G. H. Mead, Vygotsky, and Bakhtin, all of whom have shown in their various ways how our interior psychic lives are constituted through conversations among introjected social voices. Though I cannot go into this matter here,[9] it is obviously of central relevance for the understanding of ethics as a dimension of everyday life. Suffice it to note for present purposes, as emphasized by Vygotsky (1986), Vološinov (1987), and others, that this "inner conversation," and our human capacity to engage in it, are secondary products of the "outer" social one. It follows that the same is true of the relationship between "inner" ethical deliberation and its "outer" counterparts, including ethical action itself, all of these being intimately bound up with the nature of language.

### ACKNOWLEDGMENTS

For their helpful comments on various drafts of this chapter, I would like to thank Courtney Handman, Darja Hoenigman, Michael Lambek, Francesca Merlan, James and Jesse Rumsey-Merlan, and an anonymous referee. Thanks also to discussant James Laidlaw and the other participants at the Anthropology and Ordinary Ethics conference who commented on the original version there and to the conference organizers for inviting me to it and for running it so well.

---

9. See, however, Rumsey (2003a) for some relevant considerations.

# The Ordinary Ethics of Everyday Talk

*Jack Sidnell*

The juxtaposition of "ordinary" and "ethics" will, for many readers, bring to mind J. L. Austin's brilliant exposition of everyday language in "A Plea for Excuses." In the course of that discussion, Austin writes that excuses provide "a good site for field work in philosophy," for here, in this "pressingly practical matter," ordinary language is rich and subtle, having evolved in response to the infinitely varied moral and ethical contingencies of daily life. And here, moreover, according to Austin, we find an area of language that is as free as possible from infection by scientific and philosophical theories. On this point he suggests a comparison with aesthetics, which would be much better off "if only we could forget for a while about the beautiful and get down instead to the dainty and the dumpy." The idea, of course, is that a moral philosophy or at least a system is embodied in everyday talk and conduct. As such, there is no reason nor any warrant to construct an ethical or moral theory. Rather we should rediscover the one we already have by making its tacit principles explicit through a careful analysis of vocabulary.[1]

---

1. MacIntyre's (1966) consideration of adjectives of appraisal—the ancestor of English "good" among them—in Homer and writers of five centuries later can be seen as a historical application of the method.

So, on one reading, "ordinary" in "ordinary ethics" recalls the so-called ordinary language philosophy of Austin, Gilbert Ryle, and P. F. Strawson. But an objection here, a well-founded one from my perspective, would be that, for all their insight, the "ordinary language" philosophers never really did study the ordinary language of ordinary people, despite the fact that Bertrand Russell (1961) priggishly lampooned them for it. Austin's analyses were not, after all, based on his acquaintance with the ordinary language of his day—whatever that could mean—but on introspection into his own usage, coupled with consultation of the OED. The result depicts not ordinary practices of language use but rather a lexical system. Rather surprisingly perhaps, Austin's analyses, in this area at least, veer toward *langue* rather than *parole*. The studies of which "A Plea for Excuses" is one exemplar are, I contend, ultimately lexicographic—they are concerned with the meanings and uses of words and not the ordinary uses to which words are put.

An analysis of ordinary usage must begin not with the dictionary but with the details of social interaction, for it is here that words find their home: in the mouth of one person speaking to another. But more importantly, only by looking at the social interaction in which words are used can we access an arguably much more fundamental ethical domain than that revealed in vocabulary. For Austin, the moral and ethical character of talk is seen in its capacity to suture tears in the tissue of an essentially social order. If I shoot your donkey, I can either claim it was a "mistake" (I meant to shoot the wounded horse, not your healthy donkey standing next to it) or an "accident" (the gun went off inadvertently). Excuses and justifications of this sort certainly point us in the direction of an important moral and ethical domain. But consider now that when I say "I mistook your donkey for my wounded horse" I may say it through bubbling laughter or while looking sheepishly at the ground, or I may say it with obvious sincerity or clearly under pressure from my mother, who is looking on concernedly. And you, the recipient of the justification, may choose to ignore what I'm saying—with a steely gaze off into the distance—or you may receive my words with mocking laugher or studied indifference ("Oh gosh, I don't care about that old donkey") and so on. And, of course, such nuances of poise and attentiveness may inflect any and all talk—as a matter of necessity—and not just that in which we are concerned with obvious matters of morality. There is a moral and ethical dimension to all interaction, because interaction is itself a moral and ethical domain. When persons interact, they necessarily and unavoidably assess whether they are being heard, ignored, and so on. Is this person really listening to me?

Paying attention to me? And, in so doing, acknowledging me as worthwhile person who merits such attention?[2] These, I want to suggest, are some of the most basic ethical questions of ordinary social life. Admittedly, none of this is new. Questions of this sort are at the root of much phenomenological and existentialist philosophy—most famously the philosophies of Martin Buber and Jean-Paul Sartre.[3] In this essay I hope to show that they are also woven into the very fabric of ordinary conduct in a basic way.

## Goffman and the Ethics of Participation

Drawing on some suggestive remarks of Malinowski, Roman Jakobson (1980[1957], 1960) conceptualized certain basic features of social interaction in terms of a "phatic" function. The idea here is that all uses of language involve "a channel" between some speaker (or writer, etc.) and some hearer (or reader, etc.) and that this must in some sense be established. Although Jakobson was a thinker of considerable subtlety, his model of speech functions essentially reduces the diverse practices of social interaction to a singular phatic function conceived primarily as a simple, binary on-off switch.[4]

In a series of pioneering studies, Erving Goffman exploded this conception of social interaction. Rather than a simple, binary on-off switch, participation in social interaction—in a conversation, for instance—is a delicate and complex balancing act. In conversation we aim to create ease—a happy flow of words back and forth—but to do so we need to talk in just the right amount and listen in equal measure, we need to talk about

---

2. It is surely no coincidence that, in many situations, one of the most effective of all punishments is the so-called "silent treatment."

3. More recently, Forni has argued for the central importance of "attention" to ordinary ethics in his *Choosing Civility* (2002: 25). He writes: "Without attention, no meaningful interaction is possible. Our first responsibility, when we are with others, is to pay attention, *to attend to*. Etymology tells us that attention has to do with 'turning toward,' 'extending toward,' 'stretching.' Thus attention is a tension connecting us to the world around us. Only after we *notice* the world can we begin to care for it. Every act of kindness is, first of all, an act of attention. We may see a coworker in need of a word of encouragement, but it is only if we pay attention that we may do something about it. We may hear a child cry, but again, our help is contingent upon our stopping and taking notice."

4. This idea has held sway within certain quarters of linguistics, anthropology, and linguistic anthropology up to the present day, resulting in an often massively impoverished view of social interaction.

the right topics and formulate them in just the right way, with a valence that our interlocutors will be able to align with. At the same time, we can't be overaccommodating, since to do so would be obsequious. And somehow, while doing this, we have to convey just the right amount of attention to our interlocutor—if you look too long at the other you'll make her uncomfortable; if you look too little you'll give the impression you're uninterested, bored, preoccupied, and so on. Underlying our use of language, then, is a set of practices of interaction that are inferentially rich. Subtle shifts in our attention are understood by others to reveal the contents of our minds, our emotions as well as our feelings toward others.

As a conversation analyst, my method for studying the world involves close inspection of audio or video recordings of people going about their business. I won't dwell here on the specifics (see Sidnell 2010), what I need to clarify, though, is that the emphasis in conversation analysis is not on the psychological motives of the individuals involved but on the organization of the interaction itself and specifically on the stable and recurrent practices—the machinery, as Harvey Sacks (1995) sometimes described it—of speaking, hearing, gesturing, and so on of which it is composed. With apologies to the other half of the world, we are concerned, as Goffman (1967: 3) once suggested, not with "men and their moments. Rather, moments and their men."

So here is a moment involving three men, two women, one child, and a dog. The moment is embedded in a backyard picnic, in Ohio in the 1970s. The recording was made by Chuck and Candy Goodwin and is commonly known as "auto discussion," in reference to the fact that the talk eventually turns to racing and vintage cars and the various people involved in these pursuits. It is an extremely rich source of conversational data and has provided materials for many academic papers and countless examples of conversational practices. Part of this richness is a product of the highly nuanced and subtle transcript that Gail Jefferson made to accompany the recording. Before turning to the recording itself, I must say something about the transcription conventions, as these can be a bit overwhelming on first exposure.

Key for present purposes are the conventions for marking overlap and laughter. Figure 2 is an excerpt from the talk we are going to examine that illustrates both. At line 06, Gary is continuing to talk, saying "like that eh!" This is produced with laughter, which is indicated by the "(h)" in "li(h)ke" and "tha(h)t." As Gary says this, Carney starts speaking in overlap, saying, "Thank heaven the camera was'n o(h)o(h)o(h)n." Her talk is produced simultaneously with laughter ("Ehh hu:h huh! .hh") from Curt.

FIGURE 1. The Auto Discussion.

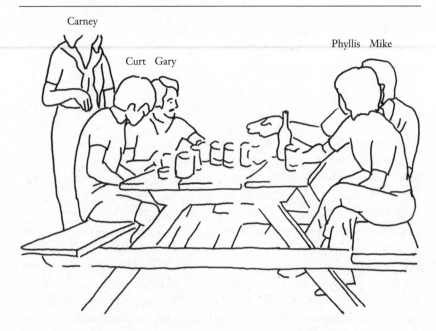

Carney

Phyllis   Mike

Curt   Gary

This begins just as Carney reaches the "n't" in "wasn't" at line 07. There's obviously more that could be said both about the production of the talk here and the transcription conventions we use to represent it, but this very brief overview should suffice for present purposes.

The fragment of talk I'm going to focus on comes from the very first part of the auto-discussion recording. In it, Carney comes over to sit on her husband Gary's knee. After a few seconds of talk about Carney's motivation for moving from one side of the table to the other, the couple readjust slightly, and Carney falls off Gary's knee onto the ground. Gary, who apparently still has his arm around Carney, falls part of the way with her, perhaps attempting to break her fall. In the moments after the fall, Curt remarks of Carney, who is still holding a drink, "never spilled a drop," in this way appreciating Carney's fall as a "trick" or accomplishment. Gary

FIGURE 2. Auto Discussion, Excerpt, "like that eh!"

```
06   GAR:   =li(h)[ke tha(h)t eh!
07   CAR:         [Thank heaven the camera was['n o(h)o(h)o(h)n
08   CUR:                                       [Ehh hu:h huh! ·hhh
09   CUR:   [(I don'know I think it's-)]
10   GAR:   [ Y o u    r e a l i z e ] I c'd'v broke my ba:ck,
```

then complains to Carney, saying, "You realize I could have broke my back?" The talk that follows concerns the injuries sustained and the responsibility for the mishap. After this, there is some talk between Carney and Gary about what happened and specifically what caused the fall.

## Before the Fall

The talk that forms the focus of the analysis here comes very near the beginning of the recording, which starts with Pam insisting to one of the other participants, "Oh yeah you've gotta tell Mike tha:t. Uh-cuz they want that on fi:lm." Whatever "that" refers to, it is not immediately told (whether it is told later in the recording we do not know), and after some talk about why Gary didn't find the story or joke funny, Carney gets up, walks around the front of the table (between the participants and the camera) and comes over to the other side, at which Gary and Curt are sitting. On her way over, Carney speaks to what is possibly a dog ("move"), and as she does this Gary realigns his body so that he is visibly attending to her. Carney continues to move toward Gary, who is now looking directly at her. As she reenters the camera field, Mike remarks: "Oh look-eh-she gonna g'm down here'n break those two u:p. see:?" It's obvious that Mike is ascribing a motivation or intention to Carney's moving over to the other side of the table and sitting on Gary's knee—specifically, Mike suggests that this is being done to "break those two up." What's not obvious is the precise way he builds this in and around Carney's bodily movement. Note, then, that Mike begins his turn well before Carney actually sits down and at a point when it's not entirely clear just what she intends to do. However, by the time he reaches "those two," Carney is visibly starting to sit down. And by the time Mike says "see," she's halfway completed this action. K. Kendrick (2009) has studied this use of "See?" and he suggests speakers may use it to claim "evidential vindication." This is a stable and recurrent practice, identifiable across different configurations of participants, engaged in different activities, talking in different contexts. Kendrick's analysis shows that this "See?" treats a prior turn or action not as the action it was designed to be in its local context but as evidence for some earlier claim or assertion. Here in the case before us, by positioning his talk in the way he does and by his use of "See?" Mike casts Carney's sitting on Gary's knee as evidence of his just-prior assertion that she intends to break Gary and Curt up.

FIGURE 3. Auto Discussion, Excerpt, "she gonna g'm down here'n break these two up."

```
06   MIK:   Oh look-eh-she gonna g'm down here'n break those two u:[p.
07   CAR:                                                          [ehhhh!
08   MIK:   se[e:?
09   CUR:     [Aw[: ma:n,]
10   MIK:        [hah hah] hah hah[hah.
11   GAR:                        [(You)talk about[j e alous.]
12   CUR:    .                   [°(           ).[          ]
13   CAR:                                        [I'm gonna-]
14   CUR:   ehh he:h he:h,
15   CAR:   S::
16   CUR:   [hn
17   CAR:   [cramp yer sty:le [(  )
18   CUR:                     [ehh!
```

Mike's motivational ascription sets up further talk by both Gary and Carney—each of them uses it as fodder for insulting the other. So Gary, looking at Curt but pointing at Carney, remarks "(You) talk about *jeal*-ous." This accepts and reinforces Mike's motivational ascription, while elaborating the stereotype of a controlling and possessive woman who in-terferes in male "friendships." Carney's "I'm gonna cramp your style" is more subtle. While with this she embraces the characterization of a med-dling spouse, she uses it to develop homosocial overtones implicit in Mike's suggestion that she is attempting to break up the two men.[5]

Consider now Curt's contribution at line 09: "Aw: *ma*:n,." This is de-signed as a response to Mike's description of Carney sitting on Gary's knee. That description is, of course, a joke that employs irony. Specifically, the expression "break those two up" implies a romantic or at least intimate relationship, but Mike is not suggesting that Gary and Curt actually are a same-sex couple (the implication is ironic). So this utterance has multiple targets—perhaps most obviously Carney, but also Gary and Curt. Curt's "Aw: *ma*:n," is an expression of disappointment and it well illustrates one practice for responding to an irony or joke such as Mike's. Specifically, "Aw: *ma*:n," builds onto the joke—goes along with it—by performing a relevant next action in the pretend world or situation it has established (Drew 1987, Holt 2006, Sidnell 2010).

Already we are into some fairly complex ethical territory: this is the ordinary ethics of telling jokes and appreciating them, of being able to laugh at one another and at oneself (Sacks 1974). There is a darker side here as well, involving the ethics of describing an action as the action of

---

5. The *Oxford English Dictionary* lists, as one use of "cramp": "c. Phr. *to cramp one's style*: to restrict one's natural actions or behavior."

an interfering, controlling woman. And of course there is, just below the surface perhaps, but nevertheless palpable, the ethics and morality of sexuality—in this case what is now known as "heteronormativity" (Kitzinger 2005). Jokes like this invoke and police "ordinary" or "normal" male-female relationships and the stereotypes of how it is that men and women (should) act. That's ten seconds of talk, and we've only begun an analysis of it. In one respect, then, Austin was quite correct—there is embedded in the ordinary language of ordinary people an ethical system of sorts, or perhaps a patchwork of multiple systems butting up against one another.

## The Fall

Continuing on, Carney falls from Gary's knee, and a complex sequence of action, laughter, and talk ensues. It's obviously not possible to deal with all of this in any detail—instead, I'll just consider a few aspects, relating, first, to Carney's saying Gary's name at line 28, second, to Curt's characterization of the fall as a successfully accomplished "trick," and, third, to the laughter that infiltrates much but not all of the talk. First, then, notice that, just as she lands at line 28, Carney says Gary's name. A speaker can use another's name to accomplish a variety of actions (Schegloff 1968, Lerner 2003), one of which is to admonish the person so addressed for something they have just said or done and thereby to mark that something as a misstep. The misstep may be in the talk, as in the case below, from a family dinner, or otherwise, as in the case we are considering here. In the following example, Virginia has been pleading for a raise in her allowance, and Mom has refused on the grounds that she doesn't have any extra expenses to warrant this. In the first fragment, Mom is asking Virginia how she spends her allowance. A short while after this, Wesley, Virginia's brother, jokingly suggests she is spending her allowance on marijuana. In response to this, Prudence, Wesley's girlfriend, uses his name and then continues by rejecting the suggestion that Virginia uses marijuana. In the case from Virginia, then, we have two kinds of evidence that the recipient's name is being used to admonish him. First there is the evidence provided by the context of use—Wesley has just done something (suggested that his sister uses marijuana, thereby teasing their mother) that is worthy of admonishment. Second, we have the evidence afforded by Prudence's subsequent talk, which elaborates the admonishment and articulates the grounds for it (i.e., that it is untrue). The point

FIGURE 4.  Auto Discussion, Excerpt, "cramp yer style."

```
17   CAR:    [cramp yer sty:le [(   )
18   CUR:                       [ehh!
19           (0.4)
20   GAR:    Mh, mh-[-mh-[-mh-mh-[-mh-
21   ???:         [°Mh [        [
22   CUR:              [eh-huh,[huh-huh!
23   CAR:                      [((little shriek)) Ohh!=
24   GAR:    =[ah!ah!ah![ah! ah!=
25   PHY:    =[ehhuh-h- [-huh huh
26   CUR:          [hhah: hha:=
27   GAR:    =[ah! ah! ah! ah! ah! ah! ah! ah! ah! ah!=
28   CAR:    =[Ga(h)ry(h)y haha
29   CUR:    =[hha:huh,  °hn-n-hn!
30   GAR:    =[ah! ah! ah!
31   CUR:    =[Never spilled a[dro:[p=
32   CAR:                    [·hh [·hhh[h! ·huh-
33   CUR:                         =[Look it that.
34   MIK:                         =[ah ah ah- hah!
35   GAR:                         =[ah! ah! ah! ah! ah! [ah! ah! ah!=
36   CUR:                                              [Outstanding.
37   CAR:                                              [Wahddiyuh mea::n!
38   GAR:    =[ah! ah!
39   CUR:    [Neh[hu:h hu:h huh.
40   PHY:        [°hmhh.
41   GAR:    (Ho[ho(h)ne(h)stly) ·hhhh
42   CAR:       [Oh::[::,
43   CUR:            [eh-heh eh-heh.
44   GAR:    (hh)He (h)hed(h)['ner inniz lap=
45   CUR:                    [heh huh huh,
46   GAR:    =li(h)[ke tha(h)t eh!
47   CAR:          [Thank heaven the camera was['n o(h)o(h)o(h)n
48   CUR:                                       [Ehh hu:h huh! ·hhh
49   CUR:    [(I don'know I think it's-)]
50   GAR:    [ Y o u    r e a l i z e ] I c'd'v broke my ba:ck,
```

here is that saying a recipient's name in this context (and with a particular intonation, see Sidnell 2010, chap. 13) is another of those stable and recurrent practices identifiable across different occasions of interaction and different configurations of participants.

Returning to the example from auto discussion, we can see that, by saying Gary's name, Carney attributes responsibility for the fall to

FIGURE 5.  Virginia, Excerpt, "W'll what do you spend your allowance on."

```
01 MOM:     W'll what do you spen:d your allowance on.
02          That's [what I have |NEVER b]een able tuh find out.=
03 VIR:            [E  V  R  Y  |THA:n:'!]
04 MOM:     =·hh·hh ((holds breath)) You get it on Satihday¿ (0.7)
05          Wensdee? You nevuh have a penny.
06 VIR:     I know.That's 'cause we go ta McDonald's, an:' goes places,
07          'n (0.7)
```

FIGURE 6. Virginia, Excerpt, "they chargin' more on thuh nickel."

```
01 WES:     [They- they char[gin' more on thuh- thuh uh nickel=
02 ???:                      [((hiccup?))
03 WES:     =ba:g now.
04          (0.7)
05 MOM:     A [ba:g?
06 PRU: ->    [W(h)e(h)sl(h)e(h)y s(h)he d(h)oe(h)s(h)n't u(h)se
07          [a(h)ny marajuana! 'ih[h! eh huh huh [^huh huh!=
08 WES:     [ehhhh 'ih!           [(    ?)      |
09 WS?:                                         [khhh!
10 WES:     ='ihhh! hih [(hmh)
11 MOM:                 [Wesley I'M tellin' you, I: don'[t think I=
12 PRU:                 [^'IH uh huh huh huh huh 'ih   |
13 WES:                                               [ihh ((hoarse))
14 MOM:     =c(h)a[n  st(h) a (h) n d] 'hhh [coming from=
15 PRU:           ['uhhh! eh huh huh!] 'ih [m'hh (    ) huh!
16 MOM:     =[both  s i : : d es,]
17 VR?:      [(    ) Wesley I don]'t [do tha:t!
18 PRU:                             [huh!
```

him—by virtue of the fact that to admonish someone presupposes that he is, in some sense, responsible for what has happened. What seems particularly important about this is that it is the *first* such attribution. This means, of course, that any *subsequent* attribution by Gary will necessarily be a "counter"-attribution, and it seems that attributions and counter-attributions are rather different things, involving quite different constraints. Here I just want to register that what Max Gluckman (1972) describes as the attribution of responsibility happens in time (and in sequences of talk) and that this has consequences for the way those attributions are done.

There is an added nuance to the way this is produced; specifically, it is infiltrated by laughter. Many years ago Gail Jefferson noted that, although Goffman, Freud, and others tended to think of laughter as a spontaneous and largely uncontrollable occurrence—a "flooding out" (Goffman 1961)—the precise placement of laugh tokens within particular parts of talk and not others suggests that it is purposively, though not consciously, put in. In this respect, looking just at Carney's talk here, we can notice that "Gary" at line 28 is produced through laughter while "Wahddiyuh mea::n!" at line 37 is not. Looking at Carney's saying of "Gary" next to the example from Virginia (in which Prudence similarly produced "Wesley" through bubbling laughter) helps us to see that, by introducing laughter into the saying of a name in this position, the speaker modulates the admonishment. By introducing laughter, the speaker can do two things at once—admonish the person whom the name addresses for something he has just done or said and, at the same time, appreciate what he has done as something laughable, funny.

This points to another key aspect of "ethics in interaction," if I may put it that way. Very often, it seems, when someone admonishes another, criticizes another's behavior, challenges the accuracy of what another has said, in short, when someone engages in some obviously ethically loaded action—she does not do it plain and simple, but rather in a way that is ambiguous, equivocal, or, as here, multiply valenced.

If we now consider Curt's talk, we can notice that he initially appreciates the fall as something laughable, whereas Mike and Phyllis, on the other side of the table, do not. The thing to which I want to draw attention though, is that, with "never *s*pilled a dro:p," at line 31 Curt makes of the mishap an accomplishment by Carney. Moreover, as we've already seen, the fall has the potential to promote discord between Carney and Gary. Curt's talk comes at it from another angle—rather than highlight the problem of who is responsible for the fall, Curt characterizes it as a successfully accomplished gymnastic feat—something to be appreciated not as funny but as remarkable and laudatory. Interestingly "never *s*pilled a dro:p," and "*outs*tanding." appear to be produced without laughter—it is only after Carney contests this with "Wahddiyuh *mea*::n!" that Curt rejoins the laughter. That may be important precisely because, in a situation like this, Curt could easily be heard as "laughing at" Carney rather than "laughing with her." So Curt makes of the fall something to be appreciated—and his "never *s*pilled a dro:p," in fact elicits laughter from Mike, who is otherwise pretty much silent throughout.

Goffman thought of face-to-face interaction as simultaneously its own institution and the foundation of everything else in society. This "interaction order," as he called it (1983), is itself a moral ordering—a complex web of standards, expectations, rules, and proscriptions, by which people orient their attempts to show deference, adopt a demeanor appropriate to a given situation, avoid embarrassing themselves and others, and so on. According to Goffman, face-to-face interaction is an incredibly delicate thing. To maintain the fiction and the feel of ease, each participant must dutifully do his or her part: attending to the right things at the right moments, conveying just the right degree of involvement, and so on. In his first published paper—"Alienation from interaction"—Goffman (1957) describes this delicate balancing act by which we engage "in a reciprocally sustained communion of involvement." One wrong move, one slip of the tongue, one chance happening in the vicinity, can set off a chain of problems, and like so many falling dominoes, the whole thing may collapse.

Given this view of the world, one can see that what Curt does here is nothing less than the exercise of virtue, for with it he manages to integrate

Carney's fall off of Gary's lap into what is otherwise happening. Goffman (1961:48) writes of one who does this:

> By contributing especially apt words and deeds, it is possible for a participant to blend embarrassing matters smoothly into the encounter in an officially accepted way, even while giving support to the prevailing order. Such acts are the structural correlates of charm, tact, or presence of mind. These acts provide a formula through which a troublesome event can be redefined and its reconstituted meaning integrated into the prevailing definition of the situation. . . . What is involved is a kind of grounding of disruptive forces, an alteration of a frame for the benefit of those who are framed by it.

This brings us to another important point about "ethics in interaction." What Curt does here emerges within a particular configuration of participants—a framework of participation (see Goodwin and Goodwin 2004, Sidnell 2009). Specifically, Curt's "Never *s*pilled a dro:p," and "Look it that" position Carney as a performer and Mike, Phyllis, and himself as an audience. This is an essential, indeed constitutive, feature of the action he uses the talk to accomplish.[6]

## *"You're the one that did it!"*

The next segment of talk begins with Carney's "Thank heaven the camera was'n o(h)o(h)o(h)n" and continues with Gary complaining that he could have broken his back. So here we see the laughter continuing and Carney saying, mistakenly, "Thank heaven the camera was'n o(h)o(h)o(h)n." Two things to notice about this are: first, that it finds something lucky or positive in the mishap, specifically, that it wasn't recorded for posterity; second, it is once again infiltrated by laughter. In one of her earliest discussions of laughter, Gail Jefferson notes that one participant's laughter may serve as an invitation to others to laugh. She goes on to note that a recipient who declines such an invitation typically does more than not laugh—rather, she will actively pursue alternative matters. Here's a rather clear case of that from a telephone conversation:

Here Lisa has been describing the work she has done in grooming Ilene's dog. After Ilene notes (at line 01) that there was a big knot behind

---

6. As Helen Tartar points out, Curt's "Never spilled a drop" draws on another stereotype—that of the ideal mate or girlfriend, a woman who does everything she can to promote the good time had by her male companion(s).

FIGURE 7. Auto Discussion, Excerpt, "like that eh!" extended.

```
46  GAR:  =li(h)[ke tha(h)t eh!
47  CAR:       [Thank heaven the camera was['n o(h)o(h)o(h)n
48  CUR:                               [Ehh hu:h huh! ·hhh
49  CUR:  [(I don'know I think it's-)]
50  GAR:  [ Y o u    r e a l i z e ] I c'd'v broke my ba:ck,
51  CAR:  (°eh-k-heh)/(0.3)
52  CUR:  W-well that's a'least a'her worries, sh-[she's always got me tuh=
53  GAR:                                          [Uh-hu:h,
54  CUR:  =(        [         [          ) eh-huh
55  GAR:           [u h!  u h! [uh! uh![uh!=
56  CAR:                      [A  (h) [ (      )=
57  CUR:                             [=eh hu[::h
58  ???:                                    =[°(is yer leg [alright?)
59  BR?:                                                   [°(whajer=
60        =[wajerajerajer).
61  GAR:  [Yer her cousi[n.
62  CUR:                [eh hheh!
63  CAR:  No:,[just my a:rm,
64  CUR:      [That's ruh- It's all in the fam'ly,
65        (0.2)
66  CAR:  Thanks hon,
67        (0.1)
68  CAR:  W'make a good=
69  GAR:  ME::=
70  PHY:  =°Go sit by [Curt.
71  CAR:             =[couple.
72  GAR:  Yer the one thet did it!
73        (0.5)
74  CUR:  C'mmere Bo,kih-jus' kick im Phyllis,
75  GAR:  hhOh m[y  G o:d.hh]=                                  (01:00)
76  CUR:        [C'mon! Hey!]=
77  GAR:  =hh I've got m[y, sacroilliac twisted all the way arou[:n
78  CUR:               [·pw! Comon,                              [
79  CUR:                                                    [Comon Bo,=
70  MIK:  =°G'wan.=
```

FIGURE 8. Heritage I3, Excerpt.

```
01  Ile:  There wz a big one behi]nd the left ear yes. Yes, yes.
02         (.)
03  Ile:  [.hhh
04  Lis:  [Yeh ah I'll tell you I'll give you chapter'n verse,
05  Ile:  Right.
06  Lis:  ↑ehh heh heh[heh he-]hh=
07  Ile:              [U h : m]
08  Ile:  =Well now look d'you want me ti[h come over'n get her? or wha:t.
```

the left ear, Lisa promises to give Ilene "chapter'n verse" (which is to say, a fully detailed account) and subsequently breaks into a bout of vigorous laughter. Ilene, however, disattends this and produces, in overlap, an item with which a participant can convey the intention to speak next (see Sacks, Schegloff, and Jefferson 1974). Lisa stops laughing, and Ilene introduces the issue of how the dog will be returned.

We can see something similar in what Gary does at line 50 of Figure 7. Specifically, Gary does not just decline to laugh, he actively pursues a nonlaughable matter. Notice also that, whereas Carney finds something positive in the mishap—that it wasn't recorded—here Gary insists on its seriousness, its possible consequences for his back. This is, of course, a complaint—a complaint not only about what Carney might have done to his back but also about her failure to appreciate this (notice the "you realize").

A complaint like this establishes a place for its recipient to respond in some way—with, for instance, an excuse, an apology, a counter-complaint, a remedy, etc. (see Schegloff 2007). It thus has the potential to initiate a particular kind of sequence. But before anything of this sort can happen, Curt once again comes to the rescue, attempting to "integrate" the complaint into the situation with a joke.

Rather than respond to Gary's complaint, Carney produces one of her own. Specifically, at line 66, Carney says to Gary, "Thanks hon,." We thank people for actions they have done (and so one response is to demur, saying, "I really can't take the credit for that"). Here, by thanking Gary, Carney is attributing responsibility for the fall to him. He hears that and responds to it, saying "*ME::*"—"Yer the one thet did it!" Earlier I suggested that accusations, or attributions of responsibility, occur in time, within sequences of action, and that this positioning as attributions or counter-attributions has consequences for their design. There could be no clearer evidence of that than Gary's talk here. Specifically, here the counter-accusation character of Gary's talk is seen in his use of repetition (broadly understood). Specifically, Gary's turn begins with a repetition of the "you" in Carney's "thank you," realized, of course, as "me." Clearly, such repetition is not possible for accusations but only for counter-accusations.[7]

---

7. Although I do not always provide the evidence to show that it is the case, all the parts of the talk I discuss here—e.g., use of format (repetition) + rejection in counter-accusations—are stable and recurrent practices identifiable across different episodes of interaction, involving different parties, and so on.

## "Well wuh were yihdoin"

And so, finally, we come to the matter of excuses—here in the final bit of talk I'll examine. Gary, under questioning by Carney, folds and accepts responsibility for the fall by offering an excuse of sorts. It's hard to make out what Gary is saying here at lines 05–06, 08, and 11—even with the transcription—but here are the words that Gail Jefferson has attributed to him: "I was sitting here. All of a sudden I had an arm—my arm behind something that was falling off." Austin famously distinguishes between excuses in which a person admits that the action in question was wrong but insists that it isn't quite correct to say that he did it from justifications

FIGURE 9. Auto Discussion, Excerpt, "Come on."

```
01  CUR:  =Come on.
02  MIK:  °Go ah[ead.
03  CAR:       [Well wuh were yih[doin ·hh
04  PHY:                         [Don't you spray yer do[g Curt,
05  GAR:                                                [A(h)h-ha-ha wz
06        [sa(h)ettin he(h)e(h)e(h)ere ·hh!=
07  RYA:  [°Over here c'mere
08  GAR:  =A(h)a(h)ll'v a sudden.·hh![I had en [a:rm,] m u h    a : r m
09  CUR:                            [Smells like [m  e.] That's why(h)y
10  PHY:                                         [°(            )
11  GAR:  =be[hind something et wz fa:(h)ll(h)i(h)n o(h)o(h)off=
12  ???:     [eh-heh!
13  GAR:  =o(h)f ih eh! eh! ah! ah! ah! ah!  ·hhh You dumb she[ck,
14  RYA:                                                      [e:gh.
15  GAR:  ((sniff))
16  CAR:  Oh:(                   [Gary)=
17  GAR:                         [M-
18  GAR:  =One good thing about bein du:mb,
19        (0.8)
20  GAR:  You show it very obv[i o u s [ly.
21  CUR:                      [Mm-mmhhh[mmm
22  CAR:                               [ehhhhhhhhhhh
23  GAR:  eh-heh-heh-heh-heh-heh!  ·hhh
24  CUR:  °hhnh!
25  CAR:  °uh-nh!
26  ???:  °hh hn-hn ·hh[hn
27  GAR:               [Ain't no sense'n bein dumb if you can't sho[w it once
28        'nawhile=                                                [
29  RYA:                                                           [Here Bo,
30  RYA:  =Bo:,
31  CAR:  That's ri:ght.
32        (0.3)
33  CAR:  Do:n't step on my-
34  ???:  hhh
35  CAR:  dri:nk.
36        (0.7)                                                    (01:30)
37  CUR:  [Mm.
38  GAR:  [S:trink?=
39  CAR:  =What there is left'v it,
```

in which an accused person admits that he did the thing in question but argues that it was not quite the wrong or bad thing that is supposed. On this definition, what Gary says here incorporates elements of both excuse and justification. It is an excuse insofar he characterizes this as something that happened to him rather than as something he himself has done. At the same time, "something that was falling off" seems to treat what happened as less than it was. The more general point here is that, in the details of actual talk-in-interaction, Austin's distinctions provide relatively little traction. But again, there's something more important, about which Austin seems to have been quite unaware: Gary delivers his excuse through laughter, and he thereby modulates the action he performs and establishes particular kinds of relevancy for any response to it.

The problem with Austin's dictionary exercise, then, is that it presupposes you can have an excuse in isolation from everything else that is going on. But that never happens—the examples we have considered are no more and no less complex than any other I might have selected. Excuses are produced within the context of social relationships and action, and for this reason are multiply inflected by humor, resentment, concern, and a range of other contingencies that are not in the word but rather in the world.

So, to summarize, I've tried to make three points about the intersection of action in interaction and "ordinary ethics"—indeed these points bear on all action in interaction—not exclusively on explicitly "ethical action."

1. The ordinary ethics of interaction happens in time—in sequences of action. Whether something is a first attribution, a counter-attribution, or an $n$th attribution of responsibility has consequences for the way it is formed, for the way it is constructed, and for the way in which a recipient responds to it (on time and action, see Goodwin 2002).

2. The ordinary ethics of interaction happens together with a host of other goings on, simultaneously in several modalities. Excuses, attributions of responsibility, accusations, and so on may be inflected by laughter, by tears, by a smirk, or by whatever else. That simultaneity, that multivocality, is clearly important to the people who produce and respond to those actions, and so it must be important to us if we are going to understand what is going on.

3. The ordinary ethics of interaction happens within particular configurations of participants (Goodwin and Goodwin 2004, Goffman 1981, Sidnell 2009). This is not something that can be dealt with as

an added-on feature, as an afterthought, because these configurations are actually constitutive of the action as such (Curt's "never spilled a drop").

I have suggested that the ordinary ethics of everyday talk runs deeper than a study of vocabulary suggests. Underlying all talk is the more fundamental and more profound moral order of social interaction. While some of this moral and ethical domain can be recovered from what people say to one another and how they say it, it cannot be reduced to language or to ways of speaking.

# PART THREE

# Responsibility and Agency

# Agency and Responsibility: Perhaps You Can Have Too Much of a Good Thing

*James Laidlaw*

Considerations of the rightness and wrongness of action, of what we owe to each other, of the kinds of persons we aspire to be, and of what we do by way of trying to bring this about—considerations, in short, of the ethical—are pervasive in human life. As Michael Lambek points out in his Introduction to this volume, the ethnographer's experience confirms this as a general rather than a culture-specific truth, and many of the best works of ethnographical description vividly convey what he calls the ubiquity of ordinary ethics. But as I have suggested elsewhere (Laidlaw 2002, 2010), certain rather entrenched features of social theory will need to be rethought if this recognition is to inform anything like systematic anthropological commentary and reflection on ethics, or sustained dialogue with philosophers and others on the subject. In this essay, I enlarge on some brief earlier remarks on anthropological invocations of "agency" (2002: 315–16) and suggest in provisional terms how that concept might be reformulated so as to accommodate proper recognition and facilitate perspicuous description of ethical life.

Two versions of a concept of agency dominate anthropological writing today. The first, and by some measure the more widely influential, uses the term *agency* to designate the creative and assertive capacities of individuals, as against the constraints of what are conceived as "larger" structures (discourses, ideologies, cultures, and so on). This general approach is commonly referred to as "practice theory," following Sherry Ortner's (1984, 2006) influential syntheses of the writings of Bourdieu (1977), Giddens (1979), Sahlins (1981), and others, and I shall adopt this usage here (although "practice theories" would be more judicious). But as Webb Keane (2003a) has pointed out, this concept of agency has become extremely widespread and is employed by many authors who would not use the term "practice theory" to describe themselves.

A series of connected problems with this conception are evident, however. First, there is a confusion between empirical specification of the capacities people may have to be efficacious in their actions and interactions, and so to pursue their goals or desires successfully, and what are generally unspoken presumptions about what those goals are and ought to be. Because an opposition to structure, and therefore to existing systems of values and power, is built into its definition, this conception of agency recognizes as efficaciousness only actions conducive toward certain ends and outcomes: empowerment, liberation, equality, and so on, these ends being imputed as values and interests to all members of the human race as such. For this reason, this conception of agency muddles rather than clarifies matters when applied to any form of life or project whose ends differ markedly from these imputed values: for instance, soteriologies such as Jain renunciation (Laidlaw 2002: 326), or, as Saba Mahmood concisely puts it (2005: 15), any that involve a striving toward actively inhabiting, rather than resisting, prevailing norms and that therefore elude the prescriptive teleology of progressive politics (2005: 9).

A further problematical feature of this conception of agency is that this supposedly universal capacity cum desire to achieve the anthropologists' own preferred forms of human flourishing is assumed to be always and everywhere advanced by the authentic expression of individual subjectivity. In this conception, the sources of the creative and transformative capacities of individuals, as against cultural determination or structural constraint, lie in individual intentionality. So Ortner, for instance, distinguishes agency from merely routine practices by saying that the former is "more intentionalized action" (2006: 135). Keane (2003a) shows that influential figures in anthropology as apparently diverse as Lila Abu-Lughod, in her (1991) critique of the concept of culture, and Akhil Gupta and James Ferguson, in their (1992) argument for the role of larger forces of political economy in the creation of local spaces, share a common concern to emphasize the capacity of human beings to change the structural systems in which they live by means of authentic self-expression. Shared also is the rhetorical move of claiming, as an advantage for this or that conceptual formulation, that it, to a greater extent than its rivals, allows these transformative capacities to be rendered visible and "recognized" (Keane 2003a: 234).

Thus practice theory's agency smuggles rather specific values into a concept of the individual's efficaciousness, imagines this to consist of a creative force deriving from the interior of the human individual, postulates a zero-sum relationship between this and sociocultural structures, and finds moral as well as analytical virtue in discovering where the former prevails over the latter.

The second, still rather less widespread and influential use of "agency" is that associated with Actor-Network Theory (ANT). In the writings of Bruno Latour and others (the most systematic exposition is Latour 2005), we find an agent conceived simply as any entity that plays a causal role in bringing about change. In contrast to practice theory, in ANT, because nonhuman and inanimate entities can be causally significant in networks of relations, they can be agents just as much as persons can. The ascription of agency rests on the empirical question of whether in any particular network of relations an entity participates in an entirely transparent and predictable way in chains of cause and effect or whether it makes an unpredictable difference in how things go. In the former case, in Latour's terminology, it is a mere "intermediary," in the latter, it is a "mediator." This is for him all there is to being an actor.

To illustrate (this example is adapted from Venkatesan 2009): ordinarily, when I write on my computer, I can predict with considerable accuracy, from the way I press the keys and manipulate the mouse, the operations the computer will perform. In these circumstances it is an intermediary, an instrument through which my capacity to act is extended in ways that are within my control. When I am running up against a deadline, however, and it inevitably plays up or crashes, it appears in the chains of cause and effect in which I now find myself no longer merely as an intermediary but as an independent actor in its own right, capriciously or maliciously eating up the nearly complete final draft of my paper. It is in these circumstances, in Latour's terms, that the computer becomes an agent in its own right. As with the *Anopheles gambiae* mosquito, which Timothy Mitchell, in an important exemplar of this genre (2002: 19–53), asserts was one of several important nonhuman agencies determining the course of events in Egypt during the Second World War, its being so does not depend on the possession of a consciousness or subjectivity but derives instead contingently from its causal relations with other entities at a particular time and place. In short, to be an actor is just to have a relatively independent causal role in a chain of events.

This approach seems to smuggle fewer unwarranted assumptions into the picture and will inform a good deal of what follows here. In particular, it seems right to emphasize that causal efficacy of persons needs to be explained in terms of their contingent relations and interactions, rather than a postulated inner quality of which they can be said to have more or less. And it is therefore important not to presuppose that in any given situation all the significant actors will be human. But the determination of what is and is not causally significant is not, as the rhetoric of ANT sometimes suggests, a straightforwardly factual matter but a matter of interpretation. Explanation is intentional: that is to say, whether any causal account in fact illuminates and explains always depends on whom the explanation is for. (What are his or her presuppositions, interests, existing knowledge, and so on?) For this reason, the most causally salient factors in explaining any particular state of affairs or happening will depend upon the significance that state of affairs has for those to whom the account is being offered. Something different will need to be said, in order to explain an event, to someone for whom it is an unprecedented outrage than to someone who was expecting and looking forward to it all along.

Actor-Network Theorists have their own reasons (no doubt not always the same reasons, and I shall not try to characterize them here) for emphasizing the significance of nonhuman actors. The important point, for my purposes here, is just that those interests, whatever they are, are those theorists' interests, and not necessarily those of the people (or mosquitoes!) they describe. And when anthropologists engage in the business of deciding whose presence and interventions have been causally significant in bringing about states of affairs, and assigning agency accordingly, they will not find themselves alone. They will find, indeed, that they have been preceded in this by the people themselves (though probably not by the mosquitoes) whose business they seek to describe. We all do this all the time. Our routine, everyday interaction is shot through with, and its course is pervasively affected by, our ongoing judgments about whose presence or absence, whose actions or omissions, whose words or silences, have contributed in which ways to things turning out as they are doing, and by our assigning responsibility accordingly. And here lies ANT's blind spot.

Since P. F. Strawson's now classic paper "Freedom and Resentment" (2008 [1962]; see also see Watson 2004; Baker, this volume), philosophers have generally recognized that our practices of assigning responsibility for what occurs among us are not underpinned by some external and objective fact of the matter about who is responsible for what. To think that there is a natural fact or quality of "moral responsibility" against which our judgments and attributions might be measured, even in principle, is a category error. Just as the adequacy of explanations of causality depends on the interests that motivate an inquiry, so attributions of responsibility depend upon the interests, and what Strawson called the "reactive attitudes," that characterize human interactions: reactive attitudes such as gratitude and resentment, indignation, approbation, guilt, shame, pride, hurt feelings, forgiveness, or love. Assessing and assigning responsibility flow from just the considerations that excite or inhibit these reactive attitudes: "Did she say that in front of everyone?" "Did he know they're my closest friends?" "Was she under the influence?" "Is he always like that?" "She said that out of spite!" "How calculating!" The causalities that make a difference to the attribution of responsibility, which are those that excite or inhibit reactive attitudes, are inseparable from questions of intention and motivation. A purported causal account of a grievous misfortune I have endured, however minute and detailed a catalogue of causes and connections and circumstances it contains, will not feel even remotely adequate if it omits the fact that just one of those constituent causes was motivated by personal hostility. My interpretation of not only why but actually what has happened is inseparable from, because partly constituted by, my judgments about responsibility for it.

This is why the fiction of tracing cause and effect as if no meaning or significance were involved, as Latour's "flat description" seeks to do, is so effective in highlighting the agency of inanimate objects. It re-presents things to us in a form that is designed to keep us indifferent to them. It is also why it is so difficult. We are not used to finding such flat descriptions explanatory. So it takes an effort, even when describing the role of inanimate objects, to exclude attributions of the kinds of intentionality that determine responsibility, as indeed I failed to do above, in ascribing malevolence to my malfunctioning computer and as Mitchell also does (2002: 38) when he describes how his mosquitoes "took advantage" of new reservoirs and river movements to advance their progress down the Nile.

But difficult as it is, I hope to show that at least something like ANT's flat description will make it possible to show how agency is created, not as an inherent quality of which individuals may have more or less but as an aspect of situations in which people may find themselves, and how this effect is created by attributions of responsibility.

Practice theory's conception has hardly affected ordinary language (though it still might, of course, as equally muddling social-science concepts such as "culture" have already done). We do not routinely speak, except as social scientists, of people as having "a lot of agency" (as if it were a character trait roughly similar to "initiative"). Most of how we do normally use the word *agent* and related forms has been strangely neglected in social theory. Management experts and politicians do talk, for instance, of someone being "an agent of change," and in other ways we speak of an agent as someone who does something *to* someone or something else. These expressions refer to agent-patient relations. But in everyday speech an agent is normally one who acts, certainly, but one who does so specifically on behalf of someone else. So advocates, tax accountants, lobbyists, the people through whom we buy and sell houses, and so on, as well as on occasion our friends, are our "agents" precisely because, and insofar as, they undertake to act for us or as our proxy, to be an instrument of our interests and wishes, to exercise their efforts and capacities on our behalf. In other words, one qualifies as an "agent" in these terms ("agent-principal" relations) precisely by tending to be a Latourian intermediary.

Stanley Milgram (1974) conducted a celebrated series of psychological tests in which subjects were told they were taking part in an important scientific experiment and asked by a white-coated figure to inflict electrical shocks on someone else. In fact, the shocks and the pain displayed by the subjects of these putative experiments were feigned, the point of the tests being to discover how willing people were to do something just because they were acting on instructions from a figure of authority. And the study showed that they did so strikingly often. When he came to speculate about why this might be so, Milgram postulated that his subjects entered what he called an "agentic" state: a stance in which they saw themselves not as the authors of their own actions but as acting as the agents of the white-coated scientists. It is striking that even Milgram's conspicuously unlovely neologism is closer to the ordinary meaning of the word *agent* than is its use in much social theory. So, for instance, a firm or corporation will be held liable for the actions of one of its employees, even if these actions are unauthorized or negligent, insofar as the employee can be shown to be acting as an "agent" of the firm. In other words, the concept of agency comes into play here precisely when the identity asserted by ANT is put in question: where human arrangements and relationships create a possible separation between the causally effective doer of a deed (or the proximate cause of a state of affairs), on the one hand, and, on the other, its responsible author. We have a prima facie case, then, for beginning a reexamination of the concept of agency by attending to the ways in which responsibility or accountability for actions and their effects are attributed to persons or things.

In *Shame and Necessity* (1993), Bernard Williams offers a helpful analysis of responsibility. His starting point is disagreement with a number of authors who had argued that the ethical thought of the ancient Greeks was rudimentary or deficient because it lacked "our" concept of responsibility, according to which, allegedly, moral blame attaches only to actions that are in a strong sense voluntary. Williams agrees that the ancient Greeks had no such conception, but not that their ethical thinking was any the worse for this. On the contrary, he follows Nietzsche (1994) in maintaining that an overemphasis on and attempt radically to "deepen" the notion of the voluntary (encapsulated in the idea of "free will") is one of the deformities of the particular and largely modern version of the ethical life that he elsewhere (Williams 1985) calls "morality: the peculiar institution." This institution does affect our thinking and our practice, but only in some contexts and to a certain extent, and where it does so the result is considerable confusion. For the most part, we operate in everyday life with a different and more complex conception of responsibility.

The understanding of responsibility we mostly use is essentially similar in structure to that of the Greeks. This Williams reconstructed from an analysis of the descriptions and evaluations of conduct in the heroic epics and classical tragedies, and according to him it consists not of a single and exclusive emphasis on intention but of four separable but interrelated questions that in any social setting anywhere will have to be addressed and understood in relation to each other. These four elements of responsibility are cause, intention, state, and response, and Williams glosses them as: (1) the idea that, in virtue of what he or she did, someone has brought about, let us say, a bad state of affairs; (2) the question of whether he or she did or did not intend that state of affairs; (3) the question of the state of mind or condition he or she was in when doing so; and (4) the idea that it is his or her business, if anyone's, to do something to make up for it. The distinction between intention and state, for instance, is clear in Agamemnon's explanation, in the *Iliad*, for the action of his that initiated his quarrel with Achilles. Agamemnon's claim not to have been responsible for this rests not on denying that he took Achilles' prize, Briseis, from him or that he did so intentionally, intending to keep her. What he suggests is that when he had that intention he was in an abnormal state of mind (one in this case induced by the gods) and for that reason and to that extent the action was not wholly his.

Williams emphasizes that, while these four elements are rooted in such general and banal features of human social life that we may expect them to occur in any conception of responsibility anywhere, we should not expect that they will be interpreted, weighed, or related to each other in any determinate way: "There are many ways of interpreting the elements, of deciding what counts as being the cause, for instance, or enough of a cause, of a given state of affairs; what is an adequate response in a given kind of case, and who can demand it; what states of mind might be strange enough to dissociate the act from the agent" (1993: 56). The Greeks understood (and so do we, except when trying to be philosophers) that we have to recognize responsibilities that extend beyond merely our normal purposes or what we intentionally do.

This analysis is helpful because it neatly shows why neither exclusively the practice-theory emphasis on subjectivity, nor the ANT attention to causality, nor even these two factors somehow combined encompasses all that is involved in ascribing agency for a state of affairs. As J. L. Austin (1961b) points out in his examination of what excuses tell us about such matters, many attempts to attenuate or mitigate liability for misdeeds involve claiming not that one did not do the thing in question, nor that one did it simply unintentionally, but rather that one did do it, "but only in a way." The especially interesting possibility that Williams's dissection of responsibility enables us to explore is that his four elements (cause, intention, state, and response) need not coincide within the same individual, or for that matter the same collectivity. They may be distributed among the entities involved in a network or a chain of events.

Let me introduce a few simple scenarios to illustrate this, some of which are adapted from an excellent though somewhat differently oriented discussion by Meir Dan-Cohen (1992). Some of these relate to legal matters, and I use some legal examples partly because questions of responsibility are very explicitly addressed in such contexts. The law of tort, as Austin observed (1961b: 136), affords the richest existing storehouse of varieties of excuses. Furthermore, in the Common Law tradition, at least, there is a fairly explicit individualist ideology, so when we find, as we shall, that responsibility and agency are nevertheless distributed among persons and groups in various ways, this is particularly telling. But these scenarios do not all concern the law, and my claim would be that in those that do the reasoning deployed is continuous with more general common sense and moral judgment.

You are attending a drinks party, and, while you are engaged in conversation, someone unseen by you places a glass of wine on a table, perilously close to your elbow. You knock it over accidentally, and the wine spills, whereupon you begin to apologize, to reach for your handkerchief to mop up the wine, and anxiously to wonder aloud if the surface of the table will be damaged. This practical and unself-conscious attribution to yourself of the agency for what happened did not refer to your state of mind or subjectivity. Quite spontaneously, and even though what you did was unintentional and would not have happened but for someone else's arguably careless action, you take responsibility for the effects of your bodily motion. So far, so ANT, and so un–practice theory.

But you may also find yourself responsible for states of affairs that are caused not by your body but by your property. A freak wind catches the curtains at your apartment window. They knock over a vase, which in turn falls on a passer-by's head. As you and a friend with whom you have been sitting in the room rush to the window and look out helplessly at the injured man below, your mortification will be the more intense of the two, and you will be expected to try to help with the greater urgency, because the damage has been caused by your property. It stands in this respect in a qualitatively similar relation to your self as does your body in the earlier example. It is close enough to being identified with you that it functions for these purposes as your agent and is therefore a conduit through which responsibility for what happens passes to you. You are responsible not simply because of a chain of cause and effect but because these entities stand in a particular "agentive" relationship to you. It is for this reason that we may both feel and be held responsible to varying degrees for actions by people under our care, dependents or children, pets and other animals we own, employees, and other agents.

In the 1970s the filmmaker Stanley Kubrick had *A Clockwork Orange* withdrawn from distribution in the U.K. This followed several news reports and a court case in which it was claimed that young people, inspired by and emulating scenes from the film, were committing violent crimes. At the time it was generally believed that remorse over these copycat crimes motivated Kubrick to arrange the ban, which he maintained forcefully for the rest of his life. After his death, however, it was claimed on his behalf that actually he had followed police advice, after threats of retribution against him and his family for the violence committed by these members of his audiences. Both possibilities serve my purpose here. Whether Kubrick voluntarily accepted some measure of responsibility or whether he merely acquiesced when it was aggressively attributed to him, either way his film became acknowledged to be an agent of his and he to be answerable to some extent for the effects it had on others (more so, of course, once those became reasonably predictable), since he had made it such that it had those effects, albeit unintentionally. Alfred Gell's *Art and Agency* (1998) exploits just this sort of possibility and argues that it explains much of the social importance of art.

So, although in many circumstances we are held responsible only or especially for intentional actions, this is by no means uniformly so. The efficacy, and hence the responsibility, of an individual may be extended by the agency of his or her body or body parts, property, dependents, or works, and this happens either because these entities are intrinsically connected to or are a part of him or her as a socially recognized, responsible self or because they have become so as a result of his or her decisions and actions, as when we use a piece of technology (plant a landmine, for example) or engage another person to act as an agent on our behalf.

A professional football player rejoices in "our" victory, in a match won by his team but at which he, as it happens, was not present (he was injured that day). Although he was causally at best tangential to the achievement of this particular success and although it might be slightly risible for him to claim equal credit with the players who were on the field, his membership in the squad means that we do not regard it as absurd that this success was to some degree a success of his and that he should share in the credit and celebrate to the full with his teammates. Correspondingly, a bank robber who attempts to deny responsibility for a murder committed by his accomplices, even though he might have been at some distance from the scene—waiting to drive the getaway car, perhaps—will meet with only very partial success. The doctrines of conspiracy and accomplice liability are the other side of the kind of acceptance of collective agency that makes the footballer's attitude seem reasonable.

What makes any particular action, effect, or state of affairs someone's responsibility is not a matter exclusively of any characteristics that adhere in or belong to that person. Agency has sources other than those "inside" the individual. Through intermediating agencies, we can be responsible for things we did not or could not have carried out, and significant among these are our connections to and relationships with others and our membership in groups. So to see agency as something that belongs to an individual as such, and insofar as he or she is autonomous in relation to "larger" structures, as in practice theory, must be an error. Our efficacy may be extended through the agency of things extrinsic to the body and the mind but to some degree intrinsic to "us."

The converse is also the case. A man who had brutally killed his own ten-year-old son was successfully defended in the ensuing murder trial

(*Regina versus Charlson*) when it was argued that this wholly out-of-charac-
ter behavior had been caused by a brain tumor. The defense depended
on the conceptual detachment of the tumor from the "self" that was the
defendant, on the idea that it was a distinct, detachable, hostile, and intru-
sive object that was not part of him. This defense of "involuntariness" is
related to but different in detail from Agamemnon's, from the notion of
"crimes of passion," and from that of "duress." A defendant accused of
criminal action committed under threat of violence or blackmail may
argue that these circumstances give rise to a period of time or an episode
during which his or her actions do not issue from his or her normal self.
This period of time, like Charlson's tumor or like a successfully repudiated
or fraudulent agent, may be detachable, so that the putative principal is
not responsible for its effects.

One thing to notice about these examples is that the claims by means
of which responsibility is embraced or repudiated, and attributed or refused to others, work in part by means of claims about the constitution
and extension of the self: Does the fact that the vase is my vase make its
effects into actions of mine? The entity to which responsibility may be
assigned is complex and malleable—sometimes excluding parts of the
body, sometimes including a good deal else—and there is no reason why
Williams's four elements (cause, intention, state, response) need be confined inside the same biological individual (or object). The "response"
implied by an acceptance of responsibility might come from some entity
other than the locus of the cause (a filmmaker is responsible for what his
movie prompted other people to do; I feel responsible for my dog's biting
you). The agency that lies behind an action that brought about some, let
us say, bad state of affairs and to which responsibility is therefore assigned
might be distributed between different persons, objects, or groups.

Such interpretive flexibility enables the very identity of an act to be
redefined insofar as responsibility for it is variously attributed, asserted, or
denied:

> Should we say, are we saying, that he took her money, or that he robbed
> her? That he knocked a ball into a hole, or that he sank a putt? That he
> said "Done," or that he accepted an offer . . . what is *an* or *one* or *the* action?
> For we can generally split up what might be named as one action in several
> distinct ways, into different *stretches* or *phases* or *stages*. (Austin 1961b: 149)

Where dramatic or consequential matters of criminal responsibility are
at stake, these claims as to just what has been done, by whom (or what),
with what intentions, or in what state may be the subject of intense and

focused contest, but in less highly colored ways we quite routinely refine and redefine who and what we are, as we accept or not responsibility for the things we claim or are held to have brought about (for anthropological treatments see Hill and Irvine 1993, and Humphrey and Hürelbaatar 2005 on "agent regret").

This is a good reason, we should note, to reject easy portrayals of "the Western conception of the person" as, to take one supremely influential example, "a bounded, unique, more or less integrated motivational and cognitive universe, a dynamic center of awareness, emotion and judgment and action organized into a distinctive whole and set contrastively both against other such wholes, and against its social and natural background" (Geertz 1983: 59). This is a much more accurate description of the postulates of certain brands of social science than it is an ethnographic description of "the Western self," for which latter purpose it is no better empirically grounded than the philosopher's "moral responsibility."

As several of the social theorists who have striven to "reconcile" structure and agency (Bourdieu perhaps most extensively) have remarked, their efforts closely parallel those among moral philosophers to demonstrate the compatibility of determinism and free will: attempts to maintain at the same time the truth of the claim that human action is amenable to causal explanation and the apparently incompatible truth that we are different from the rest of the natural world in a way that consists in our choosing or deciding how to act. Set up in this way, the philosophical project is malformed because incomplete, and the same is true of its parallel in social theory. Williams once again illuminates matters for us, in a discussion of compatibilism in moral philosophy. He points out (1995: 3–21) that any attempt at reconciliation has to deal, in fact, with three rather than two kinds of terms. These are: (1) determinism, which is to say, some kind of causal account of why people act as they do; (2) a set or range of psychological items, notions such as choice, decision, intention, and so on, by which we understand the workings of human action; and (3) a set of ethical terms, such as blame and responsibility. And crucially, as we have seen, the terms under (3) cannot be assumed merely to be singular inner psychological states. They are complex, and not just psychological. It follows that the supposed duality between structure and the "acting subject" is not a duality at all. We are not simply more of an agent the less effectively we are incorporated into supposedly larger structures. And it follows also that agency belongs not with the first of these sets of terms, in a merely causal account, as ANT would have it, nor in the second set, as an internal characteristic of the individual, as practice theory assumes it must be, but to the third, along with blame and responsibility, as an aspect of the relational processes whereby stretches, phases, or stages of people's ongoing conduct are interpreted as acts for which distinct agents (of varying shape and size) are accountable.

To illustrate this, I should like to offer a partial redescription of some very familiar ethnography, by suggesting that Evans-Pritchard's book on Zande witchcraft (1937) can be read as an essay on the production and distribution of agency. Discussion of this work has been dominated by the so-called "rationality debate," but Max Gluckman (1972) and Mary Douglas (1980) produced two powerful and unjustly neglected readings of it in relation, as they respectively put it, to the allocation of responsibility and the tracing and fixing of accountability. (These themes are not of course neatly separable from those of reason and belief, but they do emerge as salient from a different angle of approach to that in the rationality-debate literature.) I shall draw freely on both these authors (largely ignoring points of divergence and disagreement) in what follows.

Evans-Pritchard makes quite clear that what "witchcraft" explained for the Azande was not the occurrence of events or circumstances as such but specifically their moral quality; if an event or circumstance were caused by witchcraft, what this meant was that it was an act of human malevolence and therefore that someone, and someone other than the sufferer, was to blame for it. In addressing an oracle or a witch doctor and in attempting to identify who was bewitching him, an aggrieved Zande man was not seeking merely to identify a proximate cause. As in the famous case of the collapsing granary, he knew that already. (Termites ate through the supports.) What he was seeking was someone to hold to account, someone from whom a response, in Williams's terms, might be elicited. Thus, as Evans-Pritchard remarked, witchcraft was not "a necessary link in a sequence of events but something external to them that participates in them and gives them a peculiar value" (1937: 72). The "peculiar value" was that they were not just bad luck or one of those things and not one's own fault, but the fault and responsibility of some specific other agent: "Witchcraft is the socially relevant cause, since it is the only one which allows intervention and determines social behaviour . . . it is the ideological pivot around which swings the lengthy social procedure from death to vengeance" (ibid.: 73).

That this is so becomes clear if we look at the circumstances in which the sufferer of misfortune was precluded from looking to divination as a way of seeking redress or recompense (ibid.: 63–83). If what happened could be attributed to your own technical incompetence or lack of skill, then you could not blame witchcraft. Evans-Pritchard reports that of course people did try to do just this—to avoid responsibility for failure by claiming to be victims of witchcraft—but such claims were generally rejected (ibid.: 78). In other words, witchcraft might be an explanation for things that befell you, but not for your personal limitations. And so you could not cite someone else's witchcraft to account for the fact that you had committed a moral offence: "if you tell a lie, commit adultery, steal, or deceive your prince" (ibid.: 74). So if you had acted in such a way as to put yourself in a state of moral culpability—if you had broken a taboo, for example—then you could not invoke witchcraft to try to blame someone else for misfortunes that befell you in that state. It makes sense, therefore, that it was a capital offence for the relatives of a man who had been put to death on the orders of the king to consult an oracle to determine if their kinsman had been bewitched (ibid.: 75). Such a move was a challenge to the king's justice by seeking to show that it had led to unmerited punishment, since only undeserved misfortune implied witchcraft.

Although Evans-Pritchard makes clear that hostility and mistrust of others, and so the suspicion of witchcraft, were highly prevalent among the Azande, a decision was taken actually to try to identify a culprit only where there seemed to be a practical point in doing so: if compensation could be got, a sickness cured, or an ongoing or deteriorating misfortune ameliorated or removed (ibid.: 84–87). In other words, there had to be some reasonable expectation of the "response" aspect of responsibility. So death or injury in war was not attributed to witchcraft, since anyone from an opposing force identified by divination could not in any case be held to account.

The fact that commoners did not accuse aristocrats of bewitching them can be understood in the same way. Although commoners were prepared to say privately that they thought some of the noble class might be witches, they never made accusations against them. It was not a credible way of assigning responsibility because such people could not in practice be held to account (ibid.: 32–33). And contrariwise, where more direct and reliable means of redress were available, the Azande resorted to them without bothering to consult oracles: thus to the courts in cases of theft, adultery, or murder, where the culprit was known. Punitive magic was resorted to where the perpetrator could not otherwise be identified (ibid.: 113–14).

In sum, then, to claim your misfortune as an instance of witchcraft was to declare that it wasn't an accident or coincidence and that it wasn't deserved or unavoidable. It was to see yourself as a victim of an agent who could in principle be held to account, a victim, that is, of a responsible self, connected to you via an unseen agency. To be a victim of witchcraft implied the existence of a perpetrator and a demand for redress.

Evans-Pritchard went to some trouble (e.g., ibid.: 220) to insist that, as a way of managing one's affairs, these practices for seeking redress for misfortune worked perfectly well (this is one point that was picked up in the "rationality debate"). But he was a good deal more ambivalent about the moral climate these practices sustained and reflected among the Azande: the prevalence of mistrust, suspicion, and jealousy between neighbors (ibid.: 37, 100–3, 293). No one ever just died in Zandeland; their doing so was never just an accident. Someone was always to blame (ibid.: 268). To Evans-Pritchard's eyes, the Azande found blame, created culprits, and demanded redress—in general, created responsibility—for events about which he "at home" would not have thought that any moral blame need be attached to anyone:

> Where Zande moral notions differ profoundly from our own is in the range of events they consider to have a moral significance. For to a Zande almost every happening which is harmful to him is due to the evil disposition of someone else. . . . In our own society only certain misfortunes are believed to be due to the wickedness of other people. . . . But in Zandeland all misfortunes are due to witchcraft, and all allow the person who has suffered loss to retaliate along prescribed channels. (ibid.: 113)

Gluckman (1972) attributes the prevalence of witchcraft beliefs and practices in Africa to what he calls an overemphasis on social connectedness and interdependence. I think we can safely reject Gluckman's implication that there is somehow a correct degree of social connectedness about which these societies were in error; the insight I take from him is that mechanisms for the allocation of responsibility (such as witchcraft accusations and so on) create their own distinctive kinds of interconnectedness. So an increase in witchcraft accusations does represent an intensification of just those connections. People can be held accountable for actions that are simply not conceivable as actions without the practices, such as divination and accusation, through which culprits are identified. Witch finding, as a practice of allocating responsibility, turns what might otherwise be an accident or random misfortune into an action. It therefore creates agency, so to speak retrospectively.

The attribution of responsibility (cause, intention, state, response) involves postulating unseen entities (intention, will, malevolence, ill temper, etc.), and accusations of witchcraft involve this too. Here there are other and different unseen entities, some but not all located "inside" an individual, and not necessarily simply psychological. There is "witchcraft substance," of course, and also the poison oracle, which Evans-Pritchard (1937: 321) describes as "a material agency." By postulating parts of the self from which the requisite action might issue, or entities through which it might have been carried out, such practices create kinds of wrongdoing that would not be imaginable otherwise. What otherwise looks like just one of those things can become someone's fault, insofar as it can be construed as an action. In other words, they bring about an expansion of agency.

Douglas (1980: 82) points out that, by the time Evans-Pritchard came to write his Zande book, he had already completed his Nuer fieldwork, so comparisons and contrasts between the two societies would have colored how he viewed and wrote about both. It is worth, then, following Douglas in briefly comparing the processes of allocation of responsibility among the Azande with the situation, as Evans-Pritchard also described it (1940, 1951, 1956), among the Nuer.

With the Nuer, we have a very different moral world, in which the attribution of responsibility happens quite contrastingly. Whereas among the Azande everyone was more or less perennially the victim of someone else's malevolence, among the Nuer, Evans-Pritchard describes a strong ethic of self-help and personal responsibility. If someone did observably do you harm, then that was a fault of theirs and you were expected to act to hold them responsible, to demand and claim compensation, and to exact retribution as appropriate (1940: 151–52). This was affected by the question of how intentional the harm that they did you had been. If it was unintentional, this lessened but never eliminated the compensation considered appropriate (1956: 107). Instead of the prevalence of distrust, the Nuer institution of feud relied on people being willing to support their kin and neighbors. One's ability to claim and obtain compensation depended on the maintenance of healthy relations of reciprocal obligation and the perceived justice of one's case.

The difference between the Azande and the Nuer in terms of notions of individual personal responsibility was expressed in a contrast between their ideas about sin and the supernatural. Where the Azande were surrounded by people, including whole kin groups, who secretly possessed sinister powers and occult techniques, the Nuer were surrounded by spirits that were not in anyone's control but were instead all manifestations of a basically benevolent and, above all, a fair and just god. So there was a strong presumption that most misfortune was merited. If you suffered a misfortune, this was probably because you had done something you should not have done or had not done something, such as consecrating an ox to a spirit, which you ought. So a very common response to misfortune was simply to recognize that one must have sinned and to make a sacrifice in atonement (ibid.: 12). As Douglas (1980: 97) remarks, "their resignation when God was seen to have intervened was as brave as their resistance to damage caused by another person. The two kinds of accountability support each other by their grounding in the concept of 'being in the right.'"

Contrast this with the Azande, for whom taking action by citing witchcraft and recognizing a fault of your own were mutually exclusive alternatives. But more than this, and in most direct contrast with the Azande, the Nuer regarded most instances of misfortune as probably just an accident. You could not always be sure, so it was a good idea to make a sacrifice anyway. Not that the sacrifice would have any direct effect—it would not lead to a magical undoing of the misfortune you had suffered, and it would not lead to anyone else (including god) compensating you in any way. It was a way of accepting what had happened in a spirit of trusting submission to god and thereby determining to try to live as one should.

I have a very limited heuristic purpose in citing this contrast. The point is simply that institutions and practices can work so as to proliferate the kind of connections that sustain attributions of responsibility or they can tend to constrain them. They may expand and distribute agency, or they may contract it. In case this argument might seem to be limited to Evans-Pritchard's moral imagination or to mid-twentieth-century Africa, I should like to end this paper by suggesting that in the U.K. in recent decades we have witnessed an expansion of agency, comparable to that which would be produced by an increase and intensification of witchcraft accusations in a context such as the Azande, but of course by different means. These changes, in these particular respects, have made us more like the Azande than the Nuer. Here, the unseen entities by means of which new connections are made between people and the effects for which they may be held responsible are produced not by a witchcraft substance identified by means of oracles but are instead the products of institutionalized statistical reasoning.

My purpose, again, is limited and illustrative. I do not deny that there might simultaneously have been other trends that have tended in quite different directions. My claim is not about what has happened, in the round, in British society. It is about what we learn conceptually from the fact that certain things have turned out to be possible and what kind of concepts we need to describe such things, as and when they happen.

We are familiar with the way statistics are used in our legal system in ways that tend to undermine individual responsibility: the defense counsel for a child sex murderer enters, as part of his plea, the claim that "a person physically and sexually abused as a child by both parents becomes an abuser with probability 87 percent," and so on. Arguments citing the statistical regularity of crime rates, in order to claim that it is "society" that causes a crime, of which the individual perpetrator is merely "the instrument who executes it," date back to the influential Belgian statistician Adolphe Quetelet in 1832 (Hacking 1990: 114–18). And there is still no real agreement on how in the law, or in moral judgment more generally, we might make sense of and deal with this kind of "statistical extenuation."

It is less frequently observed that uses of statistical analysis have worked in the opposite direction, to create hitherto unimaginable responsibilities. What looks, at the level of an individual event, to be an accident, mishap, or misfortune—a traffic accident, for example—can be shown by means of such analysis to be part of a previously unperceived misdeed, for which a responsible agent may be identified. If the kind of accident you have been involved in or the unexplained illness from which you suffer can be shown to be part of a statistically significant fact or trend, then responsibility for this larger phenomenon may be assigned, and some kind of response (compensation, perhaps) demanded. This is what transforms a set of symptoms into a syndrome (such as "Gulf War Syndrome") and links it to a cause (a particular set of events). So if you have been injured at work in what seems like an accident (or in a hospital, or let down by a "failing school," and so on), and if this kind of accident happens more in your firm than in an otherwise comparable competitor, or in a firm of one type more than another, then you have at least the beginnings of a claim to be a victim of a culpable misdeed.

This effect of statistical analysis in creating or discovering new misdeeds and culprits is especially powerful where it is used to create new kinds of responsibilities, including and increasingly attaching to collective agents, that simply would not have been possible or even conceivable without it. Consider, for example, the idea of "indirect discrimination." A whole range of agents—individuals, private institutions, and public bodies—insofar as they are deemed to be performing "public functions" in the U.K., are now charged with a responsibility to contribute to certain statistical effects being measurable in the world (in terms, for instance, of sex or race equality in employment). This means that we can imagine an event or action—a decision to employ or promote this person rather than that—which, viewed as a single event in its own right, seems not to be in any way reprehensible: fortunate for the person employed or promoted and a misfortune for the others, without these misfortunes being something for which anyone could be held to be culpable. But now imagine that the combinational effects of many decisions or actions of this kind is to create a statistical effect, more men being employed or promoted than women, for example. Now the woman who did not get the job or the promotion may be considered to be a victim, not so much of the individual decision, since that may remain unimpeachable in its own terms, as of the aggregate relative misfortune produced by the fact that there are many decisions of a similar kind being made. This fact, invisible and even unimaginable without statistical reasoning, creates an injustice where otherwise there might only be an individual misfortune. Legislation requiring employers to carry out the kind of statistical analysis needed to reveal effects of this kind thus constitutes a requirement to deploy a technology not only for the creation of calculating selves and calculable spaces (Miller 1994) but also for the proliferation of responsible agency.

The employer may now be held accountable for contributing to a regrettable statistical trend. The rejected woman's victimhood and the employer's culpability depend upon this hitherto unknowable entity, where formerly there had been only bad luck. Now there is moral luck (Williams 1981). Like witch finding (cf. Evans-Pritchard 1937: 148), where audit-derived statistical analysis of this kind expands, as it has been doing recently, it does so at the expense of notions such as luck or fate, which are squeezed out or reduced at its expense (Hacking 1990, P. L. Bernstein 1996, Desrosières 1998).

Statistical analysis and its use in processes of audit is therefore the medium for arguments about where responsibility lies for states of affairs or effects that are only imaginable in the first place through these very techniques. Once again, there are parallels with the Zande case. Evans-Pritchard comments that much of the misfortune people suffered was caused by unseen powers, and the only basis for action against those powers was knowledge derived in similarly occult ways (1937: 267). He writes: "The oracle is consulted on matters referring to witchcraft, sorcery, and the ghosts, and the information it gives refers to mystical forces for the existence of which it is likewise the sole evidence" (ibid.: 342–43).

These developments all tend toward a proliferation of agency, namely, the detection of new kinds of acts and new injuries and faults, and they also tend toward increasing ascription of agency to entities other than individual human beings. (Moves to introduce "corporate killing" into the criminal law also have this quality.) Of course, the entities whose culpable agency is being so industriously uncovered in this way tend to be those, such as corporations and public bodies, able to pay substantial damages. Like Zande witchcraft (and largely unlike our criminal law) this is a strictly practical set of governmental techniques. Accountability is traced to entities from which a worthwhile response, in Williams's terms, may be expected.

We should note one further and rather far-reaching point about these processes and practices for the proliferation of responsibility, which is that, contrary to the assumptions built into practice theory, an augmentation to one's agency is not necessarily an empowering or liberating experience.

In the case of the Azande, practices, such as divination, that created and distributed responsibility so productively were to some extent balanced by others whose effect was to soften and disperse it, in a sense blurring or lessening the severity or weight of the responsibility involved. The first of these was the notion that witchcraft was hereditary. This meant that it was not entirely your fault if you were a witch, although it might be your fault that you were an active one. In any case, this meant that obligations arising from your status as a witch were shared to some extent by your kin group, and in that sense lessened (1937: 26–27). Second, there was the notion that bewitching might be an unconscious act: not just unintentional, but entirely unknowing, until it was revealed by divination (ibid.: 109). This left it open to a discovered witch more or less to wipe out the blame attached by accepting the accusation with resignation, rather than appearing to confirm it by reacting aggressively. The stereotype of a witch was a mean, resentful, ill-mannered person, so reacting politely to an accusation was partially to disconfirm it. Even in the absence of an accusation, it was polite, when visiting a sick friend, to perform a simple ceremony, saying, "if it is I who am killing him with my witchcraft let him recover" (ibid.: 126). The suspicion that all sickness must be someone's responsibility is softened, in terms of the practical demands it places on those held to be responsible, by the possibility that the fault might be unintentional.

There are parallels to these mitigations in the case of statistically generated responsibility. The recent development of powerful mechanisms for assigning responsibility by means of statistical reasoning has been balanced by complementary institutions and practices that, like the factors just mentioned in the Zande case, soften or disperse the blow when responsibility is assigned and response demanded. Insurance is the most powerful and important of these, and it is no coincidence that it also depends upon, and has indeed been a principal site for the development of, the same techniques of statistical and risk analysis that are employed in creating or discovering the kinds of liability for misfortune against which insurance itself is used to protect people and organizations. Widespread use of insurance means, of course, as does the heredity of witchcraft among the Azande, that the costs of these new kinds of faults and responsibilities (and the protection of people from, or at least their compensation for, an increasing range of misfortunes) are dispersed very widely through society. The cost of paying compensation falls directly on newly discovered culprits— mostly employers and public bodies—but some of these costs are indirectly distributed fairly widely through the pricing of insurance premiums (although, of course, not all responsibility is dispersed in this way: blame can still stick, sometimes to the institution and sometimes to individuals within it). These processes work through market rather than state institutions, but this should not conceal from us the fact that this is a powerful way in which the response element of responsibility has been increasingly effectively collectivized as more or less loosely socialist techniques for doing so in liberal polities have dwindled (Ewald 1991, O'Malley 1996).

I began this paper by distinguishing two general conceptions of agency: that found in practice theory and that in ANT. For the most part, I have deployed a modified version of the latter against the former and have tried to press home that "agency" is not helpfully to be thought of as a capacity for efficacy inherent in individuals or derived from their subjectivity, but rather as a matter of relations that reach both into and beyond the individual by means of mediating entities, be they body parts, property, artworks, tools or weaponry, witchcraft substance, or statistical effects. If this is correct, then any discussion about how much agency "the acting subject" may or may not have is, roughly speaking, meaningless. Where persons experience an augmentation to "their agency," this is not an increase in their general capacity to get what they want done. It comes instead, as we have seen, as responsibility for particular happenings or states of affairs, and these may include states of affairs that they have rather limited capacity to influence.

### ACKNOWLEDGMENTS

I am very grateful indeed to Michael Lambek, Jack Sidnell, and Paul Antze for their invitation to participate in the 2008 Toronto symposium Ordinary Ethics and to all the participants for a stimulating set of discussions and challenging and thought-provoking comments on my paper, including especially Webb Keane's characteristically insightful discussant's commentary. A revised version was presented to the Anthropology Department at University College London. I am grateful also for a very helpful discussion at that gathering, and especially for Martin Holbraad's generous and penetrating commentary and for helpful suggestions from Allen Abramson. For comments on written drafts, I should like to thank Susan Bayly, Matei Candea, Caroline Humphrey, Michael Lambek, and Jonathan Mair.

# Abu Ghraib and the Problem of Evil

*Steven C. Caton*

I want to think about the prison abuses committed in Abu Ghraib during the U.S. military counter-insurgency in the Iraq War of 2003 to 2005 within the framework of ordinary ethics.[1] In some ways this is easier said than done, not least because there was hardly anything "ordinary" about what is alleged to have transpired behind the walls of Abu Ghraib. Yet we must be mindful that those who committed acts we might call evil were, by and large, ordinary men and women in the U.S. armed services who were thrown into extraordinary circumstances. By stressing this, I by no means wish to exonerate authorities stretching from the White House to

1. For help in formulating some of the ideas in an early version of this paper, I want to thank Ramyar Rossoukh. All participants in the Ordinary Ethics Conference at the University of Toronto in October 2008 gave insightful comments on this draft, but I especially want to single out for gratitude Joshua Barker, the principal discussant, and Michael Lambek, who also gave helpful written comments. At Pitzer College on April 9, 2009, at the kind invitation of John Norvell and Leda Martens, I gave a lecture on the same topic and received invaluable feedback from the former as well as from their colleagues Dan Segal and Claudia Strauss. From their reactions I was encouraged to pursue the conceptualization of "situational evil" more precisely, which I have endeavored to do in this essay. I thank Dan Segal for taking the time to give this version a final critical reading before it went off to press.

the Department of Defense and generals in the U.S. army of responsibility for possible war crimes. Their culpability is now being explored in a number of different works.[2] What I find compelling is not that there were powerful actors behind the scenes responsible for the evil committed in Abu Ghraib but that there were "ordinary" ones.

Another way in which this essay tries to work within the framework of this volume, albeit uneasily, is in its address to what might be called "the problem of evil." Ethics, even ordinary or perhaps especially ordinary ethics, is ultimately about how to do good and avoid evil in life and the world, and yet it is striking that, in modern anthropological and philosophical discourses on ethics, "evil" is hardly ever raised as a question for reflection (as in "What is evil?" "How do we understand it?" "What can be done about it?"); rather, it is subsumed under the more general category of the unethical. Perhaps Abu Ghraib (the metonym I will use for the abuses committed therein) represents a limit case of our thinking on ethics, for, to my mind, there is something profoundly unsatisfying in calling what happened in Abu Ghraib "unethical" (though surely it was that) as opposed to "evil." To put the same point differently, Abu Ghraib exceeded what we might call the "unethical" and might be better captured under the category of evil.

If the category of evil is necessary for understanding Abu Ghraib, it bears repeating that modern philosophy and anthropology have all but abandoned it as an analytical construct.[3] It would seem that, after Kant, the problem of evil was consigned to theology and after that largely ignored in philosophy, with the possible exception of Nietzsche or Hannah Arendt, whose work on the subject I will examine later.[4] As for anthropology, any number of ethnographic works have talked about "evil" (e.g., Evans-Pritchard's 1937 classic on Azande witchcraft and the conundrum of why a particular granary should have fallen on a particular individual sitting beneath it, with mortal consequences), but they have not asked whether

---

2. See Jane Mayer (2008), a careful critique of the Bush administration's systematic assault on anything that curtailed presidential power and that administration's handling of the war on terror, including its designation "enemy combatant" for terrorists or terrorist suspects that, it was was argued, would circumvent prisoner treatment according to the Geneva Conventions, to which the United States is a signatory. For the confusing and often contradictory ways in which the U.S. military interpreted the administration's dicta and tried to implement them, see also Gourevitch and Morris (2008: 45–56).

3. Though see Ricoeur (1967).

4. See Nieman 2002 for an attempt to recuperate the category of evil for philosophical analysis and for singling out Arendt in that project.

evil ought to exist as a category of analysis or theory in its own right. That is to say, in most such works, evil is a cultural category, something that belongs to local cosmological systems and as such is an object of description or cultural interpretation, not of theory. To talk about evil in contemporary anthropology, then, is to talk about it in relation to a particular belief system.

I intend to think about evil here as an analytical category, but I also ask whether this requires an ontological commitment to universals (evil as a transcendental category, as in Kantian philosophy), and if not, whether the alternative must be relativistic (that is, evil is part of a particular belief system or cosmology). Must we be caught between the Scylla of universalism and the Charybdis of relativism? I propose as an alternative the concept of "situational evil" and argue that Abu Ghraib was an instance par excellence of such a category.

Another question this essay asks is: "How do we understand guilt or culpability for such evil?" As I will demonstrate, there have been two concepts in philosophy, broadly speaking, through which guilt has been determined: intentionality and contingency. The first argues that, if one did not intend to commit evil, one is not judged culpable or evil in turn; the second argues that contingencies or circumstances may have caused one to commit evil, which is why one *can* be morally excused for what one did. Both of these concepts are at work in moral judgments about Abu Ghraib, and yet I argue that, once again, there is something profoundly absent in this discussion of moral judgment, which has to do with a notion of responsibility. For our understanding of this concept, the work of Arendt is particularly salient (Arendt 1963, 1971, 2003, and 2006).

Closely linked to the problem of evil and responsibility is moral judgment, or the capacity to judge a situation as evil and determine what to do about it. Here, I would argue, philosophy, and again the work of Arendt, has been more helpful than anthropology in clarifying the terms of our discourse, though the essay by Michael Lambek in this volume is an important contribution and I will enter into a conversation with some of its ideas.

One caveat. Perhaps the most unusual thing to have come out of Abu Ghraib is the haunting, disturbing images documenting prisoner abuse committed by its Military Police. To be sure, atrocities have been caught on camera before by innocent bystanders or journalists (for example, during the Spanish Civil War), but it is rarer (though not unprecedented) to find ordinary men and women carrying out what are deemed abuses and to be the ones taking the pictures of them, with themselves as the perpetrators in the camera frame. This is obviously an important aspect of the history of photography, which, to my knowledge at least, has yet to be written. In Abu Ghraib, what we might call a reflexive documentation, in the sense that the abuser documents himself or herself committing the abuse, was not ad hoc or occasional but prolific and systematic, numbering in the hundreds if not thousands of acts and made over a period of weeks. There has been endless speculation as to why it was done, and to date no completely satisfying or convincing explanation has been given (or may ever be forthcoming). I will describe the abuses performed through taking pictures, but I will not analyze those images in this essay. I have attempted to do so elsewhere (Caton 2006; see also Eisenman 2007). The circulation of these images expanded from within the prison walls via the Internet to family members and friends, and from there eventually to mass newspapers and television news networks around the world. In May 2009 the Obama administration decided not to release the full archive of these images deposited with the U.S. military, arguing that this would further incite Arab and Muslim anger against U.S. troops, particularly in Afghanistan. The reaction that the initial release of these images provoked in various interpretive communities both within the United States and especially in the Muslim and Arab worlds has yet to be thoroughly analyzed (though see Caton 2006 for a start), but it is in part this history that supposedly influenced the administration's decision. It is not entirely clear, however, that Arabo-Muslim reaction would have been as the administration claims.

## Background: The Legal and Administrative Codes Behind Abu Ghraib

Before embarking upon a philosophical/anthropological discussion of evil in Abu Ghraib, it is important to understand, insofar as it is possible to do so, the multiple problems—legal, bureaucratic, and military—that beset the "war on terror" and entities like Abu Ghraib created to combat it. This understanding forms the background from which to judge moral responsibility and the difficulty of moral judgment.[5]

---

5. There have been cases in which the U.S. army has been implicated in atrocities committed during times of war, for instance, the My Lai Massacre in the Vietnam War, in which Lt. Calley gave the orders to shoot mostly old people, women, and children at a village called My Lai, for which crime he was convicted and sent to prison, though no one higher in the army chain of command was

Shortly after the attacks of September 11, 2001, Vice President Dick Cheney gave a now famous interview on *Meet the Press* in which he explained how the administration would respond to the terrorist threat: "We'll have to work sort of the dark side, if you will." Over the next several months, the administration's tactics in response to the terrorist threat were developed and carried out, some in deepest secrecy. The designation of the attacks on the United States as a war, not a crime, justified President George W. Bush, at least in the eyes of his administration as well as many in Congress, to assume extraordinary powers and take extraordinary actions based on them, all with the supposed aim of safeguarding the nation in a time of war against further attacks. Such tactics included: a domestic e-mail and telephone surveillance program, which the Department of Justice argued could be conducted against citizens and noncitizens alike without first obtaining a court order and which Congress was only too ready to grant the President in the Patriot Act; allowing rendition to countries where torture is routine (Egypt, Morocco, and Jordan), often with air bases in western European nations serving as intermediary stopping-off points or with assistance from those nations' security forces in rounding up suspects for deportation (a program the Obama administration has decided to continue, though pledging to monitor prisoner treatment); and the indefinite incarceration of these "illegal enemy combatants" without trial in off-shore penal colonies such as Guantánamo (which the Obama administration has decided to close down, moving prisoners to other installations and allowing some defendants to stand trial).

A legal structure, put in place by the Justice Department and legal counsel to the President of the United States, made possible—though did not explicitly condone—abuses like the ones in Abu Ghraib. First and foremost was the designation of terrorists as "illegal enemy combatants," a category not recognized in international law and therefore not covered by the Geneva Conventions. This would allow agents to operate on what Dick Cheney called "the dark side" (until the Supreme Court began to overturn some of the Bush administration's assumptions, particularly with regard to Guantánamo and its status, that would have repercussions for the application of habeas corpus). Numerous investigators of crimes against

---

charged. In Vietnam some soldiers took pictures of civilians being beaten or otherwise mistreated by members of the U.S. army, and the Abu Ghraib images brought back these memories in the minds of some soldiers. See Nelson 2008 for an account of how U.S. soldiers are or are not confronting the truth about atrocities committed in Vietnam by the U.S. army, a process that has not yet begun with veterans of the Iraq and Afghan wars.

humanity have pointed out that part of the process through which people are socialized, as it were, into accepting and perpetrating exceptional acts of one sort or another is first made possible by "language rules" (Arendt 1963).

Of course, the rules were far more than linguistic. As Abu Ghraib was a military prison, what are called Standard Operating Procedures, or SOPs, had to be formulated for the treatment of illegal enemy combatants. (They were compiled from previous experience in Vietnam and Afghanistan.) These bureaucratic rules also spelled out how the ordinary soldier was supposed to react to any possible contingency inside prisons, ranging from prisoner riot to inclement weather. It should be noted that the MPs in Abu Ghraib received these SOPs rather late in the counter-insurgency (Gourevitch and Morris 2008: 91), and they were not always properly instructed or trained in them. One of the gray areas in question, as we shall see, had to do with the mandate of the MPs to "soften up" detainees before they were handed over to MIs (Military Intelligence) for interrogation. (It was these "softening up" tactics that were captured in the Abu Ghraib photographs.) It is now coming to light in recently released documents that the C.I.A. authorized and supervised many interrogation techniques later judged to be abusive (Mazzetti and Shane 2009).

Let us now turn to the bureaucratization of work within the prison. MIs were trained in gathering up suspects and bringing them to the prison, where another subgroup of them extracted information presumed to be valuable in efforts to suppress the insurgency. MPs were the guards and wardens of the prison, and they too were differentiated according to roles and functions. The social-psychological literature on authoritarian organizations, like the army or the police, that inherently use force and violence to carry out their objectives suggests that this piecemeal distribution of work, an outcome of the rationalization of bureaucracies, can give an individual the impression that he or she is merely a "cog in the machine"; more importantly, it makes it difficult for that individual to see himself or herself as being responsible in any large way for the wrongdoings that that organization commits (Kelman and Hamilton 1989). But what is peculiar about Abu Ghraib is that these roles and functions, rather than being kept discrete, were often blurred, a fact lamented by military experts commenting on what went wrong in the prison. What became blurred, specifically, was the distinction between the operations conducted by MIs and by MPs. MPs were asked to "soften up high-value targets" before they were interrogated by the MIs, the assumption being that information could be more rapidly extracted in the interrogation phase after the "softening up" had taken place. The MPs were not trained in such techniques, and though many of these were approved by the C.I.A., as already noted, the MPs ended up *improvising* many of them as well, by demeaning the prisoners. These attempts drew on assumptions concerning Arab and Muslim shame regarding the naked body or religious concerns with impurity and desecration.

Besides the legal system and the bureaucratic organization of work, other factors to consider in weighing the soldiers' reactions were the extreme conditions in Abu Ghraib, especially overcrowding. The "gathering up" of suspects routinely covered a wide sweep of individuals who might have been present or nearby some "incident" that had occurred (though, as it turned out, they more often than not had nothing to do with causing it, let alone any involvement with the insurgency). Among the suspects who were interrogated, tortured, and even killed, some were determined to be innocent "after the fact." (It is difficult if not impossible to give accurate figures or percentages for such cases.) Due to the fact that suspects were taken in faster than they could be registered, many ended up in prison without any official record of their incarceration, making it extremely difficult for families and others to track them down or for the military prison system to examine their cases when complaints arose and to discharge them if they were held without cause. Like other detention centers inside Iraq, Abu Ghraib soon became overpopulated, both worsening the squalor and exacerbating the stress on inmates and MPs alike. A peculiarity of Abu Ghraib was that it was inside the field of military operations and thus was subjected to almost daily attack and bombardment (another violation of the Geneva Conventions, which stipulate that prisoners of war must be held far enough behind the line of combat so as to be safe from military fire—but then they were not designated prisoners of war). Not only were MPs exhausted from having to deal with an overcrowded prison, their physical well-being was in constant danger because of insurgency attacks.

## The Abuses

Many different kinds of abuses were committed. Among these were: being shackled naked in a cell for hours at a time, sometimes with a derisive female present or with female underwear pulled over the prisoner's head; facing snarling dogs, which at times were allowed to charge and attack the naked prisoner; and sleep deprivation. Physical restraint meant to cause extreme discomfort and pain included being "trussed" with hands behind the back and hoisted above the head, sometimes causing dislocation of the joints and even asphyxiation. In addition, prisoners were verbally assaulted or subjected to extremes of noise and temperature. None of the above-mentioned tactics is sanctioned by the Geneva Conventions (but then, because the prisoners were designated as "illegal enemy combatants," it was not clear to the MPs whether the Conventions applied).

Finally, one must consider the use of the camera, or more exactly, taking pictures as an instrument of abuse. Among the pictures taken in Abu Ghraib are scenes of soldiers on the "stage" on which the physical torture or psychological humiliation was taking place, snapping pictures or wielding a camera as if they were taking pictures and doing so with the prisoner's cognizance. In other words, in these scenes the camera is itself an instrument of abuse, as much as the collar and leash, the female undergarment pulled over the face, and the snarling dog. The thinking behind it was presumably that an Arab, due to cultural notions of honor and shame, is terrified of having images of his humiliation made public, especially to his family, and to avoid that he would be willing to be compliant or cooperative. What did not emerge until months after the release of the photographs is that some acts of prisoner abuse captured on film were actually staged. This was the case, for example, for one of the most iconic images from Abu Ghraib, the picture of a prisoner in black poncho and hood who was made to stand on a box with "electrodes" running from his extended arms, the presumption being that he would have been electrocuted had he stepped down or fallen from his makeshift platform. Once the soldiers had taken their picture of him in this costume and bodily position, he was allowed to step down and change clothing. It is unclear whether the prisoner knew all along that his torture was faked, but even if he did, he presumably had no choice but to go through with this "ritual" of humiliation. Nevertheless, the picture was taken to be "real" by the press and the public at its initial release. For me, what is most interesting is the question of the picture's ontological status. It is not a document of abuse in the same way as many other prison photographs were, because the abuse was staged specifically for the camera; the photograph itself is the abuse, or is *performing* the evil, and as such is different from the others.

One last point before we go on to our philosophical discussion of the problem of evil in Abu Ghraib has to do with the model of a security apparatus of power. Caton and Zacka (2010) explain why Abu Ghraib is perhaps best understood not as a prison in the disciplinary sense as Foucault (1977) elaborates it, but as a nodal point in a security apparatus as

Foucault (2007) also discusses. A security apparatus had been hastily and haphazardly put in place in Iraq almost immediately after the insurgency began. It was meant to sweep up "dangerous" elements, contain them for interrogation, and then either release them back into the population or send them to other, more permanent security locations in Guantánamo and elsewhere. Much has been made of the fact that, if only the rules of engagement with "enemy non-combatants" had been made clearer and put in place in Abu Ghraib sooner, the prisoner abuses we saw might have been avoided entirely. In other words, it was a technical glitch, a failure in the "rational" processes of bureaucratic institutions. It turns out, as noted above, that the Bush administration's legal counsel was obsessed with the problem of rationalizing (in the Weberian legal sense) the physical and psychological punishment of prisoners so as to extract the maximum of intelligence information while avoiding "torture" or "abuse," and so this argument about a lapse of bureaucracy seems tenuous at best. In fact, Foucault's model of the security apparatus presupposes an *improvisatory* power, a creative and often ad hoc performance of prisoner treatment much in the way the MPs created abuses in Abu Ghraib, suggesting that this was due less to a flaw in the prison system, a dearth of rules, or a few "rotten apples" among the soldiers than to the entailments of a security apparatus built to fight an insurgency. With this model, it is important to bear in mind that unforeseen contingencies and unique events are the rule rather than the exception for soldiers and intelligence gatherers in the field (or what Foucault called the milieu). It is this *eventfulness* and the *emergence* of relatively innovative responses to it by of soldiers in the Iraqi counter-insurgency that are essential to understanding the evil soldiers perpetrated and their prisoners confronted.

## Evil and Responsibility in Abu Ghraib

A transcendent ethic, at least as formulated by Kant in his notion of radical evil (see his *Religion Within the Boundary of Mere Reason*), presupposes categories of judgment that are beyond particular situations. As I understand it, Kant's notion entails two concepts of the radical: one with the meaning "root," derived from the Christian doctrine of inherited sin, which makes us all inherently tempted by evil; the other with the meaning "exemplary" and "hyperbolic," as we might say of Hitler that he was the exemplar of radical evil in the modern world—the limit case, if you will—against which all other evil is to be compared and judged (Pol Pot, Slobodan Milošovič,

Idi Amin, Saddam Hussein, etc.).[6] A Kantian or transcendent notion of good and evil informs contemporary rights discourse when it speaks of "human rights" of one sort or another whose violation must be punished by "international law." Ethics in this view is supposedly derived a priori (by a rational human subject, who is seen to be at the heart of ethical judgment), and anyone who challenges its universality must be "backward." The lesson often drawn from Abu Ghraib, for example, is that we had "forgotten" the American (and by extension universal Geneva) doctrine of rights by which this country has conducted itself in war (in spite of the many documented counter-examples when America did not so conduct itself in war). In other words, our failing was due to our forgetfulness of the laws, not to the possibility that our laws need to be questioned.

What is missing in these transcendent views of good and evil is the possibility that ethical conduct is not simply assured by following an ethical code, but that such conduct *emerges* in a given situation. This is true in any instance of ethical conduct, but particularly so in cases like Abu Ghraib, in which unforeseen circumstances and unique events, as I have argued above, are the rule rather than the exception for security apparatuses confronting insurgencies. I do not mean to suggest that soldiers go into these situations without any knowledge of ethical codes, quite the contrary, for the MPs held to various ethical convictions ranging from Christianity to the U.S. military code of conduct to prison or correctional codes, none of which condone the abuses that were committed. Yet it is startling that these were put in abeyance or temporarily forgotten on the grounds that the evil being faced by counter-insurgents was exceptional (in Kantian terms "radical"), thus seemingly justifying the evil treatment of prisoners as exceptional or even regrettable but necessary and unavoidable. This was U.S. Vice President Dick Cheney's reasoning in his expression, "the dark side": to combat evil requires evil deeds in turn, though supposedly harnessed to a greater good. I am certainly not saying that evil does not exist or that the U.S. counter-insurgency in Iraq did not confront evils at the same time that it was committing them, but what I am saying is that it is not helpful or particularly illuminating to invoke a transcendent category of evil by which to know and judge them, just as it is not particularly helpful to invoke a transcendent category of good. The whole point is to understand the singularity or particularity of both the evil and the good we condemn or espouse. The Bush administration's invocation of the "axis

---

6. I thank Judith Baker for pointing out to me the differences in meaning Kant intended by the term *radical evil*.

of evil" is indicative of the problem of thinking about evil in capital letters, or EVIL, that is, as a universal or transcendent category, however effective a rhetorical tool it might have been. To be sure, there was quite a lot of evil committed by the Saddam regime, as there is by many another, but the question to ask was: "How was it *singularly* evil?" How was it linked to the historical challenges faced by a government trying to rule this particular country, to a particular totalitarian regime and the cult of personality developed around its leader, and so forth. To put the point more generally, I am asking whether, as in certain discourses that speak of "situational truths," we can also speak of "situational evil" or an "evil of singularity."

To some my arguments will smack of "relativism," thus of giving up on the problem of evil altogether. To reiterate, I am not saying that moral judgment is simply a matter of applying a particular cultural ethic to a given situation, with the result that people with different ethical calibrations of the situation will inevitably conduct themselves differently in it. I am concerned with singular *events*, unpredictable and haphazard, which exceed the instituted ethical codes and institutions available to individuals caught up in them. Again, this is not to say that codes of conduct are not relevant (or as Michael Lambek says, in his essay in this volume, that "criteria" are not relevant) or that they will not be invoked retrospectively to justify what ought to have been done, but only that they will ineluctably fall short in giving answers to individuals confronting problematic situations. As such, events require of actors to *think* critically about the situation the event has thrown them into, and, further, it requires them to *construct a truth or truths about the evil of the situation and their responses to it.*

Now let me turn to another theme in my discussion of the problem of evil at Abu Ghraib, that of moral responsibility. That the MPs at Abu Ghraib did not (and do not) *profess* moral responsibility is stunningly apparent in the film *Standard Operating Procedure* (2008, directed by Errol Morris), which is based on their paid testimonies. Though they express all kinds of other feelings about what they did, remorse or contrition (a sense of responsibility for what happened inside the prison) is not one of them, and this is even after they have served prison sentences and can no longer incriminate themselves. Here is an instance where ordinary language, as used in this volume, fails. They express shame for having let down the honorable tradition of their military families (Jeremy Sivits), or resentment for having become scapegoats for the higher ups who are "really responsible" for the moral wrongs committed in Abu Ghraib (Ken Davis), or resentment of having been sexually violated and psychologically manipulated by male commanding officers (Lynndie England). But they do not confess to any moral responsibility for the abuses they committed. Even when Sabrina Harman entertains that possibility (Gourevitch and Morris 2008: 273), she understands her actions as a "dereliction of duty" (of not following military rules of conduct by reporting what appeared to be criminal acts), not as a lapse of conscience. The question here is not whether MPs like Ken Davis thought what they were doing in Abu Ghraib in the name of the war on terror was immoral, for some of them clearly did (Gourevitch and Morris 2008: 104). The question, rather, is to what extent, if any, he and others like him felt any responsibility for those immoral actions because of not doing anything or not doing enough to stop them. It is a matter of performance or action, precisely in the terms Lambek talks about in the Introduction to this volume.

Of course, there was an MP, Joseph Darby, who did do something by turning in to military command the pictures taken by Harman, Graner, Ambuhl, and others. He was honored with the John F. Kennedy Profile in Courage Award and became the only "hero" of Abu Ghraib. Yet even his actions seem ambiguous to some. Soldiers who were familiar with Darby later doubted his motives or intentions, suggesting they were more self-serving than altruistic. Though it was reported in the press at the time that he had seen the pictures for the first time in late December 2003 and turned them in to military command several weeks later, in mid-January of 2004, the interval was in fact much longer. He later said he had hesitated for a number of reasons: a conflict of loyalty with his fellow MPs at the prison; a conflict with military command, his own morals, and the U.S. army code of ethics; a fear of reprisal by his comrades or the military authorities; and the loneliness of being the only soldier who seemed to think that the pictures were wrong (which was in fact not the case, as others had their doubts as well). What he did not say was that, by having delayed the reporting of the pictures by six weeks, he helped to perpetuate the evil inside the prison that much longer, and he knew it. This gets us to the problem of intention: Does it matter what Darby's motives were, so long as he did the right thing in the end? Why do individuals like Darby act responsibly? Must they rely, first of all, on adherence to a universal code of good versus evil?

Let us examine the problem of intention more closely, for it is one basis by which guilt can be determined in the law. Jurisprudence views crimes done with malice and forethought as being heinous. John Yoo, deputy chief in the Justice Department's Office of Legal Counsel (2001–3) and one of the architects of the Bush administration's policies regarding the use of torture on "illegal combatants," emphasized that intent was crucial in determining criminality in war crimes (Mayer 2008: 256). According to this reckoning, the intentions of the men and women who abused prisoners in Abu Ghraib were not evil because they never *meant* to inflict harm beyond what was "instrumentally necessary," and there is no prima facie reason to doubt the assertions about their intentions. This conceit of the kindly intentioned soldier, for example, is behind the construction of Specialist Sabrina Harman, the woman who took most of the photographs of the Abu Ghraib abuses: it was said by her comrades in arms that she literally "couldn't hurt a fly" (her sobriquet being Mother Theresa) and that she was simply "the wrong person in the wrong place." And indeed, vicious or gratuitously sadistic treatment of prisoners seems to have been relatively rare. The closest to a manipulative sadist and diabolical figure, a radically evil person in Kant's sense, is Charles Graner, who said to one confederate, "The Christian in me knows it's wrong, but the corrections officer in me can't help but love to make a grown man piss himself" (Gourevitch and Morris 2008: 127). Most of the time, however, the guards did not seem to enjoy the pain or humiliation they thought had to be inflicted on prisoners to obtain "valuable" intelligence (to be sure, it has long been known by intelligence services that testimony extracted under torture is of questionable intelligence value, given that a person will say anything in order to stop the pain). Sometimes it is claimed that the MPs hated their prisoners because of racist attitudes towards Arabs and Muslims, supposedly ingrained in American culture. Literature on authoritarian organizations stresses the importance of such "dehumanizing" stereotypes of the Other (Kelman and Hamilton 1989), yet there is little evidence of such hatred in the Abu Ghraib case. "None of the MPs who spent their working hours doling out affliction on the MI block spoke of such hatred for their prisoners. They regarded them as enemies, with varying degrees of fear, anger, hostility, and contempt" (Gourevitch and Morris 2008: 157). On the basis of intention, therefore, few of the soldiers who committed abuses at Abu Ghraib would be viewed as culpable of evil acts.

Another basis for judging culpability is contingency or circumstance. One of the most pervasive of these in the twentieth century, with its massive bureaucracies, is the "cog in the machine" argument Adolf Eichmann adopted in his defense, as analyzed by Arendt in her *Eichmann in Jerusalem* (1963). A central insight of her book, one of the most important twentieth-century texts on evil, is that evil can often be "banal" in its face, or take ordinary forms. Despite his own (and the prosecution's) representation of his power, Eichmann, according to Arendt, was such a person, a nonentity. How does one match the enormity of the war crimes with which he was charged to someone who appears to be merely a cipher?

Intentionality also became relevant to Eichmann's trial in a big way. His defense claimed that he had never been a "Jew hater" (indeed, several witnesses testified to the "civility" with which he ordinarily treated the Jews with whom he came into contact, in contrast to the brutish behavior of many other Nazi officials) and that he had never willed the murder of human beings. It was circumstance or contingency that was his most salient defense, in which Eichmann described himself as a selfless bureaucrat, a victim, so to speak, of a murderous regime, not a culprit. It was the heads of state, the formulators of a heinous policy (e.g., Adolf Hitler, Reinhardt Heydrich, and Heinrich Himmler), who ought to have been held accountable and punished, not the hirelings like himself, who were simply "doing their duty" or, like true civil servants, being "obedient to the state's laws."

It is tempting to talk about the soldiers in Abu Ghraib as "cogs in the machine," though, as we have seen, perhaps a not very well-oiled machine at that, embodying what Arendt called the banality of evil even if they were not guilty of atrocities of the same scale and viciousness as those committed by Eichmann. The fact that the C.I.A. obsessed about interrogation techniques seems to bolster this view. But if Foucault's model of the security apparatus is credible, then Abu Ghraib was a nodal point in it, and the description of the soldiers as mere ciphers in a counter-insurgency machine is less convincing.[7] They were supposed to be left to their own devices, to be given space for improvisation in their treatment of the prisoners, so long as the desired intelligence was obtained by the MIs in the next round of abuses. There is willfulness or agency here, not mere obedience to orders. That is also why Abu Ghraib bears only superficial resemblance to the sort of situation Stanley Milgram (1974) created in his famous experiments on obedience to scientific authority. The soldiers were authorized to improvise, not to follow instructions blindly.

Closely connected to the "cog in the machine" argument, in fact an extension of it, is the replacement or substitution argument. The army has a term, *replacement*, to refer to a soldier who takes the place of another in a military unit, either because of loss or to complete a quota. Individuals are not replaced, holders of functions or work are. Following this line of reasoning, it is sometimes said that it would hardly have mattered if one

---

7. I thank Bernardo Zacka for this insight.

of the MPs in Abu Ghraib had objected to the treatment of its prisoners, for he or she would have been replaced by someone else who could be counted on to toe the line. The same cog-in-the-wheel reasoning came up in the Eichmann trial, of course, and Arendt had no difficulty in poking holes in the "argument":

> If the defendant excuses himself on the ground that he acted not as a man but as a mere functionary whose tasks could just as easily have been carried out by anyone else, it is as if a criminal pointed to the statistics on crime— which set forth that so-and-so many crimes per day are committed in such- and-such a place and declared that he only did what was statistically expected, that it was mere accident that he did it and not somebody else, since after all somebody had to do it. (Arendt 1963: 289)

Arendt broke with moral reasoning according to intentionality and contingency by insisting that there is an ethic of responsibility—an ethic that had not been worked out very clearly in philosophy or law to date—under whose rubric judgments of culpability, or sin, have to be judged (Nieman 2002: 277).

Besides the "cog in the machine," the argument based on contingency or circumstance can take another version, namely, "the fog of war," apparently coined by former Secretary of Defense Robert S. McNamara and made famous in another documentary bearing this phrase in its title.[8] The awful conditions at Abu Ghraib, exacerbated by daily enemy bombardment, which threatened prisoner and jailer alike, could cloud a soldier's practical judgment. Of course, some circumstances can be extenuating, as when oneself or a family member might be killed for not following orders, even if the orders be heinous. But one might argue that one still has a choice—albeit a horrible one—even in such circumstances, which were not applicable to Abu Ghraib in any case. (At most, MPs faced imprisonment and/or discharge from the army for dereliction of duty.) This argument is often coupled with another having to do with the "ordinariness" of human beings and the conviction that one cannot expect too much of them under terrible circumstances. Nevertheless, the U.S. Government saw fit to award Joseph Darby, the whistle blower on Abu Ghraib, a special citation for courage.

In spite of the fact that Eichmann did not present the face of evil in the form one might have expected, Arendt was nevertheless convinced that he

---

8. *The Fog of War: Eleven Lessons from the Life of Robert S. McNamara* (2004), directed by Errol Morris (Sony Pictures).

should hang for war crimes (as indeed he did). If the legal basis was not exactly clear (if not intention or circumstance, then what?), one thing was clear to her: the peculiar form or presentation of evil in modern, highly bureaucratized, and totalitarian society needs to be recognized and understood:

> When I speak of the banality of evil, I do so only on the strictly factual level, pointing to a phenomenon which stared one in the face at the trial. Eichmann was not Iago and not Macbeth, and nothing could have been farther from his mind than to determine with Richard III "to prove a villain." Except for an ordinary diligence in looking out for his personal advancement, he had no motives at all. . . . *He merely*, to put the point colloquially, *never realized what he was doing.* (Arendt 1963: 287; emphasis in the original)

If neither intentionality nor contingency, the two bases on which moral judgments of evil have existed in philosophy, seemed altogether plausible or sufficient to convict Eichmann, then perhaps one was left with the concept of moral responsibility to do so. The philosopher Susan Nieman (2002) argues that Arendt's way of formulating the question, in terms of responsibility rather than intentionality or circumstance, is what makes her text both original in moral philosophy as well as important for understanding evil in modern society. That said, a fully worked-out theory of responsibility is not what one finds in *Eichmann in Jerusalem*. For that one needs to turn to a later work, *Responsibility and Judgment* (2003), an anthology of lectures and essays written by Arendt toward the end of her life in which she wrestles with the questions of personal responsibility and moral judgment.

## Judgment and Will

A key essay in that volume is "Personal Responsibility under Dictatorship," in which there is an important passage I will cite at length. Arendt asks whether there is any difference between those who fully supported the Nazi regime and those who, although they did not rise in full rebellion against it, refused to collaborate or give public support to Nationalist Socialism, and she answers the question in the affirmative, saying that

> the non-participants, called irresponsible by the majority, were the only ones who dared judge by themselves, and they were capable of doing so not

because they disposed of a better system of values or because the old standards of right and wrong were still firmly planted in their mind and conscience. On the contrary, all our experiences tell us that it was precisely the members of *respectable* society, who had not been touched by the intellectual and moral upheaval in the early stages of the Nazi period, who were the first to yield. They simply exchanged one system of values for another. I therefore would suggest that the non-participants were those whose consciences did not function in this, as it were, automatic way—as though we dispose of a set of learned or innate rules which we then apply to the particular case as it arises, so that every new experience or situation is already prejudged and we need only act out whatever we learned or possessed beforehand. Their criterion, I think, was a different one: they asked themselves to what extent they would still be able to live in peace with themselves after having committed certain deeds; and they decided that it would be better to do nothing, not because the world would then be changed for the better, but simply because only on this condition could they go on living with themselves at all. Hence, they also chose to die when they were forced to participate. To put it crudely, they refused to murder, not so much because they still held fast to the command "Thou shalt not kill," but because they were unwilling to live together with a murderer—themselves. (Arendt 2003: 44)

The passage is interesting not least because it envisions a context in which moral judgment is made without holding on to preconceived standards, norms, or general rules ("Thou shalt not kill") under which the particularities of the case are to be subsumed. In other words, circumstances or events can be unprecedented and not foreseen in the general rules, even as exceptions. If not by application of a rule to a case, how, then, is moral judgment possible under such circumstances? Here Arendt evokes a quasi-Socratic method: one asks oneself, "Can one live with oneself after having acted in such and such a way?" Moral conduct, in this view, depends on a person conducting a colloquy with herself, a colloquy that depends on a *thinking* subject, which Arendt adapts from the Platonic dialogues:

even though I am one, I am not simply one, I have a self and I am related to this self as my own self. This self is by no means an illusion; it makes itself heard by talking to me—I talk to myself, I am not only aware of myself—and in this sense, though I am one, I am two-in-one and there can be harmony or disharmony with the self . . . as I am my own partner when I am thinking, I am my own witness when I am acting. (Arendt 2003: 90)

She goes on to argue that the subject who goes through such a thinking process or act and arrives at moral judgments becomes a person.

Arendt went on to devote an entire book to the philosophical understanding of thought and the will (Arendt 1971), a full investigation of
which would go beyond the scope of this essay. It is important to note,
however, that in her view, just as philosophy had neglected the problem
of evil and responsibility, so too had it ignored the question of will (both
in the sense of choice and of creating something new or unprecedented),
on the grounds that it applies to subjective experience only and could always be explained away in terms of cause or determinism. Arendt (1971)
attempted to write a "history" of the will's "discovery" (or what we might
call its "invention"), showing along the way how closely a concept of the
will is tied to evil and to ethics more generally. In that sense, for contemporary students of ethics who ground their analyses in Aristotle, who made
little if any room for will in a world where matter was due either to chance
or to necessity, the voluntarism behind ethical action will be back-
grounded or denied. Yet ethical action is not only a matter of judgment—of applying "criteria," in Lambek's words—to particularities or
situations, it is also the *will* to apply them (or not). The Darbys of this
world have to decide to act responsibly. The problem of voluntarism,
however, is as neglected as the problem of evil in contemporary anthropological thought.

Arendt's notion of the subject accords with Bakhtin's notion of the "dialogical self" (Bakhtin 1981; see also Vološinov 1973 [1928]), as well as an
older pragmatist notion of the reflexive individual whose attention is
caught by something in the situation that is unexpected or new and who
then has to think about that eventfulness (my term) to determine his or
her active relationship to it. The pragmatist philosopher George Herbert
Mead (1964) stressed long ago in his reflexive, interactionist sociology this
ability of the individual to think critically about what he or she thinks is
right in a given situation. Such moral conclusions are, however, always
provisional and never infinite or closed. Finally, there is no way to determine in advance which individuals will act ethically or even evilly in given
situations; in the sense that this is "spontaneous," the individual, as Kant
insisted, is free to choose.

No doubt the possibilities for a process of moral judgment like that I
have sketched out are severely curtailed in a military or warlike situation,
where following orders is at a premium, but that is also an argument for
why these situations are morally the most "dangerous" and require the
greatest vigilance. It may be argued that there is no time to think under
fire, let alone to think critically or to question and evaluate, but this is
precisely what leaders who formulate evil policies are counting on, so that

the obedient civil servant or soldier will blindly carry out their orders. If heroism under fire may be the exception but hardly a rarity in war, then why not also critical moral judgment and responsible action in cases of war's abuses?

## Conclusion

In this essay, I have tried to develop, however schematically and provisionally, a notion of situational evil and to argue that it is helpful in understanding Abu Ghraib. This concept contextualizes evil, making us realize its singularity, as well as its connection to specific events. In spite of efforts by the C.I.A. to routinize prisoner torture and by the military administration to rationalize the softening up of terror suspects, Abu Ghraib, by virtue of being part of a security apparatus, always exceeded the rules by which it was supposed to be ruled. In fact, improvisation and making things up as one went along were a creative response for the soldiers in such a situation. Knowing what to do that is also what is right is an emergent knowledge, a matter of judgment in regard to particularities and can never be merely a following of ethical rules.

How does one apply practical as well as moral judgment to that which is unexpected and novel? How does one judge personal responsibility for acts committed in such a situation? I have argued that transcendent ethical categories, though not entirely irrelevant, are, in fact, not particularly useful in such a situation. More than one system or code is likely to be applicable, and conflicts between them rife. Moreover, as we saw in the Abu Ghraib case, several soldiers sensed or even understood that what they saw happening during the softening up phase was wrong, by either a religious standard or the army code of conduct, and yet only one in the end did anything to stop it. The rest voiced no personal responsibility for remaining silent or acquiescent.

Intentionality and contingency, for long the two most prominent criteria for determining culpability in philosophy, are not particularly satisfying for judging the Abu Ghraib abuses. Many of the soldiers did not intend to do harm; they also were operating within a bureaucratic chain of command. Does this then exonerate them? We are left with a notion of personal responsibility that depends on a particular kind of subject (what Arendt calls a person), a thinking and critical subject, who is able to attend to a problematic situation and make a personal judgment about it. Even that is not enough, for that person has to *will* to do what he or she deems right. If we think of ethics on the model of the Austinian performative ("I confess that . . .") or of the Aristotelian notion of *technē* ("I am a virtuous citizen"), the problem of will, which I argue is fundamental to ethics, may be obscured, though for different reasons, given that the performative requires an intentional as opposed to a willing subject, the notion of *technē*, educability or discipline. But to do right and to avoid evil requires more; it requires the will and the courage to do right. Thus, in the end what is important is not inculcating the person with a particular code of ethics but inculcating him or her with a particular kind of moral thinking and action.

# PART FOUR

# Punishment and Personal Dignity

# The Punishment of Ethical Behavior

*Charles Stafford*

During my first period of anthropological fieldwork in rural Taiwan, I went through the—literally unfortunate—experience of becoming spiritually polluted through participation in a funeral. Much could be said about this incident, but here I want to focus on some questions it raises about ethical *thinking*.[1]

In considering these questions, I will follow the lead of Bernard Williams and others in drawing—at least provisionally—a distinction between ethics and morals. Williams points out: "By origin, the difference between the two terms is that between Latin and Greek, each relating to a word meaning disposition or custom. One difference is that the Latin term from which "moral" comes emphasizes rather more the sense of social expectation, while the Greek [from which "ethics" comes] favors that of individual character" (1985: 6).[2] Using a different language, we might say that morality (defined as the rules, norms, and conventions against which

---

1. I will not address the question of professional ethics, which—however relevant to the events I describe—was not the main focus of the Ordinary Ethics conference.

2. Williams goes on to treat morality as a "peculiar institution" of the West, something we should not confuse with ethical life in general (cf. the summary and discussion in Laidlaw 2002).

human behaviors are judged good or bad) is structure, whereas ethics is agency. But what I want to explore in particular here is the notion that the domain of ethics is somehow deliberative, reflective, and thoughtful in a way that the domain of morals is not. The more we think about morals—whether prospectively or retrospectively—the more we are shifting into the domain of the ethical.

Of course, distinguishing ethics from morals in this way is not unproblematic, but it does have two virtues. First, it helps draw attention to the role of thinking and judgment in moral life, something stressed by Michael Lambek (2000, this volume), James Laidlaw (2002), Bernard Williams (1985), and others. Second, it helps remind us that via (ethical) thinking and judgment we sometimes end up breaking (moral) rules, norms, or conventions, even intentionally opposing them.

To put this last point differently, it is possible, and perhaps even common, for us to behave ethically and immorally at the same time—that is, to do what we think is right, even if the rules say otherwise. This conflation of the ethical and the immoral raises interesting questions about punishment, for it is surely a special kind of learning experience, or so I want to suggest, to be at the receiving end of punishment for acts that we ourselves consider to have been "good" in some sense.

## A Literary Preface

Before turning to the spiritual pollution incident, I want to remind readers—by means of a brief literary preface—that in modern China (and in Taiwan via a shared but distinctive history) there has been a hugely strong current of antitraditionalism, culminating in the Cultural Revolution. This current is in some ways problematic, one feels, for anthropologists, who, while typically not believing in such things as ancestors, spiritual pollution, etc., are professional suspenders of disbelief and rarely adopt an explicitly "anti-culture" stance. As Laidlaw (2002) observes, anthropologists have, at least to some extent, followed Durkheim in equating the collective with the good.

In any case, a few years after my initial fieldwork in Taiwan (during which the pollution incident happened) I spent a year in northeast China, where I was affiliated with a teachers college. I explained to a professor there that I was interested in traditional customs and practices, and almost immediately he handed me a couple of things to read by the influential writer Lu Xun (1881–1936), including a very famous short story, "The

New Year's Sacrifice."[3] Lu Xun was a key player, as it happens, in the history of reformist/radical thought that led many ordinary people in China and Taiwan to take what might be called an "ethical" stance against traditional Chinese culture and morality.[4]

Briefly, "The New Year's Sacrifice" is narrated by a thoughtful young scholar (someone presumably not unlike Lu Xun himself) who returns to his native place in the countryside during the New Year festival and stays with an uncle, Mr. Lu. While there, the young scholar bumps into an old woman known simply as "Xiang Lin's wife," who formerly worked for his uncle's family but is now in a terrible state, reduced to begging in the streets. She unexpectedly approaches the young scholar and asks him some awkward questions about ghosts and the afterlife, which he finds impossible to answer. The next day she dies "of poverty"—right in the middle of the New Year festivities. As the scholar's uncle, Mr. Lu, puts it: this timing is "a sure sign of bad character." It transpires that Xiang Lin's wife, born in another community, had been literally plagued by misfortune. Her first husband died, after which she began to work for Mr. Lu. But her in-laws had not approved this arrangement, and eventually they took her back by force and sold her into a second marriage. She fiercely resisted this, but eventually settled into a new life and gave birth to a son. Then, incredibly, both her son and her second husband died. After this, she returned to work for the Lus. But her mental state deteriorated, and local people began to avoid and then to ridicule, her. Also, although Mr. Lu agreed that she could work again for his family, he warned his wife that:

> while such people may be pitiful they exert a bad moral influence. Thus although it would be all right for her to do ordinary work she must not join in the preparations for [ancestral] sacrifice; they would have to prepare all the dishes themselves, for otherwise they would be unclean and the ancestors would not accept them. (Lu 1960)

Aware that such things were being said, Xiang Lin's wife spent a year's wages buying a "threshold" in a local temple, in the hope of remedying her morally dubious status. But Mr. Lu still considered her unfit to help with the sacrifices, and eventually—as she became incapable of any work

---

3. Lu Xun (1960[1927]); see also the interesting commentaries by Huters (1984) and Jenner (1982).

4. Although Lu Xun, embraced by the Communists, was initially deemed too radical for readers in nationalist Taiwan, the wider reformist/radical tradition of which he was a part has had a huge impact there too.

at all—they told her to leave and return to her in-laws. She instead became a beggar, and then she died.

Lu Xun's story can obviously be read as an attack on traditional culture, more specifically, on the "superstitions" that were felt (by Lu Xun and many others) to exploit vulnerable people like Xiang Lin's wife. She herself did not, however, oppose this culture in any obvious way in the story; she was merely its victim. She did not intend to do bad things, she was above all remarkably unlucky, and she made efforts to justify herself to those around her. Local people, it seems, got fed up listening to her account of her incredibly bad luck (a point I will come back to later on). It was as if they did not want to think about this case any more, whereas she thought about it so much that eventually it drove her mad.

The interesting ethical narrative in the story, however, focuses not on her or even on Chinese traditions as such but on the young scholar/narrator. He seems likeable, reasonable, good. On returning home, he is dismayed to see Xiang Lin's wife in such a state and to learn of her decline. But he also seems paralyzed: incapable of answering her questions (about ghosts, etc.) with either clarity or honesty; incapable of denouncing superstition; incapable of confronting directly his own conservative relatives. In short, we are led to conclude that the narrator should have behaved ethically (in Lu Xun's terms, but also in the narrator's own terms) by showing his opposition to traditional morality—something he signally fails to do, even when the punishment of Xiang Lin's wife reaches its cruel climax. By the end of the story, we may wonder how good he really is.[5]

## The Polluted Anthropologist

Now let me take up the case of my own spiritual pollution. When I first encountered Chinese popular religion in the Taiwanese fishing community of Angang, I was struck among other things by the extent to which it

---

5. As Huters observes, Lu Xun places the young scholar in the story, "but at the same time [holds] this character up to scrutiny in such a way as to withdraw gradually the sympathy and identification that the reader initially feels for him. To the extent that the reader has come to accept the narrator as a reliable moral guide, the process of withdrawing faith has the effect of causing the reader to look to himself for those flaws that elicited the identification in the first place" (Huters 1984: 66).

did not seem focused on moral/ethical problems as such.[6] The people I met made offerings to spirits and participated in collective rituals and feasts. But they were not expected to listen to long-winded sermons (there were no such things), nor did most of them study religious texts. The point, so far as I could tell, was to seek help from gods and ancestors, not to criticize or punish the failings of mere humans. But I was soon to learn otherwise.

One morning when I was still living in the local school (I later moved to a house in the village), I heard amplified music coming over the schoolyard fence. Two teachers explained to me that a funeral was being held. I said I was keen to see a ritual of this kind, but that I worried it might be inappropriate for me to attend, and in particular that the family would object. They replied that the family would certainly not object, however, funerals were "a little bit dangerous" (*you yidian weixian*)—and they themselves would not care to go. What did they mean, I asked. It could be "bad for me," they said, because spirits were involved. But they made this point rather lightly. I told them I was worried about bothering others, not about personal danger, and then left the schoolyard, alone.

The funeral was being held in the courtyard of a private home and in the surrounding vicinity. At a quick glance, it seemed an elaborate affair involving several dozen people, including priests and performers of various kinds. However, it was clearly an event the entire community was not required or expected to attend. I stood off to the side and then spoke with a woman who seemed to be involved, probably as a member of the family. (These people were complete strangers to me, and I to them.) I said that I would like to observe, but that I didn't want to bother anybody or be in the way. She said it was no problem, I was very welcome, but that I should be careful (*xiaoxin*) because it could be dangerous.

With her comment in mind, I stayed off to the side for a while; however, I soon found myself pulled, by participants, into more of the action. Among other things, I was encouraged to offer incense at the foot of the deceased's coffin. I learned that she had been an elderly woman with many grandchildren, and her eldest son later told me, with some emotion, that I had honored his family by being there. The occasion was a curious mix

---

6. I have discussed popular religion, and more generally my fieldwork in Taiwan, in Stafford 1995, 2000, and 2008. An excellent introduction to Chinese funerals is the volume edited by Watson and Rawski (1988), which includes discussions of spiritual pollution.

of sadness, celebration, and almost slapstick humor. I sat with the (very funny) funeral troupe for many hours, ate a couple of meals with the family—the funeral lasted two days—and then accompanied them on the walk behind the coffin out to the burial place. For a novice anthropologist, it was an exhilarating experience.

Not long afterwards, as I was falling back into the school routine, I once again heard music coming from the village. Recognizing the laments, I followed the sound until I came upon another funeral. Again, I asked if anyone minded if I observed—they did not, and this time there were no comments about "danger." The welcome was a bit less warm, and the experience less exhilarating; however, I did feel that I was learning a great deal. I was asked, at one point, if I would be willing to help (*bangmang*) with something—to which, of course, I said yes. The request did not come from the family but rather from some local men who were helping organize the event. They asked me to carry a (rather heavy) parcel of food and other offerings in the procession to the burial place, where it would be given to the deceased at the end of the rites. This I did.

Shortly after participating in the second funeral, however, I learned that I had become spiritually polluted, literally "not clean" (*bu ganjing*), possibly because of this helpful act. This was revealed to me when a woman I knew, a local shopkeeper, unexpectedly took me to visit a spirit medium's altar behind her shop. I had yet to attend a spirit medium session, and this was another remarkable event to observe—one filled (not unlike the funeral) with high seriousness, theatricality, and humor. The medium dealt with many things but at one point turned to me—acting and speaking as the god by whom he was possessed—and commented on my arrival in the community. He said, in brief, that he thought it a good thing I had come so far to study in this place and to learn how local people lived. He recommended I should think carefully about what I saw. He had also noted my presence at the funerals. He knew I was "good-hearted" and that I wanted to help. But funerals were dangerous, and I had become unclean through my actions. (My heart sank, at this point.) Never mind, he said, he would cleanse me, provided I made an offering to him the next day, and then of course I should be much more careful in the future.

## Aftermath and Reactions

I soon found out that things were not so simple. Indeed, I began to realize that, in my enthusiasm, I had made a serious error of judgment. The handful of people I knew at that early stage of research told me not to worry, but even they made it clear that my actions had been rash. They also began to restrict my movements, not only banning me from funerals for the duration of my fieldwork but also keeping me from places in the countryside local people considered "dangerous" in some way (e.g., because someone had met a violent death there). Moreover, as the days went by, I learned that I was not, after all, considered free of pollution through the spirit medium's intervention, at least not by everyone. Some people were unclear exactly what I had done: Had I touched the coffin, or perhaps even the corpse? Then the pollution would be very serious indeed. Carrying the offerings to the graveyard was bad enough: I had participated in a part of the funeral (moving the corpse from house to grave) that causes most local people to close and even lock their front doors—normally kept wide open in this community—as a precaution against possible harm.

One day the shopkeeper, who was very friendly to me, let it be known (through her daughters) that I should not touch the religious items sold in her shop, incense and "spirit money," in case her customers might stop buying them. And a local fisherman seemed irritated when some friends and I came upon him conducting rituals to protect his boat before going out to sea. I sensed he wanted us to leave, but my friends would not tell me why. As you might expect, I found these experiences painful. It had never occurred to me—given what I thought I knew of myself—that I could fall into a trap of this kind. Had I been insensitive? Professionally incompetent? I found it such an uncomfortable topic that I mostly avoided raising it with anyone and to a remarkable extent—given its "anthropological interest"—even left it out of my fieldnotes.

Piecing things together, however, I came to learn that local people had various reactions to what had happened, some of which may be summarized as follows:

1. It was a cultural misunderstanding. The foreigner doesn't know how things work here, and—somewhat like a child—can't be held responsible for his actions. Furthermore, he is a "good person" who was trying to help.

Note that in this theory intentions (specifically, my good intentions) matter. Also note that the argument from cultural relativism was made easily and spontaneously by my informants, all of whom have experience of Taiwan's cultural diversity. This suggests that, although the situation I'm describing may seem unusual, it was in some respects a rather ordinary one from the point of view of my informants.

2. It doesn't matter how ignorant someone is or how good: this foreigner has become spiritually unclean, which is simply a technical matter related

to coming into contact with death. Also, the kind of person who would let this happen to himself is not without moral fault.

In this theory, it's important to stress that intentions may still matter in various ways—but that actions also matter a great deal. In brief, in this moral system it makes little sense to say that a ritual (or ritual infraction) could be completely insignificant or "empty" simply because of the thoughts that accompany, or don't accompany, it.[7] Actions count.

Some of the local commentary about the pollution incident focused on the possible cure, rather than my fault in the matter, as such:

3. He may or may not have become unclean, but the rituals performed by the spirit medium after the funeral will, in any case, have made him clean again—so it isn't a problem.

4. The purification rites can work, but *that* spirit medium (and/or the god for whom that spirit medium speaks) isn't effective enough to sort out a problem of this kind.[8] He remains unclean.

5. Even with help from an effective spirit medium, death pollution lingers, just as it does for the family of the deceased, no matter what is done. For one hundred days he is potentially dangerous to those around him.

A further important consideration was whether some other agent—that is, someone other than me—might be held accountable (or jointly accountable) for what had occurred. Why had no one stopped me? The explanation for this, in my view, is that at this early stage of fieldwork no one felt responsible enough for me to care one way or another what I did. However, I *had* been warned of the dangers I faced. I'm also confident that the family members who encouraged me to join in the funeral would not have sought to cause me harm. Yet it does seem possible that the men organizing the second funeral (again, strangers to me) thought it would be interesting or funny to ask a foreigner to help out. Further to this, I learned that another local view was that:

---

7. Note James Watson's suggestion (in Watson 1988; cf. the commentary in Feuchtwang 2001, chap.1) that in the Chinese tradition, at least at some historical moments, "orthopraxy" (correct practice) has had priority over "orthodoxy" (correct belief and/or thoughts).

8. I never actually heard this said with reference to my situation. However, I later learned that, in this community, clients of given spirit mediums (and there were many such mediums) routinely suggested that *other* mediums were ineffective when it came to sorting out their clients' problems.

6. It was a bad thing for this outsider to have been allowed or encouraged, by people from this community (either the families involved or the ritual organizers), to do something of this kind.

Finally, in reporting such theories, I should stress that some local people simply don't believe in "spiritual pollution" at all. Among them are the older men—mostly Christians, of whom there are a handful in this place—who show up to actually carry the coffin during funerals and are paid for it. And then there are quite a few others who, because of education or personal inclination, accept the long-standing argument—linked to the history of reformism/radicalism that I have already mentioned above— that Chinese religion is either pure "superstition" (*mixin*) or has a lot of superstitious elements in it, which have, furthermore, done a great deal of harm to ordinary people. From the point of view of those holding (some version of) this perspective, it might be added that:

7. Spiritual pollution doesn't exist. It is therefore a good thing for a foreigner to participate in a funeral, and especially for him to publicly participate in a funeral, so that everyone can see his indifference to the supposed "dangers" involved.

My own reaction to these events was highly changeable, but combined elements of (1) and (6) plus, if I am honest, a bit of (7). That is, I felt this had been a textbook case of cultural misunderstanding—but also one that local people might well have done more to help me avoid. And while I felt guilty for possible lapses in sensitivity, professionalism, etc., I equally felt (as did most local people, it seems) that my underlying intentions had been "good." I was asked to help, and I helped. For this reason, I found the punishments I was given—relatively light ones, to be sure—vaguely unjust and, in fact, quite wounding. Thus, in my resentment, I felt a bit of (7).

## Punishment

A person who is spiritually polluted becomes a partial outcast, temporarily restricted from activities such as making offerings to gods or attending banquets to mark joyous occasions. In theory, this applies equally to women who are "unclean" while menstruating, to people who must attend the (dangerously polluting) funerals of close relatives, or to someone like me who has simply stumbled into uncleanness. In most cases, this status isn't considered a huge problem, and the direct impact on me was relatively short-lived. But, as noted above, when news of my situation spread,

I was asked not to touch religious items, and it was implied I should not bring my uncleanness into other people's lives at significant moments (as with the fisherman who was ritually purifying his boat). Moreover, I was barred from attending funerals, and my movements around the country- side were constrained. This wasn't simply for my protection. If I were to become polluted again, there was a risk I would contaminate everyone else, bringing misfortune into the lives of those with whom I interacted.

I was also subject to a degree of public ridicule and gossip. Importantly, this is not something that would attach to a menstruating woman or to people who are required, through Confucian norms, to take on pollution at the funerals of their relatives. The shopkeeper's daughter told me that by walking through the streets as a participant in the funeral, and espe- cially by carrying things to the burial place as if I were a "helper," I had become the object of laughter (*gei ren xiao*). This was, in brief, a face- losing (*diu lian*) matter. The mere fact of people gossiping about it, and about me, was a humiliation, and something that should have led me to avoid it in the first place. Moreover, as with spiritual pollution, the con- tamination from this could be said to affect all those associated with me— and in particular my friends and those who sought to help me.

In sum, then, I was punished by having my activities and movements restricted, to some extent, and through a loss of reputation, to some extent. And, strange as it may sound, this unwanted experience of punish- ment—of feeling that society had imposed itself on me, in the Durkheim- ian sense—is what forced me to recognize that my informants took their religion seriously. They were not kidding.[9]

Speaking of Durkheim, in a passage on moral education he makes a fascinating observation: "It is idle to think that we can rear our children as we wish. There are customs to which we are bound to conform; if we flout them too severely, they take their vengeance on our children" (1972: 204). Surely this possibility of social vengeance—that is, of punishment, which in Durkheim's scheme is explicitly linked to learning—has signifi- cant implications for the anthropology of ordinary ethics. As Durkheim might have it, we unfortunately cannot turn ourselves, through ethical reflection, into just anything we wish—that is, without paying a price if in doing so we cross the line and act immorally.

---

9. I should perhaps note that I myself had a very religious upbringing—so I don't find the fact of holding religious beliefs, as such, surprising. My point is that the pollution incident really shifted my perspective about my informants' level of commitment to particular aspects of their religion (in this case, beliefs about pollu- tion) that I might otherwise not have taken very seriously.

## The Hydraulics of Ethics and Morals

The events I've described illustrate what may seem obvious: that people think, judge, reason, and talk about moral/ethical situations. As Lambek suggests, we could even say that this thinking, judging, etc. really *is* morality, that is, that the moral/ethical always is a field of judgment.[10]

However, in many cultural accounts the moral—by my definition, the rules, norms, and conventions against which human behaviors are judged "good" or "bad"—is precisely *not* taken as subject to contingencies, including those of human thought. To some extent it is not permissible to (really) think about the moral, which is a special kind of cultural-historical artifact. This helps explain why anthropologists typically get content-poor answers when they ask informants explicitly moral questions (such as "In your society, how should children treat their parents?").[11] Nevertheless, the same informants are surrounded by any number of ethical questions (in my terms) that emerge from the actual circumstances of life. These questions catch their attention, it seems, causing them to philosophize, sometimes deeply. Indeed, such questions are the subject not only of their individual thoughts but also of the shared gossip, stories, soap operas, etc. that fill much of their waking hours. What seems odd is the extent to which this detailed individual and collective thinking leaves (or often appears to leave) "the moral" untouched.

In an imaginary quantification of this ideal type contrast between the moral and the ethical, we might suggest that, as a matter of course, for every $n$ hours we spend thinking about "the moral" we spend, say, $10n$ hours thinking about "the ethical." Let's assume, as well, that an increased

---

10. Lambek observes that: "From the perspectives of both Aristotle and Rappaport morality is not a coherent, imposed system, a specific set of rules, an unequivocal code, or an uncompromising disciplinary order to which people are obliged to submit unqualifiedly—as in effect, simply another form of power—but the forms and acts by which commitments are engaged and virtue accomplished—the practical judgments people make about how to live their lives wisely and well and, in the course of making them, do live their lives, albeit in the face of numerous constraints (Lambek 2000: 315).

11. Obviously, the issue of how such questions are framed is crucial: as every anthropologist knows, a well-framed question about morals might provoke interesting replies. My point is simply the anthropological truism that the more a question is framed with reference to "the rules," the more one typically receives a rule-bound, by definition nonimaginative, reply. This suggests not only that such questions are badly framed but also that people do not spontaneously improvise around morals-oriented questions.

quantity of thinking correlates with increased learning and with content-rich thought (so that we would expect informants' replies to "ethical questions," in contrast to their replies to "moral questions," to be content rich).

But of course there's a further issue in measuring quantity of moral/ethical thinking: namely, the extent to which a given individual will actually be drawn (or not) to reflect on a given situation. So, let's imagine that for a given ethical situation, the quantity of attention will be $10n$ hours if it involves me directly (as one of the key agents); $5n$ if it involves me indirectly (say, as an observer, or as someone linked to one of the key agents, e.g., as friend or enemy); but only $2n$ if the situation does not involve me and I simply hear of it. This formulation implies, in effect, that the less directly I am involved with an ethical situation, the more my thinking about it will be content poor, almost as poor as if I were thinking about "the moral." But what does it really mean here to be involved? Even ethical situations that do not involve me directly may become very engaging if I feel sorry for one of the agents or angry at him—psychological states that may, by the way, come into existence if the story of the situation is told to me in an especially compelling manner. So a compelling story might increase the quantity of my attention to a situation in which I have no involvement—say, in one case, from $2n$ to $4n$. We might further hypothesize that the presence or absence of punishment will be a key factor in terms of level of interest (this on the grounds that punishment is attention grabbing because it is a potential resolution of a situation, but one that is often problematic or disputed in some way). Let's say a story that does not involve real or threatened punishment is basically not a good ethical story—so merits only attention of $1n$. And in a real-world situation, if I receive punishment as a result of some act, I would spend, say, $15n$ hours thinking about the situation rather than $10n$, while for those who do the punishing, the figures would go up as well, perhaps from $5n$ to $10n$.

The point I am getting at by elaborating this (I hope not too tedious) hydraulic model—which could be endlessly problematized—is relatively simple: that ethical life may partly be construed as a matter of attention, driven by such factors as personal involvement, quality of narrative, existence of punishment, etc.

With respect to the pollution incident in Taiwan, note that I was torn between talking about what had happened—partly in order to justify myself, not least to myself—and saying nothing at all, in the hope that other people would stop thinking about it, thus making it go away. And for me there was a certain element of surprise in discovering that people could, indeed, be bothered to focus attention on what was, by any standard, a relatively minor incident in local life. Why, in short, did they bother to react to this moral/ethical situation rather than letting it pass them by?

Edward Westermarck's answer, in part (the other, more detailed, part of his answer relates to socialization or enculturation), is that we have evolved to do just this, that is, to have moral reactions.[12] He was struck in particular by the strong emotions that attach to moral disapproval across otherwise very different cultures. He was struck, in other words, by the fact that people appear to care so much when they see morality contravened.[13]

Westermarck draws a sharp contrast, however, between emotional reactions, such as feelings of indignation, and rational thought, suggesting that moral disapproval usually engages the former much more strongly than the latter.[14] He also points out that moral judgments—significantly, the prelude to punishment—are often (intrinsically?) cursory:

> It is true that moral judgments are commonly passed on acts without much regard being paid to their motives; but the reason for this is only the superficiality of ordinary moral estimates. Moral indignation and moral approval are, in the first place, aroused by conspicuous facts, and, whilst the intention of the act is expressed in the act itself, its motive is not. (Westermarck 1906: 208)

---

12. Of course, the study of moral thought from evolutionary perspectives has expanded dramatically in recent years (e.g., Hauser 2006), and in this sense Westermarck was ahead of his time. But it's worth stressing that, unlike many evolutionists who have followed him, Westermarck had a profound understanding of cultural variation in moral systems and an ethnographer's eye for the complexity of "real world" moral/ethical situations. See the thought-provoking comparison of Westermarck and Durkheim by Roos (2008) and the edited volume and review article by Stroup (1982, 1984). Also note the comprehensive empirical study of (evolved) incest aversion by Arthur Wolf, based primarily on materials from Taiwan and China, which is directly inspired by Westermarck's theory of the moral emotions (Wolf 1995).

13. "As public indignation is the prototype of moral disapproval, so public approval, expressed in public praise, is the prototype of moral approval. . . . But of these two emotions public indignation, being at the root of custom and leading to the infliction of punishment, is by far the most impressive" (Westermarck 1906: 122).

14. This was long before the neuropsychologist Damasio and other writers problematized this distinction, arguing that human reason actually evolved from, and relies upon, our systems for responding "emotionally" to events around us (Damasio 2006 [1994]).

So it is as if we are judged by "emotional" others who do not know, and possibly even prefer not to reflect on, the details (such as "good intentions" or underlying circumstances) that might mitigate our wrongdoing and thereby constrain the punishment we are given. In fact, this phenomenon has been widely discussed by psychologists in recent years.[15] To return to Lu Xun's account of Xiang Lin's wife: as I noted, her neighbors actually do not want to hear what she has to say about her pitifully bad luck.

But this clearly complicates the model of attention outlined above. In Westermarck's scheme, attention might be taken as a function of emotional reaction: for example, we pay a lot of attention to a given situation because we are indignant about it. And yet emotional reactions, almost by definition, push us in the direction of conceiving a situation in "moral" rather than "ethical" terms. That is, while they focus attention on a problem, they simultaneously constrain us from thinking about this problem very much—by means of the rule, found in most if not all human societies, which says that to (really) think about the moral is not allowed. If we are to punish wrongdoers, we have to battle within ourselves not to construe the situation as an ethical one, because this tends to mitigate wrongdoing and make it harder to punish.

J. L. Mackie, building on Westermarck, refers to this as the "paradox of retribution":

> The paradox is that, on the one hand, a retributive principle of punishment cannot be explained or developed within a *reasonable* system of moral thought [that is, in my terms, a system based on "ethical" reflection], while, on the other hand, such a principle cannot be eliminated from our moral thinking [because underlying emotional reactions, which call for retribution, are at the root of all ethics and morality]. As Westermarck says, "It is one of the most interesting facts relating to the moral consciousness of the most humane type [meaning the most reflective, and thus the farthest removed from innate emotional reactions], that it in vain condemns the gratification of the very desire from which it sprang." (Mackie 1982: 145, emphasis added)[16]

---

15. The discussions in psychology of the "fundamental attribution error" and the "correspondence bias" are relevant here. Very briefly, it is suggested that people are often uncharitable in interpreting the actions of others (specifically, that they are less likely to give weight to contextual circumstances that might justify the behavior of others), whereas they tend to interpret their own behaviors charitably (i.e., they understand perfectly well the circumstances that "force" them to act as they do). See, e.g., Gilbert and Malone 1995, Jones and Harris 1977, Nisbett 2003, Ross 1977.

16. The quote is from Westermarck 1932: 86.

## Against Morality?

Obviously, Mackie's paradox is framed from the viewpoint of those who punish—not from the viewpoint of the punished. For the latter, there is arguably a different kind of paradox, or at least problem. Briefly, punishment based on "moral" rules might teach us, if you like, that society exists, is impressive. Indeed, some evolutionary anthropologists have suggested that the evolution of the willingness to punish—as a means of both teaching the rules of the game and enforcing them—plays *the* crucial role in the emergence of cooperation in human societies, and indeed the emergence of "anything else" (i.e., any other kind of joint human activity; Boyd and Richerson 1992).

However, because we tend to conceive of moral situations involving ourselves in "ethical" rather than "moral" terms (first, because by definition we care enough about these situations to reflect on them, and second, because by definition we know all about the background to whatever it is that we do), to be punished might simultaneously draw our attention to the—sometimes unreasoned—nature of social vengeance. From society's point of view, I want to ask, is this dangerous? Is there a risk that we—the punished—will be led to think too much about "the moral," construing it as "ethical" and then wondering what our punishment is all about?

But here it may help to distinguish between three very different scenarios:

1. I set out to break the rules for "bad" reasons, for example, I do not share food with others because I am selfish, I only care about myself. Here my punishment might be unwelcome, but it is hard to complain about it, and I might even feel that my punishment is deserved.

2. I break the moral rules, yes, but arguably for "good" reasons: for example, they are broken by accident, or through ignorance, or because in my present, special circumstances I have no choice but to break them. Perhaps I fail to share food with unrelated people, for example, because right now my own children are going hungry. I am a good person. Note that while *my* punishment might seem unfair in these circumstances, I could still believe that *others*, for example, those who break the same rules intentionally but without good excuses, should be punished.[17]

---

17. Note the thought-provoking discussion of the problem of "moral luck" by Williams (1981), Zimmerman (2002), and others.

3. I explicitly set out to break the rules, because "ethical" reflection has led me to conclude that "moral" rules *should* be broken; they are bad.

My pollution incident seems, at first glance, to match scenario (2): unintended rule breaking. However, I did have mixed feelings about it, of course, and felt that I might, after all, have behaved "badly," as in scenario (1). Moreover, scenario (3) is also relevant because it is possible, as I've explained, that I was actually set up to break the rules by local people who believe that "superstitions" are harmful and who thought it would be good for me to (publicly) flout local anxieties about spiritual pollution. In fact, I wonder whether scenarios (1) and (2) might not have a general tendency to slip into being explained, after the event, in terms of scenario (3)—for example, by protagonists who are trying to make sense of the fact of being punished and/or by those who (because of this punishment) have had their attention drawn to "unreasonable" aspects of morality. And on the surface, at least, (3) seems by far the most radical scenario.[18]

In order to reflect further on this radical potential, I'd like to briefly consider two cases of moral/ethical dilemmas found in the anthropological literature on China before concluding. The first is James L. Watson's study of adoption in a powerful Chinese lineage. Briefly, the moral rule here is that, whenever possible, one should adopt agnatically (e.g., adopt one's brothers' sons) in order to maintain lineage purity, keep lineage property intact, etc. Someone who is forced or who willfully decides, in spite of this rule, to adopt an outsider (generally by purchasing a son from strangers) is, among other things, put through a very expensive banquet initiation ceremony, "during which he [the adopting father] is humiliated by his peers":

> The whole tone of the banquet is different [from those accompanying
> happy events such as weddings] because the adopting father must
> compensate his fellow members for accepting an outsider into their midst.
> The guests try their best to humiliate the host by shouting insults about his
> inability to produce his own heirs. During the banquet any guest may seek

---

18. One interesting question that follows on from this is whether those who—for whatever reason—identify closely with the person being punished may *also* read things ethically rather than morally and have increased doubts about the validity of moral rules. This is arguably the case with the narrator in Lu Xun's story; that is, the young narrator identifies with Xiang Lin's wife, sees her pitiful circumstances, and then clearly finds the punishment she has been given to be unacceptable—even if he holds back from doing anything about it.

out the host and borrow money on the spot. This done with full knowledge that the lender will never ask for repayment, for it would only be an embarrassing reminder of the initiation. (J. Watson 1975: 298)

In spite of this punishment, a significant proportion of men do, nonetheless, decide to "defile" the lineage by adopting outsiders—that is, they intentionally contravene lineage morality. More specifically, although they are generally happy to adopt close agnates, they find the adoption of complete outsiders a better (in this case, less risky) strategy than the adoption of more distant agnates, who might have divided loyalties and eventually disappoint or abandon their adoptive parents.

In explaining such decisions, Watson says that an adopting father "has more at stake than his own pride since he is responsible for producing heirs who will carry on the worship of his immediate ancestors" and because his own old-age security depends largely on procuring—somehow —a filial descendant (ibid. 303). In my terms, then, a father who adopts an outsider in this system might be said to be acting immorally in terms of lineage rules, but he could also be said to be acting ethically, that is, based on his reasoned judgment that a loyal outsider son will help him fulfill his duties to his own ancestors and immediate family. Of course, this could also be described as selfishness. But reading Watson's account, I imagine that anyone paying the price of the humiliating banquet ceremony would, nevertheless, describe his motivations and actions as having been "good."

In terms of the scenarios outlined above, then, although other lineage members might (at least publicly) treat this as a scenario (1) situation—and certainly that is the legal position, as it were—the protagonist would be more likely, so far as I can tell, to treat it as a scenario (2) situation *and/or* scenario (3) situation. That is, the adopting father himself might well feel that it was really bad luck—as in scenario (2)—that put him in the position of having to adopt a son in the first place, and this consideration is more important than his good or bad intentions. But if intentions have to be taken into account, then he is, from his point of view, acting "ethically" against the morals of the lineage (3).

A separate question is whether, having been punished, a person in this situation (and perhaps also those who identity with him, or who can imagine the situation he faces) might resent the social. Is there something intrinsically radical about being willing to face down punishment in this way, and then having it actually happen? Interestingly, Watson points out that in such cases the adopted sons—that is, the outsiders—far from seeking to overturn convention, sometimes actually "try to overcompensate for their ambiguous position by becoming the staunchest upholders of lineage traditions" (ibid. 299). More generally, the humiliating banquet ceremony that their adoptive fathers go through—whatever these men may think about it—can be seen as producing the effects noted by Bourdieu in his short essay "A Paradoxical Foundation of Ethics." That is to say, such ceremonies are one of the means by which a person who is breaking a rule—something that happens in all societies, often as a matter of routine—ostentatiously declares respect for it.[19]

Still, strategies of officialization don't always work, of course, especially over the long term. This brings me to a second example, this one from Yunxiang Yan's research in a Heilongjiang village (Yan 2003). Very briefly, he charts the decline in this community, since 1949, of patriarchal power and the rising influence of young people—especially young women—over kinship and family life. As with the adoption example outlined by Watson, some of the behaviors of the young people in Yan's fieldwork community may be described as "immoral" (e.g., when elders are treated disrespectfully or left to fend for themselves) or "selfish" (e.g., when sons, on behalf of their fiancées, demand very high marriage payments from their own parents). As Yan records, such immoral or selfish behaviors have been punished in various ways over the years, not least through public criticism and gossip (even, in extreme cases, through the suicides of aggrieved parents).

And yet two things must be noted. First, kinship and family life have changed dramatically. The reasons for this are complex, of course, but the change is certainly in part (as Yan stresses) due to the actions of individuals who, at key moments, were willing to face down criticism—and punishment—in order to act in new ways. Second, as Yan shows, many of these "immoral" and "selfish" people clearly feel that, in the terms of my definitions, they have behaved ethically: that is, in their judgment (and sometimes in the judgment of the wider community) their actions have been justified and at least partially "good." One of the well-known moral dilemmas of modern Chinese kinship, for instance, is the extent to which traditional filial piety can be sustained under new socioeconomic circumstances. Yan notes that the married sons among his male informants tended to formally endorse the notion of elder support while making up "excuses for avoiding the obligations" of elder

---

19. "These strategies of officialization, by which agents express their reverence for the official beliefs of the group [while contravening them], are strategies of universalization which accord the group what it demands above all else, that is, a public declaration of reverence for the group and for the self-representation it presents to others and to itself" (Bourdieu 1998: 141).

support in practice. But he also shows that, for example, they engage in ethical reflection on traditional views of parent-child relationships and reciprocal obligations. Among other things:

> Many of them rejected the traditional idea that giving life to a child is the parents' *enqing* [a gift of emotion, intimacy, and kindness] to the child and that the child cannot repay this highest debt. They argued that giving birth to a child is just a natural event that transforms a couple into parents, not a great favor to the child [i.e., not something that would necessarily oblige this child to support his parents in old age], because the child has no choice about birth. Once a child is born, it is the parents' duty to raise the child, they said; everyone will do the same, and even animals give the greatest love and care to their children. (Yan 2003:176)

This could, of course, be taken simply as an excuse for avoiding elder support—as yet more selfishness. (Yan details many actual cases of elder neglect and even abuse.) But I doubt that most of the young people thinking their way through a complex moral/ethical field would see it in this way, and I doubt they are happy to be punished (as they sometimes are) for taking what are genuinely difficult decisions about how best to live. In other words, for their social critics this is at least partly a situation of "immoral intentions," as in scenario (1), whereas for them it is a situation in which circumstances often force them to do what they do, as in scenario (2), *and* one in which a new kind of "ethics" is posed against traditional "morals," as in scenario (3).

This leads me to a question: Is it not, in fact, quite ordinary for people to object—as I did in the case of my funeral pollution—to the fact of being punished, and specifically for them to object to this on what might be called "ethical" grounds, either because they feel that the rules are flawed in some way and deserve to be broken or (and perhaps this is more common) because they feel that breaking them in a particular set of circumstances should have been at least somewhat forgivable? Again, I want to ask what people learn when—these ethical objections notwithstanding—they are punished. We tend to think that punishing "immoral" behavior is what helps create the social, by enforcing moral rules. This is the Durkheimian stance, but also—coming from a very different angle—the stance of evolutionary theorists. I'm sure this is basically right, but punishment also entails some danger. I'm suggesting that what we often punish is, in fact, "ethical" behavior from the point of view of those who are punished. So we need to study the learning that follows from *this* type of punishment—that is, in circumstances where the ethical and the immoral are conflated, as happens all the time—if we want to understand ordinary ethics.

### ACKNOWLEDGMENTS

I am grateful to a number of friends and colleagues who have given me comments on this essay, including Stephan Feuchtwang, Maurice Bloch, and Michael Lambek. In particular, I'd like to thank Judith Baker for the very insightful comments she made about my presentation during the Toronto conference. I can't claim to have taken Judith's comments (which are published in this volume) fully into account in this essay, but her thoughts have directly influenced other things that I'm thinking about and writing in relation to Chinese ethical life. I would also, of course, like to thank the people of Angang, in Taiwan, who treated me with great warmth and kindness in spite of my shortcomings.

# Ordinary Ethics and Changing Cosmologies: Exemplification from North Australia
*Francesca Merlan*

## Cosmological Morality

In this essay, I will be discussing issues of continuity and change in relation to ethics among Aboriginal people I have known over the past three decades in the region of Katherine in the Northern Territory of Australia. The historical baseline for my discussion is a social scene before the Second World War, in which Aboriginal persons and groups experienced an intimate and differentiated attachment to portions of country, performed ritual, and related according to intra-Aboriginal norms of sociality. As elsewhere in Australia, Aboriginal people who grew up under these conditions were given to citing "Law" as the moral basis of right and wrong. Law—whether named using the now widely known English term or indigenous-language antecedents—denotes a body of concepts concerning right and wrong conduct that these people have taken to be ancestrally laid down and includes ideas of proper ways of relating to others and to the country itself, redolent as it is or was with the aura of creator ancestors, as well as persons. For many such Aboriginal Australians, Law comprehends a wide range of normative conduct with respect to the social categories of marriage, observance of appropriate behavior having to do with places and ceremony and their gender-restricted or otherwise special

character, and proper conduct toward persons (normally part of an extended universe of kin). People tend not to cite concepts of Law in the
explicit form of rules or explicit guides for conduct. Rather, they are general doctrinal precepts and tend to weigh most heavily and be invoked
most frequently when people sense a problem or see a reason for a
prohibition.[1]

Although the prewar baseline period persists in memory, the lives of
Katherine-area Aboriginal people I have known have been characterized
by profound, ongoing social transformation. For many, the relations to
country that they consider to be in some sense their own have become less
intense and much less an ongoing context of formative experience (Merlan
1998). Their engagement in ritual has likewise tended to become irregu-
lar, to have ceased, or to occur rarely and in locations distant from their
normal places of residence. They have become notionally included in, but
are effectively disfavored subjects of, a largely welfare- and money-based
general economy and an often hectic circulation of cash, purchased food,
and other commodities, which takes place largely within and among sets
of Aboriginal people at specific times determined by government welfare-
payment scheduling (Merlan 1991). A handful have been recipients of
training and schooling that have enabled them to enter, at least for periods
of time, into jobs and paid work (for, e.g., national parks, Aboriginal organizations, tourist ventures, and sometimes private enterprises along environmental, cultural, and related lines). But, importantly, many such people
have grown up in what we may call "indigenous" social contexts, influenced most directly by the behavior of family and close kindred. The comportment of many such people—perhaps, generally speaking, varying
directly with age and thus particular epochs of experience—is distinctive
compared with other Australians and, I would argue, exhibits distinctive
kinds of ethical orientation coming from within that social universe.

In this essay I will describe and try to conceptualize aspects of these
distinctive "ordinary" ethics that are no longer so clearly or so strongly
entwined with the cosmologically totalizing earlier formation. Before I
turn to ethnographic material, I want to take up, from a perspective useful

---

1. To give examples, a place considered off limits or restricted in some way
because of its sacred character falls within the constraining purview of Law, as may
the injunction to marry within proper social categories and limits (and disapproval
when they are breached); the same holds for the imperative that different categories of people take differentiated roles with respect to the protection and management of places or "country."

to me, two themes that are amply discussed in other chapters: the ethical and the ordinary.

## The Ordinariness of Ethics: Toward Action and Change

Michael Lambek (this volume) argues cogently that "ethics" is not a separate domain, distinct category, or module but a dimension, function, or modality of action, of which speech itself is one important moment. In this view, ethics is not specialized or esoteric, and it should become an ordinary part of our interest in what people do. This aspect of his discussion causes us to focus on questions of action. Recognizing ethics to be an inevitable moment leads us away from overly rigid notions of reason and what James Faubion calls the established principles of systemic organization. I find this approach congenial in that it makes us more concerned with action, doing, as the medium of our explorations of social life. It perhaps also gives us more scope to understand people, like those of whom I speak in north Australia, who do not tend toward explicit discursive reasoning and accounting for what they do.

Lambek goes on to argue that judgment is realized on the basis of criteria entailed in speech and action, and also that the criteria are inherent in "forms of life." Focus on the "ordinariness" of ethics implies that it is a dimension of every kind of action. We need to consider further what the "ethical" moment in action is. Faubion (this volume) addresses this directly in his discussion of the "sovereign actor." Nietzsche's "blond beasts" and Weber's charismatics are examples of figures with no one to "serve as an ethical other" to them. Ethics emerges, Faubion argues, at the moment when the charismatic leader recognizes and accommodates the chrism of the other. But this act of accommodation does "not yet constitute an act of routinization, the establishment of normativity." Ethics has to do with the recognition of others and with forms of accommodation and displacement linked to that recognition. This occurs in a space somewhere between established forms of normativity that actors can access and the pragmatics of action. This relationship is only intelligible as a process participating both in a dimension of "becoming" and in what has already been established. This formulation helps us to see that ethics is one of the important dimensions through which we can address the perennial questions of sociocultural reproduction and transformation. It is part of what is necessarily indeterminate and in flux in every particular circumstance.

I find this kind of formulation, in raising questions of reproduction, useful for the kind of situation I am considering. I attempt to characterize relations among Aboriginal people (previously modeled in the ways I have briefly outlined) and the great asymmetry between them and other Australians. Their lives are unacceptable according to many viewpoints in wider Australian society. Aborigines' very ways of doing and being are subject to constant disapproval and critique as being too bound by existing relationships and loyalties and repellent in some respects (Povinelli 2002). Many of these Aboriginal people can interact freely only with their "own," with whom they reproduce distinctively "Aboriginal" forms of behavior.

If we emphasize ordinariness and focus on action, Lambek suggests, we may dispense with a difference between ethics and morality. The contrast between ethics and morality is usually taken to be a distinction between forms of behavior or action and standards or norms. Faubion refers to this as a distinction between an order of becoming or production and a homeostatic one. Webb Keane suggests that we may understand the order of ethics as tacit and morality as what people are able to put into words. Morality may be understood as degrees of objectification when the subject gives reasons, makes judgments, about his own and others' actions. Both these dimensions—the taking of action and objectifications that necessarily occur as moments of this—must be taken into account. Each has a different kind of temporality, but both are pragmatic dimensions of action.

The question of the tacit versus the explicit is poignant for north Australian Aboriginal people because of the changing conditions of their lives. Although many still have entered into a form of life in which Law is seen as cosmologically totalizing, with its greatest intensity in ritual performance, this has an ever less substantive role to play in how they view themselves and their everyday lives. For many of them, some of the main substantive contents of Law are now often felt to be increasingly out of range, beyond the limits of regular experience—even though there is a strong tendency to believe that Law is still powerful, to hold that someone must know about its related *sacra* (such as aspects of country), and to attribute knowledgeable status on the bases of age and family position to people who do not claim it for themselves. A sense of unrecoverability is perhaps strongest among younger people, but in certain ways the oldest also share it. I have often heard an older man say, "They died too quickly," referring to his elders, so that he had no chance to attend a particular ceremony or move with them through a particular stretch of country. This may not be entirely new, but I suspect it is an increasingly common perception. Law is still often cited by some people as weighty and situationally of great importance, but experiences of many contexts seen as focal to it are receding, and some people explicitly recognize this.

Recognizing ethics as ubiquitous and seeing it as a dimension of people's actions (and not simply of their normative statements) are two moves toward locating the ethical in the everyday. If we take ethics to be an ever-present dimension of action and are especially interested in its everyday character as part of regard for others, then we may recognize as ethically laden certain forms of unfamiliar behavior.

## An Aboriginal Ethics of Regard

In July 2008 I visited an Aboriginal man I had not seen for nearly five years. Seeing Frank[2] again after an unusually long interval threw into relief some of the things about him and our ways of interacting that seem to me typical of many of his Aboriginal age-mates in northern Australia. I also realized the extent to which, having interacted for long periods in town, camp, and rural community settings with Aboriginal people, I had come to take some of these forms of behavior for granted and that I involuntarily enact them myself on many occasions.

The circumstances of our latest meeting were both usual and unusual. They were unusual in that Frank was in jail in Darwin (several hundred kilometers north of the area in which I had spent considerable time with him and his kin), and so the meeting could only take place by permission of the authorities, in a room near the guard station and under video surveillance. But it was usual in that he, like many other of my older Aboriginal kinsmen and close associates over several decades, has been in jail several times and is no stranger to it. At the time of my visit, there were several other relatives and close countrymen in the jail, Frank noted, and still others had come and gone recently. Despite everything, the jail had some homely associations. Frank was in for drunk driving. Because of prior convictions, he'd been sentenced to four years, of which he had already served nearly two at the time of the visit.

At the time, I was in the north on some matters relating to long-running land claims involving Frank and his close kin. For years Frank has seen me as involved in these things,[3] and he takes it as part of my continuing connection to the area and to people and not (I believe) as separate from my attachment to people.

---

2. Personal names have been changed.

3. Over about three years before my involvement with land claims began, I spent a great deal of time with Frank, his relatives, and other people with whom

In my first field research in northern Australia, in 1976, I was taken into Frank's first cousin Stanley's camp as an adoptive daughter. From this grew my relationships with many people in the wider kindred. Being my father's first cousin, Frank was my uncle. Frank and his wife, though they had their own camp, were frequent companions in ours and on many short- and long-term trips into the countryside north of Katherine that all of these people considered their own country.

Unlike his cousins, Frank never speaks an Aboriginal language, though he understands at least two. He has a composed, quiet, and courteous manner. In the region from which he comes, Frank is a man of considerable status; he is considered an "old man" by his circle of relatives, in recognition of social position rather than simply in terms of age, though his hair is now streaked with gray. Kinds of knowledge (e.g., of country) are regularly attributed to him, though he does not claim them for himself. He is the last surviving son of a man who enjoyed great prestige on ceremonial, territorial, and other grounds. Though Frank was a little more reserved than others about admitting me into the kindred circle in the late 1970s, after a time he began calling me "my girl," the Kriol equivalent of niece (which is not used). Over the years we have spent a lot of time in each other's company, and he knows my own immediate family too.

On our meeting in jail recently,[4] after an unusually long period of not seeing each other, I felt myself involuntarily sliding into our accustomed decorous familiarity. We shook hands, saying nothing, and sat. After a while we talked in an unhurried way about what he was in for and what he did while in jail. He said he'd been through a course in "rehab," but that was over. He expressed no embarrassment about being in jail, saying simply that he'd try not to drink when he got out. He expressed no urgency about getting out. We talked over some old times. He eventually mentioned a trip to the Arnhem escarpment that we'd shared some twenty years before and asked one question: Did I remember if his (then) wife, my aunt, had been with us on that trip? I said I thought so, and he said yes, he did too. We confirmed a shared memory of her making a fire by the river there. We did not refer directly to certain other people who had been with us then, especially my close "father," who had died a few years before. He was Frank's first cousin and a key person within that close

---

they lived. In fact, our long-term relationships were at the basis of all my work on claims.

4. Another person was present, not from the jail but from the Land Council, whom Frank knew somewhat.

kindred. It was on my mind that the guards had said I could stay about an hour. As I was getting ready to go, I asked if Frank wanted anything. He thought carefully for about a minute and named a Slim Dusty cassette and a Johnny Cash cassette. I said OK, I would get them. He said, "See you, my girl," and I left.

On this occasion and in the main, Frank comes across as controlled, almost serene. Two things about the visit were particularly striking to me. One was that he did not mention the restraint that he was living under. To this may be linked the fact that he expressed no self-condemnation. He is not your average citizen-subject who can easily be made to feel that he has done something reprehensible by driving while drunk, even though he knows it is illegal and is aware that others feel strongly about it. He said he would try not to drink when he got out, but there was no moral absolutism in what he said.[5] The other was that he asked me nothing about myself. No question phrased in terms of where I had come from, nor where I had been in the meantime. He was able to presuppose commonality between us, but what he said and did indicated no interest in going beyond it. The many things that might lie outside the sphere of our established commonality were not part of the orientation that we had toward each other, and I did not try to introduce any. I return below to some other aspects of the character of his life and that of others with whom he has lived it out, in which such restraint is familiar. Though there may be many things that were unusual about our meeting, I was struck by how similar it was to many interactions I have had with other Aboriginal people like Frank. It might be possible to read his calm and uninquisitive behavior as passive or even depressive. But it is too much of a piece with the behavior of others of his age and similar background for me to see it that way. And there were signals that it should be read otherwise. In his talking and asking me about his former wife, it was obvious that he was thinking about the past. He spoke with interest of relatives and countrymen who showed up in jail, and he asked me to get another niece to ring him. His parting "my girl" was his only explicit indication of our relationship, a deployment that was neither instrumental nor casual but a sign of recognition, something he knew I would be alert to.

I have thought about some of these forms in the past, such as the regularity with which known people who have been away from Aboriginal

---

5. I saw Frank again a few months later, out of jail, working in a groundsman's job in a small regional center within the area he considers home. We had a similarly quiet encounter, in which he mentioned trying to stay "off the grog" and away from anybody who would tempt him.

camps and scenes are reintegrated without question or comment and—unless something dramatic has happened, such as a death—without any fuss or explicit giving of news. I have come to see these as forms of ethical behavior and particular modes of regard for others. They are often taken by outside observers to be evidence of deficits of interest or awareness, and indeed such modes of behavior may have the effect of screening or limiting interactions. But even if this is so, I am convinced that elements of these ways of acting result from the internalization of dispositions concerning self-other relations and are ethical forms.

## Models of Consociate Worlds

Practices and modes of constituting self-other relations certainly differed across the Australian continent, so no single description would be apt for all social groups. It is also important, from the outset, to be very clear that the social situations and practices of Aboriginal people have for some time been affected in complex ways by interaction with settlers, and every Aboriginal community and person has a sense of how this interaction has been over time and that it involves social distance and difference. Given that schooling, changed consumption practices of all kinds, money, new forms of housing, and many other practices and institutions are now becoming widely though variably distributed, any description must take them into account. Despite differences, some aspects of enmeshment in regional social networks and forms of connection to territories people regard as their home country do seem to show strong similarity across the continent; these are of interest to any attempts to understand ethical behavior among people who lived the general form of life in which these practices developed and are becoming modified.

Probably the best-known interpretation of forms of personhood and interrelationship is Fred Myers's (1986) account of the Pintupi (Western Desert), among whom ritual and other practices of Law as authority continue to be substantively reconfirmed. Most Pintupi still live in remote communities and outstations. Though patterns of behavior differ somewhat regionally, overall theirs are similar to ones once found across the continent and still found in communities where interaction is principally among indigenous people. Specifically, kinship and other social classifications can be extended to anyone who comes to be meaningfully known to a member of the group, This circle of kinship is surrounded by a horizon of those less well known but potentially knowable, that by a further horizon of unknowns too distant physically and socially to be reckoned as kin. In earlier times, the last were often considered hostile and even nonhuman in type.

Myers characterizes Pintupi life as pivoting around dimensions of relatedness and autonomy. "Relatedness" is an interpretation of Pintupi concepts and behaviors to which *waltyja* (roughly "kin," "family"), is central. The term connotes shared identity, grounded partly in sharing with others connections to places and their ancestral creators, partly in common experience, which coincides significantly with being (close) kin, partly in practices and expectations of openness, sympathy, support, and outward relationship toward others (Myers 1986: 22). The result is a formation of the self that is not isolated but substantially identified with others (ibid. 124).

Given such overarching connectedness, "autonomy" is not the opposite of relatedness but an expression of personal differentiation from within it: "genuine autonomy is not a product of private will, but results only through successful negotiations with others" (ibid.). Myers uses the term *autonomy* for a spectrum of positions within such socially defined personhood, including people's rejection of the imposition of authority upon themselves and close others and forms of self-assertion. Autonomy, he notes, is not "cheap coin" (ibid. 16): people are quite prepared to fight for themselves and those with whom they identify. Children are accorded autonomy, understood as self-assertion and freedom from direction by others. Myers sees Pintupi as oriented toward asserting equality rather than lasting hierarchy in relation to each other (reminiscent of Collier and Rosaldo's 1981 generalizations about expressions of power in "simple societies"). He sees ritual, in its psychic enormity, as the key setting within which tension-laden dimensions of the polity can play out: some (juniors, or people on whose behalf ritual is notionally being performed) gain autonomy through it. Pintupi understand the contributions of ritual seniors or directors, even if authoritarian or severe, as appropriate "nurturance," "looking after others" in these contexts (Myers 1980). Ritual confirms and upholds a realm of final authority, or Law, and resolves what Myers sees as the ever-present problem of constituting an authoritative center (1986: 22) outside human compass in a polity oriented toward shared constructions of the self. In this polity, Myers argues, people protect their autonomy by hiding it (ibid. 125).

Jane Goodale (1971), who was Myers's Ph.D. supervisor, also wrote of autonomy and self-direction among the Tiwi. Her focus on women's lives moved her to explain that women as well as men could be self-directed, and she also saw such assertiveness as being objectified in the form of baby-animating "child spirits," who cannot be controlled or directed. Some academic generational continuity is evident in their efforts to come to conceptual grips with a dimension of personhood that earlier accounts had submerged within normative descriptions of the structure and content of relationships.

Myers's characterization emerged from traditions of social description that naturalize notions of the "individual person," focusing on individual distinctiveness and images of the concrete individual person against a ground of commonality. The history of theorizing—the opposition between notions of "relational" and "individual" self, or models of "dividual" and "partible" persons—indicates that a difficulty in social theory is to portray the person as socially constituted in the face of a taken-for-granted notion of "individuals." The most difficult part in theorizing the person is the question of his or her "social" character. The structuralist reaction to this problem in anthropology was to seize upon recurrent "structures" (of kinship, clanship, tribe, or whatever) and to take these as foundations of the self. This rendered "individuality" anomalous in these settings, sometimes creating the primitive as structural robot. Various other traditions in anthropology have labored against this, as in the re-emergence from time to time of biography and more literary modes of writing. Accounts of partible personhood and the like have attempted fuller portrayals of cultural models and acknowledgment of the multiplicity of the sources of the person but have not resolved the underlying issue: that socially conditioned, oriented, and multiply sourced personhood is the universal situation. If that universality is acknowledged, then perhaps one can return to a favored kind of anthropological question: the range of difference within social systems and the differing theoretical and conceptual means needed to account for them.

In the history of such efforts within anthropology, sociology, and allied disciplines, much has been made of the notion of "face-to-face" relations. It has often been assumed that relations in societies variously termed "simple," "primitive," or "hunting and gathering" largely involve direct engagement. In the terms of Alfred Schütz, these are people of *Umwelt* rather than *Mitwelt*, consociates rather than contemporaries. I would suggest that much that is structural within Aboriginal modes of sociality works against the relevance of such a distinction; that "structure," in these small-scale settings as elsewhere, brings with it forms of typification through which people grasp the other (rendering less immediate than we might think the notion of the face-to-face), and that an assemblage of modes of such grasping needs to be made more explicit in order for us to be able to understand what this form of life is or was like, how it is changing, and the terms in which we may begin to attune ourselves to the ethical behavior of people like Frank. Various intersecting modes of orientation toward others within Aboriginal settings, in their totality, leave room for both typification and differentiation. While Myers's model of relatedness and autonomy has been illuminating, one cannot forget that these generalizations exist at a level abstracted from ordinary practice, as Myers himself would readily acknowledge. More detailed accounts of how people act would give us a basis for considering how widely applicable these generalizations continue to be and where they may need to be modified.

## *Kinds of Typifications, Structural and Experiential*

Aboriginal societies have long been famous for their systems of kinship and social categorization (moieties, semimoieties, subsections, etc.) and for intersections between these inclusive forms. All who came into regular contact were kin,[6] with normative typifications built into each form of relationship (e.g., the categories simultaneously understood as having normative implications for correct marriage, for ceremonial organization, and as associated with physical, temperamental, and other characteristics considered to inhere in the particular categories). Such frameworks of kin and category shape living connections among people: each faces others in terms of relationships that are relatively continuous, transgenerational, and horizontally extended (in the sense that all persons are known in terms of their ascending, descending, and presently ramifying relations to others), carry some load of normative expectation (concerning how one should behave toward certain kinds of relatives), and involve varying depths of shared experience of persons in relation to others. Such systematization thus allows for degrees of continuity in any person's relationship to others, replicability or renewability through time of relationship to the other, and a general situation of reciprocity of perspectives among people located within kindreds (such that I can expect my relationship toward others to be reciprocated in terms of our specific mutual relationships and

---

6. This must be qualified in differing degrees for the present, of course, depending on Aboriginal people's current way of living and the extent to which they regularly deal with non-Aborigines.

general terms of shared experience and involvement through time by those
others).

The genius of this kind of structuration is that it is expressed in vocabularies of relatedness (kinship) and inclusive categorization that permit continuity and recoverability even in mobility and dispersion, in this way
suppressing social differentiation of the order that Schütz attempted to
grasp through his contrast between consociates (face-to-face) and contemporaries (those with whom one shares time but not space). There is a
thoroughgoing presence of structuring categories that enable people to
grasp each other in such terms but do not entirely dominate the field of
interrelationship. This structuring also subtends the continuing possibility
of making less-known persons better known, as well as both the continuity
and the renewability of relationship in conditions of lesser and greater co-
presence of persons to each other. It may in part account for something
very noticeable in many Aboriginal settings: people position themselves in
relation to each other often without expressing much curiosity about each
other. The presupposition of continuity and renewability of relationship
damps radical curiosity in relationship; norms of etiquette further discour-
age overt expression of curiosity.

Across the continent, there is evidence of indigenous imaginative efforts to compress time and space in relations with other persons. Moreover, some imagined mobilities actively defy space-time and matter.
"Spirit travel" allows rapid and unrestricted movement to locations and
people (Tonkinson 1970), and magical means of bringing places "up close"
(Merlan 1992). Other modes of spatiotemporal binding of persons (who,
as we now see, when concretely present are simultaneously typified in a
number of ways) include naming children after particular older kinsmen
(grasped both in their concreteness and in their typicality as certain kinds
of kin), in ways congruent with other aspects of their social categorization
and kin status (e.g., naming a child after one's father's father's sister). The
junior so named is understood to "follow" or re-present the elder. The
name subsumes both junior and senior in its continuous linkage to specific
places and objects in the landscape and is itself not a mere name but a
dimension of the creative forces (totemic ancestors) of that place (Merlan
1982).

In some social settings, practices continue to bind people, places, and
natural forms in consubstantial relationship, in typical forms of identification between them. One man I know, for example, has a mark that is
understood to show his consubstantiality with black cockatoo, the "dreaming" associated with the place from which he is understood to have

emerged as a child spirit. In this way, all across Australia relationships are regularly encoded and mapped on the body, so that, for example, in systems of southern Arnhem Land I know the category father is embodied in one's right shoulder, that of father's sister in one's left shoulder, one's father's father in the right lower leg, and one's father's father's sister in the left, and so on.[7] In practice, through this conventional schematization people interpret their own bodily sensations relationally and communicatively. An ache or twitch in my right shoulder makes me think of my father(s) and what may be happening to him or them. In this way bodily events have an other-orientation, but this does not preclude their also having various additional kinds of both other- and self-directed values: as news, as particular forms of communication that some people receive more regularly and in ways attributed greater significance than others, and so on.

However, while I have emphasized certain structurally representable modes of grasping other persons, to show how ubiquitous and various they are—and how many ways of understanding and approaching others they entail and provide—any account would be incomplete if it did not also mention their being intertwined with modes of relationship that presuppose and rest upon both immediacy and typification of face-to-face experience with others. In Aboriginal settings, for example, people's smells and sweat, their bodily shapes and characteristic ways of moving, their habits, their footsteps, their lovable, unpredictable, comical, and other characteristics make an enormous difference in how others relate to them, in copresence and beyond. In Aboriginal settings in which I have worked, people typically have nicknames that reflect aspects of these personal characteristics. Frank and I, for instance, over the years, spent much time together with my grandfather, his uncle, who was known to us all in camp by a changing series of nicknames: Na-Burned-Grass (in English, for comical effect, with Jawoyn masculine prefix *na-*), after an episode in which he, returning drunk, nearly burned up in his swag (bedroll) and the entire nighttime camp was convulsed in laughter at his antics and awkwardness as this near miss transpired (except for his wife Queenie, who swore and "growled" throughout); Na-Gun-Fighter (again, in English, for his mock, usually jocular bellicosity, often also on display when he was drunk, a high-voltage, high-decibel version of his typically serene and fairly even, pleasant, and stoical temperament).

---

7. See Stanner (1937) for one of the early anthropological recognitions of these systems of coding, and Kendon (1988) for a comparative survey.

Bodiliness, body presence, smells, being together, knowing each other's habits and personal characteristics—all partly channeled by awareness of normative expectations in kin relationships and particulars of prior experience—are also partly systematic in foregrounding certain modes of grasping the other. It is in terms of this multiplicity of channels and the high degree of people's awareness of and orientation toward others that I have often understood another noticeable phenomenon: that people in this kind of formation seem relatively little concerned with what we might call an aesthetic of "looks." People are aware of and concerned with others as young, mature, and old; as fecund and sexual beings or not; or as personally characterful in certain ways, but they are not highly concerned with and do not tend to express an aesthetic of "good looks," beauty or ugliness as outsiders might see it. In keeping with this, the recent onset of obvious and widespread obesity among Aboriginal people does not occasion as much remark or notice as one might imagine.

I have been trying to give some sense of how Aboriginal modalities of grasping persons entail, simultaneously, dimensions of typification and moments that overflow them to include what is essentially grasped and remembered as personal, particular, experienced in co-presence (even if such moments also have their conventional or typical aspects). Together, these modes allow for degrees of both novelty and continuity in relationships. How continuous a relationship is may be tested (e.g., by demand; see Peterson 1993), and in any case people hold many kinds of ongoing expectation of each other. Many of the more highly structured forms of relationship imply a certain normativity and, for those embedded in these social environments, involve certain kinds of attitudes: for example, respect, duty, greater constraint versus greater familiarity, and often "shame" and a desire not to be the object of ridicule. Thus people always face others as particular kinds of person with high expectations of reciprocity in their relationship: that is, to the extent that they mutually acknowledge each other and accept some of the kinds of terms I have described.

When people like Frank face some of the institutions of the wider society that now exist all around them, there is often an incongruence between forms of action he is accustomed to and some of those he encounters. Frank's illustrious father died when he was very small; he remembers nothing of him. His mother remarried, and he was raised by a man of another, well-known, and territorially proximate southern Arnhem group in fringe camps around Katherine. When he was a small boy, Frank was sent to school at an Aboriginal community, formed after the war, about sixty kilometers from Katherine. This was Frank's first experience of school schedules and school authority. Even though he was staying with people he could consider distant kin, he ran away, back to the Katherine River camp where his stepfather and mother were. On his parents' days off and on weekends, they could all walk downriver to hunt and fish. He never went back to school. Although he remained around towns and places where his relatives worked, Frank was never inducted into ceremony, whose practice has over the decades declined around towns and has become centered in remoter Aboriginal communities; even in many of those it is becoming less regular. Like many of his contemporaries who have made their lives around towns, regional mines, and pastoral properties, Frank has lived largely in the immediate company of other Aborigines, not Europeans, though he has worked for a range of Europeans, some of whom he has encountered as individual "bosses," others as changing personnel in institutions (as when he worked for the police as a tracker).

Urged into wage labor in part by Department of Aboriginal Affairs (DAA) personnel, Frank first worked in stock camps, some of them to the south and west, outside the normal range of Jawoyn people like himself. In those days, when DAA was trying to mobilize Aboriginal workers, many ranged further than they would have otherwise. Aborginals have always lived under conditions of mobility, and these new working arrangements did not diminish the importance of kin and social connections. Talking to me about his work experience at a station southwest of Katherine, my "father"—the person Frank and I avoided mentioning at our meeting— once recalled running into Frank in that relatively unfamiliar country. Who should be unexpectedly brought by authorities to work there? he asked. "My full *barnga* [cross-cousin]," he said with satisfaction, referring to Frank, who was sitting quietly by. Something of the same emotional tone was palpable to me when Frank said to me, on my departure from the jail, "See you, my girl."

Some combination of typification and immediacy, whereby one grasps a person as simultaneously concrete and categorized, seems to me the modality in which one may understand the attentive yet circumspect, reciprocity-attuned modes of relating to others that constitute the ordinary and the ethical in the kind of behavior I seek to explore, understand, and value here.

Commenting on a large range of "modes of address and reference" among people of the Daly River region (names of several kinds, kin usages, signs, etc.), William Stanner characterized many of them as "the conversational counterpart of a circumspect formality which marks all the face-to-face approaches of natives in commonplace social relations" (1937: 314).

Practiced with decorum and restraint, these usages, he argued, "dampen the impact of one personality on another" (ibid.), and many characteristically involved a degree of what he saw as "indirection." From Stanner's insights—and my experiences—I have come to grasp something unexpected: that embeddedness in complex relationships of these kinds does not simply produce continuous relationality. From the constitutive combinations of typification and emergence, the orientations toward both immediacy and the potential inherent in these structures for continuity and renewability, there arises an ethical tenor of due regard and circumspection that Stanner was attempting to characterize. I believe this kind of characterization helps us see into the ethical dimensions of the ordinary person-oriented yet modulated behavior of people such as Frank. The way he is can be described neither as a voluntary effort nor as a lack of attention; rather, it is the product of long-term social engagement, one that should not be dismissed as either passive or inattentive. Complementing the more abstract notions of relationality and autonomy, my depiction is intended to show both what is other oriented about such behavior and how it builds and requires some kind of space from within which one attends to others.

Myers (1986: 22) describes the dimension he calls "autonomy" as reluctance to allow others to direct their authority toward the self and imprint it there. The space I have described is one aspect of this. So too is the common Kriol phrase "I'm boss for myself," understood as an assertion of self-direction (see Goodale 1971, Bell 1983, Martin 1993). While this phrase undoubtedly conveys a certain pertness, when properly contextualized it cannot be understood in simplistic terms of "resistance" or some total struggle of a presumed preexisting independent self seeking the removal of restraints. We often say *in vino veritas* and see what people do when drunk as very telling. If so, then one of the most telling expressions of the ethos I have described is the repeated, aggrieved accusations by drunken people that others are "rubbishing" them: the most deep-seated complaint and articulated source of resentment is that others are not practicing due regard, not caring for one.

Another aspect of that ethos is the idea that independence and competence at being oneself are learned from others—but in a certain way, not only in the dramatic and more authoritarian contexts of ritual but, more commonly, in everyday life, through watching and copying. People feel that by walking through country with others they internalize understanding of it. Importantly, and sometimes without any clear foundation in demonstrated knowledge, they attribute understanding acquired this way to others. Despite the importance of being with others in the experience of coming to understand, I have known even the most knowledgeable people to deny having been taught or shown.

In keeping with ideas of understanding as experienced, not taught, children are not restrained from doing many things that adults do, despite their lesser experience (cf. Hamilton 1981). They are allowed to express desires and commandeer resources (like money) in ways that are entirely at odds with more directive child-minding practices. Competences and understandings are expected to come from within the attuned experiential self. This is tragically problematized in the context of substance abuse, which is treated as expression of preference that others should not impinge upon (Burbank 2006).

Understanding and capabilities shaped in these ways produce a sense of competence—self-direction—that is not to be equated with "freedom" understood as the removal of constraints or the absence of constitutive relationships. Such ethical stances of due regard and understanding are fundamental and continue to be reproduced in Aboriginal settings now removed or remote from the practice of ceremony, though that remains a key referent of Law in certain communities.

## Conclusions

The inclusive structures of kinship (and usually but now sometimes less consistently social classification) that typify many Aboriginal social settings are not rigidly determining. The ability to understand and grasp others in terms of them, however, forms a decisive boundary between those who belong locally and those who are marginal or outside local belonging. These structures carry normative behavioral expectations, which become most noticeable when transgressed. Rather than being rigidly determining, these relationships are, it seems to me, oriented toward spatio-temporal continuity, restorability, and an open potentiality for further inclusion. Though potentially they can be extended, social systems so constituted work best on a relatively small regional scale. Any such regional network is surrounded by outer, lesser-known, or foreign fringes. Mobility was and remains both a means of livelihood and a social strategy. Networks of relationship are not characterized by complete equality among persons—notably, there are differences in gender and seniority. But they are characterized by some particularity in relationships within a familiar field and an understood or expected reciprocity of perspectives and attentiveness between those in particular relationships with each other and among closely related and/or closely associated people in these fields.

Aboriginal people who live according to these terms are able, in general, to treat a limited number of outsiders—like myself—within them, so long as the latter accept to some degree norms of reciprocity and behavior within relationships, including observing a kind of withholding—a certain reserve, respect, and nondirectiveness—in relation to others. There are balances to be struck. Engaging in expected reciprocities often means close physical proximity to some people and not others, sharing of utensils, spaces, swags, and so on, but still without transgressing boundaries of due regard according to the nature of certain relationships.

Aboriginal people like Frank experience a problem that I called, again playing upon a phrase from Schütz, the "incongruence of systems." The first place Frank truly experienced such incongruence was, I gathered, when he was sent to school. He was confronted with people who directed him, demanded compliance in dress and comportment, and did not see it as their business to find any terms of reciprocity in which to address him, terms in which he might be recognized as the person he otherwise was within a regional kindred. Instead, he was made to operate in terms of functions and competences that were to be taught to him directly, without leaving him the expected space in which he was already recognized and nothing would be demanded back directly. Being in the care of an Aboriginal family was no consolation. His reaction, like that of several of his kinsmen and classmates I have known, was to run away.

Men like him and my "father" judged former white stock camp and mining field bosses in terms of the kinds of values I have been exploring. A key one was allowing others to do things themselves. With the question of incongruence clearly aggravated by the racial divide, these men talked about one white boss who remained *baranggu* ("cheeky, aggressive"), though he worked with them "out bush" (i.e., out in a remote rural setting) himself: eventually, they belted him with a stirrup. Another station boss was recalled positively for letting blackfellas do things in their own way; yet another, for urging them to eat at a common table, not outside. Such bosses clearly made better kinds of accommodations with Aboriginal workers than many others, finding spaces of regard within ordinary whitefella ethics without, for the most part, entering more fully into Aboriginal ones.

### ACKNOWLEDGMENTS

Thanks to Judith Baker for her comments on the conference version of this paper, to Michael Lambek for subsequent comments, and to Alan Rumsey for editorial suggestions.

# Philosophical Comments on Charles Stafford and Francesca Merlan

*Judith Baker*

Charles Stafford's interesting essay "The Punishment of Ethical Behavior" starts from an important insight: it is not just philosophers who engage in thinking about morals. Stafford takes ethics to be the philosophical study of morals by ordinary people, including the behaviors that directly follow on, or precede, this philosophizing. He understands morals to be the rules, norms, or conventions against which human behaviors are judged good or bad. While he voices qualms about his distinction, he believes it helps make salient the role of thinking and judgment in moral life and the fact that ethical thinking can lead us to break or oppose moral rules.

I hope to recognize the insights of Stafford and the issues he raises, while using a different terminology. I don't myself distinguish between ethics and morality. I do recognize that distinctions between ethics and morality can be useful, but I do not believe the questions that interest me in Stafford's account can be formulated either with his distinction or with the one developed by Bernard Williams and other philosophers. This is because I think the interesting dilemmas of the essay arise just because morals, moral rules, insofar as they are regarded by agents as creating obligations, as indeed moral, need to be accepted by the individual as more than social policy or elements of control. (Stafford himself recognizes this.) We—ordinary people—not only ask whether a particular action is right or wrong, required or simply commended, and the like but also question whether what supports or favors an action or its prohibition is a genuine moral/ethical reason or something else (prejudice, personal taste, superstition, and the like). That is, in moral/ethical deliberation of the first order, concerning what to do, there is always the possibility of what I would call meta-ethical thought, whose object is the structure, or structural elements, of morality. There is a divergence of opinion in the United States, for example, not so much about whether or not young people should be chaste (whether certain sexual behavior is right or wrong) but rather about whether the reasons that support chaste behavior should be understood as moral. Deliberations and discussions with others, from adolescence on, highlight the need to distinguish our family's or culture's preferences from genuine moral reasons.

Such discussions are not confined to us. Stafford's illuminating list of responses to his attendance and behavior at funerals in Taiwan include those by members of the community who believe the idea of spiritual pollution is merely superstition. Superstition yields reasons that are not moral/ethical. Other responses also express meta-views: on what one can hope to remedy or repair once one has violated a certain kind of injunction. Moreover, deliberation about what to do, which does not always appeal to what I have called meta-ethical questions, requires that one weigh competing or conflicting considerations and obligations. Within deliberation, to the extent that an agent believes that particular obligations are outweighed, disregarding them is not immoral. While our most general reflections may sometimes lead us to break a particular moral rule, it is, I believe, misleading to suppose that ordinary individuals' reflection on what to do stands opposed to their, our, sense of obligation.

Recent philosophical distinctions will not help us formulate Stafford's conflicts, either: Williams and others have introduced a use of the term ethics as distinguished from morality. They wish to correct what they regard as a narrowness of vision in some philosophical studies of morals. Williams thinks Aristotle had it right—the basic question is how to live, what is a worthwhile human life. Wisdom allows us to see when some rules yield obligations that are more important than other considerations or other obligations. We do not, strictly speaking, break moral rules in doing what is the right thing, for we do not hold ourselves required or obliged to act on what is of lesser weight.

Williams views morality as a subspecies of ethical thought that forms part (albeit an incoherent part) of our ordinary thinking as well. He thinks morality is characterized by a certain spirit: a tendency to regard obligation, moral obligation, to be inescapable and unconditional. Unlike ordinary obligations, which may give way to various sorts of considerations, moral obligations never do. This kind of thinking does not, however, allow for "immoral but ethical" behavior. For those who fully believe that moral obligations have these stringent characteristics, there is no ethical apart from the moral; ethical thinking does not oppose, but collapses into morality.

In the course of his essay, Stafford raises two questions of particular interest to me, which I read as follows: Why do we mind so much when we are even lightly punished when we have acted in a way we regard as good? and Why are we so interested in the wrongdoing of others? I want to connect them by talking about a certain line of philosophical thinking, which is to a great extent indebted to the work of Peter Strawson. In 1960 Strawson gave an address to the British Academy entitled "Freedom and Resentment" (1962). He sought to resolve certain philosophical issues involved in the metaphysical debate about determinism and free will (in particular, whether it could make sense to punish anyone if determinism were true) by looking at our practices of punishing, moral condemnation, and approval, but he thought that this required first looking at very common personal emotional attitudes and reactions of people directly involved in transactions with each other. Whatever the success of the hoped-for resolution of the metaphysical issues, his examination of emotional attitudes has been enormously influential.

It is of particular relevance to the question of ordinary ethics, for Strawson has influenced a generation of philosophers who have begun to write on such topics as forgiveness, loyalty, trust, radical hope, the nature of good hope, moral vulnerabilities, and moral repair—who have extended our continuing examination of moral principles, of the nature of moral reasoning, of moral obligations, and of what we owe to others. Many contemporary philosophers have in greater or less depth explored morality/ethics in terms of relations with others, normative expectations of others, and the capacities, including emotions, that make these possible. The emotional reactions and attitudes first discussed by Strawson have been more or less important to these analyses. Since his article, we have learned (perhaps again) that they cannot be dispensed with.

All Strawson's remarks rest on this commonplace: the very great importance we attach to the attitudes and intentions toward us of others, how much we mind, how much it matters whether their attitudes to us reflect good will, affection, and esteem, or contempt, indifference, and malevolence. The kind and degree of attitudinal reaction to someone stepping on my foot will be different, even if the pain is the same, if it is an accident

or if someone treads on my foot out of contemptuous disregard or malevolence. My resentment of another's disregard is an illustration of what
Strawson calls a personal participant reactive attitude. Gratitude to someone whose action expresses her good will or affection is another example.
There are two other kinds of participant reactive attitude. The first of
these is what he variously calls a sympathetic, impersonal, generalized,
or vicarious (not essentially so, "vicarious" is suggestive) reaction to the
attitudes of others' will to people other than myself. When that will is
malevolent, we react with indignation, which is called moral because our
own interests and dignity are not involved, because we experience resentment on behalf of others. This involves an expectation or demand for
others, for those attitudes of esteem, good will, or at least the absence of
ill will and disregard that I demand for myself. The second of the two
other kinds comprises self-reactive attitudes associated with demands
made by others on oneself, such as feeling obliged, guilty, or remorseful.
The three participant reactive attitudes are contrasted with detached, objective attitudes.

Strawson gives an example of an objective attitude that is relevant here:
the objective attitude, he says, views the practice of punishment with the
operative notions of policy, treatment, and control. This attitude, he
claims, excludes not only the moral reactive attitudes but also the essential
elements of the concept of moral condemnation and moral responsibility.
Social utility leaves out something vital in our practices and the notions of
desert, responsibility, guilt, and justice.

Why do we care about wrongdoing? Strawson holds that the three
types of reactive attitudes I have sketched are both logically and humanly
connected. (Unfortunately, his remarks are mainly suggestive.) He thinks
it would be an abnormal egocentricity to hold the first-personal reactive
attitudes but not the vicarious or impersonal second type. Someone who
manifested the personal reactive attitudes in a high degree (resented, was
grateful, etc.) but showed no inclination at all to their vicarious analogues
would appear as an abnormal case of moral egocentricity, as a kind of
moral solipsist. If we suppose him to be susceptible to self-reactive attitudes and to fully acknowledge the claims to regard that others have on
him but to lack impersonal (vicarious) attitudes, he would see himself as
unique, both as the only one who had a general claim to human regard
and as the only one on whom human beings in general had such a claim.
Strawson thinks this barely more than a conceptual possibility, if that. He
thinks all three types of attitude alike have common roots in our human

nature and our membership in human communities. But he does not explain further.

Strawson wishes to answer philosophers who might think we couldn't give up our personal reactions, though we might give up the vicarious ones under the threat of universal determinism. Other philosophers might hold that we cannot give up our desire or demand for the good will of others toward us. But perhaps we need not demand that people show esteem or good will for others. Strawson, however, clearly thinks people's reactions to broken rules, to the disregard shown by people not toward oneself but to others, is in some way connected with demands and expectations for ourselves, but not because this serves our personal interest or expectations that others should have due regard for us.

Obviously, Strawson's insight does not preclude another source of the importance we place on the breaking of community norms: our own security is threatened both by acts of violence and by violations of rules we think maintain an orderly social world. I am hesitant to call our reactions moral indignation when social, but not moral, norms are threatened. Nonetheless, we need to take seriously people's reactions to what they view as threats to themselves as members of a community, when their community's standards are violated.[1]

Strawson suggests an answer to the first question as well: Why do I respond in a particularly resentful way to punishment of behavior I regard as good? Punishment, as the deliberate infliction of what a person regards as painful or treatment limiting her freedom, will be a source of resentment as well as morally problematic if it is not justified. The individual punished needs to acquiesce or accept that it is justified in order not to resent society as showing toward her an absence of good will. She will be unable to feel remorseful for this action or have a sense of obligations to others if she is inhibited in forming reactive attitudes of the third sort.

So far, my answer in Strawson's name does not explain any difference in resentment in various cases of unjustified punishment of myself— whether I am acting in a way I regard as good or when I, more simply,

---

1. Margaret Walker (2006: 146) notes that resentment is neither irrational nor necessarily less fervent when it is a response to forms of order that do not raise moral issues, indeed, even when it arises from violations of morally unacceptable norms that people mistakenly but fervently hold to be the right way to live. In Walker's view, people can feel the security of their lives to be threatened when the norms of their societies are violated. Her focus is on norms, but she preserves Strawson's insight, provided that threats to norms are viewed as manifestations of individuals' attitudes of ill will or indifference to us.

have not done anything wrong. I will resent being punished in both cases. What I suspect, but cannot really argue, is that resentment is worse when one thinks one is acting ethically. If one is punished by others who admit one is a good type or who disallow the role of intention because only a certain sort of individual would let such things happen to him, one faces an implacable social disregard or malevolence. How could one expect esteem or good will from people like that?

Contemporary philosophers have understood punishment to be essentially expressive of a community's attitude, of its desire to draw a line regarding acceptable behavior. I would like to add one more idea from my philosophical background. In recent years, the resurgent popularity of retributivism has prompted more philosophical thought about its possible justification. In 1982 J. L. Mackie represented many of his contemporaries in finding our retributive ideas both common and yet hard to justify. He thought that the idea that the guilty deserve to suffer in proportion to the pain that they have caused has for us an "immediate, un-derived moral appeal or moral authority" and that without such a reason for imposing a penalty, no future benefit would make it morally right to inflict suffering. Yet he thought that there was no readily understandable way of making sense of this idea. Jean Hampton (Murphy and Hampton 1988), some years later, attempted to defend a moral basis for retribution. Starting from the acknowledged idea that punishment is expressive or communicative, she understands the message underlying retributive punishment to be one of affirming, or vindicating, the value of the victim. Hampton's response, that the point of retribution is to affirm the value of the victim, has had some influence on anthropologists, notably in John Borneman's (2005) explanation of the work done by apologies.[2]

I can unfortunately make only a few comments on Francesca Merlan's essay. I have, however, much appreciated her rich examples of the ethics of Australian aboriginal ordinary life. These are placed within a theoretical framework, but one that happily seems to make minimal metaphysical assumptions. Some political philosophers have distinguished the liberal view of the self as unencumbered, existing apart from its ends and relations, a view that is then contrasted with nonliberal, communitarian views of the self as embedded or situated in existing social practices, including social

---

2. Borneman cites Hampton's account in arguing that states must repair the damaged self-worth of wronged persons. Apologies are a form of performative redress that, in Hampton's words, seek to defeat the wrongdoer's claim to mastery over the victim.

roles and relationships, leading some to talk of a relational sense of self. While liberal theories emphasize the self's ability to reflect on its ends and the practices and relations of its society, liberals would deny that this leads to any metaphysical view of an independent, unencumbered self. We need not, however, engage in that debate to appreciate the anthropologists' characterizations of societies in which an individual's sense of self and others is manifested in practices and interrelationships. As Merlan implies, we need not assume there is a "partible" or "dividual" self.

Her examples are particularly interesting insofar as they may be unexpected. To use an idea from an earlier draft of hers, aboriginal people think of themselves and others in terms of interrelationships of many kinds. But we find in Merlan's examples practices that exhibit a regard for what we might call an individual's need for her own space apart from others and her freedom to develop and learn for herself (albeit in connection with others). We can see forms or practices that differ from those of liberal societies but that, like them, respond to a demand for autonomy and due regard as an individual. Merlan's examples show us individuals who act out of ethical due regard for others insofar as they act in light of these needs. She does not see her "uncle" Frank's absence of questions regarding what she does in the world that exists apart from their common experiences as manifesting indifference to her. Frank's behavior, rather, recognizes her private life and (in some sense) private person. The refusal to teach children or others by explicit directives and individuals' pride in what they termed learning by themselves, namely, watching and imitating others, expresses a different vision of how one can become autonomous, can attain the required capabilities for what we see as a human and moral excellence.

The practices she describes—not questioning others, not directing others while fostering their learning—are not those of most of us in the West. Just as teachers of Aboriginal children in Australia regarded the children as merely unruly, Rupert Ross reminds us Canadians of European ancestry of similar misinterpretations. We tend to regard Canadian aboriginals as uncaring parents, failing to see their parental lack of directiveness as expressions of ethical regard. While Merlan is persuasive in allowing us to see the expression of due regard in these situations, it does not seem possible for us to do the same, to allow our children the freedom that might result in various harms. We do not see how to show our care, concern, and interest in friends without the variety of questions we pose. By contrast, we need no interpretive help to understand the assertions of aggrieved Aboriginals that others are "rubbishing them." Like our own minorities' assertions that others are "dissing them," these are pure and pungent expressions of the common and familiar demand for autonomy and due regard.

# PART FIVE

# Ethics and Formality

# Natural Manners: Etiquette, Ethics, and Sincerity in American Conduct Manuals

*Shirley Yeung*

What can the rules of etiquette that govern speech reveal about broader models of good conduct? And what is the broader relationship of etiquette to ethics? In a North American context, it might appear that the seemingly arbitrary constraints upon everyday conduct posed by etiquette (in the form of table manners or proper forms of address, leave-taking, apologizing, etc.) stand at a firm arm's length from enduring ethical inquiry into what is good, what is right, and considerations of the kind of life one ought to live. It is unlikely, after all, that the occasional forgetting of one's table manners will be considered unethical behavior. Yet, to the extent that "etiquette" might be considered an attempt to articulate a body of rules concerning proper conduct in everyday encounters, a look at the relationship of etiquette to ethics is fruitful. As multiple "prescriptions governing comportment in life's [ordinary] interactions" (Scapp and Seitz 2007: 2), do notions of proper etiquette overlap or answer to broader ethical questions that might outline the contours of a good life? Is etiquette merely "ethics in the diminutive—a set of smaller, less binding terms of conduct"? (MacKendrick 2007:199). Or are understandings of ethical conduct more closely tied to etiquette than they initially appear? In what ways do these considerations relate to speech, and to learning and teaching the "art of conversation"? In considering some of these questions, I look to nine-teenth-century American etiquette manuals with an eye toward how cer-tain understandings of the "good conversationalist" can shed light on the connection between manners and "morals," outlining what some etiquette experts have called an "ethics of talking" (Hervey 1853). I focus here on a number of key mid- to late-nineteenth-century conduct texts, including titles such as *Rhetoric of Conversation* (1853), *Plain Thoughts on the Art of Living* (1868), and *Frost's Laws and By-Laws of American Society* (1869), that aimed to impart the principles of propriety to a largely middle-class Amer-ican readership. This genre is interesting for the sheer number of texts produced during this time—which, from the 1820s onward, can be traced to middle-class anxieties about social mobility and the need for social "gate-keeping" practices (Hemphill 1999)—but also because of the com-monsense understandings of proper etiquette that we, in the present day, have arguably inherited from these early sources.

I will briefly situate late-nineteenth-century etiquette manuals in the context of the historical rise of an American middle class and will focus on a few general principles of conversational etiquette across a series of texts. By contrast to the notion of etiquette as an "artificial" external form or merely a set of gate-keeping rituals, I hope to show how manners were inextricably linked to morality and standards of authenticity and sincerity. Discourses on how to learn the habits of good etiquette placed emphasis not only on acquiring a set of procedures for social interaction but on acquiring the qualities of character that etiquette was intended to express. This might be considered a model of "natural manners," in which speech would not only serve as a direct reflection of an individual's moral and ethical commitments but, when disciplined, could also "act on the heart and reform it" (Hirschkind 2001: 627) effectively—and perhaps also af-fectively—transforming a speaker's ethical disposition. I suggest that learning "manners" was not merely a matter of managing strategic im-pressions but entailed a practical form of ethical self-cultivation and im-provement—one that aimed to discipline moral reflexes through the "externals" of speech, gesture, and other embodied dispositions, some-what similar to the printed and aural materials of Islamic ethical discipline described by Charles Hirschkind (2001, 2006) and Saba Mahmood (2005). I frame this "ethical side of manners" with reference to prior discussions of "sincerity" (Keane 2007) and "conviction" (Lambek 2007a), and con-clude with a brief discussion that reconsiders the broader relationship of ethics to etiquette.

## Learning to Behave

In their simplest form, American etiquette books published during the mid to late nineteenth century offered no shortage of directives for the reader desiring to "learn to behave" (Newton 1994), providing scripts for face-to-face interaction in ordinary situations. Hazel Barnes (2007: 240) points out that the connotation of the French *étiquette* links its English counterpart to notions of the "ticket" or the "label"—one that allows an individual entry or admission into an otherwise closed-off social circle.[1] Proper etiquette, as such, was largely the preoccupation of a "liminal" and emergent middle-class.[2] As Micki McGee (2005) writes in her study of self-help literature in America, the display of propriety during the late nineteenth century allowed individuals to evidence their position as members of "good society" precisely at a time when social classifications were in flux. The proliferation of etiquette texts, in other words, mediated and helped to define shifting class relations, drawing a clear dividing line between the middle and lower classes, while implying that the line between the middle and upper classes was porous and permeable. Proper etiquette provided one way of enacting the ascendance of an American middle class that, given the successes of commercial and industrial capitalism, was assuming an ever greater position of cultural authority, but one accompanied by a degree of ambiguity about questions of relative social positioning and status (Hemphill 1999). As ordinary rituals of access, manners provided an answer to the liminality of middle-classness; the ritualization of the everyday was "necessary to clarify the emerging social order" (ibid. 157).

According to some historians of manners, etiquette literature also provided a venue for the expression of a distinctly American and republican code of conduct—one in which it was possible to espouse democracy and market imperatives at the same time (ibid. 130) and in which personal

---

1. In this vein, the anonymous author of *The Laws of Etiquette* (1836), "A. Gentleman," writes: "Every man is naturally desirous of finding entrance into the best society of his country, and it becomes therefore a matter of importance to ascertain what qualifications are demanded for admittance."

2. This is evident from the advice literature itself: for instance, following a discussion of lower- and upper-classes manners, Frost writes: "there is another exceedingly large class of society, which . . . from circumstance lacks the cultivation which alone will bring conduct into such training as will fit it practically for exhibition in society. To the persons comprising this class, it is not only a source of regret, but of absolute pain, to be ignorant of the rules which make society cohere. It is for such persons . . . often at fault upon questions of detail . . . that this code of Modern Etiquette has been prepared" (1869: 8).

wealth and professional success were equated with civic virtue, merit, and divine election (McGee 2005). The "self-made man" was the well-known protagonist of this national dream—having read an etiquette manual or two, he would master the rules of proper comportment and gain entry into the right social circles. The codification and proliferation of daily rituals of conduct might be considered, in this light, a partial answer to the contradictions inherent in American society before the turn of the twentieth century—those between the cultural ideals of personal freedom, equality, and the individual pursuit of happiness, on the one hand, and the acknowledged social and material inequalities and differentials upon which capitalist logics of accumulation necessarily rest. Quite simply, as Hemphill (1999) observes, nineteenth century Americans cherished democracy while inhabiting a world of increasing economic disparities.[3] It is not surprising, to invoke Bourdieu, that many conduct authors considered the proper display of manners to consist in practiced forms of social currency that, if wisely invested, could promise returns in the form of upward mobility. For etiquette expert William Mathews, "the little courtesies which form the small change of life may appear, separately, of little moment, but, like the spare minutes, or the penny a day which amount to so enormous sums in a lifetime, they owe their importance to repetition and accumulation" (1872: 146).

Since the self-made gentleman was distinguished from the well-mannered lady, the rules of etiquette also mirrored and constituted an increasingly gender-segregated society sectioned into private and public spheres. When addressing gentlemen, the rules of etiquette and decorum aimed to ensure success in public life and enterprise; the public rituals of greeting in the street, leave-taking at social gatherings, and making introductions among the unacquainted therefore took up considerable space in men's guidebooks. Consider the character traits embodied in the proper (or improper) handshake: "In shaking hands, do not try to wring them off the wrists, nor press them as in a vise, nor pull them as though they were bell-handles. . . . Let the palms grasp each other firmly, but without any display of energy. . . . Shake the hand moderately for a moment, then release it" (Frost 1869: 25). Similarly, when out for a stroll, it was only proper etiquette for a gentleman to "always return a bow made to him in the street,

---

3. As Kelly's (2001) discussion of Soviet advice literature reminds us, however, etiquette and self-improvement discourses can just as easily be mobilized in the service of ideals of collective elevation and egalitarianism as they can be employed as tools for maintaining a "myth of mobility" within an otherwise fixed social hierarchy, as in the American case.

even if he fails to recognize the person who makes it" (ibid. 28). By contrast, advice literature addressed to late-nineteenth-century women offered counsel on embodying the model of the "virtuous maid" and stressed domestic duty and occupations, piety, obedience, modesty, charity, and sobriety (Newton 1994: 66). In fact, women were counseled to be more vigilant than men of their possible breaches of etiquette and to master the laws to a finer degree. According to *Frost's Laws and By-Laws of American Society*, a woman "must be even more upon her guard than a man in all those niceties of speech, look and manner, which are the especial and indispensable credentials of good breeding. Every little drawing-room ceremonial, all the laws of society, the whole etiquette of hospitality must be familiar to her" (1869: 15).

The manners historian C. Dalett Hemphill (1999) notes that, among their multiple meanings in American history, manners constitute a system of social regulation and are a form of government that enacts and enforces a particular hierarchical social order. In particular, Hemphill suggests that notions of propriety have played an important role in maintaining divisions of gender and class in a society that, as discussed above, has historically refused to acknowledge social stratification in its narratives of success and citizenship. By this light, the classic nineteenth-century etiquette book presents a role-teaching tool in the "conduct of conduct" (Gordon 1991: 5). Some conduct authors would have agreed with this description. For Sarah Annie Frost, the history of etiquette is one in which "manners were originally the expression of submission [of] the weaker to the stronger . . . every salutation is to this day an act of worship. Hence, the commonest acts, phrases, and signs . . . date from those earlier stages when the strong hand ruled, and the inferior demonstrated his allegiance by studied servility" (1869: 28).

However, given these arguments for etiquette as a necessary and regulatory tool of stratification by both authors and historians, it is crucial to note that etiquette experts often counseled against an overly rigid adherence to the imperatives of propriety. For all of their concern with the social laws and by-laws of conduct, authors acknowledged that manners, like any system of law or governance, ultimately violates if employed to an excessive degree: "Etiquette, like every other human institution, is of course liable to abuse; it may be transformed from a convenient and wholesome means of producing universal comfort into an inconvenient and burdensome restraint upon freedom and ease" (ibid. 9). But what does it mean to say that etiquette can be abused? And which freedoms does this abuse potentially violate? If we accept that propriety was understood merely as outward performance, as purely formal procedure, or as a cosmetic veneer applied to polish behavior, then talk about the hazards to freedom and ease seems unwarranted (perhaps akin to advising an amateur cook against following a recipe too perfectly in order to safeguard his personal freedom).

In place of promoting a speaking subject who could perfectly reproduce scripted utterances, I suggest that the model subject of the etiquette manual would not merely reproduce written imperatives but engage in actions that would reflect personal virtue and moral development. This is especially clear in common pieces of advice about conversational etiquette, the role of speech in acquiring certain moral dispositions, and the importance of being earnest or sincere in one's words. In the next section, I discuss how manners were not merely modeled as unquestionable prescriptions but were the very tools that could constitute certain kinds of freedom, virtue, and ethical personhood.

## Naturally Speaking: Etiquette as Sincerity

> In private, watch your thoughts; in your family, watch your temper;
> in society, watch your tongue.
>
> —Rhetoric of Conversation (1853)

> Sincerity embellishes every virtuous action.
>
> —The Gentleman's Book of Etiquette (1873)

The prescriptions above reveal an enduring paradox that continues to haunt our ordinary understandings of speech and action: Quite simply, how is it possible to "watch our tongues" while speaking and acting sincerely? As Webb Keane (2002) points out, sincere speech in the context of Protestant conversion was (and for us, continues to be) a normative ideal in which spoken words have the capacity to express inner states of being. Sincerity, as self-conscious practice, also reveals something about the speaker—sincere speech evidences not only full self-knowledge but the intention to make "external" words align and correspond with "internal" thoughts (Keane 2002, 2007). Historically, the view that language could act as a tool of transparent transmission not only enabled notions of scientific objectivity but, in the missionary context, held out the promise of a

personal relationship to the transcendent, liberation from social entangle-
ments, and the presence of an inner "self" inaccessible to authority, effectively freed from compulsion or external coercion (ibid.).

When held up against this standard of sincerity, the external rules governing conversational etiquette might be seen as a barrier to authenticity,
if not a form of outright deception. If language should only be used to
reveal inner truths, then prescriptions for proper speech can only derail
sincerity, since etiquette, like any script, can be perfected regardless of
individual sentiment. Often taking on the tone of commandment, some of
these rules evince this ethic of restraint and concealment whereby etiquette is what one *does not* do:

Avoid gossip and flattery. (Hartley 1873: 27)

In public, never differ from anybody, nor from anything. The agreeable
[person] is one who agrees. (Gentleman 1836)

It is a breach of etiquette to laugh at your own wit. If others will not do
that for you, you had better let your remark pass unnoticed. (Frost 1869:
171)

We should not speak against a vice which individuals of the party are known
or suspected to be guilty of. (Hervey 1853: 80)

When you begin to lose your temper, stop talking. (Gladden 1868: 65)

Never criticize any dish before you. If a dish is distasteful to you, decline
it, but make no remarks. (Hartley 1873: 55)

It is better to please in conversation than to shine in it. (Gladden 1868: 71)

Never interrogate a person whose mouth is full. (Hervey 1852: 231)

These rules included the now nearly ubiquitous caution that "Political and
religious topics are not in good taste" (Frost 1869: 41). The sentiment that
"society is a harlequin stage in which you never appear in your own dress,
nor without a mask" (Gentleman 1836) might capture the spirit of these
directives; the importance of refraining from criticizing an unappetizing
dish, singing your own praises, or losing your temper underscores the concealment of inner states and the maintenance of vigilance and self-consciousness—regardless of our thoughts and sentiments, we must hold our
tongues against impulse so as not to spoil the party.

Discourses on etiquette present another model for speech, however,
which I would like to emphasize. In this model, sincerity, not deception,
could result from good manners and a properly cultivated heart. Indeed,

the end goal for many advice writers—and perhaps also for polite practitioners—was to make manners sincere, blurring distinctions between
character and outward comportment, authenticity and artifice, virtue and
veneer. However strict and exacting the "management of the tongue"
(Hervey 1853) may have been, several authors maintain a distinction between a false or deceptive propriety consisting only of outward forms and
a truer or more natural grace, which would spring from moral disposition.
The former might constitute what Austin (1963) has called "abuse" in his
discussion of performatives; the latter suggests that manners, once mas-
tered, become natural expressions of the kind of person one has become.
To illustrate, Robert Tomes's *Bazar Book of Decorum* warns disapprovingly
against employing easy forms of "deceit which fashion seems to sanction":

> It is astonishing the number of falsehoods one has to utter to make a
> respectable figure in what is called society. . . . If anyone should drop the
> lying words of love, friendship, esteem, and admiration, and use only those
> expressions which denote the actual relations of ordinary mortals, he or she
> would be speedily thrust out . . . this confirms the social necessity of the
> lie, for in the most ordinary relations of life, we are compelled to make use
> of it . . . [But] where the conventional falsehood is most in vogue, there
> genuine truth is least common. . . . When people are asked to "stay," to
> "call again," [or] "to drop in to dinner" it is seldom wished that they should
> do either. These are the polite lies . . . of society which cannot be justified
> by any principle of morals. (1870: 130, 131)

Other authors criticized the single-minded perfection of one's utterances to the exclusion of a lived devotion to cultivating "spiritual graces"
(Frost 1869: 15), of which artful speech should be the natural reflection.
Interestingly, I suggest that writers were as concerned about correct execution as they were with whether or not practice was tethered to an abiding commitment to authenticating good manners. Given this anxiety, it
can clearly be seen how speech runs the risk of being wrongly wielded or
"abused" in the form of elegant but empty utterances. In the *Principles
of Courtesy*, for instance, Hervey criticizes the so-called "poser," whose
"concern is not whether an action be right, but whether it be gracefully
performed; not whether a remark be true, but whether it be elegantly
expressed. . . . Since manners consist much in appearances, those who are
anxious to preserve their place in the good opinion of others are tempted
to *exhibit the symbol when they cannot show the substance. . . . But manners can
never be divorced from morals*" (1852: 90, emphasis added). Likewise, in the
*Laws and By-Laws*, Frost argues for the "absurdity" of social interactions
in which

a regard for formal mannerism takes the place of the easy grace that is the mark of true politeness which [is] habitual [and] never offensively prominent. . . . The mere form over-riding and hiding the spirit which should control and guide it . . . must inevitably produce discomfort. . . . *Nature is thus made the slave of Art, instead of Art taking its proper place as the handmaid to Nature.* (1869: 10, emphasis added)

And where words were considered forms of exchanged currency ("words are coins . . . they who do not have them suffer a more pitiable poverty than others who have not a penny in their pocket"; Burgess 1873: 10), a general caution was issued against words "of the wrong stamp . . . [and persons] possessed only of counterfeit cash" (ibid. 10).[4] Why, we might ask, did authors put painful effort into detailing the everyday laws of proper conduct only to caution against the threat of counterfeit courtesy, or the "the supposed excesses of ritual" (Keane 2007: 199)?

I suggest that at the heart of a seemingly external etiquette lies, quite simply, ethics—that is, the imperative to align principle with habitual practice in bringing about, paradoxically, one's own virtue and sincerity through disciplined effort. Through practice, one could acquire the nine-teenth-century American virtues that mattered: modesty, politeness, kind-ness, charity, courage, humility, unselfishness, generosity, gratitude, indeed, Christian piety itself. In the ideal, the practice of manners was aimed at cultivating habitual social graces that would become natural and authentic with time. Cecil Hartley expresses this sentiment clearly in *The Gentleman's Book of Etiquette*:

If you wear [the mask of politeness] with the sincere desire to . . . make all the little meetings of life pass smoothly and agreeably, it will soon cease to be a mask, but you will find that the manner which you at first put on to give pleasure has become natural to you. . . . Where ever you have assumed a virtue to please others, you will find the virtue becoming habitual and natural and part of yourself. *Do not look upon the rules of etiquette as deceptions. They are just as often vehicles for the expression of sincere feeling as they are the mask to conceal a want of it.* (1873: 32, emphasis added)

Frost echoes this sentiment: "Etiquette, it is sometimes urged, is used to cloak what is hollow, unmeaning and false, yet may it not also drape grace-fully what is true and important? . . . Is truth, then, a hedgehog, always

---

4. The notion that words and acts constitute a form of currency is interesting in light of everyday English idioms concerning social graces. These include no-tions of "paying a compliment," "paying a visit," "paying respect," "paying hom-age," and "putting your money where your mouth is.'

bristling and offensive?" (1869: 13). More than the capacity to persuade, to impress, or to engage others with one's speech, artful conversation "is a reflex of character . . . strive as we may, we cannot always be acting. Let us, therefore, cultivate a tone of mind and a habit of life, the betrayal of which need not put us to shame in the company of the wise, and the rest will be easy" (ibid. 48). For George Hervey, masterly speakers "succeed because they speak just what they mean" (1853: 272). And according to Washington Gladden, we enjoy the company of a good conversationalist "without being constantly on our guard against irony or double-entendre. Sincerity is a distinguishing quality of the good talker" (1868: 65). Simply put, "if you would talk well, you must live well" (ibid. 72).

What emerges as critical here is the *sincere desire to become sincere*, where sincerity is as much the result of disciplined cultivation as it is the quality of outright earnestness. The mimetic speech of manners might be said here to possess the power to "infiltrate the soul" and transform it (Hirschkind citing Burnyeat 2001: 639). Sincerity is, further, much more than talk unbridled or the blunt expression of all passions; it is itself already ethically charged. Frankness might be considered a necessary but insufficient quality of "artful speech" because honesty is only applauded as sincerity when a speaker upholds some notion of right conduct.[5] If sincerity, being intentional and self-consciously practiced, says something about the very character of the speaker (Keane 2007: 211), then the notion of a sincere boaster, a sincere cynic, a sincere gossip, or of sincere selfishness puts communicative transparency at the service of impropriety, throwing its virtue into question. "Sincerity," then, is arguably synonymous with "sincerely good." The rules of conversational etiquette, in this light, create a model for practice in which artful speech is both "the index of the soul" (Frost 1869: 15) and the means by which speakers become sincere and ethically attuned. In this way, conduct manuals might be considered "ethical materials" (Mahmood 2004: 82) akin, in a secular context, to the Islamic pedagogical literature described by Mahmood (2004) and the cassette-tape sermons discussed by Hirschkind (2001, 2006)—that is, they address practical questions of virtuous conduct in the everyday and assist practitioners in creating certain moral sensibilities and embodied or gestural dispositions. Quite simply, mastering etiquette held the promise of both virtuous authenticity and authentic virtue.

---

5. This reading partly draws on the suggestion made by Austin that "sincerity . . . does not suffice to set [a performative utterance] beyond the reach of all criticism" (1963: 30). There is still the remaining question about whether a sincerely issued (performative) utterance is good, just, or fair (ibid. 32).

Because sincerity is, here, less the cause than the consequence of artful speech, we might look at this art of speaking as one model for acquiring seriousness or "conviction" (Lambek 2007a) in speech and action. Like sincerity, the notion of conviction assumes that one begins with a degree of seriousness toward one's conduct, but it reminds us that self-knowledge and seriousness are not always present at the outset of a course of action, though they can come about as its result. The notion of conviction underscores how, rather than "doing what one means," oftentimes "one means what one does" (Lambek 2007a). By this light, if the common present-day remedy for insincerity or hypocrisy is the injunction to "practice what you preach" (to compel actions to fall in line with avowed commitments), then the notion of conviction recognizes the converse—that "practice makes perfect" or, simpler yet, that "practice perfects" (or that avowed commitments can also follow upon actions). Perhaps it is in this fashion that the mimetic formalism entailed in manners might "soon cease to be a mask" (Hartley 1873: 32). If acquiring conviction is a "habit of life" (Frost 1869: 48) that can be discerned only restrospectively, and if manners "become natural" through ongoing practice, what more might be said about the relationship between the seemingly minor practice of manners and the ongoing practice of ethical habits of living?

## Etiquette and Ethics: Do Manners Matter?

So far, my focus has been on accounts of what might be called "sincere etiquette" or natural manners—with how a preoccupation with seemingly external formalities could include a concern with "the heart," inner qualities, and dispositions. Among their maxims and imperatives, etiquette books conveyed a will to be "sincerely good." This standard of authenticity not only prompted authors to warn against the hollow mimicry of fashionable but deceptive modes of comportment but was also what etiquette training promised. The ongoing exercise of etiquette could be the means to both social mastery and personal virtue. While this essay has been limited to a treatment of texts, and I have not been able to address the gap between written rules and the practice of manners in the everyday, this very gap between prescription and practice opens up a space for reflecting on the broader relationship between etiquette and practical ethics.

Etiquette has been described as a form of minor ethics, situated midway between ethics, concerning the kind of life one ought to live, and aesthetics, concerning what is beautiful or pleasing (Scapp and Seitz 2007: 4). In other words, manners might be nothing more than the meeting place between grace and goodness. Our understanding of manners also largely depends on whether they are viewed as a means or an end. As a means, etiquette is "the place to turn for advice on what to wear to a wedding or a funeral, but hardly the source for counsel on matters of life and death" (ibid. 2). The occasional violation of certain rules of etiquette (laughing at your own jokes, interrupting someone mid-sentence, neglecting to offer a timely "thank you," etc.) is rarely labeled "unethical." Conversely, impeccable manners do not provide a sure sign of what is commonly understand to be ethical conduct. If the process of learning social engagement through forms of etiquette is little more than strict adherence to a set of handed-down rules, then manners might even be considered an obstacle to ethical conduct to the degree that a model of ethics also presupposes a particular understanding of human freedom (Laidlaw 2002: 315).

Yet etiquette, as a set of guidelines, is meant to be practiced. The suggestion that one should live well in order to speak well implies not only that etiquette engages with a particular model of ethical living but that manners are an important aspect of its habitual and practical realization. As in the earlier discussion of "seriousness" (Lambek 2007a), one's words and gestures not only reflect prior thoughts or sentiments but can be the means through which the contours of ethical conduct can later be discerned. In addition, social gestures, rituals, and habits also acknowledge, enact, and recreate a certain social order (Newton 1994: 4), irrespective of the views of those individuals who constitute it. As Rappaport points out in his discussion of ritual and liturgical performance, participation in and acceptance of a particular order through ritual is independent of inner states of belief or doubt: "it is the visible, explicit, public act of acceptance, and not the invisible, ambiguous, private sentiment which is socially and morally binding" (1999: 122). To the degree that manners are everyday rituals that participate in constituting social orders, this suggests that even a thoroughly insincere politeness leaves intact an acceptance of the order in which it is performed (and which it thereby creates). Perhaps in implicit recognition of this aspect of etiquette, some present-day thinkers have advanced the notion of "resistant comportment," whereby new manners (non-manners?) can signal refusal of one social order or another. And if "questioning contemporary etiquette is already to risk disappropriating oneself from the domain of propriety, thereby rendering oneself as either inappropriate, incoherent . . . or psychologically dysfunctional" (Hamann 2007: 62, 65), then certain questions emerge as salient: Who, after all, defines the terms of "rudeness" and to what end? If ostensible rudeness resists and repudiates not only "politeness" but the social order that defines propriety itself, when and where does this become an ethical question? Where is impropriety ethical?

But etiquette is linked to ethics and matters of judgment in a much simpler way. To the degree that the discipline of etiquette is the result of ongoing practice, even the strictest follower of Miss Manners must determine when one rule or another is appropriate—whether, given a particular context, an otherwise golden silence borders on cold reserve, whether the brilliant anecdote begins to grow tiresome, whether frankness is bound to injure, or whether, quite simply, the rules of polite conversation have reached their limit, as in the speech genre Stanley Cavell (2005a) calls "passionate utterance." These are instances in which we speak to single one another out, demand a response (whether forgiveness, love, an apology, etc.), and in doing so subject ourselves and our words to the vulnerabilities of a situation whose outcome we can neither calculate nor predict. Unscripted, the passionate utterance is not polite "participation in the order of law, [but] an invitation to improvisation in the disorders of desire" (ibid. 19). In this light, even a model sincerity must contend with the question posed by Cavell of how it is bearable to lay claim to a voice or signature "that always escapes us, or is stolen" (ibid. 65), whereby what we say and mean (and thus what we are held responsible for) might not be what others understand, nor necessarily what we will understand ourselves to have meant in hindsight. This is an awareness that even sincere speech can and does "become the prey of external forces which attach to it something totally different from what it is explicitly, and drive it into alien and distant consequences" (Hegel 1945: 80). Etiquette is, here, a concern for ethics, because there appear to be no remedies for this "incessant and unending vulnerability of human action" (Cavell 1995a: 53)—even the virtuous practice of propriety is itself a form of ethical improvisation. A world of difference lies, after all, between knowing when to keep quiet and when to speak up, when to mind our p's and q's and when to risk rudeness—but these are all questions that manners manuals cannot adequately address. If learning the difference, and thus learning both artful and ethical speech, consists of more than a reliance on procedural knowledge (Lambek 2007a) or conformity to a set of precepts, and if it is possible to "do things with words" (Austin 1963), then etiquette already is inherently ethical—part of mastering a rule, method, or maxim is knowing when it has arrived at its limits. Of the perfectly executed performative, one might still ask, as Austin does, "Agreed, I spoke in all sincerity . . . I was fully justified perhaps, but was I right?" (ibid. 31).

## Conclusion

The relationship between manners and morals, or etiquette and ethics, is complex. Etiquette is not merely a set of postures and precepts, nor is it "ethics-lite." As I have tried to show, nineteenth-century courtesies were surely aimed at governing comportment but were also portrayed as the means by which certain moral dispositions could be acquired and cultivated. This was a vision in which speech could infiltrate and transform the heart and where sincerity was as much a perfectible capacity as it was a characteristic belonging to the already virtuous. But my account of "natural manners" provides only one way of linking etiquette to the ethical. If speech participates in constituting social orders and if no regime of speech can completely eliminate the vulnerabilities (or the possibilities) entailed in becoming intelligible—and thus never eliminate the need to weigh the ethical consequences of our and others' words—then a consideration of manners reinvites us not only to consider the philosophical question of whether or not perfect sincerity is possible but to consider what models of ethical personhood are embodied and materialized in everyday words and gestures. We might, then, shift focus from whether we and our interlocutors really "say what we mean" to looking at what ordinary utterances accept, achieve, complete and create. Invoking Austin, this calls for an attentiveness to how we do things with words, and in turn, to how words do things with us.

### ACKNOWLEDGMENTS

My (sincere) interest in sincerity was first inspired by the seminar Speaking Subjects: Topics on the Borderland of Anthropology, Linguistics, and Philosophy, co-taught in Fall 2006 by Michael Lambek, Jack Sidnell, and Paul Antze at the University of Toronto. This paper draws directly on that stimulating and spirited discussion. I am also indebted to Michael Lambek for his encouragement and comments throughout and for very generously extending the opportunity to give an earlier draft of this paper at the Anthropology of Ordinary Ethics symposium, which he hosted with great warmth at the Center for Ethics at the University of Toronto. I am additionally grateful for the incisive discussion and comments of discussant Veena Das and other workshop participants, and for the support of the Social Sciences and Humanities Research Council of Canada. All oversights remain my own.

# "They Did It Like A Song": Ethics, Aesthetics, and Tradition in Hopi Legal Discourse

*Justin B. Richland*

In early November 2000, just after I had moved to the Hopi reservation for the year, I found myself confronted with the tumult that can be Hopi tribal politics, and the role that language ideologies and metadiscourse play in it. At the time I was living in the home of a member of the Hopi Tribal Council, the tribe's legislative body, who had been selected to head a committee investigating the actions of a staff assistant to the vice chairman of the tribe. The council had received complaints that the assistant in question had repeatedly misrepresented himself and the tribe, telling various tribal department heads that they were under investigation when they weren't, demanding access to files he was not authorized to examine, and taking other actions in an effort to get information relevant to his personal interests. After hearing evidence in this matter, the committee recommended to the council that the staff assistant be reprimanded and/or terminated by the vice chairman. The committee also recommended that the vice chairman be required to come before the council within the next five days to report on the actions he had taken to resolve this matter. The council approved the recommendations and gave the vice chairman orders to act pursuant to them. However, those five days passed with no word from the vice chairman's office regarding these matters.

I learned from my friend that the vice chairman's refusal to report was part of a larger pattern of defiant behavior that he had displayed toward the Tribal Council after it had passed a resolution reducing the powers of his office. She told me this as we sat after dinner with her elder brother in their late mother's home, warming ourselves by a fire to fight the chill of a fall desert evening. It seems that the reason why the powers of the vice chairman's office had been reduced in the first place was that he had failed to fulfill the responsibilities that came with them. At the same time, the vice chairman never missed a chance to speak in public. During these speeches, she explained, he'd almost always invoke his authority as a member of his village's Bear clan, its founding clan, and thus claim a considerable seat of traditional authority. And without fail he would follow this with what my friend described as "the most beautiful prayer," in which he reiterated his responsibility, as a member of a founding clan, to protect the welfare of the entire Hopi population, referring to them in Hopi and English in the traditional refrain as "our children." Given these performances, the irony of the vice chairman's truculent responses to her committee's investigation was not lost on my host. Nor was it lost on others. She explained, "People are going up to him at all levels in the government saying that what he is doing now goes against those very words."

As she told me this story, she seemed rather shocked by the whole affair. But when her older brother—a leading figure in both Hopi tribal governance and his village's ceremonial life—finally chimed in, his ironic reflections showed more weariness than surprise. He suggested that this is a well-known problem within the Hopi community, one that regularly appears not only in its tribal political arenas but in its ceremonial ones as well. "Well this is nothing new," he said, "I go to the *katsinkiy* [where ceremonial participants rest between performances] to smoke, and there are these guys who give long, elaborate statements . . . using very impressive words. And then they leave . . . because that is why they came. My grandfather used to say that these guys just did these things *like they were songs.*"

It is not particularly surprising that he would compare the problems with the vice chairman and his staff to those he had faced in the course of his extensive ceremonial experience. Despite the number of pickup trucks crossing the Hopi reservation with stickers on their bumpers screaming "No Politics in the Kiva!" or the regular requests by litigants in Hopi tribal court to postpone their oral arguments during the kachina ceremonials, the fact is that Hopi ritual life is deeply political and often contentious. Nor is it surprising that his comments would involve a metadiscursive comparison between political discourses and Hopi ritual performance. Paul Kroskrity and others have argued eloquently for a robust ideology across the Pueblo communities of the Southwest, in which ceremonial practices and their highly formalized language, kinesics, and built spaces are understood as an ideal against which all other communicative events are measured (Kroskrity 1993, Ortiz 1972).

What did strike me was the extent to which my host's brother was willing to interrogate the talk of both contemporary Hopi politicians and the ceremonial actors he had observed for their apparent lack of sincerity—and, moreover, that this lack of sincerity was somehow revealed in their otherwise quite appropriate use of ceremonial speech and the ideologies of strict conventionalism that surround it. This seems to suggest that anthropological themes of Pueblo ritual conservatism (Dozier 1970, Ortiz 1972), in which "innovation is neither desired nor tolerated" (Kroskrity 1993: 36), tell only part of the story, explaining what might be necessary but not sufficient to the efficacious execution of ceremonial acts. It also gives support to recent efforts to rethink certain shopworn conceptualizations of Pueblo personhood that, since Mauss, have argued that these peoples understand the self through tokens of a ritual type (dramatis personae, positional identities) rather than as an individuated, fully intending agent (Mauss 1985 [1938], but see Whiteley 1998). How, and under what circumstances, can Hopi social actors like my host's brother pierce the ideological valorization of the proper performance of ritual formulas to demand that such speech also come from the speaker's "heart" (as Hopi regularly say)? What relation do Hopi see between formulaic action and individual intention, a view that seems, under some conditions, to equate aesthetics and ethics, beauty and moral worth, but in others holds them apart?

Building on linguistic anthropological research that explores the relationship between intentionality and speech activity generally, and the formality of ritual oratory in particular, I will argue that these metadiscourses of Hopi aesthetics and ethics, and the manner in which they are applied in actual moments of political speech and interaction, suggest no simple or fixed reconciliation between Hopi notions of sentiment and speech. Rather, they are deployed by Hopi social actors as interpretive frames for evaluating the sociopolitical significance of speech acts. I will try to ascertain the circumstances in and through which Hopi seem willing and able to evaluate the discourses of others for their aesthetic value, and when they judge them for sincerity. I will ask when and how Hopi see these two metrics as reposing on each other, so that evidence of a speaker's ethics can be located in his or her oratorical performances. I will then ask when and how they are disentangled by Hopi, as in the evaluation offered by my host's brother, in which deployment of the proper speech formula by a speaker offers no purchase for evaluating his or her intentions. In this sense, and to the extent that I will support these claims with analyses of Hopi courtroom argumentation, this essay develops earlier inquiries I have made into what I have called the *multiple calculations of meaning* that Hopi make in their political and juridical discourses (Richland 2006), here extending the analysis to consider the multiplicity of Hopi normative evaluations and their consequences, both microinteractional and macropolitical.

## *Formality and Intentionality in "Traditional" Oratory*

In the introduction to his groundbreaking edited volume on "traditional" political oratory, Maurice Bloch endeavors to map a relationship between the exercise of sociopolitical power and the formal character of ritualized speech. He argues that formalized speech acts—those characterized by patterned prosodics (pitch contours, meter, and rhyme), reliance on textual formulas (proverbs, tropes, scripture), specialized grammatico-syntatic forms and usages (co-occurrence rules, collocation), and other rarefied stylistics (when compared to everyday conversation)—constitute a kind of "impoverished language" whose restrictions on form create a speech-event context within which speakers can constrain how others might respond to them (Bloch 1975: 13). Joining an analytic concern with turn-taking sequences in conversation and linguistic-anthropological notions of politeness, Bloch suggests that formal speech works to constrain what can count as a felicitous response, restricting not just *how* such responses can be fashioned but by *whom* they can be uttered and *what* they can mean. He describes a request scenario, for example: "if a superior addresses an inferior, the latter, if he accepts to answer within the formalized code imposed on the situation (and he will rarely be in a position to do anything else) will find himself in a position where he cannot say 'no'" (ibid. 19).

Indeed, says Bloch, the constraining power of formalized speech is efficacious in multiple ways. At the very same time that respondents must enact a limited repertoire of utterances that have been prompted by the formal speech, the speaker elides his or her own interests and intentions through usages that mark the speech as nothing more than iterations of traditional formulas that have been demanded of those occupying their social roles "from time immemorial" (ibid.). In conjunction with the fact that access to formalized oratory resources in traditional societies is restricted to certain subgroups, Bloch argues that its political power is virtually always hegemonic in its effects: "Formalisation is thus a form of power for the powerful rather than simply a tool of coercion available to anybody" (ibid. 23). For those who would wish to stand against the coercions of formal speech, says Bloch, the only option is to reject the usage in toto: "A total refusal of the power of formalisation . . . is necessary since only total refusal is possible in the face of total imposition" (ibid. 25).

Subsequent critiques of Bloch's analyses of traditional oratory (Irvine 1979, Meyers and Brenneis 1984) have taken him to task for eliding different dimensions of formality—linguistic and pragmatic, social structural, and event contextual—and assuming a one-to-one relationship (causal or correlational) between them. When these are disentangled, as in Judith Irvine's cross-cultural analysis of oratory among the Wolof, Mursi, and Ilongot, what emerges is the extent to which ritualized events of political oratory actually reveal a cline of formalization, in which only certain aspects of formality are ever deployed by social actors in particular speech events and are invoked to accomplish rather different communicative functions. As such, she suggests, "the argument that formalizing a social occasion reduces its participants' political freedom can hold true only in limited ways" (Irvine 1979: 780), and certainly not in ways that are ever wholly determined by the use of formal speech alone, as Bloch seems to argue.

Fred Meyers and Don Brenneis, likewise, suggest that Bloch's analyses belie an underlying ambiguity about the power of formalization. While Bloch speaks as if this power is a coercive one deployed by the already powerful, he nonetheless acknowledges "that such 'formal' speech constrains the speaker's alternatives as well" (Meyers and Brenneis 1984: 9). Given his argument that formal speech relies so heavily on received textual formulas "of an eternal and fixed [i.e., traditional] order" as to make it all but impossible "to communicate messages concerning particular events," he implies that those who might use such speech are constrained in their capacity to press their own political intentions and influence. Nonetheless, these critics say, Bloch insists on speaking about formalized speech "at the level of action, referring to agents' capacities of achieving outcomes" (ibid.). Therefore, his approach makes it hard to see the power in such formalization as "more than individual strategies, as deeply involved in the reproduction of structures of social relations" (ibid. 10).

In raising these questions of intentionality, Myers and Brenneis link up with a broader, abiding theme in linguistic anthropology, one that involves the centrality of speaker intentions in meaning making more generally (see Duranti 1993b for a good review). In large measure, this scholarship emerged both in the spirit and with the aim of refuting the principles of speech act theory proffered by John Searle (1969) and claims to the universality of intention-driven models of meaning making.

Elsewhere I have argued that Hopi calculations regarding the meaningfulness of speech acts do not involve a single uniform metric across the varying contexts of everyday interaction (Richland 2005). Rather, and in a manner that echoes many of Irvine's insights above, I have suggested that Hopi interpretive practices afford multiple, competing, and only indeterminately related modes for evaluating the significance of particular social acts and events. This reflects an array of deeply held Hopi ideational complexes, some foregrounding the significance of traditional knowledge and ceremonial formalism for sociopolitical authority, but others giving voice to a multiplicity of intentionalities that Hopi see as operative in the world (not just human, but vegetable, animal, and even supernatural forces; Whiteley 1998, A. Geertz 1990, Brandt 1954, Whorf 1956). I have argued that the relationship between these two ideational complexes and the ways they are deployed to make sense of communicative acts and events are worked out only in piecemeal fashion across moments of actual interaction. Finally, I have suggested that the discourses of the Hopi tribal court—that is, a particular communicative context in contemporary Hopi society where discourses of social conflict and dispute are the explicit topics of social action (Llewellyn and Hoebel 1943)—provide a uniquely explicit site for considering the multiplicities of meaning as they are worked out by and between Hopi social actors.

In this essay I extend this argument to suggest that only in accounting for such interpretive complexities and indeterminacies, as well as their metadiscursive expression, can we begin to approach a productive understanding of the ways in which Hopis deploy normative judgments in contemporary juridical and political contexts. As I shall reveal, this is in large part due to the efforts of the court to strike a balance between the Anglo-American-style juridical norms and practices that constitute much contemporary Hopi tribal law and local notions of Hopi custom and tradition, which judges have also been mandated to consider and rely upon in resolving disputes. But I will not suggest that what emerges in Hopi courtroom interactions is a multiplicity of normative calculations that neatly aligns intention-driven theories of interpretation with those enacting "Anglo" style legal claims and appeal to ritual convention with those making claims in Hopi tradition to press their interpretations of disputed events. Nor do I see them mapping, a la Rappaport (1999; see also Lambek in this volume), onto some discernable distribution of Hopi speech genres or contexts that could be uncontroversially measured against each other for their relative degrees of formality. Instead, as is evident in evaluative statements made in and about Hopi ritual, political, and juridical claims, I argue that Hopi actors bring to bear an array of Hopi ideologies regarding ritual formalism and intentionality to propose multiple evaluative frames in which norms of Hopi aesthetics and ethics are sometimes complementary, sometimes opposed, when measuring the import of Hopi social events and actions.

To this end, and for the purposes of this essay, I remain agnostic regarding the longstanding scholarly debates that have raged over efforts to define and distinguish between aesthetics and ethics. Such considerations, while important, are both beyond the scope of this essay and well outside my own expertise (see Bourdieu 1984, Scarry 1999 for good discussions). Indeed, the very possibility of distinguishing between the two, particularly in Hopi (where the adjective *loloma* is used to convey the English sense of "good" as often as "beautiful") is a central theme here. Thus, and for heuristic purposes that I know may oversimplify, I intend my use of *aesthetics* to refer generally to Hopi normative assessments of events and practices in terms of their form, while my use of the term *ethics* concerns Hopi normative assessments that turn on evaluations of the good, fair, or just.

## Hopi Sociopolitical Organization

Of the nearly 11,200 Hopi tribal members, just over half (approximately 6,500) today call the Hopi reservation their primary residence (United States Census 2000), while most all Hopi, says Hopi historian Matthew Sakiestewa, "wherever they live, call the reservation home" and expect to return regularly every year (personal communication, April 2008). This is true because, unlike other tribal peoples in the United States, the Hopi have never been relocated or removed from their homelands, though the current 1.5 million acre reservation includes only a fraction of what they claim as their aboriginal territory. Residents occupy twelve villages located on or around three mesas. Before the 1930s, nine of these villages operated under autonomous village leadership, and there existed no tribal organization nor any tribal governance structure. After 1936, and pursuant to the

Indian Reorganization Act (25 U.S.C. 479; 1934), Hopi villages were federated into a Hopi Tribe to be governed by a representative Tribal Council. Tribal governance was elaborated again in 1972 with the creation of the Hopi judiciary, which includes both trial and appellate courts.

In large measure, Hopi tribal law relies heavily on the procedures of Anglo-American-style adjudication when enumerating the operations of the Hopi tribal courts. Generally speaking, the Hopi tribal legal process is adversarial—litigants submit written briefs and present oral arguments, including taking witness testimony and providing closing arguments. Final decisions are made either by juries of members of the tribe or by judges, and such decisions can be appealed to the Hopi Appellate Court if some judicial error can be shown. At the same time, however, more recent tribal law requires the court to give a preferential place to Hopi customs, traditions, and culture. In Resolution H-12–76, the Hopi Tribal Council mandated that Tribal Court give more "weight as precedent to the . . . customs, traditions and culture of the Hopi Tribe" than to U.S. state and federal law.[1]

This effort to strike a balance between Anglo-style notions of governance and Hopi traditional forms is a feature of Hopi tribal governance generally. The Hopi Constitution includes an explicit reservation of power to village leaders, giving them power over intravillage matters, including family disputes, child custody and adoption, the assignment and inheritance of farming land, and the resolution of property disputes. Thus, while the tribal institutions established by the 1936 Hopi Constitution have become "the de facto political form for the majority of Hopi people" (Whiteley 1988: 230), Hopi villages and their institutions still occupy a central place in Hopi tribal governance and in the life of tribal members.

In Hopis' idealized image, villages are constituted of several matrilineal, matrifocal, exogamous groups, including phratries, clans, lineages, and sublineages (Titiev 1944, Eggan 1950). But only clans are understood to be an explicit category of kinship. Indeed, "clanship continues to give the [Hopi] individual a primary identity that supersedes village or mesa membership or more general 'Hopi' identity" (Whiteley 1988: 177). Each clan has its own sacred, secret origin story, but anthropologists claim they share certain underlying themes. In all these accounts, the ancestors of each clan emerged from below—the third world—into this, the fourth world, through a hole or *sipaaponi* ("navel") at the center of the earth on the

---

1. On file in the Office of the Secretary of the Hopi Tribal Nation, Kykotsmovi, Arizona, May 2002.

Grand Canyon's floor. The clans then dispersed in separate directions and began their slow migrations to their mesa-top homes. Along the way, the narratives go, each clan acquired certain magico-religious knowledge from a supernatural being that would become its totemic ancestor. That knowledge, or *navoti*, comprised ritual formulas effective for bringing rain via proper invocation of and supplication to their ancestor spirits. Upon arrival at their present locations, each clan gained admittance to the village community, being given land for homes and farming, only after they could display their willingness and ability to contribute to the community welfare by bringing rain. The ceremonial cycle that occupies the Hopi calendar today constitutes the enactment, every year, of each clan's contribution to their community and in this sense is an assertion of the village charter and each clan's position in it.

Hopi people thus generally agree that their clans are the corporate holders of land, ceremonial homes, ceremonial power, and its corresponding offices of ritual authority. Though the ideology of clan corporate ownership remains strong, ethnographic evidence has long suggested that the actual distribution of resources regularly occurs along different, sub- and even interclan lines (Whiteley 1988, 1998). Little surprise, then, that issues regarding the distribution of property loom large in Hopi members' concerns about law and order in their village communities, or that discourses of tradition, ceremonial responsibility, and clan relations are a frequent and recurrent feature of both the written texts and the oral arguments proffered by litigants, witnesses, lawyers, and judges in Hopi property disputes. A review of the forty-nine property cases on file with the Hopi court, reveals that thirty-three include recurrent statements by one or more legal actors regarding rights to the property at issue or requests for how the dispute should be resolved that invoke some aspect of Hopi custom and tradition. And of the twenty-seven hearings held before the court since 1995, for which over ninety hours of audio recordings were available and analyzed for this paper, in only one did parties not argue a matter of Hopi tradition or culture. I will now turn to an analysis of interactions from those recordings.

## Aesthetics and Ethics in Hopi Tribal Court Discourse

Much like other aspects of their religion, which Hopis "spend a lot of time discussing and debating . . . in the kivas and councils" (A. Geertz 2003:

324), metadiscourses about ritual speech and its strict adherence to formulaic patterns are a regular topic of talk that turns on both aesthetic and ethical evaluation of Hopi social action. But even though "ceremonial speech is elevated to a linguistic ideal . . . manifested in everyday speech preferences" (Kroskrity 1993: 36), I did not regularly hear Hopis reciting ritual formulas in nonreligious contexts. The demands of ritual secrecy and the threats of sanction that support them militate against such uses, and, as I have written elsewhere (Richland 2005), are themselves often the topic of everyday metadiscourses about *navoti*.

Courtroom discourse is no exception to this. In the courtroom interactions I observed, discourses invoking notions of traditional knowledge, who can express it, and how were a frequent and recurrent feature of both written texts and oral arguments. In some instances, tradition is constituted through explicit reference, like the claim I heard made by a Hopi advocate in a property-dispute hearing before the court in December 2001, when he said, "Since that evidence will favor my clients, it's very likely that under Hopi custom and tradition that they will succeed on the merits of the case."

Other times tradition is indexed through talk about clan relations and ceremonial and other social obligations, as in the following exchange between a Hopi judge and a witness concerning the clan relations between a litigant and her grandfather, who the litigant claimed had given her an orchard:

> JUDGE: And was she from the same clan as the grandfather that worked the orchard?
> WITNESS: No, because you won't be the same clan as your grandpa . . . as you are aware at Hopi clanship.

Such discourses suggest the extent to which Hopi and non-Hopi interlocutors are able to deploy *navoti*, and metadiscourses about it, to articulate principles of ethical behavior and social status, expressing what Kroskrity has called an ideology of "regulation by convention" (1993), which is a key element in the idealization of ritual formulas as a model for Hopi speech generally. But without more information, it would be impossible to discern whether these references also index for Hopi the ethical quality of the people, and their intentions, whose actions are at issue in these disputes.

In fact, in other moments within and across Hopi courtroom interactions, concerns with the intentions of particular persons do seem to enter into arguments being formulated in and around notions of Hopi tradition and ritual responsibility. A man claiming that his mother had made an oral bequest of her home to him, for example, explained that, to him, "Hopi tradition is—is speaking and letting people know your intention and your wishes." How might we account for this apparent indeterminacy? Why do the evaluations constituted through these traditional discourses sometimes imply the positive aesthetic value of attending to the formulas of ceremonial convention and clan relation but at other times are oriented to a concern with a particular actor's ethical intentions? I suggest that the metadiscursive elevation of ritual formulas as an ideal for everyday interaction, when understood from a Hopi perspective, can be deployed to capture either, or both. Therefore, these metadiscourses blur divisions between individual intention and social convention, the moral and the beautiful, in ways that provide an array of evaluative resources with which Hopi people engage each other in court.

## Aesthetics, Ethics, and the Multiple Intentionalities of Hopi Ritual Action

The Hopi follow a well-described pattern of Pueblo ceremonial and cultural "conservatism," in which the felicitous execution of ritual activity "comes only from letter-perfect attention to detail and correct performance, . . . [with] emphasis on formulas, ritual, and repetition" (Ortiz 1972: 143). For the Hopi, as for other Pueblo peoples, such formulas dictate ritual action on a number of different scales of practice—from the larger-scale sequencing of events over the course of each multi-day ceremony (e.g., when and how participants enter and exit the ritual space, display ritual paraphernalia and altars, smoke and prepare prayer offerings, etc.), to the requirements for sanctifying the built space in which these events occur (e.g., the underground meeting chambers or *kivas*), to the most minute details of kinesic and discursive components of ritual actions and oratory, including, most importantly, kachina songs (*katsintawi*) of the kinds alluded to by my Hopi friends described at the outset of this essay. Moreover, access to and possession of the traditional knowledge that informs these ritual formulas and their performance is a key source of social power among Hopi. As Peter Whiteley explains, "one of the most distinguished terms for a man is *navoti'ytaqa*, 'a man of knowledge'" (Whiteley 1998: 94). It is because of this, he argues, that for Hopi "ritual knowledge is a 'strategic resource'" (ibid. 71), serving as "the 'currency,' perhaps, of power" (ibid. 74).

For most Hopi, then, possession of *navoti* and performance of the ritual formulas it informs are highly salient as idealized models for social action. While this idealization of ritual practice has suggested to some scholars (most famously, Mauss 1985 [1938]) a concomitant diminishment in Hopi concern with individuated personhood and agency, the opposite is actually the case. Whiteley and others have argued that the Hopi notion of "*Tuna-tya*, 'intending,' 'intention,' constitutes a central concept in Hopi philosophy of action" (Whiteley 1998: 39). The centrality of *tunatya*, along with the notions of *pasiwni*, "planning," and *natwani*, "self-practice" (Whiteley 1998: 41), leads Whiteley to claim that Hopi possess a "triune principle of intentionalism," an ideational complex "of what we might call 'self' and 'mind'" that is both fundamental to Hopi ontology and "foregrounded in Hopi discourse" (ibid.). Whorf writes, "The verb *tunatya* contains in its idea of hope something of our words 'thought,' 'desire,' and 'cause,' . . . it is the Hopi term for subjective" (Whorf 1956: 61–62).

This abiding Hopi concern with intentionality has an explicitly ethical valence. Indeed, the very term *Hopi* is an adjectival noun phrase used in discourse as "an ethical term at least as often as an identity maker" (Whiteley 1998: 38). It generally carries the sense of "well mannered, well behaved" and describes an action or event that is ethical insofar as it is consistent with *Hopivötskwani*, or the Hopi way of life (lit., "good, straight path"), as laid out by their ancestors. Likewise, unethical behavior is often called *qahopi*, literally "not Hopi."

At the same time, Whiteley, Whorf, and others commenting on Hopi intentionality are careful to point out that these notions are not isomorphic with the concepts of self in Western secular humanism. This is true insofar as Hopi notions of intentionality are situated within a metaphysics of action that also includes "supernatural agencies, cosmic forces, and fateful processes as well as goal oriented human pursuits" (Whiteley 1998: 42). Whorf is again eloquent on this point. He writes, "The subjective or manifesting comprises . . . everything that appears or exists in the mind, or as the Hopi would prefer to say, in the heart, not only the heart of man, but the heart of animals, plants, and things, and behind and within all the forms and appearances of nature in the heart of nature" (Whorf 1956: 59).

In many ways, these notions of Hopi intentionality appear to come together seamlessly with the strict formalism of Hopi ceremony. When tribal members evaluate ritual performances, they measure performers' adherence to ritual formulas not for their own sake but as indexes of the participants' intentions. Ritual acts that deviate from the norm are understood as expressive of the performer's improper *unangwa* ("heart"). A.

Geertz describes statements he heard after one ceremony that was plagued by a series of malfunctions, including a ritual marionette whose strings had been damaged. The poor performance was not blamed on mere bad luck. Instead, the ceremonial leader "was accused . . . of a number of moral sins, such as vanity, ambition, and inattention" (A. Geertz 2003: 330).

Ritual formulas are seen as icons of the intentionalities that are central to Hopi metaphysics (ibid. 326), and specifically of their ethical deployment. Indeed, says Geertz, "The Hopi ritual person is expected to be the ideal person, embodying all of what being Hopi means" (A. Geertz 1990: 317). As one performer explained, "A person wants to complete the ceremonial in a beautiful way, to complete it with goodness" (A. Geertz and Lomatuway'ma 1987: 164). In this sense, strict adherence to the formulas that undergird Hopi ceremonial aesthetics are not just an expression of Hopi ethics, they are its embodiment (Glowacka 1998: 386).

But, as I have described elsewhere (Richland 2006), from a certain perspective there seems to be an abiding ambiguity here. A world full of intentionalities both human and nonhuman would seem to provide little space for discerning when and how an action is the result of some particular individual's wants, wishes, and desires. Likewise, if adherence to established formulas is the key metric for evaluating whether a particular ritual activity is not only beautiful but moral, how and under what circumstances can one be sure that such acts, even if properly performed, are in fact the reflection of the ethical intentions of this particular performer at this particular moment?

Whiteley contends that, in fact, "there are . . . two intentionalisms in Hopi metaphysics" (Whiteley 1998: 43). He calls one the "meta-intentionalism" of social structure and convention that grounds Hopi metaphysics and the other a "more direct sense of intentional action by conscious agents." He explains their interrelationship, suggesting that even "if all, at the level of essential metanarrative, was intended, the manifesting-manifested trajectory is not a lockstep matching of event to structure." Instead, and in a manner that directly implicates Hopi notions of ethical action, "individuated fragments of consciousness, granted subjectivity and life, have free will—particularly in their capacity for moral action—to perform acts adherent to models of the social good, or, conversely, to depart from this to further selfish interests" (ibid.).

Yet there still seems something unresolved here. And Hopis like my host's brother seem to point to this indeterminacy when making comments, like the one above, about Hopi tribal leaders who say things "like a song." That is, such statements seem to point to the possibility that, for all their accurate performance of ritual formulas, "based on a lifetime of training" (Glowacka 1998: 386), such speech acts need not be performed with the proper intentions, either because the speaker does not really know (i.e., actually possess the *navoti* for) what he is saying or, worse yet, may be making such prayers to advance his own personal interest rather than that of the community.

I would like to suggest that, while (at least) the two intentionalisms identified by Whiteley do in fact operate in Hopi metaphysics and centrally inform the evaluations that Hopis make regarding the ethics and aesthetics of everyday speech, they do not necessarily articulate in any fully systematic or nonconflicting way. Rather, they constitute independent and distinct theories for evaluating the ethical character of actions and events in the world, which sometimes align with each other, but not always. As such, the competing and conflicting grounds of these two theories may be hidden in an indeterminacy that is overlooked in the successful flow of most everyday Hopi interaction, ritual or otherwise but that, in certain social contexts of conflict and dispute, can be strategically invoked by Hopis to perpetuate a quite stark juxtaposition of evaluative judgments of actions and events.

To reveal more fully how this is the case in the context of Hopi property disputes, and hence to capture the full spectrum of normative multiplicity that emerges there, it is necessary to consider how such practices unfold in the adversarial interactions over the course of a single courtroom proceeding. To do that, I now turn to the details of a hearing was held in the summer of 2000.

### The Multiplicities of Aesthetics and Ethics in a Hopi Probate Dispute

The hearing in question concerned a challenge raised by a woman (re-named "Jean" here) to the appointment of an administrator for the purported will of her adopted mother ("Nellie"), who was recently deceased. Jean's opponent, "Dan," the man named in the will to be the administrator, had, like her, been adopted as a child by the decedent. Under the terms of the will in question, both parties were bequeathed one of three homes controlled by Nellie. The home that Dan was promised, which he would presumptively distribute to himself if appointed administrator, was the house that Jean was already occupying.

Jean's house was one of only two "ceremonial homes" in her village, specifically, the one where *Kooyemsi* ("Mudhead katsinas") came to announce the *Niman* ceremony ("Homedance," held in mid June). Such homes, along with other forms of clan property, are generally believed to pass from mothers to their daughters. At the time of the dispute, villagers generally recognized Jean as the one who bore the primary responsibility for ritually greeting the *Kooyemsi* when they emerge from the kivas, as well as for opening the home to nonresident clan and nonclan visitors during the two days of the dance itself. Many of Jean's fellow villagers were therefore disturbed when they heard that Nellie had apparently willed the home to Dan, an unmarried man whose birth clan was other than the one to which both Nellie and Jean belonged.

On the day of the hearing, present in the tribal courtroom were Jean, her daughter Arlene (her co-complainant), Dan and his non-Hopi legal advocate, and several relatives of both parties and the decedent. Also present were the court clerk and bailiff, two Hopis from a village different from that of the parties. The judge presiding over the hearing was a Hopi woman from yet another village.

After opening the proceedings, the judge states the principles that will guide her determination as to whether Dan should be named administrator of the estate. Importantly, these principles turn on whether the will is a valid expression of Nellie's testamentary intent, closely following Anglo-American probate law in presuming that the terms of the will are valid "unless if you can show that at the time this will was written . . . Nellie was mentally incap—could not understand what the contents of the will was . . . or was not fully aware of what was happening."

But when the judge then asks Dan to explain "how [he] was to be appointed the administrator of the estate of . . . How that came about," he doesn't testify to facts that might offer indexes of Nellie's intentional state on the day she actually wrote the will (e.g., Was Nellie of sound mind on that day?). This is strange, at least from what one might expect in the context of such a proceeding in U.S. state court, insofar as these facts were clearly in Dan's favor. Dan's advocate had evidence that the will was witnessed by two disinterested, non-Hopi lawyers, each of whom attested to Nellie's soundness of mind on that day.

But rather than testifying to these facts, Dan explains how he came to be the named administrator in the will by describing his relationship with Nellie and how his dutiful execution of the responsibilities that attend to that relationship likely led to her trusting him to distribute her estate. He states:

FIGURE 1. Explaining How Dan Was Appointed Administrator of Nellie's Estate.

---

| 001 DAN: | I call her "Mom." |
|---|---|

[some lines omitted]

| 033 | I worked the cattle, |
|---|---|
| 034 | worked the fields, |
| 035 | and everything else. |
| 036 | Same old thing. |
| 037 | And hhh I guess |
| 038 | when you do things for people |
| 039 | they tend to look at ya and say, |
| 040 | "I think you deserve something." |

He doesn't fully ignore the role that Nellie's intentions might have played in the formation of wills or the distribution of property. But note how the reference to her thoughts is constituted within conventions of Hopi social responsibility. Thus Dan casts his understanding of the motivations behind the will as merely the habitual assessments (line 039 "they tend to look at ya and say") of a generic set of human subjects—those people who give gifts of property to people who have acted on their behalf. Indexed in this statement are an idealized set of social relations described and ritually inscribed in a multitude of formulas that inform Hopi ceremonial responsibilities and ritual behavior. But also present are certain kinds of calculations of ethical intent. Dan implies a set of clan obligations, indexed by the fact that he calls Nellie "Mom," an aesthetic/ethic of proper social relations that Dan explicitly claims to have fulfilled by taking care of the cattle and the fields. Indeed, what he did is exemplary of the social conventions (line 036 "Same old thing") that all ideal Hopi sons engage in for their mothers.

Thus what Dan hears the Judge asking him to describe is not a recitation of the events of April 15, 1999—not just proof that Nellie intended what was written in the will on that day—but rather a request for some ethical justification, according to the norms and expectations of Hopi social convention, that makes meaningful the terms of the will that have the illocutionary force of appointing him administrator. Even for Dan, then, the party with most to gain by proving the testamentary validity of the will, the significance of that document cannot fully be accounted for merely by reference to the decedent's intentions but must also be measured in light of Hopi social convention, of formulas of traditional responsibilities.

Here, then, the two Hopi intentionalities Whiteley describes both emerge in Dan's discourse, and they might be said to merge Hopi ethics with aesthetics. Indeed, that is the very essence of Dan's point. Nellie's intentions regarding Dan are easily knowable as nothing more than the usual response to a son who has so dutifully attended to his mother, fulfilling that role as it has been intended to be played from the origins of Hopi social structure and practice.

When Jean proffers her challenge to the validity of the will, the distinctness of these calculi of Hopi ethics is starkly visible. At first Jean seems both willing and able to inquire into Nellie's intentions at the time the will was written. Because she is not represented by an attorney, she is allowed to cross-examine Dan directly on these issues. The following interaction transpires

FIGURE 2. Jean's "Examination" of Dan: Part 1

| | | |
|---|---|---|
| 001 JEAN: | But you di—But she is not in her right mind. | |
| 002 | How do you know | |
| 003 | she's in her right mind? | |
| 004 DAN: | Because I know the lady. | |
| [Some lines omitted] | | |
| 030 | You know, | |
| 031 | because I work | |
| 032 | and I take her here and there. | |
| 033 | You know, | |
| 034 | because she asked me to do it. | |
| 035 JEAN: | Yeah in return for what? | |
| 036 DAN: | I'll take off— | |
| 037 JEAN: | In return for all this stuff? | |

At the center of Jean's questioning of Dan is a concern with intentional states, both of Nellie and Dan, at the time the will was written. Thus Jean starts with a direct challenge regarding Dan's assessment of Nellie's mental health, at line 001. And Jean's ultimate turn ("Yeah, in return for what? . . . In return for all this stuff?") can only be understood as an accusation that Dan exerted an unethical influence on Nellie to write the will, so that the terms of the document must not be an expression of her free testamentary intent.

But in her very next turn Jean makes a statement in which issues regarding Nellie's intentions, if alluded to at all, are only obliquely under consideration. The interaction continues:

FIGURE 3. Jean's "Examination" of Dan: Part 2

| | | |
|---|---|---|
| 038 DAN: | And I— |
| 039 JEAN: | I thought |
| 040 | I was supposed to be the daughter. |
| 041 | I thought they adopted me. |
| 042 | How come I'm not getting anything |
| 043 | and you're getting everything— |

[some lines omitted]

| | | |
|---|---|---|
| 046 DAN: | They—she did give you |
| 049 | the house up top. |
| 050 | You and the girls. |
| 051 JEAN: | But I want more than that. |
| 052 | Because I'm the one |
| 053 | that's taking care of everything *at* the village. |

The full force of Jean's statement that she "was supposed to be the daughter. I thought they adopted me" (lines 040–41) echoes much of the same concern for Hopi social convention as Dan's claim that he calls Nellie "Mom." By foregrounding kin relationships, Jean is indexing conventions of clanship that are central to ideologies regarding the distribution of material resources at the village and her expectation that this would result in her being the recipient of one of Nellie's homes upon her death. Indeed, her use of the demonstrative in the phrase "the daughter" (rather than the possessive "her" or the possessive suffix "Nellie's") adds to the force of this statement as alluding to the normative role of being a Hopi "daughter" and the sets of duties and expectations that go along with it. And it is by virtue of this "supposed" status that Jean expresses her incredulity in her complaint that she is "not getting anything." (line 042).

The second of Jean's two turns here (lines 051–53 "But I want more than that") reveals even more starkly that she objects to the will on grounds of social convention and ritual obligation—that she is the person "taking care of everything *at* the village," a reference to her role as the clanswoman responsible for receiving the *Kooyemsi* and others when they arrive.

This is made even more explicit a few turns later, via a discursive turn that not only announces but performs Jean's elevation of ritual convention over individual intention. When the judge asks Jean to restate her objections to Dan's claims, Jean switches to Hopi to say:

FIGURE 4. Jean's Response to the Judge's Request to Restate Her Objections

| 001 WOMAN: | *Pu'* | | *i' [DAN]*, | | | |
|---|---|---|---|---|---|---|
| | Here/Now this [DAN] | | | | | |
| | Now DAN, | | | | | |

| 002 | *Pam* | *pay* | *taaqa.* | | | |
|---|---|---|---|---|---|---|
| | He | merely | man | | | |
| | He is just a man. | | | | | |

| 003 | *Pam* | *son* | *put* | *ang* | | *hinmani* |
|---|---|---|---|---|---|---|
| | He | NEG | that | | along there/then be carrying along. EXP | |
| | He won't be able to carry that out. | | | | | |

| 004 | *Pi* | *qa* | *tiimaytongwu!* | | | |
|---|---|---|---|---|---|---|
| | Truly | not | witness dance HAB | | | |
| | He doesn't even come to the dances! | | | | | |

| 005 | *Pam* | *yaw* | *yep* | | *sinmuy* | *oo'oy'ni?*[2] |
|---|---|---|---|---|---|---|
| | He | QUOT | at this point | | people | be serving FUT |
| | Will he (as they say) be receiving the people? | | | | | |

| 006 | *Pam* | *yaw* | *yep* | | *sinmuy* | *amungem noovalawni?* |
|---|---|---|---|---|---|---|
| | He | QUOT | at this point | | people. | for them prepare food FUT |
| | Will he (as they say) come and prepare food for the people to eat? | | | | | |

| 007 | *Pangsosa* | | *sinom* | | *ökiwisngwu* | |
|---|---|---|---|---|---|---|
| | To then/there | | people | | be approaching HAB | |
| | The people all come to that house. | | | | | |

| 008 | *I'* | *yaw* | *pantini?* | | | |
|---|---|---|---|---|---|---|
| | This | QUOT | do it that way FUT | | | |
| | Can he (as they say) do all that? | | | | | |

| 009 | *Qa'e!* | | | | | |
|---|---|---|---|---|---|---|
| | No. | | | | | |
| | No! | | | | | |

Instances of everyday speech that index ceremonial activities and ritual formulas that Hopi recognize as traditional are linguistically marked as speech that quotes the prior speech of others. Traditional discourses are replete with clause-by-clause repetition of either English verbs of saying ("it is said"/"they say"), Hopi verbs of saying ( e.g., *kita*, *pangqawu*, "they have said," "they say"), or, most typically, the Hopi quotative particle *yaw* ("it is said"). At other times, speakers implicitly invoke these prior discourses by generating temporal frames within which particular normative claims are deemed to operate in seemingly "timeless" ways, encompassing the past, present, and future, as if it has always been and always will be governed by these norms and the discourses that constitute them. In these ways, these lexical, syntactic, and pragmatic forms "traditionalize" the narrative and its performance (R. Bauman 1992). They thereby instantiate Hopi language ideologies of "regulation by convention" (Kroskrity 1993) and the ritual authority that speakers claim through adherence to those conventions by indexing how the information being conveyed reports talk related at some prior communicative moment, moments that are for Hopi implicitly governed by the ritual formulas of esoteric ceremonial and clan interactions.

Note how Jean does all this here, in a real economy of traditionalization, combining repetitive use of the Hopi tradition genre marker *yaw* ("they say" or "it is said") with verbs inflected with the future tense suffix -*ni*. Note also her use of parallel clause structure, a form that echoes the poetics of repetition that Ortiz and others describe as a regular feature of Pueblo and Hopi ritual speech formulas. In all these ways, then, she conveys within single clauses at lines 005–8 the sense of a past-present-future temporality that frames her present claim as reporting the timeless talk of traditions that have occurred and are occurring from some point in the past to now and that reach forward to anticipated social moments in her brother's potential violation of those conventions.

In these turns, I would contend, we can observe Jean proposing a challenge to Nellie's will that is informed by an evaluation of its propriety in light of Hopi ceremonial aesthetics, with less concern for her intentions behind the will. Moreover, Jean seems to argue that, whatever the outcome, the home should certainly not go to Dan, for by virtue of the sexual division of ceremonial labor (line 002 "He's just a man") Dan is unfit, according to the strictures of ritual convention, to perform the duties of the house (line 003, "He won't be able to carry that out"). There is here no reference to the intentions that may have been behind the will. Nor can we read Jean's statements regarding these conventions and consequences as attempting, as I have described above, to show that Nellie could not have intended to give the home to Dan. Here, then, we do not see the two Hopi intentionalisms reposing on each other. Jean's argument against the validity of the will is evaluated through a normative lens entirely distinct from the theory implied in Dan's, the judge's, and even Jean's own statements regarding the intentions informing the purported will. Here Hopi aesthetics *are* ethics, but not in any way that can be said to reflect an individual actor's intentions. As such, and in a way that echoes my friend's concerns that some people can perform ritual formulas "like a song," here Jean's calculation of what is the proper distribution of clan property reveals the extent to which Hopi can and do hold distinct the normative valuation of ritual convention from the ethics of individual intention.

## Conclusion

In his analysis of what he calls "Hopi traditional literature," David L. Shaul notes the quality with which Hopi understand and perform ritual songs, as simultaneously expressions of social convention and individual intention. Shaul is careful to point out that Hopi do in fact distinguish between those ceremonial performers who learn and rehearse songs through rote recitation (*tawkosi,* "learn a song/learn orally") and those who are deemed to have composed them (*yeewa,* "creative plan/idea" about a song). But, he says, the difference between recitation and innovation is elided in the ways Hopi understand the process by which these songs are eventually made ready for public performance. As he explains, "After one composes a song poem, it is revealed . . . to a group of potential performers. A song which gains acceptance is then rehearsed. The notion of rehearsal is an extended sense of *wuuwa,* 'think/ponder.' The entire fabric of the song poem is considered as the group edits the contribution" (Shaul 2002: 192). He suggests that this fundamental blurring of the difference between the individual intentions of song composers and the impositions of social convention through the rehearsal/editorial process (a process that is itself intentional) reflects a fundamental trope of "Hopi culture [as] cooperation without surrender" (ibid. 189, quoting Sekaquaptewa).

The problem that my host's brother saw in the beautiful speech of Hopis who made speeches "like a song" is perhaps the flip side of this unique mixing of intention and convention in the process of Hopi ceremonial performance. Indeed, when he first uttered it, I was surprised that in evaluating their speech as "like a song" he, and possibly his grandfather before him, meant something negative. What is bad about beautiful speech?

What is bad, it seems, is that the conventions of Hopi aesthetics, conventions that in general are understood to serve as indexes of the moral value of individual intentions, are actually rather ambiguous. They can be used by Hopi actors to hide other intentions—intentions that are ill informed at best, or thoroughly unethical at worst. Of course, as is also evident in his use of such a phrase, such ambiguities can be exploited by the audiences of such speech acts, as well. The elision of aesthetics and ethics serves as an opportunity to cast doubt on the actions of performers of Hopi ritual speech—whether ceremonial or political—regardless of what they may say are their own intentions. In the case of the vice chairman, indeed, it was his opponents, like my host and her brother, whose evaluations would carry the day. His performance, no matter how beautiful for its close adherence to Hopi ritual formulas, was unable to save him from removal from office for ethical violations.

In this essay I have endeavored to tease out the ways in which the blurring between evaluations of the morality of individual intentions and the beauty of social-ceremonial performative formulas, ethics and aesthetics, plays out in how Hopi legal actors evaluate the everyday actions and events that are the source of their disputes before the Hopi tribal court. To this end, I have built upon theories and insights from linguistic anthropology regarding the fundamental indeterminacies of meaning making generally, and of ritual formality more specifically. I have argued how interactions in property disputes before the Hopi court both suggest and display the multiple, distinct, and sometimes competing theories of ethics that are available to members of the Hopi speech community. Whereas such multiplicity is often elided in the smooth flow of everyday Hopi interaction, it is in moments of conflict and contestation, and in the degree to which such conflicts emerge around the normative evaluation of an action or event, that very different and even competing ethical metadiscourses can be worked up by Hopi interlocutors for strategic rhetorical advantage in the heat of dispute-resolution discourses. I hope, through this analysis, to have provided some purchase for an anthropology of ethics that is prepared to reckon with the complex, competing, and even indeterminate manner in which ethics, like so many other normative discourses, emerges in the actual details of everyday social life.

# PART SIX

# Ethical Subjects: Character and Practice

# People of No Substance: Imposture and the Contingency of Morality in the Colombian Amazon

*Carlos David Londoño Sulkin*

This essay addresses the conditions and entailments of strategic imposture among People of the Center (Colombian Amazon). It examines individuals' accounts and evaluations of moral subjectivity and action, which often cited elements of coherent narratives and nondiscursive practices that bring together their social organization, livelihood practices, perspectival cosmology, and understandings of subjectivity. I will claim that persons are in part constituted by their self-interpretations against a backdrop of distinctions of worth between different kinds of being, action, and subjectivity, and that People of the Center's accounts of personhood reproduce and reveal just such a background. While arguing that explanations of human behavior need to attend to persons' self-consciousness and strategic intentions, the essay preempts the resurgence of radically efficacious humanist subjects endowed with an overarching grasp of their own constitution by insisting on the contingency, temporality, and *différance* (slippages of meaning) that characterize the symbolic deployments constitutive of persons.

During my fieldwork among People of the Center in the Colombian Amazon,[1] I was struck by the sheer number of morally evaluative claims

---

1. The fuzzy category "People of the Center" includes patrilineal clans of the Middle Caquetá-Putumayo region of Colombia who speak Muinane, Uitoto,

individuals made, portraying themselves as competent, admirable persons and others as ignorant, uncontrolled, or otherwise flawed miscreants. Often, people's moral portrayals were at some level rejected; others would express doubt about the truthfulness or authenticity of their expressions, particularly their self-representations, though rarely to their faces. I sometimes wondered: Were individuals simply persuaded that they were indeed admirable beings when they portrayed themselves as such, or did they describe themselves in those fashions with some sense that it was strategically advantageous to do so, whether they were persuaded that they were indeed admirable beings or not?

People of the Center's evaluative expressions allow me to consider the matter of imposture both in my terms and in theirs. In their most frequent accounts of social life and morality, imposture—the usurpation of proper human subjectivity by immoral, extrinsic subjectivities—was a key practical and existential problem, tied to the conditions for constituting a self. From my own theoretical standpoint, imposture—presenting oneself as a kind of person one is not, is not perceived as, or is not persuaded one is, or somehow claiming to have certain qualities one might not have—is of interest for three reasons. First, self-aware intentionality may be one of imposture's constitutive sins and enabling conditions, and I believe that worthwhile explanations of human action and social life must bear in mind what people understand themselves to be and to be doing. Second, imposture, especially when it is unsuccessful, helps highlight that the intentions and understandings that motivate symbolic action do not determine the effects of such action.[2] Finally, imposture and talk about impostors, in my experience, highlight people's sense of what is admirable, worthy, and despicable in subjectivity, appearance, and action.

I find that persons are partly constituted by our understandings (and misunderstandings) of ourselves. We come to be ourselves by performatively mirroring socially available linguistic and other symbolic forms. Others' iterations of these forms interpellate us, providing us in time with the forms and associations with which we achieve our sense of who and what we are and can be, what kind of world we inhabit, and what qualities are to be esteemed or despised. These forms allow us to perceive and to classify persons, actions, objects, and appearances, among other things, as

---

Okaina, Andoque, Nonuya, Bora, and Miraña. I carried out fieldwork mostly with speakers of Muinane and Uitoto along the Caquetá and Igaraparaná rivers and in the city of Leticia, between 1993 and 2008.

2. See Laidlaw's critique of the conflation of intentionality and efficacy (this volume).

of a certain kind, in terms of qualitative distinctions of worth. This enables people in this or that time or place to *be* an observant child of Jehovah, or a macho man, or a streetwise cynic, or, among People of the Center, a tobacco-imbued, productive man and to perceive aspects of the self or of others as classy or tacky, nasty or sweet, righteous or sinful, among other possibilities. People who deploy other vocabularies and symbols may make different distinctions of worth.[3] For the purposes of this volume, I treat this motivating sense of qualitative worth as morality and see it as encompassing ethical evaluations of what constitutes "doing the right thing."

Our selves—which are to a great extent constituted by our ongoing interpretations of our biographies, our relationships with others, and our own bodies, thoughts, and emotions—are bound to the intrinsically temporal and contingent social interactions that make the symbols we use available to us. In the intrinsically temporal process of sociality, groups pick up certain forms and associations more consistently than others. Individuals cite the forms in question, interpellating and making sense of situations and of each other, and making these forms available anew for others to cite. In this view, the main concerns of the individual members of a group, the matters they tend to subject to morally evaluative attention, are also the sedimented (or epidemiologically most widespread) product of contingent, performative citations; as social life goes on, however, the moral and aesthetic concerns of groups and of individuals change.

In this process, there is an important difference between the understandings and intentions that motivate subjects' production of symbolic forms, and the effects of these forms. People may know what they are doing when deploying symbols, may intend to do it, and may know why they are doing it, but they cannot really have a clear-sighted, overarching grasp of or control over the effects of what they do. The forms people mirror often interpellate others, but what those others make of these interpellations—how they interpret, cite, and transform them—is not determined by the interpellator's intentions. These interpretations are contingent upon those others' own symbolic constitutions and the particularities of the circumstances.

Methodologically, this view calls for interpretive attention to individuals, for it is individuals—or historical persons, if you will—who actually iterate symbolic forms (see Cohen 1994). This view presupposes that other individuals are thinking, feeling selves to whom things matter; I assume

---

3. My discussion here is inspired in part by Taylor (1985: 277–80).

this, recognizing that I cannot ultimately distinguish between others' consciousness and my invention of their consciousness, and that my understanding of others' selves will always be based on my (critical and ironic, I hope) understanding of myself. The emphasis on individuals does not entail that this is a less than sociological approach, however; "thick" anthropological descriptions of institutions, groups, and categories also depend at some point on attending to individuals' conscious understandings of them as expressed in dialogue and other interactions.

In this essay, I will describe People of the Center's often-cited accounts of moral personhood, which link phenomenological experience, cosmology, social organization, and livelihood. I find it important to underscore the coherence and phenomenological plausibility of these accounts, for I will argue that individuals among People of the Center produced many of their moral self-portrayals, critiques, and other discursive and nondiscursive actions in part on the basis of reflections upon themselves in terms of these accounts.[4] I will report on instances of talk about virtues, transgressions, and infelicities, specifically concerning key ritual and alimentary substances constitutive of persons, a matter of much moral solicitude by People of the Center and concerning which a contrast between authenticity and imposture often arose. Finally, I will attend to imposture in my sense of the word, in the case of an individual who portrayed himself as a kind of person others thought he was not; his unsuccessful citation of forms that in other circumstances could be part of felicitous performances highlighted these forms starkly.

## People of the Center's Production of Morality

In this section I present what I interpret to have been a common, general picture of moral personhood among People of the Center; it is an abstraction from and summary of claims and accounts that I witnessed them produce between 1993 and 2008. In this general picture, Real People (human beings, the most paradigmatic of whom were usually the lineage or clan fellows of whoever was telling the story) were intentionally and materially

---

4. People of the Center are alive and well at the time I am giving this essay its final editorial touches—July 2010. I insist upon using the past tense in my descriptions in order to be coherent with my emphasis on the contingency, and especially the temporality, of the symbolic deployments that constitute social life in an ongoing fashion.

fashioned by their parents and other kin out of key substances of divine origin. The most important of these substances was tobacco paste, the semen/sweat of the creator deity Grandfather of Tobacco. Other key substances include manioc starch and juice, hot chilies, certain "cool" herbs, and, for men, *mambe*.[5] These substances were the main components of well-made persons' flesh and bodily fluids; being agents in themselves, the substances "spoke," and their speeches constituted persons' thoughts/ emotions.[6]

Moral thoughts/emotions stemming from good substances led people to speak and otherwise interact with others sociably. The Muinane man Pablo, for instance, explained to me that the esteem one felt for one's kin when one looked at them was nothing other than one's tobacco—the tobacco constitutive of one's body—recognizing itself in others' bodies and saying, "That is my own body." The term in Muinane for this kind of recognition was *ésikinihi*, which denoted both "remembering" and "discerning appropriately." Pablo and others also told me on different occasions that tobacco would say "My brother." This was part of their explanation for the thought/emotional discernment of kin, conceived as an experience of remembering or being reminded that somebody was in fact kin. Tobacco's purported utterance, "My brother," was the vocative term of address for one's kinsperson and a metonymical reference to caring, respectful treatment of him in general. Other substances also participated in the creation of moral subjectivity: for instance, basil and other cool herbs created tranquil states of mind and motivated women to work hard to nourish their kin.

Proper substances also led people to seek to produce new generations of Real People featuring healthy, competent bodies and sociable thoughts/ emotions that would enable them to live well together and perpetuate the cycle. New people were made out of and through the agency of proper substances: proper semen (understood to be another form of tobacco) coming from a man who had behaved well and carefully avoided polluting practices and foods; proper foodstuffs consumed by the mother during her pregnancy and by the child throughout her life but especially during the

---

5. *Mambe*, also known as coca, is the Spanish term for a mildly stimulating green powder made of toasted coca leaves and the ashes of Cecropia leaves. Adult men who consumed it were called *mambeadores* (singular *mambeador*), and the exclusively male circle of seats where they consumed it ritually was known as the *mambeadero*.

6. People of the Center did not speak of thoughts and emotions as mutually distinct kinds of entity or experience.

early years; and healthful, cold water, in which the child was counseled to bathe. Children were also supposed to undergo numerous body-shaping rituals involving a variety of substances that were incorporated into the body or otherwise impinged upon its form.

As persons grew, their own and others' actions instilled competencies and flaws in their bodies. The young man who wove a basket, or made *mambe*, or helped fell the forest for the first time had to work diligently and carefully, without laziness or rest but also without haste, for his demeanor, skill, and speed would become embodied and he would thenceforth continue to work in that fashion. If he left the basket unfinished and went to sleep, this would become a part of his body and his way of working, and he would forever be a slow, inconsistent weaver. A girl who was lazy and who often interrupted her first attempts to grate manioc would also incorporate this flawed way of proceeding. My friend Lazarus once proudly pointed out his own efficacy and speed at making vegetable salt for his tobacco paste, telling me that he was like this because "that's how I grasped [or became set]"; that is, that was how his body had been shaped. They explicitly likened the processes of embodiment of skills and attitudes to making pottery; bodies, like pots, would set and harden in the shape and with the features given to them while in their early stages of fabrication.

Well-made Real People were capable of contributing to pleasurable community life. This ideally involved living in close-knit patrilineal settlements, where siblings, parents, in-marrying women, and children interrelated respectfully and caringly because they had true substances inside them, where there was an abundance of food and ritual substances, because people's bodies were properly fashioned and so were healthy, hardworking, and productive, and where dance rituals were frequent and enjoyable. In such circumstances, individuals' thoughts/emotions and general bodily states would be "cool," a term that encompassed the virtues and states of tranquility, judiciousness, and bodily well-being.[7]

The achievement of the good life and the production of new Real People were accomplished against the grain of the surrounding hostile cosmos, most of whose denizens were eager to sabotage Real People's existence and reproduction. Animals in particular, fearful of human predation upon them and jealous of Real People's morally productive ways and communities, were the origin and cause of a great many human tribulations. They too had originally been created by the Grandfather of Tobacco. Early in creation they had been human in appearance, and like the

---

7. See Lambek (this volume) on Aristotle's very similar account of the cultivation of virtuous dispositions.

Real People that would come after, they received tobacco and counsel from the creator. Unlike Real People, however, animals did not hearken to the creator's prescriptions. They misbehaved in myriad fashions and therefore could not achieve the cool, pleasurable, productive, sociable existence that Real People would eventually achieve. They were variously sleepy, lazy, horny, incestuous, indiscriminately playful, confused, surly, murderous, or otherwise miscreant and corrupted their tobaccos. The indignant creator then transformed them into their beastly shapes, consigned their corrupted and pathogenic tobaccos into them forever, and warned them that they would thenceforth be the game of Real People. Ever after, these beings had deployed their substances and other warped accoutrements against human beings, and the latter had been obliged to use rituals to extirpate evil substances from each other.

People of the Center's stories about these matters featured certain perspectival premises: namely, that each kind of being perceived the members of its species—others with bodies like its own—as human and those of other species as nonhuman. So an animal could in a variety of ways deposit its subjectivity-making substance into a member of the human species and cause that person to think/feel and behave toward other persons as an animal would toward its co-specifics. This was a common explanation of violence and anger; people attributed to angry others the subjectivity of animals: for example, I recall a woman tearfully screaming at her husband, who had just mistreated her, that he had a big-toothed animal inside and that he should kill it. Because of perspectivism, though, the claim in cases like this was not that angry people perceived others as animal bodies, which would have been phenomenologically implausible as an explanation of everyday tribulations, but rather that the person perceived other persons in the same way an animal perceived its co-specifics—namely, as human—but failed to have the loving, humane thoughts/emotions toward them that a Real Person had. Instead, they would abuse their fellows in the sundry fashions that jaguars, coatis, and other beasts mistreated theirs.[8]

## Substances, Social Organization, and Livelihood

People of the Center's most frequent expressions of moral solicitude cohered well with this general picture of the cosmos, of personhood, and

---

8. See Viveiros de Castro (1998) and Londoño Sulkin (2005) for in-depth discussions of perspectivism.

of social life; many of them were articulated in terms of persons' bodily composition, particularly whether their actions manifested human or inhuman substances. With these terms, they addressed whether people were pleasurable or even healthy to reside with, productive, knowledgeable, or competent, whether their thoughts/emotions—especially their anger— were truly human, and especially whether they behaved in the proper fashion kinspersons should. People of the Center cited this picture piecemeal in many of their activities, such as their accounts of the counsels children should receive, their quarrels with each other, a variety of rituals, and some of their practices of livelihood and of social organization.

The imagery of tobacco, selfhood, and group membership infused the talk and other practices that reproduced People of the Center's patrilineal emphasis. Their kinship terminology, though positing the transmission of kinship along both female and male lines, favored the patrilineal. Patrilineality had corporate implications: most of these people resided in settlements constituted by sets of male siblings with their unmarried sisters, their wives, and their children, and each of their frequent dance rituals was organized as an exchange of foodstuffs and esoteric services between the patriline segment hosting it and the patrilines of guests who came to sing and dance. They often articulated their patrilineality in terms of tobacco, claiming, for instance, that the bodies of the members of their lineages were made up of their patrilineal ancestors' strains of tobacco. Given tobacco's subjectivity-creating nature, consubstantiality implied that people of the same clan, and especially of the same lineage, shared the same thoughts/emotions and moral inclinations; at a meeting of clans who spoke different languages, I recall that several men stressed in hortatory speeches that their tobacco and therefore their thoughts/emotions were "the same" and that therefore they all shared a common purpose. On other occasions, in the privacy of their own *mambeadero*, a set of men would stress instead the distinctiveness of their own strain of tobacco and the consequent differences between their own virtuous ways and those of other lineages and clans.

One conversation with a Muinane man suggested that he evaluated the virtue of possible courses of action in terms of values tied to this account of masculine selfhood in relation to patrilineality. Ariel, reporting troubles with his older and notoriously authoritarian brother David, told me he often thought about uprooting and leaving the settlement. Nonetheless, he said, he knew brothers should stay together and feared the weakness that would ensue from being away from his patriline. As I read his claims, he feared he would become a less capable agent and a less admirable one.

The centrality of cultivated substances to People of the Center's understandings of moral personhood linked as well to their talk about livelihood
practices such as gardening.[9] In fact, one way in which Muinane *mambeadores* spoke about the morality of practices was by situating them in a metonymical "Cool Path," whose more literal referent was the path that led
from the *maloca*—the large, multi-family residential and ceremonial
house—to the garden in which the vital work of growing tobacco, manioc,
and other key cultigens took place. Abstract counsels state that people
should "stay on the Cool Path" and never wander from it lest they step
on thorns; this was a prescription to the effect that youths should not seek
knowledge or pursue endeavors other than those that led to the production of desirable material abundance. "Wandering from the path" into the
jungle stood for miscreant pursuits such as sorcery and adulterous relations, and "stepping on thorns" corresponded to the tribulations that
would result from the miscreancy.

Another horticultural trope concerning moral personhood was that of
baskets; People of the Center wove a wide variety of these, ranging from
some made to be beautiful, tough, and durable to others fashioned haphazardly for immediate, hasty use. These were used to carry coca leaves, manioc tubers, tobacco, and all sorts of garden produce. The abdominal and
chest cavity of the human body was also a basket, however: the "Basket of
Knowledge." A well-made person's Basket of Knowledge was well woven
through esoteric body-making rituals, so that good speeches would stay in
it and not fall through; it had to be kept clean through dietary practices,
daily vomiting, and good counsel. Productivity and other features of a
desirable lifestyle were evidence that a person's Basket of Knowledge was
the real thing and not an animalistic version.

Moral knowledge—part of the Cool Path, in one trope, and something
kept in individuals' Baskets of Knowledge, in another—included myths,
charms, dance-ritual protocols, and songs, which people claimed were variously intended to make gardening practices effective, to shape, nourish,
and heal people, to hunt, and to produce a propitious climate for human
endeavors. Knowledge of this kind was intrinsically tied to tobacco and
to patrilineality. First, each patriline had its own knowledge and ritual
responsibilities; second, the patriline's tobacco was the source and incarnation of knowledge and purportedly what made that knowledge effective.

An important aspect of all the key substances—and hence of personhood—in relation to livelihood was that their most salient capability was

9. People of the Center subsisted mainly by hunting, fishing, gathering, and
slash-and-burn horticulture.

for predatory action. This was particularly so for tobacco. In many narratives, it appeared as a virtually omniscient being, invulnerable to all evil and threats, which it could proscribe, burn, cook, or kill. Being a central component of Real People's bodies, it generated their awareness and their capacity for action in the world, a kind of action that more often than not involved predatory transformations. People of the Center treated a great many of their livelihood and ritual activities, such as felling the forest to make gardens, healing the sick, making tools, building a house, and holding a dance ritual, as involving death-dealing deployments against trees and other forest beings. The knowledge to carry out these tasks was consigned to tobacco, and it was in itself dangerous. It had to be acquired, transmitted, and used carefully and with proper protocol, lest its capability to burn, kill, or otherwise harm turn upon the deployer, learner, or teacher, or his family. In their moral self-portrayals, men among People of the Center likened themselves to tobacco, speaking approvingly of their tobacco's and their own predatory capabilities.

People of the Center spoke of yet other virtues in terms of substances: thus, people should be productive, like tobacco and coca; or "cool" and unfazibly calm, like sweet manioc, certain herbs, and tobacco; or consistent, like certain strains of chili, among other virtues with substantial exemplars.


### False Substances and Spurious Baskets

Just as tobacco paste and other properly produced substances axiomatically generated moral subjectivity and actions, animals' and other nonhuman beings' substances generated miscreant thoughts and actions. Proper tobacco, though a predatory substance, for example, was the source of the capacity to recognize kin as such and of the consequent thoughts/emotions of loving care, whereas animals' tobaccos were the source of socially disruptive thoughts/emotions. The Muinane man Jonás explained that the tobacco of a jaguar "does not say 'My brother,'" a claim to the effect that the tobacco of beasts did not generate awareness of the proper way in which one should address another—a metonymy for how one should treat them—but instead generated murderous anger.

One way in which Muinane people referred to animals and their tobaccos when these impinged upon human subjectivities was as "those who walk in others' names": in a word, impostors. I often posed to them the question of intentionality: Was the miscreant aware of his or her miscreancy? Did the foreign tobacco usurping a person's real tobacco know itself to be evil? Did it sense that it was an impostor sabotaging humanity intentionally? My interlocutors were split about this. In some cases, they stated that, when a person misbehaves, out in the forest the animals who had placed the false tobacco in the person would laugh; after all, they hated, envied, and feared Real People and wanted to harm them. In other cases, however, the impostor constituted by the usurping tobacco speaking through a person's body was persuaded of his or her own authenticity. My friend Pablo explained to me that this was why miscreants often failed to see their own acts as miscreancy, as gestures that were not really their own.

One of the central existential problems for the *mambeadores* was the discrimination of Real speeches, substances, and baskets from their false counterparts. They spoke, both in myths and in explanations of particular instances of action, of tobaccos and other beings who appeared to be the real thing but were not. The mythical Anaconda of Food, for instance, had a beautifully woven basket filled with an abundance of wholesome-looking manioc, coca leaves, tobacco, and fruit. He spoke beautifully in the *mambeadero*, and his words sounded wise and appealing. And yet no good came of it all; the basket was a false basket, all appearance but no true substance. His speeches, though they spoke of productive work and abundance and thus were supposed to create these, produced only strife and tribulations.

The tobacco and coca of the False Woman—a sexually indiscriminate mythical being, mother of vanity, incestuous desires, and other flawed thoughts/emotions—similarly looked like the real thing. The *mambeadores* who spoke to me about her stated that those who spoke her speech felt themselves to be speaking well, but their speech was carried off by the wind, remaining "unfixed" and thus never being fruitful. I heard Muinane elders blaming her false substances for people's preference for white men's knowledge and ways, contrasting this with the perspicacious steadfastness of the firmly seated *mambeador*, who, counseled and made strong by his own tobacco, stuck fast to Muinane speeches and ways.

In several myths, one or another false tobacco would claim "I am invincible!" but would then be vanquished by Real Tobacco in some contest. These tobaccos spoke through bodies and caused people to think/feel that they were powerful, wise, unbeatable Real People and to make the same kind of self-aggrandizing, unsupported claims. Part of the problem with these tobaccos, a man once explained to me, was that their angry, sometimes profane speeches tasted fatty and delicious; they were a pleasure to say and caused people to wish to continue to use them.

People of the Center's use of chilies in their rhetoric exemplifies well their talk about moral failures and achievements in terms of substances, with statements to the effect that particular instances of thoughts/emotions, talk, and other actions revealed proper, false, or no substance. Chilies were apposite for talk about anger, the thought/emotion that most solicited People of the Center's attention. Anger was an object of great ambivalence, for it was treated as either the most salient symptom of animalistic subjectivity or as an indicator of predatory capabilities.

Chilies, the Muinane elder Pedro once explained to me, were spicy hot because of the sun that shone upon them and entered them. Like chilies, women got red-faced working in the garden under the sun, and they too got hot and therefore sometimes scolded others. Nevertheless, he said, women were supposed to consign the heat and anger they received from the sun into their chilies and chili pot, and not direct it against their husbands and children. Embodied in foods prepared with these chilies, women's anger could make it into people's very flesh, where its angry spiciness would ward off evil.

Pedro's wife Sara told me that when a woman's chili paste was hot, others would say "This woman is angry in truth! She is painful [spicy hot], like her chili paste!" Yet if her chili paste, chili pot, and other preparations with chilies were not hot, people would scorn any anger she showed, saying "How can you claim to be angry, when you do not have hot chilies?" or "Your anger is empty . . . you have not 'shown' yet!" The latter expression pointed out that the woman had not materially proven that she had proper thoughts/emotions. One of Sara's points was that a woman who was bad tempered, but whose chilies proved not to be hot, thereby showed her lack of moral substance. Others could point to her scolding or her incensed gossip as the empty, fruitless speech of a lazy woman who had not worked as much as she should have. Such a woman's blustering—which lacked an underlying predatory substance—could be treated with little fear, unlike the effective anger of someone constituted by proper substances and unlike the truly dangerous and immoral fury of someone with an animalistic substance inside her.

## On Unproductive Impostors

Talk of substances sometimes conflated the stuff constitutive of bodies and subjectivities and the already-processed but still unincorporated products of livelihood practices, such as tobacco paste, *mambe*, and cooked food-stuffs. These unincorporated substances were treated as important, tangible evidence of the propriety of the embodied stuff. Material productivity was thus a matter of much moral solicitude among People of the Center.

I witnessed a serious negotiation of morality in terms of substances while doing my first stint of fieldwork at a Muinane community in 1993. Jonás's wife Lilith announced that she was convoking a drinking bout. She had prepared a large vat of starchy plantain drink, and people would pair off and give each other gourdful after gourdful of the stuff in a contest to see who could drink the most. As we headed toward the *maloca* (the multi-family residential and ceremonial house) to drink, David, the leader of that community, explained to me that several weeks earlier he had thrown at Lilith's doorstep a wild pig he'd shot, saying to her, "There's your gossip." I inquired into the affair and gathered that Lilith had been talking about another woman in the community and that this had generated some tribulations. David's gesture of giving her the pig with the claim that the carcass was her gossip was a complex challenge and insult, as well as a purported favor. It basically suggested that her talk had been gossip or lies, generated by the antisocial substance of a wild pig inside her, and that David's killing of the pig had been a transformation and removal of the substances inside her and a violent reconsignment of them into the animal. As I interpret such claims, he was not claiming that *she* had behaved in an ill-intentioned manner; rather, his claim was that it had not been her but a spurious (im-postorial) self who had misbehaved.

By killing the pig, David had purportedly healed her of her antisocial, ultimately inhuman gossiping ways. By giving her the transformed sub-stance of her false talk, now in the form of nourishing game, he obliged her to reciprocate with the product of her own hard work. By working hard and successfully on a nourishing endeavor and producing a tangible, consumable substance, she showed that she had proper corporeal sub-stance—after all, it made itself manifest in her productivity—and that therefore her talk was not empty bluster or animalistic sabotaging of com-munity life. From participation in similar events, I gather there had also been room for Lilith to turn tables on David; should he have found himself full before she did and unable to swallow any more of the drink she prof-fered, she could well have scornfully told him not to challenge a real woman, when he himself could not deal with her response.

Elsewhere (Londoño Sulkin 2006: 214) I discuss an anecdote that seems to me particularly eloquent on the matter of substances in relation to mo-rality, and concerns imposture in the sense of contrived pretense. Lazarus, a Muinane man in his mid-forties, described a recent conversation he had had with Jonás's son Abel, a young man who was visiting Lazarus's settlement. According to Lazarus, Abel had addressed him in the *mambeadero*, saying "Yo ya tengo mando" (roughly, "I already have power"), which constituted a claim to the effect that he had knowledge and esoteric capabilities. Lazarus had asked him who had given him that knowledge and legitimized his use of it. Abel had responded with the names of four older men, all more or less recognized as knowledgeable. Lazarus had then responded, "So let's see, where is it? Where is that of which you speak?" This was an unequivocal request for tobacco paste and *mambe*, the prime manifestations of a young man's knowledge and capabilities. On that occasion, the request amounted to a harsh put-down. Abel had moved around a lot in recent years and therefore did not have a garden in which to produce *mambe* or tobacco. He had to admit that he had none, whereupon Lazarus continued: "One should never say that if one has nothing to show . . . and less so to me, who just had to give you *mambe* and tobacco paste because you have none of your own. Never again talk to me thus, saying trash like that." Lazarus reported that he had then warned Abel against the shame of making such serious claims, only to fail to live up to them, and that Abel had stated that he had learned an important lesson that day.

I had known Abel since he was sixteen or so and had always found him eager to present himself as a man of competence in all fields. Claims like his—a form of gendered bragging—were actually quite typical of men there; a great many times one or another had spoken, in the context of conversations with me or with a small group of people, about their great knowledge and exceptional competence in matters esoteric or otherwise. In my experience, only a few older men could speak confidently in this fashion even in large meetings, knowing they would not be challenged. Youths who tried this often "passed"; others would somehow signal their acknowledgment of the claims, or at least remain silent and not challenge them. There was always, however, the risk of being put down or challenged. Occasionally, older men would refer to "the young men of today" in general, protesting that these behaved as if they were elders and sages, forgetting that their fathers were still alive and thus merited their sons' deference. Abel seemed to me paradigmatic of such men, being rather more intense than others in his production of claims to competence beyond his years.

As a sixteen-year-old in the settlement where I first met him, his classificatory uncle David referred to him once as "my nephew, that white dog," that is, as a weakling incapable of much. Years later, in another settlement, he had managed to achieve some standing as a schoolteacher and was often outspoken in settlement meetings. From conversations with Lazarus, I can only say that he found Abel overbearing and despised the way some elders seemed to acknowledge Abel's competence and even deferred to him on some settlement issues. It was in the context of a conversation about this that he reported on the interaction he'd had with Abel.

Refracted through Lazarus's account, Abel's claim—though formally very similar to claims he and other men often made—seems to me to have been singularly infelicitous. Lazarus frankly rejected the other's presentation and self-portrayal as a man of knowledge and, furthermore, rejected the footings of equality that Abel's demeanor and claims seemed to have been trying to establish. Lazarus's anecdote, however, was still a series of citations that reproduced a certain ideal of admirable agency, one that incorporated the explicit sense that ostensible material productivity, specifically, of key substances, was the critical evidence of morality and competence. The anecdote also had other interesting features: Lazarus was portraying himself to me as a no-nonsense, knowledgeable elder who came out on top in a confrontation on matters of proven knowledge and morality. His utterances at that moment were felicitous, if you will; I indeed treated him as a respectable, efficacious man of knowledge.

Was Abel persuaded that he was in fact already a man of knowledge? Or was he posturing, trying on the desired trappings of adult manhood, with some sense that his claims might be contested and that he was not really, or not yet, what he claimed to be? The closest I came to having a Muinane answer this question was when Lazarus's brother Pablo told me, after a meeting in which Abel had been particularly overbearing, that Abel was "sick." He explained that it had not been Abel's own true speech we had heard him produce but some pathogenic animal's. Producing ostentatious claims to knowledge and esoteric capability were likely candidates for this kind of accusation, both in myths and in daily life. If there was an impostor, it was the animal, not Abel himself.

## Contingency, Citationality, and Morality

A thick description of People of the Center's social existence—who they married, where and with whom they lived, how they spoke and otherwise treated each other, and a great many other aspects of their everyday lives— must consider individuals' own interpretive sense of what it was that they were doing and what kind of being they were, could, or should be, where this kind of being was defined by more or less articulated distinctions of worth. Their expressions of this sense seemed to me to have been shaped, and in turn to have reproduced, very coherent, phenomenologically persuasive accounts of self, much like those I described above. They manifested their conviction that human bodies were indeed constituted by cultivated substances, and that their own and others' behaviors, whether human or inhuman, had been caused by human or inhuman substances of extraneous origin.

Individuals seemed to perceive intimately the moral worth of persons, events, subjectivities, and actions, in at least some of the terms of these accounts, and to be motivated by this perception. I believe that they *saw* that predatory capability of an esoteric kind—and the anger that came with it—was profoundly admirable, and that lack of productivity, and the anger that came with it, was despicable, much as some of us might *see* that a man is being cruel when he kicks a dog or that a certain person is beautiful. By "seeing" I mean here the sense individuals have of the straightforward obviousness or givenness of the moral and aesthetic quality of something they observe or consider, a sense that I would insist is the product of our own contingently constituted understandings of self.

Lazarus and other full-grown men expressed an intimate sense that they were constituted by tobacco and that they had effectively matured into capable substance producers and esoteric predators. Young men like Abel at times deployed some of the same narratives and symbolic forms that made manifest such older men's self-understandings. My take on this, informed by my theoretical preferences but also by memories of my own little posturings and impostures, was that Abel in particular was citing forms—namely, producing quite typical forms of narrative self-portrayal, in a certain institutional setting—that he and others had deployed in the past to pass more or less successfully as men with esteemed qualities, but that he did not take for granted that he was indeed that virtuous kind of fellow. He knew that some people in fact did not perceive him as such, but he clearly desired to be understood and treated in those terms. In general, people expressed keen awareness of the likelihood that their actions and subjectivities would be questioned and criticized, because in fact at the time it was a common practice to question and criticize; this probably constituted a further motivation for them to seek to preempt that their subjectivities and actions be treated as the product of less than human substance.[10] I thus interpret Abel's claims along these lines, as being his

---

10. See Keane (this volume) and Zigon (2008: 165) on conflicts and moral breakdowns enabling conscious reflection on moral/ethical matters.

reflexive fabrication. Nonetheless, I found no evidence to suggest that he himself was reflective and reflexive about the very fact that he admired a certain kind of person.

The gist of my argument is that People of the Center evaluated subjectivity and action with intelligence, at times planning their own gestures strategically or even histrionically, but that this does not entail that they were free, utilitarian agents with a radically clear-sighted grasp of the conditions and processes of their own constitution. Rather, they thought, planned, evaluated, interpreted themselves, and developed their concerns through symbolic forms acquired in historical social interaction. This is in line with my claim that subjects do not decide what it is that matters to them, as, in my experience, I don't *choose* to find that a certain person is beautiful, or a certain style cool, or a certain act admirable or cruel. I just do, doubtless as a product of the infinitely complex and mostly opaque process of my becoming who I am, in my unique social and historical context.

I witnessed no instances in which People of the Center objectified or questioned reflexively their admiration for virtues such as predatory capability and productivity. Having said this, I very much wish to elide the picture of a monolithic culture that travels through the generations as a heavy, stable mass programming entire populations to perceive themselves and their world in a certain way, or to admire or despise certain qualities. This is a mirage produced by numbers of individuals citing more or less similar forms in a certain period of time. The same applies to any "system" of morality or ethics; it is a contingent, historical product of people using a particular vocabulary, establishing and reproducing certain institutions, and otherwise citing symbolic forms. Some narratives, nondiscursive practices, institutions, and other symbolically constituted forms are cited more often, making them all the more available and perhaps therefore more compelling. But because they are made of symbols dependent on temporal citations by persons, they cannot be perfectly shared or monolithic, or protected from objectification or reflexive rearticulation. After all, contingent events—accidents, deaths, the arrival of new neighbors with a different vocabulary—can lead us to articulate, understand, and perceive distinctions of worth differently.

In their accounts of personhood, People of the Center cited different elements of the overall account I have given, doing so selectively, transformatively, strategically, or contradictorily. Some made use of other symbolic resources altogether, to interact, to account for, or to evaluate their

own and others' subjectivities and actions. Young men, for example, sometimes produced frankly admiring descriptions of incorrigible young indigenous leaders who stole the government's monetary subsidies to
indigenous communities and spent them on trips to urban centers to in-
dulge in prostitutes and booze and who generally knew how to come out
on top in legal skirmishes, debates, arguments, and fights with their elders
or with "white people," while ignoring judiciousness and propriety.

An example of variety and contestation in accounts of substances and
selves was a case in which Jonás, who had briefly been trained as a missionary, reflected upon an Evangelical Protestant's claim years before that
Jonás's necklace with a cross constituted idolatry. Jonás told those of us
present that the same could be said of coca and tobacco, for what were
these, if not mere plants? However, like the cross, they served to "remind
him of God" and "made him feel closer to Him." Jonás was amalgamating
the tobacco and Christian deities, and objectifying his own thoughts in a
manner that did not treat these as stemming from substances. After Jonás
had left, Pedro, an older man, made manifest the more prevalent local
semiotic ideology, with its attributions of agency to substances, telling me
that Jonás's talk would upset his own coca and tobacco, which would cease
to work for him.[11]

A final example is that of People of the Center in the diasporic setting
of the Amazonian city of Leticia, who seemed to me to be citing less often
the discursive and nondiscursive forms that reproduced ideals of personhood that privileged membership in patrilines and compliance with corresponding values. Men there were more likely to move away from their
kinsmen than their counterparts in the Medio Caquetá; women often
chose, after marriage, to reside with their mothers and sisters (Nieto 2006;
something rare in the Medio Caquetá), and many stereotypified *malocas* as
authentic markers of indigenous tradition in the face of acculturation,
rather than treating them as structural symbols of patrilineal groups.

People of the Center's understandings of the kinds of beings they were,
could be, or should be, and of what constituted the good life, were causally
and symbolically tied to practices of livelihood and social organization.
Changes in any of them—for whatever reason—entailed indeterminate
changes in the others. These understandings and practices were symbolic

---

11. Christian references did not constitute an overarching theme in People of
the Center's morally evaluative talk, despite the presence of Catholic missionaries
since the 1930s and Evangelical missionaries in the 1960s. Keane's discussion of
Christian semiotic ideologies (this volume) suggests interesting research questions,
however.

deployments, and as such, material, temporal, contingent, and subject to *différance* or slippages in the meanings individuals made of them. This precludes treating People of the Center's social life and the changes intrinsic to it—for instance, changes in their desires, their enactments of leadership, or their ways of building or engaging with *malocas*—as products of the efficacious intentions of agents endowed with a clear-sighted and overarching grasp of the process. Yet it was on the basis of their interpretations of themselves and of each other that individuals deployed symbolic forms in the interactions that constituted their social lives. This is why I see People of the Center's social life as a contingent process that shaped individuals' moral reflections, reflexivity, and intentions, and in which these in turn played a causal but in fundamental ways nonteleological role. [12]

## ACKNOWLEDGMENTS

SSHRC and the Wenner-Gren Foundation funded my latest research and writing opportunities; Joanna Overing shaped my interest in anthropological approaches to morality; and Jessica Boyachek, Amy McLachlan, Charles Stafford, and the editor and contributors to this volume provided pertinent comments on this essay. Thanks!

---

12. Social life is subject to the causal effects of the materiality of signs (Keane, this volume), but this does not entail that human beings have an overarching grasp of the process. I depart from the Marxian anthropological view (e.g., Bloch 1977), according to which social change may result from individuals' episodic emancipation from false ideology, by virtue of a universally shared human cognitive capacity that grants them clear-sighted access to a presymbolic, unconstructed "real world."

# Ethics Between Public and Private:
# Sex Workers' Relationships in London

*Sophie Day*

## Love and Money

In the U.K., as in other places, we learn from a young age that love and money do not and should not mix. Love belongs to a sphere that is threatened even by association with money acting as a conduit, a set of practices, habits, and relationships that might contaminate all that love stands for. From the perspective of a denigrated female occupation, love stands paradoxically both for the reproduction of the social world and for its transcendence. Love sustains relationships of mutual care within which children and adults cultivate their human capacities. Love also fuels a quest for perfection, which points toward a hereafter. These two aspects of love, reproductive (although not necessarily procreative) and transcendent, are bundled together through deep-seated opposition to the worldly, dirty, corrupting, and self-interested qualities of money. Given the counterfactual nature of an opposition between love and money in everyday life, certain qualities of money that are attached to certain types of people and activities sustain the fiction that love makes the world go round and, simultaneously, stands above and beyond it. Such people and activities come to carry responsibility for the fragility and vulnerability of love. It is they who are to blame and their activities that elicit disgust.

It is wrong to mix love and money. When government or church offi-cials "sell" love, this love becomes venal and corrupts the wider insti-tutions. When competitions such as sports fail to reach an ascetic detachment because money changes hands, questions are asked about human fallibility. Such evidence of immorality rarely calls the practice of love into question in these institutions overall, for it is only some individu-als and some activities that are castigated. When a woman sells sex, how-ever, not only are her activities damned, but so is she herself and all others like her. Women who sell sex are seen as less than human.

Sex workers are damned for their temerity in stepping outside the ar-chitecture for life in which sex belongs with love; it cannot be sold without losing core attributes of personhood. Prostitution is thus constituted as a shadow or shame that confounds the boundaries between public and pri-vate as well as those between love and money, undermining the proper order of social reproduction, in which women have sex only "at home." The sense of disgust with which prostitutes are greeted suggests a serious transgression: it seems that women should desire a reproductive world that gives sex to a domestic and conjugal love capable of populating and sustaining the world at large.

During the 1980s and 1990s, together with Helen Ward I conducted research in a health and drop-in service known as the Praed Street Project, which we established for sex workers in London. The project is currently managed by Jane Ayres within the U.K.'s National Health Service. We established the service in 1986 to look at the risks of HIV and other sexu-ally transmitted diseases, combining epidemiological and anthropological research with the development of services. Initially, we developed specific clinic sessions and, on the basis of our early experience and further re-sources, expanded from 1988 in two key directions through a drop-in facil-ity and fieldwork to provide a range of other support services. Working outside the clinic presented difficulties, including the effect of heavy polic-ing and the fear of prosecution that made agencies and saunas reluctant to allow us onto their premises. We relied extensively on word of mouth and the introductions offered by sex workers' colleagues who had visited the project in building a cohort of women that we followed initially for seven years.[1] Subsequently, we conducted a second study and managed to follow up 130 women from the original cohort during the period 1998 to 2002. (Day and Ward 2004).

---

1. See Ward and Day 1997 for further details. The ethnographic material in this essay derives from Day 2007 unless otherwise indicated.

Drawing on fieldwork from these and other projects, I explored ethical practices among sex workers and investigated a particular dimension of ordinary ethics, which I gloss in relation to the "work of time" (Das 2007 and in this volume). Veena Das has shown how individuals come to inhabit a world in which they have been administered poisons, poisons that they digest as they continue to live; how they live next to neighbors whom they find terrifying and incomprehensible; how they strive nonetheless to live among these strangers, who might annihilate them. I present the work of time in relation to a notional career in sex work. Following women from 1986 to 2002, we found that a career typically developed through three phases, as I summarize below. Our generalizations, however, make it much easier to perceive the moral and political worlds that women negotiated than the ethical judgments made by individuals. Approaching the ethical as a process of inhabiting the world, I explore a single biography in the second part of this chapter in order to illustrate my notional career and, more critically, what I consider to be distinctive qualities of an ordinary ethics. Ethics overlaps the political and the moral but remains unique and intrinsic to an individual story. It brings into view the inevitable discriminations entailed by speech and action, such that even anthropologists entering a field learn to recognize and enter into judgments of particular practices and behaviors. Several contributors to this volume show how ethics involves critical reflexivity, choice, and judgment, and these qualities evoke Hannah Arendt's emphasis on the individuality of action. The words of an exemplary individual might move others to act in concert, precisely because her history is unique and thereby constitutes what Arendt calls an example.[2]

A woman joining the occupation—my notional sex worker—knows that she will attract disapproval, for breaking the rule Thou shall not mix love and money, just as she knows that she will be selling sex, even if she has but a vague notion of the actual contours of these novel relations of stigma and labor.

### Joining the Occupation: The Question of Morality

Women we met during the 1980s and 1990s were familiar with gender stereotypes, and they knew that you could not claim to be both Madonna

---

2. Arendt argues that the story, through remembrance, completes an act. We learn ethics through narratives that tell, for example, how Socrates staked his life

and whore, or at least not at the same time. They were aware of the opprobrium elicited by prostitution and the boundaries drawn between the spheres of love and money. A neophyte sex worker thus begins with questions of morality.

There is a world of difference, she observes, between sex and love. Sex, like many other activities, can be alienated through processes of costing, timing, and the deployment of an impersonal and instrumental rationality. These tend to be embedded in distinctive places and relationships. Sex can become a matter of money, not love, and, the novice sex worker asserts, a form of work. Her own job, she might explain, is comparable to others. She might have been working in a factory, a shop, or a home; she might have been engaged in what people consider manual, mental, or emotional labor. But, as it happens, she is working in the sex industry, doing a job that is strictly equivalent to the activities that other people undertake for money. Love has nothing to do with it. The novice sex worker explains carefully how she observes the norm.[3] She accepts the conventional postulate that love and money do not mix, and she explains time and again, with great care, that sexual services can be exchanged readily, even happily, for money in exactly the same way as all those other bodily pursuits that we call work.

A sex worker's first move on joining the industry is to assert her own morality in relation to governing fictions of love and money. She rejects the charge against her and, she hopes, steps out of her newly acquired status as pariah. This move has consequences and, judging from research findings dating from the 1980s to the 2000s, these consequences tend to be shared by sex workers and to happen sequentially.

Although a woman new to the job says she is working, she may also wonder whether or not she has sold her soul to the devil, in the words of one research participant. The novice straddles two worlds. She comes from an environment that vilifies sex workers, and she joins those who have been cast out. The words "I am simply working" simultaneously describe and call forth an ordinary morality associated with the dignity of work and with a wide range of activities that attract money.

As Goffman wrote of stigma, individuals who are dishonored are thereby reduced "from a whole and usual person to a tainted, discounted

---

on the truth; "these examples teach or persuade by inspiration, so that whenever we try to perform a deed of courage or of goodness it is as though we imitated someone else" (1993: 248).

3. See further Mahmood (2005) on the pious subject.

one" (Goffman 1974a: 12).[4] My *On the Game: Women and Sex Work* (Day 2007) presents a number of sex workers' reactions to this vertiginous loss of place. Some doubted their own morality and asked whether they had sacrificed their very lives. Most expressed anxiety about their new status, as they wondered what in fact they had transgressed. All hid what they did, since it was only when their activities became known outside the milieu that they became indelibly and permanently shamed. Everyone we met also probed the vague and pervasive moralities or fictions about love and money through which they had been damned. Through this process of scrutiny, previously unarticulated moralities were explicated little by little in political terms.

## Skilled Practice and Political Action

A novice sex worker's counter-morality soon becomes a matter of politics. Even as women experienced viscerally the weight of disapprobation, they socialized the stigma and learned to work in concert with other sex workers and associates. Some began to see their transgression as a misplaced disagreement over etiquette, and others, as a serious failure of justice. The counter-position they developed was never purely an internal rearticulation of conventional morality; it was also a collective dispute over definitions of work, especially women's work, and over the contours of occupational, civil, and human rights. In other words, the personal blemish also becomes a collective badge of identity, constituted interactively and intersubjectively.

As sex workers felt the effects of stigma, they learned a discretion that deflected this sense of revulsion. Associates at work, whether sex workers, clients, or agents, recognize you as a worker. Outside work, you are a mother, a citizen, a neighbor, and, most likely, a woman known to work in some other job. Settling into the occupation, women assumed that widespread disapproval of their job might be confined to the world of

---

4. I do not discriminate in this chapter between *stigma* and *dishonor* or a range of cognate terms, including *humiliation*, *shame*, and *disgrace*. I prefer the more processual and encompassing "politics of dishonour," however, in the light of several important analyses (for example, Das 2007, Haeri 1995, Wikan 2008). Building on an earlier anthropological tradition in the analysis of honor and shame, with particular attention to gender, these contributions focus more extensively on political action and its consequences for the boundaries of state and society.

work. Every day, they left work behind, and soon, they hoped, they would leave the industry altogether in favor of a more respectable job.

After a matter of weeks, women had begun to learn how to partition their lives, to distribute themselves across several "public" or legal identities and to hide their work from most people. All manner of distinctions were routinely deployed to set sex for money on one side and sex for love on another. At work, women used condoms and other forms of prophylaxis. They admitted only particular categories of men into a rule-bound environment, where they typically insisted on payment in advance for carefully specified activities, which were subjected to a second process of accounting in the minutes that were counted, one by one, as they passed by.

All research participants knew that sex is very generally sold and that love includes dealings with money, but they soon found that they had to conceal many of their activities outside as well as in the workplace. They learned to launder their earnings. Spending money on other adults, for example, turned these individuals into accomplices and in effect made them "pimps," that is, people who live off immoral earnings. Only money spent on children seemed clean enough to stand in association with love, and parents found that they could, for once, spend their earnings without threatening to contaminate significant personal relationships. The very process of spending money on children might even demonstrate that you were a good and loving parent. In practice, however, parenthood was often deferred, since sex workers found themselves unable to use their earnings to secure a fit home for their family.

The rearticulation of conventional morality led sex workers to dispute the immorality of sex work while intent on preserving fragile and vulnerable fictions about love, to which they were often as committed as anyone else. As a common courtesy, they worked discreetly and partitioned their lives, hoping that they might effectively deflect the thoroughgoing dishonoring of their persons. These women, however, rarely controlled processes of publicity. Practices of dishonoring were in the hands of state officials, media publicists, and other people, such as neighbors. Associates in what had become a subterranean world of sex work, as well as those living next door, might simply be careless, or they might have been seeking leverage to win a dispute. Whatever the precise mechanisms, a worker often found herself exposed after a short while in the sex industry and publicly shamed by an arrest, a criminal record, a media "outing," or a revelation to family and friends. Surveillance, policing, and idle gossip reasserted the status of pariah. All the activities that women had separated with such care were reassembled and publicized as aspects of a person who degrades herself through shameful activities.

In such circumstances, our interlocutors often became even more insistent and surrounded the language of sex with ever more elaborate circumlocutions. They insisted upon distinctions so rigid and inflexible that I came to interpret them in a different way. It seemed futile to attempt to judge whether the reports and claims pointed to differences or to continuities between the realms of "love" and "money," and whether they revealed an oppressive, systematic structure of inequality or an inner, continual, nagging anxiety that you might indeed have given yourself away. Sex workers could not argue convincingly about the dignity of work in a context where they found themselves excluded so completely from everything that mattered.

A novice sex worker may initially have been concerned about a blemish on her character, insofar as she shared views about a "whore stigma" that are common inside and outside prostitution. She may rapidly reconfigure this disapproval in terms that deflect dishonor by attending to the obvious differences between sex and love, and she may also avoid unsettling foundational fictions by conforming to etiquette (Elias 2000) and keeping her insights hidden from public view. Soon enough, however, she will be undone by other people, over whom she has no control and to whom she can offer no response that will win her back the status of a person who is recognized. All at once, she is unraveled into the pariah she never was.

Initial affirmation of the moral rule not to mix money with love typically has such consequences. The counter-position that the neophyte articulated should have proved persuasive and constituted a more inclusive moral universe. Similarly, the observation of common etiquette, where the differences between sex and love are best left unspoken, should have concealed effectively any aspects of sex work that unsettle an arbitrary but highly significant symbolic order and cemented the process of mutual recognition based on proper discretion. But conformity to the rules of morality and etiquette finds no purchase at all and, when the sex worker exhausts these matters of conventional observance, experience leads her to step outside the norms that degrade her into various forms of political dispute with practices of shaming.

After a short time, the experience of sex work led women to represent dishonor in political terms, which show how the whore stigma is produced and reproduced through policy, law, gender relations, and the organization of work. After even limited experience—as little as six months— women spoke more and more about their structural position and the social relationships in which they were marginalized. In this phase, the individual sex worker becomes maximally involved in the more formal and obviously political activities of the sex work movement: the whore stigma is credited to the external world, which must be changed.

In practice, few of the women we knew expressed identities as sex workers in public. But participants in the Praed Street Project joined sex-worker rights groups, voted at meetings, attended conferences, performed music and theater, and wrote against the whore stigma. They had a variety of views and styles of organizing as volunteers, as NGO employees, in creative work, and at meetings with other sex workers, as well as efforts to change public and especially governmental views. Very little of the public engagement, however, was visible to other people, since women generally participated in the sex-work movement through alternative identities. They continued to hide their "socially dead" persons or at least restricted information to those who shared their predicament.

Now, even if she had not before, the sex worker becomes a political actor, who speaks and interacts with others to dispute and repudiate the status of pariah in and beyond prostitution, who argues against unjust, unethical, and immoral exclusions that render all manner of people less than human and, by selective attention if not outright abhorrence, more or less dispensable. And now she finds herself, at least at times, outside the "normal" or "majority" society whose morality and etiquette she has affirmed for so long and with such ardor, and within which she has lived so much of her life.

If practices of dishonoring sex workers almost inevitably initiate and instill an oppositional politics, they simultaneously provoke a defensive reaction that by and large contains this politics within a particular compartment of life. A sex worker will have learned to deflect shame as far as possible by turning her one self into many, each with a distinct biography. These practices of partitioning constitute parts that love and are loved, that embody the skills of a valued and experienced worker, that negotiate with officials, hold distinct legal identities, belong as a citizen in one country or another, and so forth. I characterize this combination of skilled concealment and political opposition as a mid-career phase, albeit one that develops after only a few months in the job.

## The Recalibration of Morality and Politics

In my earlier research during the late 1980s and early 1990s, I often wondered what would happen to these women, for they appeared to have become stuck in their own counter-morality and oppositional politics. They were unable to build the lives they wanted. Accordingly, Helen Ward and I conducted the follow-up study noted above to track as many women as we could into middle age and beyond. Between 1998 and 2002, we succeeded in following up a third of the original cohort and found these women working in equal numbers inside and outside the sex industry. Our research was necessarily biased against those who may not have known whether they sold sex or who may have experimented ephemerally with sex work. It was biased toward full-time workers and their associates, whose activities permitted contact with us in a workplace, during a public process of naming, such as a magistrate's court or the space of the Praed Street Project, defined by a particular building, telephone line, and Internet connection. But none of the sex workers we met in London found she could efface her dishonored status, even after leaving the occupation. I once telephoned a woman I had met some years previously on several occasions, and she responded from another city and another life as a sports instructor. Her tone expressed how fervently she expected to find that the past had been sealed away forever and how much she wanted to ensure that it no longer existed. My telephone interlocutor had accomplished the uncommon feat of saving enough money to leave sex work and sediment it in the past; she had begun a new life in another town as a self-employed entrepreneur. Whether or not this development represented a permanent rupture with the past, everyday practices in the London sex industry during this period led the majority to look for the security, usually in the form of savings, that would allow them to shut their own front doors against dishonor. Women invested huge efforts in fixing their present occupation within identities that would disappear over time. Yet those who stayed in sex work ultimately found the cultivation and pursuit of such respectability less and less attractive.

We found that more experienced and older women stopped hiding. They stopped lying. Thus, a research discussion convened specifically to elicit stories from long-time workers in groups of three or four during the early 2000s dwelt on issues of honor and dishonor. It led to a general agreement that it was better to tell people what you did: "I've got to the stage where if someone can't handle that I do this as a job, if they can't handle that I have a deviant sexuality, I don't want to know them. They are not worth knowing." The same woman had just insisted upon the dignity of her working life, her profession, by referring to a television program about the legalization of prostitution. She explained the plot: a woman who had worked as a prostitute, saved her money, and gone back to college had apparently moved on in life:

This guy is saying, you know, the cliché, well now we've heard from a
working girl who's gone on to better things, . . . I mean I have been to
college but I have chosen this. I am trained in a profession. . . . Other
people I know are trained in a profession—nursing, teaching, or
whatever—and they choose. I choose to do this work and I see it as a
profession and I see it as something I continue to do.

Such women realized that their arduous, unremitting practices had not
succeeded in changing the views of other people, who still blamed them
for stepping across a key social boundary in taking up sex work. Moreover,
it was not the effects of this disapproval but their own practices that had
effectively deprived them of a brighter future that remained sealed in a far
distant realm of life. Eventually, they came to acknowledge these consequences, to reject an imaginary future and to live in the present. This
stance involved feelings of loss for some women but conferred a sense of
freedom on others. In one discussion, for example, a woman whom I had
known for some fifteen years spoke bitterly about the prospect of aging
alone. She was appalled at the thought of two women she knew who were
still working in their late fifties. While she agreed that they seemed reasonably happy, she also said, "I wouldn't want to be sixty with a tiny flat
. . . I don't know . . . not married and living with two cats and, it's like, I
find it just a bit sad." But her regret was no more typical than the freedom
expressed by her interlocutors during this conversation. They reacted
strongly. One exclaimed, "It's my idea of heaven," and the others laughed.
The first woman explained, "Well, it's obviously too late for her to have
kids, and she's got into that single way of life and she's now . . . I just
wonder when she's on her death bed, I think, is she going to regret it all?
I mean, I have been doing it seventeen years, and I'll probably be here
twenty or thirty years later, but I'd hate to be on my dying breath and
think, 'oh God.'" Two of the others continued to disagree, "But maybe,
with a great deal of respect, there is more to her life than her job. . . .
[There may be] more to her life." It's "so personal. That's everyone else's
perception of this person's life. I mean she might be having a fabulous life
for all you know."

We presented three typical stages in our analysis of women's careers.
New recruits felt dishonored and disgraced. After minimal experience and,
typically, over a period of several years, the sex workers we knew began to
qualify their earlier statements by reference to the organization of everyday life and social interactions at work and outside. They represented
stigma in terms of social processes that discriminated against them in ways

that they had not even anticipated. These women reported both hiding and fighting. They told about the partition of their lives, about concealing the work they did, and about joining the political opposition. In retrospect, however, a more experienced sex worker might look back on her mid career in less descriptive and factual terms. She might judge that she had simply become stuck in an unpalatable present, committed to a better future in one of her many lives that she could not realize and battling for justice and recognition that were likewise repeatedly deferred to some other time. She might consider that she had created or at least agreed to an unlivable situation. With extensive experience of the sex industry and the benefit of hindsight, women we knew chose a more unitary life, oriented to their present circumstances rather than to a remote future. Sex workers did not necessarily abandon an earlier counter-morality or the politics of opposition, but they generally became more and more unwilling to partition their lives and to downplay issues of the moment.

## Ordinary Ethics

According to Aristotle, the virtuous state "needs time and experience . . . [and is] the result of habit" (*Ethics* 2.1, 1103a14–b1). Long-time sex workers reflected on their careers and reconsidered the past in relation to the present as the realization dawned that it is simply impossible to argue with the ritual order exemplified in conventions of morality, which create such visceral, embodied, and enduring dishonor.[5] While this ethics overlapped with the political and moral aspects of sex work, it unfolded in the particularities of an individual's life as I illustrate with a short biography, drawing on Arendt's concept of the example.

Tina had worked in the sex industry for some twenty years, and we met periodically over more than half this period. Long ago, she had been a model. Unlike other women we met, Tina said that she had deliberately and explicitly stepped across a key social line in order to counter the social hypocrisy that she had found so distasteful in the world of modeling. Thus, she challenged conventional morals earlier than other neophytes included in my summary above and explained that she had decided to sell sex "up front" instead.

---

5. As Michael Lambek indicates in his contributions to this volume, submission to the ritual order is a necessary entailment of particular events and choices in Rappaport's formulations.

Working part time, she learned her new job, and she did well. Upholding the precept that love and money do not mix, Tina found the daily routines as demanding as other women, and, with the benefit of hindsight, she explained how long it had taken her to realize that she had transgressed the scope of "normal" life. She thought she was following a common morality, but her practices never elicited widespread recognition. Tina was surprised by the consequences of her much earlier exercise of good judgment.

Unlike many of her colleagues, Tina never sought the money that others imagined would bring success and respect. Early on in our acquaintance, not long after Tina described her move into sex work, I came to understand that she worked only sporadically. Even though she partitioned her affairs, Tina did not aspire to a future that would be radically different from the present, like the colleagues she saw working ceaselessly so as to amass the wherewithal to assimilate at last. In the mid 1990s, Tina noticed a lot of women who faded away:

> I think especially among older women there is a lot more shame and stigma and "I have got to be a mother now" and "I have to get a husband before I get too old" and "Can I actually do that?" I knew women in their forties who were working the game, and one of the things they would say is, "Have a child now, because you won't be able to later or you won't want to later. You might have all sorts of health problems, or you'll never find a man to stick to you because you have been on the game." You see all this stupidness in films. You know an older prostitute can only marry a client.

To my eyes, Tina was linking an interest in money to a series of troubling ethical predicaments. Sex workers were stuck because they subscribed to what Lee Edelman has called reproductive futurism (2004). They wanted what they thought most other people wanted: a home of their own, full of children and relations that mattered. Tina disputed stereotypes about women, sex, and fantasies about romantic love that in her experience denigrated sex workers.[6] Like many other sex workers with some experience of prostitution, she became a feminist and joined an international sex-worker movement, as well as other forms of political opposition, but she found once more that she did not fit. As with the extensive

---

6. Tina might recognize Lauren Berlant's perspectives on this fantasy: "Reciprocity is a morally laden, actuarial, and at the same time lovely, fantasy-based concept of what mutuality in love might actually be like" (Berlant 2008: 15–16). Berlant's analyses of ordinary processes of bargaining with what there is, of survival and disappointment in place of a politics of transgression and refusal, are generally relevant to my account in this essay.

sense of division in sex work, which might allow women to preserve their honor and the repeated deferral of its fuller realization, Tina found that organized politics occluded present realities through the very passion and energy that activists invested in bringing about a better future.

Tina turned toward other forms of cultural production and education. In 2000 she spoke at length about her past, explaining how hard it had been to stay in school. She did not learn anything and left home young:

> And now particularly when I think about it, I don't regret it, it's just the way it went, but the number of books I didn't read, you know, the number of authors that people talk about in the variety of writing groups that I might go to. I always say to everyone, "Listen, I haven't read any of this. I don't know any of it. I am the ignoramus. So."

Tina's sister had just died, and the prospect of dealing with her grief alone, the last of her family alive, was daunting. She had now left sex work and reflected once more: "I am not really a greedy person. I have been described as a person who walks after money. I walk after money. I don't run after it." Over a period of some years, she had bought a home and made investments through a single relationship with an older man, a client who became a close friend. It was only when he, predictably, fell in love with her that they parted: "You know, in this life, you don't get into those sort of routine life styles. You are working different hours, you are meeting different people, and you are an outlaw. You are very much an outlaw, so you learn to make your money in different ways. And invest it and use it. You are an outlaw." I understood this reference to imply that Tina wished it had been different. She had saved her client's life long ago: he had a chronic illness, and Tina happened to be at hand in a crisis to take him to the hospital and then nurse him back to health. Subsequently, he told Tina, "You know I can't give you anything for what you have done, but the least I can do is give you a home." So he bought her a house, and she felt the loss of his friendship acutely when they parted.

Tina was now financially independent. Her sister's death led her to mourn the loss of family while still repudiating her unhappy childhood and much else about her upbringing that she considered to be modeled on conventional practices of dishonoring other people. Despite her assiduous efforts to treat her client as a close friend and a near neighbor, this man had sought to rehabilitate Tina into a world that might erase all recognition of her history as an outlaw ever since she had found herself unable to subscribe to the hypocrisies of everyday life. Tina could not help being a rebel. And soon enough, she happened to find a soul mate. In her late forties, she shared a home for the first time in her life and came to know the man's two children. I asked how they dealt with her previous history, and Tina admitted that they did not discuss it:

> I don't think it is important. Both of us, well, he's fifty plus . . . so I don't really want to hear his whole life story. . . . He came out of a very unhappy long marriage with two kids, and he doesn't want to waste any more time on pettiness and nonsense. So, and also I think it is just a totally unnecessary subject; it's like if you said to me, "By the way, I did ten years in the nick [prison]." I'd go, "Yes, that's good, what did you learn?" So I don't think it is necessary to discuss it. . . . I always said to myself if, when, I met men outside of work that, if they behaved like a client or if they treated me like a whore, then I would treat them like a client.

I learned that Tina and her new partner shared childhood experiences. Tina was trying to learn the language she knew as a five-year-old, planning a trip home to a country where it had been impossible to live. Surviving somehow, part of her family had fled, and, as far as I could tell, her parents' marriage had promptly disintegrated in the U.K. Now, Tina said, she was nervous but excited about the proposed trip, and she explained that she might even track down her family or find records about them. Tina said again that it had been hard leaving sex work: "You're used to being an outlaw—you know where you are, where you stand. Once you come back into society, so to speak, you feel you don't fit in many ways. It's hard to adjust to it. All [these] questions come into your mind and you don't know." Tina's love of freedom has elicited a response, but I do not know what happened subsequently, as we finished this research project in 2002.

## The Work of Time

Tina reevaluated her life with the benefit of hindsight and experience. Her judgments and those of other women we knew had no doubt always been unique but they were constrained less and less by a defensive armor against stigma as time passed. The monolithic disapproval of prostitution in the U.K. and other countries creates entire political and moral worlds to which dishonored sex workers perforce have to respond and to which they react initially in equally uniform ways. Bit by bit, however, women acknowledged their own unique histories and found particular ways to live in the world. I have referred above to Arendt's attention to the example, and, in the context of practices of dishonoring sex workers, I have since explored a particular example of Arendt's with Victoria Goddard (Day and Goddard, forthcoming). We looked at the biography of Rahel Varnhagen, where Arendt outlines a move in three stages from the status of pariah to parvenue and back again. This history suggested similarities with the idealized career Helen Ward and I had sketched in sex work.

Because of anti-Semitism, Rahel was a pariah in nineteenth-century Berlin. Fleeing dishonor, she found herself mired in another set of exclusions from history and the world at large, as well as from her co-religionists. Therefore, she eventually returned to her pariah status. In her account of Rahel's decision to inhabit the world, despite its violence toward her and others like her, Arendt offers a perspective on ordinary ethics and the work of time in sex work.

Rahel's attempts to assimilate as a parvenue succeeded only in converting her shared social dishonor into a personal defect. Arendt considers identification with the status of pariah the only possible route to worldliness and associated responses to things of the world, such as children, love, the seasons, and the weather (1997: 226). And yet, for sex workers, it proves difficult simultaneously to deflect shame by hiding from the world and to fight practices that dishonor certain categories of people and affirm the honor of their ostensible superiors. Tina's story shows how she, like other women, came both to repudiate and to embrace the world. Moreover, her commitment to the world as a totality reinforced the isolation that Arendt associates with introspection and with the status of parvenue. In Arendt's view, Rahel could deny aspects of reality and retreat through introspection, but her love of a free existence threw her back upon a world that promised things that only that totality can give (1997: 93). In other words, Arendt suggests, we might perforce accept the "fact" of birth and inhabit a world that also accords us a pariah status in a plural society. In the terms used by Das, this identification implies a process of digesting the world's poisons (Das 2007). The work of time in my example indicates what might be at stake in ordinary attachments to the world, where Tina waits but does not expect others to acknowledge or recognize her commitments.[7] It suggests that Tina's ethics both are very ordinary and also radically repudiate the existing order.

The taint becomes, in Arendt's account, a source of Rahel's distinction through self-realization and public action, which rejects any particularistic identification. If Tina likewise acknowledged a taint, she remained isolated

---

7. See further Steven Caton's discussion of Arendt's ethic of responsibility in this volume.

in the status of outlaw during the early 2000s, as she insisted upon the very totality that Arendt so valued. Her friend left, and Tina was, it seemed, more alone than ever. Tina might have referred to the worldliness that made Rahel an incorrigible rebel, incapable of assimilation, however sincere her attempts. Assimilation risked turning Tina and other women into observers rather than "daughters of the earth." Such isolation deprived them of the capacity to act, and Tina was left for a while without a single interlocutor. In what sense did she, then, inhabit the world? It was only shortly after this time that Tina found a soul mate.

## Concluding Remarks

Tina has left the occupation, at least for the time being. She stands as a particular and perhaps exemplary individual, whose speech might move others to act. Tina is a pioneer (Rapp 2000), who comes to ask about the very possibility of politics in such a world, refusing the goal of ends over the actuality of means and thereby illustrating precisely what Arendt considers (contrastively) intrinsic to political action: an approach that insists on new beginnings, insofar as the future can neither be read from nor determined by the past.

I have outlined various words and actions in the London sex industry that are simultaneously moral, political, and ethical. But I have drawn particular attention to the work of time, which leads an initial morality into an oppositional politics and then an ordinary ethics defined by accumulated experience and habitual skill. The work of time is a work of unique individuality. Tina could not have known the consequences of refusing ordinary hypocrisy. Her decisions might have secured her a place to live in the world as a whole. But other people considered that she had transgressed, and perhaps it was through their perception of extraordinary nonobservance that they glimpsed their own dignity and honor. In *The Politics and Poetics of Transgression*, Peter Stallybrass and Allon White argue that we should attend to the symbolic significance of the social margins, citing Foucault's comment: "Transgression. Perhaps one day it will seem as decisive for our culture, as much a part of its soil, as the experience of contradiction was at an earlier time for dialectical thought. But in spite of so many scattered signs, the language in which transgression will find its space and the illumination of its being lies almost entirely in the future" (Foucault 1977: 33). Exploring the production of the grotesque in the "taboo-laden overlap between high and low discourse" through symbols that remap bodies including, in the nineteenth century, those "around the figure of the prostitute [where] the gaze and touch, the desires and contaminations, of the bourgeois male were articulated" (1986: 137), Stallybrass and White draw attention to the disgust elicited in a politics of dishonoring sex workers. In effect, they argue against a "thin ethics" and against misrecognition of the world. Not only is this disgust a thoroughly embodied, visceral relationship, it incorporates what is excluded at another level. As they argue, dishonor is embodied in the singular (bourgeois or non-sex-working) subject, whose unconscious remains a messy heterogeneity.

Conventional understandings of political, moral, and ethical projects convey a communicative transparency that Tina never encountered. Stallybrass and White speak to her experiences when they conclude that the bourgeois democracy that emerged, "whilst indeed progressive in its best political aspirations, had encoded in its manners, morals and imaginative writings, in its body, bearing and taste, a subliminal elitism which was constitutive of its historical being. Whatever the radical nature of its 'universal' democratic demand, it had engraved in its subjective identity all the marks by which it felt itself to be a different, distinctive and superior class" (ibid: 202).

The novice sex worker has not transgressed. In her eyes, she conforms to the same moral rule as everyone else. With time, she formulates actions with other people in opposition to state rules and social discrimination. Having distinguished work and money again and again from love, she has turned an opaque and largely counterfactual prohibition into a formal guide that can be observed. And yet she remains dishonored. Tina stood by her earlier judgment and lived as an "outlaw." She looked for a place in the world with other pariahs in a struggle for honor. Political activism constructs a clear argument about the status of work that renders all workers equivalent and consequently points to the arbitrary nature of social arrangements, which are therefore amenable to reform. Informal and formal alliances across a variety of interests join in challenging the apparently natural and taken-for-granted hierarchies of social life. Political actions by sex workers in an international movement initiated in the 1970s have unmasked the inequity of a politics of dishonor that implicates corrupt officials, double standards, and fictions about the love that might as though by magic transcend the realities of this world.

However, Tina found this politics of opposition to be overly concerned with identity, in other words, sectarian. No doubt, she also tired of political activism and despaired of the increasingly repressive climate in the

U.K. and other states, which has radically reduced any prospect of emancipation. She also found that politics reproduced many of the present's problems simply by holding up the beacon of a brighter future. I have stressed Tina's skepticism about a better future because it points toward the consequences of decisions that Tina locates back at the beginning of her story. If the future for which many sex workers and political activists struggle is based upon denial as well as repudiation of the world, then it is not surprising to find that the work of time led Tina and others to mistrust and reconsider their previous judgments. It seems to me that such women came to reject all teleologies, since they inevitably bypass "the example"—histories and biographies of what remain unique and contingent works of time.

Without the promise of a redemptive future, Tina continued to recognize the world she knew and to which she attuned herself, binding worldly realities to her own life. Little by little, she has fashioned her biography as she lives through the consequences of earlier commitments, decisions, and chance events. Despite assiduous observance of difficult daily routines, it seems that she has failed to reproduce a core postulate of social life. Navigating the rule that serves both to denigrate and to guide her activities, Tina waits for affirmation and, from time to time, encounters other people who turn out to be near at hand, despite the opacity of their point of meeting. Her story ends in the year 2002, when we completed this research, as she began anew once more.

Tina's story resonates with others. To my recollection, none of these women, whether or not they still worked in the sex industry, spoke of ethics. In my interpretation, however, an ordinary ethics that overlaps with equally ordinary moral and political practices can be identified in the work of time, where a pariah insists on the reality of her experiences and acknowledges the unanticipated entailments of previous speech and action.

ACKNOWLEDGMENTS

My thanks to workshop participants and especially Michael Lambek and Naisargi Dave for their comments, as well as to Helen Ward and Victoria Goddard for their many contributions to my thoughts on these life trajectories. My debt to research participants and Praed Street Project staff spans many years, and I am grateful to AVERT and The Wellcome Trust (grant 053592) for their support.

# On the Pragmatics of Empathy in the Neurodiversity Movement

*Paul Antze*

Most of us would agree that ethics involves caring about the experience of other people. The Golden Rule points in this direction, and it is implicit in Kant's injunction to respect the dignity and humanity of persons as distinct from things. And yet there are times when this prescription fails us.

In an interesting article on Kant's view of friendship, Rae Langdon elaborates the distinction between persons and things in a way that nicely points up its limits. Drawing on the work of P. F. Strawson, she contrasts the moral or "interactive" standpoint we commonly assume toward our fellow human beings (especially those close to us) with the more practical or "objective" attitude we take toward things. In the former case, she says, "we are involved," and this involvement shows up in the way we communicate and cooperate with others. And yet, she adds, "we don't adopt the moral standpoint—the interactive standpoint—toward everybody, all the time" (Langdon 1992: 487). By way of illustration, she invites the reader to imagine a neighbor who vandalizes her car at night. When she confronts him the next day, he responds, not with an apology or an explanation, but "with bulging eyes and a torrent of incoherent invective." She now sees that he is "a badly shell-shocked war veteran," and with this realization her indignation turns to alarm. "I stop thinking of him as an agent whose reasons, mysterious as they might be, I can come in principle to understand." My neighbor becomes a problem to be managed, an obstacle to be avoided, not a person to be argued with. "This," she says, "is the attitude we have to things, items in the natural order, whose behavior is explicable under causal laws, and manipulated if you know enough about them. To adopt it is to see a person as, perhaps, 'an object of social policy; as a subject for what, in a wide range of senses, might be called treatment; [someone] to be managed or handled or cured or trained" (ibid. 487–88).

Langdon's example is compelling, but it points to a problem that was probably far from her mind. The lines between reason and madness, between a moral agent and a phenomenon to be explained or managed, are not always so clear. Given some context and a little more patience, there's always the chance that her neighbor's babblings might have made sense. In the real world of mental illness, first impressions can be misleading. The more we know about someone's cultural background and personal circumstances, the better the chance of seeing unusual behavior as something plausibly human. This may be the reason why numerous studies have shown that cultural and economic differences between psychiatrist and patient can have a direct bearing on severity of diagnosis (Littlewood 2002).

The point here is that the difference between phenomena calling for personal engagement and those calling for management or treatment is hardly obvious. It depends very much on what we bring to the encounter—on our own background and prejudices, but also on our ability to enter imaginatively into the experience of the other person. In her book *Upheavals of Thought*, Martha Nussbaum uses the term *empathy* to describe this latter capacity. For Nussbaum, empathy alone doesn't lead us to ethical conduct, though it helps to point us in that direction. "By reconstructing in my own mind the experience of another," she says, "I get a sense of what it means for her to suffer in that way, and this makes me more likely to see her prospects as similar to my own" (Nussbaum 2001: 331). It is important to note that, for Nussbaum, the ability to empathize is not just a personal characteristic; it depends on knowledge and can be a focus of education. Indeed, she envisions a future curriculum for citizenship that would "provide the knowledge of social conditions, not just as a collection of facts about diverse ways of life, but as a way of entering into those lives and seeing the human meaning of the issues at stake in them" (ibid. 441).

Whatever we might say of empathy as a basis for ethics, it is clearly indispensable to the practice of moral rhetoric. In fact it's hard to imagine

any form of moral appeal, whether for help, for justice, or for simple understanding, that doesn't aim for empathy in Nussbaum's sense of the
word. "Put yourself in my shoes," we say. "Imagine how she must have
felt." As even these bare phrases reveal, such appeals involve stories. Since
there are many ways to reconstruct the experience of another person, there
are many possible stories, and any given version is highly contestable.

In that case, we may ask, why do some stories succeed when others fail?
What makes a given story persuasive? In the case of third-person appeals,
the answer probably involves the same factors that account for other forms
of rhetorical success: a compelling storyline, effective use of evidence,
knowing and pitching to the biases of the audience. These are the arts of
the trial lawyer or crusading journalist, and they can be applied in many
ways—to elicit sympathy in some cases and the certainty of guilt in others.

When we look at first-person appeals, however, the picture becomes
more complex. By their very nature, such appeals are alike in aiming for
sympathy or at least understanding. At the same time, because the person
making the appeal is also its object, the whole transaction takes on an
added dimension. In fact, we might say that it operates in two registers at
once, corresponding roughly to the constative and performative dimensions of language. On the one hand, there is the story I tell you about
myself, subject to the usual tests of plausibility, consistency, and so on. On
the other hand, there is me telling the story, and thus a series of questions
about the "felicity" of my whole presentation. Do I seem to be sincere?
In claiming remorse, do I actually sound remorseful? Or, when I insist on
my mental and moral competence, do I perform that competence or subtly
undermine it? This is the gamble that lawyers take in putting their clients
on the stand. There's always the danger something in the client's bearing
will betray the most carefully scripted testimony.

This essay examines a particular type of first-person appeal, one that
involves this tension between what is said and what is performed in the
saying of it, but with an additional twist. It deals with the kinds of stories
told in groups whose members all share a common condition—stories told
in the context of advocacy or consciousness raising or mutual help. The
interesting point about appeals of this kind is that they carry an additional
performative burden: while ostensibly personal and singular, their real interest is communal and plural, so that my story matters only because it is
ours. In cases of this kind, the criteria for "felicity" or success are more
complicated. On the one hand, persons making an appeal on behalf of a
whole condition or category must—as in individual cases—invite empathy
and appear to be what they say they are. On the other hand, they must

also credibly embody the condition they represent. For some categories of people (women, persons of color, the physically disabled) mere physical appearance may be enough to authenticate the author's voice. In many others, however (trauma victims, alcoholics, or victims of oppression), credibility may hinge on a more complex (and often contested) cultural performance.

My concern in this paper is with the appeals to empathy made by advocates for people suffering from autism, a condition that has been defined in part as an incapacity for empathy. As I shall try to show, both the changing nature of autism and the rise of the Internet have helped to open the way for autism self-advocacy. However, in doing so they have placed advocates in a curious bind, one involving a tension between what they say about themselves and what they "perform" in the saying of it. The problem is rooted not only in conflicting claims about the nature of autism but also in the peculiarity of the Internet as a site for first-person moral claims. The end result is that, while autism advocates have been very successful in presenting themselves on-line as persons or moral subjects in Langdon's strong sense of the term, their very success in doing so has called their credibility into question.

## Autism: A Failure of Empathy?

In 1943 Leo Kanner first used the word *autism* to describe a specific childhood disorder, applying it to children who seemed unable "to relate themselves in the ordinary way to people and situations from the beginning of life" (Kanner 1943). Kanner noted that these children had other problems as well, including a failure to respond when held or picked up, delays in learning language, and a failure to use language in social ways. The meaning of the term has changed somewhat in the meantime. Today the American Psychiatric Association's Diagnostic and Statistical Manual (DSM-IV) applies it to children who show "qualitative impairment" in social interaction and communication (including language) and a propensity to "stereotyped patterns of behavior, interests and activities," including repetitive movements like hand flapping.

In the years since Kanner, there have been other changes as well, two of them especially striking. First, the view of autism as a rare and severe disorder of early childhood has given way to the notion of a "spectrum disorder," with effects ranging from severe to very mild. Indeed, the possibility that the milder forms can go undetected has led a small but growing number of adults to diagnose themselves retrospectively. It has also led to the suggestion that many so-called "geeks" (people who are good at math and socially inept) may have mild autism or its less debilitating cousin, Asperger's syndrome. This idea has lately been applied to a wide array of eccentric geniuses, including Ludwig Wittgenstein, Alan Turing, Glenn Gould, and Bill Gates (Griswold 2007).

The second change is a little more mysterious, though it may owe something to the first. Autism is much more common today than it was in Kanner's time. According to the Center for Disease Control, in fact, the chance that a child born today will fall somewhere on the autism spectrum is one in 166, more than twice the rate a decade ago and more than ten times the estimated rate in 1970 (Center for Disease Control 2007).

Predictably enough, the spread of the diagnosis has created a large and highly visible parents' movement dedicated to awakening public awareness and marshalling more support for research and treatment. Over the past decade, organizations like the National Autism Association, Autism Speaks, and Cure Autism Now have established a strong presence on the Internet, where they present their own compelling moral appeals. Although their agendas may vary, what these groups share is a common sense of urgency about autism as a severe medical problem requiring aggressive action at many levels. They often exhort readers to put themselves in the place of families overwhelmed by the "nightmare" of this "devastating diagnosis" (NAA website). Sometimes the language is more extreme. Thus, for example, in his forward to a popular account of a mother's life with an autistic child (McCarthy 2007), Jerry Kartizinel likens the condition to a demonic force that "steals the soul from a child; then, if allowed, sucks life's marrow out of the family members, one by one." A promotional video for CAN (Cure Autism Now) invites the viewer to "imagine that aliens were stealing one in every two hundred children. That is what is happening in America today" (quoted in Hacking 2009: 44). It is interesting that, in the moral appeals mounted by these groups, autistic children themselves never appear (one might argue they *cannot appear*) as moral agents in their own right. (Indeed, sometimes, as in the cases above, the whole point is their *absence*.) Where they do appear, it is as classic targets of Langdon's second, or "objective," standpoint, that is, as objects of social policy or treatment, in need of more resources in order to be adequately "managed or handled or cured or trained," as Langdon might put it.

The "objective" view of autistic children implicit in the language of parents' groups draws added support from much of the expert writing on autism. It seems to follow directly, in fact, from Simon Baron-Cohen's highly influential claim that these children lack what he calls a "theory of mind." By this he means that the core impairment underlying their many problems is "an inability to attribute mental states to oneself and to others and to interpret behavior in terms of mental states" (Baron-Cohen 1995: 55). In a landmark paper, Baron-Cohen, together with Alan Leslie and Uta Frith (1985), described the results of an experiment comparing relatively high-functioning autistic children with normal and mentally retarded control groups. In the experiment, each child is shown a drama with two dolls, Anne and Sally. Anne puts a marble into a basket while Sally looks on. Then Sally leaves the room, and while she is out Anne takes the marble from the basket and puts it in a box. When Sally returns the researcher asks the child where Sally will look for the marble. The authors found that normal and retarded children over three years of age uniformly answered that she would look in the basket, showing that they understood the difference between what they knew and what was in Sally's mind. Nearly all the autistic children failed this test. The authors concluded that the autistic children's failure to appreciate the difference between their own and the doll's mind reflected their inability to represent mental states. "As a result of this," they said, "the autistic subjects are unable to impute beliefs to others and are thus at a grave disadvantage when having to predict the behavior of other people" (ibid. 43).

Baron-Cohen later coined the word *mindblindness* (1995) to capture this central feature of autism, arguing that it applies equally to children and to adults. He has more recently (2002) proposed that this difference makes autistic persons "emotion-blind" as well, citing evidence that they share an "extreme male brain" that is far better at systematizing than empathizing. He concludes that even high-functioning adults with autism suffer from a fundamental incapacity for empathy that explains many of their difficulties in navigating the social world.[1]

---

1. Autism research remains a complex and highly contested field. While the work of Baron-Cohen has been central to both expert and popular understandings of autism over the past two decades, it has also been criticized as failing to account for the range and variability of autistic behavior. At the same time, recent studies by a number of researchers have begun to converge around a more optimistic view of autism, which emphasizes differences in perceptual processing rather than higher-order cognitive deficits (Edelson 2006; Mottron, Dawson, et al. 2006; Soulières, Dawson, et al. 2008). This work also called attention to the presence of specific above-average intellectual skills even in low-functioning autistic children. One implication is that there may be ways to use these skills to work around their perceptual limitations.

Theories like Barron-Cohen's have contributed to a popular view of autism as a condition of profound impairment, relieved in just a few cases by narrowly circumscribed savantlike abilities—as seen, for example, in the film *Rain Man*. More to the point here, they contribute to the view that autistic persons cannot qualify as moral agents in the ordinary sense of the word, because they lack the basic capacity to imagine the experience and mental states of others. In other words, viewed in light of Langdon's Kantian distinction between our "interactive" relations with persons and our "objective" treatment of things, they put autistic people very firmly in the latter category. In doing so, they may be further reinforcing the "empathy wall" separating autistic experience from the rest of the world, a wall propped up on one side by neurological deficit, on the other by pessimistic assumptions about the mental capacities of persons whose behavior offers few direct clues about what they are thinking.

Luckily, in recent years some important cracks have opened in this wall, beginning with the publication of Temple Grandin's autobiography, *Emergence: Labelled Autistic* (co-written with Margaret Scariano), in 1986 and followed by a second memoir, *Thinking in Pictures*, in 1995. These candid and lucidly written books offered the first public glimpse into the experience of autism, while conveying a sense of the author as a determined and resourceful person who gradually found ways to work around her limitations and build a successful career. A further set of memoirs by Donna Williams, *Nobody Nowhere* (1992) and *Somebody Somewhere* (1994), offered a very different perspective, more emotionally colored and focused on the author's gradual progress toward a sense of self and connection to other people. In addition to what they have conveyed about the experience of autism, both Grandin and Williams have done a great deal to promote a more optimistic view of their condition and its possibilities.[2] At the same time, the narrative trajectory of both sets of books—from autistic chaos to something like a normally ordered life—has undercut their value as accounts of autism as an ongoing way of being.

### The Neurodiversity Movement

A far more important opening for autistic adults came with the rise of the Internet. While dedicated Web pages and chat lines have been a boon to

---

2. These two books have opened the way for a series of other, more recent works, including T. R. Mukhopadyay's *Beyond the Silence: My Life, the World and Autism* (2000), Kamran Nazeer's *Send in the Idiots: Or How We Grew to Understand the World* (2006), and Daniel Tammet's *Born on a Blue Day: A Memoir of Asperger's*

all sorts of grassroots movements, in the case of autism sufferers they seem to have provided something more: a form of communication uniquely suited to the autistic's social and perceptual disabilities. In contrast to face-to-face interaction, which many autistics find a confusing blur, keyboard chatting takes place at a rate easily controlled by participants, and it leaves a permanent trace. Even more important is the fact that the keyboard restricts communication to a single narrow channel of words, dispensing with all the signals—tone of voice, gestures, and facial expressions—that autistics find so hard to read. The information missing from these encounters has another fringe benefit as well: it allows autistic people to communicate without betraying their autism. In effect it has enabled them to leave their autistic bodies behind, so that revealing their condition or level of functioning becomes a matter of personal choice. For autistics who are able to use a keyboard, the result has been nothing less than revolutionary. Today, in the words of one influential advocate, "the Internet is for high-functioning autistics what sign language is for the deaf" (Dekker, n.d.).

The Web has given many autistic people a way of taking on new, more "able" personae and forming new connections to one another independent of family and caregivers. In doing so, it has given rise to what many participants describe as the Neurodiversity Movement, located not in any geographical region but in a proliferating series of websites, chatlines, and blogs. The movement has its own lingo: "auties" and "aspies" are people with autism and Asperger's syndrome, respectively; "curebies" are those, parents usually, who advocate for a cure; "neurotypicals" (NTs) are the rest of us.

To the extent that this movement had a founding moment, it was probably a 1992 meeting between Donna Williams and Jim Sinclair (another high-functioning advocate), which led to the creation of Autism Network International and its very popular email list, ANI-L. Today other major sites include Autistics.org, which hosts an excellent library of written commentaries by autistics spanning the past fifteen years, The Real Voices of Autism, "a social network for the autistic community," and The Autism Hub, which promises "the very best in autism blogging." Links on each of these sites lead quickly to a host of others, many with evocative names: "Autism Diva," "Posautive," "Oddizm," "Wrong Planet," and "The League to Fight Neurelitism," to name just a few. These sites even extend into the virtual world of "Second Life," where an island called Brigadoon is home to "The Autistic Liberation Front."

---

*and an Extraordinary Mind* (2006). When taken together, they offer a compelling answer to any lingering illusions about the uniformity of autism as a condition.

The postings one finds on these sites are mainly of two kinds—individual exchanges on a variety of subjects (many of them tucked away in members-only mailing lists), and a more highly visible array of declarations, confessions, manifestos, proposals, and pleas, usually directed to fellow autistics, parents, professionals, and sometimes the public at large. While these latter contributions vary widely in tone from earnest entreaty to righteous indignation, most could be described as moral appeals—for respect, understanding, and support, but above all for a new and more empathic view of autism. Because these appeals draw their authority from the authors' personal experience of autism, they provide vivid examples of the speech acts in which the "I" is actually a "we" and the true predicate of personal stories or insights is an entire condition, category, or movement. As I shall try to show, however, there is a basic tension between what is claimed in these appeals and what is implicitly performed in them. The tension is implicit in the central idea underlying nearly all these appeals: the concept of *neurodiversity*.

At the most basic level, neurodiversity is simply the idea that the human brain can be wired in a variety of ways, none of them inherently superior. However, as it plays out in the moral rhetoric of autism activists, this idea involves an uneasy marriage between two different appeals. The first is a call to see autism as not a disease or disability but just another way of being human. Drawing analogies to the history of gay rights and the struggle to defend deaf culture against medical interventions, neurodiversity advocates have railed against the search for a "cure" favored by many parents' organizations. Not only are autistics not in need of curing, they say, the very idea is demeaning and dangerous in ways that smack of eugenics. In an essay responding to a letter from a cure-oriented parents' organization, the activist Amanda Baggs writes:

> One cannot love someone . . . and simultaneously wish that they were someone else or that people like them should not be born. And those are exactly the messages that cure and prevention send out. . . . But they are not the result of autism. They are in fact the result of . . . the idea that it is better to eliminate autism and autistic people rather than adjust to our existence. (Baggs, n.d.a)

In a similar vein, here is Jim Sinclair, co-founder of Autism Network International:

> What are the goals of medical research on autism? To "cure" me—to make me fit the world better by altering my ways of sensing, perceiving, thinking,

feeling, and relating, until I'm no longer the same person? To even out my autistic friends' oddnesses so that they're no longer the same people I know and care about? . . . To create a world that has no people like me in it? These are the goals that I'm supposed to demand increased funding for? (Sinclair, n.d.d [1995])

In a somewhat lighter vein, the "different, not diseased" theme informs a wide array of postings that relativize differences between autistics and neurotypicals, while poking fun at the biased stereotypes underlying NT views of autism. One of the most striking is a mock-serious website, "The Institute for the Study of the Neurologically Typical." Posing the question "What is NT?" the homepage delivers the following grave response:

> Neurotypical syndrome is a neurobiological disorder characterized by preoccupation with social concerns, delusions of superiority, and obsession with conformity. Neurotypical individuals often assume that their experience of the world is either the only one, or the only correct one. NTs find it difficult to be alone. NTs are often intolerant of seemingly minor differences in others. When in groups NTs are socially and behaviorally rigid, and frequently insist upon the performance of dysfunctional, destructive, and even impossible rituals as a way of maintaining group identity. NTs find it difficult to communicate directly, and have a much higher incidence of lying as compared to persons on the autistic spectrum. (Institute, n.d.)

The site goes on to note that "NT is believed to be genetic in origin" and that the brain of the neurotypical "may have overdeveloped areas related to social behavior." "Tragically," it adds, as many as 9,625 out of every 10,000 individuals may be neurotypical." Other entries include an on-line NT screening test, a parody of Baron-Cohen's theory of mind experiment, and an elaborate DSM-style diagnostic protocol for "Neurotypic Disorder."

Rhetorically speaking, a parody of this kind, produced by self-identified autistics, strikes at two levels. At an explicit or "constative" level, it raises questions about the prejudices embedded in expert characterizations of autism. At a performative level, it reinforces this message through its evident command of humor and the very "theory of mind" that autistics are supposed to lack. The effect is to suggest—and in a sense show—that the expert view of autism is an arbitrary prejudice, akin to ethnocentrism.

Jim Sinclair takes up a closely related point in a brief essay, "Some Thoughts about Empathy." Confronting the standard view that "autistic people lack empathy," he counters that "it might be more fair to say that

autistic people lack certain expressive and receptive communication skills
. . . and that this, combined with any cognitive or perceptual differences,
means that neurotypical and autistic people do not share each others' perceptions."[3] In this respect, autistics and NTs face each other across a barrier of mutual incomprehension. And yet there is a difference:

> When I am interacting with someone, that person's perspective is as
> foreign to me as mine is to the other person. But while I am aware of this
> difference and can make deliberate efforts to figure out how someone else
> is experiencing a situation, I generally find that other people do not notice
> the difference in perspectives and simply assume that they understand my
> experience. . . . If I know that I do not understand people and I devote all
> this energy and effort to figuring them out, do I have more or less empathy
> than people who not only do not understand me, but who do not even
> notice that they do not understand me? (Sinclair, n.d.a [1989])

As these examples suggest, the first version of neurodiversity tends to
discount the impairments associated with autism and to evoke a kind of
empathy that sees autistics as a misunderstood minority, perhaps not so
different from us once we take the trouble to speak their language and
appreciate their distinctive needs. To the extent that there is an ethical
argument implicit in these appeals, it is to a classic liberal universalism
with obvious precedents in the civil-rights and women's movements: autistics are people like the rest of us and thus are entitled to the respect and
autonomy that come with full membership in society.

The second version of neurodiversity, which appears side by side with
the first (often in the same authors), takes almost the opposite tack. Here
the appeal is still to view autistics as "different, not diseased," but now the
accent is on "different." This appeal reaches out in two directions, toward
autistics themselves, who struggle unhappily to fit into the neurotypical
world, and toward the parents and professionals who still see normality as
a goal. On the autistic side, the message is that trying to appear normal is
an exercise in frustration and, worse, a kind of self-betrayal. Again, in the
words of Sinclair:

> Some autistic children internalize this message and accept "being normal"
> as their major goal in life. And it's been my observation that the more
> deeply invested an autistic person is in being normal, the more likely it is

---

3. Sinclair's point is consistent with the emerging research cited above (n. 1)
and with a central idea developed in Hacking's recent article "Humans, Aliens and
Autism" (2009). See also n. 4 and n. 6, below.

that he or she suffers from anxiety, depression, and low self-esteem. It's a natural consequence of making one's top priority to become something other than oneself. (Sinclair, n.d.b [1992])

Autism chatlines often carry personal stories about the dangers of "faking NT." One anonymous contributor, for example, writes of an unhappy childhood and adolescence in which he was coerced to meet the expectations of parents and peers to behave normally:

> Now, at 35, after spending a lifetime of "faking NT," I fear I may be coming to the end of my rope. The depression is overwhelming. . . . I have already attempted suicide once and am currently in grave danger of attempting to do so again. . . . I've been in and out of therapy a fair amount of my adult life—therapists are anxious to "teach me social skills" and learn how to "play the NT game," which is simply another way of saying that they want to turn me into someone that I'm not. . . .
>
> All this, just so the NTs don't have to be uncomfortable with seeing me talk to myself, or drum my fingers on the back of my head, or perseverate on topics that they find boring or weird. Is my mental health—my very life—really worth that? (Anonymous, 2003)

Directed to parents, the same concern becomes a call for a different and more demanding kind of empathy. In an address to the Autism Society of America in 1995, Jim Sinclair argued that the real challenge is not learning to see the child hiding behind the autistic symptoms, but coming to accept the fact that this child is not and never will be "normal":

> Autism isn't something a person has, or a "shell" that has a person trapped inside. There is no normal child hidden behind the autism. Autism is a way of being. It is pervasive; it colors every experience, every sensation, perception, thought, emotion, and encounter, every aspect of existence. It is not possible to separate the autism from the person—and if it were possible, the person you would have left would not be the same person you started with. (Sinclair, n.d.c [1993])

To succeed with their autistic children, Sinclair concluded, parents need a special attitude, one that does not come easily:

> Take a look at your autistic child sometime, and take a moment to tell yourself who that child is not. Think to yourself: "This is not my child that I expected and planned for. . . . This is not that child." Then go do whatever grieving you have to do—away from the autistic child—and start learning to let go. After you've started that letting go, come back and look at your autistic child again, and say to yourself: . . . "This is an alien child who landed in my life by accident. I don't know who this child is or what it

will become. But I know it's a child, stranded in an alien world, without parents of its own kind to care for it. It needs someone to care for it, to teach it, to interpret and to advocate for it. And because this alien child happened to drop into my life, that job is mine if I want it.

Other advocates have urged a similar attitude, not just to parents of autistic children, but to anyone encountering autism:

> Talk to autistic people—communicate with us as if we were aliens, not as if we were damaged versions of yourself. Forget what you think you know about us, and learn about us and, most importantly, from us. You might be surprised, at the combination of differences and similarities between what we want in life and what you want in life. Approach us without the preconceptions of what you have been taught about autism, and what you believe about people in general, and you will see a lot. Explore the uniqueness and beauty that is autism, in all its forms, respect it, and don't try to eliminate it. (Baggs, n.d.a)

This figure of the autistic as alien appears repeatedly in neurodiversity postings and has even inspired the creation of a whole website, wrongplanet.net, which features a little cartoon alien as its mascot.[4] As Sinclair's words above suggest, however, this term implies a call to a specific type of empathy, one that abandons preconceptions and tries to meet the autistic on his or her own ground. To the extent that this call implies its own ethical theory, it is clearly no longer the liberal universalism noted above. The insistence that autistic persons be appreciated precisely in and through their difference from neurotypicals (rather than by reference to their hidden similarity) seems more in keeping with the ethical attitude espoused by the philosopher Emmanuel Levinas, who called for a radical openness to "the alterity of the Other" and warned against all reductions of "the Other" to "the Same" (Levinas 1989).[5]

There is something very appealing in these calls by autistics themselves to approach them with the same lack of preconceptions we might bring to an encounter with aliens. However, it is hard to read them without a

---

4. Hacking (2009) has shown that the figure of the alien actually appears very widely in popular representations of autism, albeit in many different ways. He suggests that, while this term has been a source of controversy (some find it attractive, others offensive), it draws its resonance from the sense of strangeness that autistics and neurotypicals experience in trying to read each other's behavior. That experience applies in the present case as well, but Sinclair's claim is that it calls for a specific type of moral sensitivity.

5. For a more explicitly Levinasian perspective on communication with autistic persons, see Pinchevski (2005).

lingering doubt. Exhortations of this kind draw their authority from the fact that they are written *inside* autism; they are saying, in effect, "here is what you need to do to reach us," where "us" denotes the whole range of autistic persons. This is a very diverse group; are they all equally "alien"? And more to the point, to what extent do the authors themselves, the neurodiversity activists, qualify as the kinds of aliens they describe? Certainly they can't be said to speak with an alien voice. Their writings, in fact, seem to be vivid examples of the classic hazard of first-person testimony mentioned earlier: sometimes what is said can be undermined in the very saying of it. At a performative level they can't fail to leave the reader with a nagging question: Are these people really autistic?

This is certainly a question raised with some vehemence by parents' organizations, who have criticized neurodiversity activists as "a handful of noisy people . . . who do not represent a broad swath of the autism community" (Solomon 2008). One parent writes to complain that "the Neurodiversity Movement is ashamed of the lower functioning members of the autism world. . . . Content with themselves, they wish to deny the opportunity for lower-functioning autistic persons to be treated and cured" (Doherty 2007). Another sharpens the point further:

> Don't you question the fact that these people are highly verbal and intelligent, many of them successfully employed and in relationships, yet many of them claim not to be fully toilet-trained? Lack of self-help skills and self-injurious behaviors are usually associated with people who are lower functioning who are unable to express their wants and needs. These are the facts. I question strongly as to whether these people are being truthful.
> (Quoted in Baggs, n.d.b)

Neurodiversity advocates parry this charge with a compelling rebuttal. Writing for the on-line journal *Ragged Edge*, Cal Montgomery points out that objections to the verbal fluency of neurodiversity advocates create a requirement that would bar any advocate from speaking. According to the critics, she writes, "if you are capable of making your opinions known, then you're obviously not autistic, because autistic people can't communicate. And if you're not autistic, obviously you aren't qualified to pontificate on what autistic people believe. [So] if you are capable of making your opinions known, you aren't qualified to have them" (Montgomery 2005). Jim Sinclair bolsters this point with examples of similar objections from the history of the disability rights movement and even the history of slavery. He noted that Frederick Douglass, the former slave who became an eloquent abolitionist, "was suspected of being an impostor because he was too educated and too well-spoken to fit prevailing stereotypes about the ignorance of slaves" (Sinclair 2005).

It is interesting that, while these responses make a telling polemical point, they remain less than wholly convincing. There seem to be two reasons for this. The first is the well-known diversity of the "autistic spectrum," which raises doubts about anyone's right to speak about autism in general on the basis of personal experience. The second arises from the very freedom that the Web as a text-based medium has afforded autistic people, a freedom to leave their bodily and social limitations behind as they establish newly competent on-line personae. The problem is that, once it leaves the body behind, first-person speech loses much its testimonial weight. "I" on the Internet does not point to a speaker or even a known writer whose embodied presence might vouch for what is said. "I" on the Internet could be anyone. In fact, the only indexical information attached to an on-line testimonial lies in the language itself—its tone, its style, perhaps the knowledge it reveals—and of course even these are questionable. Unfortunately for on-line neurodiversity advocates, nothing in their language serves to authenticate their autism—indeed, their very eloquence appears to speak against it.

If it is true, as I have been suggesting, that this problem arises from the text-based limits of the Internet, then today these limits no longer strictly apply. The advent of Internet video applications like YouTube has opened the way to new modes of self-presentation that permit a more complex relationship between what is said and what is performed. Neurodiversity advocates have been quick to seize this opportunity. Of their various efforts to date, the most interesting remains a nine-minute YouTube video by Amanda Baggs entitled *In My Language*, which has drawn more than eight hundred thousand hits since it was posted in 2007. Its content bears directly on the issues at stake in this paper.

The video opens on a short, overweight young woman with close-cropped hair, her back toward the camera, standing before a window, rocking slowly and waving her arms as she sings or wails aimlessly in rising and falling tones. The vocalizations continue as the camera cuts to a series of close-ups of the woman's hand making various repetitive movements: scraping a loop of wire against a door, brushing her hand over a computer keyboard, twirling a telephone wire, playing with a stream of water, rattling some wire on a door handle, making a Slinky bounce up and down. This goes on for just over three minutes (though it seems much longer), accompanied only by the tuneless singing. Then a title appears against a black screen: "A Translation." The repetitive motions continue, but now we hear a computer-synthesized woman's voice:

> *The previous part of this video was in my native language. Most people assume that when I talk about this being my native language, that means that each part of the video must have a particular symbolic message. . . . But my language is not about designing words or even visual symbols for people to interpret. It is about being in a constant conversation with every aspect of my environment, reacting to every aspect of my environment.*

The voice goes on to explain that:

> *Far from being purposeless, the way I move is an ongoing response to what is around me. Ironically, the way I move when I respond to everything around me is described as "being in a world of my own," whereas if I . . . only react to a much more limited part of my surroundings, people claim I am "opening up to true interaction with the world."*

There is a shot of her typing rapidly at a keyboard, and a few seconds later the voice comes from the computer's speaker: "*As you heard, I can sing along with what is around me, [but] it is only when I type something in your language that you refer to me as having communication.*"

The monologue continues in this vein, building toward its central point:

> *The way I naturally think and respond to things looks and feels so different from standard concepts . . . that some people do not consider it thought at all. . . . And since their definition of thought defines their definition of personhood so ridiculously much, they doubt that I am a real person as well. I would like to honestly know how many people, if you met me on the street, would believe I wrote this.*

As the video nears its end the voice reminds us that it "has not been intended as a voyeuristic freak-show" but:

> *as a strong statement on the existence and value of many different kinds of thinking and interaction in a world where how close you can appear to a specific one of them determines whether you are seen as a real person. . . . And in a world where those determine whether you have any rights, there are people being tortured, people dying, because they are considered non-persons, because their kind of thought is so unusual as not to be considered thought at all. Only when the many shapes of personhood are recognized will justice and human rights be possible.*

The concluding disclaimer offers a good point of entry to the meanings at play in this video, since it tacitly implies that the author is making a deliberate display of her own strangeness. She certainly succeeds in this, since the opening minutes of the video are indeed strange and puzzling to most viewers. However, her aim, as she points out, is not to stage "a freak-show" but to join the strangeness of her autism with her activist identity and goals. At a very basic level this conjunction gives her first-person appeal the embodied authority needed to speak for autistics in general. It also creates a performance that conveys the "diversity" of the neurodiversity movement in an unexpected way, by combining its extremes in someone who appears to be "high functioning" and "low functioning" at once. This is more than a symbolic statement, since many neurodiversity advocates argue that the contrast between the two ends of the spectrum has been overdrawn and that every autistic person is a curious amalgam of strengths and incapacities. At the same time, in presenting her repetitive singing and gestures as her "language," Baggs is saying that they are more than mere symptoms of her condition, that they are a medium of experience essential to her way of being. In doing so she tacitly reinforces the neurodiversity theme of autistics as aliens who deserve the same effort of understanding that they extend to us. The fact that she tells us these things not in her own voice (which makes only wordless sounds) but through a keyboard and voice synthesizer makes even her "translation" into a kind of alien speech.

Quite beyond these effects, the real importance of *In My Language* may lie in the larger question it poses for the issues we have been considering here and for ethical theory in general. Like the appeals of other neurodiversity activists, it compels us to think beyond the simple Kantian dichotomy that separates persons we intuitively recognize as moral agents from those whose strangeness confines them to thinglike status as objects of policy or treatment. More than that, it invites us to question the source of that "strangeness" and to reconsider its moral implications. In a recent article, Ian Hacking (2009) has argued that what autistics typically lack is not a basic cognitive faculty for grasping other minds but simply the ability to read the feelings and intentions of other people directly from their facial expressions and behavior.[6] This view finds strong support in a growing body of research that understands autism as arising more from differences

---

6. Hacking's discussion draws extensively on the work of Wolfgang Kohler, who pointed out that ordinarily we are able to read the facial expression and physical bearing of other people, especially those close to us, in such a way that we "just see" what they are experiencing. While Kohler regarded the ability to form a such a direct picture of another person's experience as "the common property and practice of mankind" (quoted in Hacking 2009: 53), Hacking argues that this is precisely what autistic people lack and hence why they are often described as alien.

in perceptual processing than from the absence of higher cognitive faculties.[7] The implication is that autistics who do succeed in communicating are those who have found a way of working around their perceptual limitations, often, as their own accounts suggest, through a laborious process of guesswork and inferential learning.

To see autism in this way is also to recognize a problematic ambiguity in the concept of empathy as it bears on moral agency. There is an important—perhaps even fundamental—difference between "empathy" as an immediate perceptual skill and the kind of empathy that matters morally, the kind we achieve by "reconstructing in our own minds the experience of another," to use Martha Nussbaum's phrase. The absence of the former tells us nothing about a person's capacity for the latter, except perhaps that achieving it may not come so easily. By the same token, our failure to make intuitive sense of someone's behavior is not a prima facie basis for "objective" recourse to management or treatment, as implied in Langdon's dichotomy. It can be taken just as readily as a call for the hard work of inference and imagination needed for access to a different experience of the world. This is a lesson that applies not just to encounters with strangeness imposed by neurological differences, but to those arising from cultural differences as well.

ACKNOWLEDGMENTS

I am grateful to Naisargi Dave, Michael Lambek, and an anonymous reviewer for their suggestions in response to an earlier draft of this paper.

---

7. See n. 1, above.

# Being *Sadharana*: Talking about the Just Business Person in Sri Lanka

### *Nireka Weeratunge*

The ethics of business is a very old problem, debated extensively by philosophers, writers, and social scientists, and it underpins current concepts of social justice within a market economic system. In rural societies, where most people engage in agriculture or fishing, disdain for those who make a living by trade has a long history. Sri Lanka is no exception. Current global discourses on business ethics and the profit motive tend to focus on the practices of large corporations rather than on micro, small, and medium businesses, which form the economic fabric of most countries. In this essay, I examine the discourse of *doing sadharana* ("just")[1] business in order to determine how rural people perceive and talk about businesses in their communities and regions, and what it is about business and business people that they find problematic. I will also examine how business people respond to these perceptions by talking about *being* a *sadharana* business person. These discussions about exchange relations constitute an intuitive

---

1. The term *sadharana* in colloquial Sinhalese translates as "fair," "just," or "reasonable." It is used as an adjective or adverb in relation to a transaction, decision, judgment, argument, or behavior. This is in contrast to its usage in Vedic Hindu texts and in colloquial Hindi as "ordinary," "common," or "basic." The Sinhala term does not imply that *sadharana* is "ordinary"; it signifies both a desirable norm in transactions and a sense of rising above the ordinary.

approach to one strand of ordinary ethics in the social life of people in Sri Lanka. To some extent, I follow the anthropology and political economy tradition of the "moral economy" of peasant societies (Scott 1976, 1985, Popkin 1979) and of trade (Evers and Schrader 1994, Southwold-Llewellyn 1994a,b) from an interpretive perspective (Keesing 1981).

I will combine an anthropological perspective on the person with philosophical concepts of justice and virtue to explore the relationship between business people and others. By "person," I refer to society's confirmation of the individual's identity as socially significant (La Fontaine 1985). Personhood is defined, measured, and valued differently across cultures. South Asian notions of the person are embedded in social relations—while personhood is often seen as fluid (Daniel 1984), most anthropological literature (Trawick 1992, Lamb 1997) on the region emphasizes an individual's relationships to and feelings toward other persons over his or her own qualities or attributes. I will attempt to determine how a business "person" is constituted by his or her social relations and transactions, and how this might reflect on his or her business practice and self-identity as a business person. This addresses questions of the status and identity of business people within their communities in terms of local notions of justice connected with the virtuous human being, grounded partially in the religious traditions practiced in Sri Lanka, as well as gender and ethnic constructs.

## *Justice and Virtue: Unraveling the Threads*

In *Nicomachean Ethics*, Aristotle distinguishes between justice and virtue, perceived as not the same in "essence": justice is a "relation to one's neighbors," and virtue is a "certain kind of state without qualification." He also distinguishes between "particular" justice, referring to voluntary and involuntary transactions between people, and "general" justice, being the prescribed laws that govern people's lives. "Grasping" or taking too much of what is good was considered a "particular" form of injustice. The just was equated variously with the proportional or the commensurate, as well as seen as equal, intermediate, and relative, consistent with the Principle of the Mean. "Therefore, the just is intermediate between a sort of gain and a sort of loss, including those which are involuntary; it consists of having an equal amount before and after the transaction" (Nicomachean Ethics 5.4). "Equal" here is meant in relative terms. In this essay, I am interested specifically in Aristotle's notions of "particular justice" and "virtue" as they relate to understanding the ordinary ethics of business relations in rural Sri Lanka. From an anthropological perspective, the Aristotelian concept of particular justice deals with relational aspects of personhood, whereas virtue deals with the qualities attributed to personhood. Moreover, the Aristotelian notion of justice, being intermediate and proportional, is indeterminate. Thus, I will look at how justice is negotiated in everyday transactions between business people and their clients, focusing on what might be imbued in local discourses of business justice from a wider, complex moral universe, shaped by various understandings of virtue.

This begs the question of the extent to which Aristotelian notions are commensurate with notions of just business in Sri Lanka. The idea of not grasping is very much part of everyday notions of fair business practice and is consistent with the Buddhist notion of eliminating desire. In a society asked to believe that the root cause of suffering in the world is desire, the business person, like everyone else, is expected to demonstrate virtue as a human being by following the Middle Path toward curtailing desire. Thus, in the Sri Lankan context, the Aristotelian perspective of "grasping" or "greed" is not merely a particular form of injustice that characterizes transactions but in its wider sense of "fulfilling desire" could also be considered as a lack of virtue. In other words, grasping within transactions between individuals, shaped by underlying norms and values, has some relationship to virtue as a "certain kind of state without qualification." This link between individual grasping and the quest for curtailing desire as a social goal is evident in G. Nanayakkara's (1997) argument that Buddhist societies have been relatively slow to generate accumulation and economic growth, while being relatively quick in the egalitarian distribution of growth, referring not only to Sri Lanka but also to Thailand and Burma. The significance of *sadharana* is discussed by Nanayakkara (1997: 227) in terms of the Buddhist moral of congruity. By "congruity" he refers to a cluster of notions, which include the maintenance of balance, avoidance of extremes, and following the Middle Path. This resonates with the Aristotelian concept of justice as the "Mean" or as intermediate and proportional. This is affirmed by many respondents engaged in the business-development sphere in Sri Lanka.

> People follow the Buddhist teaching of limiting your greed. We're not a very ostentatious people. We don't display our wealth, compared to other South Asian countries. Except for the gem traders—they have a huge facade to show sellers that they have sufficient money to buy gems. (Janaka, male Sinhala Buddhist business development professional, Colombo)

While the Aristotelian concept of particular justice is useful in making sense of everyday business transactions, his notion of virtue is helpful in understanding the embeddedness of these transactions within a wider Buddhist moral universe of maintaining balance and avoiding extremes. These two notions also intersect with the relational and qualitative dimensions of personhood in anthropology. My essay will attempt to bridge the distinction made by Aristotle between justice and virtue by looking at the understandings of entrepreneurs' personhood and their business practices, as articulated by rural people in Sri Lanka. In doing so, I will also explore the commensurability of the Aristotelian principle of the Mean with the Buddhist imperative of the Middle Path.

Moderation and satisfaction with the nonmaterial virtues of life are prescribed in the Buddhist concept of the Middle Path. Business is perceived to undermine this ethic, because it implies gain for one party and loss for the other.

> Buddhists think business is inferior because it's taking something illegally. All persons are equal in Buddhism. . . . Buddhism says to be satisfied with what you have—don't search for other things. (Suranjith, male Sinhala Buddhist provincial-level government official, Puttalam)

Thus, outdoing someone or competing against someone becomes an ordinary ethical problem.

> In our country, there is no competition. If somebody goes forward, that person, who is now in front, doesn't compete any further. It is sufficient for them if they get something. (Malini, female Sinhala Buddhist preschool teacher, Nuwara Eliya)

However, some respondents interviewed during my research argued that most people are pragmatic about what they follow in Buddhism. Several referred to a Buddhist code for business in the sutras and pointed out that effort, positive thinking, and economic development are not contrary to Buddhism. Thus, Buddhists are seen to have a capacity for business as much as adherents of other religious groups, implying a lack of a contradiction between being a skilled or just business person and a virtuous human being.

> If all are good Buddhists they would go to the jungle and forget everything; they'll eat whatever they get, wear one robe. . . . It would be a peaceful life without stress. . . . There is a clear code for business in Buddhism—keeping aside portions for consumption, investment, savings, and donating to the

poor. (Chamath, male Sinhala Buddhist business development official, Colombo)

Confronted with these underlying notions of congruity and of the Middle Path, of contesting views on the material and nonmaterial dimensions of life, the everyday ethics of business transactions always entails a tension that is commensurate with the Aristotelian notion of justice, as a relative sense of not grasping, of both parties not suffering a sense of too much loss or gain. In a predominantly Buddhist society[2], the larger moral universe applies to entrepreneurs of other ethnic groups, following different religious orientations, as much as to Sinhala Buddhists. Thus, discourses around business transactions in Sri Lanka reveal an inextricable link between the Aristotelian concepts of particular justice and virtue.

The terms *business person* and *entrepreneur* are used interchangeably in this essay, although a distinction between the two would be made in business studies (McClelland 1961, Cochran 1971, Timmons 1989, Luczkiw 1998). In Sri Lanka, however, there are no well-accepted colloquial forms to differentiate between the two English terms.

My essay is based on material gathered over the last five years in the course of working on several enterprise and entrepreneurship development projects, which attempted to identify cultural strengths and barriers, supportive and nonsupportive sociocultural contexts for starting or expanding micro and small enterprises in farming and fishing communities in Sri Lanka (Weeratunge 2001, 2008; Reinprecht and Weeratunge 2006). Most of the research was done through qualitative, open-ended questionnaires with a range of respondents—entrepreneurs, farmers,

---

2. According to the 2001 Sri Lanka Census, around 70 percent of the Sri Lankan population are Sinhalese Theravada Buddhists, while 15 percent are Tamil Hindus, 8 percent are Tamil- and Sinhalese-speaking Muslims, and 8 percent are Christians, cutting across both the Sinhalese and Tamil ethnic groups. The conflict between the Sinhalese-dominated government military forces and Tamil militants of the Liberation Tigers of Tamil Eelam (LTTE) in the last thirty years is often portrayed as a primordial ethnic conflict between two separate linguistic groups practicing different religions. However, Buddhism and Hinduism are related religions, both originating in India. Both ethnic groups share a syncretic tradition, and therefore respect for each other's religion generally overrides religious animosities. While Hindu Tamils might question the practice of Buddhism by the Sinhalese, especially the contravention of the principle of nonviolence, they do not necessarily challenge the Buddhist ethics that constitutes its moral universe. In the same vein, many Hindu beliefs and practices are incorporated into the form of Theravada Buddhism practiced by rural Sinhalese in Sri Lanka.

fishers, workers, state employees, government officials, community leaders, and representatives of organizations working on business development. In two projects, life histories and decision-making trajectories were collected from micro and small entrepreneurs, as well. While the interviews covered the entire spectrum of types of business (trade, services, and manufacturing) and sizes (micro, small, medium, and large), the respondents were mainly those engaged in micro and small trading and service enterprises, as they comprise the numerical majority within the business landscape of Sri Lanka.

## A History of Otherness

Business people have been looked upon as "outsiders" (Moore 1997) by the predominantly rural *Goigama* (farmer) caste of the Sinhalese population of Sri Lanka because they tended to come from particular ethnic groups and/or castes in the past. The historical development of capitalism in Sri Lanka is identified with the "Indian Trading Groups" (Indian Muslims, Bohras, Gujaratis, Sindhis, Parsis, Colombo Chetties) and the Sinhalese castes of *Karawa-Salagama-Durawa* (KSD), with customary occupations as fishers, cinnamon peelers, and toddy tappers, respectively, originating in South India (Roberts 1982, Arseculeratne 1991). While some of the *Goigama* Sinhalese have always been involved in trade (Jayawardena 2000) and had joined the ranks of the country's fifty "most wealthy businessmen" by the 1980s, the Sinhalese KSD castes, the "Indian Trading Groups," and Muslims remain "over-represented" among this group of fifty in relation to their share of the population (Moore 1997).[3] By the 1990s, the *Goigama* had managed to make considerable inroads into business, often by using political support (Moore 1997).

There is a vast global literature in anthropology on the relationship between ethnicity and entrepreneurs (Geertz 1963, Firth and Yamey, eds., 1964, Barth 1967, Babb 1984, Cohen 1974, Cook 1984, Ueda 1992, Maegawa 1994, Larsen and Harris 1995). Particular ethnic groups and castes are perceived as "middlemen minorities" and have been able structurally to occupy specific trading niches because they were mobile, were considered to be foreigners, outsiders, or strangers (Simmel 1967 [1908]), and were not permitted to own land by local rulers. Thus, ethnicity and caste,

---

3. Muslims in Sri Lanka are considered to be both a separate ethnic group and adherents of a separate religion.

particularly the long experience of these particular groups in trading, are salient factors in their entrepreneurship. This is because dense social linkages within ethnic/caste networks provide information and trust, two vital ingredients in business success (Moore 1997, Landa 1994). First-generation entrepreneurs in Sri Lanka have come disproportionately from minority castes or ethnic groups, often with unknown class origins. Most successful entrepreneurs have had no higher education or formal training of any kind and value loyalty and commitment over educational qualifications (Ranasinghe 1996). Although men have generally dominated the small, medium, and large business spheres in Sri Lanka, many women traders are involved in buying and selling local produce at the micro-level. Thus, notions of the entrepreneur as a person are deeply embedded in local social, cultural, economic, and political networks and structures.

The extent of antipathy toward business varies among regions and ethnic groups in Sri Lanka. According to the first national survey on corporate social responsibility (International Alert 2005), significant majorities believed that businesses exploited consumers (69 percent) and destroyed cultural values (58 percent). These perceptions were particularly high in regions with predominantly Sinhalese populations (except in North Central Province) and lowest in Northern Province, with a predominantly Tamil population. While a large majority (76 percent) agreed that businesses help society by providing employment, only a minority (46 percent) believed that they helped by providing goods and services to communities. The social responsibility of business was reiterated by a large majority (77 percent)—they believed that businesses need to take into account the impact of their decisions on employees, local communities, and the country, in addition to making profits.

Moreover, in identifying the characteristics of businesses that would contribute to the betterment of society, the second most important factor for people was "conducting business in the most honest and fair manner" (72 percent)—after "providing many employment opportunities" (73 percent) and before "taking the environment into consideration" (71 percent), "respecting the cultural and religious identity of the country" (68 percent), "providing good value for money" (67 percent), and "caring about consumers and product quality" (66 percent). The least important were "having well-recognized brand names" (34 percent), "being a leader in innovation and technology" (44 percent), and "releasing reliable information about business activities" (49 percent). Thus, business in Sri Lanka is judged as much by sociocultural expectations as by economic expectations. The anticipation that business will be conducted honestly and fairly was high across most regions, with the lowest expectation in the urbanized western province.

### *Particular Justice: Being Reasonable and Fair in Transactions*

What does "conducting business in the most fair and honest manner" imply? In qualitative studies, many respondents talked about doing "*sadharana* business" as something both nonentrepreneurs and entrepreneurs value. The corporate social responsibility survey was framed to some extent around the cultural discourse of doing *sadharana* business. The word *sadharana* primarily refers to being "reasonable," "fair," or "just." In terms of a business transaction, it designates a range of practices encompassing fair prices and fair play. It includes offering what is perceived to be a good price, restricting the margin of profit, offering good-quality or unadulterated wares, writing out accurate bills, and not hoarding goods in the expectation of a better price later on. In Aristotelian terms, this would be not grasping—not taking more than one's rightful share of a good thing.

Following the time-honored practice of Aristotle, who defined justice by working backwards from injustice, local notions of justice in business practices can also be approached by considering their opposite. Injustice does not refer merely to the margin of profit, an important consideration—profit margins of 100 to 200 percent are considered excessive. Malpractices relating to quality, treatment of employees, and hoarding were all considered unethical business practices. Not everyone thought business people in their communities were unjust. Reasonable prices, convenient access, and employment opportunities were aspects used to define the just business person. Some people pointed out that business is not always about justice, given that profit is a more important consideration, and business people were not judged negatively on this aspect.

Entrepreneurs often consider other entrepreneurs to be unfair or unreasonable, while considering themselves to be just. Competition, rivalry, and envy are underlying dimensions of their relationship to other entrepreneurs. Some entrepreneurs held positive notions about their peers in their village, although they were critical of "traders from outside." Ideas of fairness in terms of sustaining established relationships were emphasized. This was considered as an indication of prioritizing human values over individual profit.

The people who do business in the village are not unfair—we don't hoard goods, but sometimes traders from outside can be unjust. We always sell to a permanent person whom we know, even for a lesser amount—rather than to the person who offers the highest price. There are both traders from the village and outside who buy from us. We're ahead in our values, although we might have an average amount of money in our hands, rather than big money—we live well. (Ariyapala, male Sinhala Buddhist farmer and entrepreneur, Puttalam)

Entrepreneurs are used to the idea that they might be considered unjust by others and provide the counter-argument of unfairness of producers, who sell at high prices and falsely accuse traders of nonpayment. Thus, the yardstick of fairness or justice is used by both entrepreneurs and customers to assess their day-to-day transactions, and each party will readily fault the other for being unreasonable, unfair, or unjust.

To gain a more rigorous understanding of local notions of transactional fairness, a version of the ultimatum game (also known as the "fairness" game) was played at a number of workshops involving entrepreneurs and representatives of organizations involved in business development (Reinprecht and Weeratunge 2006). Participants were divided into two groups—those offering and those receiving money. A hypothetical sum was offered individually to members of one group on the condition that he or she would receive it only if he or she shared it with a party in the other group. The person who received the money could decide what he or she would offer the other party. However, if the other party did not accept his or her offer, no money would be forthcoming. Thus, the person with access to the money had to gauge what would be considered an acceptable share by the other person.

The results were consistent with those obtained in most industrialized and agrarian societies internationally (Henrich et al. 2001).[4] They indicated that the majority of those offering and receiving among all ethnic groups in Sri Lanka considered sharing 50/50 of an amount they had received to be the fair option.[5] However, the study was less concerned about experimental and controlled conditions that can generate robust statistical

---

4. Even through global results show overall that reciprocity and fairness are more important than economic maximization, cross-cultural results show noteworthy deviation on what is considered fair, especially in some tribal and nomadic societies. See Henrich et al. 2001.

5. Because a rigorous quantitative sampling procedure was not used, statistically valid results were not calculated for each workshop, though dominant patterns were recorded. The purpose of these workshops was to understand the rationale for the decision making, rather than to calculate standard deviations.

findings than about the explanations provided by participants for their decisions. Offers and acceptances were explained on the basis of both fairness and an equal partnership in a venture. Those who offered half of their share explained this in terms of the recipient's expectations, the necessity for equity, mutual benefit and cooperation, and avoiding anger or recalcitrance. Those who accepted the offer also referred to expectations, mutual benefit, equity, fairness, and happiness. It was pointed out that "it is an injustice to give too little or too much."

Only a few participants offered more or less than 50 percent of the sum they had received. Of these two options, the higher amount was more suspect and was refused by recipients, who questioned the motive for offering a larger share. The reasons offered were that this would lead to dependency and lack of trust, the need for further discussion and negotiation, and the uncertain rationale for receiving a larger share. This is consistent with the Aristotelian notion of giving or taking too much of a good thing, where the lack of equivalence places one party at a moral disadvantage vis-à-vis the other: "It is plain too that the distributor acts unjustly, but not always the man who has the excessive share; for it is not to whom what is unjust appertains that acts unjustly, but he to whom it appertains to do the unjust act voluntarily, i.e. the person in whom lies the origin of the action, and this lies in the distributor, not in the receiver" (Aristotle, *Nichomachean Ethics*, 5.9).

Offers of less than 50 percent were refused by some and accepted by others. Those who made such offers argued that they were entitled to the larger share, as they were the first beneficiaries. Those who accepted said that "something was better than nothing." Those who refused said that a smaller share indicated selfishness, a lack of fairness, and an insecure basis for partnership, again demonstrating a lack of "proportion," in Aristotelian terms.

## Virtue: *Manushyakama*, or Being a Human Being

It is not enough to be fair and reasonable in one's business transactions to be considered a good or just business person. The importance of being a good person, a human being—*manushyakama* (literally, "being a human being") is, interestingly, most often stressed by entrepreneurs themselves. They especially judge other business people by the presence or absence of *manushyakama*.

> There are higher-level business people in the district in transport and communication. They have no time for their families, children,

society—no time for others. They don't have the humanism [*manushy-akama*] and generosity [*udavkarana gathi*] that we have among our small producers. (Ariyapala, male Sinhala Buddhist farmer and entrepreneur, Puttalam)

*Manushyakama* is often perceived not as an abstract virtue in and of itself; rather, it has to do with the relationship of people to others around them. Thus it is closer to a notion of justice, as a "relation to one's neighbors." However, it implies more than conducting business transactions in a fair and honest way. Every business transaction is imbued with understandings of justice that come from a broader moral universe, with entrepreneurs often affirming a convergence between being a successful business person and a good human being.

Whatever you do should be done properly. If you harm anybody, that is no good. Patience is very important, and you have to be a good human being. Only then can you say you are a successful business person. (Brito, male Sinhala Catholic entrepreneur, Puttalam)

By contrast, some nonentrepreneurs found an essential contradiction between business and religion, and they were not convinced that business people practiced the ethics of their religion. They indicated that religion merely served as a support mechanism in the quest for business success.

All businessmen here go to the *devale* [deity shrine]. They start business daily by lighting lamps to the deities, whether Ganesha, Buddha, or Jesus. If they really follow religion, they can't do business. They have to cheat and play out the customer sometimes. (Jayantha, male Sinhala Buddhist chamber of commerce representative, Kurunegala).

To understand the tensions between what constitutes *manushyakama* and the requirements of business transactions, it is useful first to look at how the identity of business people is constructed.

### The Problem of Identity: To Be or Not to Be a Mudalali

A wide range of business people are referred to as *mudalali* (Sinhalese) or *muthalali* (Tamil), denoting a trader or shopkeeper. Although microentrepreneurs are not generally included under this term, most business people oriented themselves to a notion of "doing business" (*business karanawa*) and worked within an underlying colloquial understanding of the *mudalali.* Literally meaning "moneyed person," the term implies making a living by buying and selling.

In S. Southwold-Llewellyn's (1994a) pioneering work on traders in the Kurunegala district, she points out that a *mudalali* was generally thought of as an "outsider exploiter" on whom rural producers and customers depended, both to sell their produce and to purchase what they needed, often on credit. *Mudalalis* were not necessarily outsiders, as they required some linkage to the community (based on kinship, friendship, or marriage) in order to start a business. They were exploiters only in the relative sense of the word, since they had to operate within the moral norms of the community. The *mudalali* gained by being perceived as an outsider, since he or she could expect the customer to pay back the credit, and the customer gained because he or she was more likely to receive credit from an outsider rather than a relative. Southwold-Llewellyn argues that, although traders did not often have social characteristics that differentiated them from the rest of the community, the outsider myth was perpetuated by both the trader and customer to reinforce the credit relationship.

Many business people complained that it was necessary to give credit to retain clients, while they had to make an effort to get the money back. Although not being indebted and thus not dependent on anyone was valued by most people, credit repayment itself was not similarly valued. The moral obligation to ensure the subsistence of poor people, referred to as "kindness," was also acknowledged.

> And if you are not kind you cannot do this type of business [grocery shop]. You must work hard to give customers reasonable prices—then everybody likes to come to your place. They do not go to other shops. If you know how to keep your customers for years you can be successful. (Karuna, female Sinhala Buddhist entrepreneur, Polonnaruwa)

Southwold-Llewellyn (1994a) points out that, in credit relationships between suppliers and copra merchants, the supplier expected a reasonable price, as well as credit for emergencies and consumption. Not an absolute criterion of reasonableness or fairness but the perception of fairness was important.

In rural Sinhalese and Tamil farming communities, the personhood of the *mudalali* was therefore regarded with ambivalence. Most business people, including newly trained ones, said they did not want to call themselves *mudalalis*, though others referred to them as such, sometimes seriously, jokingly, or as an insult. The majority did not mind others referring to them as *mudalalis* but did not want to call themselves that. Poorer respondents were more likely to take pride in the title of *mudalali*, even when they were not sure that doing business was a "proper" job.

> My present work is the food business. It's not really a job, but just what I am doing. None of my neighbors will say I am doing business. They think of me as somebody who does not have any free time. I do think of myself as a *mudalali* because I do business. I would be happy if others call me one. (Rita, female Sinhala Catholic entrepreneur, Puttalam)

A minority pointed out that they did not want to consider themselves or be considered to be *mudalalis* because it set them apart from other people.

Thus, while the idea of doing business is not necessarily seen as negative, identifying oneself as or calling someone a *mudalali* has connotations of ambivalence or resentment. This underlying resentment is manifested explicitly as envy or jealousy (*irisiyawa*), which several entrepreneurs identified as what they least like about being an entrepreneur. While most business people refrained from identifying envy as a problem, only a minority answered in the negative when explicitly asked whether anyone was envious of their business success. Most identified neighbors and relatives, rather than business rivals, as the primary adversaries.

> My neighbors said it was better to do a laborer's job than to do business. The rich people, because they wanted me to work for them as a laborer. The others said this [business] was a difficult task. When I started operating my brick kiln, someone set fire to it, and it burnt to the ground. I think it was one of my relatives. It didn't stop me from starting all over again. (Anura, male Sinhala Buddhist entrepreneur, Kurunegala)

## The Qualities of the Business Person

In exploring intersection of the Aristotelian notion of virtue and anthropological understanding of personhood, the kind of qualities and characteristics (*gathiguna* in Sinhalese, *kunam* in Tamil) associated with business people become relevant. These are mediated by gender, ethnic, and religious constructs. In discussing business success, three core clusters of important qualities emerged from entrepreneurs.[6] These were "winning

---

6. Qualities are referred to as "core" not in some essentialist sense but because a larger proportion of respondents consistently indicated them as distinctive qualities or features. These are to be considered normative, rather than empirically valid—i.e., what people believe to be true.

hearts/minds" or "talking nicely to people," patience, and aptitude or knowledge.

"Winning hearts/minds" (*hitha dinagenima*) was related to "being close to the heart/mind" (*hithavathkama*) and "cordiality," literally, "having a good heart" (*suhadakama*). This was not conceived as merely skill in persuasion and networking. Paradoxically, the business person was to become a *hithavath mudalali*, who could cultivate a relationship close to the heart/mind of the customer and be trustworthy, even though *mudalalis* in general were perceived as exploitative outsiders. Thus, a notion of trust was implicit in the relationship of *hithavathkama*. Of the three major ethnic groups, Muslims were attributed with special, even embodied, qualities in winning trust ("knowledge in their body"), acquired through tradition and habit or even "inherited," according to some. Respondents who considered women to be better at business mentioned this ability in women, enhanced by their physical attractiveness relative to that of men.

Patience with customers and business partners, as well as with suffering losses, was emphasized repeatedly. Both Muslims and women were seen to have this attribute. Given that customers always want to be served as soon as they enter the business, business people had to go through the motions of trying to satisfy everybody at once. Some clients were demanding and rude but had to be tolerated. Business partners were not always prompt with supplies or payments. Patience might mean losing time, with a corresponding loss of efficiency and transaction costs, or a tolerance for low quality. None of this was as important as hurting a relationship with somebody.

> My son gets angry easily when he has to go pick up money from the *mudalalis*, but we try to teach him to be patient. They always complain about quality, however hard we try. We have to bear it and be calm. If I get angry at what the *mudalalis* say, I lose the order and don't have any business.
> (Ahmad, male Muslim entrepreneur, Nuwara Eliya district)

Even though patience was not a competency that was taught in training programs, business trainees considered it a key characteristic. Some of them were so convinced of its significance that they even claimed that it was part of the entrepreneurial competencies that they had learned in training.

The third cluster was aptitude and knowledge, related to running a business, production of goods, and operating in markets and in society. Trainees saw this knowledge as something to be acquired, whereas other business people viewed it as part of their experience. Although some entrepreneurs emphasized continuous learning by networking, trial and error and accumulated knowledge were valued more. Muslims were considered to possess this knowledge through tradition, learning, and networks, and some thought their aptitude was inherited. People also indicated that knowledge or aptitude was a critical attribute for business success, associated with individual characteristics such as skill (*hekiyava*), effort (*uthsahaya*), courage (*dhairya*), and self-confidence (*athma vishwasaya*), irrespective of gender. Ideas about the origins of business qualities were gendered. Most men perceived these as being learned, whereas most women perceived them as a combination of learning and inheritance, often stating that knowledge was learned, but almost everything else was inherited.

Other qualities mentioned by fewer respondents—such as cunning, the ability to save, and the resilience to bear profits and losses—were attributed to both Muslims and women to a greater degree than to other ethnic groups or men. Ability to compete, risk taking, efficiency, and innovation (considered desirable entrepreneurial competencies in most entrepreneurship training programs) were mentioned by a tiny minority or not at all. Risk taking and efficiency were associated to a larger degree with Muslims and men.

The predominant qualities that were emphasized—winning hearts/ minds, patience, and knowledge—all deal with connections to other people, indicating that the person of the entrepreneur is constructed by social relationships. This is confirmed by the studies of C.T.A. Perera (1996) on the social power base of low-country Sri Lankan entrepreneurs, using D. C. McClelland's concept of the "need for affiliation." Perera has emphasized that affiliation characteristics are more pronounced in Sri Lankan entrepreneurs than achievement (risk taking, efficiency, concern for quality) and planning.

A persistent issue that emerged in the intersection of business success and virtue was *lejja bhaya* ("shyness and fear," "shame," "modesty"). Reluctance to enter and negotiate within a male business world and restrictions on mobility after dark were attributed to the *lejja bhaya* of women and considered obstacles to business success. By contrast, Muslims were considered to be an ethnic group that lacked *lejja bhaya*. Their relative lack of concern with status, expressed in their readiness to engage in small business, was seen as a distinct ethnic characteristic.

> Everything works out for them [Muslims]. They don't have the kind of minds/hearts that envy one another. Most of all they believe in their God.

Three times every day they pray to God. It [success] is what God has given them. They'll try to live well, even by selling cloth on the pavement. We look at "respect" and don't like doing something like that. (Meena, female Tamil Hindu trainee, who did not start a business, Badulla district)

Muslims, Hindus, and Catholics were more likely to feel that their religion influenced their business practice, based on faith in God or deities. However, even though Buddhists often claimed that religion had no influence over their business practice, it was clear that they also practiced a plethora of rituals to invoke business success. Taboos that function as shared abstinence among a social group (or several individuals) are considered a significant aspect of personhood in anthropology (Fortes 1966, Lambek 1993) and emerged as an important concern in business practice as well. Taboos associated with business are strongest for Buddhists and Muslims. For Buddhist entrepreneurs, the main prohibition is related to taking life or harming other beings. Livelihoods associated with rearing livestock for meat, fishing, aquaculture, and selling pesticides are considered taboo.

When I did poultry, I didn't go near the temple. I was doing well with the business, and Prima [a multinational company] supported me to expand. I started with twenty-five chickens in 1991, mainly because I wanted eggs for the family, and by 1996 I had four thousand chickens. But I didn't really like the business. My mind was not at rest, although I wanted to earn money. (Nayana, female Sinhala Buddhist entrepreneur, Kurunegala)

Sale of alcohol is also considered harmful, a restriction shared with Muslims, although intoxication, not consumption of alcohol per se, is prohibited in Buddhism. In addition, Muslims referred to *riba* (usury) restrictions, which they considered difficult to maintain without an Islamic banking system.

Most Buddhists tended to explain the influence of their religion on business in ethical terms, such as doing *dehemi* business (righteous business, literally "according to the doctrine," abstaining from stealing and lying, usually rolled into the three notions of *hora boru vancha*—stealing, lying, and deception or vice) or doing no harm, being calm and having a "strong heart/mind" ("what is in your heart/mind" or "mental peace," "mental satisfaction," "lightness of mind" ) as notions linked to Buddhism.

Religion helps me to distance myself from stealing, lies, and vice [*hora boru vancha*] and engage in a just [*sadarana*] enterprise. (Sunil, male Sinhala Buddhist entrepreneur, Puttalam)

In our religion purity of the soul [*shudda adyatma*] is not important. What matters is the courage and resolution you have in your heart/mind, what is in your heart/mind from childhood. (Samanthi, female Sinhala Buddhist entrepreneur, Nuwara Eliya)

Admittedly, the fact they say they do just business does not mean that Sinhalese Buddhists necessarily do so in practice. However, the repeated concern with justice and fair play seems to indicate that they were under more moral pressure than others to be perceived as just, to counter popular discourses that construct traders as exploitative outsiders.

By contrast, Hindus, Muslims, and Catholics are not encumbered to the same extent by their communities and thus are able to pursue their business while maintaining their identities as respectable persons.

This point is further supported by the evidence in one study that business tended to be the sole means of household livelihood for the majority of Muslim business people and around half of the Tamils, while it was so for only a third of Sinhalese Buddhist entrepreneurs. In addition to this being a risk-averse livelihood strategy, ideological notions seem to underlie the tendency of Sinhalese Buddhists to engage in part-time business, so that their personhood is not completely defined by their association with business.

### "Bravado and Generosity": Earning Respect as a Business Person

The anthropological notion of personhood is defined by others considering one's identity to be socially significant. For business people in Sri Lanka, the discussion of identity as a *mudalali*, as well as notions held about Muslim business people, reveal that the respect and status they receive from others is a fundamental concern. One way they go about achieving this is by supporting and participating in religious, community, and life-cycle events within their communities.

If you earn anything, you should help other people—the community. Then people don't want to take things away from you. (Ruwani, female Sinhala Buddhist NGO representative, Colombo)

Although most religions prescribe shares to be spent on the poor or social welfare in general, none of the respondents referred to these, with the exception of Muslims. Muslim entrepreneurs were aware that they were expected to provide 2.5 percent of their income in charity to the poor as *zakat*, considered a form of purification from greed and envy. However, most respondents indicated that they were considered too poor themselves to provide *zakat* and that the mosque was happy with any contribution they would make. In the west coast (Puttalam district) of Sri Lanka, mostly Catholic entrepreneurs pointed out that they set aside around 10 percent of their profits for contributions to the community and social welfare activities, including the church, whereas in other parts of the country this was not as precisely defined. A Catholic priest from the same region indicated that the tradition of contributing 10 percent to social welfare was waning.

Businessmen, especially those who have been in business for some time, are clearly expected to give large sums of money or contributions in kind to the community. Contributing to community events is an opportunity for a man to affirm his status, increase his prestige, and advertise his business. Businesswomen offer more modest and less conspicuous contributions. Young people who had started businesses were often not in a position to contribute financially to community events. However, they built goodwill by contributing their labor and participating in village societies instead. Members of Muslim traders' associations in Puttalam mentioned that they contributed to temple and church ceremonies and festivals just as much as to mosques. They pointed out this played a role in maintaining goodwill toward them in other ethnic communities.

Often the temple, church, or mosque can become a space where business people interact, negotiate deals, maintain relations within business and kinship networks, and affirm their status as persons. The Karumariamman temple in Badulla district was built by Pushparaj, a textile entrepreneur operating in Colombo who was born in a "line room" (quarters) to a Tamil working-class family in the nearby tea plantation. He had vowed to give a food offering to the deities and his former fellow estate workers every day of the full moon for the rest of his life because he had received the blessings of the Goddess Karumariamman to become a successful trader. On full moon days, he invites both his Tamil and his Sinhalese business partners in the textile trade in Colombo to visit the temple and worship the goddess. Some of his partners are encouraged to place their gold chains on the goddess during the *puja*, so that these will be imbued with the *shakthi* (energy or power) of the goddess. Although the temple provides a means of achieving instrumental goals for businessmen like Pushparaj, it is also the interface between the economic system and the ritual system, for the logic of prestation that Pushparaj is involved in is a not strictly a capitalist logic. Yang (2000) points out: "There is another attitude here, equally challenging to capitalist accumulation: wealth can be made, but one must display the generosity and bravado to squander it in the community for prestige."

The studies consistently revealed that most business people in Sri Lanka are well integrated into social and political networks within their communities, as well as regional and national organizations. Most were members of community-level organizations and societies, such as funeral assistance, farming, fishing, women's, rotating credit, micro-finance, and trade associations. Women entrepreneurs tend to become members of such groups more often than men do. A minority of these entrepreneurs are officeholders as well, with men generally predominating. However, some women held important offices and were actively involved in a number of societies.

Although business people constantly strove to provide sufficient support to community events and increase their goodwill, the status and respect they expected was not always forthcoming. This was often discussed by both entrepreneurs and others in terms of "social acceptance" or "social recognition." Priyanthi, a twenty-one-year-old who had started an Internet café, was one of the few entrepreneurs who mentioned as essential characteristics of business success the need for "a brain" and "cunning or shrewdness," as well as getting along with all kinds of people and "not being proud." Asked what, apart from personal qualities, a business person needs to be successful, a question that many other respondents answered with "capital" or "infrastructure," Priyanthi immediately replied "social acceptance." Earning respect is one of the biggest challenges for business people and acts as a leverage for fair business transactions.

> Social acceptance [*samaja piligenima*] of your status [*thatvaya*], what you receive from your family lineage [*paramparava*] is very important. It is very clear to us because we started our business here . . . we didn't know people here. We were outsiders to them, and they wanted to chase us out. But we overcame all those initial problems. (Priyanthi, female Sinhala Buddhist entrepreneur, Matale)

Some respondents perceived links to farming, uniqueness within a farming universe, relationships with people of occupations that were considered respectable (such as government officers), wealth, and generosity to afford social recognition to entrepreneurs. Many business people, however, contested the level of social acceptance or recognition they received. They lamented bitterly that they were treated as exploiters and black marketeers, despite their contribution to the development of their regions by providing employment, goods, and services, as well as contributions to religion, education, and health.

Entrepreneurs are the center of the economy, but increasing production is not valued. . . . At the Assistant Government Agent's office, they don't even offer us a seat. If rulers and officials don't treat us properly, farmers and other people have the same attitude. They call us "black marketeers." If an entrepreneur develops here, it's because of his own effort. . . . We should be satisfied as human beings. If we don't get respect, we don't feel happy about being in the business field. (Ruwan, male Sinhala Buddhist traders' association representative, Polonnaruwa)

Thus, the role of the business person in society and notions of status and respect afforded to the business person were issues of great concern to business people. The ambivalence of this status and the need for fulfillment as a "human being" were repeatedly emphasized.

### Conclusion: Negotiating Justice and Virtue in Everyday Business Transactions in Sri Lanka

How commensurate are Aristotelian concepts with notions of just business in Sri Lanka? This paper argues that the particular justice of not grasping in business transactions needs to be placed within a wider moral universe and discourses, related to virtue as a "certain kind of state without qualification." This Aristotelian sense of virtue is embodied in the idea of *manushyakama*, or "being a human being." *Manushyakama*, unlike the notion of doing *sadharana* business, is not tied to an understanding of the proportional or intermediate, as it intertwines transactional relations with the sphere of generosity, reciprocity, social acceptance, and respect. All these make up the stuff of the anthropological concept of personhood. At the same time, these virtues are not entirely independent of the imperative of following the Buddhist Middle Path and eliminating desire, thus placing some sense of the proportional or moderation within the fluid boundaries of "being a human being."

Both entrepreneurs and their clients understand intuitively that doing *sadharana* business is not about a determinate sense of justice or injustice.

Some do fair business, and some are exploitative. Some charge reasonable price for things that they sell. Some who give credit to other people charge excessively high interest rates. If you take ten business people, they have ten different ways of doing business. Some only think about their improvement. Many go in the wrong path when they do business. (Kusuma, female Sinhala Buddhist entrepreneur, Polonnaruwa)

However, what exactly the right path is remains somewhat hazy for almost everyone. To do just business and be a virtuous human being are a tall order in any society. Aristotle recognized that doing the right thing was not easy, even if one were to know what the right thing was. He understood that people have difficulties in applying a general moral rule, such as justice, to a particular case. It is in this sense that every business transaction is fraught with tension. Every transaction is an opportunity for the entrepreneur to assert her- or himself as a just business person. At the same time, what exactly is just is not always apparent. What matters is the construction of justice, fairness, or reasonableness—the way in which the business person and the client decide to negotiate the intermediate within their complex moral universe. The striving for and the affirmation of his or her social identity as a just business person and a virtuous human being depend upon it.

### ACKNOWLEDGMENTS

I would like to thank Michael Lambek and other participants in the symposium The Anthropology of Ordinary Ethics for their invaluable feedback on an earlier version of this paper. My appreciation also goes out to my former colleagues at the Centre for Poverty Analysis and the ILO Enterprise for Pro-Poor Growth Project, both in Colombo, as well as my current colleagues at the WorldFish Center in Penang for their support at various stages of the research and writing process that contributed to this paper.

# PART SEVEN

# Ethical Life: Encounters with History, Religion, and the Political

# Engaging Others: Religious Conviction and Irony in the Holy Lands

## *Donna Young*

This essay focuses on the ethical practices of a group of pilgrims to the Holy Lands in the summer of 2007. Most of the pilgrims participated in a month-long biblical course created by the Sisters of Zion at Ecce Homo in the Old City of Jerusalem, but there were also guests at Ecce Homo pursuing their own spiritual and political projects. The Sisters considered all of them pilgrims.[1] Collectively they included theologians, nuns, and priests, although most were deeply religious lay people. Whether Roman Catholic or not, the majority had chosen to stay at Ecce Homo because they appreciated the religious community's sensitivity to cultural differ-ence and openness to the religious traditions of others. Indeed, this recep-tivity to others guides the moral and ethical practices of this particular Roman Catholic religious order, founded in the nineteenth century by Jewish converts to Christianity. My focus here is not on the forms of bibli-cal exegesis the religious community of the Sisters of Zion espouses but rather on the ordinary ethics (Das 2007, Lambek in this volume) that the

---

1. Recent anthropological studies of pilgrimage include Badone and Roseman, eds. (2004), who emphasize the intersections of pilgrimage with tourism; and Coleman and Eade, eds. (2004), who focus on new forms of pilgrimage in which people embrace displacement as they seek meaning in a world thought to be in motion and in flux.

pilgrims at Ecce Homo articulated as they negotiated the religious and political landscape of the Holy Lands, a form of ethics informed by their particular reading of the scriptures.

With the exception of two young American Mormons, who briefly stayed at Ecce Homo on their way to a kibbutz, none of the pilgrims I spent time with interpreted biblical texts literally. Indeed, they found troublesome the young Mormons' interpretation of the current political crisis as foretold in the Bible.[2] Others have noted the ways in which "Jewish Israeli tour guides and Protestant pastors become co-producers of a mutually satisfying performance that transforms the often-contested terrain of Israel-Palestine into Bible Land" (Feldman 2009: 351; Habib 2004).[3] By contrast, the pilgrims with whom I spent time approached various holy sites with a good deal of ironic reflection and were disparaging of the historical narratives attached to various places and objects. They rejected, if you will, the dominant chronotopic reading of the Israeli landscape, which is actively promoted by fundamentalist Jews and Christians, and fuels archaeological probing into every corner. Their own interpretations of the Bible were more metaphorical, multivalent, and open-ended, primarily concerned with the narrative of Jesus Christ's life, which they considered instructive.

The pilgrims at Ecce Homo focused on Jesus Christ's relationships with the disinherited and his disdain for those who were so preoccupied with the letter of the law in ancient Israel that they had lost sight of its spirit. There is, within Judaism, an internal critique that considers such practitioners to be holy fools. Inversely, within Christianity, holy fools are considered blessed, as they shun the letter of the law, placing compassion and love above worldly matters, above politics. According to this form of interpretation, Jesus Christ was a holy fool, and Christianity ushered in a new form of ethics, in which an inclusive and universal love for others transcends old tribal authorities and traditions. The pilgrims who accept this theological position are neither secular liberals, who find in the biblical Jesus Christ a revolutionary prototype (see, e.g., Eagleton 2007 and Žižek 2003), nor woolly New Age gnostics, who accord every belief system a kernel of truth (see Žižek and Milbank 2009). Rather, the pilgrims at

2. See Crapanzano (2000) on literalism and McAlister (2005) for an analysis of popular genres that contribute to this particular way of understanding current political crises in the Middle East.

3. For an example of work that contributes to this enterprise, see Crossman and Reed (2001).

Ecce Homo were guided by a distinctly Christian moral ethos that informed their notions of virtue and judgment, and guided them as pilgrims traversing military checkpoints and separation walls to visit holy sites. Ironically, the liminality of checkpoints became the focus of their spiritual reflection, as it provided an opportunity to recognize the suffering of others and act in solidarity with the victims of political strife, both Jewish and Palestinian.

One morning at breakfast, a pilgrim was introduced to me as a professor at an American university who often brought his students to Ecce Homo. The Sister who introduced us explained that I was an anthropologist of Christianity. When I asked the professor what he taught, he replied "Christian Anthropology." An awkward silence followed. I am convinced he had a better notion of what I did than the other way around. Certainly his Christian anthropology and my secular discipline are rooted in the same Western traditions of philosophy (see Asad 1993, 2003; Gillespie 2008; Keane 2007). Although we have grown estranged at a theoretical level, now kissing cousins at best, as the summer passed, I found it increasingly difficult to distinguish between our ethical practices. Our daily engagements with others, ethics as ordinary practice, were essentially the same. I began to think there was a strong case to be made for anthropology as the holy fool of the academy.

## Ethnographic Present 2007: Twilight in Jerusalem

It is twilight and I am hurrying back to Ecce Homo, the convent and pilgrim house on the Via Dolorosa in the Old City of Jerusalem, where I am living for the summer. I have been visiting a Jewish friend in West Jerusalem, who has dropped me off at the Jaffa Gate because she is afraid to drop me off in East Jerusalem, the Arab part of the city. Her husband insists it is unsafe. So I've waved goodbye and quickly skirted the perimeter of the walled city, crossing the only too visible line that divides West from East Jerusalem, to enter the Muslim Quarter of the Old City at the Damascus Gate. It is immediately apparent that something is wrong. The steps descending to the gate are emptied of the rows of shoes, undergarments, perfume, and other sundries that one typically steps over when entering through this gate, the main entry into the Muslim Quarter. And it is quiet: no one is hawking wares; there are no women shopping, no children scurrying in and out of the crowd or cheekily flicking at the large brim of my sun hat. Even the elderly men who congregate on the benches along the gate's wall have vanished. There is always a military presence at the gate, but today this presence is increased. I am filled with a sense of foreboding. As I enter the ancient market of the Old City, I see that all of the stalls are closed, even though this is usually the busiest hour in the *suq*. Most alarming of all is the quietness, for I have grown accustomed to the sounds of the mischievous urchins who play, wrestle, work, and generally rule the streets until the wee hours of the morning, when their family's small and cramped flats have finally cooled from the heat of the day, making sleep possible.

At every turn, as I make my way to the convent, there are youthful Israeli soldiers, who nod at me as I pass by. When I reach Ecce Homo, the Palestinian porter who keeps watch in the evening hours greets me. I ask him whether something has happened, but he just sighs and shakes his head no, everything is safe. I have missed supper but go upstairs to the lower balcony, where I hope to spend the evening hours chatting with the pilgrims who are participating in the biblical studies program. I am startled to see Sister Jean stretching police tape across the balcony, to prevent all of us from peering over the railing at the activities below in the Via Dolorosa, where I noticed several army youth were stationed. Sister explains that she now does this once a month, when the people who belong to the various religious sects that support the Third Temple Movement enter the city at the Lion's Gate and proceed through the Muslim Quarter to reach the Western Wall. There they hold vigil and await the day they will be allowed to resurrect the Third Temple and reestablish the Sanhedrin, the ancient priesthood of the Jewish people. To achieve this, the gorgeous Dome of the Rock and the Al-Aksa Mosque, which together form the third holiest site in the Islamic world, the place from which Muhammad is believed to have ascended into heaven, will be demolished, and the Palestinians driven from the Temple Mount and its environs.

Sister Jean explains that a few years ago Aroon, a young and impetuous Palestinian who helps out in the kitchen, shouted to the police that the protesters were crazy, and immediately the soldiers raised their guns and "made a bead" on his head. Sister Jean wrapped herself around Aroon and screamed at the soldiers, "He is a harmless boy, he is with me, a sister in this convent." Since then she has not allowed anyone near the balcony railing on the evenings when members of the Temple Mount and Land of the Israeli Faithful Movement and their kind march. As darkness descends, I run to the upper balcony to catch sight of the protesters, who are now departing from the Holy City, mostly young families dressed in the hippielike clothing of voluminous skirts and snoods, baggy pants and brightly embroidered yarmulkes, that identify them as Jewish settlers and their sympathizers. Young parents lean their heads together in intimate conversation as they push their baby strollers down the ancient, cobbled street, their older children skipping along beside them. They appear to my eyes to be drowsy but contented families returning from a summer outing.

The following day I am invited to have a cup of mint tea in my friend's carpet and antiquities shop, and I ask him about the previous day. For once, he is too weary to spread his carpets for me, in one of his many attempts to help me part with my money. I must confess that the only times I am filled with fear and trepidation while traveling in Israel and Palestine are when the couple of merchants who have befriended me begin to show their wares. For I am a fool in the holy city, and I have already been parted from what little spending money I had. The merchant knows this, but he is desperate. His wife and four small children live on the other side of the separation wall in Ramallah, and he leaves them for long stretches of time to work in the family shop, because crossing the wall and navigating the many checkpoints is too dangerous and too onerous to do regularly. He is worried because there are taxes to be paid, or his family will lose the shop. But the wealthy tourists that once flocked to the city shy away from the Muslim Quarter; the tourists that do come are Christian pilgrims or conscientious supporters of the Palestinians. They bring their convictions and good will, not deep pockets.

The previous day the merchant remained hidden in his shop, the windows and doors boarded and locked up, with heavy furniture dragged in front of them for good measure. He could not leave the shop because he had to stay to protect the family's investments, but he was afraid of being caught there, for what could he really hope to achieve if there was an incident? Months later, he would call me in Canada to explain that he had just been released from prison, having been caught at a checkpoint without the proper documents. Small wonder he spent the day of the protest in a state of terror, hoping that the whole affair would pass without incident. "What of the others?" I asked. "My sister," he responded, "we are afraid; we are all afraid. All we want is peace, so that the tourists will return and we can support our families."

A few weeks later I journey by an Arab bus to Gilo to spend Shabbat with my Jewish Israeli friend. There is a look of incomprehension on the bus driver's face when I ask to be let off at what appears to me to be nothing more than a southern suburb of Jerusalem. When my friend picks me up at the bus stop, she explains that people who live in Gilo do not travel on the Arab buses, because Gilo began as a settlement built on land annexed by the State of Israel after the 1967 Six-Day War. She drives me past the apartment building in her neighborhood where people were shot on their balconies by Palestinians from Beit Jala at the time of the Second Intifada. She is a bit startled when I explain that I have been to Beit Jala, which is an old Christian town in the West Bank. I went to Beit Jala to visit a well-known Christian activist, who took me and a few other pilgrims from Ecce Homo on a journey to various biblical and political hot spots, which she linked together in a seamless Christian narrative of hope and suffering. Standing in caves in which I'm told the shepherds would have slept with their flocks on the night they saw the star of Bethlehem in the east and were visited by heavenly hosts, this Palestinian Christian talked about the poverty and humble circumstances of Palestinians. She deftly linked the story of Palestine's plight to the dawn of Christendom. She even took time to correct a biblical error, as she reinterpreted the story of the innkeeper who refused hospitality to Joseph and Mary. She explained that no Palestinian would ever refuse people in need of shelter. The Church Fathers, being men and unfamiliar with customs of the Middle East, misunderstood the significance of this passage, for Mary was a virtuous woman who was seeking the privacy of the animal's stall in which to deliver her child.

As we stood in the plaza in front of the Church of the Nativity in Bethlehem, our tour guide explained the hopefulness she had felt as the Millennium approached and she and other officials in Bethlehem prepared for the papal visit. It was decided that, rather than celebrate the event with fireworks, two thousand white doves representing peace would be released into the air. But the children of Bethlehem were very disappointed when they heard there would be no fireworks, so the committee decided they would reconsider and do both. On the day when the pope announced that it was time for pilgrims from around the world to gather in Bethlehem, Palestinians were filled with joy, believing that peace was upon them and their economy would soon be thriving. The doves were released, followed by the fireworks. Within moments, dead white doves began to drop from the sky, and our guide foretold there would be no peace. Before the year was over, the Second Intifada had begun.

I love sharing these ethnographic moments with my Jewish friend from Gilo. I also want to share with her the story of this woman's dilemma, as she agonizes over her family's future and considers whether or not to emigrate from Palestine. She had taken us to her terraced garden, at the edge of Beit Jala, and we saw how the separation wall had sliced through the upper terrace, cutting away the ancient olive trees that were once the pride of her garden. On the day that the bulldozers came, she and her friends mounted a peaceable protest, and she pleaded with the workmen to reconsider. She told them that for years she had taken her children to dance classes with young Jewish children so that they would meet their neighbors and learn to live in peace. "If you do this," she told the workers, "my work as a mother will be undone and my children will hate you." The workmen called in the army.

I know these stories make my Jewish friend sad and uncomfortable, for she admits that she feels safer with the separation wall and in her opinion Gilo is not an illegal settlement but a suburb of Jerusalem. By law, she is not allowed to visit the West Bank, and I am eager to tell her what it is like. I try to explain the panic we had felt on returning to the checkpoint at Bethlehem to find that it had been closed. We stood stunned among the dirt and rubble on the dark side of the wall, then turned and quickly backtracked through the warren of stiles that are used to herd Palestinians though checkpoints, hoping to reach our Palestinian tour guide before she drove off. Thankfully, she was still there, waiting to make sure we got through safely. She drove us to another checkpoint for automobiles, and we knocked on the windows of cars lined up there until we found someone with enough room to accommodate all of us. No one found our behavior the least bit strange, and the woman who picked us up graciously delivered us to the Damascus Gate, although it was out of her way. I remember commenting to my fellow pilgrims that our tour guide may have a valid point about the biblical innkeeper.

My friend is anxious that I understand that not all people who support the separation wall are monsters. But they are afraid, so afraid. At this point I have not yet been to Hebron, have not yet walked through market streets that are shrouded in netting in a feeble attempt to stop the bricks and stones that hail down upon Palestinians from the settlement walls that have been built by an unlawful group of Jewish settlers in the middle of their market. I want to be fair-minded, receptive to multiple perspectives, to various cultural logics. This is what our discipline teaches, but it seems such a foolish, even immoral position to hold on to in the face of so much pain. But I have not been to Hebron yet, and I welcome these opportunities to share in the Sabbath, to speak with the people who live in Gilo.

The following long day, as we await the appearance of the first star in the sky, which will bring Shabbat to a close, we gather with neighbors on the garden terrace. There is stillness, an unbelievable calmness in Gilo, as the normal business of quotidian life is suspended for Shabbat. I find it unbelievably restful and beautiful, although I am somewhat mystified by the complexity of the injunctions involved in keeping Shabbat. "How," I ask, "can there be an ancient taboo against turning electricity on and off?" They patiently explain the spirit of the law, which must be continuously reinterpreted and upheld over time. And they laugh at themselves, for some of the contortions involved in insuring that one will still have hot coffee in the morning without the need to turn a switch border on the ludicrous. Some, like my friend's neighbors, are more fastidious than others in their observances of the law, a system of ethics concerning right and wrong actions that requires incredible attention to minutia. I am torn between respectful fascination and thoughts that this is utter foolishness.

I entertain my friends and their neighbors with my stories of ineptitude in the marketplace. My inability to escape the company of my two Arab merchant friends without parting with substantial amounts of money is considered hilarious. To date, I have bought every member of my family a carpet, whether they want it or not, and even though I know it will only convince them that I have lost my mind, as I come from a part of the world that still embraces the ethic of Weber's Benjamin Franklin. But even here in Jerusalem, laughter soon turns to concern. I am told in no uncertain terms that all Arab merchants are dishonest and never to be trusted. When they learn that I have accepted an invitation to dinner with a member of the merchant's family in East Jerusalem, they grow alarmed. The neighbors, Mizrahim who left Morocco to make *aliyah* (i.e., migrate to Israel) after the Six-Day War in 1967, explain that Arabs care only about business and they will lie to me and tell me whatever hard-luck stories will make a sale. They are very concerned for my safety. My stories of the poverty in East Jerusalem, of the destruction and despair I have witnessed in the West Bank, create an awkward silence. They believe that the only possible way to live in peace is to live apart. At the same time, they tell me Israel is a very small country that cannot be endlessly broken up and remain viable and secure.

I am alarmed that my slowness at adapting to the rules and life of the *suq* should feed into this way of thinking about others. Surely they have refused to recognize my merchant friends as fellow humans, with all the quirkiness that attends our needs, desires, and joys. Writing of sectarian violence in India, Veena Das explains that the "refusal to accept the flesh and bloodedness of the other—hence the fate of oneself as an embodied being—gets enacted in terms of staving off the knowledge one has of the other by putting one's faith instead in the capacity for rumor" (2007: 107). The sad irony of the anti-Semitism fueling this caricature of the Arab merchant is only eclipsed by the rigid policies of containment and separation that mark daily life in Jerusalem. A system of separate neighborhoods, bus systems, highways, walls, and documents discourages consorting with the other.[4] And when people must rub shoulders, an army is brought in to police the affair. Indeed, a Jewish citizen of Israel would have to break the law to visit Palestinians on the West Bank.[5]

Yet all the Christian pilgrims who stay at Ecce Homo traverse back and forth between Jewish and Arab neighborhoods, and this experience shadows their biblical studies and spiritual journey in the Holy Lands. I want to suggest that this very "descent into the ordinary" (if I may again cite Das) animates the ethical lives of these Christian pilgrims.

## Sisters of Zion

The pilgrims and visitors at Ecce Homo are, for the most part, a highly educated lot. I spend my evenings talking to biblical theologians and scholars, journalists, and other professionals who have chosen to spend their holidays studying religious texts, either at the convent or at institutions in West Jerusalem where they can learn Hebrew and study Judaism. In this crowd, I feel decidedly undereducated, given that my biblical education stopped shortly after junior Sunday school. While my own early religious instruction was with the literally inclined fundamentalists of whom Crapanzano (2000), Harding (1987), and Feldman (2009) write, the residents of Ecce Homo eschew such interpretive practices in favor of a complex hermeneutics that requires close attention to the historicity of biblical texts and welcomes ironic reflection. When I first arrived at Ecce Homo, there was a group completing a month-long tour of the Holy Lands while reading the Gospel of John. Their days began with morning prayers, and then they took biblical instruction from a group of Christian, Judaic, and Islamic theologians. During their stay they had ritually walked the Christian Stations of the Cross and held mass in innumerable Christian holy places, had visited and prayed in mosques, had worshipped in a synagogue, and had visited the Holocaust Museum.

---

4. See Handelman (2004) for a brilliant discussion of the bureaucratic logic that informs these policies.

5. Nevertheless, many Israelis break this law, either as illegal settlers or as peace activists expressing solidarity with Palestinians. See both Shulman (2007) and Carse (2010).

Ecce Homo is owned and operated by the Sisters of Zion, a Roman Catholic religious order that was founded in France by Theodore and Alphonse Ratisbone in 1848. The brothers converted from Judaism to Christianity in 1842, after Alphonse had a vision of the Virgin Mary. In 1855, Father Mary Alphonse traveled to Palestine, then a poor province of the Ottoman Empire, to establish a religious house upon an archaeological site dating back to the First Temple Period (31 B.C.–4 A.D.). The site was, at that time, thought to contain the ruins of the Arch of the Ecce Homo, where Jesus was tried by Pontius Pilate, crowned with thorns, and presented to the crowd with the words "Ecce Homo—Behold the man" (John 19:5). The Sisters explain to all that current evidence no longer supports this claim, but since the Middle Ages pilgrims have flocked to this place as the "Second Station of the Cross," and so it has become, through Christian tradition, a holy place, a place to reflect upon the life of Christ. The need for historical and archaeological certainty, which seems to obsess so many religious groups in Israel, strikes them as unimportant, even immaterial. For them, truth does not attach to such things, and they have successfully resisted the pleas of state archaeologists who wish to connect this site to the warren of underground tunnels that spread beneath the Old City of Jerusalem.[6] They know that the residents of the Muslim Quarter consider such archaeological work an insidious encroachment of Jewish land claims, reaching back to the time of First Temple. While not being in the least antiscience per se, the theological and political implications of ongoing excavations are considered wrongheaded and politically suspect. Indeed, many Israeli archaeologists question the science behind much of what passes as biblical archaeology in Israel.[7] Ecce Homo has from its beginning navigated shifting geopolitical boundaries in Jerusalem by teaching religious tolerance for the three faiths of Abraham, serving the poor, and educating pilgrims.

In the evenings, I especially enjoy sitting with a group of spirited Sisters of St. Louis, who have traveled from California to complete a pilgrimage to the Holy Lands. As women religious, they have a close affiliation with

---

6. The Western Wall Heritage Tunnel is controlled by the Holy Sites Authority and has been at the center of controversies between Israelis and Palestinians. The excavations extend under land owned by the Islamic *waqf*, and several buildings in the Muslim Quarter of the Old City were structurally damaged and collapsed as a result. (See El Haj (2001: 216–38 and 315n22.)

7. See Benvenisti (2000), Finkelstein (1988), El-Haj (2001), and Karmi (2007) for incisive critiques of the relationship between archaeology and Zionism.

the Sisters of Zion, the founders of both orders having been contemporaries and friends (at least this is how I understood it). The sisters explain that in the past week they have held holy mass at two different tombs of Christ. Over the past few weeks, they have also visited several sacred sites claiming to be the last resting place of John the Baptist. They are beginning to find this sanctification of place completely absurd and tell me that it is difficult to feel reverent in places that have invited so much bickering and dissension. One sister told me that on their trip to Galilee she stopped in a place that seemed to her closer to nature, and there reflected upon a landscape she imagined being closer to the one Jesus inhabited. It was, to date, her only deeply spiritual moment. To this another sister, Mary, responded: "I felt an overwhelming sense of what it is to be a Christian when we deliberately got off the bus at the checkpoint in Bethlehem to walk in solidarity with Palestinians. For me, this was a deeply spiritual moment." And to my delight, all of the sisters concurred.

I sat with Sister Mary at breakfast the following Saturday, a day in which the pilgrims were free to do as they chose. I noted Sister Mary was eating an exceptionally large breakfast for such a tiny elderly woman in her seventies. She looked up and smiled: "Donna, I'm walking to Bethlehem today to visit this woman we met who is caring for abandoned children. I cannot sleep for thinking of her and those poor children. And I will not rest until I find a way to help her." "But surely you can take a bus," I responded. She laughed, "I love a long walk, it fills me with joy." I am very fond of Sister Mary, who has previously confided, "God is nothing other than the joy you experience when you look into the eyes of another and delight in their humanity." She drew closer and whispered: "This is between us; some of my Christian family would find this heretical. I have been a woman religious for over fifty years, but this is what I think. I know some of my sisters need more than this, but for me, this is enough." At supper that evening, Sister Mary looked sunburnt and exhausted. She was a bit despondent, she confessed, because the woman she had hoped to speak with was not at home. Departing for California a few days later, she told me her pilgrimage had been very significant, for she knew she had new work to do, which would give her retirement meaning. She didn't know how, but she would find a way to build an orphanage for the abandoned children of Bethlehem.

Ecce Homo seemed almost empty when the pilgrims from the month-long biblical program left, but soon others arrived. And the Sisters, who had been too busy running the biblical program to spend time chatting with me, now joined us for meals. The new pilgrims journeyed as individuals, and in the evenings we would compare our days and discuss matters both religious and political. There I found young Clara, a British university student who had just completed a month-long summer camp for Christian teenagers in the West Bank, and Gerta, a German schoolteacher on her summer holidays, who travels every day to the West Bank to teach crafts to Bedouin children. A reporter for the British press is writing a story on the worsening conditions in the West Bank. Ursula is a Lutheran priest who has returned to Jerusalem to continue her studies of the Talmud. John is a Roman Catholic priest from Australia who has spent the last two years teaching English in Lebanon and is now busy visiting political activists in Jerusalem, including an anti-Zionist Orthodox Rabbi and the secular pro-Palestinian tour guides who work out of the Jerusalem Hotel. It was with John that I traveled to Hebron, where Christian peace activists escorted Palestinians to and from the Mosque to pray. All of these pilgrims find sanctuary at Ecce Homo and claim to attend to a deeply Christian ethic. I was told time and time again that it was ordinary forms of daily encounter with Jewish and Muslim others in their midst that enlivened their sense of a Christian ethics, in which the commandment "to love one's neighbor as one's self" is considered paramount.

By contrast to their guests, the Sisters of Zion are much more reticent about their political sympathies, and I don't think anyone would consider them activists. If anything, they refuse to engage at that level at all, although they are eager to hear what their guests are doing, thinking, etc. They always show concern but never voice a political opinion, refusing to takes sides. At first I thought this simply a tactic for surviving in difficult political times, but I have come to see it as an expression of a deeply held theological position. When I tried to explain this attitude to a fellow anthropologist who began her own ethnographic fieldwork on the other side of Israel's separation wall just ahead of me, she blurted out, "Well given the situation, that is simply immoral!" She may be surprised to learn, as was I, that there is in fact a strong theological argument that Christianity should be un-moral, or amoral (may Durkheim rest in peace). As the "radically orthodox" theologian John Milbank explains, Christianity upsets the law of the land and moral imperatives that assume one's rights must be protected against another's, because such laws express a generalized feeling that there is a lack of what humans require in the world. But the Christian story of faith in God's love, a belief that God will provide, replaces a sense of scarcity with one of plenitude. Consequently, Christians need no longer heed the laws of the land or worry about the chains of reciprocity that must assume a return to one's self of that which was forfeited. In other words, one need not be calculating or politically astute; one must only give freely and love one's neighbor. Milbank concludes:

> So no, the Christian man is not a moral man, not a man of good *conscience*, who acts *with* what he *knows* of death, scarcity and duty to totalities. He has a bad conscience, but a good *confidence*: for he acts with what good he does not know but has faith in. In absolute trust he gives up trying to be good, to sustain a right order of government within himself. The Romans that Paul wrote to did this already, but they still needed a letter from Paul—to hear what? Simply to hear the other, receive the other, and through the other receive the gratuitous God. Cease to be self-sufficient in the face of scarcity. Instead to be good at receiving from the all-sufficiency of God, and acting excessively out of this excess. The three virtues alone abide: faith, hope and charity, but the greatest of these is charity. (Milbank 1997: 231)

Yet another way of thinking about this Christian form of amorality is to heed Paul's first letter to the Corinthinians, in which he writes: "Yet God has chosen what the world considers foolish to shame the wise; he has chosen what the world considers weak to shame the strong" (I Corinthians 1:27).[8] In other words, one is to become a fool for Christ.

One night I talk to the Sisters about the overwhelming fear of the other that I find everywhere in Jerusalem, about my Jewish friends' fears of entering the Holy City at the Damascus Gate, which I find so baffling. One of the Sisters says:

> Yes, it must be so terrible to live with such fear. One night when I was working in the reception room, a young Jewish man came here to the convent to meet with a friend. He was a young soldier on holidays, and he was visibly shaken. I asked him if something was wrong, and he told me he was very afraid to walk through this part of the old city. So I offered to walk with him through the city, and he accepted my offer so quickly and gratefully, I was surprised. After all, he was a young soldier and I am just a small woman. But I took him by the arm, and walked with him through the city.

After the biblical program had ended, the Sisters decided all the workers in the convent needed a holiday, and so they rented a van and headed for the West Bank to gather the Palestinian workers and their families,

---

8. Quoted from the *Christian Community Bible*, Catholic Pastoral edition. Quezon City, Philippines: Bernardo Hurault, 2005.

whom they illegally escorted through the checkpoint at Bethlehem. They spent the day at a water park, swishing down water slides, laughing, eating junk food, and chasing after the children. They and the Palestinian workers said it was the happiest day they had had in a long time. In a land where there are more ways to be righteous than one can shake a stick at, the Sisters of Zion have chosen the path of unrighteousness. They made slipping through checkpoints sound like nothing other than a jolly good time, an opportunity to delight in others. What fools!

### Of Anthropologists and Other Fools, Blessed or Not

As the weeks passed by in the summer of 2007, I had a sense of foreboding, a feeling that things were getting worse and worse, and that the sky would surely fall. I suspect that all who travel to Israel experience something like this. As the end of my journey, fieldwork, or pilgrimage was approaching, I felt unready to leave, yet afraid to stay. My Jewish friend suggested I was picking up on the vibe of liminality that accompanies the days approaching Tisha b'Av, a three-week period "between the strictures" of Tammuz and Av, when Jews mourn the destruction of the First and Second Temple, exile and spiritual loss. I am told that being between the strictures is akin to being pinched, which I understand as being stuck between a rock and a hard place. During the three weeks no weddings or joyous events are scheduled; people read the prophesies that foretold the destruction of the Temple, reflect upon their sins, and observe food taboos, culminating in a day of fast that ends with the reading of Lamentations. From the Internet, I downloaded pages of rules that cover diet, bathing, clothing restrictions, etc. to aid in rituals of purification. My friend and I agree to meet at the Western Wall on the eve of Av to read the Book of Lamentations so that we may collectively pass out of this liminal funk.

Another Christian pilgrim and I arrive at the Western Wall early to meet my Jewish friend from Gilo, knowing it will be crowded. Within moments, a woman handing out pamphlets on appropriate feminine attire books all three of us for clothing violations. This comes as a bit of shock, as we have all dressed conservatively, in a manner we thought appropriate. But my Jewish friend wore a snug sweater rather than a baggy blouse, and the Irish Catholic had too much peek-a-boo lace and a cross around her neck. As for me, I failed the "raise the leg until your thigh is at a forty-five-degree angle from your body to see if your skirt is sufficiently voluminous" test. The Christians in the crowd had also forgotten to cover their hair. We burst into unholy laughter when the woman departs, and my Jewish friend hopes that her neighbor does not get stopped, as she tries so hard to follow every law and rule. She would be utterly mortified if she failed this test. It turns out her neighbor is joining a large group that is outside the city walls, marching around the perimeter of the city. We are to meet up with her at the Lion's Gate after we complete the ritual reading of Lamentations. My friend has brought me the book in translation so that I can follow along. We enter the women's side of the wall, but notice that several families are gathered near the back and refuse to segregate along gender lines, much to the consternation of the morality police. I manage to lower my arthritic knees to the cold, hard pavement and slowly fall into the rhythm of the men who are reading Lamentations on the other side of the wall. My friend points her finger to the appropriate verse, and I am caught up in this ritual of mourning, this profound expression of loss and grieving.

All three of us are quiet as we meet up with my friend's husband and leave the square to make our way to the Lion's Gate, which is at the very end of the Via Dolorosa. The army is out in full force, and the streets virtually empty. Approaching the Lion's Gate, my friend's husband stops to chat with a soldier and learns that thousands are circling the city. We sit down to await the crowds. When they finally arrive, we find ourselves in the glare of television cameras, as Rabbis and politicians stand in front of us to deliver speeches to the masses gathered there. My friend translates as a distraught woman screams: "We made our mistake in 1967. We should not have stopped here. We should have pushed them out of the Temple Mount." I am horrified and turn to my friend to say, "Good God, what if someone I know watches a clip of this footage and sees me at this rally?" My friend turns and smiles: "Donna, you are an anthropologist. How else will you understand?" And so we stand and watch, and I try to take it in.

Like the silly princess who has stayed too late at the ball, I realize my curfew is fast approaching, and I must make haste to Ecce Homo. We turn to reenter the city, but the soldiers block our way. We all begin to talk at once, until a local police officer, who knows the Muslim Quarter, intervenes. We explain that two of us are pilgrims at Ecce Homo, and she confers with the others and says we may pass. We proceed, but the soldiers refuse to let my Jewish friends through with us. I have not properly said goodbye, and this is the last time I will see them on this trip. My eyes fill with tears, but my friends just shrug their shoulders and throw me a kiss.

This departure haunts me, for I cannot accept it, cannot accept that lives are lived this way. In "Desire to Be Gisella," the Israeli novelist and essayist David Grossman writes:

> After spending a century in all-out war and becoming accustomed to seeing anyone who threatens us as an enemy to the death, and having the concept of "enemy" engrained in us so deeply, almost from birth, and living in an environment in which the concept is so highly available, because of the hostility and the constant acts of violence—after all this eventually our compasses and healthy instincts go awry, and then, in almost any situation of conflict or disagreement, even one's brother looks like the enemy. It is enough for his opinions and habits to be different from our own, for his interpretation of a situation to be different from ours, for our brother to become, in our minds, in our fears, an enemy.
>
> When I see this, I fear that after decades of spending most of our energies, our thoughts and attention and inventiveness, our blood and our life and our financial means, on protecting our external borders, fortifying and safeguarding them more and more—after all this, we may be very close to becoming like a suit of armor that no longer contains a knight, no longer contains a human. (Grossman 2008: 47–48)

At risk here is the humanity of the person who refuses to see the other, the self in the other. Grossman advocates an ethical position articulated by Levinas (1989), one rooted in a metaphysics that bears a striking resemblance to that of my Christian pilgrims.

The following day I revisit my favorite haunts in the Old City. The second of my merchant friends swoops down on me and drags me into his shop. "You must help, sister, I have visited friends in the West Bank and they are desperate. Here, see this family quilt made of the embroidered inserts of Bedouin dresses. You must buy this. The family took this off their own bed and begged me sell it for them so they can feed their children. You must help."

"I'm sorry, Khalid, but I have no more credit. I cannot help."

"Please, please, use my phone. You are a good person. The bank will extend your credit."

I look at the mildewed and torn blanket and think that it looks as though it has crossed the desert a hundred times. I can't imagine what on earth I would do with it. But we phone the bank, and VISA graciously extends my credit.

The blanket arrives in the post the same day as the call from VISA to inform me someone has made a copy of my credit card and is using it freely. I hang up the phone and cannot stop laughing. How I wish that I had had the presence of mind to explain to my friends in Gilo, with whom I shared Shabbat on that lovely day in July, that it is wrong to hold an Arab merchant responsible for my own foolishness. Surely, in this land of the righteous, in which there are a myriad of ways to be a holy fool, I am the biggest fool of all. For I have attempted to assuage the ethical dilemmas of even attempting to carry out fieldwork in this holiest of lands, with its sacred solitudes and laws, anguish and injustices, by shopping.

# Between Queer Ethics and Sexual Morality

*Naisargi N. Dave*

The story behind this essay begins in January 2003, on the inaugural day of the Asia Social Forum (ASF) in Hyderabad. Queer and allied groups across India had spent months of fervent planning to host events that would highlight the relevance of sexuality rights to the forum's dominant themes of poverty alleviation and antiglobalization. At one of these sexuality-themed seminars, a panelist introduced himself as a believer that "sex workers' rights are human rights." He said this with chest proudly expanded, as if challenging us to counter him; what he received instead was a chorus of intense solidarity. "Sex work is a totally legitimate form of labor!" one woman said, nodding vigorously. "Sex work is about pleasure and choice," said another, smashing her fist into her palm for emphasis. Amid this celebration of agency rose from his chair a gay activist, a young Bangalorean, in a floppy red sunhat and floral print shirt. "Aren't we sidestepping a moral question here?" Tarunabh, this activist, asked. "Sex work is a form of labor under capitalism. And aren't all forms of labor under capitalism exploitative and morally problematic?" People nodded hesitantly, wondering where this was going. He continued: "We can't keep escaping the responsibility to articulate our *moral* stands. It's not enough to just celebrate and defend what *they* condemn. Just because they say sex work is morally wrong doesn't mean that we have to say that it's morally 'right.' The point—our point—is to create a *new* morality."

This was a powerful moment for me. As I listened I recalled conversations that I had sustained over the past several months. These once disparate, though dutifully noted, fragments were now suddenly given shape through Tarunabh's remarks on sex work and morality. In the activist groups I had been working with, everyone had been talking about the relationship between means and ends: whether to accept funding and the compromises that inhere in doing so; the kinds of symbolic violence and the pragmatic advantages of consciously opting for identity-based politics; whether to strike strategic alliances with groups whose politics were suspect. There were also assertions that the ways in which queer people care for and relate to one another in our everyday lives are as significant to our politics as any public, collective organizing. Listening to the speakers that morning in Hyderabad—and particularly to Tarunabh—it became clear to me that the activism I had been witnessing and documenting for the past year was centrally about the search for and cultivation of *ethics*.

This was not the project that I had initially envisioned and set out to do. My first preliminary research trip to India was in the summer of 1999, six months into the heady aftermath of the Hindu nationalist violence over commercial screenings of the film *Fire* (1996, dir. Deepa Mehta), which depicts a sexual relationship between two married sisters-in-law living in the same household. In July 1999, Campaign for Lesbian Rights (CALERI), a group that emerged out of the *Fire* counter-protests, was in the final stages of editing their manifesto titled "Lesbian Emergence." I spent several evenings with them, listening and tentatively participating as they vociferously debated the finest points of language and strategy. I eventually decided to do a research project comparing CALERI, a nonfunded, radical collective, with Sangini, an internationally funded helpline cum support group that resisted public engagement in order to protect those Indian women who accessed its services but could not risk being out or could not risk being associated with a group that might be publicly identified as queer.

However, when I returned to India to do my fieldwork, I found that CALERI had gone defunct—two of its central founding members had gone to the United States for graduate studies, while others had dropped out due to the strains and conflicts endemic to political organizing. In CALERI's place, however, had arisen a new Delhi-based collective called People for the Rights of Indian Sexual Minorities (PRISM). PRISM was another resolutely nonfunded collective, comprising men, women, transsexuals, straight, queer, and nonidentifying, all united in the cause of public queer advocacy and equal rights. I found myself at the home of two of PRISM's co-founders, a lesbian couple I had become friends with over previous summers. I would come to spend many days and nights with them outside of organizational meetings, basking in their exceptional hospitality. And their home was an exceptional place—something of a queer halfway house and a cooperative where friends from across the country and abroad would come and go, seeking solace from heartache, marriage pressure, suicide pacts, distant or abusive families, and all forms of loneliness.

As these people passed through, they would inevitably, if with some initial reluctance, become active participants in the political debates that formed the center of our lives there: funding imperatives; the limitations and possibilities of identity-based politics; whether the "Indian" in People for the Rights of Indian Sexual Minorities was too much of an appeal to nation and culture during a time when the *Bharatiya Janata Party* (BJP) was on the ascendant; and whether the term "sexual minorities" indicated that PRISM's vision extended only to gays and lesbians, rather than to social transformation on a wider scale.

All of these committed and sometimes accidental activists would become for me and for one another something similar to what anthropologist Kath Weston calls a "chosen family"—queer parents, brothers, sisters, and daily companions (Weston 1991). It was a responsibility to ethical engagement, a tireless grappling with the central question—how we might live, as queer Indians, socially unacknowledged and unschooled—that served as the moral foundation for the political life of that collective. My responsibility as an ethnographer was to grapple with an additional question—to understand and convey the complexities at stake in being a queer activist in India at this time.

I thus began asking questions different from the ones I had originally formulated. Instead of analyzing how one organization functions in a particular political field or how the strategies of one group compare with those of another, I began asking about the activists themselves: Why do activists act? Why are activists activists?

The answers I came to were within the realm of the ethical. People are drawn to activism because they have an ethical orientation to the world. They act because they nurture ethical ideals of what the world *ought* to look like. They act out of conflicted beliefs in the possibility of justice. They act in part because they desire the practice of new freedoms that they can only yet imagine, but still strive to enable. But the political institutions that activists must engage in order to effect these transformations are far from conducive to the cultivation of such radical imaginings.

I framed my research as an ethnography of precisely this tension—between the ethical and affective ideals that animate (in this case) queer activism in India and the moral and political hegemonies in the postcolonial democratic nation-state that work to subsume that potential and render "unremarkable" and commensurate the most radical aspects of this emergent world (Povinelli 2001). That constitutive tension, in other words, is between the embryonic and the ossified, between what might be and what must be. Or, possibly put another way, between the ethical and the moral.

For this reading of the concept of ethics, and of the distinction between the ethical and the moral, I draw upon the later work of Foucault, a period whose onset I mark with the second volume of *The History of Sexuality* (*The Use of Pleasure*, 1985). Foucault's "ethical turn" between the first and second volumes of *The History of Sexuality* was read by many critics as a radical, unsettling departure. His work on governmentality and modern discipline had demonstrated the ever-widening circulation and deeper penetration of power, such that subjects so formed come to exercise limits upon themselves within the space of ostensible freedom. The critique of this work, before Foucault's "ethical turn," was that the relentless omnipresence of power left no space for resistance and hope. But given that it was Foucault who pointed out in the first volume of *The History of Sexuality* that "Where there is power, there is resistance" (1978: 95), it was precisely his recognition of the depth of power's penetration that led to a recognition of the depth of possibilities for transgression, critique, and creativity.[1] This depth of radical imaginary possibility within the workings of power is the space of the ethical. For a study such as mine, this understanding of ethics—of how people act within and against socially prescribed and enforced limits—has immense potential.

One of the problems, however, of arguing for the centrality of ethics to subaltern activisms relates to the conflation of ethics and morality, in which the latter is (and thus both are) seen as the province of the unenlightened powerful—a system of codes, norms, and rules, aspiring to universality and rooted in religiosity and positivism.[2] Among the critical conceptual interventions in Foucault's later work is his distinction between

1. Bernauer and Mahon 2005. See also Davidson 2005.
2. Bauman 1993.

ethics and morality. Morality is here understood as a system of codes and norms, the space of the institutional and juridical, which mandates what *must* be done rather than what *could* be done. By contrast, ethics for Foucault comprises practices and techniques that we perform on ourselves to *become* moral subjects and (in an Aristotelian vein) to achieve happiness, brilliance, and life. This "aesthetics of existence" involves an emphasis on invention, creativity, and becoming that results from a profound recognition of the limits placed upon, and enforced through, the processes by which we come to understand ourselves as subjects (Foucault 1985).

The concept of the ethical as a process of becoming was central to Foucault's later work and also to his increasingly programmatic views on contemporary gay politics. In a 1977 interview he argued: "It's up to us to advance [into] a homosexual ascesis that would make us work on ourselves and invent (I don't say discover) a manner of being that is still improbable" (Foucault 1988: 116). This "homosexual ascesis" was not a form of identity politics or a call to embrace a new code of what (homo)sexuality is and must be. Rather, Foucault understood homosexual ascesis as "the work that one performs"[3]—the "work at *becoming* homosexuals" rather than to "be obstinate in recognising that we are."[4]

We are still left to ask: What, precisely, is this "becoming"? What is this "work"? And how does it relate to queer activism in India?

Philosopher and Foucault scholar Arnold Davidson points out that the "work" of "ascesis" requires, foremost, a form of philosophical labor (Davidson 2005: 131). Davidson refers to the first chapter of *The Use of Pleasure*, in which Foucault defines philosophy as "an 'ascesis' . . . an exercise of oneself in the activity of thought" and "the endeavour to know how and to what extent it might be possible to think differently, instead of legitimating what is already known" (Foucault 1985: 9). Davidson argues that this linking of ascesis with philosophical exercise is nowhere more vibrantly brought out than in Foucault's discussions of the radical potential of contemporary gay practice (Davidson 2005: 133).

Foucault's comments in a 1981 interview (1985: 135) exemplify Davidson's view:

> Another thing to distrust is the tendency to relate the question of homosexuality to the problem of "Who am I?" and "What is the secret of my desire?" Perhaps it would be better to ask oneself, "What relations, through homosexuality, can be established, invented, multiplied, and

---

3. Foucault 1994.
4. Ibid. 136, emphasis added.

modulated?" The problem is not to discover in oneself the truth of one's sex, but, rather, to use one's sexuality henceforth to arrive at a multiplicity of relationships.

This succinct articulation of a homosexual ascesis or, as I prefer to term it, a "radical ethic," raises three issues that pertain directly to Indian queer activisms. First is the question of a commitment to philosophical exercise, to "thinking differently," to asking new questions of oneself in order to analyze (and surpass) the limits upon what can be said and done. Foucault refers to this aspect of ethical practice as "problematization," or a critical reflection upon norms (see Faubion 2001a). Second is an emphasis not on liberation from power or a reversal of its existing structures but on the imaginative labor of *inventing* formerly unimaginable possibilities. Third is the inherently relational quality of this radical ethic—an inhabiting of one's *distance* from moral norms such that the very remove from institutional power serves as the *condition of possibility* for the creative practice of new, and multiple, affective relational forms.

This triumvirate of affective exercise, I argue, constitutes the often under-analyzed ethical center of any activism that seeks to transform and multiply existing social relations. Lesbian and gay activism in India is a case in point; and to demonstrate this claim, I briefly invoke the story with which I began this essay. First, we can recall Tarunabh's passionate *problematization* of the discursive norms by which either one mode of political speech or its opposite is intelligible—the language of for/against, right/wrong, moral/immoral, which militates against understanding the nuances of our subjections. Similarly, we can remember Tarunabh's call not only to reverse existing moral codes of proper behavior but to *invent* an ethical language more closely approximating the hope for social justice, and not only for social power. Last, we can place ourselves back in the activist household described earlier in this essay—a space of invention in which the enforced remove from the morally disciplining centers of family, law, and nation serve as the necessitating factor, as well as the *condition of possibility*, for the creative practice of new forms of affiliation and relationship. These are not modes of simple "resistance" but of radical invention.

The triumvirate of affective exercise I posit as the ethical is distinct from moralism. I understand morality to be a system of imposed codes and norms, legitimized through texts, scriptures, and custom, and deployed in order to maintain social stability and the reification of already-existing relations of power. Morality is not just one, but is multiply manifested.

My research examines the various moralities that queer activists engage: the disciplining thrust of community; the imperative of sexual identity; the global feminist concept of Third World women as sexual victims, and not as sexually aspiring; the discursive hegemony of the nation and of "Indian culture"; and the dualistic language of law. These and other moral discourses are characterized by normalizing effects, by which I mean a narrowing of human possibilities.

Ethics, however, I interpret as that which emerges from *within* subjections as a creative, disruptive response to the drive to normalization. My central question, then, is: How do radical ethics—constituted by the problematization of norms, the imaginative invention of alternatives to those norms, and the practice of new relational possibilities—emerge from, and confront, the normalizing processes that work to render the ethical impulse of activism commensurate with existing moral codes? How do we understand, in other words, the struggle activism presents between imaginative possibility and moral imperative?

My larger written work on this research is organized through the analysis of the above series of moral discourses and their normalizing, and *productive*, relationship to the ethical possibilities of queer activist practice in India. Through these analyses, I also attempt to critique an encompassing moral premise of activist labor: namely, that the value of social engagement is rooted in any actor's ability to penetrate further and larger fields of influence. I thus move from lesbian women's creation of imagined and then local communities to the burgeoning desire to form institutions and organizations, to the mandatory forging of alliances between lesbian collectives and other more established movements, to the imperative of visibility and rights claims in the public sphere, to engagement with legal reform and the state. I regard this teleology of activism *itself* as a norm that imposes certain limits on what can be said and imagined.

All these questions work together in an analysis of the primary tension between the ethical and affective ideals that animate, in this case, queer activism in India and the normalizing processes of political engagement that subtly work to absorb that potential, rendering commensurate that which is most radical about this new social world. And though moments of fraught commensuration do make up the bulk of that narrative, its spirit is derived from those many moments of radical possibility—those moments in which we do not yet know in advance the limits of what might be.

ACKNOWLEDGMENTS

This essay is an edited transcript of a presentation delivered to the Alternative Law Forum in Bangalore on June 11, 2007. The essay was first published in the Sarai Reader (Dave 2008). I wish to thank Smriti Vohra of Sarai, attendees of the Alternative Law Forum discussion, and participants of the Ethnographies of Activism workshop at the London School of Economics for comments on other iterations of this material. I am especially indebted to Michael Lambek and to the other participants of the Ordinary Ethics workshop in Toronto for giving me the opportunity to think further about the ideas in this essay.

# Engaging the Life of the Other:
# Love and Everyday Life

*Veena Das*

I begin this essay with the simple proposition that everyday life is the site in which the life of the other is engaged. I try to work out the implications of such a proposition for the moral striving I observe in low-income neighborhoods in Delhi, where, in collaboration with a group of researchers, I have been engaged in understanding urban transformations for the last ten years. What is at stake for me here is both the idea of the everyday and our picture of what is constitutive of moral striving. Due to the breadth of its semantic meanings, everyday life can be understood in many ways. Everyday life might, for instance, be thought of as the site of routine and habit, within which strategic contests for culturally approved goods such as honor or prestige take place. For others, everyday life provides the site through which the projects of state power or given scripts of normativity can be resisted (see Gardiner 2000 for a succinct discussion of these issues). I have argued in recent years that our attachment to routines and habit is inflected by another affect—that of the experience of the everyday as also the site of trance, illusion, and danger (Das 2007). The mutual shadowing of the ordinary and skepticism in my view defines the character of the everyday, so that to secure the everyday, far from being something we might take for granted, might be thought of as an achievement.

My view of moral life is deeply influenced by a notion of the everyday in which how I respond to the claims of the other, as well as how I allow myself to be claimed by the other, defines the work of self-formation. In the philosophical writings of Stanley Cavell, the realization of these moral ideas, or what he calls the picture of Emersonian perfectionism, is not premised on a pregiven, objectively agreed-upon idea of the common good or on virtues that have a vocabulary of their own but rather envisions a moral striving that in its uncertainty and its attention to the concrete specificity of the other is simply a dimension of everyday life (Cavell 1990). In this picture of spiritual becoming, what one seeks is not to ascend to some higher ideal but to give birth to what sometimes Cavell is moved to call an adjacent self—a striving in which the eventual everyday emerges in a relation of nextness to the actual everyday (Critchley 2005). Against the dominant understanding of morality as the capacity to form *moral judgments* in which the crucial requirement is that we should be able to take an abstract, nonsubjective vantage position from which we can orient ourselves to the world, I argue that recourse to such an ideal position often results in evading the imperative to be attentive to the suffering of the other. I am arguing not that there is no room for moral judgments in our lives or that people do not apply abstract standards derived from, say, a rule of conduct found in what they consider to be authoritative traditions but rather that whole areas of moral life remain obscure if our picture of morality remains tied to some version of following rules.

In order to give conceptual and empirical depth to the notion of nextness or an adjacent self as the aim of moral striving, I wish to develop what used to be called an extended case study of the marriage of a Hindu man and a Muslim woman in one of the low-income neighborhoods in Delhi. I offer this case study not as an example of larger social processes of, say, social change or social conflict but rather as a mode of engaging a singularity through which I can show how a range of complex forces brought into being by the simple fact of a boy and girl having fallen in love fold themselves into intimate relations and come to define what Henrietta Moore calls "intimate aspirations" (personal correspondence). In the later Wittgenstein we have a stringent critique of the notion that the correct projection of a concept is already laid before us—thus, he says, when we assume that we know what following a rule means, we have a picture of a rigid line or grid on which our actions will move. Yet this picture produces only the buried mythology of our language (Wittgenstein 1953).[1]

---

1. Para. 219 of *Philosophical Investigations* states: "'All the steps are already taken' means: I no longer have any choice. . . . But if something of this sort really

What would be the opposite of this notion of "projection" along the imagery of an ideally rigid rail line? We could draw upon Foucault's notion of eventalization, which he argues is a way of lightening the weight of causal thinking in our intellectual projects, of interrupting given constants and instead thinking of gestures, acts, and discourses through which the imagery of the rigid line on which action will unfold can be made to stop (Foucault 1996).[2] One ethnographic mode of writing that we could draw from Wittgenstein is to think of the scenic as capturing a particular way in which a mode of conversation or a course of action is dramatized so that various voices (that of the child, of the skeptic, of common sense, or the philosopher) are allowed expression (Wittgenstein 1953). Using the idea of a scene, I hope to show how something as simple as a Hindu boy having fallen in love with a Muslim girl becomes a seed scattered in the soil of the everyday. It carries within it the potential to unleash great violence—but also an opportunity for intimate aspirations to be realized by all who have to re-create their relations around the couple. While I will try to frame this kind of nascent happening with an account of political affects to show how such an act can morph into Hindu-Muslim violence, how it can become the subject of police investigations, court cases, and parliamentary inquiries, I will also carry it into the life of this couple, whom I call Kuldip and Saba and their relationships. My descriptions of the mode of engaging this event in the everyday will, however, take the form of scenic descriptions that evoke Wittgenstein's scenes of instruction (as in a child learning to read) or dramatizations of skeptical doubt (as in the parable of the boiling pot). I hope that, by presenting the singularity of this case in this mode, I will be able to show how the notion of nextness or the adjacent self allows for some calming of the turbulent potential of this event. It is a picture of moral perfectionism as a striving—the play of uncertainty, doubt, and the deepening of intimate relations within a whole weave of life.

---

were the case, how would it help? No; my description only made sense if it was understood symbolically. —I should have said: This is how it strikes me."

2. Foucault is worth citing in some detail here. He says that eventalization "means making visible a *singularity* at places where there is a temptation to evoke a historical constant, an immediate anthropological trait or an obviousness that imposes itself uniformly on all . . . as a way of lightening the weight of causality, 'eventalization' thus works by constructing around a singular event analyzed as process a 'polygon' or rather a 'polyhedron' of intelligibility, the number of whose faces is not given in advance and can never properly be taken as finite" (Foucault 1996: 277).

## The Explosive Potential of Hindu-Muslim Marriages

The potential for violence in Hindu-Muslim relations involving the sexuality of women is a long-standing theme of political rhetoric in India and has been addressed in administrative and judicial practices through the concern for "public order." Deepak Mehta (2009) has analyzed how exchanges of insults between Hindus and Muslims in the public sphere were articulated around the themes of the sexualized body of the Prophet, the emasculation of the men of the other group, and slights concerning the sexuality and purity of women. He analyzes the genres of insult and shows how they were written not so much to evade the British censor as to be recognized in the eyes of the colonial state as literatures of insult. However, heaping insults and humiliation on the other is only part of the story—the other part is the theme of desire that crosses the normative boundaries of religion, which has fascinated poets, writers, and filmmakers. Within this field of desire, fraught with the possibilities of tremendous violence, how are loving couples enabled to negotiate the treacherous waters of Hindu-Muslim sensibilities, the difficult realm of law, and the dense kinship universe of each person?

In her recent work on love marriages in Delhi, Perveez Mody (2008) offers the notion of "not-community" to depict the complex interaction between law, publicity, and intimacy. She argues that ideas of liberal citizenship are both enabled and punctured by new forms of intimacy, as demonstrated in the legal trajectories through which such issues are addressed in India. In a fascinating account of how the law negotiates the sensitivities around Hindu-Muslim relations, Mody's work brings out the contradictions embodied in legislative acts, such as the Special Marriage Act of 1872 in the colonial period, that, on the one hand, provided legal protection for individuals who chose to marry without parental consent and yet, on the other, constrained these choices by various other qualifications—specifically, by restricting the law's application to those who explicitly renounced membership in any religious community. Not only at the legislative level but also at the level of police procedure, adjudication, and public-interest litigation, the ambivalence regarding Hindu-Muslim marriages often bursts into publicity of one sort or another, as is evident both in the literature of the nineteenth century and in the newspaper and other reportage in our own times.[3] For such couples, negotiating the terrain of parental consent, community approval, or even a complete break

---

3. The question of dissolving a marriage in which one spouse has converted to Islam has received considerable attention in law, though at the level of adjudication rather than legislation. Thus, for instance, Basu (1949) discusses the landmark

with previous kinship relations might bring into play a whole range of affects that are the stuff of cinema and literature. Most anthropologists have been reluctant to explore the profound implications of such a situation. Even Mody, because she was constrained to follow cases that had already burst into national publicity, is not able to show us how questions of ethics, morality, and intimate aspirations are negotiated outside the realm of publicity, though she does show that, when couples are successful in getting parental consent, they are careful to maintain a fiction of "arranged marriage."

Jonathan Parry (2001) writes of the ubiquity of marriages and liaisons that cut across caste and community among the Satnamis of Chattisgarh, but he points out that these cases pertain to secondary marriages.[4] As far as primary marriages are concerned, the norms of caste endogamy are maintained. Parry seems to suggest that, within these parameters, the contrast between normative marriages and non-normative ones was not so stark in that region until the Bhilai Steel Plant (BSP), a Public Sector Undertaking, took it upon itself to intervene to ensure the stability of marriages. Parry's descriptions of such marriages leave one with the impression that there is not much affective stake in marriage until one realizes that the basis of his conclusion is "public talk" and gossip among men, which might leave little room for expressions of emotions of intimacy. It seems safe to say that one gets little help from the anthropological literature on how marriages outside the norms of caste and community create new forms of subjectivation at the level of the local. What kinds of shifts in subjectivity can one detect as marriages across caste and community become a matter that lies between kinship and politics?

In order to demonstrate that Hindu-Muslim marriages continue to carry a potential for violence, I will give a recent example from a political

---

cases from the 1920s on this issue. The legislative acts formulated to address the question of forcible abduction of women during the Partition brought a whole range of anxieties, fears, and fantasies into being around the issue of Hindu-Muslim marriages in the public domain (Das 2007).

4. The work of the historian Prem Chowdhry establishes that the tolerance for intercommunity marriages has declined in modernity, at least in north India, though reliance on cases that come up in caste *panchayatsi*, or courts, predisposes one to ignore those who continue to live in the recesses of everyday life. See Chowdhry (1997). In fact, Ravinder Kaur has argued that there are long-established traditions in certain parts of Haryana in which wives were brought from regions as far away as Bengal and Assam, though the pressure of a declining sex ratio has increased the demand for wives from outside in Punjab and Haryana (Kaur 2004).

pamphlet distributed by Akhil Bharati Vidyarthi Parishad (ABVP), the student wing of the Bharatiya Janata Party (BJP), known for its militant defense of a Hindu nationalism that has consistently put into question Muslim belonging to the nation.[5] The pamphlet shows how the anxieties around terrorism and Islamic *jihad* that have gained fresh ground due to both global and national discourses on terrorism and security are folded into the older rhetoric of the Muslim tendency to "seduce" young and gullible Hindu girls.

The pamphlet, written in English, which was distributed to students at the prestigious Jawaharlal Nehru University in 2009, following much publicity in the print and electronic media, carried the following warning:

> Few days back a Malayalam Daily; Kerala Kaumudi exposed shocking revelations about a jihadi organization named 'Love Jihad' which has been conveniently ignored by rest of the media. The allegation that Muslim men entice Hindu and Christian women into marriage for reasons other than love, as part of an Islamist conspiracy, has recently been investigated by Kerala Police and has brought out some ugly details. The August 31 issue of Kerala's foremost newspaper, Malayalam Manorama, carried an extensive report on how a Pakistan-based terrorist organization is planning, abetting and financing the enticement of college students from different communities in the State to become cannon fodder for its jihad in India. The report terms such young women as 'Love Bombs'.

The exposé continues:

> Trapping naive Hindu girls in the web of love in order to convert to Islam is the modus operandi of the said organization. Already more than 4000 girls have been converted to Islam by these Jihadi Romeos. Special branch of Police started investigation when marriages of such large scales were reported within last 6 months. As per the instructions of this organization, the recruits need to trap a Hindu girl each within the time frame of 2 weeks and brainwash her to get converted and then get married with her within 6 months. Special instructions to breed at least 4 kids have also been issued. If the target doesn't get trapped within first 2 weeks, they are instructed to leave her and move on to another girl. College students and working girls should be the prime target. Having completed their mission the organization will give 1 lakh Rupees and Financial help for the youth to start a business. Free mobile phone, bikes and fashionable dresses are offered to

---

5. I am grateful to Pratiksha Baxi for sending me material pertaining to this controversy.

them as tools for the mission. Money for this "Love Jihad" comes from the Middle East. Each district has its own zonal chairman to oversee the mission. Prior to College admission they make a list of Hindu girls with their details, and target those who they feel are vulnerable and easy to be brainwashed.

This pamphlet was based upon newspaper reports in both regional and national dailies. The issue came up when the Kerala High Court was hearing the anticipatory bail petitions of two young Muslim men, Sirajjudin and Shahan Sha, on the charges that they had abducted two girls from a local college and had forcibly converted them to Islam. The parents of the girls had brought a habeas corpus petition before the court. In the course of hearing the anticipatory bail petition, the court had observed that every citizen is entitled to "freedom of conscience and the right to freely profess and propagate religion as enshrined in Article 25 of the Constitution." "This right," the court further observed, "did not extend to the right to compel people professing a religion to convert to another religion." As this event unfolded, it spread to a hearing in the Karnataka High Court and a police inquiry into the activities of the alleged Love Jihad organization, as well as the People's Front of India, a Muslim group alleged to be involved in funding these activities. The police did not find any organization by the name of Love Jihad—nevertheless, the Deputy General of Police (DGP) reported in court that a spurt in conversions of Hindu and Christian girls was suspected and would be investigated in greater detail. A militant Hindu Rights Group, Sri Ram Sene, announced that it would send 150 party activists to keep an eye on suspicious activities of couples and immediately stop any "love jihad" activity they might identify. Members of Catholic organizations in Kerala also took notice of these events. K. S. Samson, the head of the Kochi based organization Christian Association of Social Action, announced that it would cooperate with the Vishwa Hindu Parishad (a right-wing Hindu group) to identify girls who were being forcibly converted from Hinduism and would expect reciprocal cooperation for saving Christian girls. An unnamed police officer is reported to have stated that certain fundamentalist groups that have been carrying out vigilante attacks against couples who marry outside their respective communities have now started using the label "love jihad" to justify their attacks.[6]

---

6. Details of the various episodes, including the court hearings, can be found in *Indian Muslim*, October, 27, 2009. Downloaded from http://twocircles,net/2009 Oct 27.

I point to such pamphlets and forms of publicity to indicate that an aura of suspicion surrounds marriages that cut across communities, especially the Hindu-Muslim divide. While there might be intensification of rumors and a heightened sense of danger at some moments and at others the intensity might wane, people in the neighborhoods in Delhi and other places are very aware of the potential for violence that such marriages might unleash. In two of the neighborhoods in Delhi in which I conducted fieldwork, local peace committees, composed of Hindus, Muslims, and Sikhs, have been created at the initiative of the local police, in association with the neighborhood branch of the Congress Party; they work to track down rumors and to mobilize support to defuse any violence that might escalate in response to local or even national events. I don't want to suggest that members of the police force always play a peace-maintaining role or that some political parties are more tolerant or, as the local parlance would have it, "secular" in accepting such marriages than others, but there are interesting local histories that account for different sensibilities even at the level of the neighborhood.[7]

In the context of tracking some of the publicity materials that these committees have generated, I learned about nine cases of Hindu-Muslim marriage, as well as other intercaste marriages that created considerable tension in the two neighborhoods in the last eight years. In addition, there are elopements or rumors of affairs across caste boundaries or even within the same community. For the purposes of this essay, however, I shall look only at the cases of Hindu-Muslim marriage. As I describe the manner in which social relations were continuously reconfigured in this one case, I make only occasional reference to the other cases. However, my discussion is informed by the wider field of forces that operate in them all. My technique of description is to place myself within an imminent and emerging story, depicting scenes of conversation, evasion, fear, and elation, rather than taking a transcendental view from a distance after the story has already acquired clarity. I was sometimes accompanied by my research assistant and colleague, Purshottam, who has been collecting statistical data on a panel of households in the area for the Institute for Socio-economic Research on Development and Democracy (ISERDD), a research organization dedicated to longtime research and advocacy on behalf of the poor,

---

7. It is common in north India for English-speaking persons to speak of someone as "communal" or "secular," or even to insert these English words within Hindi sentences, as in "Voh admi bahut secular hai" ("that man is very secular"). I am afraid that my own writing might have imbibed these modes of speaking, and I thank Michael Lambek for gently pointing out those errors.

of which I am a founding member. Purshottam and I often visited Bhag-
wanpur Kheda, a low-income neighborhood in East Delhi, together, and
sometimes we would end up talking to Kuldip's family together. I also
stopped often to have tea with women who were sitting in the street, making small objects for sale, chatting, or simply "taking in the sun" in the
winter months. Since 2000 I have visited these neighborhoods at least
twice a year, but the story is drawn from 1998 to 2000, when I conducted
intensive fieldwork in this area. I use the ethnographic present when I am
able to draw directly from my field notes.

## A Stranger in My House

Purshottam and I were walking down the street when Leela Devi's sister-
in-law, Savita, happened to open the door of their house. She insisted that
we come in to have a cup of tea. Leela Devi is not home today—normally,
being the eldest women in the house, she is the one to greet us and give
us news of what has been happening. It is clear that Savita is bursting to
tell us something. (This and other conversations all took place in Hindi
and have been translated by me.)

> SAVITA: Did you know that Kuldip [Leela Devi's eldest son] has gotten
>     married?
> VEENA: No, when did that happen? Congratulations. Where are the sweets?
> SAVITA: What congratulations? He has brought a Muslim girl into the
>     house [lit., has made a Muslim girl sit in the house]. No one in the
>     neighborhood knows. They are both constantly running here and there
>     [*idhar udhar bhag rahen hain*], hiding from her parents, who are threat-
>     ening to kill Kuldip and they [the parents of the girl] have also lodged a
>     police case of abduction. Didn't sister [Leela] tell you?

Over the next few days, we visit Leela Devi several times, because she
seems anxious to talk and keeps calling both of us to come and visit her—
yet when we meet, she can only skirt around the issue. Thus what we can
gather are broken fragments.

It is afternoon, and Leela Devi, Purshottam, and I are sitting in the
open courtyard while she washes some clothes. Suddenly there is a flurry
of movement, as sounds of loud knocking erupt. Before we can react, Leela
Devi has gotten up, wiped her hands, rushed us into a little adjoining
room, where old TVs and a broken sofa are piled up, and locked the door
from outside. I can hear some kind of contentious conversation taking

place. Leela Devi sounds placatory, saying he is not here—he was ill—that is why he has not returned your money, but he will. Finally the men leave, but their threats hang in the air. It turns out that these were two tough men sent by some people from whom Kuldip has taken credit. When Leela Devi finally comes to open the door of our room, I can see that she is trembling.

She tells us the following story:

You know how good Kuldip was in his studies. He got a scholarship to IIT. [The Indian Institute of Technology is an elite engineering school. As it happens, Kuldip's scholarship was not to IIT but to ITI, one of several Indian Technical Institutes set up by the government as vocational training centers. These are highly valued by families in lower-income neighborhoods, but they train students to be technicians, not engineers. This pattern of slight deception about his accomplishments was typical of Kuldip's stories about himself.] But he did not complete that degree, because he set up a tutorial college in partnership with a friend. He said, "I can make much more money setting up a college on my own." But his partner deceived him. He ran away with the money they made jointly. See how brilliant he is; his photograph is in the papers. [She shows me an advertisement in a two-sheet tabloid called *Careers Today* that has Kuldip's photograph.] Now the moneylenders are after him. What between these moneylenders and the RSS guys,[8] we are afraid to leave the house.

I mutter something about how sorry I am and say that if they need any help they should tell me. But she continues to talk, almost to herself:

For the last two years, things have just not worked out. Earlier my husband got so many TVs and cassette players to repair. [A room had been built as an extension of the house and as a storefront for the repair shop.] But now he does not get much business. For the last two years there has been this *chakkar* between my son and Saba. We did not know, but his grandfather knew. And in truth he encouraged Kuldip.

It is hard to translate the term *chakkar*, but its meaning in this context might best be conveyed as a tangled web. What did the encouragement of the grandfather mean? I had learned earlier that the grandfather, who was a retired employee of the postal department, was considered relatively well

---

8. RSS refers to the Rashtriya Swayamsevak Sangh, a Hindu nationalist organization affiliated with the BJP and generally hostile to the rights granted to Muslims in the Indian polity. On the local level, branches of the RSS are often involved in preventing cross-religious marriages by intimidation

off by local standards because he had both a regular pension and other sources of income. One of these was from a local shrine in small urban settlement (*kasba*), where the ancestral home was located. It seems that, after the Partition of India, many Muslims from this town either migrated to Pakistan voluntarily or were forced to leave because of the communal violence. One such family was the shrine keeper of a local *pir* (saintly master ), about whom not much was known. The shrine remained abandoned for awhile, but someone used to go and light a *diya* (earthen lamp) every evening on it. One day a visitor, who did not know that the overgrown, abandoned site was a shrine, had gone to relieve himself there at night, but the *diya* chased him away. The very same night, Kuldip's grandfather dreamed that the spirit of the Pir, named Bhooray Khan, had come into him, and he took upon himself the task of becoming the manager of the shrine. He cleaned up the place and slowly, through the medium of dreams, he began to construct the history of the local Pir. He has since filled in details, making his own biography of the Pir, on the model of the usual *urs*[9] stories of a Muslim saint who is handsome and pious. He is on way to his betrothed's house when some village women plead with him to rescue their cattle from a group of raiding bandits. The handsome young man agrees to do so but dies in the ensuing fight with the bandits, though he is able to restore their cattle to the women and is consequently consecrated as a Pir. According to the grandfather, he also received the boon of being able to cure various ailments. Although he has never studied Arabic, he can dream of Qur'anic *ayats* (verses); he then recites them over a glass of water or another material object, with which he can cure ailments. It is not clear from his description whether he sees the verses or hears them, but in any case he says he gets knowledge—sometimes he calls this knowledge *gyan* and sometimes *ilm*. Both terms can have generic and specific meanings in the context of healing cults but are differently anchored to Hindu and Islamic ideas of knowledge, respectively. His son, Kuldip's father, has also inherited this ability to dream cures. The family, however, considers itself to be firmly Hindu. Kuldip's mother and father are devout

---

9. *Urs* (lit. "nuptial ceremony") refers to the celebration of the death anniversaries of various *pirs*, celebrated at the site of their tombs. The saints, far from dying, are believed to reach the zenith of their spiritual life on this occasion. The biography of the *pir* is recited or sung on this and other occasions. It has a standard plot structure, which involves a journey on the occasion of the *pir*'s marriage that is interrupted to offer help to an oppressed figure and in the course of which the *pir* meets a heroic death.

worshippers of the mother goddess, Vaishno-Devi, who demands vegetarianism of them. The grandfather and the children are exempt from these requirements placed by the mother goddess. The grandchildren, Kuldip and his siblings, have not inherited this ability to dream. The grandfather believes that each grandchild will show his disposition and that nothing can be imposed by way of an impersonal religious belief.

Therefore, I suspect, when Kuldip fell in love with Saba he confided in his grandfather, relating the difficulties they were facing and the fact that they were both hesitant whether they would be able to withstand the pressures that are built into a marriage outside one's community, especially a Hindu-Muslim marriage. I will let Kuldip speak about this. The occasion was a poignant one, since, after hiding from Saba's relatives and running all over north India from one sympathetic relative to another, sometimes Kuldip's, sometimes Saba's, and living in various cheap hotels, they had run out of money. Saba was pregnant and soon to give birth. Meanwhile, negotiations between various relatives had been continuing, so that Saba felt reassured that her parents or brother would not risk a communal confrontation by killing Kuldip or her, as they had earlier threatened to do. Kuldip's mother invited them to come back. This was now more than a year after they had first eloped.

> KULDIP: When I first saw her, I did not even notice her very much. Actually, one of my friends was going out with a girl. He used to ask me to come with him, and his girl friend brought Saba along so that they would not be conspicuous—a girl and a boy alone attract the attention of all kinds of bad people. I do not know how it happened, but then I knew that she was the only one in the world for me. But I did not know if she would be able to stand the rigors of a true love [*saccha pyar*].
>
> SABA: First I was offended, but then his sincerity won me over. Still, it was difficult, because everyone in my family knows how I have immersed myself in the verses of the Qur'an. I was the first girl in my family to have learned how to read the whole Qur'an. I know only enough Arabic to recognize the verses and to recite them, but I am not like others, who learn just a few verses. So I knew how hurt and upset my father and brother would be. But once I acknowledged to myself that I loved him, I thought that this is what I must do—this is what I have to do [*yeh to karna hi karna hai*].[10]

---

10. I note a further thought here, though I cannot develop it fully for lack of space. The expression Saba used has some resonance with the upper-caste Hindu notion, popularized by popular Hindi cinema and television serials, that a chaste woman falls in love only once and that true love is to be found only once in a lifetime.

The story that followed is similar to other stories of strategies followed by couples to combine the resources of helpful kin and friends and to somehow get the protection of the law to evade the feared violence that such a marriage can generate (Mody 2008). Thus, for instance, before Kuldip and Saba eloped they took care to leave a written statement with the local police station through a lawyer, with copies in the hands of some friends, to the effect that Saba was voluntarily leaving with Kuldip in order to get married. Saba feared that her father might lodge a complaint of abduction against Kuldip (which he did), and she was advised that such a letter would come in handy against police harassment or criminal charges, were they to be levied against Kuldip. Like many other eloping couples, they had first gone to the Tis Hazari Court in Old Delhi in order to get married under the Special Marriage Act of 1954, but, as Mody has described in her book, it is not a straightforward matter for an eloping couple to get married in the court. The banns of the intention to marry have to be publicly posted for thirty days in advance, in addition to the require-ment of several official forms of certification, including one from the local police station testifying to residence of the couple in a neighborhood in Delhi.[11]

Many young men of the RSS or other Hindu fronts monitor these banns in order to prevent such marriages. Recall that the Sri Ram Sene said that they would send 150 activists to stop "love jihad" marriages and the comment of the anonymous policeman I cited earlier that this threat should be seen as a continuation of the usual strategies of threatening and intimidating couples from different religions who wish to marry. How-ever, Mody also points out that there are various kinds of services offered in the courts that are not part of the formal legal system but have neverthe-less become a part of the everyday life of the court. One of these services is that of the Arya Samaj, a Hindu reform organization that has historically combined a progressive agenda of Hindu reform with a strong anti-Mus-lim stance and a program for reconverting Muslims to their "original" Hindu state. Even *E. J. Brill's First Encyclopedia of Islam, 1913–1936*, in its chapter on India, mentions that the Arya Samaj had been active in the work of reconversion and that the Rajput Shuddhi Society (Rajput Purifi-cation Society), which was affiliated with it, had brought 1,052 Rajput Muslims into the Hindu fold between 1907 and 1910 (Houtsma et al. 1993)

---

11. Many Internet sites where couples can discuss their problems and seek advice have grown up in recent years. See http://sukh-dukh.com, for instance.

In any case, with the help of some friends, Kuldip and Saba were able to contact a local Arya Samaj priest, who offered to convert Saba to Hinduism and to perform an Arya Samaj wedding for them, which would be recognized by the court. Thus they could simply register their marriage rather than have to wait for the court procedures. Both Kuldip and Saba pointed out to me that this was not the only option they tried.

SABA: I really had no objection to being converted—I thought if one of us has to do it, why not me? They gave me a different name—Seema—not too different from my own name, so that I would not become disoriented. The priest actually told me that it is customary for all Hindu girls to get a new name on marriage. There was not much ritual or anything—just *yag* [in Sanskrit, *yajna*, fire sacrifice]—and circumambulation round the fire and putting vermilion in the parting of my hair. Kuldip said to me, "Don't take anything to heart—this is just for legal purposes. No one is going to stop you from reading the Qur'an or saying your *namaz*."[12] But still it was interesting [using the English word] that no temple would agree to marry us—only the Arya Samaj agreed.

KULDIP: Actually we also tried the mosque. I wanted to become a Muslim, but there they insisted that we must bring an affidavit signed in a court that I was willing to be converted out of my own free will. The mufti of Fatehpur Sikri told me that I would have to study the Qur'an for at least three months before I could know that I wanted to accept Islam and before they could assure themselves that it was a genuine case of wanting to convert and not simply a ruse for getting married. Actually, all these are excuses—these days no one wants to take a risk [using the word *risk* in English].

SABA: All these are just excuses for doing nothing—to cover up the fact that they don't want the hassle. They think the RSS guys will come and take panga [a colloquial expression meaning to pick a fight]. And then they don't want to deal with irate parents. The fact is that my parents are very conscious of their high caste status—we are Rajputs, and Kuldip comes from a lower caste.

KULDIP: Oh yes, this is a *kaum* [community] that should welcome those like me who genuinely want to accept Islam, because this community grew by conversions. Only later did they come to realize that someone like me who has received the light of Islam is like a gift from above [*uppar wale ki den*]—like a precious newborn—to be received on one's eyelashes

12. *Namaz* (in Urdu) refers to the five prayers offered by Muslims to Allah by reading prescribed sections from the Qur'an and is considered to be one of the five pillars of Islam.

[an expression denoting extreme delicacy]. But they were bothered about caste and parents and RSS.

I wanted to talk more, but there were always interruptions. I give some further texture to Kuldip's intriguing references to his attraction to Islam, as well as its relation to the manner in which his father's and grandfather's unstable relations to Islam played in the life of the household, by stitching together several short conversations from different times after Kuldip and Saba had moved back into Kuldip's parents' house and after the birth of a son to Saba.

> LEELA DEVI: I do not know when our days will turn. I pray day and night to Mata Rani [the mother goddess], saying, "Don't turn your face away from us." Earlier my husband used to have visions of her, and she used to guide him—do this; do that. But now there is no business—everyone gets new TVs and no one seems in need of repair.
>
> VEENA: Is she angry because something wrong has been done?
>
> LEELA DEVI: Who is to say? It is the mother's wish. I keep trying to divine what is the matter. Is it because Saba might have become a Hindu? But who can take away the *samskara* she has? [*Samskara* refers to the impressions formed on one's being from the intimate environment in which one grows up—the term also refers in more specific way to rites of passage.] So I thought maybe when she is lighting the evening lamp [at the domestic altar]—or maybe she does something not quite right in the *puja* [ritual worship]—so I tactfully stopped her from doing that. Maybe He [her husband—a common way of referring to one's husband, since it is taboo for a woman to pronounce her husband's name] has started drinking. He might even be eating meat. He is inclined that way, though the goddess has imposed very strict dietary restrictions on him. People criticize me for bringing Kuldip and Saba home—the RSS boys are after us. I told one of them, "You can get many people to defend your Hindu *dharma*. But as for me, I am a mother. Where will I get my son again if I lose him?" I say, "Mata Rani, forgive me—don't punish me for loving my son."

Here, with a different inflection, Saba:

Though I told you that, when they did all that *shuddhi* [purification] and conversion, both Kuldip and I knew that this was just for the marriage, it did have some influence on me. I began seriously to learn how to do *puja*. It moved me to think that this is what Kuldip grew up watching and doing—and then I thought that, so long as I do not perform *sajda* [the Islamic term for prostration][13] before another god, I do not offend against Allah's glory. I would fold my hands and bow my head in respect, but I would not touch my head to the altar. That is why I thought I have not rejected Islam. Allah too knows and blesses lovers. [*Aashikon par to Allah bhi fida hai*—lit., even Allah is enchanted by lovers.]

On yet another occasion, sitting in the *barsati* (a room on the side of the open terrace) that had been now assigned to Kuldip and Saba as a "Muslim" or "Islamic" space (since the family did not make the subtle distinctions that scholars make between the two) and having tea:

SABA: But then Mummy Ji [referring to Kuldip's mother] began to be somehow uneasy with my performing *puja* and all. She said, "You have learned to read the Qur'an and to say the *namaz* since you were such a little girl—how can we take away from you all your *samskara*? Maybe the goddess herself does not want us to take you away from what is dear to your heart and from your Allah.

KULDIP: Here in the *barsati* we keep the Qur'an and everyone supports Saba—they know she has to perform the rite at the right time. Anyway, women are not allowed to go to the mosque, so all that has to be done at home.

VEENA: And you, how do you relate to all this?

KULDIP Well, I have also started reading the *namaz*.

SABA (interrupting): Actually, that was really quite amazing. Papa Ji [Kuldip's father] says he can dream the right *ayat* to be read when he makes a cure. But he is under some kind of order from Mata Rani not to say *Bismillah*. I have watched him perform all this, and I cannot understand how Allah *mian* does his work.[14] But He [referring to

---

13. The rules for prostration and correct forms of worship are laid out in the 32nd *sura* of the Qur'an, entitled As-Sajda. They are also the subject of many fatawas issued by the Dar-ul-uloom and by local muftis.

14. The honorific *mian* is often added to *Allah* among South Asian Muslims. The term *Bismillah* is an abbreviation of the longer phrase *b-ismi-llāhi r-rahmāni r-rahīm*. "In the name of God, most gracious, most merciful." It is recited before every *sura* of the Qur'an except the ninth *sura*, which includes the famous sword verse, according to which Muslims are exhorted to kill any pagan they encounter—though it must be remembered that the command was given in the context of the battle of Tabuk, as my Muslim friends in this neighborhood never tire of reminding me. The fact that Kuldip's grandfather could dream of the *ayats* of the Qur'an but could not say *Bismillah* because of the command of the goddess could mean several things. It could mean that, though he recites the verses, he does not do so with full allegiance to Islam. It could have the darker meaning that the verses he

Kuldip] is like he's intoxicated with this [*is cheez ka nasha chad gaya hai*]. The other night he woke me up at three in the morning and said, "Teach me how to read the *namaz*." I said, "Now?" And he said, "Yes." I can tell you I know how long it takes even for a person born a Muslim to learn the proper way of reading the *namaz*—but he seems to pick up so fast. It is hard to know what Allah wants.

VEENA (to Kuldip): So do you think of yourself as Muslim now or as Hindu? Or does it not matter?

KULDIP: I am a Muslim now. Of-course, I stand with my mother when she performs *arti* [waving of lamps and chanting] in the evening before the image of the goddess. I too used to be a complete devotee of the goddess. And of course I will take part in the annual *shraddha* rituals to honor the ancestors. But sitting in temples or making offerings—all that is over. Now I think that something compels me to learn more about Islam. I go and hang about in the mosque. I have talked to the elders there, and they now see that the light of Islam has come into me. They now agree that a great mistake was made in not admitting me earlier—but now I have recited the *kalma* [profession of faith].

Saba corrects him to say *kalima*, and he recites for me *La Illaha Illallah Muhammadur Rasullullah*, "There is no God but God, and Mohammad is his Prophet." Then he says shyly that Arabic does not yet sit on his tongue properly.

It turned out that each person in the family was trying to make slow shifts in his or her orientation to the divine, to prayer, and to ritual performances, as well as adjustments in the question of to which community he or she belonged. Kuldip's mother became closer to the goddess as she tried to see that anything that angered the goddess in relation to the presence of a Muslim girl in the home was somehow neutralized. Her husband, who had earlier been able to dream both in an Islamic and in a Hindu idiom, felt the weight of betrayal toward the goddess. But he was losing his ability to cure, so he shifted his allegiance to a local Sufi *baba* (an honorific for a holy or wise older man) known as *khichdi baba*. Khichdi is a popular dish of rice and lentils, but in popular parlance it also refers to an

---

recites are the verses, or are seen as similar to the verses, in the ninth *sura*, in which God's anger against pagans is most evident, and that he uses these verses by trapping the anger that lies in the words to overcome the disease or perhaps to perform harmful magic. This point was somewhat dangerous to pursue, hence Saba takes leave of the interpretation by referring to the mysterious ways of Allah.

unruly mix.[15] Once when I was talking to Kuldip's grandfather, he said that, since Allah had given them small bounties such as the blessing of the *pir*, he was now demanding what was due to him (*apna hisab le rahen hain*). Kuldip took on the Islamic name Mohammad as a sign of his commitment to Islam but limited its use to the mosque or among Saba's relatives. His grandfather had a dream in which a new *basti* (settlement) was being formed, in which he saw a mosque and, like a watermark on a sheet of paper, a temple behind it.[16] Consulting a book on how to interpret dreams from an Islamic perspective, he informed me that the dream was a good omen, since if you see a new *basti* with a mosque and a market it means Allah has blessed a new endeavor—as for the temple, he could not say. Dreams, he tells me, are the last bit of prophecy Allah has bestowed on humans, provided you know how to interpret them, for Iblis (Satan) also uses dreams to delude men.

As I indicated earlier, Kuldip had something of a trickster quality, as in being able to make ITI appear as IIT or in managing his debts with the dexterity of a gambler—taking loans from one type of person (a relative) and to pay off another (a moneylender). Perhaps this is why the grandfather was relieved to have a good dream. However, Kuldip's luck did not hold for long—there was added pressure from his uncle and aunt, who shared the house with his parents, because his unsettled debts were creating a scandal in the neighborhood. Kuldip had gone a long way toward "becoming Muslim" but had neither been circumcised nor partaken of beef—the two ultimate tests in local understanding that conversion is complete. After one particularly ugly event, in which one of his creditors threatened to have him beaten up, he left with Saba and their son for Aligarh, where some of her relatives stay in a Muslim neighborhood and where he was able take on a Muslim identity (name, beard, and regular prayers in the mosque, while still avoiding beef and deferring circumcision). Although I could not meet Saba and him after they left, they maintained regular contact with the family, and his mother told me that the

---

15. In addition to well-known regional shrines of *pirs*, numerous shrines are not known outside the small *kasbas*, or urban neighborhoods. Sometimes the *pir* is known both by a Hindu name and by a Muslim name and may have functionaries from both communities. At other times, as in this case, either a Muslim family or a Hindu one might officiate as the main ritual functionary at the shrine. See Saheb (1998).

16. The analogy of the watermark is mine. He used the term *mandir ka saaya jaisa*, "as if there were the shadow of a temple"—his gesture of moving his hands

creditors had forcibly placed a family on the top floor, who paid regular rent to the creditors and were expected to stay until the debt was paid off. Kuldip's four younger bothers became the major conduits for contact between the parents and his family. In addition, tentative gift exchanges between the affines were established by each side, sending appropriate gifts of sweets from the market for *diwali* and *id -ul-nabi*, the two major festivals of Hindus and Muslims. Kuldip's younger brother laughingly told me that Kuldip was trying to put Saba in *purdah*, to observe the veil, and that Saba was vigorously resisting on the grounds that even her orthodox father had failed to do that. After a year had passed, I heard rumors that Kuldip had failed to establish himself economically, that a tutorial college he had set up with borrowed money in Aligarh had failed, and that he might be returning to his parent's house. The first indication of this was that he had sent his son to spend the summer in Delhi.[17]

Not all such marriages across religion or caste seem to show the same complexity. While marriages across communities are by no means rare, the reactions range from quiet acceptance to violent fights. Thus, for instance, Namita, a girl from the *baniya* caste fell in love with a Muslim boy from the same neighborhood, eloped with him, and converted to Islam. Her parents would have nothing to do with her and had cut all connections, but she was hopeful that over time they would forgive her. By contrast, when a Hindu girl, Sonia, ran away with a hawker, a Hindu from a similar lower-caste background, it was not caste or religion that was the issue but the sheer fact of her running away and the question of family honor. Her mother and uncle (her father had abandoned her mother) lodged a case of abduction with the police on the grounds that she was a minor. The couple was produced in court, where Sonia alleged that her mother was trying to engage her in prostitution and that was why she was opposing their marriage. Her mother was reduced to silence and amazement that such coarse language could (as she said) "come out of her daughter's mouth." The court ordered Sonia to be placed in Nari Niketan

---

in slow motion from one side to another as he talked of this scene reminded me of a watermark.

17. Their son had not yet been circumcised. However, among many Indian Muslim communities, the ritual of circumcision is customarily performed when the child is a bit older. Mehta (2000) has described how the ritual of circumcision called *Musalmani* ("making a Muslim") among the Ansaris includes a verbal statement addressed to the child to the effect that until that day he was a Hindu and now he is going to become a Muslim. The fascinating account shows how the social memory of conversion might thus be encoded in ritual language.

(a government-run custodial home for girls and women who might have been raped, who have been rescued from brothels, or who are otherwise in danger of being sexually or physically violated) until she attained legal majority. The family then relented and withdrew the case, which legally then ended in a "compromise."[18]

I do not wish to go into the full geography of these cases here, although an understanding of the changing forms of intimacy in urban India would require us to do that. Instead, my aim is to reflect more deeply on the case of Kuldip and Saba to ask what moral projects might be embedded in everyday life in the context of the agonistic belonging of Hindus and Muslims as neighbors in the same local worlds (see Singh 2009)—local worlds that are, however, inflected with national and even transnational imaginaries that shape Hindu and Muslim identities. What idea of everyday life might we propose here? And how might our understanding of the moral depart from the idea of morality as the capacity to make abstract moral judgments or to deploy a vocabulary that marks off the domain of the moral from everyday life?

## Everyday Life as an Achievement

The term *everyday* covers a wide range of meanings: it tends to perform different kinds of functions in the oeuvre of different writers. Rather than attempt to give an account of these different theoretical positions, here I will show how two specific intuitions about the everyday become important sites for understanding the sense of the moral as the generation of an

---

18. Although compromise is not legal in the case of rape, and thus court records do not ever state that a compromise was reached, Baxi (2008), in her remarkable work on the adjudication of rape in the district courts in Gujarat, notes that the courts regularly arrived at this solution, partly in recognition of the fact that parents will sometimes register criminal charges of abduction and rape against a man, even if their daughter has left voluntarily with him, in order to "punish" the girl and her lover. In such cases, courts are aware that the courtroom is being used to avenge the honor of the family rather than to seek justice. Alternatively, the courts recognize that parents might have already "recovered" the girl, who, due to the long time it takes for a case to be adjudicated in court, might now be married to someone else and settled in her conjugal home. This is not to deny that a settlement might be the result of pressure put on the courts by men in power, especially if the girl comes from a lower-status family that does not have the means to make court appearances over such a long period of time.

adjacent self, as we have seen in the case of Kuldip and Saba. In his magis-
terial work on the everyday, Fernand Braudel (1979) speaks of the coordi-
nation of the durability of the long term with the minute fluctuations of
low-level occurrences. Behind the visible institutions of state and market,
Braudel was interested in the "basic activity which went on everywhere,"
the volume of which he called "fantastic." What Braudel tries to do for
material life, covering the rich zone that he calls "infra-economics," one
could do for the moral life. The big events that become visible because of
their capacity to break into the public realm have both an antecedent life
and an afterlife. These eventologies of the ordinary in the light of what
comes after, as Shane Vogel (2009) elegantly puts it, require one to wait
patiently to track how something new might be born. In the case of Kuldip
and Saba, we see that there isn't one single conversion as a turning away
from a previous mode of life but rather a slow flowering of the discovery
of how Saba might become the daughter by marriage of a home in which
the identities Hindu and Muslim are in an unstable relation to one another. Moreover, we see that Islam holds an attraction for Kuldip, though
the specific dimensions of Islam with which he finds affinity will come
only later. Each member of the family is given an opportunity to learn
how to inhabit this newness, and I have tried to track closely and respectfully, to the extent that they would allow me, the ordinary moments inter-
woven with extraordinary events, such as Kuldip's desire in the middle of
the night to learn how to say the *namaz*, or Kuldip's grandfather's dream
that a new *basti* was being formed and his vision of a mosque and an old
ruined temple that is never completely erased, a scene that he could interpret as a harbinger of good things to come.

There is another vision of the everyday in both Freud and Austin, which
Cavell describes as "not being awake." In his words, "each harbors, within
sensibilities apparently otherwise so opposite, a sense of human beings in
their everyday existence as not alive to themselves, or not awake to their
lives"(Cavell 2005c: 214). What it is to become awake to one's life might
be thought of by analogy with Cavell's reading of Thoreau and his
pond—of Thoreau taking the time to relate a hundred details, such as the
transformation of water into ice or the significance to be found in bubbles
within the ice. This attentiveness to minute shifts in actions and dispositions is one way in which to inhabit the everyday: one sees something like
it in the changes Kuldip's mother notices through the mediation of her
mother goddess or in what Saba tries to bring about in herself so that she
can connect to Kuldip's childhood. There are, of course, pressures from
the lack of money, and one could hardly hold Kuldip up as some kind of

moral exemplar. But, beyond his attempts to elude his debtors and perhaps a bit of cheating here and a bit of misrepresentation there, his love for Saba brings a possibility for newness into being. This is the possibility that, even when the national rhetoric is vitiated by a vision of a strong Hindu state in which the presence of Muslims is barely tolerated, a small community of love can come about and, at least in some lives, break the solidity of oppositional identities.

In a provocative essay on evil and love, Leo Bersani (2008) asks whether love can overcome evil. He invites us to think of a different way to conceptualize love, and indeed relatedness. Developing Freud's great insight that, in love, to find an object is always to refind it, Bersani argues that love is inseparable from memory. Thus the loved object is already a bearer of other memories (of the mother, of an infantile idealized self)—it cannot, despite claims to the contrary, provide an openness to the other. Bersani makes the extraordinary claim that the "beloved becomes the lover as result of being loved" and thus defines the task of love as embracing the reality of the other as one's own. In other words, what one has to overcome in love is, first, the inability to love oneself and hence the inability to love the other. Without going into the full development of his argument, what I take from Bersani's remarkable essay is the idea that love provides us with the opportunity to realize our "virtual being," which is not the idealized infantile self but rather, in my vocabulary, an adjacent self that is allowed to come into being. That course entails losses that we might even mourn—the most important loss being the security of anchorage in a solid, given identity. I find it salutary to understand that, in this urban environment, in this household struggling with everyday wants and needs, this labor of opening oneself to a different vision of what it might be to receive the other should be performed. Even before the marriage, there were indications in this household that Hindus and Muslims are not completely locked inside their identities; that perhaps constitutes the condition of possibility for such love to be born and to find a home. It is a picture of the moral in which we might lose the profundity of moral statements through which much of philosophy, theology, and religion (including that of the religious experts in these very neighborhoods) stages the moral. What we gain is the simple capacity to inhabit the everyday and to perform the labor of discovering what it is to engage the life of the other.

What, then, of the scholarship on Hindu-Muslim relations that has long argued that there is a profound history of hostility between Hindus and Muslims, within which the only hope for peace lies in settling for relationships in the "marketplace"? In Louis Dumont's famous formulation:

we are faced with a reunion of men divided into two groups who devalorize each other's values and who are nevertheless associated. The association, quite inadequately studied, has had a profound effect on Hindu society and has created Muslim society of quite a special type, a hybrid type which we are scarcely in a position to characterize, except by saying that, lying beneath the ultimate or Islamic values are other values presupposed by actual behaviour . . . [there is a] permanence of psychological dispositions to the extent that each Muslim, Christian, or Lingayat has something of the Hindu in him. (1980: 211)

It is interesting that Dumont does not ask himself whether there might be a "Muslim," for instance, within the "Hindu." Nor does he imagine that a traffic in categories might be normal in the social life of nations and persons.

The thesis of "devalorization" has a strong hold on many scholars. Thus, though many scholars have provided evidence of so-called "syncretic" practices in folk religion, Peter van der Veer (1994) has cautioned against reading a history of harmony or mutual respect into these practices. Instead, he argues that Hindus seek out Muslim shrines not as an expression of devotion but because they assume that, like untouchables, Muslim healers are able to master the spirit world and to expel malign spirits. He then goes on to conclude that the Muslim practice of saint worship is thus incorporated into impure practices typical of lower castes in a Hindu worldview. A major problem with his analysis is that it slips too easily between the figure of the *pir* and the figure of the *amil*, or healer who uses the occult. Others have shown that relations between Hindu devotees and Muslim *pirs* are much more nuanced (Saheb 1998, Werbner and Basu 1998). Another problem, from the perspective of this essay, is that terms such as "the Hindu worldview" are so totalizing that they leave little room for an exploration of the moral projects people might pursue because they assume that all the steps are already taken or that following rules is like following a pregiven grid.

To pay attention to the possibilities for both hurt and care within the contentious memories Hindus and Muslims have of each other, possibilities that increase or decrease in intensity along with the larger political projects within which their identities are implicated, is to assume neither that we can find solace in such binary oppositions as faith and ideology (Nandy 1990) nor that all relationships across the Hindu-Muslim divide are doomed to failure from the start. Instead, we might pay attention to the manner in which moral striving shows up in everyday labors of caring for the other, even in contexts where a mutual antagonism defines the relation—or, as Bhrigupati Singh (2009) formulates the issue, where the relation between neighbors might be defined as one of "agonistic belonging," in which one locked in conflict with another at one level might find that there are other thresholds of life in which one becomes, despite all expectations, attracted to that other.

## ACKNOWLEDGMENTS

I am very grateful to my colleagues at ISERDD and especially to Purshottam for their help and cooperation. I thank Webb Keane and Michael Lambek for comments and discussions on the broader questions of ethics. My ongoing conversations with friends in Baltimore and Delhi, especially Bhrigupati Singh, Sylvain Perdigon, Sidharthan Maunaguru, Naveeda Khan, Deborah Poole, Michael Moon, Aaron Goodfellow, Deepak Mehta, Rita Brara, Pratiksha Baxi, and Roma Chatterji, have helped shape my thinking on issues relating to kinship, sexuality, and sovereignty. The persons I name as Kuldip and Saba and their respective families were excellent teachers on matters of religion and love, for which I am grateful for more than can be said here. My thanks to Helen Tartar for her amazing editorial eye.

# The Ghosts of War and the Ethics of Memory

*Heonik Kwon*

In *The Ethics of Memory*, the philosopher Avishai Margalit proposes two distinct ways to conceive of collective memory, particularly in regard to the tragic mass destruction of human lives and the obligation to remember and commemorate these lives. One is what he calls "thick memory," the knowledge of a past event kept and transmitted within the milieu of intimate relations such as the family (or the national community, according to Margalit). The beholders of "thick memory," according to him, constitute a community that shares an ethic of memory. The other type of collective memory takes as its site the horizon of "thin relations," defined as other than the milieu of kinship and friendship. For Margalit, these thin relations may have a morality of memory in contrast to thick relations, which maintain an ethic of memory, and he observes that the morality of memory, based on diffuse and nonsolidary relations, is largely nonexistent in the world and is bound to be weak where it does exist. He says:

> Thick relations are grounded in attributes such as parent, friend, lover, fellow-countrymen. Thick relations are anchored in a shared past or moored in shared memory. Thin relations, on the other hand, are backed by the attribute of being human. Thin relations rely also on some aspects of being human, such as being a woman or being sick. Thick relations are

in general our relations to the near and dear. Thin relations are in general our relations to the stranger and the remote. (Margalit 2004: 7)

Margalit distinguishes morality from ethics in terms of the relations each informs and describes and in a specific analytical way, following Bernard Williams (see James Laidlaw's chapter in this volume). His privileging of the ethics of memory over the morality of memory has raised some controversies. It has been argued, for instance, that Margalit's rumination on the ethics of memory is oblivious to the crucial domain of the politics of memory (Bell 2008). This objection concerns particularly the way in which Margalit portrays the national community as a community of thick relations. Another question relates to the statement "Thin relations are in general our relations to the stranger and the remote." Although this statement seems to point to an obvious fact of life, I doubt whether extending this point to a conclusion about thin memory will be that obvious and whether the relations to the stranger and the remote necessarily entail thin memory.

Researches in history and anthropology show that thin relations are not merely other than thick relations but can also be constitutive of them. Janice Boddy describes how a spirit cult in northern Sudan incorporates myriad foreigner or stranger spirits and how this local religious form of a specific cosmopolitan orientation coexists with the dominant institutional Islamic belief (Boddy 1989: 165). Marilyn Strathern has shown that the traditional Melanesian vision of the intimate world incorporates a sense that appears to European observers as cosmopolitan sensibility and raises an objection to the assumption in the contemporary literature about traditional social forms that the cosmopolitan ethos necessarily means transcending parochial local cultural horizons (Strathern 1992: 98–99).

John Gillis, referring to the parallel existence of a feudal agrarian world and a multicultural urban civilization throughout the late medieval and early modern periods, states that collective memory in old Europe, before it was incorporated into national memory, was either highly "localized or relatively cosmopolitan" (Gillis 1994: 5). In a history of Salonica, Mark Mazower (2004) describes how, although this northern Greek city sits on an archaeological heritage of intense exchanges among Islamic, Jewish, and Christian cultures, this heritage goes unrecognized in its contemporary life and has been denied by nationalist claims. In an engrossing analysis of Vietnamese historiography, Keith Taylor emphasizes the local horizons of intercultural fusion and the "fluid surface of mass culture" in contradiction to the imagined genealogical depth and homogeneity of Confucian elite culture (Taylor 1998: 974).

In this essay, I want to address the problems involved in reducing the ethics of memory to a community of thick relations. My point of reference will be how the Vietnamese villagers of Quang Nam Province today commemorate victims of the country's recent war. For the Vietnamese, the Vietnam War was at once an international, a national, and a local conflict; the memory of this war, likewise, has local, national, and global dimensions. I will examine how this multidimensional history of war is manifest in Vietnamese ritual commemorative practices, which consist of memorials to the nation's heroes, family ancestors, and a variety of displaced spirits, including some of foreign origin, and I will explore the possibility of conceiving of "relations to the stranger and the remote" as an integral part of the ethics of memory. As a way of situating this inquiry in broader debates about the politics of war and the morality of death commemoration, I will review relevant conceptions from two separate philosophical traditions: the Kantian notion of universal hospitality as a condition of perpetual peace and Hegelian ethical questions about modern political life that address a critical moral dilemma in war commemoration.

## Two-way Commemoration

My case material focuses on the form of ritual commemoration observed in contemporary Vietnam. The 1990s was a time of formidable change for Vietnam. The country was transformed during this relatively short time, in the view of the outside world, from a poor and isolated country ravaged by successive wars to a politically stable, vibrant economy. Mired in a deep economic crisis, with high inflation and low productivity, in the late 1980s Vietnam's political leaders embraced a program of general economic renovation (*doi moi*), swinging toward a regulated market economy. The shift in economic ideology involved a growing political tolerance for communal and associational activities, including religious worship. As a result, one of the most notable changes in Vietnamese society during the 1990s was "a nationwide resurgence of religion and ritual" (Malarney 2003: 225; see also Luong 1993).

In the province of the central region, Quang Nam, where I studied the local history of the war in the second half of the 1990s, the revival of ancestral rituals took place in parallel with the reinvigoration of ritual activity meant for the opposite category, which may be called, for the sake of convenience, "ghosts." In many communities of this region, when people began to renovate domestic ancestral shrines and communal ancestral temples, they extended the development project to include shrines for displaced, unknown spirits of the dead (Kwon 2006: 79–81). These ghost shrines are usually located on the opposite side of the ancestral temple or shrine, although some are scattered around the village without a clear pattern, according to where a given ghost may have appeared. As the seasons passed, by the end of the decade these ghost shrines became aesthetically the most audacious material objects in some villages of this region, sumptuously decorated with various colorful offerings.

As a result of this development, domestic ancestral rites in this region typically involve two distinct shrines. One is the newly refurbished tilted altar, holding memorabilia of family ancestors. It is located at the center of the house. Opposed to it, usually where the front garden borders on the street, there is an external shrine, popularly called *khom* in the language of the Quang Nam province. This shrine for ghosts typically looks like a large birdhouse, a small roofed structure standing on a tall, single column, although it may take variant forms, such as an empty Coca Cola can hanging on a tree, which is popular in poor areas. Within this dual concentric ritual organization, consisting of ritually appropriated ancestors and other deities settled on the house side (called *ong ba*, meaning "grandfathers and grandmothers"), and unsettled, placeless ghosts on the street side (addressed as *co bac*, "aunts and uncles"), the act of commemoration is highly alacritous. Participants offer incense and kowtow toward the house-side ancestral shrine, then turn their bodies in the opposite direction to repeat their gestures of remembrance to the street-side shrine. Through this two-sided act of worship, the commemorator engages with two separate religious symbols and the two different milieus of memory they represent.

Within this system of dual structure and two-sided practice emerge two distinctive ways to imagine social solidarity. On the house side, we may say, following Durkheim, that the commemorative act affirms solidary relations between the living and the dead, thereby generating a sensation of mutual belonging and the sense of a coherent social whole—whether we call it genealogical unity or the lineage paradigm (Durkheim 1995 [1912]). This is particularly evident in the periodic ceremonies held at the communal house (*dinh*), which is usually the most important site of worship in a rural village, dedicated to its founding ancestors. All family and lineage groups of the village are expected to take part in these occasions or at least to contribute to them, including people of village origin who happen to live in faraway places. Participants listen to oratory about the founding ancestors' legendary history of migration and settlement and make gestures and offerings of tribute to their memory, according to order of seniority and lineage status.

The organization of this village-wide ancestral rite also includes ritual-ized interactions with wandering spirits. After the house-side worship is over, the participants turn in the opposite direction, walk to the external shrine for ghosts, and pray and make offerings on behalf of displaced spir-its who, unlike the ancestors believed to be settled inside the temple, do not have the privilege of a home in which to reside. The street-side wor-ship does not follow a strict order of seniority like that prominent in the house-side worship and hence has a comparatively chaotic appearance. Prayers for ghosts may also, on certain occasions, be accompanied by po-etic addresses. When this happens, the village ritual specialists recite the traditional incantation of spirit invitation and consolation, calling in all the different categories of tragic or displaced death and urging the spirits to receive the villagers' gestures of sympathy and hospitality. The incanta-tions are often improvised versions of a famous classical poem, called *Van chieu hon* or *Van te co hon* ("Calling the wandering souls"), composed by an eminent mandarin scholar of the eighteenth century (Nguyen 1993: 130–32; Tan 1994: 105–14).

This ritual performance is not an affirmation of solidarity between the living and the dead, as Durkheim has it, but rather an act of hospitality to the unknown and unrelated: from the moral community of settlers (the ancestors and their descendants) to the crowd of strangers who are imag-ined to exist in proximity to the community (Kwon 2008: 87–88). The *co bac* as a ritual category refers to spirits of the dead who are not the ances-tors of the ritual actors. These spirits stand as social outsiders to the ances-tors and as cosmological strangers to the community when the community demonstrates its spiritual solidarity with ancestors and other specific dei-ties. They are not relationally part of the community but nevertheless are existentially close to the life activities taking place there. The street-side worship acknowledges the ghosts' existential status and their right to exist in the village world but distinguishes their social standing from that of the ancestors.

## Political Ghosts

The categorical distinction between ancestors and ghosts is an important element in Durkheim's sociology of religion. Durkheim assigned supreme social value to ancestral spirits, with and through whom the living generate the sacred notion of a social whole. By contrast, he relegated ghosts to a sociologically irrelevant category that plays no meaningful function in the symbolic construction of social order (Durkheim 1995: 276–77). Elsewhere I review Durkheim's definition of ghosts as a socially marginal, sociologically insignificant category (Kwon 2008: 21–24); for the purpose of this essay, let me raise another important issue at stake in the categorical distinction between ancestors and ghosts. Ghosts are cosmological strangers in social classification, as noted previously, but their phenomenological existence, by definition, is inseparable from a particular history of death. The category of ghosts is a product of the interplay between cultural concepts and historical reality—the spirits of the dead fall into this category through a crisis in the social organization of commemoration and the historical events that cause this crisis. The proliferation of ghost-related actions in contemporary Vietnamese cultural life should therefore be considered in relation to the proliferation of violent death in recent Vietnamese political history.

The Vietnam War, for people in central and southern Vietnam (what was South Vietnam during the war) was not a single war. It was a revolutionary struggle against foreign aggressors, but also a vicious civil war and a domestic confrontation. People in this region were forced to fight against the revolutionary movement as well as in support of it. Those who want to assert genealogical unity in this region must therefore deal with the legacy of political disunity left by the bifurcated mobilization on both sides during the Vietnam War. When the war was over and the nation was reunited under the revolutionary state, the memory of the dead from "that side"' (*ben kia*, meaning "the American side," against *bent ta*, "our side" or "the revolutionary side") was banned from the new political community of the nation and, by extension, from the moral community of family ancestral worship. As a result, after the war a large number of war dead became politically engendered ghosts who, according to an observer, "dying unmourned, constantly haunt the living in an attempt to force their way into the consciousness of the community, to be acknowledged as worthy of being remembered if only because they once walked the earth" (Tai 2001: 228).

The war dead whose memory was excluded from the postwar institutions of commemoration were not merely fallen soldiers on "that side." The huge civilian sacrifice during the war also posed many difficulties in the postwar politics of memory. The Vietnamese revolutionary state made enormous administrative efforts to battle what it considered feudal and backward customs and encouraged the population to internalize "revolutionary sentiments." This policy resulted in a wide-scale destruction of traditional ancestral temples and other sacred places of the village world, on the one hand, and, on the other, conversion of the traditional familial and communal institutions of ancestral death remembrance into political shrines meant exclusively for the commemoration of the heroic revolutionary war dead (Malarney 2002).

For local communities in the southern and central regions, this postwar politics of memory meant that a large number of family ancestors, beyond the chosen few endorsed by the state, were stripped of home (a place where they are remembered according to appropriate rituals) and thus relegated to the category of ghosts. These politically engendered ghosts are not the same kind of ghosts Durkheim wrote about. They are not a categorical opposite to ancestors but rather constitute a crowd of categorical ancestors uprooted and displaced from their homes. For many ancestral spirits, this displacement was caused by the politics of national memory; for others, it resulted from the total destruction of homes in a violent war. There had been widespread mass killings of civilians, which resulted in the termination of family lines and the consequent loss of the social basis of death commemoration.

## The Diversity of Ghosts

Whether these ghosts became ghosts of war because their home was destroyed or through political exclusion from a home that still existed, a simple scheme of moral symbolic opposition to the status of ancestors cannot explain their status. Instead, we must examine their status in terms of how the destructive forces of modern warfare include the force to destroy the social foundation of remembrance as well as human lives. Today, Vietnamese villagers are relatively free to interact with diverse spirits of the dead in their everyday life, and they increasingly do so, in the central region, within the concentric spatial organization consisting of the interior shrine for ancestors and the external milieu of ghosts. This organizational form in part manifests the complications in social memory caused by the experience of a violent war and the postwar politics of heroic death. In striving to renovate both sides of the ritual complex, people today must grapple with a historical reality in which the distinction between ancestors and ghosts has been violently ruptured and coercively confused.

The last point is well illustrated by the situation at the seaside community of Cam Re in Quang Nam Province south of Danang. This community used to be famous for an architecturally sophisticated communal house that sheltered the village's founding ancestors. That communal house was blown up in a military action in 1967. Unlike other neighboring villages, this poor fishing village has not been able to restore its ancestral temple, which remains in ruins to date. Around the ruins, the villagers have placed a number of makeshift shrines of various shapes, and they regularly leave incense or other small offerings on these shrines. Although these acts of worship are meant for the honorable ancestors of the village, villagers refer to the makeshift roadside shrines as *khom* or *thang tho*, that is, shrines for ghosts. The village ancestors have, in their view, lost their homes and are enduring a destitute life on the street, and this is a great shame to the village.

Not far from the ruins of the communal house is a stone ghost shrine in the shape of a birdhouse. Some of the Cam Re fishermen regularly visit this place, which is dedicated to seventeen fishermen and their children who were ambushed by a convoy of U.S. soldiers on an early morning in 1967. Some of the dead fishermen have surviving relatives and thus benefit from family-based death day or other ceremonial occasions, whereas others have no surviving family and are thus pure ghosts. However, living relatives offer prayers at this shrine too, because the place is known to have an auspicious power to protect fishermen from storms at sea. When they offer prayers, people do not distinguish the spirits in the shrine who are also their ancestors from those who are not.

There are many other isolated ghost shrines in Cam Re and its vicinity, and they all have a distinctive history of death and apparitions. These include a site associated with an unknown revolutionary fighter from the time of the Vietnam War and another place identified with an unknown patriot from the earlier war against France. I also visited a small stone memorial dedicated to the spirit of a child who, stranger to the village, died in the chaos of the war in the early 1960s. This ghost, originally a small girl, has been so responsive to the villagers' prayers that the community elders decided to enshrine her in the early 1990s as one of the guardian spirits held in the community temple, which is nominally dedicated to Ca Ong—"the spirit of the whale" and the protector of fishermen. Close to the whale temple, there is a humble shrine built in memory of the ghost of a man who, as an apparition, is believed to appear standing on his head. He had been accused of a counter-revolutionary act, and, as punishment, was buried alive upside down by a Vietcong hit squad. The ghost asserts, according to the villagers who encounter his apparitions, that the accusation and punishment were totally unjust. The villagers also associate a number of places in the vicinity with foreigner ghosts. These include two American GI ghosts, several ghosts of French combatants, and the ghost of what people believe was originally a colonial conscript from Algeria during the war against France, as well as that of a South Korean marine from the ensuing Vietnam War.

The village ghosts in Cam Re all have unique historical backgrounds of death and displacement, and they constitute a highly diverse group of beings in terms of race, nationality, and political grouping. The Cam Re villagers regularly pray and make offerings to this composite group of ghosts, irrespective of their secular origins. The diversity of ghosts is an aspect of the history of the recent wars that has turned the village space inside out, transforming it into a fierce and confused battlefield on an international scale. This diversity also distinguishes the milieu of ghosts from the official sites of war heroes, which characteristically exclude foreign elements, defined in terms of nationality and political unity, as well as from the sites of family and communal ancestors, defined in terms of genealogical unity.

The contemporary ritual landscape in communities of central Vietnam can be summarized as a transition from a politicized, centralized composition focused on the heritage of heroic war death to a decentralized, localized composition anchored in the cult of ancestors. In the new composition, local genealogical memory can coexist with nongenealogical, foreign traces of the past, and the latter are given a sovereign status of their own in the horizon of historical memory. When the villagers of Cam Re distribute offerings to places of apparition or the unknown graves within the neighborhood, they do not ask which spirits belonged to which side in terms of nationality or political loyalty. When people in other villages gather for the annual or seasonal opening ceremonies of their newly reconstituted ancestral temples and make offerings to the shrine for ghosts built within the premises, they imagine that all the diverse walks of death would associate with their act of remembrance, irrespective of their origins in life. In both contexts, ritual ties with the ghosts demonstrate a principle of hospitality and pose no fundamental contradiction to the ritualized expression of intimacy and unity with the ancestors.

## The Ethics of Memory

Alluding both to the Hebraic tradition of the "city of refuge" that welcomed and protected targets of vengeance and to the premodern European institution of sanctuary, Derrida engages with Kant's philosophical concept of "the cosmopolitan right" and "the law of universal hospitality" (Derrida

2001: 18; see also Honig 2001). In an attempt to reconcile conceptually the civil order and the international order (the freedom of the individual within a state and the autonomy of the state in inter-state relations), Kant defines hospitality as "the right of the foreigner not to be treated with hostility when he arrives on the soil of another," and he envisages the condition of "universal hospitality" as the ethical foundation for a peaceable international political order (although he clearly distinguishes the ideal condition from the historical reality in which European countries claimed the right of conquest overseas; Kant 1983 [1775]: 118–19). Derrida reflects on what the principle of hospitality had been like in the premodern, pre-Enlightenment Europe, before the principle was enlightened and reinvented by Kant according to the conditions of the eighteenth century.

Derrida discusses questions of cosmopolitan ethics mainly with reference to the plight of political refugees and asylum seekers in the contemporary world. However, the principle of hospitality is an equally critical issue for collective memory. It is not merely the living who experience coerced displacement from home. The dead can also fall into the status of refugees and stateless people, and, as Hegel showed, the pariah status of the dead and the displacement of the living are often closely interrelated questions in modern history.

The experience of the Cold War as a violent civil conflict resulted in a political crisis in the moral community of kinship. It resulted in a situation that Hegel characterizes as the collision between "the law of kinship," which obliges the living to remember dead kinsmen, and "the law of the state," which forbids citizens to commemorate those who died as the enemy of the state (R. Stern 2002: 135–45). The political crisis was basically about a representational crisis in social memory, in which a large part of family ancestral identities was relegated to the status that I earlier called political ghosts, whose historical existence is felt in intimate social life but nevertheless is without a trace in public memory.

If Kant is concerned with the ethical foundation of a peaceful order among sovereign states, it is the ethical foundation of a just political order within a state that concerns Hegel. Drawing upon the legend of Antigone in Sophocles' Theban plays, Hegel explores the philosophical foundation of the modern state partly through ethical questions involved in remembering war dead. Antigone is torn between the obligation to bury her two dead brothers, according to "the divine law" of kinship, on the one hand, and, on the other, the reality of "the human law" of the state, according to which she is prohibited from giving burial to the enemy of the city state (Stern 2002: 140). She gives burial to her brother who died as the hero of the city and proceeds to do the same for the brother who died as an enemy of the city. The latter act violates the edict of the city's ruler, and she is subsequently condemned to death. Invoking this mythic tragedy from ancient Greece, Hegel reasons that the ethical foundation of the modern state is grounded in a dialectical resolution of the clashes between the law of the state and the law of kinship (Avineri 1972: 132–54; Williams 1997: 52–59). For Judith Butler, the question is about the fate of human relatedness, suspended between life and death, being forced into the liminal situation of having to choose between the norms of kinship and subjection to the state (Butler 2000: 1–25).

Part of what I have described in this essay may be considered in the light of Hegelian ethical questions. Many individuals and families in southern and central Vietnam have been torn between the familial obligation to attend to the memory of their kin killed in the war and the political obligation not to do so for those who fought against the revolutionary state. Today these families are concerned about giving a proper home to the hitherto stigmatized ancestral memory from "that side" and thereby enabling this memory to coexist with the memory of death on "this side" in their domestic and communal ritual space. These concerns are materialized in changes in the domestic space. In a growing number of households, it is now common to see that the family's ancestral altar is shared by former political foes or that a hero's death certificate shares wall space with the picture of another young man, who also fell in the war, but on the opposite side from his hero brother. The act of repairing brotherly relations between these two fallen soldiers is at once a moral and a political practice. It is political to the extent that the act works against the towering moral hierarchy of death in the state politics of memory and in the sense of recovering the right to have rights, which Arendt describes as "the right to have a political home" (Villa 1999: 36). In domestic ritual space, one brother's identity is removed from the organization of national memory, which allows only holders of revolutionary patriotic merit, excluding the soldiers of "America's puppet army" who fell on the other side of the civil war. The invitation is also a moral act, in the sense that the democratization of memory is based on the empowerment of traditional norms about death remembrance and the revitalization of family-based ritual activity. The efficacy of the act as a political practice is based on the fact that it assumes a culturally familiar and morally legitimate form.

The parallel empowerment of ancestors and ghosts in contemporary Vietnam should be considered in the context of the history of coexistence between these two categories on the margins of the village social life and in the exteriority of national memory. The politics of hero worship caused critical problems in the southern and central regions by alienating many ancestors from the communal institution of commemoration and relegating them to the political status of ghosts. A distinctive feature of this modern political history is that the milieu of ghosts has become in part a space for genealogical identity, kinship memory, and what Durkheim (1995: 277) calls the "true spirits" of the place.

Going back to Hegel's law of kinship, it is important to note that the epic heroine in Sophocles' play had two brothers; one died as a war hero of Thebes and the other as the enemy of the city. The body of the hero brother is buried according to an appropriate rite and his name is enshrined on the city's public altar, whereas the body of the "traitor" brother is left abandoned outside the city wall, forbidden funerary rites, and his name is not called upon in public lamentations for the dead. Hegel does not pay much attention to this dual concentric symbolism of death, which constitutes, in my opinion, a core element of the epic narrative, nor do more contemporary commentators on *Antigone*, including Butler, who delves instead into the element of incest she finds hidden in Antigone's love for her dead brother (Butler 2000: 12–25). Considering this element, it appears that Antigone's predicament relates not merely to the conflict of kinship norms with the moral claims of the state, as Hegel describes it, but also, more specifically, to the bifurcation of kinship obligations into outside and inside, within the structure of concentric moral symbolic dualism. Butler argues, "Antigone represents not kinship in its ideal form but its deformation and displacement" (2000: 24). I will argue that the condition of displacement relates above all to the dispersal of the memory of the dead across the traditional moral boundary of inside and outside, good death and bad death, which is the typical social consequence of a civil war.

In *Antigone* (verses 570–90), the city's ruler, Creon, interrogates Antigone, demanding that she explain how she can fail to differentiate between her two brothers, the hero from the traitor, given that in the eyes of her hero brother, according to Creon, it would surely be an impious act to render his enemy the honor of burial (verse 575). Antigone defends her act, saying, "Death longs for the same rites for all. Who, Creon, who on earth can say the ones below [Hades, the god of the underworld] don't find this pure and uncorrupt?" (Sophocles 1984: 85, verses 580–85). Antigone declares that the rights of the dead are universal and part of "the great unwritten, unshakable traditions" (verse 505). Later in the story, the prophet Tiresias upholds her claim that divine law prescribes burial for all dead men. Seen in this light, Antigone's claim is not merely an expression of "family love" and blood relationship, as Hegel understood it (Hegel 1962: 264), nor is it necessarily an allegory for "the limits of kinship," relating to incestuous affection and illegitimate love, as Butler (2000: 23) describes it. Rather, we should consider it also to be an assertion of a particular ethics of memory relating to the inalienable rights of the dead to be properly buried and grieved. This religious imperative becomes part of the assertion of the law of kinship through the specific experience of a civil war, which divides the family in political terms. In other words, the act of claiming the rights of kinship to remember the dead, against the backdrop of a civil war, empowers a universal ethics of commemoration.

We may imagine, therefore, that the ritual milieu involving the ghosts of war is in touch with both kinship norms and universal ethical, religious values. Ritual relations with ghosts of war relate to the representational crisis in genealogical memory caused by the displacement of death and afterlife from home. In Vietnam, the recent war made displacement in death a generalized phenomenon rather than an isolated event, and the postwar state politics of heroic death added further, politicized conditions of afterlife displacement. Displacement in death thus presents a challenge to the law and moral power of kinship, as these are defined by Hegel. However, in cultural practice, ritual interactions with ghosts point to a moral and ethical dimension beyond the morality of kinship, though in relation to it. Within the dual structure and two-sided practice of Vietnamese ritual commemoration, which encompasses the symbolic domains of inside and outside (or house and street), the displaced spirits of the dead on the street side are entitled to acts of social recognition from living neighbors, just as are the ancestral spirits placed on the house side. The composition of this ritual landscape entails that the law of kinship (manifested in the form of ancestral worship on the house side) can coexist with the principle of hospitality (for the unknown, displaced spirits of the dead on the street side). It entails further that the rights of kinship (to remember dead kinsmen), against the historical backdrop of generalized mass displacement, can be guaranteed only in interaction with efforts to guarantee the rights of the dead to be remembered beyond the narrow sphere of kinship.

Thus today's vigorous ritual interactions with ghosts are not only an expression of the "law of hospitality," but also, in part, a moral practice based on what Hegel calls "the sacred law" of kinship. Ritualized hospitality for unknown foreign spiritual entities has its own particular history of coming to terms with native spirits who were forced to become strangers to the political community. In this context, the ethics of memory manifest in the ritual act of hospitality, being open to diverse traces of past destruction, does not contradict the morality of communal solidarity. On the contrary, ritual interaction with "the stranger and the remote" is, in practice, a way to preserve the law of kinship.

The law of hospitality and the law of kinship are separate domains of values in Vietnamese ritual order, as well as in Western philosophical discourse; yet this should not obscure the fact that these two separate moral and ethical domains of rights and obligations can, in practice, interact closely with each other in dealing with the ruins and remains of modern political history and the politics of memory. When Vietnamese villagers engage in death commemoration today and move between the shrine for ancestors and the milieu for ghosts in doing so, their actions associate both with the true spirits of the community and with spiritual identities foreign to it. On the surface, these actions appear to have different meanings on each side of the ritual organization: the affirmation of moral solidarity on one side and the expression of universal hospitality on the other. "Thick" memory and the "thin" memory coexist in the ritual complex but nevertheless exist separately in the structure of worship.

The separation of ghosts and ancestors on the surface of the ritual order, however, exists within a history of their undifferentiated coexistence in the periphery of postwar public memory. The villagers of Cam Re do not find it problematic that they kowtow to the errant spirits of their ancestors and at the same time make offerings to the displaced spirits of foreign combatants. The problem they have now is, rather, how to mobilize enough resources to settle their errant ancestors in a proper place. When they will have succeeded in reinstating the ancestral temple, they will have an interior shrine for ancestors and a separate, external shrine for foreign spirits. They will then, like people in other villages, be able to commemorate their honorable founding ancestors in a place of their own and will relate to them separately from the multitude of other village ghosts. This process of communal development involves an equivalent process in the sphere of domestic life, where the ancestral altar is renovated and the memories of those who fell on the wrong side of the Vietnam War are cautiously invited into the sacred space as part of the renovation. This general dynamics of family repair and social renovation is advancing in parallel with growing dynamism in ritual interactions with the displaced, unknown, and diverse ghosts of war. The coexistence of "thick" and "thin" memories is not an issue for the people of Cam Re; it has been part of village life since the war started. The real issue for them is how to bring the coexisting but different groups of spirits into the center of the village's ritual life and demonstrate their existences in a separate, structured way, according to cultural tradition.

Abu-Lughod, Lila. 1991. "Writing Against Culture." In *Recapturing Anthropology: Working in the Present*, ed. Richard G. Fox, 137–62. Santa Fe: School of American Research Press.

Agha, Asif. 2007. *Language and Social Relations*. Cambridge: Cambridge University Press.

Allerton, Catherine. Forthcoming. "Visible Relations and Invisible Realms: Speech, Materiality and Two Manggarai Landscapes." In *Landscapes Beyond Land: Routes, Aesthetics, Narrative*, ed. A. Arnarson, N. Ellison, J. Vergunst, and A. Whitehouse. Oxford: Berghahn.

Anonymous. N.D. *What is NT?* Institute for the Study of the Neurologically Typical. http://isnt.autistics.org/.

———. 1911. "Hartmann, Karl Robert Eduard von." In *Encyclopedia Britannica*, Volume 13. Eleventh edition. Cambridge: Cambridge University Press.

———. 2003. *Faking NT vs. Being Yourself.* Autistics.org; Autism Information Library. file:///Users/paulantze/Library/Favorites/Mydox/mental%20health/Autism/autism%20on%20the%20web/fakingnt.html.

Appiah, Kwame Anthony., 2008. *Experiments in Ethics*. Cambridge: Harvard University Press.

Archetti, Eduardo. 1997. "The Moralities of Argentinian Football." In *The Ethnography of Moralities*, ed. Signe Howell, 98–123. London: Routledge.

Arendt, Hannah. 1963. *Eichmann in Jerusalem: A Report on the Banality of Evil.* New York: Penguin Books.

———. 1971. *The Life of the Mind*. San Diego: Harcourt.

———. 1993 [1954]. "Truth and Politics." In Arendt, *Between Past and Future: Eight Exercises in Political Thought*, 227–64. Harmondsworth: Penguin.

———. 1997 [1957]. *Rahel Varnhagen: The Life of a Jewess*. Ed. Liliane Weissberg. Trans. R. and C. Winston. Baltimore: Johns Hopkins University Press, in cooperation with Leo Baeck Institute.

———. 1998 [1958]. *The Human Condition*, 2nd ed. Chicago: University of Chicago Press.

———. 2003. *Responsibility and Judgment*. Ed. and introd. Jerome Kohn. New York: Schocken Books.

————. 2006. "What is Freedom?" In Arendt, *Between Past and Present: Eight Exercises in Political Thought,* 142–69. New York: Penguin.

Aristotle. 1934. *The Nicomachean Ethics.* Trans. H. Rackham. Cambridge: Harvard University Press.

————. 1976 [1953]. *The Nicomachean Ethics.* Trans. J. A. K. Thomson. Introd. J. Barnes. Rev. Hugh Tredennick. Harmondsworth: Penguin.

Arseculeratne, S. N. 1991. *Sinhalese Immigrants in Malaysia and Singapore, 1860–1990: History Through Recollections.* Colombo: K. V. G. de Silva.

Asad, Talal. 1993. *Genealogies of Religion: Discipline and Reasons of Power in Christianity and Islam.* Baltimore: Johns Hopkins University Press.

————. 2003. *Formations of the Secular: Christianity, Islam, Modernity.* Stanford: Stanford University Press.

Austin, J. L. 1961a. *Philosophical Papers.* London: Oxford University Press.

————. 1961b. "A Plea for Excuses." In Austin, *Philosophical Papers,* ed. J. O. Urmson and G. J. Warnock, 123–52. Oxford: Oxford University Press.

————. 1963. "Performative-Constative." In Austin, *Philosophy and Ordinary Language,* ed. C. Caton. Urbana: University of Illinois Press.

————. 1965 [1955]. *How to Do Things with Words.* New York: Oxford University Press.

————. 1975 [1962]. *How to Do Things with Words.* Cambridge: Harvard University Press.

Avineri, Shlomo. 1972. *Hegel's Theory of the Modern State.* Cambridge: Cambridge University Press.

Babb, F. 1984. "Women in the Marketplace: Petty Commerce in Peru." *Review of Radical Political Economy* 16:45–59.

Badone, Ellen, and Sharon Roseman, eds. 2004. *Intersecting Journeys.* Urbana : University of Illinois Press.

Baggs, Amanda. N.D.a. *Love, Devotion, Hope, Prevention, and Cure.* Autistics.org Autism Information Library. http://www.autistics.org/library/love.html.

————. N.D.b. *To the Kit Weintraubs of the World.* Autistics.org Autism Information Library. http://autistics.org/library/ambweintraub.html.

————. N.D.c. *In My Language.* YouTube video. http://www.youtube.com/watch?v=JnylM1hI2jc.

Bakhtin, Mikhail M. 1981. *The Dialogic Imagination: Four Essays.* Ed. Michael Holquist. Trans. Caryl Emerson and Michael Holquist. Austin: University of Texas Press.

————. 1984. *Problems of Dostoevsky's Poetics.* Ed. and trans. Caryl Emerson. Minneapolis: University of Minnesota Press.

Barker, John, ed. 2007. *The Anthropology of Morality in Melanesia and Beyond.* Aldershot: Ashgate.

Barnes, Hazel E. 2007. "Take Clothes, for Example." In *Etiquette: Reflections on Contemporary Comportment*, ed. R. Scapp and B. Seitz, 239–48. Albany: State University of New York Press.

Baron-Cohen, S. 1995. *Mindblindness: An Essay on Autism and Theory of Mind.* Cambridge: MIT Press.

———. 2002. "The Extreme Male Brain Theory of Autism." *Trends in Cognitive Science* 6(6):248–54.

Baron-Cohen, S., A. M. Leslie, et al. 1985. "Does the Autistic Child Have a 'Theory of Mind'?" *Cognition* 21:37–46.

Barth, F. 1967. *The Role of the Entrepreneur in Social Change in Northern Norway.* Bergen: Oslo Universitetsforlaget.

Basu, K. K. 1949. "Hindu-Muslim Marriages." *Indian Law Review*, 24–36.

Bateson, Mary Catherine. 1979. "The Epigenesis of Conversational Interaction: A Personal Account of Research Development." In *Before Speech: The Beginning of Human Communication*, ed. Margaret Bullowa, 63–77. Cambridge: Cambridge University Press.

Bauman, Richard. 1992. "Contextualization, Tradition, and the Dialogue of Genres: Icelandic Legends of the Kraftaskald." In *Rethinking Context: Language as an Interactive Phenomenon*, ed. Alessandro Duranti and Charles Goodwin, 125–45. Cambridge: Cambridge University Press.

Bauman, Zygmunt. 1993. *Postmodern Ethics.* Cambridge: Blackwell.

Baxi, Pratiksha. 2008. *The Hostile Witness and Public Secrecy in Rape Trials in India.* Paper presented at the panel "Interrogating the Governance of Intimate Violence: Social Movements, State Presences, Legal Process." Law and Social Sciences Research Network (LASSNET) Conference, Delhi, January 10.

Beckett, Jeremy. 1994 [1965]. "Kinship, Mobility and Community in Rural New South Wales." In *Being Black: Aboriginal Cultures in Settled Australia*, ed. Ian Keen, 117–36. Canberra: Aboriginal Studies Press.

Bell, Diane. 1983. *Daughters of the Dreaming.* Melbourne: McPhee Gribble/ George Allen and Unwin.

Bell, Duncan. 2008. "Agonistic Democracy and the Politics of Memory." *Constellations: An International Journal of Critical and Democratic Theory* 15(1):148–66.

Benedict, Ruth. 1959 [1934]. *Patterns of Culture.* Boston: Houghton Mifflin.

Benhabib, Seyla. 2003. *The Reluctant Modernism of Hannah Arendt.* 2nd ed. Lanham, Md.: Rowman and Littlefield.

Benveniste, Emile. 1971 [1966]. *Problems in General Linguistics.* Coral Gables: University of Miami Press.

Benvenisti, Meron. 2000. *Sacred Landscape: The Buried History of the Holy Land since 1948.* Trans. Maxine Kaufman-Lacusta. Berkeley: University of California Press.

Berlant, Lauren. 2008. *The Female Complaint: The Unfinished Business of Senti-mentality in American Culture*. Durham, N.C.: Duke University Press.

Bernauer, James W., and Michael Mahon. 2005. "Michel Foucault's Ethical Imagination." In *The Cambridge Companion to Foucault*, 2nd ed., ed. G. Gutting, 149–75. Cambridge: Cambridge University Press.

Bernstein, Peter L. 1996. *Against the Gods: The Remarkable Story of Risk*. London: John Wiley.

Bernstein, Richard J. 1983. *Beyond Objectivism and Relativism: Hermeneutics and Praxis*. Philadelphia: University of Pennsylvania Press.

Bersani, Leo. 2008. "The Power of Evil and the Power of Love." In Leo Bersani and Adam Philips, *Intimacies*, 57–89. Chicago: University of Chicago Press.

Biever, Celeste. 2007. "Web Removes Social Barriers for Those with Autism." *New Scientist*, June 27, 2007:26–27.

Bloch, Maurice. 1975. "Introduction." In *Political Language and Oratory in Traditional Society*, ed. Maurice Bloch, 1–28. London: Academic Press.

———. 1977. "The Past and the Present in the Present." *Man*, n.s. 12 (2):278–92.

———. 1989 [1974]. "Symbols, Song, Dance, and Features of Articulation: Is Religion an Extreme Form of Traditional Authority?" In Bloch, *Ritual, History, and Power*, 19–45. London: Athlone Press.

———. 1992. *Prey into Hunter*. Cambridge: Cambridge University Press.

Boddy, Janice. 1989. *Wombs and Alien Spirits: Women, Men, and the Zar Cult in Northern Sudan*. Madison: University of Wisconsin Press.

———. 1994. "Spirit Possession Revisited." *Annual Review of Anthropology* 23:407–34.

Borneman, John. 2005. "Public Apologies as Performative Redress." *School of Advanced International Studies Review of International Affairs* 25(2):53–66.

Bourdieu, Pierre. 1977 [1972]. *Outline of a Theory of Practice*. Trans. Richard Nice. Cambridge: Cambridge University Press.

———. 1984. *Distinction: A Social Critique of the Judgement of Taste*. Trans. Richard Nice. Cambridge: Harvard University Press.

———. 1998. "A Paradoxical Foundation of Ethics." In Bourdieu, *Practical Reason: On the Theory of Action*, 141–45. Cambridge: Polity Press.

Boyd, Robert, and Peter J. Richerson. 1992. "Punishment Allows the Evolution of Cooperation (or Anything Else) in Sizable Groups." *Ethology and Sociobiology* 13:171–95.

Brandt, Richard. 1954. *Hopi Ethics: A Theoretical Analysis*. Chicago: University of Chicago Press.

Braudel, Fernand. 1979. *Civilization and Capitalism, 15th to 18th Century: The Structures of Everyday Life*. Trans. Sien Reynolds. Rev. ed. Berkeley: University of California Press.

Brown, Roger, and Albert Gilman. 1960. "The *Pronouns of Power and Solidarity*." In *Style in Language*, ed. Thomas Sebeok, 253–76. Cambridge: MIT Press.

Buber, Martin. 1971. *I and Thou*. Trans. Walter Kaufman. New York: Free Press.

Burbank, Victoria. 2006. "From Bedtime to On Time: Why Many Aboriginal People Don't Especially Like Participating in Western Institutions." *Anthropological Forum* 16(1):3–20.

Burgess, Walton. 1873. *Five Hundred Mistakes of Daily Occurrence in Speaking, Pronouncing and Writing the English Language, Corrected*. New York: James Miller.

Burridge, Kenelm. 1960. *Mambu: A Melanesian Millennium*. London: Methuen.

———. 1969. *New Heaven, New Earth*. Oxford: Blackwell.

Butler, Judith. 1989. *Gender Trouble: Feminism and the Subversion of Identity*. New York: Routledge.

———. 1993. *Bodies That Matter: On the Discursive Limits of "Sex."* New York: Routledge.

———. 2000. *Antigone's Claim: Kinship Between Life and Death*. New York: Columbia University Press.

Carse, Henry Ralph. 2010. *No-One Land: Israel/Palestine 2000–2002*. London: Ziggurat Books.

Caton, Steven C. 2006. "Coetzee, Agamben, and the Passion of Abu Ghraib." *American Anthropologist* 108(1):114–23.

Caton, Steven, and Bernardo Zacka. 2010. "Comment on Abu Ghraib, the Security Apparatus, and Occular Evil." *American Ethnologist*.

Cavell, Stanley. 1976. *Must We Mean What We Say?* Cambridge: Cambridge University Press.

———. 1979. "Criteria and Judgment." In Cavell, *The Claim of Reason*, 3–36. Oxford: Oxford University Press.

———. 1988. "The Uncanniness of the Ordinary." In Cavell, *The Quest of the Ordinary: Lines of Skepticism and Romanticism*, 153–78. Chicago: University of Chicago Press.

———. 1990. *Conditions Handsome and Unhandsome: The Constituion of Emersonian Perfectionism*. Chicago: University of Chicago Press.

———. 1995a. *Philosophical Passages: Wittgenstein, Emerson, Austin, Derrida*. Oxford: Blackwell.

———. 1995b. "What Did Derrida Want of Austin?" In Cavell, *Philosophical Passages: Wittgenstein, Emerson, Austin, Derrida*, 42–65. Oxford: Blackwell.

———. 1996. *A Pitch of Philosophy*. Cambridge: Harvard University Press.

———. 2004. *Cities of Words*. Cambridge: Harvard University Press.

———. 2005a. *Philosophy the Day after Tomorrow*. Cambridge: Harvard University Press.

————. 2005b. "Performative and Passionate Utterance." In *Contending with Stanley Cavell*, ed. Russell B. Goodman, 177–98. New York: Oxford University Press. Also in Cavell, *Philosophy the Day after Tomorrow*, 155–91.

————. 2005c. "Thoreau Thinks of Ponds, Heidegger of Rivers." In Cavell *Philosophy the Day after Tomorrow*, 213–36. Cambridge: Harvard Univeristy Press.

Center for Disease Control. 2007. "Prevalence of Autism Spectrum Disorders————Autism and Developmental Disabilities Monitoring Network, Six Sites, United States." *MMWR Surveillance Summaries*. http://www.cdc.gov/mmwr/preview/mmwrhtml/ss5601a1.htm.

Cesari, Chiara de. 2010. "Hebron, or Heritage as Technology of Life." *Jerusalem Quarterly* 41:6–28.

Chowdhry, Prem. 1997. "Enforcing Cultural Codes: Gender and Violence in Northern India." *Economic and Political Weekly*, May 10, pp. 1019–28.

————. 2007. *Contentious Marriages, Eloping Couples*. New Delhi: Oxford University Press.

Cochran, T. C. 1971. "The Entrepreneur in Economic Change." In *Entrepreneurship and Economic Development*, ed. P. Kilby, 95–107. New York: The Free Press.

Cohen, Anthony P. 1994. *Self-Consciousness: An Alternative Anthropology of Identity*. London: Routledge.

Cohen, Anthony P., ed. 1974. *Urban Ethnicity*. London: Tavistock.

Coleman, Simon, and John Eade, eds. 2004. *Reframing Pilgrimage: Cultures in Motion*. London: Routledge.

Collier, Jane, and Michele Rosaldo. 1981. "Politics and Gender in Simple Societies." In *Sexual Meanings: The Cultural Construction of Gender and Sexuality*, ed. Sherry Ortner and Harriet Whitehead, 275–329. Cambridge: Cambridge University Press.

Cook, S. 1984. *Peasant Capitalist Industry: Piecework and Enterprise in Southern Mexican Brickyards*. Lanham: University Press of America.

Corsín Jiménez, Alberto. 2007. *Culture and Well-Being: Anthropological Approaches to Freedom and Political Ethics*. London: Pluto.

Crapanzano, Vincent. 1992. *Hermes' Dilemma and Hamlet's Desire: On the Epistemology of Interpretation*. Cambridge: Harvard University Press.

————. 2000. *Serving the Word: Literalism in America from the Pulpit to the Bench*. New York: New Press.

————. 2004. *Imaginative Horizons: An Essay in Literary-Philosophical Anthropology*. Chicago: University of Chicago Press.

Critchley, Simon. 2005. "Cavell's 'Romanticism' and Cavell's Romanticism." In *Contending with Stanley Cavell*, ed. Russell B. Goodman, 37–55. New York: Oxford University Press.

Crossman, John Dominic, and Jonathan L. Reed. 2001. *Excavating Jesus: Beneath the Stones, Behind the Texts*. San Francisco: Harper Collins.

Damasio, Antonio. 2006 [1994]. *Descartes' Error: Emotion, Reason and the Human Brain*. New York: Avon Books.

Dan-Cohen, Meir. 1992. "Responsibility and the Boundaries of the Self." *Harvard Law Review* 105:959–1003.

Daniel, V. 1984. *Fluid Signs: Being a Person the Tamil Way*. Berkeley: University of California Press.

Das, Veena. 2007. *Life and Words: Violence and the Descent into the Ordinary*. Berkeley: University of California Press.

Dave, Naisargi N. 2008. "Between Queer Ethics and Sexual Morality." In *The Sarai Reader 07: Frontiers*, ed. Monica Narula et al., 387–95. New Delhi: Centre for Studies in Developing Societies.

———. n.d. "Ethics and Politics in India's 'Lesbian Emergence.'" Working paper delivered at the Department of Anthropology, University of Toronto, Jan. 15, 2008.

Davidson, Arnold I. 2005. "Ethics as Ascetics: Foucault, the History of Ethics, and Ancient Thought." In *The Cambridge Companion to Foucault*, 2nd ed., ed. G. Gutting, 123–48. Cambridge: Cambridge University Press.

Day, Sophie. 2007. *On the Game: Women and Sex Work*. London: Pluto.

Day, Sophie, and Victoria Goddard. Forthcoming. "New Beginnings Between Public and Private: Arendt and Ethnographies of Activism," *Cultural Dynamics*.

Day, Sophie, and Helen Ward. 2004. "Approaching Health Through the Prism of Stigma: A Longer Term Perspective." In *Sex Work, Mobility and Health in Europe*, ed. Sophie Day and Helen Ward, 161–78. London: Kegan Paul.

De Jong, Ferdinand. N.D. "In Times of Catastrophe: Temporalities of Conflict and Peace in Senegal." Paper presented to the Conflicts in Time, ESRC Seminar Number 1, University College London, May 17, 2008.

Dekker, Martijn. N.D. "On Our Own Terms: Emerging Autistic Culture." *Autistic Culture*. http://autisticculture.com/index.php?page = articles.

Derrida, Jacques. 2001. *On Cosmopolitanism and Forgiveness*. London: Routledge.

———. 2008. "Abraham, the Other." Trans. Gil Anidjar. In *Religion: Beyond a Concept*, ed. Hent de Vries, 311–38. New York: Fordham University Press.

Desrosières, Alain. 1998. *The Politics of Large Numbers: A History of Statistical Reasoning*. Cambridge: Harvard University Press.

Doherty, Harold L. 2007. "Is The Neurodiversity Movement Ashamed of Lower Functioning Autistic Persons?" Weblog, *Facing Autism in New Brunswick*, February 26, 2007. http://autisminnb.blogspot.com/2007/02/is-neurodiversity-movement-ashamed-of.html.

Douglas, Mary. 1966. *Purity and Danger: An Analysis of the Concepts of Pollution and Taboo*. London: Routledge & Kegan Paul.

———. 1980. *Evans-Pritchard*. Brighton: Harvester.

Dozier, Edward P. 1970. *The Pueblo Indians of North America*. New York: Holt, Reinhardt and Winston.

Drew, P. 1987. "Po-faced Receipts of Teases. *Linguistics* 25:219–53.

Du Bois, John W. 1993. "Meaning Without Intention: Lessons from Divination." In *Responsibility and Evidence in Oral Discourse*, ed. J. H. Hill and J. T. Irvine, 48–71. Cambridge: Cambridge University Press.

———. 2007. "The Stance Triangle." In *Stancetaking in Discourse*, ed. Robert Englebretson, 139–82. New York: John Benjamins.

Dumont, Louis. 1980 [1969]. *Homo Hieararchicus: The Caste System and Its Implications*. Chicago: University of Chicago Press.

Duranti, A. 1988. "Intentions, Language and Social Action in a Samoan Context." *Journal of Pragmatics* 12:13–33.

———. 1993a. "Intentions, Self, and Responsibility: An Essay in Samoan Ethnopragmatics." In *Responsibility and Evidence in Oral Discourse*, ed. J. H. Hill and J. T. Irvine, 24–47. Cambridge: Cambridge University Press.

———. 1993b. "Truth and Intentionality: An Ethnographic Critique." *Cultural Anthropology* 8(2):214–45.

———. 2008. "Further Reflections on Reading Other Minds." *Anthropological Quarterly* 81(2): 483–94.

Durkheim, Emile. 1938 [1895]. *The Rules of the Sociological Method*. Ed. George E. G. Catlin. Trans. Sarah A. Solovay and John H. Mueller. New York: The Free Press.

———. 1972. *Selected Writings*. Ed. Anthony Giddens. Cambridge: Cambridge University Press.

———. 1973 [1914]. "The Dualism of Human Nature and Its Social Conditions." In *Emile Durkheim on Morality and Society*, ed. Robert Bellah, 149–63. Chicago: University of Chicago Press.

———. 1995 [1912]. *The Elementary Forms of the Religious Life*. Trans. Karen E. Fields. New York: The Free Press.

Eagleton, Terry. 2007. *The Gospels: Jesus Christ*. London: Verso.

———. 2009. *Reason, Faith, and Revolution: Reflections on the God Debate*. New Haven: Yale University Press.

Edel, Abraham, and May Edel. 1970. *Anthropology and Ethics: The Quest for Moral Understanding*. 2nd ed. New Brunswick: Transaction Books.

Edelman, Lee. 2004. *No Future: Queer Theory and the Death Drive*. Durham, N.C.: Duke University Press.

Edelson, M. 2006. "Are the Majority of Children with Autism Mentally Retarded? A Systematic Evaluation of the Data." *Focus on Autism and Other Developmental Disabilities* 21:66–83.

Eggan, F. R. 1950. *Social Organization of the Western Pueblos*. Chicago: University of Chicago Press.

Eisenman, Stephen F. 2007. *The Abu Ghraib Effect*. London: Reaktion Books.

El-Haj, Nadia Abu. 2001. *Facts on the Ground*. Chicago: University of Chicago Press.

Elias, Norbert. 2000 [1939]. *The Civilizing Process: Sociogenetic and Psychogenetic Investigations*. Trans. E. Jephcott. Rev. ed. Oxford: Blackwell.

Enfield, Nicholas, and Stephen Levinson, eds. 2006. *Roots of Human Sociality: Culture, Cognition and Interaction*. Oxford: Berg.

Engelke, Matthew, and Matt Tomlinson, eds. 2006. *The Limits of Meaning: Case Studies in the Anthropology of Christianity*. New York: Berghahn.

Evans-Pritchard, Edward E. 1937. *Witchcraft, Oracles and Magic among the Azande*. Oxford: Oxford University Press.

——. 1940. *The Nuer: A Description of the Modes of Livelihood and Political Institutions of a Nilotic People*. Oxford: Oxford University Press.

——. 1951. *Kinship and Marriage among the Nuer*. Oxford: Oxford University Press.

——. 1956. *Nuer Religion*. Oxford: Oxford University Press.

——. 1969 [1955]. "Introduction." In Marcel Mauss, *The Gift: Forms and Functions of Exchange in Archaic Societies*, v-x. London: Routledge & Kegan Paul.

Evens, T. M. S. 2008. *Anthropology as Ethics: Nondualism and the Conduct of Sacrifice*. New York: Berghahn.

Evers, H. D., and H. Schrader, eds. 1994. *The Moral Economy of Trade: Ethnicity and Developing Markets*. London: Routledge.

Ewald, François. 1991. "Insurance and Risk." In *The Foucault Effect: Studies in Governmentality*, ed., Graham Burchell, Colin Gordon, and Peter Miller, 197–210. Chicago: University of Chicago Press.

Faubion, James. 2001a. "Toward an Anthropology of Ethics: Foucault and the Pedagogies of Autopoiesis." *Representations* 74:83–104.

——. 2001b. *The Ethics of Kinship: Ethnographic Inquiries*. Lanham, Md.: Rowman and Littlefield.

——. 2001c. *The Shadows and Lights of Waco: Millennialism Today*. Princeton: Princeton University Press.

——. Forthcoming. *What Becomes a Subject: An Anthropology of Ethics*. Cambridge: Cambridge University Press.

Faubion, James, and Jennifer A. Hamilton. 2007. "Sumptuary Kinship." *Anthropological Quarterly* 80:533–59.

Feldman, Jackie. 2009. "Constructing a Shared Bible Land: Jewish Israeli Guiding Performances for Protestant Pilgrims." *American Ethnologist* 34(2):351–74.

Feuchtwang, Stephan. 2001. *Popular Religion in China: The Imperial Metaphor*. Richmond: Curzon Press.

Finkelstein, Israel. 1988. *Archaeology of the Israelite Settlement*. Jerusalem: Israel Exploration Society.

Firth, R., and B. S. Yamey, eds. 1964. *Capital, Saving and Credit in Peasant Societies: Studies of Asia, Oceania, the Caribbean and Middle America*. London: Allen and Unwin.

Fischer, Michael M. J. 2003. *Emergent Forms of Life and the Anthropological Voice*. Durham, N.C.: Duke University Press.

Forni, P. M. 2002. *Choosing Civility: The Twenty-five Rules of Considerate Conduct*. New York: St. Martin's Press.

Fortes, Meyer. 1966. "Totem and Taboo." In Meyer Fortes, *Religion, Morality and the Person*, ed. J. Goody, 110–44. Cambridge: Cambridge University Press, 1987.

———. 1987. *Religion, Morality and the Person*. Ed. J. Goody. Cambridge: Cambridge University Press.

Foucault, Michel. 1977. *Discipline and Punish: The Birth of the Prison*. Trans. Alan Sheridan. New York: Pantheon Books.

———. 1978 [1990]. *The History of Sexuality*, Volume 1: *An Introduction*. Trans. Robert Hurley. New York: Vintage.

———. 1984a. "Preface" to *The History of Sexuality*, Volume 2." In *The Foucault Reader*, ed. Paul Rabinow, 333–72. New York: Random House.

———. 1984b. "On the Genealogy of Ethics: An Overview of Work in Progress." In *The Foucault Reader*, ed. Paul Rabinow, 333–72. New York: Random House.

———. 1985. *The Use of Pleasure*. Volume 2 of *The History of Sexuality*. Trans. Robert Hurley. New York: Pantheon.

———. 1988. *Power and Sex. Politics, Philosophy, Culture: Interviews and Other Writings, 1977—1984*. Ed. L. Kritzman. London: Routledge.

———. 1994. "Friendship as a Way of Life." In *Ethics: Subjectivity and Truth*, ed. Paul Rabinow, Volume 1 of *Essential Works of Foucault, 1954–1984*, 135–40. New York: New Press.

———. 1996. *Foucault Live: Interviews, 1966–84*. Ed. Sylvère Lotringer. Cambridge: MIT Press.

———. 2007. *Security, Territory, Population: Lectures at the College de France, 1977–78*. Ed. Arnold I. Davidson. Trans. Graham Burchell. New York: Palgrave.

Frost, Sarah Annie. 1869. *Frost's Laws and By-laws of American Society: A Condensed but Thorough Treatise on Etiquette and Its Usages in America, Containing Plain and Reliable Directions for Deportment in Every Situation in Life*. New York: Dick and Fitzgerald.

Gadamer, Hans-Georg. 1975. *Truth and Method*. Trans. G. Borden and J. Cumming. New York: Seabury.

———. 1979. "The Problem of Historical Consciousness." In *Interpretive Social Science: A Reader*, ed. Paul Rabinow and William Sullivan, 103–60. Berkeley: University of California Press.

Garber, Marjorie, Beatrice Hanssen, and Rebecca Walkowitz, eds. 2000. *The Turn to Ethics*. New York: Routledge.

Gardiner, Michael E. 2000. *Critiques of Everyday Life*. New York: Routledge.

Geertz, Armin W. 1990. "Hopi Hermeneutics: Ritual Person among the Hopi Indians of Arizona." In *Concepts of Person in Religion and Thought*, ed. H. Kippenberg, Y. Kuiper, and A. Sanders, 309–35. Berlin: Walter de Gruyter.

———. 1994. *The Invention of Prophecy*. Berkeley: University of California Press.

———. 2003. "Ethnohermeneutics and Worldview Analysis in the Study of Hopi Indian Religion." *Numen* 50:309–48.

Geertz, Armin W., and Michael Lomatuway'ma. 1987. *Children of the Cottonwood: Piety and Ceremonialism in Hopi Indian Puppetry*. Lincoln: University of Nebraska Press.

Geertz, Clifford. 1963. *Peddlers and Princes: Social Change and Economic Modernization in Two Indonesian Towns*. Chicago: University of Chicago Press.

———. 1973a [1966]. *The Interpretation of Cultures*. New York: Basic Books.

———. 1973b. "The Impact of the Concept of Culture on the Concept of Man." In Geertz, *The Interpretation of Cultures*, 33–54. New York: Basic Books.

———. 1973c. "The Growth of Culture and the Evolution of Mind." In Geertz, *The Interpretation of Cultures*, 55–83. New York: Basic Books.

———. 1980. *Negara: The Theatre State in Nineteenth-Century Bali*. Princeton: Princeton University Press.

———. 1983. " 'From the Native's Point of View': On the Nature of Anthropological Understanding." In Geertz, *Local Knowledge: Further Essays in Interpretive Anthropology*, 55–70. New York: Basic Books.

———. 2000a. *Available Light: Anthropological Reflections on Philosophical Topics*. Princeton: Princeton University Press.

———. 2000b [1968]. "Thinking as a Moral Act: Ethical Dimensions of Anthropological Fieldwork in the New States." In Geertz, *Available Light: Anthropological Reflections on Philosophical Topics*, 21–41. Princeton: Princeton University Press.

———. 2000c. "Anti Anti-relativism." In Geertz, *Available Light: Anthropological Reflections on Philosophical Topics*, 42–67. Princeton: Princeton University Press.

Gell, Alfred. 1998. *Art and Agency: An Anthropological Theory*. Oxford: Oxford University Press.

Gentleman, A. 1836. *The Laws of Etiquette; or, Short Rules and Reflections for Conduct in Society*. Philadelphia: Haswell and Barrington.

Giddens, Anthony. 1979. *Central Problems in Social Theory: Action, Structure, and Contradiction in Social Analysis*. London: Macmillan.

Gilbert, Daniel, and Patrick Malone. 1995. "The Correspondence Bias." *Psychological Bulletin* 117(1):21–38.

Gillespie, Michael Allen. 2008. *The Theological Origins of Modernity*. Chicago: University of Chicago Press.

Gillis, John. 1994. "Memory and Identity: A History of Relationship." In *Commemorations: Politics of National Identity*, ed. John Gillis, 3–25. Princeton: Princeton University Press.

Gladden, Washington. 1868. *Plain Thoughts on The Art of Living, Designed for Young Men and Women*. Cambridge, Mass.: Welch, Bigelow & Co.

Glowacka, M. D. 1998. "Ritual Knowledge in Hopi Tradition." *American Indian Quarterly* 22:386–92.

Gluckman, Max. 1972. *The Allocation of Responsibility*. Manchester: Manchester University Press.

Goffman, Erving. 1957. "Alienation from Interaction." *Human Relations* 10(1):47–60.

———. 1961. *Encounters: Two Studies in the Sociology of Interaction*. Indianapolis: Bobbs-Merrill.

———. 1967. *Interaction Ritual: Essays in Face to Face Behavior*. Garden City, N.Y.: Doubleday.

———. 1974a [1963]. *Stigma: Notes on the Management of Spoiled Identity*. Harmondsworth: Penguin.

———. 1974b. *Frame Analysis: An Essay on the Organization of Experience*. Cambridge: Harvard University Press.

———. 1981. *Forms of Talk*. Oxford: Basil Blackwell.

———. 1983. "The Interaction Order: American Sociological Association, 1982 Presidential Address." *American Sociological Review* 48(1):1–17.

Goodale, Jane. 1971. *Tiwi Wives: A Study of the Women of Melville Island, North Australia*. Seattle: University of Washington Press.

Goodwin, Charles. 2002. "Time in Action." *Current Anthropology* 43(Supplement):19–35.

———. 2007. "Participation, Stance and Affect in the Organization of Activities." *Discourse & Society* 18(1):53–73.

Goodwin, Charles, and M. Goodwin. 2004. "Participation." In *A Companion to Linguistic Anthropology*, ed. A. Duranti, 222–44. Oxford: Blackwell.

Gopnik, Alison, and Andrew N. Meltzoff. 1997. *Words, Thoughts, and Theories*. Cambridge: MIT Press.

Gordon, Colin. 1991. "Governmental Rationality: An Introduction." In *The Foucault Effect: Studies in Governmentality*, ed. Graham Burchell, Colin Gordon, and Peter Miller, 1–52. Chicago: University of Chicago Press.

Gould, Timothy. 2003. "The Names of Action." In *Stanley Cavell*, ed. Richard Eldridge, 48–78. Cambridge: Cambridge University Press.

Gourevitch, Philip, and Errol Morris. 2008. *Standard Operating Procedure*. New York: Penguin.

Graeber, David. 2001. *Toward an Anthropological Theory of Value: The False Coin of Our Own Dreams*. New York: Palgrave Macmillan.

Grandin, T. 1995. *Thinking in Pictures: And Other Reports from My Life with Autism*. New York: Doubleday.

Grandin, T., and M. Scariano. 1986. *Emergence, Labeled Autistic*. Novato, Calif.: Arena Press.

Grice, H. P. 1957. "Meaning." *The Philosophical Review* 66:377–88.

———. 1968. "Utterer's Meaning, Sentence-meaning, and Word-meaning." *Foundations of Language* 4:225–42.

———. 1969. "Utterer's Meanings and Intentions." *Philosophical Review* 78:147–77.

———. 1976 [1968]. "Logic and Conversation." In *Syntax and Semantics*, ed. P. Cole and J. L. Morgan, 3:41–58. New York: Academic Press.

Griswold, A. 2007. *Autistic Symphony*. Lincoln, Neb.: iUniverse.

Grossman, David. 2008. *Writing in the Dark*. New York: Farrar, Straus and Giroux.

Gupta, Akhil, and James Ferguson. 1992. "Beyond 'Culture': Space, Identity, and the Politics of Difference." *Cultural Anthropology* 7:6–23.

Gutting, Gary. 1999. "MacIntyre." *Cambridge Encyclopedia of Philosophy*.

Guyer, Paul. 1999. "Cavell." *Cambridge Encyclopedia of Philosophy*.

Habib, Jasmin. 2004. *Israel, Diaspora, and the Routes of National Belonging*. Toronto: University of Toronto Press.

Hacking, Ian. 1990. *The Taming of Chance*. Cambridge: Cambridge University Press.

———. 1998. *Rewriting the Soul: Multiple Personality and the Sciences of Memory*. Princeton: Princeton University Press.

———. 2009. "Humans, Aliens and Autism." *Daedalus* 138(3):44–59.

Haeri, Shahla. 1995. "The Politics of Dishonor: Rape and Power in Pakistan." In *Faith and Freedom: Women's Human Rights in the Muslim World*, ed. M. Afkhami, 161–73. London: Tauris.

Hamann, Trent. 2007. "Impolitics: Toward a Resistant Comportment." In *Etiquette: Reflections on Contemporary Comportment*, ed. R. Scapp and B. Seitz, 59–68. Albany: State University of New York Press.

Hamilton, Annette. 1981. *Nature and Nurture: Aboriginal Child-Rearing in North-Central Arnhem Land*. Canberra: Australian Institute of Aboriginal Studies.

Hammer, Espen. 2002. *Stanley Cavell: Skepticism, Subjectivity, and the Ordinary*. Cambridge: Polity.

Handelman, Don. 2004. *Nationalism and the Israeli State: Bureaucratic Logic in Public Events*. Oxford: Berg.

Hanks, William. 1990. *Referential Practice: Language and Lived Space among the Maya*. Chicago: University of Chicago Press.

———. 2000. "Dialogic Conversions and the Field of Missionary Discourse in Colonial Yucatan." In *Les Rituels du Dialogue*, ed. A. Monod Becquelin and Philippe Erikson, 235–54. Nanterre: Société d'Ethnologie.

Harding, Susan F. 1987. "Convicted by the Holy Spirit: The Rhetoric of Fundamentalist Conversion." *American Ethnologist* 14:167–81.

Hartley, Cecil B. 1873. *The Gentlemen's Book of Etiquette and Manual of Politeness: Being a Complete Guide for a Gentleman's Conduct in All His Relations Towards Society*. Boston: De Wolfe, Fiske & Co.

Hatch, Elvin. 1983. *Culture and Morality: The Relativity of Values in Anthropology*. New York: Columbia University Press.

Hauser, Mark. 2006. *Moral Minds*. New York: Harper Collins.

Haviland, John. 1979. "How to Talk to Your Mother-in-law in Guugu Yimidhirr." In *Languages and Their Speakers*, ed. Timothy Shopen, 166–239. Cambridge, Mass.: Winthrop.

Hegel, G. W. F. 1945 [1821]. *Philosophy of Right*. Trans. T. M . Knox. Oxford: Oxford University Press.

———. 1962. *Lectures on the Philosophy of Religion*. Trans. E. B. Speirs and J. B. Sanderson. New York: Humanities Press.

Hemphill, C. Dallett. 1999. *Bowing to Necessities: A History of Manners in America, 1620–1860*. Oxford: Oxford University Press.

Henrich, J., R. Boyd, S. Bowles, C. Camerer, E. Fehr, H. Gintis, and R. McElreath. 2001. "Cooperation, Reciprocity, and Punishment in Fifteen Small-scale Societies." Unpublished paper.

Hercus, Louise, and Isobel White. 1973. "Perception of Kinship Structure Reflected in the Adnjamathanha Pronouns." In *Papers in Australian Linguistics*, no. 6, ed. Bruce Schebeck, Louise Hercus, and Isobel White, 47–72. Canberra: Pacific Linguistics.

Hervey, George Winfred. 1852. *The Principles of Courtesy: With Hints and Observations on Manners and Habits*. New York: Harper and Brothers.

———. 1853. *Rhetoric of Conversation; or, Bridles & Spurs for the Management of the Tongue*. New York: Harper and Brothers.

Hill, Jane H. 1995. "The Voices of Don Gabriel: Responsibility and Self in a Modern Mexicano Narrative." In *The Dialogic Emergence of Culture*, ed. Dennis Tedlock and Bruce Mannheim, 97–147. Urbana: University of Illinois Press.

Hill, Jane H., and Judith T. Irvine, eds. 1993. *Responsibility and Evidence in Oral Discourse*. Cambridge: Cambridge University Press.

Hill, Jane H., and Ofelia Zepeda. 1992. "Mrs. Patricio's Trouble: The Distribution of Responsibility in an Account of Personal Experience." In *Responsibility and Evidence in Oral Discourse*, ed. Jane H. Hill and Judith Irvine, 197–225. Cambridge: Cambridge University Press.

Hirschkind, Charles. 2001. "The Ethics of Listening: Cassette-Sermon Audition in Contemporary Egypt." *American Ethnologist* 28(3):623–49.

———. 2006 *The Ethical Soundscape: Cassette Sermons and Islamic Counter-Publics*. New York: Columbia University Press.

Hobson, Peter. 2004. *The Cradle of Thought*. Oxford: Oxford University Press.

Hollis, Martin, and Steven Lukes, eds. 1982. *Rationality and Relativism*. Oxford: Blackwell.

Holt, E. 2006. "'I'm eyeing your chop up mind': Reporting and Enacting." In *Reporting Talk: Reported Speech in Interaction*, ed. R. Clift and E. Holt, 47–79. Cambridge: Cambridge University Press.

Honig, Bonnie. 2001. *Democracy and the Foreigner*. Princeton: Princeton University Press.

Houtsma, Martijn, Thomas A. J. Wesnick, E. Lévi Provençal, H. A. R. Gibb, and W. Heffening, eds. 1993. *E. J. Brill's First Encyclopedia of Islam, 1913–1936*. Leiden: Brill.

Howell, Signe. 1997. "Introduction." In *The Ethnography of Moralities*, ed. Signe Howell, 1–24. London: Routledge. Howell, Signe, ed. 1997. *The Ethnography of Moralities*. London: Routledge.

Hubert, Henri, and Marcel Mauss. 1964 [1898]. *Sacrifice: Its Nature and Function*. London: Cohen and West.

Hume, David. 1957 [1751]. *An Inquiry Concerning the Principles of Morals*. New York: Liberal Arts Press.

Humphrey, Caroline. 1997. "Exemplars and Rules: Aspects of the Discourse of Moralities in Mongolia." In *The Ethnography of Moralities*, ed. Signe Howell, 25–48. London: Routledge.

Humphrey, Caroline, and Altanhu Hürelbaatar. 2005. "Regret as a Political Intervention: An Essay in the Historical Anthropology of the Early Mongols." *Past and Present* 186:3–45.

Huters, Theodore. 1984. "Blossoms in the Snow: Lu Xun and the Dilemma of Modern Chinese Literature." *Modern China* 10(1):49–77.

Institute for the Study of the Neurologically Typical, The. N.D. http://isnt .autistics.org/.

International Alert. 2005. *Peace Through Profit: Sri Lankan Perspectives on Corporate Social Responsibility*. Colombo: IA.

Irvine, Judith T. 1979. "Formality and Informality in Communicative Events." *American Anthropologist* 81:773–90.

———. 2009. "Stance in a Colonial Encounter: How Mr. Taylor Lost His Footing." In *Stance: Sociolinguistic Perspectives*, ed. Alexandra Jaffe, 53–71. Oxford: Oxford University Press.

Jackson, Michael. 1989. *Paths Toward a Clearing: Radical Empiricism and Ethnographic Inquiry*. Bloomington: Indiana University Press.

Jakobson, Roman. 1960. "Linguistics and Poetics." In *Style in Language*, ed. T. Sebeok, 350–77. Cambridge: MIT Press.

———. 1980 [1957]. "Metalanguage as a Linguistic Problem." In *Contributions to Comparative Mythology: Studies in Linguistics and Philology*, Volume 7 of Jakobson, *Selected Writings*, ed. S. Rudy, 113–21.The Hague: Mouton.

Jakobson, Roman, and John Lotz. 1949. "Notes on the French Phonemic Pattern." *Word* 5:151–85.

Jay, Martin. 2005. *Songs of Experience: Modern American and European Variations on a Universal Theme*. Berkeley: University of California Press.

Jayawardena, K. 2000. *Nobodies to Somebodies: The Rise of the Colonial Bourgeoisie in Sri Lanka*. Colombo: SSA.

Jefferson, G. 1979. "A Technique for Inviting Laughter and Its Subsequent Acceptance/Declination." In *Everyday Language: Studies in Ethnomethodology*, ed. G. Psathas, 79–96. New York: Irvington Publishers.

———. 1985. "An Exercise in the Transcription and Analysis of Laughter." In *Handbook of Discourse Analysis*, Volume 3, ed. T. A. Dijk, 25–34. New York: Academic Press.

Jeganathan, Pradeep. 2004. "Checkpoint: Anthropology, Identity, and the State." In *Anthropology and the Margins of the State*, ed. Veena Das and Deborah Poole. Santa Fe: School of American Studies Advanced Seminar Series.

Jenner, W. J. F. 1982. "Lu Xun's Last Days and After." *China Quarterly* 91:424–45.

Joas, Hans. 1996. *The Creativity of Action*. Chicago: University of Chicago Press.

Johnson, Paul Christopher. Forthcoming. "An Atlantic Genealogy of Spirit Possession." *Comparative Studies in Society and History*.

Jones, Edward, and Victor Harris. 1977. "The Attribution of Attitudes." *Journal of Experimental Social Psychology* 3:1–24.

Jurecic, A. 2006. "Mindblindness: Autism, Writing, and the Problem of Empathy." *Literature and Medicine* 25(1):1–23.

Kanner, L. 1943. "Autistic Disturbances of Affective Contact." *Nervous Child* 2:217–50.

Kant, Immanuel. 1983 [1775]. *Perpetual Peace and Other Essays on Politics, History, and Morals*. Trans. Ted Humphrey. Indianapolis: Hackett.

———. 1998. *Religion Within the Boundary of Mere Reason*. Ed. and trans. Allen Wood and George di Giovanni. Cambridge: Cambridge University Press.

Karmi, Omar. 2007. "In the City of David: How Jerusalem of the Bible Is Reshaping the City of Today." *Jerusalem Quarterly* 29:12.

Kaur, Ravinder. 2004. "Across Region Marriages: Poverty, Female Migration and the Sex Ratio." *Economic and Political Weekly* 39(25):2595–603.

Keane, Webb. 1997. *Signs of Recognition: Powers and Hazards of Representation in an Indonesian Society.* Berkeley: University of California Press.

———. 2002. "Sincerity, 'Modernity,' and the Protestants." *Cultural Anthropology* 17(1):65–92.

———. 2003a. "Self-Interpretation, Agency, and the Objects of Anthropology: Reflections on a Genealogy." *Comparative Studies in Society and History* 45(2):222–48.

———. 2003b. "Semiotics and the Social Analysis of Material Things." *Language and Communication* 23(2–3):409–25.

———. 2007. *Christian Moderns: Freedom and Fetish in the Mission Encounter.* Berkeley: University of California Press.

———. 2008a. "Modes of Objectification in Educational Experience." *Linguistics and Education* 19(3):312–31.

———. 2008b. "Market, Materiality, and Moral Metalanguage." *Anthropological Theory* 8(1):27–42.

———. 2008c. "The Evidence of the Senses and the Materiality of Religion." *Journal of the Royal Anthropological Institute* 14(1):110–27.

Keenan, Elinor Ochs. 1976. "The Universality of Conversational Postulates." *Language in Society* 5:67–80.

Keesing, R. 1981. "Theories of Culture." In *Language, Culture, and Cognition: Anthropological Perspectives,* ed. R. W. Casson, 42–66. New York: Macmillan.

Kelly, Catriona. 2001. *Refining Russia: Advice Literature, Polite Culture, and Gender from Catherine to Yeltsin.* Oxford: Oxford University Press.

Kelly, Raymond C. 1993. *Constructing Inequality: The Fabrication of a Hierarchy of Virtue among the Etoro.* Ann Arbor: University of Michigan Press.

Kelman, Herbert C., and V. Lee Hamilton. 1989. *Crimes of Obedience: Towards a Social Psychology of Authority and Responsibility.* New Haven: Yale University Press.

Kendon, Adam. 1988. *Sign Languages of Aboriginal Australia: Cultural, Semiotic and Communicative Perspectives.* Cambridge: Cambridge University Press.

Kendrick, K. 2009. *Finding Evidence in Interaction: "See?" as a Retrospective Claim of Vindication.* MS. University of California, Santa Barbara.

Kitzinger, C. 2005. "Heteronormativity in Action: Reproducing the Heterosexual Nuclear Family in 'After Hours' Medical Calls." *Social Problems* 52(4):477–98.

Kockelman, Paul. 2004. "Stance and Subjectivity." *Journal of Linguistic Anthropology* 14(2):127–50.

Kresse, Kai. 2007. *Philosophising in Mombasa: Knowledge, Islam, and Intellectual Practice on the Swahili Coast.* Edinburgh: Edinburgh University Press.

Kripal, Jeffrey J. 2001. *Roads of Excess, Palaces of Wisdom: Eroticism and Reflexivity in the Study of Mysticism*. Chicago: University of Chicago Press.

Kroskrity, Paul. 1993. *Language, History and Identity: Ethnolinguistic Studies of the Arizona Tewa*. Tucson: University of Arizona Press.

Kuipers, J. C. 1990. *Power in Performance: The Creation of Textual Authority in Weyewa Ritual Speech*. Philadelphia: University of Pennsylvania Press.

Kulick, Don. 1992. *Language Shift and Cultural Reproduction*. Cambridge: Cambridge University Press.

Kwon, Heonik. 2006. *After the Massacre: Commemoration and Consolation in Ha My and My Lai*. Berkeley: University of California Press.

———. 2008. *Ghosts of War in Vietnam*. Cambridge: Cambridge University Press.

La Fontaine, J. S. 1985. "Person and Individual: Some Anthropological Reflections." In *The Category of the Person: Anthropology, Philosophy, History*, ed. M. Carrithers, S. Collins, and S. Lukes, 123–40. Cambridge: Cambridge University Press.

Laidlaw, James. 1995. *Riches and Renunciation: Religion, Economy, and Society among the Jains*. Oxford: Oxford University Press.

———. 2002. "For an Anthropology of Ethics and Freedom." *Journal of the Royal Anthropological Institute* 8:311–32.

———. 2010. "Social Anthropology." In *The Routledge Companion to Ethics*, ed. John Skorupski. London: Routledge.

Lamb, S. 1997. "The Making and Unmaking of Persons: Notes on Aging and Gender in North India." *Ethos* 25:3.

Lambek, Michael. 1981. *Human Spirits: A Cultural Account of Trance in Mayotte*. Cambridge: Cambridge University Press.

———. 1988. "Graceful Exits: Spirit Possession as Personal Performance in Mayotte." *Culture* 8(1):59–69.

———. 1992. "Taboo as Cultural Practice among Malagasy Speakers." *Man* 27:19–42.

———. 1993. *Knowledge and Practice in Mayotte: Local Discourses of Islam, Sorcery, and Spirit Possession*. Toronto: University of Toronto Press.

———. 1996. "The Past Imperfect: Remembering as Moral Practice." In *Tense Past: Cultural Essays in Trauma and Memory*, ed. P. Antze and M. Lambek, 235–54. New York. Routledge.

———. 1998. "Body and Mind in Mind, Body and Mind in Body: Some Anthropological Interventions in a Long Conversation." In *Bodies and Persons: Comparative Perspectives from Africa and Melanesia*, ed. M. Lambek and A. Strathern, 103–23. Cambridge: Cambridge University Press.

———. 2000. "The Anthropology of Religion and the Quarrel Between Poetry and Philosophy." *Current Anthropology* 41(3):309–20.

————. 2002a. *The Weight of the Past: Living with History in Mahajanga, Madagascar*. New York: Palgrave Macmillan.

————. 2002b. "Nuriaty, the Saint and the Sultan: Virtuous Subject and Subjective Virtuoso of the Post-Modern Colony." In *Post-Colonial Subjectivities*, ed. Richard Werbner, 25–43. London: Zed Books.

————. 2002c. "Fantasy in Practice: Projection and Introjection; or, the Witch and the Spirit-Medium." In *Beyond Rationalism: Rethinking Magic, Witchcraft and Sorcery*, ed. Bruce Kapferer, 198–214. New York: Berghahn.

————. 2003a. "Rheumatic Irony: Questions of Agency and Self-Deception as Refracted through the Art of Living with Spirits." In *Illness and Irony*, ed. M. Lambek and P. Antze, 40–59. New York: Berghahn.

————. 2003b. "Memory in a Maussian Universe." In *Regimes of Memory*, ed. Susannah Radstone and Katharine Hodgkin, 202–16. London: Routledge.

————. 2004. "The Saint, the Sea Monster, and an Invitation to a Dîner-Dansant: Ethnographic Reflections on the Edgy Passage—and the Double Edge—of Modernity, Mayotte, 1975–2001." *Anthropologica* 46(1):57–68.

————. 2007a. "On Catching Up with Oneself: Learning to Know That One Means What One Does." In *Learning Religion*, ed. David Berliner and Ramon Sarró, 65–81. Oxford: Berghahn.

————. 2007b. "Provincializing God? Provocations from an Anthropology of Religion." In *Religion: Beyond a Concept*, ed. Hent de Vries, 120–38. New York: Fordham University Press.

————. 2007c. "Sacrifice and the Problem of Beginning: Reflections from Sakalava Mythopraxis." *Journal of the Royal Anthropological Institute* 13(1):19–38.

————. 2008. "Value and Virtue." *Anthropological Theory* 8(2):133–57.

————. 2010. "How to Make Up One's Mind: Reason, Passion and Ethics in Spirit Possession." *University of Toronto Quarterly* 79, no. 2, Special issue *Models of Mind*, ed. Marlene Goldman and Jill Matus, 106–28.

Lambek, Michael, and Jacqueline Solway. 2001. "Just Anger: Scenarios of Indignation in Botswana and Madagascar." *Ethnos* 66(1):1–23.

Landa, J. T. 1994. *Trust, Ethnicity and Identity: Beyond the New Institutional Economics of Ethnic Trading Networks, Contract Law and Gift Exchange*. Ann Arbor: University of Michigan Press.

Langdon, Rae. 1992. "Duty and Desolation." *Philosophy* 67:481–505.

Larsen, B., and O. Harris. 1995. *Ethnicity, Markets, and Migration in the Andes: At the Cross-roads of History and Anthropology*. Durham, N.C.: Duke University Press.

Latour, Bruno. 2005. *Reassembling the Social: An Introduction to Actor-Network Theory*. Oxford: Oxford University Press.

Laugier, Sandra. 2005. "Rethinking the Ordinary: Austin *after* Cavell." In *Contending with Stanley Cavell*, ed. Russell B.Goodman, 118–40. New York: Oxford University Press.

Leach, E. R. 1954. *Political Systems of Highland Burma*. Boston: Beacon.

Lear, Jonathan. 1988. *Aristotle: The Desire to Understand*. Cambridge: Cambridge University Press.

———. 2006. *Radical Hope: Ethics in the Face of Cultural Devastation*. Cambridge: Harvard University Press.

Lerner, G. 2003. "Selecting Next Speaker: The Context Sensitive Operation of a Context-free Organization." *Language in Society* 32:177–201

Levinas, Emmanuel. 1989. "Ethics as First Philosophy." In *The Levinas Reader*, ed. Seán Hand, 75–87. Oxford: Blackwell.

———. 1998. *Entre Nous: Thinking-of-the-Other*. Trans. Michael B. Smith and Barbara Harshav. New York: Columbia University Press.

———. 2003. *The Humanism of the Other*. Trans. Nidra Poller. Urbana: University of Illinois Press.

Levinson, Stephen. 1977. "Social Deixis in a Tamil Village." Ph.D. dissertation. Department of Anthropology, University of California, Berkeley.

Lévi-Strauss, Claude. 1950. "Introduction à l'oeuvre de Marcel Mauss." In Marcel Mauss, *Sociologie et anthropologie*. Paris: Presses Universitaires de France.

———. 1966 [1962]. *The Savage Mind*. Chicago: University of Chicago Press.

Lewis, I. M. 1971. *Ecstatic Religion: An Anthropological Study of Spirit Possession and Shamanism*. Harmondsworth: Penguin.

Littlewood, R. 2002. *Pathologies of the West: An Anthropology of Illness in Europe and North America*. Ithaca, N.Y.: Cornell University Press.

Llewellyn, Karl N., and E. Adamson Hoebel. 1941. *The Cheyenne Way: Conflict and Case Law in Primitve Jurisprudence*. Norman: University of Oklahoma Press.

Løgstrup, Knut Ejler. 1997. *The Ethical Demand*. Notre Dame, Ind.: University of Notre Dame Press.

Londoño Sulkin, Carlos David. 2005. "Inhuman Beings: Morality and Perspectivism among Muinane People (Colombian Amazon)." *Ethnos* 70(1):7–30.

———. 2006. "Instrumental Speeches: Morality and Masculine Agency among Muinane People (Colombian Amazon)." *Tipiti* 4(1–2):199–222.

Lu Xun. 1960 [1924]. "The New Year's Sacrifice." In *Selected Stories of Lu Hsun*. Trans. Yang Hsien-Yi and Gladys Yang. Beijing: Foreign Languages Press. English version available online at http://web.archive.org/web/2004 1204234335/www.eldritchpress.org/hsun/hsun.htm (accessed 6 November 2009). Chinese version available online at http://www.xys.org/xys/classics/ Lu-Xun/Panghuang/zhufu.txt (accessed November 6, 2009).

Lucy, John A., ed. 1993. *Reflexive Language: Reported Speech and Metapragmatics*. Cambridge: Cambridge University Press.

Luczkiw, E. 1998. *Global Enterprise: Instilling the Spirit; Learning Strategies for the New Millennium*. St. Catherine: Institute for Enterprise Education.

Luhmann, Niklas. 1989. *Ecological Communication*. Trans. John Bednarz, Jr. Chicago: University of Chicago Press.

———. 1996. "The Sociology of the Moral and Ethics." *International Sociology* 11:27–36.

———. 2001. "Morality and the Secrets of Religion." In *Religion and Media*, ed. Hent de Vries and Samuel Weber, 555–67. Stanford: Stanford University Press.

Luong, Hy Van. 1993. "Economic Reform and the Intensification of Rituals in Two North Vietnamese Villages, 1980–90." In *The Challenge of Reform in Indochina*, ed. Borje Ljunggren, 259–92. Cambridge: Harvard Institute of International Development.

Lutz, Catherine. 1988. *Unnatural Emotions: Everyday Sentiments on a Micronesian Atoll and Their Challenge to Western Theory*. Chicago: University of Chicago Press.

Lutz, Catherine, and Lila Abu Lughod, eds. 1990. *Language and the Politics of Emotion*. Cambridge: Cambridge University Press.

MacIntyre, Alasdair. 1966. *A Short History of Ethics*. New York: Macmillan.

———. 1984. *After Virtue*. 2nd ed. Notre Dame, Ind.: University of Notre Dame Press.

———. 1990. *Three Rival Versions of Moral Inquiry*. London: Duckworth.

———. 2007. *After Virtue: A Study in Moral Theory*. 3rd ed. Notre Dame, Ind.: University of Notre Dame Press.

MacKendrick, Karmen. 2007. "Make It Look Easy: Thoughts on Social Grace." In *Etiquette: Reflections on Contemporary Comportment*, ed. R. Scapp and B. Seitz, 199–206. Albany: State University of New York Press.

Mackie, J. L. 1982. "Morality and the Retributive Emotions." In *Edward Westermarck: Essays on His Life and Work*, Volume 34, ed. T. Stroup, 144–57. Helsinki: Acta Philosophica Fennica.

Macpherson, C. B. 1973. *Democratic Theory: Essays in Retrieval*. Oxford: Oxford University Press.

Maegawa, K. 1994. "Strategic Adaptation of Entrepreneurs as Middlemen in Badu, Torres Strait." *Man and Culture in Oceania* 10:59–79.

Mahmood, Saba. 2005. *Politics of Piety: The Islamic Revival and the Feminist Subject*. Princeton: Princeton University Press.

Malarney, Shaun K. 2002. *Culture, Ritual, and Revolution in Vietnam*. Surrey: Routledge Curzon.

———. 2003. "Return to the Past? The Dynamics of Contemporary Religious and Ritual Transformation." In *Postwar Vietnam: Dynamics of a Transforming Society*, ed., Hy Van Luong, 225–56. Lanham, Md.:Rowman and Littlefield.

Malinowski, Bronislaw. 1922. *Argonauts of the Western Pacific: An Account of Native Enterprise and Adventure in the Archipelagoes of Melanesian New Guinea*. London: Routledge and Kegan Paul.

————. 1939. "Group and Individual in Functional Analysis." *American Journal of Sociology* 44:938–64.

Margalit, Avishai. 2004. *The Ethics of Memory*. Cambridge: Harvard University Press.

Marriott, McKim. 1976. "Hindu Transactions: Diversity Without Dualism." In *Transaction and Meaning*, ed. B. Kapferer, 109–42. Philadelphia: Ishi Press.

Martin, D. 1993. "Autonomy and Relatedness: An Ethnography of Wik People of Aurukun, Western Cape York Peninsula" Ph. D. dissertation. Canberra: Australian National University.

Mathews, William. 1872. *Getting On in the World; or, Hints on Success in Life*. Chicago: S.C. Griggs and Co.

Mauss, Marcel. 1967 [1925]. *The Gift: Forms and Functions of Exchange in Archaic Societies*. Trans. Ian Cunnison. New York: W. W. Norton.

————. 1985 [1938]. "A Category of the Human Mind: The Notion of Person; The Notion of Self." Trans. W. D. Halls. In *The Category of The Person: Anthropology, Philosophy, History*, ed. M. Carithers, S. Collins, and S. Lukes, 1–25. Cambridge: Cambridge University Press.

————. 1990 [1925]. *The Gift: Forms and Functions of Exchange in Archaic Societies*. Trans. W.D. Halls. London: Routledge.

Mayer, Jane. 2008. *The Dark Side: The Inside Story of How the War on Terror Turned into a War on American Ideals*. New York: Doubleday.

Mazower, Mark. 2004. *Salonica, the City of Ghosts*. New York: HarperPerennial.

Mazzetti, Mark, and Scott Shane. 2009. "Investigation Is Ordered into C.I.A. Abuse Charges." *New York Times*, August 25, pp. A1 and A7.

McAlister, Melanie. 2005. "Prophecy, Politics, and the Popular: The *Left Behind* Series and Christian Evangelism's New World Order." In *Palestine, Israel, and the Politics of Popular Culture*, ed. Rebecca Stein and Ted Swedenburg, 288–312. Durham, N.C.: Duke University Press.

McCarthy, J. 2007. *Louder than Words: A Mother's Journey in Healing Autism*. New York, Dutton.

McClelland, D. C. 1961. *The Achieving Society*. New York: Van Nostrand.

McGee, Micki. 2005. *Self-Help Inc.: Makeover Culture in American Life*. Oxford: Oxford University Press.

Mead, George Herbert. 1964. *Selected Writings*. Ed. and introd. Andrew J. Reck. Indianapolis: Bobbs-Merrill.

Mehta, Deepak. 1996. "Circumcision, Body and Community," *Contributons to Indian Sociology*, n.s. 30 (2):215–43.

————. 2000. "Circumcision, Body, Masculinity: The Ritual Wound and Collective Violence." In *Violence and Subjectivity*, ed. Veena Das, Arthur Kleinman, Mamphela Ramphele, and Pamela Reynolds, 79–102. Berkeley: University of California Press.

————. 2009. "Words That Wound: Archiving Hate in the Making of Hindu and Muslim Publics in Bombay." In *Crisis and Beyond: A Critical Second Look at Pakistan*, ed. Naveeda Khan. New Delhi: Routledge.

Meneley, Anne. 1996. *Tournaments of Value*. Toronto: University of Toronto Press.

Merlan, Francesca. 1982. "A Mangarayi Representational System: Environment and Cultural Symbolization in Northern Australia." *American Ethnologist* 9(1):145–66.

————. 1989. "Jawoyn Relationship Terms: Interactional Dimensions of Australian Kin Classification." *Anthropological Linguistics* 31(3–4):227–63.

————. 1991. "Women, Productive Roles and Monetisation of the 'Service Mode' in Aboriginal Australia: Perspectives from Katherine, Northern Territory." *The Australian Journal of Anthropology* 2(3):259–92.

————. 1992. "Male-Female Separation and Forms of Society in Aboriginal Australia." *Cultural Anthropology* 7(2):169–92.

————. 1998. *Caging the Rainbow: Places, Politics, and Aborigines in a North Australian Town*. Honolulu: University of Hawai'i Press.

Merlan, Francesca, and Alan Rumsey. 1991. *Ku Waru: Language and Segmentary Politics in the Western Nebilyer Valley, Papua New Guinea*. Cambridge: Cambridge University Press.

Milbank, John. 1997. *The Word Made Strange: Theology, Language, Culture*. Oxford: Blackwell.

————. 2006. *Theology and Social Theory: Beyond Secular Reason*. Oxford: Blackwell.

Milgram, Stanley. 1974. *Obedience to Authority: An Experimental View*. New York: Harper Collins.

Miller, Peter. 1994. "Accountancy and Objectivity: The Invention of Calculating Selves and Calculable Spaces." In *Rethinking Objectivity*, ed. Alan Megill, 239–64. Durham, N.C.: Duke University Press.

Mills, C. Wright. 1959. *The Sociological Imagination*. New York: Oxford University Press.

Mitchell, Stephen. 1988. *Relational Concepts in Psychoanalysis: An Integration*. Cambridge: Harvard University Press.

Mitchell, Timothy. 2002. *Rule of Experts: Egypt, Techno-Politics, Modernity*. Berkeley: University of California Press.

Miyazaki, Hirokazu. 2006. "Economy of Dreams: Hope in Global Capitalism and Its Critiques." *Cultural Anthropology* 21(2):147–72.

Mody, Perveez. 2008. *The Intimate State: Love Marriages and the Law in Delhi*. New Delhi: Routledge.

Moeller, Hans-Georg. 2006. *Luhmann Explained: From Souls to Systems*. Chicago: Open Court.

Montgomery, Cal. 2005. "Defining Autistic Lives." *Ragged Edge Online.* http://www.raggededgemagazine.com/reviews/ckmontrubin0605.html.

Moore, M. 1997. "The Identity of Capitalists and the Legitimacy of Capitalism: Sri Lanka since Independence." *Development and Change* 28(2):331–66.

Morgan, M. H. 1991. "Indirectness and Interpretation in African-American Women's Discourse." *Pragmatics* 1:421–51.

Morris, Errol. 2008. *Standard Operating Procedure.* Film. Sony Pictures.

Mottron, L., M. Dawson, et al. 2006. "Enhanced Perceptual Functioning in Autism: An Update, and Eight Principles of Autistic Perception." *Journal of Autism and Developmental Disorders* 36(1):27 –43.

Mukhopadhyay, T. R. 2000. *Beyond the Silence: My Life, the World and Autism.* London: National Autistic Society.

Mulhall, Stephen. 1996. "Introduction." In *The Cavell Reader.* Malden, Mass.: Blackwell.

Murphy, Jeffrie, and Jean Hampton. 1988. *Forgiveness and Mercy.* Cambridge: Cambridge University Press.

Myers, Fred R. 1980. "The Cultural Basis of Pintupi Politics." *Mankind* 12:197–213.

———. 1986. *Pintupi Country, Pintupi Self: Sentiment, Place and Politics among Western Desert Aborigines.* Canberra and Washington, D.C.: Australian Institute of Aboriginal Studies and the Smithsonian Institution.

———. 1988. "The Logic and Meaning of Anger among Pintupi Aborigines." *Man* 23(4):589–610.

Myers, F., and D. Brenneis. 1984. "Introduction." In *Dangerous Words: Language and Politics in the Pacific,* ed. D. Brenneis and F. R. Myers, 1–29. New York: New York University Press.

Myhre, Knut. 1998. "The Anthropological Concept of Action and Its Problems: A 'New' Approach Based on Marcel Mauss and Aristotle." *Journal of the Anthropological Society of Oxford* 29(2):121–34.

Nanayakkara, G. 1997. "Some Reflections of Buddhism on Morality in Business and Management." *Sri Lankan Journal of Management* 2(3):217–32.

Nandy, Ashis. 1990. "The Politics of Secularism and the Recovery of Religious Tolerance." In *Mirrors of Violence: Communities, Riots and Survivors,* ed. Veena Das, 69–93. New Delhi: Oxford University Press.

Nazeer, K. 2006. *Send in the Idiots; or, How We Grew to Understand the World.* London: Bloomsbury.

Needham, Rodney. 1972. *Belief, Language, and Experience.* Chicago: University of Chicago Press.

Nehamas, Alexander. 1998. *The Art of Living.* Berkeley: University of California Press.

Neiman, Susan. 2002. *Evil in Modern Thought: An Alternative History of Philosophy.* Princeton: Princeton University Press.

Nelson, Deborah. 2008. *The War Behind Me: Vietnam Veterans Confront the Truth about U.S. War Crimes*. New York: Basic Books.

Newton, Sarah E. 1994. *Learning to Behave: A Guide to American Conduct Books Before 1900*. Westport, Conn.: Greenwood Press.

Nguyen, Khac Vien. 1993. *Vietnam: A Long History*. Hanoi: The Gioi.

Nieto, Valentina. 2006. "Mujeres de la Abundancia." Master's thesis, Maestria en Estudios Amazónicos, Universidad Nacional de Colombia, Sede Leticia.

Nietzsche, Friedrich. 1956 [1887]. *The Birth of Tragedy and the Genealogy of Morals*. Trans. Francis Golffing Garden City, N.Y.: Doubleday Anchor Books.

———. 1994 [1887]. *On the Genealogy of Morality*. Trans. Carol Diethe. Cambridge: Cambridge University Press.

Nisbett, Richard. 2003. *The Geography of Thought: How Asians and Westerners Think Differently . . . and Why*. London: Nicholas Brealey.

Noddings, Nell. 1984. *Caring: A Feminine Approach to Ethics and Moral Education*. Berkeley: University of California Press.

Nussbaum, Martha. 1992. *Love's Knowledge: Essays on Philosophy and Literature*. New York: Oxford University Press.

———. 2001. *Upheavals of Thought: The Intelligence of Emotions*. Cambridge: Cambridge University Press.

Obeyesekere, Gananath. 1981. *Medusa's Hair: An Essay on Personal Symbols and Religious Experience*. Chicago: University of Chicago Press.

Ochs Elinor. 1984. "Clarification and Culture." In *Meaning, Form, and Use in Context: Linguistic Applications, Georgetown University Round Table on Languages and Linguistics 1984*, ed. D. Schiffrin, 325–41. Washington, D.C.: Georgetown University Press.

———. 1988. *Culture and Language Development: Language Acquisition and Language Socialization in a Samoan Village*. Cambridge: Cambridge University Press.

Ochs, Elinor, and Tamar Kremer-Sadlik. 2007. "Introduction: Morality as Family Practice." *Discourse & Society* 18(1):5–10.

O'Malley, Pat. 1996. "Risk and Responsibility." In *Foucault and Political Reason: Liberalism, Neo-Liberalism and Rationalities of Government*, ed. Andrew Barry, Thomas Osborne, and Nikolas Rose, 189–207. London: UCL Press.

O'Neill, Onora. 1991. "Kantian Ethics." In *A Companion to Ethics*, ed. Peter Singer, 175–85. Oxford: Blackwell.

Ortiz, Alfonso. 1972. "Ritual Drama and the Pueblo World View." In *New Perspectives on the Pueblos*, ed. Alfonso Ortiz, 135–61. Albuquerque: University of New Mexico Press.

Ortner, Sherry B. 1984. "Theory in Anthropology since the Sixties." *Comparative Studies in Society and History* 26:126–66.

————. 2006. *Anthropology and Social Theory: Culture, Power, and the Acting Subject*. Durham, N.C.: Duke University Press.

Overing, Joanna. 2000. *The Anthropology of Love and Anger: The Aesthetics of Conviviality in Native Amazonia*. London: Routledge.

Overing, Joanna, ed. 1985. *Reason and Morality*. London: Tavistock.

Palmer, Frank. 1986. *Mood and Modality*. Cambridge: Cambridge University Press.

Parkin, David, ed. 1985. *The Anthropology of Evil*. Oxford: Blackwell.

Parry, Jonathan. 1986. "The *Gift*, The Indian Gift, and the 'Indian Gift.'" *Man* 21:453–73.

————. 2001. "Ankalui's Errant Wife: Sex, Marriage and Industry in Contemporary Chhattisgarh." *Modern Asian Studies Review* 35(4):783–820.

Parry, Jonathan, and Maurice Bloch. 1989. *Money and the Morality of Exchange*. Cambridge: Cambridge University Press.

Paxson, Heather. 2004. *Making Modern Mothers: Ethics and Family Planning in Urban Greece*. Berkeley: University of California Press.

Perera, T. 1996. "The Need for Affiliation as a Moderator in the Behaviour of Entrepreneurs." *Sri Lanka Journal of Management* 1(3):252–61.

Peterson, Nicolas. 1993. "Demand-Sharing and the Pressure for Reciprocity among Foragers." *American Anthropologist* 95(4):860–74.

Pinchevski, A. 2005. *By Way of Interruption: Levinas and the Ethics of Communication*. Pittsburgh: Duquesne University Press.

Pitt-Rivers, Julian. 1977. "The Law of Hospitality." In *The Fate of Shechem; or, The Politics of Sex: Essays in the Anthropology of the Mediterranean*, ed. Julian Pitt-Rivers, 94–110. Cambridge: Cambridge University Press.

Poovey, Mary. 1998. *A History of the Modern Fact: Problems of Knowledge in the Sciences of Wealth and Society*. Chicago: University of Chicago Press.

Popkin, S. 1979. *The Rational Peasant: The Political Economy of Rural Society in Vietnam*. Berkeley: University of California Press.

Povinelli, Elizabeth. 2001. "Radical Worlds: The Anthropology of Incommensurability and Inconceivability." *Annual Review of Anthropology* 30:319–34.

————. 2002. *The Cunning of Recognition: Indigenous Alterities and the Making of Australian Multiculturalism*. Durham, N.C.: Duke University Press.

Rabinow, Paul. 1996. *Essays on the Anthropology of Reason*. Princeton: Princeton University Press.

Radin, Paul. 1957 [1927]. *Primitive Man as Philosopher*. New York: Schocken.

Ranasinghe, S. 1996. "Entrepreneurship Education and Training in Sri Lanka." *Sri Lankan Journal of Management* 1(3):262–77.

Rapp, Rayna. 2000. *Testing Women, Testing the Fetus: The Social Impact of Amniocentesis in America*. New York: Routledge.

Rappaport, Roy. 1999. *Ritual and Religion in the Making of Humanity*. Cambridge: Cambridge University Press.

Rasch, William. 2000. *Niklas Luhmann's Modernity: The Paradoxes of Differentiation*. Stanford: Stanford University Press.

Read, Kenneth. 1955. "Morality and the Concept of the Person among the Gahuku-Gama." *Oceania* 25(4):233–82.

Reinprecht, K., and N. Weeratunge. 2006. *Enterprise for Pro-poor growth: Design of a Strategy to Promote Enterprise Culture in Sri Lanka—Socio-cultural Assessment Results*. Colombo: ILO.

Richland, Justin B. 2005. " 'What are you going to do with the village's knowledge?' Talking Tradition, Talking Law in Hopi Tribal Court." *Law and Society Review* 39:235–71.

———. 2006. "The Multiple Calculi of Meaning." *Discourse and Society* 17, no. 1: 65–97

Ricoeur, Paul. 1967. *The Symbolism of Evil*. Trans. Emerson Buchanan. Boston: Beacon Press.

———. 1992. *Oneself as Another*. Trans. Kathleen Blamey. Chicago: University of Chicago Press.

Robbins, Joel. 2004. *Becoming Sinners: Christianity and Moral Torment in a Papua New Guinea Society*. Berkeley: University of California Press.

Roberts, M. 1982. *Caste Conflict and Elite Formation: The Rise of a Karawe Elite in Sri Lanka, 1500–1931*. Cambridge: Cambridge University Press.

Roos, J. P. 2008. "Emile Durkheim Versus Edward Westermarck: An Uneven Match." In *The New Evolutionary Social Science*, ed. Tamas Meleghy et al., 131–42. Boulder, Colo.: Paradigm Publishers.

Rorty, Richard. 1989. *Contingency, Irony, and Solidarity*. Cambridge: Cambridge University Press.

Rosaldo, Michelle. 1980. *Knowledge and Passion: Ilongot Notions of Self and Social Life*. Cambridge: Cambridge University Press.

———. 1982. "The Things We Do with Words: Ilongot Speech Acts and Speech Act Theory in Philosophy." *Language in Society* 11:203–37.

Ross, Lee. 1977. "The Intuitive Psychologist and His Shortcomings: Distortions in the Attribution Process." In *Advances in Experimental Social Psychology*, Volume 10, ed. L. Berkowitz, 174–221. Orlando, Fla.: Academic Press.

Rousseau, Jean-Jacques. 1979 [1762]. Emile. Trans. Allan Bloom. New York: Basic Books.

Rumsey, Alan. 1982. "Gun-gunma: An Australian Aboriginal Avoidance Language and Its Social Functions." In *The Languages of Kinship in Aboriginal Australia*, ed. Jeffrey Heath, Francesca Merlan, and Alan Rumsey, 161–82. Sydney: Oceania Publications.

———. 2000. "Women as Peacemakers: A Case from the Nebilyer Valley, Western Highlands, Papua New Guinea." In *Reflections on Violence in Melanesia*, ed. Sinclair Dinnen and Allison Ley, 139–55. Annandale, Canberra, and Sydney: Hawkins Press and Pacific Studies Press.

———. 2003a. "Language, Desire, and the Ontogenesis of Intersubjectivity." *Language and Communication* 23:169–87.

———. 2003b. "Tribal Warfare and Transformative Justice in the New Guinea Highlands." In *A Kind of Mending: Restorative Justice in the Pacific Islands*, ed. Sinclair Dinnen, Anita Jowett, and Tess Newton, 79—93. Canberra: Pandanus Press.

———. 2008. "Confession, Anger and Cross-Cultural Articulation in Papua New Guinea." *Anthropological Quarterly* 81(2):455–72.

Russell, Bertrand. 1961. "The Cult of Ordinary Usage." In *The Basic Writings of Bertrand Russell, 1903–1959*. New York: Simon and Schuster.

Ryle, Gilbert. 1949. *The Concept of Mind*. London: Hutchinson.

Sacks, Harvey. 1974. "The Analysis of the Course of a Joke's Telling in Conversation." In *Explorations in the Ethnography of Speaking*, ed. Richard Bauman and Joel Sherzer, 337–53. Cambridge: Cambridge University Press.

———. 1995. *Lectures on Conversation*. Oxford: Blackwell.

Sacks, Harvey, E. A. Schegloff, and G. Jefferson. 1974. "A Simplest Systematics for the Organization of Turn-taking for Conversation." *Language* 50:696–735.

Saheb, S. A. A. 1998. "A Festival of Flags: Hindu Muslim Devotion and Sacralising of Localism at the Shrine of Nagar-e-sharif in Tamilnadu." In *Embodying Charisma: Modernity, Locality and Performing of Emotion in Sufi Shrines*, ed. Pnina Weber and Helene Basu, 51–62. London: Routledge.

Sahlins, Marshall. 1972. "The Original Affluent Society." In Sahlins, *Stone Age Economics*, 1–39. Chicago: Aldine.

———. 1976. *Culture and Practical Reason*. Chicago: University of Chicago Press.

———. 1981. *Historical Metaphors and Mythical Realities: Structure in the Early History of the Sandwich Islands Kingdom*. Ann Arbor: University of Michigan Press.

———. 1985. *Islands of History*. Chicago: University of Chicago Press.

———. 1988. "Cosmologies of Capitalism: The Trans-Pacific Sector of 'The World System.'" *Proceedings of the British Academy* 74:1–51.

———. 1996. "The Sadness of Sweetness: The Native Anthropology of Western Cosmology." *Current Anthropology* 37(3):395–428.

Said, Edward. 1975. *Beginnings: Intention and Method*. Baltimore: Johns Hopkins University Press.

Sansom, Basil. 1982. "The Aboriginal Commonality." In *Aboriginal Sites, Rights and Resource Development*, ed. Ronald M. Berndt, 117–38. Academy of the Social Sciences in Australia. Nedlands: University of Western Australia Press.

Sartre, Jean-Paul. 1952. *Existentialism and Humanism*. London: Methuen.

Scapp, Ron, and Brian Seitz. 2007. "On Being Becoming." In *Etiquette: Reflections on Contemporary Comportment*, ed. R. Scapp and B. Seitz, 1–6. Albany: State University of New York Press.

Scarry, Elaine. 1999. *On Beauty and Being Just*. Princeton: Princeton University Press.

Schegloff, E. A. 1968. "Sequencing in Conversational Openings." *American Anthropologist* 70:1075–95.

———. 2007. *Sequence Organization in Interaction: A Primer in Conversation Analysis*. Volume 1. Cambridge: Cambridge University Press.

Schieffelin, Bambi. 1990. *The Give and Take of Everyday Life: Language Socialization of Kaluli Children*. Cambridge: Cambridge University Press.

Schmitt, Carl. 1985 [1922]. *Political Theology: Four Chapters on the Concept of Sovereignty*. Trans. George Schwab. Cambridge: MIT Press.

Schneewind , J. B. 1998. *The Invention of Autonomy: A History of Modern Moral Philosophy*. Cambridge: Cambridge University Press.

Schütz, Alfred. 1967 [1932]. *The Phenomenology of the Social World*. Trans. George Walsh and Frederick Lehnert. Evanston, Ill.: Northwestern University Press.

Scott, James C. 1976. *The Moral Economy of the Peasant: Rebellion and Subsistence in Southeast Asia*. New Haven: Yale University Press

———. 1985. *Weapons of the Weak: Everyday Forms of Peasant Resistance*. New Haven: Yale University Press.

Searle, J. 1969. *Speech Acts: An Essay in the Philosophy of Language*. Cambridge: Cambridge University Press.

———. 1983. *Intentionality: An Essay in the Philosophy of Language*. Cambridge: Cambridge University Press.

Sen, Amartya. 1999. *Development as Freedom*. Oxford: Oxford University Press.

Sharp, Lesley A. 2000. "The Commodification of the Body and Its Parts." *Annual Review of Anthropology* 29:287–328.

Shaul, David L. 2002. *Hopi Traditional Literature*. Albuquerque: University of New Mexico Press.

Shiner, Roger. 1986. "Canfield, Cavell and Criteria." In *Criteria*, ed. John Canfield, 353–72. London: Garland.

Shoaps, Robin. 2004. "Morality in Grammar and Discourse: Stance-Taking in the Negotiation of Moral Personhood in Sakapultec (Mayan) Wedding Counsels." Ph. D. dissertation. Department of Linguistics, University of California, Santa Barbara.

———. 2007. " 'Moral irony': Modal Particles, Moral Persons and Indirect Stance-Taking in Sakapultek Discourse." *Pragmatics* 17(2):297–336.

Shryock, Andrew. 2008. "Thinking about Hospitality, with Derrida, Kant, and the Balga Bedouin." *Anthropos* 103:405–21.

Shulman, David. 2007. *Dark Hope*. Chicago: University of Chicago Press.

Sidnell, Jack. 2009. "Participation." In *The Pragmatics of Interaction*, ed. J. Verschueren and Sigurd D'hondt, 157–73. Amsterdam: John Benjamins.

———. 2010. *Conversation Analysis: An Introduction*. Oxford: Blackwell.

Silverstein, Michael. 1976. "Shifters, Linguistic Categories, and Cultural Description." In *Meaning in Anthropology*, ed. Keith Basso and Henry Selby, 11–55. Albuquerque: University of New Mexico Press.

———. 1993. "Metapragmatic Discourse and Metapragmatic Function." In *Reflexive Language: Reported Speech and Metapragmatics*, ed. John A. Lucy, 33–58. Cambridge: Cambridge University Press.

———. 2003. "Indexical Order and the Dialectics of Sociolinguistic Life." *Language and Communication* 23(3–4):193–229.

Simmel, G. 1967 [1908]. "The Stranger." In *The Sociology of Georg Simmel*. Trans. K. Wolff. New York: Free Press.

Sinclair, Jim. N.D.a [1989]. "Some Thoughts about Empathy." Jim Sinclair's Website. Online at http://web.syr.edu/~jisincla/empathy.htm.

———. N.D.b [1992]. "What Does Being Different Mean?" Jim Sinclair's Website. Online at http://web.syr.edu/~jisincla/different.htm.

———. N.D.c [1993]. "Don't Mourn for Us." Jim Sinclair's Website. Online at http://web.syr.edu/~jisincla/dontmourn.htm.

———. N.D.d [1995]. "Medical Research Funding?" Jim Sinclair's Website. Online at http://web.syr.edu/~jisincla/research.htm.

———. 2005. "Autism Network International: The Development of a Community and Its Culture." Autism Network International. Online at http://web.syr.edu/~jisincla/History_of_ANI.html.

Singh, Bhrigupati. 2009. "Gods and Grains: Lives of Desire in Rural Central India." Ph.D. dissertation. Department of Anthropology. Johns Hopkins University.

Smith, Adam. 1976 [1759]. *The Theory of Moral Sentiments*. Oxford: Oxford University Press.

Sohm, Rudolph. 1970 (1892). *Kirchenrecht*. Volume I. Berlin: Duncker & Humblot.

Solomon, Andrew. 2008. "The Autism Rights Movement." *New York Magazine* online edition, May 25, 2008. http://nymag.com/news/features/47225/.

Sophocles. 1984. *The Three Theban Plays*. Trans. R. Fagles. New York: Penguin.

Soulières, I., M. Dawson, et al. 2008. *Neural Underpinnings of Autistic Reasoning and Novel Problem Solving*. London: The International Meeting for Autism Research.

Southwold, M. 1983. *Buddhism in Life*. Manchester: Manchester University Press.

Southwold-Llewellyn, S. 1994a. "The Creation of an Outsider's Myth: The *Mudalali* of Sri Lanka." In *The Moral Economy of Trade: Ethnicity and Developing Markets*, ed. Hans-Dieter Evers and Heiko Schrader, 175–97. London: Routledge.

———. 1994b. "Mapping and Manipulation of Traders in Sri Lanka." In *Financial Landscapes Reconstructed: The Fine Art of Mapping Development*, ed. Frits J. A. Bouman and Otto Hospes, 249–69. Boulder, Colo.: Westview Press.

Sperber, Dan. 1996. *Explaining Culture: A Naturalistic Approach*. Oxford: Blackwell.

Stafford, Charles. 1995. *The Roads of Chinese Childhood*. Cambridge: Cambridge University Press.

———. 2000. *Separation and Reunion in Modern China*. Cambridge: Cambridge University Press.

———. 2008. "What Is Interesting about Chinese Religion." In *Learning Religion*, ed. R. Sarro and D. Berliner, 177–89. Oxford: Berghahn.

Stallybrass, Peter, and Allon White. 1986. *The Politics and Poetics of Transgression*. London: Methuen.

Stanner, William Edward Hanley. 1937. "Aboriginal Modes of Address and Reference in the North-West of the Northern Territory." *Oceania* 7(3):300–315.

Stasch, Rupert. 2008. "Knowing Minds Is a Matter of Authority: Political Dimensions of Opacity Statements in Korowai Moral Psychology." *Anthropological Quarterly* 81(2):443–53.

Steiner, Franz. 1956. *Taboo*. New York: Philosophical Library.

Stern, Daniel. 1985. *The Interpersonal World of the Infant*. New York: Basic Books.

Stern, Robert. 2002. *Hegel and the Phenomenology of Spirit*. New York: Routledge.

Strathern, Marilyn. 1988. *The Gender of the Gift*. Berkeley: University of California Press.

———. 1992. "Parts and Wholes: Refiguring Relationships in a Post-plural World." In *Conceptualizing Society*, ed. Adam Kuper, 75–104. London: Routledge.

Strawson, P. F. 1962. "Freedom and Resentment." *Proceedings of the British Academy* 48:1–25. Oxford: Oxford University Press.

———. 2008 [1962]. "Freedom and Resentment." In Strawson, *Freedom and Resentment and Other Essays*, 1–28. London: Routledge.

Stroup, Timothy. 1984. "Edward Westermarck: A Reappraisal." *Man* n.s. 19(4):575–92.

Stroup, Timothy, ed. 1982. *Edward Westermarck: Essays on His Life and Work.* Helsinki: Acta Philosophica Fennica, vol. 34.

Sykes, Karen. 2005. *Arguing with Anthropology: An Introduction to Critical Theories of the Gift.* London: Routledge.

Szafraniec, Asja. 2008. "Inheriting the Wound: Religion and Philosophy in Stanley Cavell." In *Religion: Beyond a Concept,* ed. Hent de Vries, 368–79. New York: Fordham University Press.

Tai, Hue-Tam Ho. 2001. "Commemoration and Community." In *The Country of Memory: Remaking the Past in Late Socialist North Vietnam,* ed. Hue-Tam Ho Tai, 227–30. Berkeley: University of California Press.

Tammet, D. 2006. *Born on a Blue Day: A Memoir of Asperger's and an Extraordinary Mind.* London: Hodder and Stoughton.

Tan, Viet. 1994. *Tap Van Cung Gia Tien* (Prayer book for ancestor worship). Hanoi: Nha xuat ban van hoa dan toc.

Taylor, Charles. 1985. *Human Agency and Language.* Cambridge: Cambridge University Press.

———. 1989. *Sources of the Self: The Making of Modern Identity.* Cambridge: Harvard University Press.

———. 1993. "To Follow a Rule . . ." In *Bourdieu: Critical Perspectives,* ed. Craig Calhoun, Edward LiPuma, and Moishe Postone, 45–60. Chicago: University of Chicago Press.

Taylor, Keith W. 1998. "Surface Orientations in Vietnam: Beyond Histories of Nation and Religion." *Journal of Asian Studies* 57(4):949–78.

Taylor, Lawrence J. 1995. *Occasions of Faith: An Anthropology of Irish Catholics.* Philadelphia: University of Pennsylvania Press.

Timmons, A. Jeffry. 1989. *The Entrepreneurial Mind.* Amherst, N.H.: The Brick House.

Titiev, M. 1944. *Old Oraibi: A Study of the Hopi Indians of Third Mesa.* Cambridge, Mass.: Peabody Museum of American Archaeology and Ethnology, Papers, 22(1).

Tomasello, Michael. 1999. *The Cultural Origins of Human Cognition.* Cambridge: Harvard University Press.

Tomasello, Michael, Melinda Carpenter, Josep Call, Tanya Behne, and Henrike Moll. 2005. "Understanding and Sharing Intentions: The Origins of Cultural Cognition." *Behavioral and Brain Sciences* 28:675–735.

Tomes, Robert. 1870. *The Bazar Book of Decorum: The Care of the Person, Manners, Etiquette, and Ceremonials.* New York: Harper and Brothers.

Tomlinson, Matthew. 2006. "Retheorizing Mana: Bible Translation and Discourse of Loss in Fiji." *Oceania* 76:150–72.

Tonkinson, Robert. 1970. "Aboriginal Dream Spirit Beliefs in a Contact Situation: Jigalong, Western Australia." In *Australian Aboriginal Anthropology,* ed. Ronald M. Berndt, 277–91. Perth: University of Western Australia Press.

Trawick, M. 1992. *Notes on Love in a Tamil Family*. Berkeley: University of California Press.

Trevarthen, Colwyn, and Kenneth Aitkin. 2001. "Infant Intersubjectivity: Research, Theory and Clinical Applications." *Journal of Child Psychology and Psychiatry* 42:3–48.

Turner, Bryan. 1992. "Preface." In Emile Durkheim, *Professional Ethics and Civic Morals*, ed. Bryan S. Turner, xiii–xlii. London: Routledge.

Turner, Victor. 1969. *The Ritual Process: Structure and Anti-structure*. Ithaca, N.Y.: Cornell University Press.

Ueda, Y. 1992. "Characteristics of Local Entrepreneurs in Nakhon Ratchasima City." *Southeast Asian Studies* 30(3):331–72.

Urban, Greg. 1989. "The 'I' of Discourse." In *Semiotics, Self and Society*, ed. B. Lee and G. Urban, 27–52. Berlin: Walter de Gruyter.

Vallely, Anne. 2002. *Guardians of the Transcendent: An Ethnography of a Jain Ascetic Community*. Toronto: University of Toronto Press.

Veer, Peter van der. 1994. *Religious Nationalism: Hindus and Muslims in India*. Berkeley: University of California Press.

Venkatesan, Soumhya. 2009. "Rethinking Agency: Persons and Things in the Heterotopia of 'Traditional Indian Craft,'" *Journal of the Royal Anthropological Institute* 15:78–95.

Villa, Dana R. 1999. *Politics, Philosophy, Terror: Essays on the Thought of Hannah Arendt*. Princeton: Princeton University Press.

Viveiros de Castro, Eduardo. 1998. "Cosmological Deixis and Amerindian Perspectivism." *Journal of the Royal Anthropological Society* 4(3):469–88.

Vogel, Shane. 2009. "By the Light of What Comes After: Eventologies of the Ordinary." *Women and Performance: A Journal of Feminist Theory* 19(2): 247–63.

Vogt, Evon, and Ethel Albert, eds. 1966. *The People of Rimrock: A Study of Values in Five Cultures*. Cambridge: Harvard University Press.

Vološinov, V. N. 1973 [1928]. *Marxism and the Philosophy of Language*. Trans. Ladislav Matejka and I. R. Titunik. New York: Seminar Press.

———. 1987 [1927]. *Freudianism: A Critical Sketch*. Trans. I .R. Titunik. Bloomington: Indiana University Press.

Vries, Hent de. 2008. "Introduction: Why Still 'Religion'?" In *Religion: Beyond a Concept*, ed. Hent de Vries, 1–98. New York: Fordham University Press.

Vygotsky, Lev. 1986 [1934]. *Thought and Language*. Cambridge: MIT Press.

Walker, Margaret. 2006. *Moral Repair: Reconstructing Moral Relations after Wrongdoing*. Cambridge: Cambridge University Press.

Ward, Helen, and Sophie Day. 1997. "Health Care and Regulation–New Perspectives." In *Rethinking Prostitution*, ed. G. and A. Scambler, 139–64. London: Routledge.

Warneken, F., and Michael Tomasello. 2006. "Altruistic Helping in Human Infants and Young Chimpanzees." *Science* 31:1301–3.

Warner, Michael. 1993. "Tongues Untied: Memoirs of a Pentecostal Boyhood." *The Village Voice* 38(6):73–75.

———. 2008. "Is Liberalism a Religion?" In *Religion: Beyond a Concept*, ed. Hent de Vries, 610–17. New York: Fordham University Press.

Watson, Gary. 2004. *Agency and Answerability: Selected Essays*. Oxford: Oxford University Press.

Watson, James L. 1975. "Agents and Outsiders: Adoption in a Chinese Lineage," *Man* n.s. 10(2):293–306.

———. 1988. "The Structure of Chinese Funerary Rites: Elementary Forms, Ritual Sequence, and the Primacy of Performance." In *Death Ritual in Late Imperial and Modern China*, ed. James L. Watson and Evelyn Rawski, 3–19. Berkeley: University of California Press.

Watson, James L., and Evelyn Rawski, eds. 1988. *Death Ritual in Late Imperial and Modern China*. Berkeley: University of California Press.

Weber, Max. 1946. "The Sociology of Charismatic Authority." In *From Max Weber: Essays in Sociology*, Ed. and trans. Hans H. Gerth and C. Wright Mills, 245–52. New York: Oxford University Press.

———. 1947. *The Theory of Social and Economic Organization*. Trans. A. M. Henderson and Talcott Parsons. New York: The Free Press.

———. 1958 [1905]. *The Protestant Ethic and the Spirit of Capitalism*. Trans. Talcott Parsons. New York: Charles Scribner.

———. 1978 [1956]. *Economy and Society: An Outline of Interpretive Sociology*. Ed. Guenther Roth and Claus Wittich. Berkeley: University of California Press.

Weeratunge, N. 2001. *Micro-entrepreneurs and Entrepreneurial Cultures in Sri Lanka*. Colombo: CEPA.

———. 2008. "Enterprise for Pro-poor Growth Project: Impact Assessment of the Enterprise Culture Component." Unpublished report. Colombo: ILO.

Wellman, Henry M. 2002. "Understanding the Psychological World: Developing a Theory of Mind." In *Blackwell Handbook of Childhood Cognitive Development*, ed. Usah Goswami, 167–87. Oxford: Blackwell.

Werbner, Pnina, and Helene Basu. 1998. *Embodying Charisma: Modernity, Locality and Performing of Emotion in Sufi Shrines*. London: Routledge.

Westermarck, Edward. 1906. *The Origin and the Development of the Moral Ideas*. Volume 1. London: Macmillan.

———. 1932. *Ethical Relativity*. London: Kegan Paul, Trench, Trubner & Co.

Weston, Kath. 1991. *Families We Choose: Lesbians, Gays, Kinship*. New York: Columbia University Press.

Whiteley, P. M. 1988. *Deliberate Acts*. Tucson: University of Arizona Press.

———. 1998. *Rethinking Hopi Ethnography*. Washington, D.C.: Smithsonian Institution Press.

Whorf, B. L. 1956. *Language, Thought, and Reality*. Ed. J. B. Carroll. Cambridge: MIT Press.

Wikan, Unni. 2008. *In Honor of Fadime: Murder and Shame*. Chicago: University of Chicago Press.

Williams, Bernard. 1981. *Moral Luck*. Cambridge: Cambridge University Press.

———. 1985. *Ethics and the Limits of Philosophy*. Cambridge: Harvard University Press.

———. 1993. *Shame and Necessity*. Berkeley: University of California Press.

———. 1995. *Making Sense of Humanity and Other Philosophical Papers, 1982–1993*. Cambridge: Cambridge University Press.

Williams, D. 1993. *Nobody Nowhere: The Extraordinary Autobiography of an Autistic*. Toronto: Doubleday Canada.

———. 1994. *Somebody Somewhere: Breaking Free from the World of Autism*. New York: Times Book.

Williams, Robert R. 1997. *Hegel's Ethics of Recognition*. Berkeley: University of California Press.

Wilson, Bryan, ed. 1970. *Rationality*. Evanston, Ill.: Harper and Row.

Wittgenstein, Ludwig. 1922. *Tractatus Logico-philosophicus*. Trans. C. K. Ogden. London: Kegan Paul, Trench, Trubner.

———. 1953. *Philosophical Investigations*. trans. G. E. M. Anscombe. New York: Macmillan.

———. 1958. *Philosophical Investigations*. 2nd ed. Trans. G. E. M. Anscombe. New York: Macmillan.

———. 1961. *Tractatus Logico-philosophicus: The German Text of Ludwig Wittgenstein's Logisch-philosophische Abhandlung*. With trans. by D. F. Pears and R. F. McGuinness. London: Routledge and Kegan Paul.

Wolf, Arthur. 1995. *Sexual Attraction and Childhood Association: A Chinese Brief for Edward Westermarck*. Stanford: Stanford University Press.

Yan, Yunxiang. 2003. *Private Life under Socialism*. Stanford: Stanford University Press.

Yang, M. M. 2000. "Putting Global Capitalism in Its Place: Economic Hybridity, Bataille, and Ritual Expenditure." *Current Anthropology* 41(4):477–509.

Zelizer, Viviana. 2005. *The Purchase of Intimacy*. Princeton: Princeton University Press.

Zigon, Jarrett. 2007. "Moral Breakdown and the Ethical Demand: A Theoretical Framework for an Anthropology of Moralities." *Anthropological Theory* 7:131–50.

———. 2008. *Morality: An Anthropological Perspective*. Oxford: Berg.

Zimmerman, Michael. 2002. "Taking Luck Seriously." *Journal of Philosophy* 99(11):553–76.

Žižek, Slavoj. 2003. *The Puppet and the Dwarf: The Perverse Core of Christianity*. Cambridge: MIT Press.

Žižek, Slavoj, and John Milbank. 2009. *The Monstrosity of Christ: Paradox or Dialectic?* Cambridge: MIT Press.